HOHOKAM HABITATION SITES IN THE NORTHERN SANTA RITA MOUNTAINS

by

Alan Ferg
Kenneth C. Rozen
William L. Deaver
Martyn D. Tagg
David A. Phillips, Jr.
David A. Gregory

With Contributions by

Margaret Glass
Robert S. Thompson
Kurt Dongoske
Karl J. Reinhard
Richard H. Hevly
Richard C. Lange
Bruce B. Huckell

Submitted by

Cultural Resource Management Division
Arizona State Museum
University of Arizona

Prepared for

ANAMAX Mining Company

1984

Archaeological Series No. 147, Vol. 2, Part 1

CONTENTS

xii   Contents

xvi   Contents

TABLES

xxxviii   Contents

PREFACE

Bruce B. Huckell

This, the second volume of the report series on the ANAMAX-Rosemont Project, presents the results of investigations at a series of Tucson Basin Hohokam sites in the northern Santa Rita Mountains. Due to the level of detail presented in the various specialized analyses, it has been necessary to divide this second volume into two parts. The first part contains an introduction, the research design, and the site descriptions, together with chapters on the pottery and flaked stone artifacts. In the second part are chapters dealing with the utilitarian and nonutilitarian ground stone artifacts, shell artifacts, the factors involved in site locational patterning, and the summary and conclusions. Also in the second part are appendixes reporting the faunal and floral remains, pollen studies, physical anthropological examination of the cremations and inhumations, an attempt to identify parasites from soil samples secured from inhumations, and a brief discussion of the archaeomagnetic dating of project samples.

The Rosemont Hohokam sites are interesting for a number of reasons. First is their location in a montane or upland environment, a setting that one does not normally associate with the Hohokam. Second, these sites lie on or very near what must be the southeastern frontier or Tucson Basin Hohokam territory, and in many ways reflect this isolation from the main stream of the Tucson Basin. Third, the sites chronicle the struggles of the Hohokam to adjust to this rich but unfamiliar environment, from the early colonists who founded a few relatively large sites to the last hangers-on living in small groups at a few dispersed localities. Finally, the ANAMAX-Rosemont Project offered the first opportunity to examine in detail a large group of sites in a single geographically restricted area, and as such illustrates the variability and adaptability of Tucson Basin Hohokam society that cannot be addressed at scattered single sites.

In many respects the investigation of the Hohokam sites was the most complex part of the entire project. The developmental history of the ANAMAX-Rosemont Project and its attendant logistical difficulties have already been detailed in the preface to the first report volume (Huckell 1984a: xiii-xv). The successive changes in the size and configuration of the exchange area probably most significantly affected the Hohokam sites research, at one point including over 70 ceramic period sites in portions of two drainage basins, and finally consisting of a total of 34 sites in part of one drainage basin. Further, problems generated by extremely limited surface artifact assemblages, survey recording of highly variable accuracy, and the complex topographic locations of many sites combined to make planning and investigation logistics difficult. Temporal and budgetary constraints also figured into the work, as they always do in responsible contract archaeological projects. Final frustrations, in the form of a near lack of absolute chronological control and extremely small artifact assemblages at several sites, also were endured. Nevertheless, the people whose work appears in this volume successfully overcame these difficulties to produce what I believe is an excellent picture of the Hohokam who called the Rosemont area home over a 700-year period.

ACKNOWLEDGMENTS

Alan Ferg

Memories of the mitigation phase work at the Hohokam sites of the ANAMAX-Rosemont Project, which began about two and one-half years ago, often focus on particular events. Overall, however, three things come to mind. The beauty of the Rosemont area made it a special place in which to work. For some, the thought of exploring Hohokam culture in an ecological setting previously thought not to contain such sites, made the work doubly exciting. Finally, archaeology is inseparable from the people doing it, each shaping the other's character to some degree. Grandiose as that may sound, it is true, and from a personal viewpoint, one of archaeology's virtues is in its doing. Zahniser (1966: 192-200) rightly discussed the humanistic values of archaeological work for the people doing it. In the end, the work at Rosemont was more than just a job to all involved, and presumably the work and interaction have broadened us all. All of the people below not only made the physical completion of the project possible, but made it an exciting and often fun way to spend 30 months. It is a pleasure to acknowledge all who contributed to the project's execution and completion.

Primary thanks must go to ANAMAX Mining Company for sponsoring the work and providing assistance of all kinds throughout its duration. Company President Gene Wyman, Chief Counsel John Frankovich, Geologist Wilson McCurry, and Land Records Administrator Bert Reid all helped make the project run smoothly.

Coronado National Forest Archaeologists Donald Wood and Patricia Spoerl helped the project run smoothly and the interest of Forest Supervisor Robert Tippeconnic was greatly appreciated.

In and out of the field, and throughout the report preparation, Project Director and Co-Principal Investigator Bruce B. Huckell provided advice, labor, and the occasional prod needed to keep the work moving. His involvement with the ANAMAX-Rosemont Project began with the close of the survey work, and it is largely through Bruce's input and persistence through the testing phase, additional surveys, and planning of the mitigation research that the whole project has come to fruition. Likewise, David A. Gregory provided valuable guidance in formulating the mitigation phase research design. Lynn S. Teague, Co-Principal Investigator, also bent her managerial skills to the task of seeing the project through the mitigation phase.

John and Paige Gayler of the VR Ranch extended project personnel any number of courtesies which made the field work easier, including putting up with temporarily sprung fences and water lines.

Field crews will make or break a project; both crews deserve special thanks for their continued hard work throughout a nearly six-month field season. Crew Chiefs William L. Deaver and Kenneth C. Rozen handily ran their respective crews, with the assistance of Richard G. Ervin and Martyn D. Tagg; all exhibited substantial skill at repeatedly shifting crews and equipment to new sites and excavating each in a professional manner. They also bore the burden of keeping laborers, volunteers, visitors, and cows out of each other's way and behaving as each ought. Laborers, each bringing certain abilities to the project, included: Richard Anduze, Allan Bannister, James Bayman, Ronald Beckwith, Martin Biedermann, Kathy Corcoran, Kurt Dongoske, Wayne Ferguson, Cynthia Graff, Kathlene Greene, Carolyn Groome, David Gunckel, John Herron, William Hohmann, Edward Kaler, Banks Leonard, Doak McDuffie, Steve Maher, Geoffrey Purcell, Sam Shepard, Carol Sullivan, Susan Wells and Mark Ziem. We would also like to thank Terence Thomas for returning the Brunton compass.

Volunteers are a valuable commodity, and the Hohokam excavations were blessed with quite a few; their willing labor made the excavations more complete than they might have been. Maria Abdin, Daryl and Brian Adams, Richard Ahlstrom, Kim and Ron Beckwith, Kathy Corcoran, John Conyers, Rick Ervin, Michele Farritor, David Gregory, Clarrisa Gregory, Lisa and Bruce Huckell, William, Mary and Nicki Hohmann, Richard King, Charlotte Morris, Bob Robb, Ken Rozen, Marylin Saul, Marty Tagg, Miki Tagg, Sharon Urban and David Wilcox all contributed their time in the field. Paul Fish's University of Arizona field school class and Mike Bartlett's cadre of volunteers derived largely from Tucson Public Library patrons both came out, and both got rained out, but their willingness was appreciated.

Special mention must be made of Kathlene Greene, Alan P. Sullivan, III, and Heather and Bill Deaver, whose combined volunteer person-days totalled several months.

Bob ("Backhoe Bob") Foote and his son, Ken, of Foote Excavating provided the best backhoe trenching seen to date, and substantially expanded the author's knowledge of the kinds of places a backhoe can go given the right operator. Bob's good humor was also much appreciated.

Out of the field, laboratory duties were supervised by Arthur Vokes. Carol Heathington, Alan Sullivan, and Donald Graybill managed various aspects of the computer manipulation of the data. Much of the report was produced by personnel who had also participated in the field work, bringing to bear, I think, a greater understanding of the archaeology to the process of artifact analysis and report writing. I think all can be said to have done an extremely thorough job, often clearly exceeding the highly variable "standards" of contract archaeological work. Bill Deaver wrote up the ceramic assemblage, Ken

Rozen the chipped stone, Marty Tagg the ground stone, and Kurt Dongoske the human skeletal material. Cynthia Graff assisted with the chipped stone analysis. Ron Beckwith drafted most of the charts and prepared many of the figures for publication, particularly all of the pottery drawings and new whole vessel photographs in Chapter 4; Rozen drafted his own charts. Charles Sternberg did many of the field maps, and drafted all of the site and feature maps which appear in this report.

Additional authors include David A. Phillips, Jr., who took on the onerous task of interpreting all of the survey data, Margaret Glass analyzed the faunal material; Charles H. Miksicek analyzed the flotation and wood samples; Robert Thompson analyzed the pollen samples, and Richard Lange and Barbara Murphy dealt with the archaeomagnetic samples. Special thanks to Karl J. Reinhard and Richard H. Hevly for their contribution of time and effort to look for parasites and pollen in burial contexts.

Robert O'Haire kindly identified many of the mineral specimens from the project, and Walter H. Birkby, Marylin Saul, and Richard Harrington provided help with some of the human skeletal material. Ellen McGehee, Jannelle Weakly, Alice Moffett, Patricia Crown, David Abbott, Henry Wallace, Karl Reinhard, David Wilcox, Chris Downum, and Doug Craig lent their expertise to various facets of the ceramic analysis. Bill Hohmann, Paul Fish and Rich Lange kindly allowed photography and publication of newly recovered restorable pots from Red-tail Village and Los Morteros Site. Special thanks also to Amadeo M. Rea for his identifications of bird bones.

Arizona State Museum Collections Division personnel, including Jan Bell, Mike Jacobs, Steve Rogers, Ellen Horn and Kathy Hubenschmidt provided needed access to artifacts and photographs. Helga Teiwes took all of the artifact photographs used in the volume, and printing of many of these and the field photos fell to Michael Barton. Sharon Bartlett, Dola Moore, Diann Blair, and Martha Barrow all managed to keep track of personnel changes and paychecks, for which all of us were quite thankful.

In the actual production of this volume, Carol Heathington served as principal editor and coordinator for all typists and authors, ably assisted by Bruce Huckell and Gerald Harwood of Cave Canyon Associates. Their supervision and editing contributed much to the clarity and timely production of the entire volume. Typing and corrections were all patiently carried out by Jeanne Witt, Michaline Cardella, Robin Dysor, and Cathy Carver. Candy Schreiber carefully typed most of the oversized tables.

The author of Chapter 4 would like to specially thank his wife, Heather, for her help in the field and repeated proof-reading and editing of the pottery manuscript. Finally, the senior author would like to thank Beth Rogan Ferg who cheerfully put up with a lot during this project, and who did in fact supply lentils when things were critical.

ABSTRACT

Excavations at 22 ceramic period sites in the Rosemont area of the northern Santa Rita Mountains, Coronado National Forest, are described. Investigations have established that these sites were occupied by the Tucson Basin Hohokam more or less continuously from approximately A.D. 500 until abandonment of the area at approximately A.D. 1200.

The ceramic period prehistory of southeastern Arizona is outlined in the first chapter, and the research design for work at the Rosemont sites is presented in the second chapter. Next each site that received investigation is briefly described, including discussions of the features, artifacts, and length of occupation of each. This is followed by a series of six chapters which present the results of specialized analyses of various classes of material culture. The first of these discusses the pottery from the sites. Detailed definitions and descriptions of the plain, painted, and red ware pottery types are presented, and a model of decorative stylistic development of Tucson Basin painted pottery is introduced. Potential and temporal changes are explored as well; a few temporal trends are noted, but no functional differentiation was identified. The flaked stone artifacts are rigorously described, and both the implements and debitage are subjected to detailed technological, formal, and functional examinations. This study demonstrates that the assemblages display a great deal of consistency in all attributes, and that there is little evidence of technological, formal, or functional variability among the sites. Only projectile point styles exhibit change through time. The ground stone artifacts, divided into utilitarian and nonutilitarian forms, are treated in the next two chapters. A series of formal and functional classes is defined for both, and the various classes are described in detail. Possible functions are discussed, and each class is compared to similar classes from other sites and other areas. It is noted that the Rosemont ground stone artifacts are generally simple, unembellished forms made of local materials, and that the assemblages from all sites are quite similar. Shell artifacts are next described and discussed, and are again found to be relatively simple forms, probably entering the area as finished items. Comparisons show them to be similar to forms known from other Hohokam sites.

In the ninth chapter an analysis of the factors influencing settlement location is presented. Variables such as topography, soils, vegetation, elevation, and distance to permanent water are found to have low correlations to site location, but location of sites is highly correlated to stream profile gradient. Comparisons with sites located

in similar areas in southeastern Arizona suggest that this variable may
have considerable explanatory and predictive power. The last chapter
pulls together all available data to examine the nature of the Hohokam
occupation of the Rosemont area. Functional site types and intrasite
organization are first discussed. Three categories of functional site
types (new farmsteads, stable or growing farmsteads, and one site with a
ballcourt) are recognized, as is a pattern on intrasite organization
which is probably based in part on Hohokam customs and in part on local
topography. Economy and subsistence are next examined, and from the
meager data available it is proposed that maize agriculture supplemented
by hunting and gathering of upland fauna and flora supported the area's
inhabitants. Examination of areal and regional relationships indicates
principal contacts with the Phoenix Basin Hohokam, the Mogollon, and the
Trincheras cultures. Intrusive decorated pottery is the primary
evidence for contact, although the presence of a large number of
inhumations and certain aspects of architecture provide further
documentation of intercultural contact. The nature of the Tucson Basin
Hohokam occupation of the area is next traced in terms of site
distribution, population distribution, and intersite organization.
Possible organization of the Rosemont "local system" is discussed, and
reconstructions of temporal trends in settlement and population numbers
are presented. Unstable climatic conditions, in conjunction with over-
exploitation of the local resource base, is suggested to be the ultimate
cause of abandonment of the Rosemont area.

Chapter 1

THE ROSEMONT STUDY AREA AND PREVIOUS RESEARCH
IN SURROUNDING AREAS

Alan Ferg

Study Area Location

The Rosemont study area and proposed land exchange presently encompasses approximately 23 square miles in the northernmost portion of the Santa Rita Mountains (Fig. 1.1). The study area was named after Rosemont, an abandoned mining town located near the center of the area.

The Rosemont study area is located adjacent to the western edge of a large watershed known as the Cienega or Empire Valley, which ranges from an elevation of about 3800 feet (1158 m) to 9453 feet (2881 m) at the top of Mt. Wrightson in the Santa Rita Mountains. The valley is fringed on the west by the Santa Rita Mountains, on the north by the Empire Mountains, and on the east by the Whetstone and Mustang mountains. Cienega Creek, flowing north through the valley, is the major drainage. At the head of this creek, two major drainages form the southern end of the watershed. One of these is Sonoita Creek, which flows south and west past the towns of Sonoita and Patagonia to its confluence with the Santa Cruz River near Calabasas. The other major drainage, the Babocomari River, flows eastward past the town of Elgin to its confluence with the San Pedro River near Fairbank. The Santa Cruz and San Pedro river watersheds are among the most important in southeastern Arizona.

About 70 percent of the Rosemont study area (Fig. 1.2) is located east of the ridgeline of the Santa Rita Mountains; the remaining area is west of the ridgeline. The southern base of Mt. Fagan (elevation 6186 feet or 1886 m), a prominent landform of this range, forms the northern boundary of the study area. The mouth of Box Canyon, which separates the northern mountain range from the higher, larger range to the south, lies at the south-central edge of the study area. State Highway 83 runs along the eastern portion of the study area.

Within the study area, the elevation ranges from 4000 feet (1231 m) to 6312 feet (1924 m). A number of important drainages flow through parts of the study area. The most prominent is Barrel Canyon, which heads near the south-central boundary and drains

1

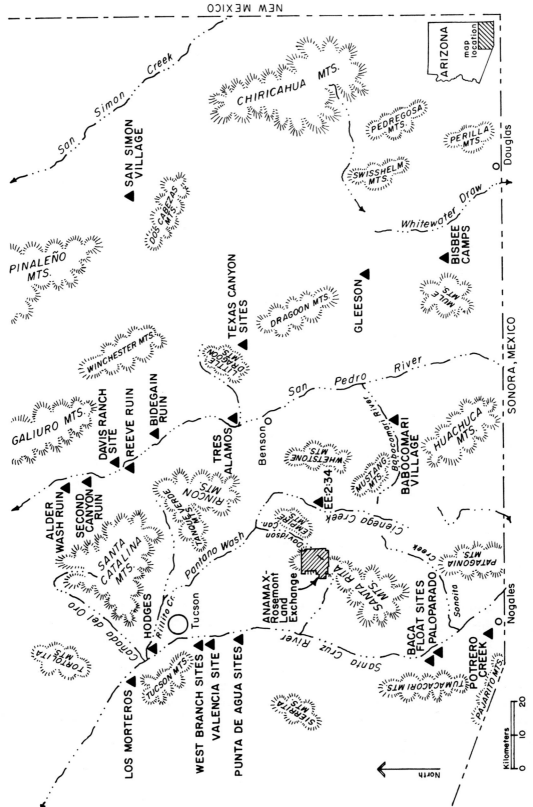

Figure 1.1. Southeastern Arizona, showing the location of the ANAMAX-Rosemont land-exchange area and the archaeological sites discussed in this volume.

2

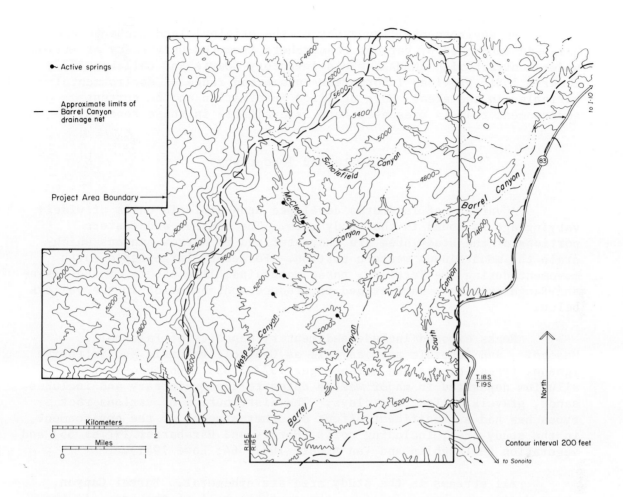

Figure 1.2. Topography and named drainages of the land-exchange area.

northeastward, where it meets Davidson Canyon outside the study area.
The latter is an important tributary of Pantano Wash, which drains part
of the Tucson Basin. Four major tributaries of Barrel Canyon also head
in the study area. The northernmost is Scholefield Canyon, named for a
pioneer rancher in the region. It drains eastward from the north-
central part of the study area past the eastern boundary, where it joins
Barrel Canyon. McCleary Canyon, named for the founder of the historic
town of Rosemont, meanders from the west-central part of the study area
to its junction with Barrel Canyon in the east-central boundary area.
The third major tributary is Wasp Canyon, which heads in the southwest
corner of the study area and drains to the northeast, joining Barrel
Canyon just east of the historic town of Rosemont. The fourth
tributary, which we have named South Canyon, drains a high escarpment at
the southern and eastern edges of the exchange area. It joins Barrel
Canyon near the east-central part of the exchange area.

Study Area Environment

An environmental inventory of the original land exchange area has been conducted by various researchers from the University of Arizona under contract with ANAMAX. This inventory (Davis and Callahan 1977; Cockrum 1981) provides information on a broad range of environmental variables in the area. More detailed information on the current environment than is presented here is available in those reports.

Climate and Topography

A variety of landforms developed upon geologic units of widely varying age is found in the study area. The central and eastern portions of the study area are characterized by narrow canyons which drain the mountainous western portion. Formed by large-scale earth movement during the Tertiary, these mountains, like others of the Basin-and-Range province, have eroded to produce sedimentation in the valleys below.

Rocks exposed include sedimentary deposits of Paleozoic, Mesozoic, and Cenozoic age, as well as Cenozoic volcanic and intrusive igneous types (Hargis and Harshbarger 1977a: 43). Unconsolidated alluvium deposited in major washes dates to the Quaternary and includes sands, gravels, silts, and clays. The distribution of various rock types has had a significant effect on other aspects of the environment in the study area, including soils (Hargis and Harsbarger 1977a: 55) and vegetation (McLaughlin and Van Asdall 1977: 64; Lowe 1981).

All streams in the study area are ephemeral. Barrel Canyon, which drains northeastward from the southern half of the area, is the most prominent drainage. Major tributaries already mentioned are Wasp, McCleary, and Scholefield canyons. These are characterized by narrow floodplains usually not exceeding 30 m in width.

There are seven major active springs in the Rosemont study area, five of these in McCleary and Scholefield canyons (Hargis and Harsh-barger 1977b: 34). Numerous smaller springs are also found in Wasp Canyon and smaller, unnamed canyons to the south. Rosemont Spring, currently used by the VR Ranch, is found in a small tributary branch of Barrel Canyon.

At present, the Rosemont area averages between 16 and 18 inches of precipitation annually, concentrated in the months of July, August, and September (Sellers 1977). Frosts occur between mid-November and mid-April, producing an average growing season of about seven months at elevations between 4400 and 5400 feet. Sellers (1977: 4) estimates that the average variability of maximum temperatures is 3.5° to 5° F (1.96° to 2.8° C) per 1000 feet in elevation, so that lower elevations in the study area are up to 10 degrees warmer on the average than are higher elevations.

Vegetation

McLaughlin and Van Asdall (1977: 82-84) recognized four major types of plant communities in the study area: woodland, grassland, limestone scrub, and riparian communities (Fig. 1.3). Woodland communities are composed of evergreen oaks and junipers with rosette shrubs and a dense cover of grasses. These communities are located on north-facing slopes at most elevations and in mountain drainages. Grasslands occur on ridge tops and xeric slopes and include, in addition to a variable grass cover, scattered woody plants and many cacti and shrubs. Limestone scrub communities, with a high density of woody plants and cacti, and a low grass cover, are found on all limestone substrates. These represent the westernmost occurrence of essentially Chihuahuan Desert vegetation. Riparian communities of deciduous trees and shrubs are found in low-elevation washes.

The overall pattern is one of interspersed grasslands and woodlands in the eastern and central portions of the study area, with riparian environments along most of the drainages. Limestone scrub communities occur at the base of the mountainous western area. The mountains themselves display grasslands and woodlands in areas where the substrate is not high in carbonates. Figures 1.4 and 1.5 convey an impression of the vegetation patterns in the area.

Within each community type there is significant variation, depending on elevation, slope, aspect, and other localized conditions. In general, however, the total coverage of herbaceous plants decreases from woodland to grassland to riparian to limestone community types (McLaughlin and Van Asdall 1977: 82).

Fauna

Various studies included in the overall environmental assessment of the study area (Davis and Callahan 1977; Cockrum 1981) discuss in detail the insects, noninsect invertebrates, fishes, amphibians, reptiles, birds, and mammals of the Rosemont area. The invertebrate fauna was found to be quite sparse, represented by a small number of very common species. Thirty-seven species of reptiles and seven amphibian species were noted (Lowe and Johnson 1977: 165; Lowe and Schwalbe 1981). A total of 141 species of birds was identified, with the greatest diversity in riparian habitats (Russell, Mills and Silliman 1977: 193; Russell and Goldwasser 1981: 102). The mammalian fauna is basically that of grassland environments (Roth 1977: 195); however, desert and woodland species are also present. The 45 identified species represent 29 genera (Roth 1977; Petryszyn 1981: 107). Eighteen species previously observed in the area are now presumed to be locally extinct.

Hungerford's (1977) study of game species is of special interest in that many of the animals in this category may have been of economic importance to the prehistoric occupants of the area. Deer and javelina

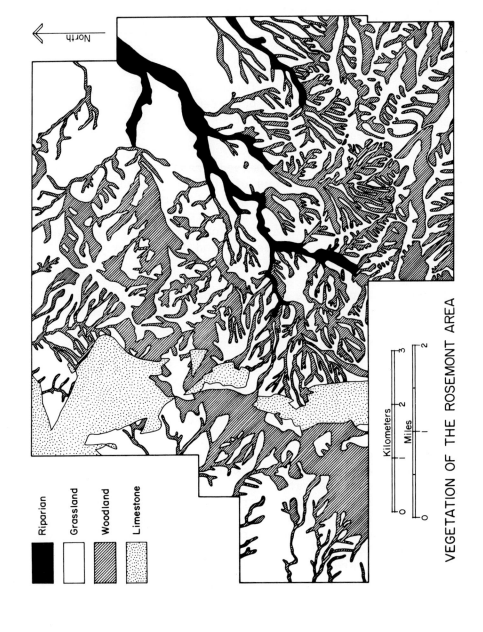

VEGETATION OF THE ROSEMONT AREA

Figure 1.3   Map of the plant communities within the ANAMAX–Rosemont land exchange area (after McLaughlin and Van Asdall 1977).

Figure 1.4 (left). Looking west at the Gayler (VR) Ranch on the flood-plain of upper Barrel Canyon, with the crestline of the Santa Ritas in the background. Arrow indicates the location of AZ EE:2:76. Trees are primarily juniper, with oaks in the drainage bottoms. Rosemont Springs is located in the heavily wooded area immediately behind the ranch.

Figure 1.5 (right). Looking northwest down the ridge on which AZ EE:2:106 is located (light areas are backhoe trenches) with the crestline of the Santa Ritas in the background. The Barrel Canyon floodplain is below he line of sight in the middle distance. Trees visible are primarily juniper, with a few intermingled, darker oaks.

are among the listed species of larger mammals. Bighorn sheep are assumed to have existed in the study area but are now absent. Other game species present include: quail, dove, pigeons, and, in the higher elevations south of the study area, wild turkeys. Hungerford notes that the Rosemont area satisfies the principle criteria for good game habitat:

> It encompasses several vegetative types, and the diversity or amount of edge between types is increased by the nature of the topography. The numerous small drainages with intervening ridges offer both north and south exposures, and the more mesic semiriparian conditions in the water courses provide additional habitat diversity. Also, the origin of soil types is variable enough across the area to cause differences in vegetation. This variability increases the total amount of boundary between vegetative types and results in additional diversity. Water is available to game species at natural springs (1977: 219).

When discussing the past and present distributions of animal species in the Rosemont area, and in southern Arizona in general, it should be kept in mind that javelina, coatimundi and black vultures appear to be relatively recent immigrants. These are neotropical species which appear to be expanding their range northward (Rea 1983: 87-90; Ferg 1983a). The importance of this information to the present study is that javelina, for example, would not have been available as a game species to the prehistoric inhabitants of the Rosemont area. To date, none of these species has been recovered from Hohokam sites, a single bone from the middle Santa Cruz River Valley notwithstanding (Doyel 1977a: 49).

Summary

In essence, the land exchange encompasses an area in the Upper Sonoran Life-Zone (Lowe 1964) with desert grassland faunal and floral communities at the lower elevations grading into oak woodland faunal and floral communities in the higher elevations. Linear patches of riparian woodland can be found around springs and in various canyons. The area receives more precipitation than the Lower Sonoran Life-Zone areas surrounding it, and yet is not so high in elevation that the growing season is seriously curtailed. Hence, despite the somewhat limited supply of water, the body of the exchange area is rich in plant and animal resources; the relative abundance of prehistoric sites in the area is not surprising. Only in the drier portions of the exchange area, notably Sycamore Canyon on the north, does this natural bounty decline, with the presence of essentially Sonoran desert scrub communities from the Lower Sonoran Life-Zone of the Tucson Basin. Ceramic period site density drops dramatically here.

Previous Research in the Land-Exchange Area

Prior to the archaeological survey of the ANAMAX-Rosemont project area, little was known of archaeological remains within the project area itself. In 1961, the Historic Sites Committee assigned Arizona State Museum (ASM) site number AZ EE:2:49 to Rosemont, the abandoned mining town located in the center of the study area. Apparently the site was never actually surveyed and adequately recorded, since no other archaeological information is to be found in the files. In 1971, James Ayres and Adrienne B. Anderson recorded two sites for ASM Site Survey Files. One, AZ EE:2:52, was a sherd and lithic scatter near the VR Ranch (Gayler Ranch). The second, AZ EE:2:53, was recorded as a sherd and lithic scatter with a historic adobe dwelling. Both sites were pointed out to Ayres and Anderson by local ranchers.

From late 1975 to late 1976, some 25 square miles were intensively surveyed by the Cultural Resource Management Division of the Arizona State Museum (CRMD) under contract with the ANAMAX Mining Company. By the end of this field work, just over 750 archaeological manifestations had been recorded; more than 100 of these were isolated artifacts (Debowski 1980). The sites recorded included Archaic, ceramic, protohistoric and historic sites, with the area apparently abandoned between each of these major periods. This assumption was based on survey data, but subsequent testing and additional survey have not produced any contrary evidence. No Paleo-Indian sites were found; however a late Pleistocene paleontological locality was recorded. Recorded site types range from isolated artifacts to lithic quarry sites over 9000 square meters in extent, from large pit house villages to small scatters of less than 10 artifacts, and from an entire historic town site to single tent platforms.

It was readily apparent from the survey phase that the site density in this mountainous area was higher than anticipated, and that these cultural resources were potentially a source of important new data. To further assess this body of sites, a testing program was designed (Debowski and Huckell 1979) and carried out during the summer of 1979 (Huckell 1980). Over 40 archaeological localities representing six major classes of sites were investigated during the testing phase. These classes are: Archaic, Hohokam, Protohistoric (Upper Piman or Sobaipuri), historic (European), unknown aboriginal lithic resource exploitation sites and unknown aboriginal biotic resource exploitation sites. The paleontological locality was tested as well. These investigations greatly enhanced the understanding of the nature of the resources in the area, and provided sufficient information with which to determine their significance and to develop plans for the mitigation of the adverse effects of the passing of this public land into private ownership. Significance was documented for most of the archaeological resources in the land-exchange area (Huckell 1980: 224-238), and two districts were proposed for inclusion in the National Register of Historic Places, the Barrel Canyon and Davidson Canyon archaeological districts.

Testing at the Hohokam sites (Huckell 1980: 41-136) generally confirmed the inferences based on survey data. The Hohokam occupation of the Rosemont area was found to be largely confined to the Rillito and Rincon phases (A.D. 700-1200), and cultural affinities were determined to lie primarily with the Tucson Basin.

In 1980 and 1981, approximately 7 sections of land were dropped from the exchange area, and another 4 1/2 sections added and surveyed on the southwestern and western (Huckell 1981a), and northern (Ferg 1981) edges of the original exchange area. Both surveys disclosed a small number of sites.

Regional Culture History

Tucson Basin

The Tucson Basin can be defined as the area bounded by the Santa Catalina Mountains on the north, the Rincon Mountains on the east, the

Santa Rita and Empire mountains on the south and southeast, respectively, the Sierrita Mountains on the southwest, and the Tucson Mountains on the west. It is bisected by the Santa Cruz River, and contains other major drainages, such as Pantano Wash, Rillito Creek, and Cañada del Oro, along which many archaeological sites have been found.

Tucson Basin ceramic period culture history exhibits a sequence related to the Phoenix Basin sequence (Fig. 1.6). The Phoenix Basin was occupied as early as 300 B.C. In contrast, the earliest certain evidence for Hohokam settlement in the Tucson Basin is represented by ceramics, and at least one pit house, of the Snaketown phase (A.D. 300-500) at the Hodges Ruin (Kelly 1978). Potentially earlier materials are represented at the Hodges Ruin only by Phoenix Basin, Sweetwater phase ceramics, and two pit houses which may predate the Snaketown phase (Kelly 1978: 16). Ceramics were found in stratified contexts, but were not associated with structures. The Snaketown phase was also represented in the ceramics from the Hardy Site, AZ BB:9:14 (Gregonis and Reinhard 1979; Gregonis 1983). Subsistence and settlement pattern data for this time period in the Tucson Basin are practically nonexsistent.

By A.D. 500, materials from the Tucson Basin are sufficiently different from those in the Phoenix Basin to merit separate designations. The earliest of these is the Cañada del Oro phase, defined at the Hodges Ruin on the basis of four pit houses and their associated ceramics (Kelly 1978). At the Punta de Agua sites, Greenleaf (1975) notes the presence of a small sample of Cañada del Oro Red-on-brown sherds that appear to represent transitional materials between typical Cañada del Oro Red-on-brown and Rillito Red-on-brown. Again, subsistence and settlement pattern data for this time period are sparse.

Sedentary village sites first become the norm during the Rillito and Rincon phases (A.D. 700-900 and A.D. 900-1200, respectively). During this period, a significant number of small villages were established along primary and secondary drainages in the Tucson Basin. During the Rillito phase, most villages were located in secondary drainages rather than in the primary drainage of the Santa Cruz River; the Rincon phase is characterized by settlements throughout the valley. These villages were composed of shallow, rectangular pit houses and the associated assemblages included red-on-brown painted pottery, and lithic artifacts including numerous grinding implements for processing plant foods, probably both wild and domesticated.

Rillito and Rincon phase pit houses were identified at the Hodges Ruin, the Punta de Agua sites and the Hardy Site. At the Hodges Ruin, few Rillito phase houses could be identified; construction of the later Rincon and Tanque Verde phase houses had destroyed the majority of the earlier occupation phase. The chronological relationship between the Snaketown, Cañada del Oro, Rillito, and Tanque Verde phases was exhibited by house superposition; however, there was no definite structural relationship between Rincon and Tanque Verde. This ordering was demonstrated, however, in the stratified trash deposits. Based on recent work at the Valencia Site combined with a reexamination of

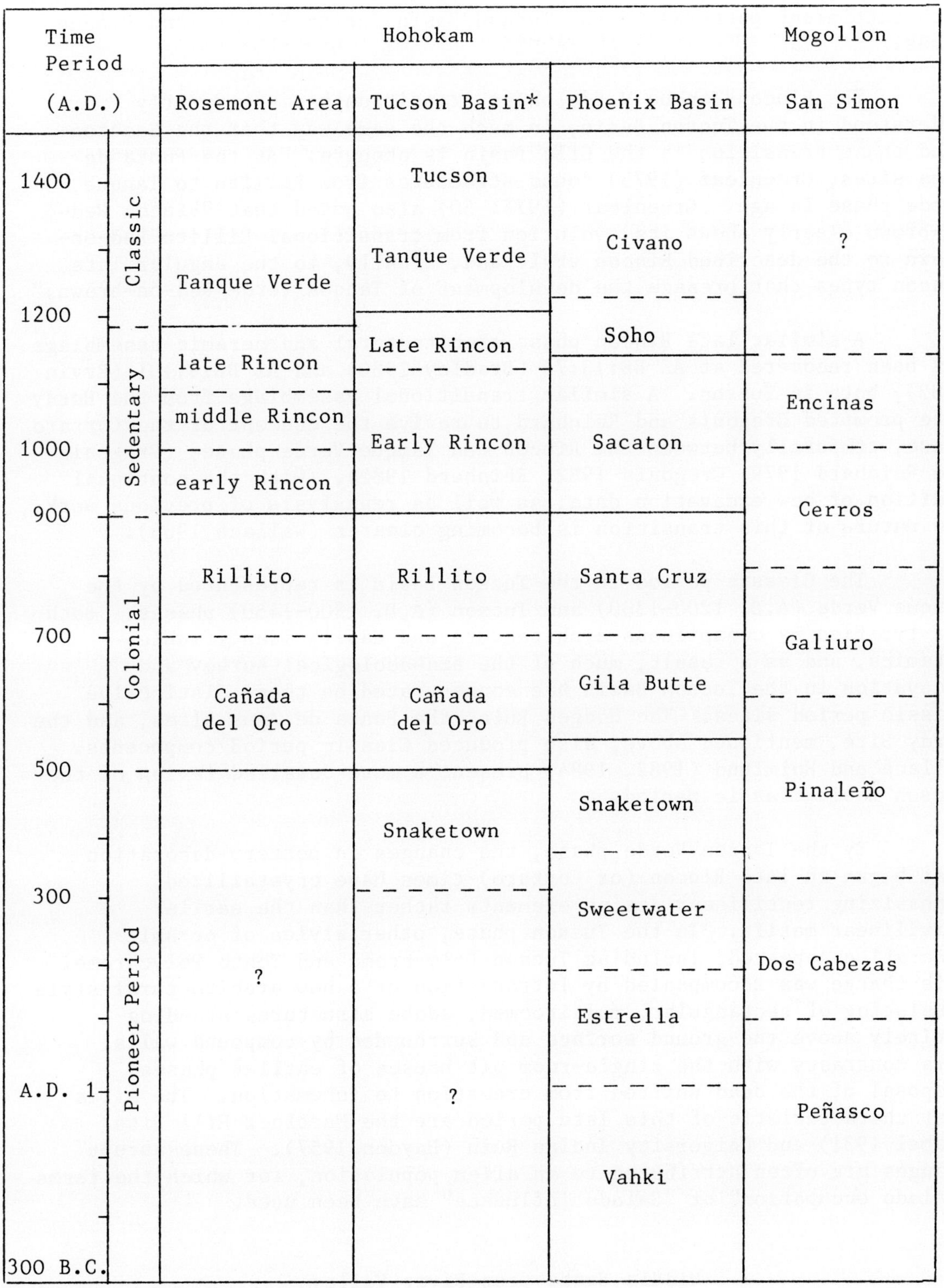

Time Period (A.D.)		Hohokam			Mogollon
		Rosemont Area	Tucson Basin*	Phoenix Basin	San Simon
1400	Classic	Tanque Verde	Tucson	Civano	?
1200			Tanque Verde		
	Sedentary	late Rincon	Late Rincon	Soho	
1000		middle Rincon	Early Rincon	Sacaton	Encinas
900		early Rincon			Cerros
700	Colonial	Rillito	Rillito	Santa Cruz	Galiuro
		Cañada del Oro	Cañada del Oro	Gila Butte	
500					Pinaleño
			Snaketown	Snaketown	
300	Pioneer Period	?		Sweetwater	Dos Cabezas
A.D. 1			?	Estrella	Peñasco
				Vahki	
300 B.C.					

* after Greenleaf 1975

Figure 1.6 Regional culture-historical sequences.

earlier data Doelle (1983) has presented several new arguments concerned with settlement patterns in the Tucson Basin during Rillito and Rincon times.

The Rincon-Tanque Verde phase transition has been poorly understood in the Tucson Basin, in much the same way that the Sacaton-Soho phase transition in the Gila Basin is obscure. At the Punta de Agua sites, Greenleaf (1975) found structures from Rillito to Tanque Verde phase in age. Greenleaf (1975: 50) also noted that "Rincon Red-on-brown clearly shows its evolution from transitional Rillito Red-on-brown to the described Rincon style and, finally, to the angular late Rincon types that presage the development of Tanque Verde Red-on-brown."

A similar late Rincon phase architectural and ceramic assemblage has been recovered at AZ BB:13:74 (Bradley 1980) and AZ BB:9:101 (Ervin 1982), both in Tucson. A similar transitional assemblage from the Hardy Site prompted Gregonis and Reinhard to revive the concept of the Cortaro phase, temporally between the Rincon and Tanque Verde phases (Gregonis and Reinhard 1979; Gregonis 1982; Reinhard 1982). With the continual addition of new excavation data, as well as reanalysis of previous work, the nature of this transition is becoming clearer (Wallace 1983).

The Classic period in the Tucson Basin is represented by the Tanque Verde (A.D. 1200-1300) and Tucson (A.D. 1300-1450) phases. Both are typified by conspicuous architecture and easily identifiable ceramics, and as a result, much of the archaeological survey and excavation in the Tucson Basin has concentrated on these distinctive Classic period sites. The Hodges Ruin, the Punta de Agua sites, and the Hardy Site, mentioned above, also produced Classic period components. Wallace and Holmlund (1982, 1984) present a more detailed review of the Tucson Basin Classic period.

By the Tanque Verde phase, the changes in pottery decoration that began in late Rincon (or Cortaro) times have crystallized, emphasizing rectilinear design elements rather than the earlier curvilinear motifs. In the Tucson phase, other styles of ceramic decoration appeared, including Tucson Polychrome and Tonto Polychrome. This change was accompanied by introduction of a new architectural style consisting of rectangular, multiroomed, adobe structures standing entirely above the ground surface and surrounded by compound walls. This contrasts with the single-room pit houses of earlier phases. Disposal of the dead shifted from cremation to inhumation. The sites most characteristic of this late period are the Martinez Hill Site (Gabel 1931) and University Indian Ruin (Hayden 1957). These abrupt changes are often attributed to an alien population, for which the terms "Salado occupation" or "Salado influence" have been used.

Middle Santa Cruz River Valley

South of the area defined as the Tucson Basin lies the middle Santa Cruz River Valley. This portion of the river has been defined as the area from Paloparado to the Tucson Basin; it is bounded by the Sierrita Mountains on the northwest, the Santa Rita Mountains on the northeast, the Tumacacori Mountains on the southwest, and the San Cayetano Mountains on the southeast. All recent work accomplished in the middle Santa Cruz has been under salvage or contract archaeological programs, including those at Paloparado (Brown and Grebinger 1969), Potrero Creek (Grebinger 1971a, 1971b) and Baca Float (Doyel 1977a). The development of the cultural and chronological sequence for the area has been based largely on knowledge gained from the above projects, in conjunction with earlier surveys (Danson 1946; Frick 1954) and excavations (Di Peso 1956) as well as information from the Tucson Basin.

The earliest occupation in the middle Santa Cruz may have been during the Pioneer period. Sweetwater and Snaketown phase ceramics have been found at Paloparado and Potrero Creek, but none of the structures found dated to those phases. In two surveys along the Santa Cruz (Danson 1946; Frick 1954), the earliest identified settlements were attributed to the Colonial period (A.D. 500-900).

By A.D. 700-900, many settlements were located in the middle Santa Cruz and its secondary drainages. The Paloparado Site (Di Peso 1956; Brown and Grebinger 1969), Potrero Creek (Grebinger 1971a, 1971b) and three of the Baca Float sites (Doyel 1977a) were all occupied during the Rillito and Rincon phases.

Paloparado is situated on a western terrace above the Santa Cruz River. The Hohokam component at the site was summarized by Doyel:

> The Hohokam component was substantial, consisting of approximately 50 houses arranged in irregular rows, a possible ceremonial house, a possible dance area, and at least 75 cremations (Di Peso 1956: 225-227). Large quantities of various pottery types were recovered, including northern wares, buff wares, red-on-brown wares and Trincheras wares, suggesting widespread contacts. Quantities of shell artifacts of various types, carved stone vessels and eccentrics, figurines, and other artifacts were present in abundance. A canal system may have served the village. All of these attributes generally reflect the character of primary village sites in the Hohokam core area located to the north (Doyel 1977a: 98).

The Potrero Creek Site lies on the flat crest of a low hill. Architectural units at the site were characteristic of the Rillito and Rincon phases, dating between A.D. 700 and 1200. The analysis of the Potrero Creek materials focused on a distributional study of material culture aimed at delineating the structure of maintenance activities. Activities identified at the site included plant or animal-skin processing areas and cooking areas. These activities were identified on the basis of the distributions of lithic tool types, ceramics and pollen remains, and the locations of nonarchitectural features. Based on his analysis, Grebinger concluded that:

The substantial size of the site, the presence of the fully constructed dwellings and the kinds and structure of activities carried on there are characteristic of seasonal or permanent occupation. This leads to the conclusion that the Potrero Creek Site was not a temporary camp at which only one or two specialized activities were carried out (1971b: 50).

All three Baca float sites were situated on the first terrace west of the Santa Cruz River. These sites have been identified as habitation sites, with structures, and have artifact assemblages characteristic of the Rillito and Rincon phases. They produced a variety of ceramics: plain wares, red wares, local red-on-brown wares and polychromes, Nogales and Rincon polychromes, Rincon red, Trincheras Purple-on-red, and intrusive, Phoenix Basin red-on-buff wares. Lithic artifacts included a highly variable chipped stone assemblage with a low ratio of finished tools to total assemblage, almost lacking in projectile points, and a wide variety of ground stone artifacts. Shell jewelry and other nonutilitarian items were also recovered. The subsistence data indicate a strong emphasis on domesticated and wild plant processing (Doyel 1977a: 95-96).

The surveys of Danson (1946) and Frick (1954) recorded many settlements dating to the Rillito and Rincon phases in the middle Santa Cruz drainage. Both surveys concentrated on the easily accessible floodplains and river terraces, and excluded most of the foothills of the Santa Rita and Sierrita mountains. Sherd areas, compounds, and mesa-top rock enclosures were found, dating to the Rillito, Rincon, Tanque Verde, and Tucson phases. Because most of the survey was undertaken on the floodplains and terraces, these are the areas identified as having the majority of sites, most attributed to the Rillito phase. Fewer sites were found in the foothills, and were dated to the Rillito or Rincon phases. Frick also noted the presence of cleared areas, indicated by rock piles, in association with Rillito and Rincon phase materials, suggesting the practice of dry farming.

There are few sites of the succeeding Tanque Verde and Tucson phases in the middle Santa Cruz Valley. As noted above, Frick (1954) found some Classic period sites in his survey, most of which lacked architectural features. A Classic period occupation identified at Paloparado closely parallels those in the Tucson Basin to the north in terms of architecture, burial practices and, to some extent, pottery.

Empire Valley

The Empire or Cienega Valley consists of an area of approximately 1300 square kilometers, about 80 km southeast of Tucson. It is bounded on all sides by mountains: on the east are the Whetstone and Mustang mountains, on the south are the Canelo Hills, on the west are the Santa Rita Mountains, and on the north are the Empire Mountains. The primary drainage is Cienega Creek, which flows into Pantano Wash in the Tucson Basin. It is along Cienega Creek and its secondary drainages that most archaeological research in the valley has been conducted.

The earliest documented archaeological work in the valley was done by Byron Cummings of the University of Arizona. In 1926, Cummings excavated two human inhumations, buried 3.6 m below the present surface, along Cienega Creek on the Empire Ranch. These burials may date to the Archaic period (McGregor 1965: 126). Following Cummings' work, Emil W. Haury and various archaeology students, also of the University of Arizona, conducted archaeological surveys during weekend field trips. Between 1937 and 1955, Haury and his students recorded 17 archaeological sites in the Empire Valley, representing occupation of the valley during the Archaic period and the later ceramic period.

Two archaeological projects have provided information on the settlement and subsistence patterns during the ceramic period. These are Swanson's (1951) survey of the valley and Eddy's (1958) survey and excavation at the junction of Cienega Creek and Matty Canyon.

Between 1948 and 1950, Earl Swanson, then a graduate student at the University of Arizona, surveyed and recorded archaeological sites in the Empire Valley watershed and in areas southwest of Sonoita and south of Elgin. His studies resulted in the recording of 18 sites and formed the basis for his Master's thesis (Swanson 1951). It appears that Swanson concentrated his survey along the primary and secondary drainages in the valley (Swanson 1951, Fig. 1).

Swanson compared his survey findings with existing data on ceramic dates, geological associations, and other cultural traits in order to develop a tripartite ceramic period chronology for the Empire Valley. Swanson noted a lack of tradewares during the early period, and consequently did not assign a beginning date to the period. The chronology (Swanson 1951: 48) is presented in Table 1.1.

Two early period sites were found. One site, with a possible pit house, produced an artifact assemblage of milling stones, scraping tools, early Mogollon plain and red wares (none painted), and a dog skeleton which was asociated with the pit house. Bone implements, shell and projectile points were absent. The other site, a surface scatter on a small terrace above Sonoita Creek, contained Dos Cabezas Red-on-brown, San Francisco Red, and Alma Plain, which Swanson considered locally produced. The pit house site probably belongs to the Peñasco phase, and the surface scatter to the Dos Cabezas phase of the San Simon branch of the Mogollon (Sayles 1945) shown in Figure 1.6.

Middle period sites in Empire Valley, in contrast to those of the early period, generally lack Mogollon pottery types; however one site produced some Cascabel Red-on-brown. Another site, above Cienega Creek, is distinguished by Gila Butte Red-on-buff and Gila Plain. Both sites were small, had few pot sherds, and even fewer lithic artifacts (no diagnostic materials), and were assigned to the Cascabel and Gila Butte phases, respectively.

Table 1.1

SWANSON'S EMPIRE VALLEY CHRONOLOGY

Period	Phase	Date	Cultural Affinity
Late	Babocomari	A.D. 1350-1450	Babocomari Village
	Huachuca	A.D. 1150-1350	Babocomari Village
Middle	Cascabel	A.D. 900-1000	Hohokam-Mogollon
	Gila Butte	A.D. 700-900	Hohokam
Early	Dos Cabezas	about A.D. 400	Mogollon
	Peñasco	about A.D. 300	Mogollon

The late period was the time of densest occupation in the Empire Valley. This occupation was attributed to the Babocomari people (Di Peso 1951), and was divided into two phases. Huachuca phase sites, are characterized by an abundance of trade wares (Tucson Polychrome, Gila Polychrome, St. Johns Polychrome, Santa Cruz Polychrome, Trincheras Purple-on-red, Tanque Verde Red-on-brown, and Sells Red) found in association with Babocomari wares (Babocomari Plain and Polychrome). The only extensive site in the valley, located on a terrace above Cienega Creek, dated to this phase. The site contained numerous stone-lined hearths and middens, although it lacked structures. In contrast Babocomari phase sites are small in size, and lack middens or fire hearths, and structures. Artifacts present include trough metates, oblong manos, and keeled scrapers. Of the trade wares so common during the Hauchuca phase, only Tanque Verde Red-on-brown occurs in the Babocomari phase.

Swanson based his phase assignments on the co-occurrence of certain ceramic and chipped stone artifacts and on a certain type of pit house in the Empire Valley that resembled those same artifacts and features in the San Simon area. Because his middle period sites exhibited Gila Butte Red-on-buff and Gila Plain, and Cascabel Red-on-brown, they were assigned to the Gila Butte phase and Cascabel phase, respectively. Neither of the sites of this period contained any distinctive ground or chipped stone tools. For his late period, the association of Phase I and II with the Huachuca and Babocomari phases was possible due to the large number of sites and to the definition of Babocomari wares as indigenous. The Phase I (Huachuca) sites were distinguished from the Phase II (Babocomari) sites by the almost complete lack of trade wares in the latter.

Swanson concluded that settlement and subsistence from the Archaic period through Hohokam Sedentary times were primarily based not on agriculture but rather on the seasonal exploitation of wild food resources along drainages (1951: 49). He also felt that, given an apparently long history of human occupation, and such a large region, "occupation was not particularly heavy" (1951: 17).

In 1956, Frank Eddy, another University of Arizona graduate student, began the fieldwork for his Master's thesis (1958) in a V-shaped, 5-square-kilometer area at the junction of Matty Canyon and Cienega Creek. He recorded 11 sites and conducted some important excavations at Archaic period sites, working closely with geologist M.E. Cooley. This study has only recently been published (Eddy and Cooley 1983).

Eddy was primarily concerned with the interrelationship between culture and environment. In particular, he noted that cultural materials were associated with recent alluvial deposits in the study area. This suggested that the surface available for occupation was gradually rising due to alluviation (and suggests that Swanson's general lack of sites in the area is more apparent than real). Thus, because cultural remains would be vertically spread throughout the alluvial depth, Eddy hoped to be able to identify the order of cultural and environmental events and to reconstruct the environmental setting of the occupations. Using diagnostic artifacts from the archaeological sites, some of which could be cross-dated with types known elsewhere in southern Arizona, the alluvial stratigraphy was correlated with the archaeological remains.

Ceramic period materials in the Cienega Creek Basin represented possible Vahki-Estrella phase through Tanque Verde phase occupations. Recovered ceramics are affiliated with those found in the Tucson Basin, and Eddy used the Tucson Basin cultural sequence in classifying his materials, rather than Swanson's scheme. Eddy identified a shift in settlement pattern in the middle of the Ceramic period. From the earliest phase, Vahki-Estrella, through the Rillito phase, villages and campsites were most frequently located in the floodplains. With the onset of the Rincon phase, and in the succeeding Tanque Verde phase, occupation occurred more often on ridges adjacent to the floodplains.

The subsistence pattern was one of a mixed economy. Hunting, gathering, and small-scale agriculture were practiced. According to Eddy (1958: 104-105), some of the conditions considered favorable for Archaic period hunters and gatherers were actually limiting factors for Hohokam agriculturalists. Factors limiting full-scale agriculture in the Cienega Creek Basin would have been ". . . a shorter growing season, denser growth covering the alluvial flats, restricted floodplain area for farming, and isolation" (Eddy 1958: 105). Eddy also noted that evidence of trade goods is generally absent, suggesting no major surplus of goods and only a limited exchange network.

Finally, in 1972, Noel Walker and Ann Polk, archaeologists for the Arizona State Museum, crossed the eastern part of the Empire Valley

near the Whetstone Mountains on an archaeological survey of the Pantano-
Whetstone 115 kv power transmission line for the Arizona Electrical
Power Cooperative (Walker and Polk 1973). Along this 32-mile-long
strip that passes through the valley, nine archaeological sites were
found. These were divided into four categories: lithic resource sites,
abiotic and biotic resource manipulation sites, and habitation sites.

San Pedro River Valley

The San Pedro River is a major northward-trending tributary of
the Gila River. The river originates some 40 km south of the
international border in Sonora, Mexico and flows for a distance of more
than 240 km to its juncture with the Gila River at Winkelman, Arizona.
The upper portion of the river (south of Benson) has seen virtually no
work at ceramic period sites, but numerous sites of this period have
been excavated in the lower river valley (north of Benson).

A cultural hiatus seems to exist in the lower San Pedro Valley
from the end of the Archaic Cochise culture (about 300 B.C.) to the
arrival of Hohokam immigrants from the Gila River Valley during the
early part of the Christian era. This situation is most likely
artificial, being fostered in part by the paucity of systematic survey
and excavation. It is possible that an early Mogollon population such
as that noted in the nearby San Simon and Sulphur Spring valleys (Sayles
1945) will eventually be found to fill the gap.

The Hohokam appear to have settled in the San Pedro Valley
sometime prior to A.D. 500 (Franklin and Masse 1976). Evidence for this
early occupation consists of Pioneer period ceramics and diagnostic
items such as figurines at at least three large village sites in the
lower San Pedro: Sosa Wash Ruin (AZ BB:11:18), Redington Ruin (AZ
BB:11:2), and the Big Ditch Site (AZ BB:2:2). These three sites are
notable because of their long occupation spans, sizable trash mounds,
and the presence of both "Snaketown" and "Casa Grande" style ball
courts; in these respects are smaller scale models of the Hohokam type
site of Snaketown (Gladwin and others 1937). There is little doubt that
these villages must have served as integrative focal points for the
Pioneer through Sedentary period Hohokam populations in the San Pedro
Valley. While there is no direct evidence for the use of canal
irrigation at these sites, their location near the mouths of tributaries
of the San Pedro River, with their broad fertile floodplains, argues for
a subsistence pattern similar to that practiced in the Gila and Salt
river valleys.

As in other Hohokam areas, late Colonial and Sedentary
occupations are the most numerous in the San Pedro Valley (Masse 1980a).
This period is best known from survey data and the excavations at Alder
Wash Ruin, the Big Ditch Site, Redington Ruin and Second Canyon Ruin.

The Big Ditch Site is one of the largest and longest-lived of
the known Hohokam settlements in the San Pedro Valley. The site was

initially occupied during the Snaketown phase, approximately A.D. 350-550; the major occupation occurred during the following Gila Butte (A.D. 550-750), Santa Cruz (A.D. 750-950), and Sacaton (A.D. 950-1150) phases. On the basis of ceramic evidence, the Santa Cruz phase and possibly the Sacaton phase saw the largest number of occupants spread over the greatest spatial extent of the site. Presumably sometime during the Santa Cruz phase (or possibly the Gila Butte phase), a large, Snaketown-style ballcourt was constructed near the southeast margin of the site. Later, probably during the Sacaton phase, a smaller, Casa Grande-style ballcourt was built near the site center.

During the late Colonial and Sedentary periods, site settlement in the San Pedro Valley shows an interesting correlation between villages and dry farming areas. Literally thousands of acres of dry-farming fields consisting of rock piles, checkdams and contour terraces were found on the second, third, and fourth terraces between Redington and Winkelman by W. Bruce Masse of Southern Illinois University.

Not long after the Hohokam established themselves in the San Pedro River Valley, an amalgamation of the Hohokam and peripheral Mogollon populations may have taken place, producing what has been termed the "Dragoon culture" (Fulton and Tuthill 1940; Tuthill 1947; Fulton 1934a, 1934b, 1938). It is difficult to determine when this supposed cultural blending took place, but it seems to have occurred sometime between A.D. 500 and 800. By A.D. 900, the Dragoon culture, with its distinctive red-on-brown pottery, possible inhumation of the dead, and more deeply excavated pit houses, was established in southeastern Arizona. The nature of the relationship between contemporary groups of the Hohokam and Dragoon cultures has yet to be fully explored, although it appears to have been an amicable one. Whether the Dragoon culture can best be thought of as a named regional variant of Hohokam culture, in the same way that the Tucson Basin Hohokam are viewed as a distinct group within the "Hohokam regional system" (Wilcox 1979a: 78-79), or whether it should be considered part of the San Simon Branch of the Mogollon (Gladwin 1945; Sayles 1945) is probably a moot point.

The close of the Hohokam Sedentary period marked the beginning of a 150-year period (A.D. 1150-1300) of population movements throughout the Southwest and one of extensive changes in previous culture patterns. Unfortunately, this period of time is poorly known in the San Pedro Valley. Of the prehistoric sites which have been excavated and reported on, Alder Wash Ruin (AZ BB:6:9), Una Cholla (AZ BB:6:17), the Big Ditch Site (Masse 1980a), and Second Canyon Ruin (Franklin 1980) all witnessed at least some occupation during the early portion of the Classic period. These cultural manifestations are strikingly similar to contemporaneous developments in other portions of southern and central Arizona. Architecture at those sites is similar to that reported from Tanque Verde phase sites in the Tucson Basin (Zahniser 1966; Fraps 1935). The ceramic assemblages are also similar, although the San Pedro Valley sites contain only small amounts of Tanque Verde Red-on-brown. The latest occupations in the San Pedro Valley, which produced Gila

Polychrome, and are analagous to the Tucson phase in the Tucson Basin, are represented at a number of sites, including Redington Ruin (Duffen 1936; Bradley 1979) and the Reeve Ruin and Davis Ranch Site (Di Peso 1958; Gerald 1975). With the close of these late occupations comes the end of the prehistoric ceramic period in the valley.

Chapter 2

A RESEARCH DESIGN FOR THE ROSEMONT HOHOKAM HABITATION SITES

David A. Gregory and Alan Ferg

The following research design was prepared to guide the investigation of Hohokam sites in the ANAMAX-Rosemont area, and is divided into three parts. The first section presents background information necessary to an understanding of the derivation and character of the sample of Hohokam sites.

The second part defines the four major problem domains to be examined by the project: (1) functional site types and intrasite organization; (2) economy and subsistence; (3) site distribution, population distribution, and intersite organization; and (4) areal and regional relationships. An overview of each problem domain is presented, several specific research questions are posed, and a discussion of the data classes relevant to each problem domain is included.

The third section deals with the methods used to address the research concerns. Both general methods and specific archaeological techniques are discussed in terms of their relationships to the research problems. Site selection, general sampling strategies, field and laboratory techniques, and specialized analyses are all briefly considered.

The Derivation and Character
of the Present Sample of Hohokam Sites

Since the original survey of the ANAMAX-Rosemont area, various modifications to the land-exchange area have occurred and periodic reexamination and reevaluation of the archaeological materials recorded during the survey have been accomplished. These developments determined the universe of sites available and targeted for investigation during the final mitigation phase of the project. A summary of these events is presented below, followed by a discussion of the relevant characteristics of the present sample of sites.

At the completion of the initial survey in 1977, 102 ceramic period archaeological loci had been recorded within the land-exchange area as defined at that time; this total included isolated artifacts (Debowski 1980: 109-111, Fig. 2). Subsequent reevaluation of the survey forms, in conjunction with the preparation of the testing proposal for the land exchange, eliminated a number of loci of questionable character, reducing the recognized number of sites to 89 and isolated artifacts to 4 (Debowski and Huckell 1979: 17). No work was recommended for isolated artifact loci.

By the close of the testing phase excavation and analysis, continued field reexamination of sites in the exchange area determined that 14 of these sites should be eliminated because: (1) they could not be relocated, or had been destroyed; (2) their affiliation with the ceramic period (Hohokam) was doubtful; or (3) these sites were so small or dispersed as to have extremely limited research potential. These 14 were dropped from further consideration, leaving a total of 75 ceramic period sites (Huckell 1980: 258, 275).

Based on the testing phase results, Huckell (1980: 234-283) presented a proposal for final mitigation based on a sampling strategy which took into account the natural topography of the exchange area, the numbers and distributions of sites within the drainage networks, site sizes and artifact densities, and the ways these factors appeared to relate to subsurface features. In essence, this plan suggested excavation of a percentage of sites drawn from each of four site classes based on size and artifact density, within each drainage. The drainage nets of Barrel Canyon and Davidson Canyon contained the majority of archaeological sites of all ages, and all but 2 of the 75 Hohokam sites. Accordingly, Huckell defined the Barrel Canyon and Davidson Canyon Archaeological Districts as the basic units for his proposal. These districts correspond to naturally bounded drainage units, and were likely to be reflected to some extent in the archaeological materials. These districts were also of some utility as managerial tools in that State Route 83 follows almost exactly the divide between the two drainages (Huckell 1980: 234-239). Separate proposals were prepared for each district, since the final land-exchange boundaries had not yet been set. It was believed that a presentation of alternative proposals would aid in such a determination. Most of the sites (59) were located in the Barrel Canyon Archaeological District. An additional 14 sites were located in the Davidson Canyon Archaeological District; the remainder of the 75 sites (2) lie outside district boundaries.

In fact, after consideration of the testing phase report and its proposal and cost estimates, ANAMAX and the Forest Service did reduce the size of the land-exchange, defining it not along archaeological district lines, but along the north-south midlines of Sections 16, 21, 28 and 33 of T18S, R16E and Section 4 of T19S, R16E (Fig. 2.1). This eliminated all 14 of the Davidson Canyon Archaeological District ceramic period sites as well as 12 other sites in the lower end of the Barrel Canyon drainage network and Archaeological District and one nondistrict site. Twenty-seven sites in all were eliminated (Table 2.1), leaving 47

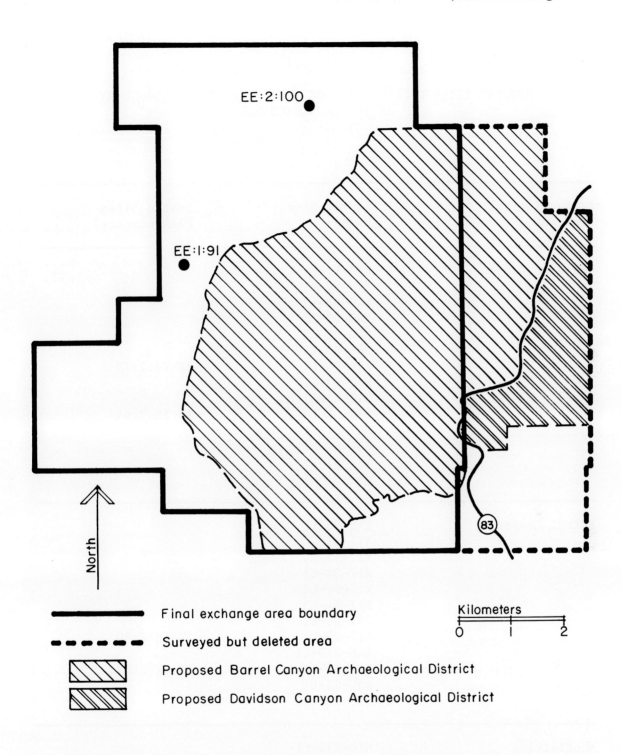

Figure 2.1. Map of the areas surveyed for the ANAMAX-Rosemont land exchange. Parcels surveyed by Huckell (1981a) and Ferg (1981) are included within the final boundary.

Table 2.1

HOHOKAM SITES LOCATED OUTSIDE THE FINAL EASTERN BOUNDARY
OF THE LAND EXCHANGE

Archaeological District	Survey Site Number	Tested Sites (ASM numbers)
Davidson Canyon	X40-S1-L1	
	X40-S2-L1	
	X40-S2-L2	
	X40-S3-L1	
	X40-S3-L2	
	X40-S3-L3	
	X40-S4-L1	AZ EE:2:78
	X40-S7-L1	
	M40-S1-L1	
	M40-S2-L1	AZ EE:2:94
	M41-S1-L1	
	M41-S2-L1	
	X84-S1-L1	
	M32-S1-L1	
Barrel Canyon	X15-S3-L2	
	X17-S1-L7	
	X17-S2-L4	
	X17-S4-L1	
	X17-S4-L2	
	X17-S4-L3	
	X17-S5-L1	
	X17-S7-L1	AZ EE:2:80
	X48-S10-L1	
	X19-S1-L1	AZ EE:2:79
	X52-S2-L1	
	X52-S3-L1	
Nondistrict	H10-S24-L1	

Total Sites = 27

sites in Barrel Canyon and one nondistrict site in the newly defined and substantially reduced land-exchange area.

After the reduction of the eastern portion of the land-exchange aproximately 4 1/2 sections of land were added on the southwest and northern edges. These areas were surveyed and two additional Hohokam sites were recorded (Huckell 1981a; Ferg 1981). Both sites lie outside the Barrel Canyon Archaeological District (Fig. 2.1) and will be discussed in further detail below.

In summary, prior to the preparation of this research design for data recovery at the Hohokam sites, a total of 50 sites had been documented within the present land-exchange area, 47 in the Barrel Canyon Archaeological District, and 3 outside this district.

Prior to the initiation of the mitigation phase, in November 1981, all recorded Hohokam sites were revisited and reevaluated. As with previous site reevaluations, this activity has confirmed the location, description, and research potential of some sites, allowed the elimination of others from consideration, and, in at least one case, considerably altered the assessed reseach potential of a site.

This latter site, AZ EE:2:105, included a previously unrecorded feature which appeared to be a ballcourt. This made the site unique in the exchange area and provided the opportunity to address an interesting set of research questions dealing with the characteristics and functions of this type of feature, the role played by this site in the intersite organization of the area, and the relationship of the Rosemont area to the Tucson Basin, the closest area where other ballcourts have been recorded. The research problems suggested by the presence of the ballcourt are discussed below.

Sites presenting obvious sampling problems were eliminated from the sample to be investigated unless circumstances indicated that they were potentially important in addressing research questions which could not be dealt with at some other site. Such sampling problems include natural or modern, man-made damage so extensive that the research potential of the site was significantly reduced. Three sites exhibiting extensive admixture of cultural materials or features of greatly differing ages, which could compromise the analysis, were also eliminated. Mixture of Hohokam artifactual, floral, and faunal materials with earlier or later materials could present interpretive problems during the analysis of ceramic period data, even though the admixture was known to exist. In addition, funding specialized analyses of samples from such sites would be a questionable allocation of resouces; such analyses would be essentially useless if the sample could not be confidently assigned to a particular component of the site. On the basis of these and other considerations, 13 of the 47 Barrel Canyon Archaeological District sites were removed from further consideration.

Of the three nondistrict sites within the exchange area, only one, AZ EE:1:91, was selected for additional, limited work. It is located outside the Barrel Canyon drainage net, and found to contain unique architectural features of apparent ceramic period age not duplicated elsewhere in the area. Investigations at AZ EE:1:91 are reported by Tagg in the fourth volume of the ANAMAX-Rosemont project series.

In summary then, the sample of sites included 34 in the Barrel Canyon Archaeological District, and 1 additional site, for a total of 35.

Table 2.2 summarizes the basic data from the 34 sites remaining in the Barrel Canyon Archaeological District. They have been broken down into four classes based on the site area and relative surface density (Huckell 1980). The first class (I) is composed of sites which are areally extensive and exhibit relatively dense surface artifact scatters. This class has only a single member, AZ EE:2:105, which has the ballcourt. The second class of sites (II) has four members. These sites are more areally restricted than those in Class I, but still have relatively high surface artifact densities. Testing phase data suggested that Class II sites consisted of several structures and a range of other features. It was not clear whether these sites were occupied on a year-round basis, seasonally, or in some combination of these modes. The 25 sites in the third and largest class (III) are small in area but still exhibit a moderate surface artifact density. It was believed likely that this class of sites was quite variable with respect to the nature of the occupation or use(s) represented, probably ranging from farmsteads of one or two structures to functionally

Table 2.2

SITES IN THE BARREL CANYON ARCHAEOLOGICAL DISTRICT,
BY CLASS AND AREA

Site Class	Huckell's Type	Area (m^2)	Number of Sites
I	H/L	6750	1
II	H/M	1250-2300	4
III	M/S	200-900	25
IV	L/L	1150-7000	4
TOTAL			34

* Artifact density/site area: H = high, M = moderate, L = low or large, S = small

specialized or limited activity loci. The final class of sites (IV) consists of four areally extensive, artifact scatters of extremely low surface density, with or without subsurface features.

As noted above and shown in Table 2.3, most of the sites appeared to fall within the time period bounded by the Rillito and Rincon phases. All of the Class I and II sites as well as eight of the Class III and IV sites produced ceramics dating to these periods. Further, of the 50 sites recorded during the project which produced decorated ceramics, 46 produced Preclassic period Tucson Basin red-on-brown types. Classic period, Tanque Verde Red-on-brown sherds were recorded at only two sites. With the exception of a single sherd of Gila Butte Red-on-buff, all of the few non-Tucson Basin ceramics recovered fall within the period represented by the Rillito and Rincon phases.

In summary, the sample of ceramic period sites is largely contained within a study area which is isomorphic with a naturally bounded drainage unit, the Barrel Canyon network, and which is situated in an upland environment, an environment that has seen little previous archaeological research. With these general characteristics of the sample of sites in mind, we may now turn to the research problems to be addressed.

Problem Domains and Research Questions

The following section presents the problem orientations which served to guide the research of the Hohokam sites. Four general problem domains were defined, with several specific research questions under each domain. General classes of data relevant to each domain were also identified.

The problem domains and research questions defined here were designed to provide organization and direction to the research and were not considered as absolutes. For example, the specific reseach questions posed here are not necessarily viewed as the only ones which might be addressed; alternatively, it could not be stated with absolute certainty that all of the questions listed here would be successfully answered by the reseach. To the degree possible, the problem domains and research questions were tailored to take into account the general character of the sample of sites, the specific information gained during the testing program, and current knowledge concerning relevant archaeological materials from adjacent areas. The problems and questions presented here were designed to provide sufficiently specific direction for the research while allowing the flexibility necessary to most productively respond to the research situation as it might unfold.

It should be pointed out that chronology and chronological problems were not specifically targeted as research problems.

Table 2.3

THE SAMPLING UNIVERSE OF HOHOKAM SITES
BY GROUP, CLASS, AGE, AND AREA

Group	ASM Site Number	Site Class	Huckell's Type	Estimated Age (A.D.)*	Area (m2)
1	AZ EE:2:113	II	H/M	700-1200	2300
	AZ EE:2:129	II	H/M		2300
	AZ EE:2:124	III	M/S	700-1200	810
	AZ EE:2:93	III	M/S		750
	AZ EE:2:84	III	M/S	700-900	700
	AZ EE:2:122	III	M/S		600
	AZ EE:2:125	III	M/S	700-1200	300
2	AZ EE:2:105	I	H/L	700-1350 (?)	6750
	AZ EE:2:77	II	H/M	900-1200	1250
	AZ EE:2:112	III	M/S		700
	AZ EE:2:117	III	M/S		600
	AZ EE:2:121	III	M/S		450
	AZ EE:2:126	III	M/S		340
	AZ EE:2:92	IV	L/L	900-1200	1200
3	AZ EE:1:104	III	M/S	900-1200	700
3a	AZ EE:2:76	II	H/M	700-1000	1350
	AZ EE:2:106	III	M/S		800
	AZ EE:2:120	III	M/S		630
	AZ EE:2:114	III	M/S		510
	AZ EE:2:118	III	M/S		425
	AZ EE:2:110	III	M/S		425
	AZ EE:2:119	III	M/S		250
	AZ EE:2:111	III	M/S		208
	AZ EE:2:123	IV	L/L		1150
	AZ EE:2:52	IV	L/L		6000
3b	AZ EE:1:101	III	M/S	800-1100	300
	AZ EE:1:102	III	M/S	900-1200	800
	AZ EE:2:107	III	M/S		630
	AZ EE:2:108	III	M/S		420
	AZ EE:2:109	III	M/S	700-1200	480
	AZ EE:1:103	IV	L/L		7000
3c	AZ EE:2:115	III	M/S		625
	AZ EE:2:116	III	M/S		630
	AZ EE:2:127	III	M/S		225

* based on surface ceramics

Obviously, questions of chronology are relevant to all of the research problems suggested below, and are an important general problem within Hohokam archaeology (F. Plog 1980; Haury 1980). Samples suitable for dating by chronometric techniques were collected whenever the opportunity presented itself. It was expected that the degree of chronological control necessary for implementation of the research concerns would be gained through temporally diagnostic ceramics and stratigraphic relationships within sites.

Functional Site Types and Intrasite Organization

One principal set of research concerns focused on the nature of prehistoric activities carried out at the sites and on the spatial and social dimensions of the organization of those activities. The major goals were: (1) to determine the range of activities which produced each site and the spatial organization of those activities within the site, and (2) to arrive at a reliable inference concerning the kinds and numbers of social groups which occupied or used each site.

Recent research in Hohokam sites in the Phoenix Basin has demonstrated the utility of the notion of site structure as a basis for inferences about social group size and composition (Wilcox and others 1981; Wilcox and Sternberg 1983; Gregory 1983; Sires 1983; Howard 1982). Further, by focusing on the distribution, size and arrangement of houses, extramural work areas, cremation areas, and trash deposits as recognizable classes of functional space, it is possible to structure the sorting and analysis of artifact assemblages and other materials in terms of behaviorally meaningful units. The application of this analytic perspective provided a means to examine the range and structure of activities once carried out at the sites, as well as a basis for inferences concerning the size and composition of the social groups which once occupied them.

Based on survey data and the results of the testing program, it appeared that site size, the range of past activities undertaken at each site, and the duration and complexity of the occupation or use of those sites would vary considerably within the sample. In addition to providing a context for the interpretation of individual sites, a focus on function and intrasite organization supplied information relevant to the other major problem domains discussed below.

The following specific research questions relating to functional site types and intrasite organization were posed:

1. What was the range of activities carried out at the site?

2. What degree and manner of patterning may be demonstrated in the distribution of features and artifacts at the site?

3. Can functionally distinct areas be identified; if so, how
    are they distributed over the site area?

4. What may be inferred about the size and composition of the
    social groups that occupied or used the site?

5. What patterns of change may be seen in the kinds of
    activities carried out at the site during its occupation or
    use?

6. What patterns of change may be seen in the number and kinds
    of social groups occupying or using the site?

and, with specific reference to the Ballcourt Site, AZ EE:2:105:

7) What role did the ballcourt play in the organization of
    space within this site?

8) What evidence is there for the existence of differential
    social status between the groups occupying this site?

Relevant Data Classes

To a large degree, the questions posed above could be addressed
with the basic data recovered in the course of the excavation of the
respective sites. Mapping of the distribution of houses, work areas,
cremations, and trash areas, and plotting various artifact class
distributions provided data relevant to these questions and were part of
the basic investigative procedures used at the sites.

Perhaps the most important implication of a concern with these
questions lies in the realm of site selection and sampling of individual
sites. The ability to examine the spatial relationships between houses
and other features within a site, for example, requires broad horizontal
exposures and relatively complete excavation of site areas, and, in
order to compare such distributions successfully, a sufficient sample of
the range of site types present in the sample must be excavated. Thus,
while the specific kinds of data needed to explore these questions would
be produced in the course of excavating the individual sites, this focus
required that a sufficient number of sites from each class, and a
sufficient sample of each of those sites be excavated. These concerns
are addressed in the section on methods.

Economy and Subsistence

Because of the upland setting of the project area, an
environment which has seen little archaeological research in the Hohokam
area, a major focus of the research concerned ecological aspects of the

Hohokam occupation. Previous research conducted in the Tucson Basin and along the middle Santa Cruz drainage has demonstrated that these people were sedentary or semisedentary agriculturalists. Seasonal gathering activities and hunting were apparently also important parts of their subsistence, and it is quite certain that the Hohokam system was more varied and complex than can be documented on the basis of present evidence. This is due in part to the skewing of previous research toward sites in the Lower Sonoran Life-Zone.

While the exploitation of montane resources has been suspected or suggested (Doyel 1977a), traditional belief has limited it to short-term foraging for wild foodstuffs, by small groups. The survey data as well as the results of the testing program suggested that the Hohokam exploitation of the ANAMAX-Rosemont areas was more substantial than this, and probably included as an important aspect the cultivation of domesticated crops. One major goal of a concern with the prehistoric economy was the specification of the nature of the Hohokam adjustment to this upland environment. By accomplishing this goal, the research could make a substantial contribution to understanding the overall nature of Hohokam subsistence-settlement systems on a regional scale. This potential contribution was recognized by Doyel during the initial survey of the project area:

> An additional aspect of the regional system which deserves
> attention are the mountain zones . . . work in progress by the
> Arizona State Museum in the Santa Rita Mountains has recorded a
> number of Rincon phase sites in higher elevations . . . future
> studies of these areas should be seen as critical to the
> interpretation of the total settlement system (Doyel 1977a: 98).

Since the ANAMAX-Rosemont survey, survey and excavation in the Tortolita Mountains by Pima Community College (Hewitt and Stephen 1981) have demonstrated a similar situation and reemphasized the integral nature of mountainous areas to the overall Hohokam settlement pattern.

Thus the project provided an opportunity to create a greatly expanded and more precise conception of the prehistoric Hohokam economy and subsistence strategies for the relevant time periods. Two separate but interrelated concerns were identified. These are: first, the nature of the environment during the prehistoric occupation and the elements of that environment which could have been exploited by the inhabitants; and second, the segments of the prehistoric environment which were actually used and the methods by which this was accomplished. In the context of these concerns, the following specific research questions were posed:

1. What is the range of natural resources, including arable land and water, which would have been available to the prehistoric inhabitants of the area? What is the distribution of these resources?

2.   What is the range of vegetable foodstuffs in evidence at each of the sites? What do these materials suggest concerning the relative importance of cultivated versus wild foods at each of the sites? Over the entire sample of sites? What temporal variability in the occurrence of vegetable foodstuffs may be shown?

3.   What is the range of animal resources present at each of the sites? Over the entire sample of sites? What do these materials suggest about the relative importance of animal resources at each of the sites? Over the entire sample of sites? What temporal variability in the occurrence of animal resources may be shown?

4)   What is the distribution of sites relative to the probable former distribution of natural resources? What correlations may be shown between the distributions of the various functional site types and the distributions of particular resources or sets of resources? What temporal variability may be shown to exist in these relationships?

5)   What evidence exists for the seasonal occupation of sites? To what extent may this seasonality be related to subsistence activities?

6)   To what extent may the occupation of the ANAMAX-Rosemont area be argued to be a self-contained subsistence-settlement system?

Relevant Data Classes

Much of the basic information concerning the ecological aspects of the Hohokam occupation was anticipated as a result of the variety of environmental samples taken from each of the sites, including pollen and flotation samples, and faunal materials. Examination of site distribution relative to available natural resources also contributed to an understanding of prehistoric subsistence practices.

Site Distribution, Population Distribution, and Intersite Organization

Both the range of site types represented in the sample of Hohokam sites and the relatively small size of the study area, with its natural boundaries, suggested that sites which were occupied contemporaneously would have been related in some way. Several features of the sample of sites, the occupation of most of them during either the Rillito or Rincon or both phases, the presence of a ballcourt at one site, and the potentially meaningful spatial clustering of those sites into three distinct groups (Fig. 2.2), suggested that systemic relationships between contemporaneous sets of sites were a feature of the Hohokam occupations. If ballcourts were indeed the focus of some sort of community ritual (Wilcox and Sternberg 1983), then the entire population of the area might, at least during some periods, have functioned as a single, dispersed community. A social unit analogous to Doyel's (1980) irrigation community might in fact be represented-- although existing under entirely different environmental circumstances and focusing on pursuits other than canal irrigation-based agriculture.

The interrelationships which may have existed between the sites and the social groups thus represented might be examined by first documenting the distribution of various site types and relating these site types to the distribution of the Hohokam population. Obviously, not all sites were considered loci of permanent population units, since seasonality and other modes of functional variability within the sample of sites was probable (Gregory 1975). Determining the nature of the sites with respect to some of these variables was a goal of both the preceding problem domains, and the answers to those questions should provide a firm basis for inferences regarding population distribution.

Patterning in both the distribution of functional site types and in the inferred distribution of population might be used to interpret the degree and character of intersite organization within the project area. Several specific research questions dealing with intersite relationships were posed:

1. What was the distribution of functional site types during the period(s) of occupation? What patterning may be seen in these distributions and how did these patterns change through time?

2. What was the distribution of population during the period(s) of occupation? What patterns may be seen in the distribution of population and how do these patterns change through time?

3. What is the distribution of population relative to the Ballcourt Site, AZ EE:2:105? To what degree was this site the central focus of the occupation of the study area?

4. What levels of community structure may be identified within the study area? To what degree did contemporaneous sites in the study area constitute a single system? What was the history of the development of that system?

Relevant Data Classes

The primary source of data relating to questions of population distribution and intersite organization is relational in character and

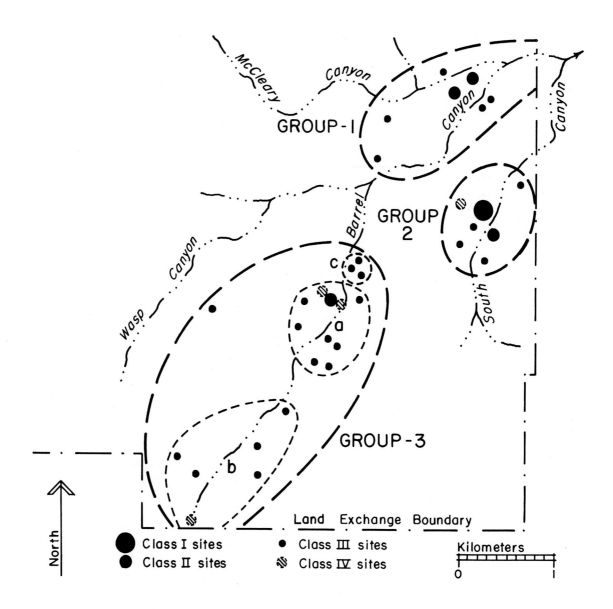

Figure 2.2. Map of the southeastern portion of the exchange area, showing the relative positions of the sites, by class and proposed geographic group.

was represented by the plotting of various kinds of information on maps of the study area. The examination of the research questions posed above depended largely on the results of the analyses proposed under the first two problem domains.

Areal and Regional Relationships

It was apparent from the existing data that the Hohokam occupation sequence in the ANAMAX-Rosemont area is much shorter than those which are apparent in adjacent areas. The available information suggested that the occupation of the area was largely restricted to the Rillito and Rincon phases and, as these phase designations suggest, showed close affiliations with Tucson Basin populations. Thus the Hohokam occupation of the area was presumably the result of movement of populations from the nearby Tucson Basin during the Rillito and Rincon phases.

From the culture histories of areas adjacent to the ANAMAX-Rosemont area, and of areas farther afield, it is clear that the Hohokam regional system achieved its greatest areal extent during the late Colonial and Sedentary periods (Wilcox 1979a; Wilcox and Sternberg 1983). It is probably not coincidental that the occupation of the study area occurred primarily during these times, and it is of great interest that a ballcourt was constructed in the area. One concern of the proposed research was a fuller understanding of the areal and regional context in which the occupation of the study area occurred, with a focus on identifying the nature of the relationships between the ANAMAX-Rosemont populations and those known to have been in place elsewhere during the same time periods. Such a concern also had obvious implications for understanding why the area was occupied originally, and why it ceased to be occupied during later periods.

The following specific research questions were then posed:

1. What is the range, frequency, and distribution of items of nonlocal origin in the ANAMAX-Rosemont area? Within individual sites? What factors, for example site function, social status, exchange, and so forth, were responsible for producing those distributions?

2. What mechanisms may be inferred to account for the presence of these items of nonlocal origin in the study area?

3. What processes were occurring in adjacent areas which may have been factors in the Rillito-Rincon focus of occupation in the ANAMAX-Rosemont area?

4) To what degree may a cultural boundary be shown to have existed between the Tucson Basin and the adjacent areas to the east and south, including the upper San Pedro drainage

and the Empire Valley? What was the nature of that boundary
and what factors may be inferred to have been important in
its creation and maintenance?

Relevant Data Classes

As is suggested by the above research questions, two very
different sets of data were important in the examination of areal and
regional relationships. The first includes those nonlocal materials
which were recovered from the Hohokam sites. The variety, frequency,
and distribution of such items as shell, lithic material unavailable
locally, and intrusive ceramics provided a basis for assessing the
nature and extent of trade relationships with other groups.

Aside from the specific documentation and analysis of nonlocal
items in the material culture inventory, the examination of areal and
regional relationships was largely a synthetic and comparative exercise
based on the total range of data recovered from the project area and on
the available data from adjacent areas. The specific analyses which
would form the basis for this synthesis and comparison were dependent
upon and designed around the materials actually recovered from the
Rosemont Hohokam sites, but it was predicted that such variables as
population and settlement distribution, subsistence strategies, and both
intercommunity and intracommunity organization would be examined in a
comparative context and on an areal and regional scale.

Methods

Site Selection

Amassing the kinds of data needed to adequately address the
questions posed in the research design depended in large part on the
sites examined being virtually or actually intact. With a few
qualifications, the 34 sites in the sampling universe of Hohokam sites
were intact or possessed some feature which justified their further
consideration. Given that among these sites there was some homogeneity,
or repetition, of archaeological information (as was indicated by both
survey and testing phase data), and that it was therefore neither
necessary nor desirable to excavate all of them, how should those sites
to be excavated be selected? The method used was a modification of that
suggested by Huckell (1980), necessitated by the deletion of the lower
end of the Barrel Canyon drainage from the exchange area, the deletion
of additional sites based on their limited research potential, and the
identification of a previously unrecorded ballcourt within the exchange
area.

Huckell (1980, Fig. 53) divided the Barrel Canyon Archaeological District into seven drainage segments: Wasp, McCleary, Scholefield, and South canyons, and upper, middle and lower Barrel Canyon. Using a sampling procedure which incorporated both probabilistic and nonprobabilistic methods, he selected a percentage of sites from each of his artifact density-site area classes for excavation (Huckell 1980: 258-265).

With the last change in the land exchange boundary, all sites in the Scholefield and Lower Barrel Canyon segments were lost. With the various deletions of low reseach potential sites, all but three of the original "low density" sites were eliminated from consideration. Huckell (1980: 264-265) noted the probable lower research potential of this class of sites (based on testing phase results), and accordingly reduced the proposed level of effort for that class; the subsequent drastic reduction in their numbers further skewed his proposal.

Finally, the discovery of a ballcourt by Huckell during a revisitation of AZ EE:2:105 reinforced the impression gained from the distribution of large, high density and medium-sized, high density sites that several large village sites in the exchange area appeared to have smaller satellite sites around them. Three such groups of a large site (Class I or II) and related smaller sites (Class II, III or IV) were posited for the Barrel Canyon sites, and are referred to here as Groups 1, 2, and 3 (Fig. 2.2, Table 2.3). The hypothesized extent and composition of each group was to some extent subjective, but was based on the geographic spacing of the sites.

Groups 1, 2, and 3, and the possible smaller clusterings of sites within Group 3, served as an alternative to Huckell's drainage segments, providing groups of sites from which samples of each site class could be drawn. None of the four low density, Class IV sites were initially targeted for investigation, but all were revisited, reevaluated, and considered for testing, during the mitigation field phase.

The Ballcourt Site (Class I) was scheduled for intensive excavation, as a thorough knowledge of its intrasite organization was considered essential to interpretation of Group 2 in particular, and the Rosemont area in general. All four Class II sites, one of which is adjacent to the Ballcourt Site, and one of which may be the nuclear site for Group III, were also targeted for intensive investigation.

Initially, one Class III site from each of the geographic groups (including the possible subgroups within Group 3) was to be excavated (Table 2.4). AZ EE:1:104, the only Group 3 site which was not part of a subgroup, was not originally targeted for excavation (although it was ultimately excavated).

The results of the excavation of these sites were then used to guide the selection of additional sites for excavation, based on two

Table 2.4

ROSEMONT HOHOKAM HABITATION SITES SELECTED FOR EXCAVATION,
BY GEOGRAPHIC GROUP AND SITE CLASS

Geographic Group	Sites Selected for Excavation*				N of Sites Excavated	N of Sites Present
	I	II	III	Total		
1	0	2	1	3	4	7
2	1	1	1	3	3	6
3	0	0	0	0	1	1
3a	0	1	1	2	3	8
3b	0	0	1	1	2	5
3c	0	0	1	1	1	3
Total	1	4	5	10	14	30

* by site class

criteria: observed or inferred intersite and intrasite patterning, and the apparent validity of the proposed geographic groups.

In summary, 10 of 34 sites (29%) were initially planned for excavation. Ultimately, the number of sites fully investigated included 4 additional Class III sites, for a total of 14 sites (41%) examined, as shown in Table 2.4. Testing and limited excavations were undertaken at another 5 sites (Chapter 3).

Intrasite Sampling

Again, in order to address the reseach questions raised, not only should the sites examined be intact (as discussed under Site Selection above), but at least some of the sites had to be totally excavated, in the sense that all features would be located and sampled, if not entirely excavated. In particular, the determination of size, shape, orientation, presence or absence of internal features, and age of all structures was critical. The bulk of the nine sites selected for initial attention would be excavated, testing extensively and systematically for features and, where found, opening up broad horizontal exposures around and between them. Thereafter, the intrasite sampling strategy would be based upon any patterning or lack of patterning of features observed at these nine sites, and between sites of the same size class or geographic group.

General Field Techniques

The field methods and excavation techniques used during the final mitigation phase were in large part the same as those employed during the testing phase (Huckell 1980). Proveniencing was done using 4-m-by-4-m grid systems, with the southwest corners serving as the datum for the site and for individual squares. If natural stratigraphy was not discernible, vertical excavation followed arbitrary levels of varying depths, as appropriate to the type of feature being excavated.

Excavations at AZ EE:2:76, EE:2:77, and EE:2:84 were begun during the testing phase; they were completed using only hand excavation of grid squares. AZ EE:1:104, also investigated during the testing phase, was completed using both backhoe trenching and hand excavation. With one exception, all other sites examined were first trenched with a backhoe, usually at 4-m or 8-m intervals; habitation areas were then excavated by hand, in 4-m-by-4-m grid units. AZ EE:2:109 was excavated entirely by hand, because it was inaccessible to the backhoe.

Regardless of whether grids, trenches or both were to be utilized, the placement of excavation units was nonprobabilistic, in that the desired effect was the discovery of all features, not just a representative sample thereof.

All excavated feature fill was passed through one-quarter-inch or finer mesh screens; screening of cultural overburden within grid squares was optional at the discretion of the field supervisor. Standard ASM excavation and feature forms were completed for all excavated areas, and all sites were mapped with an alidade and plane table. Complete photographic records were kept, including 35 mm color slides and 2-1/4 by 2-1/4 black-and-white prints.

Specialized Sampling

Environmental and subsistence-related materials were collected or sampled only in culturally meaningful units such as features or occupation surfaces. This included pollen and flotation samples, charcoal (for species identification), and animal bone. Grinding implements such as manos and metates, found in situ, were often bagged for pollen washes. Some nonsite areas which could have been agricultural areas were sampled for pollen.

Potentially datable materials were collected when appropriate, including charcoal (for either radiocarbon or tree-ring dating) and archaeomagnetic samples.

Chapter 3

SITE DESCRIPTIONS

Alan Ferg

During the investigation of Hohokam sites in the ANAMAX-Rosemont area, 14 habitation sites were intensively investigated, 2 more were trenched, and isolated features were dug in 3 other locations, all within the Barrel Canyon drainage system (Fig. 3.1). All the habitation sites were occupied for various lengths of time between approximately A.D. 500 and 1200, that is, from sometime during the Cañada del Oro phase to the end of the Rincon or the beginning of the Tanque Verde phase. Numbers of features found and excavated at each site are presented in Table 3.1. Four of these sites (AZ EE:1:104, EE:2:76, EE:2:77, and EE:2:84) were first examined during the testing phase in 1979; virtually all testing phase materials were reanalyzed with those recovered during the mitigation phase. Other habitation sites examined during the testing phase fell outside the final land-exchange boundary. These were reported elsewhere (Huckell 1980) and are not reexamined here except in the broader areal discussions in Chapters 9 and 10.

Site descriptions are often utilized not only for the primary presentation of raw data, but also interpretations and syntheses, complete in and of themselves. However, the scope of this chapter is restricted specifically to brief, summary presentations of: (1) feature and artifact data, (2) information bearing on the dating of individual features and the site as a whole, and (3) information bearing on the sequence of construction and abandonment of features. Each description includes a site map, selected feature maps, a list of feature and subfeature numbers assigned, and summary tables listing artifacts recovered, the contents and dating of all structures, and temporally diagnostic decorated pottery by provenience.

Environment

The natural environment of the project area in general has been discussed in varying detail in Chapter 1, in the first volume of the ANAMAX-Rosemont report series (Huckell 1984a), and elsewhere (Davis and Callahan 1977; Ferg and Huckell 1983). Those aspects of the environment which are particularly important to the Hohokam occupation are discussed

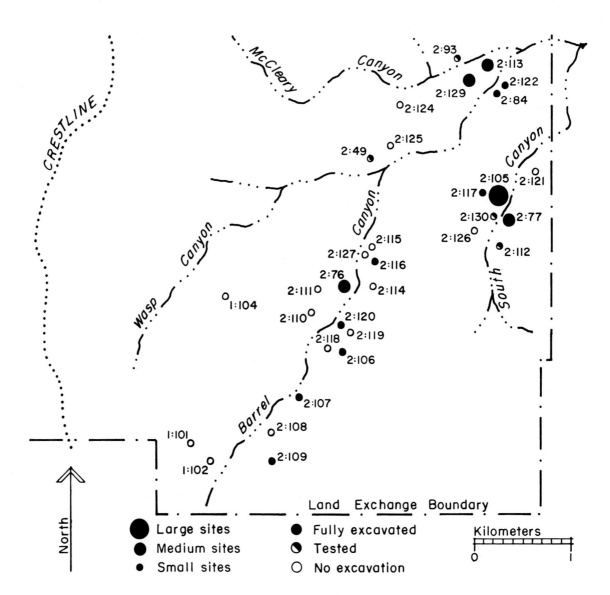

Figure 3.1   Southeastern portion of the ANAMAX-Rosemont land exchange area showing the recorded Hohokam sites by site number and treatment.

Table 3.1

EXCAVATION DATA, HOHOKAM HABITATION SITES,
ANAMAX ROSEMONT MITIGATION PROJECT

Site Number	Habitation Area (m²)	Machine Stripping (m²)	Hand Stripping (m²)	Trenches (m)	Percent of Site Stripped	Cremations/Inhumations (excavated)	Extramural Features (excavated/unexcavated)	House Pits/Pit Houses (excavated)	Number of Excavated Features	Person Days	Hand Excavation (m²) Per Person Day
AZ EE:2:49	–	0	0	10	–	0/0	1/0	0/0	1	1	–
AZ EE:2:52	–	0	0	0	–	0/1	0/0	0/0	1	2	–
AZ EE:2:76	1348	0	420	0	31	23/5	48/26	8/17	92	270	1.56
AZ EE:2:77	822	0	496	0	60	6/2	49/0	7/9	66	163	3.04
AZ EE:2:84	576	0	197	0	34	1/0	16/5	4/4	21	86	2.29
AZ EE:1:104	718	88	57	224	20	0/0	2/0	2/2	4	32	1.78
AZ EE:2:105	6970	75	1205	900	18	4/2	36/72	27/32	67	460	2.62
AZ EE:2:106	1020	0	131	300	13	0/0	5/1	5/5	10	53	2.47
AZ EE:2:107	752	0	270	222	36	2/3	6/0	5/5	16	99	2.73
AZ EE:2:109	977	0	261	27	0	0/0	4/1	5/5	9	79	3.30
AZ EE:2:112	–	0	0	62	–	0/0	0/0	0/0	0	1½	–
AZ EE:2:113	1881	0	950	218	51	14/9	104/110	8/14	141	372	2.55
AZ EE:2:116	1159	0	376	12	32	0/0	0/0	2/3	3	81	4.67
AZ EE:2:117	1454	0	147	204	10	0/0	13/2	2/2	15	61	2.43
AZ EE:2:120	573	0	184	113	32	2/0	4/0	6/7	13	70	2.63
AZ EE:2:122	386	0	54	168	14	1/0	3/0	2/2	6	23	2.35
AZ EE:2:129	1819	100	260	627	20	0/0	14/0	2/4	18	110	2.36
AZ EE:2:130	–	0	0	220	–	0/0	0/0	3/?	–	1½	–
AZ EE:2:136	–	0	0	0	–	0/0	1/1	0/0	1	1	–

below, but the natural setting of each site is not described in detail.
Ceramics, chipped stone, utilitarian and nonutilitarian ground stone,
shell, architecture, site organization, site settlement, mortuary
practices, and the various biological samples collected are all given
detailed treatment in other chapters of this volume, and are treated
with concomitant brevity in the following site descriptions. General
environmental comments, excavation methodology, and the feature
classifications employed are presented below.

Sixteen of the 19 sites examined, including all known habitation
sites, were located on ridgetops. The remaining three sites (AZ EE:2:49,
EE:2:52, and EE:2:136) were located in or immediately above the floodplain of Barrel Canyon and had been exposed by arroyo cutting, road
grading, and the creation of a borrow pit, respectively. The exposed
features, all roasting pits, were excavated; no large-scale, systematic
excavations were carried out. Thus, while drainage floodplains were
utilized for some activites, the project encountered no evidence of
structures anywhere except on ridgetops. The primary focus of village
life was on elevated, relatively flat settings, with more specialized or
restricted activities taking place in other topographic settings, as
clearly indicated by the results of the testing and mitigation phase
excavations.

Virtually all the ridges in question consist of an alluvial
gravel, cobble, and boulder substrate dissected by Barrel Canyon and its
tributaries. Sandy loams of mixed alluvial, eolian, organic, and
cultural origin, resting on argillic or calcic soil horizons, contained
the cultural materials. The excavated sites are located on relatively
flat-topped ridges ranging from 35 m to 1000 m in length and from 8 m to
60 m in width.

Water is relatively abundant in the Rosemont area in the form of
numerous permanent springs, seasonal streams, and rain fall. As a
result, the availability of water appears to have been a relatively
unimportant factor in site selection during the ceramic period.

The land-exchange area is heavily dissected; virtually all
ridges are immediately adjacent to floodplains of varying width and soil
depth. This factor is also responsible for the extensive, thorough
interfingering of soil types, three of the four main vegetation
communities (Fig. 1.2), and their attendant animal species throughout
the area at elevations below about 5400 feet; the limestone scrub
community is found at higher elevations. So, while the occupants of
each site would have had access to a host of highly localized, slightly
varying niches, the full range of faunal and floral resources and arable
land settings would, in a general sense, have been equally available to
all. Obviously, individual species occur in greater quantities in
particular microenvironments (for instance, mule deer and white-tailed
deer have differing habitat preferences, pinyons are more abundant at
higher elevations, and so forth), but the inhabitants of all sites would
have had access to resources of all kinds.

As McLaughlin and Van Asdall note:

Woodland occurs on north-facing slopes at most elevations and in
the drainages at the higher elevations. . . . Grassland occurs
on ridge tops and xeric slopes. . . . Riparian gallery forests
occupy low-elevation washes and have a dense cover of primarily
deciduous trees and shrubs (1977: 81, 87).

In essence, one can cross three vegetation communities by simply walking
from one ridgetop to the next, across a wash bottom, at any of the lower
elevations in the exchange area. While the distribution of these
communities was probably somewhat different during the Hohokam
occupation, the mosaic character of the area has probably not changed.

Excavation Methods

Specific excavation techniques used at all sites, during both
the testing and mitigation phases, were essentially the same.
Horizontal provenience was recorded within the framework of a 4-m-by-4-m
grid system laid out over the site, with one axis aligned with the long
axis of the ridgetop, regardless of compass orientation. The grid
system origin (NOEO), which served as the site datum, was located in or
just outside the southwestern portion of the site, so that excavations
would be contained within the northeast quadrant. Each grid was
identified by the Cartesian coordinates of its southwest corner.

Although it was convenient for practical reasons, the alignment
of the grid systems with topography rather than magnetic north resulted
in some confusion in the field, especially in determining which side of
a grid or quadrant should be identified with a particular cardinal
direction for proveniencing. Thus, although the topographic situation
suggested the grid layout, hindsight indicates that a grid system
aligned to magnetic north would have been preferable.

Vertical provenience was recorded as a distance below modern
ground surface rather than below an arbitrary, fixed elevational datum.
This was done in order to excavate the sites and analyze the assemblages
in units which, though not exactly natural stratigraphic units, had some
depositional integrity. Although the testing phase had shown vertical
stratigraphy to be absent in the Rosemont sites, it had also shown that:
(1) virtually all features were excavated into the argillic or calcic
sterile soils of the ridges, and (2) the thickness of the cultural fill
covering sterile was quite uniform over entire site areas, even those on
ridges with marked slopes. Therefore, measurements of depth below
surface identified the same depositional stratum at any point on the
site, whereas arbitrary elevation measurements would only create a more
complicated data record, particularly on sites on sloping ridges. When
required, relative elevations of different grid units were extrapolated
from contour maps.

Redeposited, weathered artifacts were observed on the slopes
surrounding the ridges. This material was not systematically sampled;

however, prior to the start of excavations, decorated sherds, projectile points, and ground stone and shell artifacts were collected. The sherds and points were potentially useful temporal indicators. Ground stone was collected in an effort to identify an easily recorded surface attribute which was positively correlated with the numbers of structures and features found by excavation. The usefulness of the survey data would have been significantly improved if some such predictive factor could have been identified; however, no such correlation was found. Surface collections at sites with the same number of structures produced wildly varying amounts of ground stone. Of all the habitation sites, only AZ EE:2:130 produced no surface ground stone, although trenching at that site revealed three house pits (the site was not excavated further). In contrast, AZ EE:2:112 did have surface ground stone, but trenching revealed no subsurface features.

The intensive surface collection of transects and the plotting of areas containing multiple classes of artifacts (ceramics, chipped stone, ground stone, shell, and bone), which proved relatively accurate for prediction of the site type and subsurface boundaries on the Salt-Gila Aqueduct (SGA) Project (Teague 1982a), was considered to some extent both impractical and unnecessary, at the Rosemont sites. A similar use of artifact class proportions will be attempted later in this volume, using the excavated artifact assemblage. Given the small size and restricted topographic setting of the Rosemont sites, boundaries were readily determined by visual inspection, and later refined by the use of systematic backhoe trenching.

With site boundaries relatively well defined, the mitigation phase excavations focused on locating all structures on a site and opening up as large an exposure of the prehistoric ground surface as time permitted. To this end, both 4-m-by-4-m hand excavations and backhoe trenching were systematic and nonrandom. Those sites examined during the testing phase (AZ EE:1:104, EE:2:76, EE:2:77, and EE:2:84) were among the first excavated during the mitigation phase. With the knowledge of stratigraphy and specific feature locations gained from the testing, these sites were excavated by hand, with excavation units placed as necessary to completely outline features, and to cover the habitation area in such a way that all structures would be located.

The ultimate extent and placement of excavations varied from site to site. At AZ EE:2:77 hand excavation eventually encompassed virtually the entire habitation area. At AZ EE:2:116, units were placed in a uniform checkerboard pattern over the habitation area, while at AZ EE:2:76, EE:2:84, and EE:2:109, placement and expansion of excavation units was more judgmental, but complete in its coverage. Backhoe trenching was first used on the largest sites (AZ EE:2:105, EE:2:113 and EE:2:129), as proposed in the research design (Gregory and Ferg 1982; Chapter 2, this volume). Trenches were placed at 8-m intervals, and, occasionally, at 4-m intervals, when additional information was needed.

The stratigraphy of the Rosemont sites influenced these decisions. As noted in the environmental discussion above, all the ridges were capped with orange or whitish sterile soil horizons into

which virtually all prehistoric features were dug. Feature fill was
consistently homogeneous, very dark gray or black in color, and
contrasted sharply with feature walls or floors. As a result, hand
excavation was a relatively straightforward proposition involving
stripping the overburden to expose the sterile horizon, then excavating
the dark outlines which remained. These outlines were, in general,
quite "crisp," often clearly showing feature dimensions and orientations
before the fill was removed (Fig. 3.2). Therefore, the use of backhoe
trenching as an initial exploratory device, originally planned only for
AZ EE:2:105, EE:2:113, and EE:2:129, was subsequently used at the
remainder of the small sites examined, AZ EE:1:104, EE:2:106, EE:2:107,
EE:2:112, EE:2:117, EE:2:120, EE:2:122, and EE:2:130. Because of the
notable contrast between sterile and fill, the undesirable effects of
trenching were largely avoidable. The backhoe operator consistently
felt the change in soil upon hitting the edge of a house pit about the
same time that (if not sooner than) the monitoring archaeologist spotted
the change in soil color. Consequently, the depth of the trench was
decreased and only rarely were pit house floors damaged. The skill,
length of experience in the Tucson area, and genuine interest of the
backhoe operator should also be cited as a factor in this success.

Machine stripping, using a front-end loader, was done at four
sites. At AZ EE:1:104, EE:2:105, and EE:2:129 (eastern area) small
areas were bladed to sterile to rapidly expose several pit house
outlines. At AZ EE:2:113, and between Trenches 2 and 16 at AZ EE:2:129,
about 20 cm of the thick cultural overburden were bladed off the site
areas to save excavation time, leaving from 10 cm to 30 cm of soil
covering the features and sterile. This layer was then stripped by
hand.

Initial plans called for screening a sample of the cultural
overburden, but in the first two weeks of excavation it became clear
that, except directly above features, very few artifacts were being
recovered from this stratum. Screening of stripping units was then
abandoned, although artifacts found in the course of stripping were
still collected. Feature fill was screened through one quarter-inch or
finer mesh, with the exception of occasional postholes, which were
troweled out, and the fill carefully inspected before discard.

All cremation deposits and inhumations found were fully
excavated. When it was impossible to excavate all extramural features,
efforts were made to excavate a representative sample. All house pits
were completely or partially excavated at all sites except AZ EE:2:105
and AZ EE:2:130. At AZ EE:2;105, 21 of 27 found were investigated; at
AZ EE:2:130, three house pits were found by trenching, but the site was
not subsequently excavated due to the dictates of project scheduling.
In most cases, one-half to two-thirds of each house was excavated to
floor, an area sufficient to include the entryway and locate the hearth,
if one was present and centered behind the entryway (as in Fig. 3.2) as
was usually the case. Superimposed structures and structures unusual in
size or character received more attention and were often entirely
excavated.

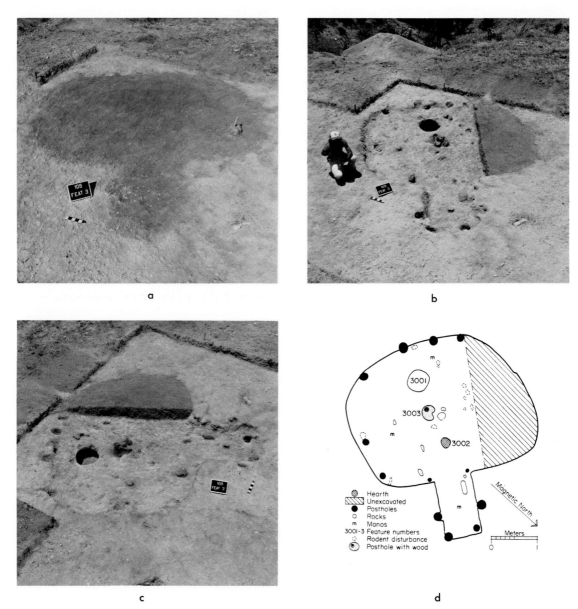

Figure 3.2   Feature 3 pit house at AZ EE:2:109. a, Overburden removed showing clear outline of structure; b, after excavation as viewed from same location as a; c, after excavation as viewed from another direction; d, map of structure. Note the numbering of the subfeatures and the symbols used to designate the various types of subfeatures.

Table 3.1 presents excavation data and effort figures for all the sites examined during the mitigation phase. The boundaries of habitation areas were estimated using the known distributions of features, and their relation to the level portions of the ridgetops. Although the habitation area figures do not include trash areas on the ridge slopes, most are probably somewhat generous in their inclusion of the break-in-slope areas on ridgetop margins. Figures for the sites with few, dispersed features, located on large, flat ridge midsections may be the least accurate, in that clearly defined habitation areas are lacking. AZ EE:2:116 and AZ EE:2:117 are extreme examples of this problem. Finally, this probable overestimation of habitation areas and the strict definition of excavated area (only those segments of trenches surrounded by hand-stripped areas were included) suggest that the figures in Column 6 are probably somewhat low. AZ EE:2:77 and EE:2:113, for example, are more completely excavated than their 60 and 51 percent figures suggest. Also, the percentage of the site stripped is not synonymous with the percentage of the site investigated. In the framework of the research goals, all the habitation sites are considered fully investigated. With one exception, all structures on each site were located either by hand or machine work. Only AZ EE:2:105 had to be sampled.

Person-days includes both crew and supervisory personnel time, as well as volunteer time. Area excavated by hand per person-day ranges from 1.56 to 4.67, with an average of 2.63. The low figure for AZ EE:2:76 is undoubtedly the result of the considerable time expended in screening dirt from stripping units. At AZ EE:1:104, the low figure reflects the fact that virtually all time on the site was spent in digging structures. The extremely high figure at AZ EE:2:116 is doubtless a result of the fairly shallow overburden (10 cm to 15 cm) and the fact that no extramural features were encountered. The high figures at AZ EE:2:77 and EE:2:109 are less easily explained; the relatively simple nature of both sites (few superimposed features, shallow overburden) and the fact that both were dug early in the 5-1/2 month span of the fieldwork may have been factors.

Comparison with excavation rates at habitation sites on the SGA Project (Teague and Crown 1981: 14; Teague and Hull 1982: 13) indicates that excavation rates were about equal: an average of 2.3 square meters per person-day on SGA, and 2.63 square meters per person-day on ANAMAX-Rosemont. Site depth and density of features will obviously affect these calculations, but the excavation rate of one cubic meter per person per day noted on SGA as a rule-of-thumb estimate appears to hold in the Santa Ritas as well.

Terms and Procedures Used in Data Presentation

The feature numbering system used gave each feature a six-digit designation. The first three digits were the primary identification for a given feature, while the second three digits were used (when needed) to identify subfeatures or superimposed features. For example, in Figure 3.2d, the pit house as a whole can be referred to either as Feature 3, or more precisely as Feature 003000. A floor pit was designated 3001 (003001), the hearth was 3002 (003002), and so forth. In the case of major superimposed features, which were not recognized as such until the excavation was already underway, the fourth digit was used. This occurred only on AZ EE:2:105 and AZ EE:2:113. For example, when three superimposed houses were defined in the Feature 6 house pit at AZ EE:2:113, they were designated 006100, 006200, and 006300, thus allowing each house, its subfeatures and associated artifacts, to be kept separate, or later recombined as needed. A list of excavated features and subfeatures is presented in the descriptions of the larger sites.

The following terms have been used throughout this report:

Pit house - a house built in a shallow excavation, usually with roof support postholes, a hearth, and an entryway.

Limited-use structure - a structure built in, or consisting of a shallow excavation, often of small size and with few internal features.

Pit - an extramural pit with no rocks in the fill.

Pit with rocks - an extramural pit, with rocks comprising up to 50 percent of the fill.

Roasting pit-hearth - an extramural pit, with rock constituting more than 50 percent of the fill.

Rock cluster - rocks (usually fire-cracked) resting on a surface, not in a pit.

Rock-lined pit - extramural pit lined with irregular rocks.

Slab-lined pit - extramural pit lined with tabular rocks.

The distinctions between, and variation within, pit houses and limited-use structures are discussed in Chapter 10. The distinctions among the various types of pits are obviously morphological. Analysis of their contents, including artifacts and animal and plant remains, provided few insights into either their functions or alternate groupings of these features. All extramural features, whether excavated or not, were assigned to some classification. These classifications are probably incorrect in an unknown number of those cases seen only in plan view. At AZ EE:2:113, for example, 60 numbered extramural features which were exposed by stripping (not cut by trenches) were subsequently excavated; 40 percent of these (25) were reclassified after excavation. Of those, two-thirds (16) were of natural origin (either rodent burrows or natural depressions). The classification of unexcavated features is undoubtedly biased towards an overrepresentation of pits, and an underrepresentation of lined pits and roasting pit-hearths, since those designations depended on the kind and quantity of rock showing after stripping to sterile. Functional interpretations of extramural features are made, when possible, in the site descriptions, with a general summary in Chapter 10.

The tables which summarize the dating and contents of structures record not only the basis for dating the structures, but other attributes which may have a bearing on the confidence with which this age assignment can be viewed. "Site ceramics" refers to the temporal range of pottery types found on the site as a whole, and which are presumed to at least bracket the age of all features. "Other" refers to archaeomagnetic or radiocarbon dates, diagnostic projectile points, and so forth.

The identification of "burned" structures was based on the presence of burned structural wood. Houses such as Feature 71200 on AZ EE:2:105 and Feature 2 on AZ EE:2:106 clearly burned down, with charred, in-place post butts or lengths of posts or beams lying on the floor. Other instances become increasingly less straightforward. For purposes of the summary table, if a structure had even a single burned, in-place post or floor-contact structural element, it was considered burned.

Designation of a structure as "trash filled" was based on the density of sherds and chipped stone in its fill, both in absolute terms as well as relative to other structures on the same site. Ground stone, bone, and shell were not figured in, nor were any floor assemblage materials. Artifact densities were compared only on an intrasite basis because even a trash-filled structure on a small, briefly occupied site might have a lower artifact density than a non-trash-filled structure at one of the larger, more intensively occupied sites. Dramatic differences in fill artifact density were considered evidence of trash fill, such as one structure having two, three, or more times the artifact density of its neighbor (unless both figures were extremely low). Artifact densities for each structure are presented in Table 3.2. Sites which had a broad range of densities with no clear breaks gave rise to the use of "?" in the summary table to denote houses which may have been trash filled. For structures largely destroyed by later, superimposed structures, "U" (unknown) is entered.

Many structures had one or several artifacts found on their floors, but only those assemblages thought to represent associated sets of items, such as the assemblages from burned houses, are identified as "floor assemblages."

Finally, the stylistic and chronological divisions of Tucson Basin Hohokam pottery are fully discussed in Chapters 4 and 10. In looking at changes through time in architecture, plant and animal use, and nonceramic artifact attributes, the temporal frameworks used were constructed with reference to the ceramic seriation of features and sites. The general occupation span of each site is shown in Figure 3.3.

Table 3.2

ARTIFACT DENSITY DATA FOR HOUSE PITS AT ALL SITES

Site Number	Feature Number	Artifacts per Cubic Meter	Trash Filled[1]	Average Density[2]
AZ EE:1:104	1	41	–	28
	2	20	–	
AZ EE:2:76	7	182	–	254
	8	222	–	
	10	431	+	
	25	136	–	
	27	291	+	
	29	308	?	
AZ EE:2:77	1	208	?	164
	2	66	–	
	3	392	+	
	4	116	–	
	31	125	–	
	56	78	–	
AZ EE:2:84	1	65	–	93
	10	111	–	
	15	93	–	
AZ EE:2:105	5	176	–	341
	6	405	+	
	7	451	+	
	9	671	+	
	10	332	?	
	11	203	?	
	12	337	?	
	38	236	?	
	41	369	?	
	50	475	+	
	71001	1030	+	
	71200	329	?	
	72	249	?	
	74	44	–	
	81	126	–	
	87	161	–	
	88	179	–	
	91	175	–	

Table 3.2, continued

ARTIFACT DENSITY DATA FOR HOUSE PITS AT ALL SITES

Site Number	Feature Number	Artifacts per Cubic Meter	Trash Filled[1]	Average Density[2]
AZ EE:2:106	1	115	−	58
	2	73	−	
	3	64	+	
	6	14	−	
	7	46	−	
AZ EE:2:107	1	71	−	103
	2	109	−	
	3	95	−	
	5	181	+	
AZ EE:2:109	1	24	−	22
	2	5	−	
	3	41	+	
	4	20	−	
	5	23	−	
AZ EE:2:113	6100	73	−	241
	6200	167	−	
	6300	270	?	
	7	211	−	
	8	190	−	
	10	438	?	
	11	263	?	
	12	209	−	
	83	180	−	
	86	329	+	
	154	167	−	
AZ EE:2:116	1	71	+	56
	2	46	−	
AZ EE:2:117	1	11	−	21
	2	36	−	
AZ EE:2:120	1	117	−	108
	3	90	−	
	6	37	−	
	7	44	−	

Table 3.2, continued

ARTIFACT DENSITY DATA FOR HOUSE PITS AT ALL SITES

Site Number	Feature Number	Artifacts per Cubic Meter	Trash Filled[1]	Average Density[2]
AZ EE:2:120, continued	8	97	–	
	11	219	+	
AZ EE:2:122	1	5	–	18
	2	28	–	
AZ EE:2:129	1	186	?	133
	2	64	–	

[1] Artifact density was not the only factor considered in identifying trash-filled structures. Explanations are provided in individual site descriptions.

[2] Average number of artifacts per house pit for each site.

In the site descriptions below, only those features contributing specific information to the reconstruction of the occupational history or dating of the site, or to the functional interpretation of certain feature types, are discussed in the text; basic information on all others appears in the various tables presented. The sites have been grouped by type, time period, and field treatment, under these headings:

Nonhabitation Sites -- AZ EE:2:49, EE:2:52, and EE:2:136

Trenched Habitation Sites -- AZ EE:2:112 and EE:2:130

Early and Multicomponent Habitation Sites -- AZ EE:2:76, EE:2:84, EE:2:105, EE:2:113, and EE:2:129

Middle Rincon Habitation Sites -- AZ EE:2:77, EE:2:107, EE:2:109, and EE:2:120

Late Rincon Habitation Sites -- AZ EE:1:104, EE:2:106, EE:2:116, EE:2:117, and EE:2:122

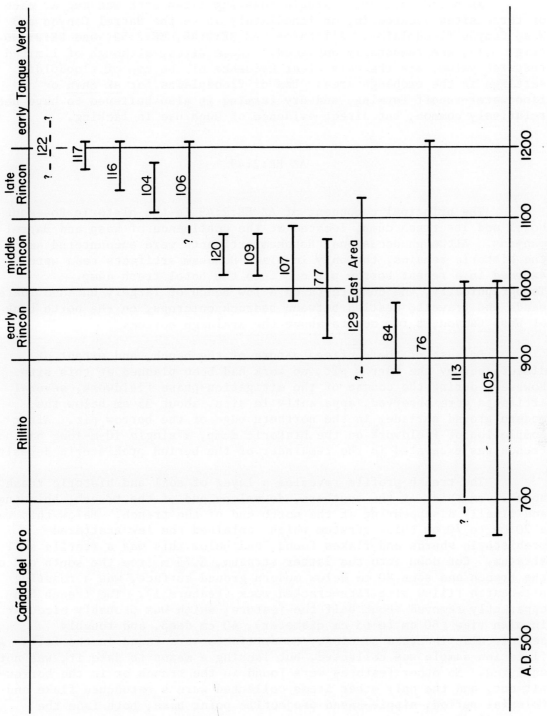

Figure 3.3 Site life-span chart for the excavated Hohokam sites.

Nonhabitation Sites

As noted earlier, a single roasting pit-hearth was dug at each of three sites located in, or immediately above the Barrel Canyon and Wasp Canyon floodplains. All three, AZ EE:2:49, EE:2:52, and EE:2:136 (Fig. 3.1), are temporally unplaced. These sites, although of limited research value, are the only clear evidence of the use of floodplain settings in the exchange area. Use of floodplains for ak chin or floodwater-runoff farming, and dry farming is also believed to have been relatively common, but direct evidence of such use is lacking.

AZ EE:2:49

The principal component of AZ EE:2:49 is the historic Rosemont hotel and its trash dump, located at the confluence of Wasp and Barrel canyons. Although occasional Hohokam artifacts were encountered among the historic remains, the only in-place Hohokam artifacts seen were exposed in a recent borrow pit cut into the hotel trash dump. Topographically, the dump rests on a low bench of largely unconsolidated sands and gravels, nestled between bedrock outcrops, on the north bank of Wasp Canyon, a few meters above the drainage bottom.

Because of the confined nature of the bench, and extent of disturbance by the borrow pit, no work had been planned at this site. However, during the course of the mitigation-phase fieldwork, several artifacts were observed, apparently in situ, about 35 cm below the modern ground surface, in the northern edge of the borrow pit. After completion of fieldwork on the historic dump, a single 10-m-long backhoe trench was excavated in the remainder of the buried prehistoric deposit.

The trench profile revealed a layer of soil and historic trash some 15 cm thick at the southern, downslope end of the trench, thinning and finally disappearing at the north end of the trench. Below this was a 20 cm to 70 cm thick stratum which contained the few scattered prehistoric sherds and flakes found, and below this was a sterile soil stratum. Cut down into the latter stratum, 2.75 m from the south end of the trench and some 80 cm below modern ground surface, was a roasting pit-hearth filled with fire-cracked rock (Feature 1). The trench had apparently removed about half the feature, which was probably circular in plan view (60 cm to 65 cm diameter), 40 cm deep, and roughly semicircular in cross section. No artifacts were found in the fill. A flotation sample was collected, but lacking a means to date it, was not analyzed. No other features were found in the trench or in the borrow-pit cut, and the only other items collected were a retouched flake and a Colonial period, nipple-based projectile point base, both from the borrow-pit face.

AZ EE:2:52

As originally recorded, AZ EE:2:52 referred to a sherd and
lithic scatter around the buildings of the Gayler (VR) Ranch. It is
used here to indicate a single roasting pit found in an arroyo cut,
immediately downslope and to the north of AZ EE:2:76 (Fig. 3.1). This
pit could be considered the lower edge of the ridge upon which
AZ EE:2:76 is located, or the very upper limit of the Barrel Canyon
floodplain in this area.

In addition to being located in an unusual setting (not on a
ridgetop), this roasting pit (Feature 1) was of interest in having seen
secondary use as a burial pit. Excavation showed that about two-thirds
of the pit and most of the human remains had already been washed away.
The pit itself was a bell-shaped roasting pit, at least 70 cm deep with
a flat, circular floor, probably originally about 120 cm in diameter.
The mouth of the pit was gone, and the uppermost portion of the pit wall
remnant was about 1 m below modern ground surface. Fire-cracked rocks
and two metate fragments were found on the floor of the pit. All that
remained of the inhumation was fragments of some lumbar vertebrae, the
pelvis, sacrum, left femur, and some rib and foot elements, about 25 cm
above the pit floor. This adult female was apparently interred in the
pit, on her back, head to the south or southwest, with the legs flexed,
knees up. The only artifacts directly associated with the body were two
tiny rectangles of worked turquoise and a shell and a bone "toggle."
Troweled out from below the pelvis, these were found in positions
suggesting that the turquoise pieces may have been attached to the
toggles, as illustrated in Chapter 7. The possible mosaic pieces are
interpreted as jewelry either worn about the hips or attached to the
woman's clothing. Similarly positioned shell jewelry was recovered in
two other inhumations in the exchange area, one of which was definitely
female. The only artifacts recovered from the pit fill were plain ware
sherds, two flakes, and a rabbit tibia (distal fragment).

AZ EE:2:76, nearby, was occupied throughout the Hohokam
occupation of the Rosemont area, and the roasting pit and inhumation
designated AZ EE:2:52 are probably related to it. However, no
temporally diagnostic artifacts were recovered from this feature, and
its age is unclear. Of the two associations of hip jewelry with
inhumations noted above, one is probably Cañada del Oro (Feature 67 at
AZ EE:2:76), and the other (Feature 10 at AZ EE:2:107) mid-Rincon phase
in age.

AZ EE:2:136

Downslope and southwest of AZ EE:2:116, a roasting pit was
exposed in a road cut as it enters the Barrel Canyon drainage bottom.
This pit, located on the east bank of the floodplain (Fig. 3.1), was
designated Feature 1, AZ EE:2:136, and was excavated. Later in the
fieldwork a second roasting pit (Feature 2) was exposed only a few
meters north when the road was regraded; it was not excavated.

Feature 1 was shaped like an inverted cone, slightly outflaring at the top, 70 cm deep and 140 cm in diameter. The upper half was filled with fire-cracked rocks and gravel, while the lower fill consisted of ashy sand. A single plain ware sherd and a small lump of hematite were recovered from the fill. Three flotation samples, one each from the upper fill, among the rocks, and the lower ash layer, produced very little other than oak charcoal (Miksicek 1984a; Appendix B).

Trenched Habitation Sites

Two ridgetop sites were trenched because of their proximity to AZ EE:2:105, the Ballcourt Site. AZ EE:2:112, substantially disturbed by a bladed dirt road, was not orginally scheduled for excavation. AZ EE:2:130 was originally recorded as part of the Ballcourt Site, but is actually isolated on a small spur coming off the main ridge on which that site is located. It was trenched to determine whether it had any characteristics that differed from the other small habitation sites which might indicate a link with the Ballcourt Site.

AZ EE:2:112

Located on a ridge segment on the eastern bank of South Canyon (Fig. 3.1), relatively sharp breaks-in-slope defined the presumed habitation area. This portion of the ridge is aligned approximately north-south; the dirt road follows the eastern edge, then cuts across the ridgetop to the west. The undisturbed portion of the ridgetop measured 10 m to 18 m wide and 25 m long. Four parallel trenches were dug, 4 m, 6 m, and 8 m apart, the uneven spacing done to avoid unnecessarily destroying trees. No features were found and the cultural deposit across the site area was thin. Given its topographic location and the presence of utilitarian ground stone on the surface, the absence of features was surprising. Based on this testing, AZ EE:2:112 is classified as a nonhabitation site, although features could have been lost to the road or missed between the more widely spaced trenches. The trenches were backfilled, and no additional work was done except for the production of a site map (not published). No artifacts were collected.

AZ EE:2:130

Ten backhoe trenches were dug on this site, from 2 m to 8 m apart, in a manner designed to thoroughly cover the ridgetop, but avoid large trees. Although cultural material was quite sparse, three house pits were located (Fig. 3.4) on the central portion of the ridge. The house-pit fills were quite dark, but only a single plain ware sherd was recovered, from the trench backdirt of the southwesternmost house. A complete slate palette (illustrated in Chapter 7) and an Archaic point

were collected from the surface. In the absence of unusual
architecture, and because of the paucity of artifacts in general, no
additional work was believed to be justified, and the trenches were
backfilled.

Early and Multicomponent Habitation Sites

Five sites were found to have either early occupations or
multiple occupations beginning in either the Cañada del Oro or Rillito
phase. AZ EE:2:76 and EE:2:129, in addition to their early materials,
have some middle or late Rincon phase materials. AZ EE:2:84, EE:2:105,
and EE:2:113 were first occupied in Cañada del Oro or Rillito times, but
all are abandoned during, or near the end of, the early Rincon phase, as
Rincon Red-on-brown, Style A pottery is replaced by Style B (Deaver,
Chapter 4).

AZ EE:2:76--The Gayler Ranch Ruin

The Gayler Ranch Ruin was recorded as a high artifact density,
moderate area site with ceramics, chipped stone, and ground stone all
present in quantity on the slopes. Located just south-southwest of the
Gayler (VR) Ranch, this site sits on a gently sloping ridge segment
overlooking upper Barrel Canyon (Fig. 3.1). The ridge has been eroded
at this particular point and drops off steeply immediately below the
site area, giving the false impression that the site is situated at the
end of the ridge. The ridge does not actually terminate for another
200 m. A ridge terminus, or "false terminus", as in this case, is the
usual setting for habitation sites in the exchange area.

The habitation area is approximately 45 m long and 30 m wide
(Fig. 3.5), and contains at least 7 house pits, a possible limited-use
structure, at least 27 cremation deposits and inhumations, and at least
74 extramural features (Table 3.3). Artifacts recovered are tabulated
in Table 3.4, and Table 3.5 presents a list of the features and
subfeatures.

Structures

Seven house pits (Features 3, 7, 8, 10, 25, 27, and 29)
representing 15 or 16 pit houses, and one pit which may be a limited-use
structure (Feature 16) were partially or completely excavated (Table
3.6). While no other structures are known to be present, given the
proximity of Feature 27 to the eastern edge of the ridgetop, another

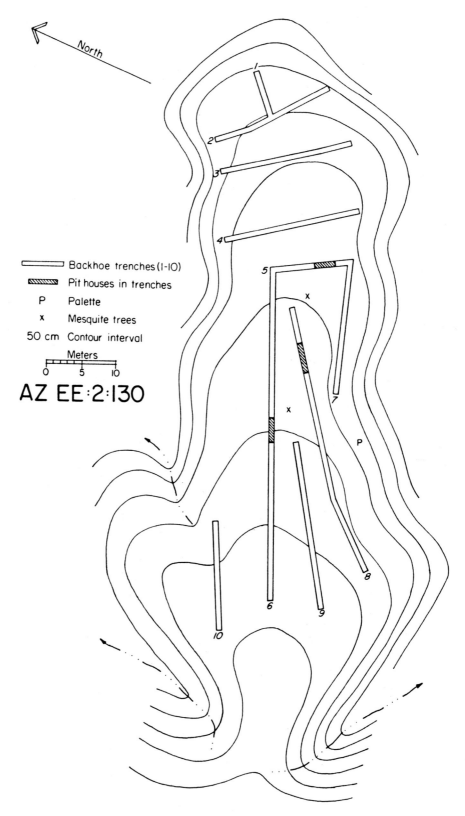

Figure 3.4   Site map, AZ EE:2:130.

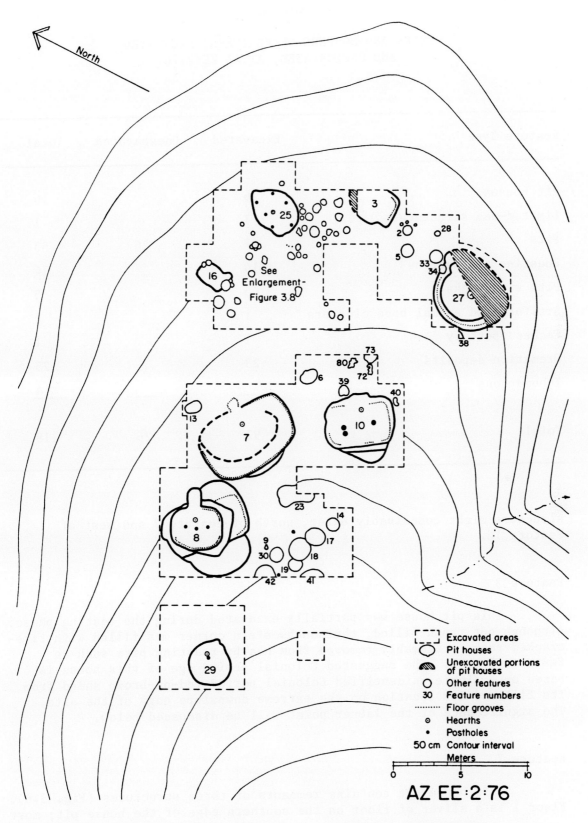

North

25
3
16
See
Enlargement—
Figure 3.8
20
28
5
33
34
27
38

73
80
72
6
39
13
40
7
10
23
14
17
8
9
18
30
19
41
42

29

Excavated areas
Pit houses
Unexcavated portions
of pit houses
Other features
30 Feature numbers
Floor grooves
Hearths
Postholes
50 cm Contour interval
Meters
0   5   10

AZ EE:2:76

Figure 3.5 Site map, AZ EE:2:76 -- the Gayler Ranch Ruin.

Table 3.3

TYPES AND NUMBERS OF FEATURES, EXCAVATED
AND UNEXCAVATED, AT AZ EE:2:76

Feature Type	Excavated	Unexcavated	Total
Pit houses	16		16
Limited-use structures	1		1
Pits	27	26	53
Roasting pit-hearths	14		14
Pits with rocks	5		5
Artifact and animal bone clusters	1		1
Caches: pottery	1		1
Cremation deposits	23		23
Inhumations	4		4
Total	92	26	118

structure might conceivably exist, north of Feature 7 and west of
Feature 16.

Feature 3

This pit house was partially excavated during the testing phase.
Although not trash filled, the southwestern corner was filled with fire-
cracked rock, presumably removed from nearby roasting pits such as
Features 2 or 5. The suggested Colonial period age of this house is
based on a single unidentified Colonial period red-on-brown sherd from
its fill and its location on the extreme downslope edge of the site.
The significance of the latter point will be discussed below.

Feature 7

This house pit contains remnants of three structures (Fig. 3.6).
Floor 1 is a sliver of floor on the southern edge of the house pit; most

Table 3.4

ARTIFACT TOTALS BY CLASS FOR AZ EE:2:76

Artifact Type	Count	Category Total	Percent of Assemblage
Ceramics		8455	68.2
Decorated sherds	2573		
Red ware sherds	155		
Plain ware sherds	5724		
Figurine fragments	3		
Chipped Stone		3693	29.8
Debitage	3350		
Retouched pieces	284		
Cores	40		
Hammerstones	18		
Utilitarian Ground Stone		120	1.0
Metates	38		
Mano-handstones	63		
Polishing stones	2		
Tabular knives	8		
3/4-grooved axes	2		
Other	7		
Nonutilitarian Stone		32	0.3
Palettes	6		
Worked slate	1		
Bowls	3		
Jewelry	4		
Crystals or minerals	16		
Other	2		
Shell		73	0.6
Bracelets	44		
Bead lots (N = 291)	9		
Other	20		
Worked Bone		17	0.1
Awls-hairpins	8		
Antler flakers	1		
Other	8		
Total		12,390	100.0

Table 3.5

EXCAVATED FEATURE INFORMATION, AZ EE:2:76

Feature or Subfeature Number	Interpretation and Description
1	cremation deposit
2	roasting pit-hearth with three small pits around it
3	pit house
4	collective designation for two cremation deposits in Feature 25 pit house
4001	urn sitting on floor of Feature 25 pit house
4002	cremation pit dug into floor of Feature 25 pit house
5	pit with rocks which apparently intruded a cremation deposit
6	pit with rocks
7	collective designation for three pit houses, the upper (Floor 1) is the earliest, and the latest (Floor 3) is a series of postholes dug into Floor 2
7001	roasting pit-hearth intruded into the fill and floor of the pit house
7002	floor pit (?)
7003	roasting pit-hearth intruded into the fill and floor of the pit house
7004	huge floor pit associated (?) with three postholes
7005	floor pit or posthole (?)
7006	floor pit or intrusive disturbance (?)

Table 3.5, continued

EXCAVATED FEATURE INFORMATION, AZ EE:2:76

Feature or Subfeature Number	Interpretation and Description
7009	floor pit (bell-shaped) (intrusive ?)
7012	floor pit
7014	floor pit
7015	floor pit
7016	probable hearth (unlined pit); Floor 2
7023	floor pit ? posthole ?

8	collective designation for what is definitely four and probably five superimposed pit houses; from earliest to most recent they are designated:
	
	    Floor 1
	    Floor 2a
	    Floor 2b
	    Floor 3
	    Floor 4

8001	hearth plastered; Floor 4
8002	double (?) posthole (?); probably one of three main roof support postholes in Floor 4
8003	floor pit; Floor 4
8004	floor pit that probably originated with Floor 3, but could have been used during the use of Floor 4 as well
8005	floor pit in Floor 1; cut by Floor 3
8006	floor pit in Floor 1
8007	floor pit in Floor 1

Table 3.5, continued

EXCAVATED FEATURE INFORMATION, AZ EE:2:76

Feature or Subfeature Number	Interpretation and Description
8008	floor pit in Floor 4 entryway
8010	floor pit in Floor 4
8011	one of three main roof support postholes in Floor 4
9	artifact/animal bone cluster
10	collective designation for three superimposed pit houses; upper (earliest) is Floor 1, and deepest (latest) is Floor 3
10001	circular depression in the middle of the Floor 3, within which is a smaller, offset circle of postholes
10005	floor pit
10010	hearth (unlined pit) intruded by a posthole that is part of the circle of postholes in the Subfeature 10001 depression
10011	hearth (unlined pit); Floor 3
10012	floor pit or major posthole in the Floor 1 remnant
10014	posthole with post remnant in it, which is part of the circle of postholes in the Subfeature 10001 depression; Floor 3
11	roasting pit-hearth
12	roasting pit-hearth
13	roasting pit-hearth

Table 3.5, continued

EXCAVATED FEATURE INFORMATION, AZ EE:2:76

Feature or Subfeature Number	Interpretation and Description
16	four (?) limited-use structure (?), intruded by features
16001	pit
16002	pit with 1 whole bowl
16003	cremation deposit
16004	roasting pit-hearth intruded into the upper fill of Subfeature 16003
17	pit with rocks
20	pit with three posthole (?) impressions in the bottom
21	inhumation (infant under smashed jar)
22	cremation deposit
24	roasting pit-hearth
25	pit house intruded by 2 inhumations, 10 cremation deposits
25001	floor pit (heavily rodent disturbed)
25002	floor pit with posthole
25003	floor pit (heavily rodent disturbed)
25004	floor pit with posthole
26	rock-lined roasting pit-hearth, connected to Feature 60 by cultural (?) disturbance

Table 3.5, continued

EXCAVATED FEATURE INFORMATION, AZ EE:2:76

Feature or Subfeature Number	Interpretation and Description
27	collective designation for two superimposed pit houses; upper (earlier) is Floor 1, lower (later) is Floor 2
27001	floor pit (hearth ? - unlined pit); Floor 2
27002	articulated hawk skeleton in the fill of the Floor 2 entryway
28	roasting pit-hearth
29	pit house
29002	hearth (unlined pit)
29003	single main roof support posthole
31	roasting pit-hearth
32	cremation deposit
35	cremation deposit, Feature 25 fill
36	pit
37	pit
39	pit with one large rock in it
40	roasting pit-hearth
43	pit
44	cremation deposit
45	cremation deposit

Table 3.5, continued

EXCAVATED FEATURE INFORMATION, AZ EE:2:76

Feature or Subfeature Number	Interpretation and Description
46	inhumation placed in an old roasting pit-hearth; inhumation may have intruded an earlier cremation deposit placed in this feature
47	cremation deposit
48	pit
49	cremation deposit, Feature 25 fill
50	pit
51	cremation deposit
52	cremation deposit
53	cremation deposit ?
54	cremation deposit, Feature 25 fill
55	cremation deposit, Feature 25 fill
56	cremation deposit (urn type) atop rock covered inhumation intrusive into the floor of the Feature 25 pit house
57	collective designation for three superimposed pits and a cremation deposit; absolute ordering of the deposits not possible
57001	cremation deposit, cut definitely by 57002 and possibly by 57003
57002	pit
57003	pit

Table 3.5, continued

EXCAVATED FEATURE INFORMATION, AZ EE:2:76

Feature or Subfeature Number	Interpretation and Description
57004	pit
58	pit
59	rock cluster above pit
60	pit, connected to Feature 26 by cultural (?) disturbance
61	pit
63	pit
64	cremation deposit, Feature 25 fill
65	cremation deposit, Feature 25 fill
66	pit
67	inhumation intrusive into the floor of the Feature 25 pit house
68	cremation deposit; floor of the Feature 25 pit house
69	pit
70	collective designation for what appears to be two superimposed pits
71	pit
72	roasting pit-hearth
73	pit
74	pit with rocks

Table 3.5, continued

EXCAVATED FEATURE INFORMATION, AZ EE:2:76

Feature or Subfeature Number	Interpretation and Description
80	pit
86	pit
91	pit
92	pit

of it was destroyed when the Floor 2 house pit was dug down through it. A surface remnant with three postholes at the northeast corner of the house pit is also probably part of Floor 1. Floor 2 creates the bulk of the house pit outline, and is the largest intact house found, measuring 6.85 m across. A groove encircled the floor and entryway. Floor 3 has been inferred from a series of postholes enclosing a small oval area within Floor 2 (Fig. 3.6). Finally, Subfeatures 7001 and 7003 are extramural roasting pit-hearths which are intruded into Floors 2 and 3, postdating the Floor 3 structure.

Only Floor 3 is securely dated by a partial Rincon Red-on-brown, Style C jar found on the floor within the Floor 3 posthole outline. The suggested ages of Floors 2 and 1 (Table 3.6) are based on two factors: (1) they predate Floor 3, and (2) Rillito Red-on-brown and Rincon Red-on-brown, Styles A and B sherds were found in the house pit fill (Table 3.6).

Feature 8

With remnants of four or possibly five pit houses (Fig. 3.7), Feature 8 was the most complex series of superimposed structures encountered. Because each new building episode did <u>not</u> remove most of the preceding house, as was so often the case, the dating of the various Feature 8 floors is also the best documented series of superpositions.

Floor 1 is a partial floor, entryway orientation unknown, on which several manos and three partial plain ware jars were found. Floor pit 8005 contained a sherd of Snaketown Red-on-buff. An in-place wall

Table 3.6

STRUCTURE DATING AND CONTENT SUMMARY, AZ EE:2:76

Feature Number	Age Assignment	Basis for Dating									
		Site Ceramics	Floor Ceramics	Fill Ceramics	Superimposition	Other	Burned	Trash Filled	Floor Assemblage	Intrudes Features	Intruded by Features
003000	Colonial ?			+		+		+			
007000 (Floor 1)	Rillito or early Rincon			+	+		u	u	u		+
007000 (Floor 2)	early or middle Rincon			+	+				+		
007000 (Floor 3)	late Rincon	+			+				+	+	+
008000 (Floor 1)	Colonial				+	+	+		+		+
008000 (Floor 2) a & b	Rillito	+			+				+	+	+
008000 (Floor 3)	early Rincon ?				+					+	+
008000 (Floor 4)	middle Rincon	+			+	+	+		+	+	
010000 (Floor 1)	Rillito ?			+	+		u	u	u		+
010000 (Floor 2)	early Rincon ?			+	+		u	u	u	+	+

Table 3.6, continued

STRUCTURE DATING AND CONTENT SUMMARY, AZ EE:2:76

Feature Number	Age Assignment	Basis for Dating									
		Site Ceramics	Floor Ceramics	Fill Ceramics	Superimposition	Other	Burned	Trash Filled	Floor Assemblage	Intrudes Features	Intruded by Features
010000 (Floor 3)	middle Rincon			+	+			+		+	
016000	Colonial			+	+	+					+
025000	Cañada del Oro			+	+						+
027000 (Floor 1)	Colonial ?			+	+			?			+
027000 (Floor 2)	Rincon ?			+	+			+		+	
029000	Colonial ?			+		+		?			

post associated with Floor 1 produced a radiocarbon date of 1070 + 70 B.P. (A-3559), A.D. 880 + 70, and is discussed below under "Ceramics and Dating."

The Floor 2a structure may have had an entryway oriented to the north or north-northeast, and had a partial Rillito Red-on-brown jar on its floor. Floor 2b is that portion of the floor "outside" the floor groove on the northeast (Fig. 3.7, upper right); whether Floor 2a precedes or follows 2b, or whether these represent a single structure is unclear.

Floor 3, the smallest of the floor surface remnants, also appears to have been oriented to the northeast. No artifacts could be directly associated with Floor 3.

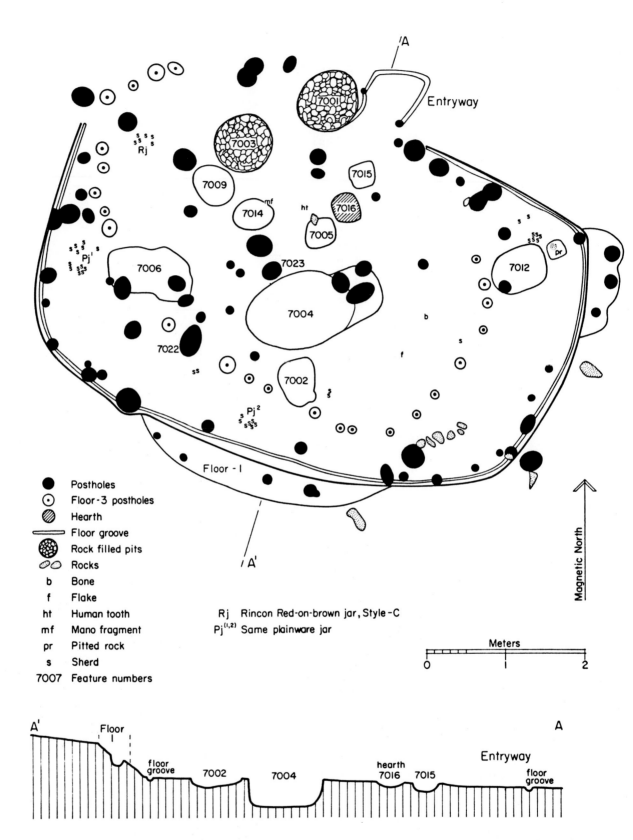

Figure 3.6   Plan view and cross section of the three house floors in the Feature 7 house pit, AZ EE:2:76.

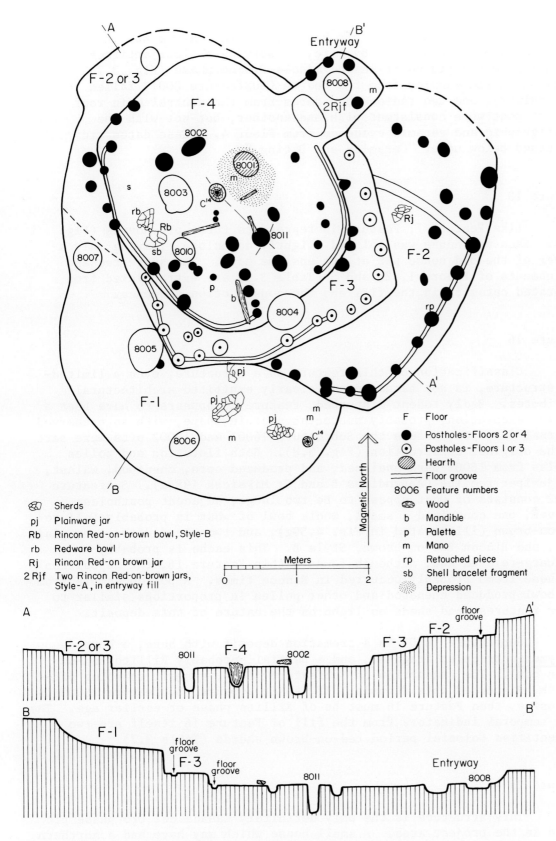

Figure 3.7 Plan view and cross sections of the four house floors in the Feature 8 house pit, AZ EE:2:76.

Floor 4 is the final pit house built in Feature 8. It is complete, and was destroyed by fire, preserving a floor artifact assemblage which places it in the middle Rincon phase (Fig. 3.7). Archaeomagnetic samples from the hearth (Subfeature 8001) failed to date (Appendix F), and two radiocarbon dates from the central main roof support post were consistent with one another, but not with the stratigraphic and ceramic evidence from Floor 4. These dates are discussed below under "Ceramics and Dating."

Feature 10

Like Feature 7, Feature 10 represents three pit houses (Fig. 3.5). Each new house was shifted slightly downslope, leaving only a sliver of the old house pit at its upslope edge. The suggested age assignments of Floors 1, 2, and 3 (Table 3.5) are extrapolated from decorated ceramics in the fill and the construction sequence.

Feature 16

Classification of this feature as a structure, even a limited-use structure, is not based on any clearly exhibited architectural attributes. Badly rodent disturbed, Feature 16 appears to have been a shallow excavation, probably subrectangular in shape, with no preserved internal features, unless the Subfeature 16001 and 16002 pits were part of the original construction (Fig. 3.8). Both flotation and pollen samples from 16001 were analyzed, and produced corn, chenopod, walnut, and juniper remains (Appendixes B and C; Miksicek 1984a). Subfeature 16002 consists of what appear to be two large, adjacent postholes; however, one contained a small, whole bowl of what is probably Galiuro Red-on-brown (illustrated in Fig. 4.59g), and two sherd disks, one plain ware, one Rincon Red-on-brown, Style B. This cache is probably mortuary-related and, although found within Feature 16, the deposition of these items probably occurred in Rincon times. A pollen sample from the bowl produced chenopod and other pollen in proportions similar to other features, and sheds no light on the nature of this deposit.

Subfeature 16003 is a cremation deposit with bone, a burned Glycymeris bracelet fragment, and a partial, probably Rillito Red-on-brown bowl. The excavation of Subfeature 16004, a small roasting pit-hearth, disturbed this deposit. If, as it appears, Subfeature 16003 is intrusive, then Feature 16 must be of Rillito phase or earlier age. The only temporal indicators from the fill of Feature 16 itself are two unidentified Colonial period red-on-brown sherds (Table 3.7).

Feature 25

This structure is the only definitely Cañada del Oro phase pit house in the project area. A small house which may have had a northern entryway, its fill and floor were intruded by two inhumations and ten cremation deposits (Fig. 3.8). The Feature 56 inhumation cut through

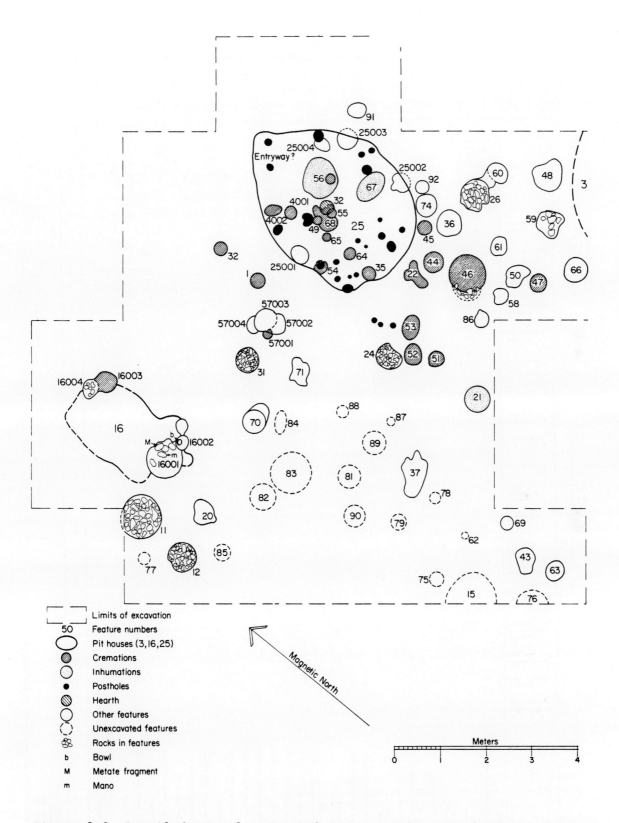

Figure 3.8 Detailed map of excavated area on ridge toe showing concentration of extramural features, the cemetery area, and the Feature 3, 16, and 25 structures.

Table 3.7

DECORATED POTTERY TYPES FROM AZ EE:2:76

Provenience	Cañada del Oro Red-on-brown	Rillito Red-on-brown	Unidentified Colonial	Rincon Red-on-brown, Style A	Rincon Red-on-brown, Style B	Rincon Red-on-brown, Style C	Rincon Red-on-brown, Style ?	Rio Rico Polychrome	Sahuarita Polychrome	Tanque Verde Red-on-brown	Sweetwater Red-on-gray	Snaketown Red-on-buff	Gila Butte Red-on-buff	Santa Cruz Red-on-buff	Sacaton Red-on-buff	Dos Cabezas Red-on-brown	Galiuro Red-on-brown	Trincheras Purple-on-red	Nogales Polychrome	Total
Stripping	1	11	11	15	24	35	63	6	2	3		1		11	1		3	1	1	189
Feature 3 pit house			1																	1
Feature 7 pit houses		1	1	1	7	2 PJ	4	2						3		1		1		23
Feature 8 pit houses	1	3 PJ	5	5 2PJ	10 PB	4	15	7				1	1	11					3	66
Feature 10 pit houses		5	2	9	14	1	27	2						1			4		2	67
Feature 16 limited-use structure			2																	2
Feature 25 pit house			1				2													3
Feature 27 pit house		7	6	8	17	6 PB	41			4	1			3	6			1	2	102
Feature 1 cremation deposit		WB																		WB
Feature 4 cremation deposit		WJ																		WJ
Feature 5 cremation deposit?				PB PJ																PB
Feature 7003 roasting pit-hearth							1													1
Feature 16001 pit				2			3													5
Feature 16002 pit					1															1
Feature 16003 cremation deposit			12																	12
Feature 26 roasting pit-hearth					1															1
Feature 31 roasting pit-hearth				4																4
Feature 32 cremation deposit	WB																			WB
Feature 39 pit				1																1
Feature 44 cremation deposit					PB		WJ													PB,WJ
Feature 45 cremation deposit		PJ																		PJ
Feature 46 inhumation														2						2
Feature 47 cremation deposit														PB						PB
Feature 50 pit			1																	1
Feature 51 cremation deposit				WJ																WJ
Feature 56 cremation deposit	WJ																			WJ
Feature 57001 cremation deposit		PJ																		PJ
Feature 74 pit with rocks		1																		1
Total	2	28	42	45	74	48	156	17	2	7	1	2	1	31	7	1	7	3	8	482

PJ = Partial Jar
PB = Partial Bowl
WB = Whole Bowl
WJ = Whole Jar

Note: Whole and partial vessels are not included in totals.

the Feature 25 floor and was in turn surmounted by a cremation deposit
in a late Cañada del Oro or early Rillito Red-on-brown jar (illustrated
in Fig. 4.17b), making both the inhumation and the Feature 25 pit house
Cañada del Oro phase or earlier in age.

Feature 27

       This feature consists of two pit houses which were partially
excavated. It appears that the second, smaller house was placed
directly inside the first, leaving a concentric ring of Floor 1 intact
(Fig. 3.5). The remarkable thing about this house is that its fill
contains sherds representing the known Hohokam occupation span of the
Rosemont area, from the only sherd of Sweetwater Red-on-gray found on
the project, through Tanque Verde Red-on-brown (Table 3.6). The actual
ages of Floors 1 and 2, however, are unclear (Table 3.5), and the
astonishing span of ceramic types is presumably attributable to repeated
use of the house pit as a trash pit.

Feature 29

       This structure produced one identifiable decorated sherd, which
is probably Snaketown Red-on-buff. This, combined with its similarity
in size and shape to the Colonial age, Feature 25 pit house, led to a
tentative Colonial period age assignment.

Slope Trash

       Trash was abundant on all areas of the ridge downslope of the
habitation area, but was densest on the eastern side. The high artifact
densities in the fill of Features 10 and 27 also suggest that trash was
commonly dumped on this side of the site.

Extramural Features

       Seventy-four extramural features were found, including 53 pits,
5 pits with rocks, 14 roasting pit-hearths, 1 artifact and animal bone
cluster, and 1 probable mortuary cache (Feature 16002) discussed above.

Pits and Hearths

       Pits are found in all areas where extramural features occur.
Excavated roasting pit-hearths, on the other hand, are restricted to
downslope areas. Cremations and inhumations are clearly restricted to
the extreme downslope edge of the habitation area.

       Flotation samples from eight roasting pit-hearths yielded
primarily corn, chenopod seeds, and occasional pieces of an
unidentified, columnar-celled shell (Miksicek 1984a). Both flotation

and pollen samples from one pit and one pit with rocks (Features 16001 and 16017), and pollen samples from two additional pits were analyzed. None produced any unusual results (Appendixes B and C, Miksicek 1984a).

Artifact and Animal Bone Cluster

Feature 9 consisted of a cluster of rabbit bones and sherds representing about half of a red ware bowl. All were resting on the prehistoric ground surface just southeast of the Feature 8 house pit. Whether this is an intentional deposit such as is present at AZ EE:2:113, or represents the random disposal of trash is uncertain.

Burials

Twenty-three cremation deposits (Features 1, 4001, 4002, 5, 16003, 22, 32, 35, 44 through 47, 49, 51 through 56, 57001, 64, 65, and 68) and four inhumations (Features 21, 46, 56, and 67) were found on AZ EE:2:76, clustered at the downslope edge of the habitation area (Fig. 3.8). This is the largest burial population at any of the exchange-area sites. As already noted, the inhumation recovered from AZ EE:2:52 (near the base of the AZ EE:2:76 ridge) may also be related to the occupation of AZ EE:2:76.

Cremation Deposits

The large number of cremation deposits recorded for AZ EE:2:76 may be misleading in that several separate deposits could represent a single individual, what has been termed "serial cremation", or "partition burial." Conversely, although serial cremation has yet to be demonstrated in Hohokam assemblages, numerous instances have been found of more than one individual being represented in a single cremation deposit. Some of the "cremation deposits" at AZ EE:2:76 may also be fortuitous associations of rodent-moved, cremated bone with artifacts (Features 5, 46, and 68). Only complex or culturally disturbed deposits are described below; information on the remainder can be found in Chapter 10.

The 10 cremation deposits in the fill or floor of the Feature 25 pit house do not appear to be a subgroup of the burial population, that is, they are no more similar to one another than to any deposits outside the pit house. Most, if not all, were interred after Feature 25 was completely filled in, and burial inside or outside the house pit was probably of no concern, if the existence of the pit house was even recognized at the time of burial. Comparison of the plain ware jar sherds from Features 4002, 35, 65, 68 and several sherd clusters on the pit house floor shows them to be unrelated.

Feature 4002. This deposit consisted of an oval pit dug through the floor of the Feature 25 pit house, which was then lined with 11 plain ware sherds from a single jar, filled with cremated bone, and capped with a burned rectangular sandstone slab.

Feature 5. Classified as a "pit with rocks," this feature is probably a partially cleaned-out roasting pit. In its fill were found a partial bowl and jar of Rincon Red-on-brown, Style A, a miniature plain ware jar, and a few grams of cremated bone. Whether the roasting pit intruded the cremation deposit, or whether a cremation was placed in an existing roasting pit and subsequently disturbed is unclear. The apparently accepted practice of placing burials in abandoned roasting pits (see Feature 46 below, Feature 1 at AZ EE:2:52, and Feature 7 at AZ EE:2:84), and the fact that the miniature jar was intact, suggest the latter inference is more probable.

Feature 46. This feature was originally a roasting pit, into which a cremation deposit had been intruded. It, in turn, was disturbed by an inhumation, with burned bone and artifacts thrown back into the fill of the burial pit. This sequence of events is inferred from the jumble of sherds of at least two plain ware vessels, two burned Glycymeris bracelet fragments, and miscellaneous cremated bone found in the fill of the Feature 46 inhumation, primarily above the chest. Additional details may be found in the description of the Feature 46 inhumation below.

Feature 52. This unusual deposit contained a small amount of bone and 122 shell disk beads. The beads are unburned, and were scattered throughout the undisturbed pit fill. Almost all (119) are unidentified marine shell, while the reddish color of three suggests they may be made of Spondylus shell. The presence of somewhat unusual, unburned offerings in this deposit prompted analysis of a pollen sample from the bottom of the pit. The results, however, show no unusual proportions of pollen types nor are any unusual species represented (Appendix C).

Feature 56. As noted earlier, the age assignment for the Feature 25 pit house was based on the Feature 56 Cañada del Oro or early Rillito Red-on-brown cremation jar. This vessel was found in place above an inhumation which had been intruded through the pit house floor. The cremation deposit was that of an infant, and is itself unusual in having had a miniature plain ware bowl and jar placed inside the large urn, along with the cremated bone, four unburned shell disk beads, and a burned Glycymeris bracelet fragment. Also present, mixed with the cremated bone, were a few unburned infant bones, and the feature may represent a multiple interment. Poor cleaning of the crematory could explain such a mixture of two individuals, but would not explain why some of the infant bones were not burned. Even though the cremation urn was upright and essentially intact, two rim sherds and the shell beads were found inside the vessel (which are identical to those recovered from the Feature 56 inhumation), suggesting that rodent disturbance may have mixed these deposits. As with the Feature 52 cremation deposit, the unusual offerings prompted the analysis of a pollen sample from the lower fill of the large jar, but the results were similarly unenlightening (Appendix C).

Feature 57001. This deposit consisted of the sherds of a smashed Rillito Red-on-brown jar placed in a small pit with cremated bone and an unworked, unburned fragment of a Laevicardium elatum valve. This deposit was subsequently cut by one or two pits (Subfeatures 57002 and 57003), but the bone and sherds presumably disturbed were not found nearby.

Inhumations

Feature 21. This feature consisted of a fetus inhumation in a pit which was apparently positioned with the body on the eastern side of the pit, head to the south. The head was covered with 24 sherds from a single plain ware jar, and four rocks had been placed along the eastern edge of the pit.

Feature 46. This adult female inhumation was semisupine, slouched against the southern wall of the burial pit, chin on chest, with the legs completely flexed and spread apart, the knees at the shoulders. The left arm was slightly bent with the hand in the lap, palm up; the right arm was bent under the body. This inhumation apparently disturbed a cremation which had been deposited in what was probably a bell-shaped roasting pit. When the inhumation was interred, the pit may have been cleaned and enlarged, leaving only an undercut remnant of the roasting pit (Fig. 3.8) and a few rocks in the fill. Santa Cruz Red-on-buff sherds in the feature fill may have originated with the roasting pit, the cremation deposit, or the inhumation.

Feature 56. This adult female was lying on her right side, tightly flexed with both arms bent and the hands near the right shoulder. The head was oriented to the northeast. The body had been placed in a pit dug through the floor of the Feature 25 pit house, and covered with eight large rocks, upon which the Feature 56 cremation jar was subsequently set. A pinkish bead-pendant (probably Spondylus shell) was found in the chest area, and 35 unburned shell disk beads were scattered around the hips.

Feature 67. This 5-or-6-year-old child was placed on its back with the legs tightly flexed and turned to the left. The head was oriented to the northwest. Both arms were at the body's sides, left hand palm up, right unknown. This burial clearly postdates the abandonment of the Feature 25 pit house as indicated by its disturbance of the floor and a posthole. Grave goods consisted of 124 unburned shell disk beads; most were rodent-scattered in the chest and pelvis region, but 10 were found side-by-side under the left innominate, as they were presumably strung.

Ceramics and Dating

As already noted, AZ EE:2:76 is the longest-lived of the Hohokam sites examined. The Sweetwater Red-on-gray, Snaketown Red-on-buff, and Cañada del Oro Red-on-brown sherds are all presumed to indicate an initial occupation somewhere between A.D. 500 and 700. Rillito Red-on-brown, all three defined styles of Rincon Red-on-brown, and both early and late intrusive types are present. Occupation of the Rosemont area in general, and AZ EE:2:76 in particular, drew to a close just as the Tanque Verde phase was beginning, probably around A.D. 1200-1225. Only a very few sherds of Tanque Verde Red-on-brown were found on AZ EE:2:76, scattered in feature fill and sheet trash.

All the pit houses represented in Features 7, 8, 10, 25, and 27 could be placed in time with varying accuracy, based on floor or fill ceramics (Table 3.6), structural superposition, or both. Features 3, 16, and 29 each had a few sherds in their fills from which early dates were inferred. An intrusive Rillito phase cremation deposit (16003) appears to corroborate the Colonial period dating of Feature 16. Another, more speculative line of evidence supporting Colonial period ages for Features 3, 16, and 29 is the site layout. There appear to be two arcs of four structures each, both dating to the Colonial period: a downslope arc, Features 27 (Floor 1), 3, 25, and 16; and an upslope arc, Feature 10 (Floor 1), possibly Feature 7 (Floor 1), either Floor 1 or 2 of Feature 8, and Feature 29 (Fig. 3.9).

Feature 8, with its superimposed floors, floor assemblages, structural wood from Floors 1 and 4, and a plastered hearth on Floor 4, was selected for archaeomagnetic and radiocarbon dating in an attempt to apply some absolute dates to these pit houses and the Tucson Basin ceramic sequence in the Rosemont area. The archaeomagnetic samples from the Floor 4 hearth (Subfeature 8001) failed to date (Appendix F). Radiocarbon samples consisted of a completely carbonized, in-place post from Floor 1, and the uncarbonized, outermost preserved rings of the butt of the middle roof support post from Floor 4 (see Fig. 3.7). The Floor 1 sample, known to be of Rillito or earlier age (based on the Rillito jar from Floor 2), dated A.D. 880 $\pm$ 70 (A.D. 770-1190 at a 95 percent confidence interval). Floor 4 dates to middle Rincon times, based on the floor ceramics. A radiocarbon assay, however, produced a date of 1360 $\pm$ 60 B.P. (A-3560), A.D. 590 $\pm$ 60. The relative ages of these two radiocarbon dates contradict both information derived from the floor assemblages and from the stratigraphic order of the floors. To be sure that the two samples had not been accidentally switched, thorough checks of field notes and maps were made, and finally a second sample of the roof support post was submitted for dating. This second sample produced a date of 1250 $\pm$ 60 B.P. (A-3891), A.D. 700 $\pm$ 60, with the amounts of ^{13}C and ^{14}C statistically indistinguishable from the first

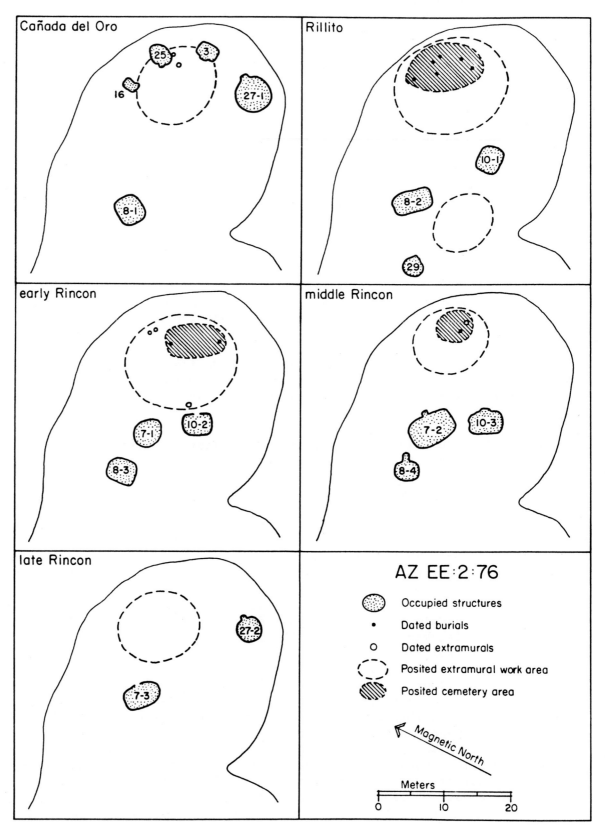

Figure 3.9 Possible pit house occupation sequence, AZ EE:2:76.

sample, according to Austin Long, of the University of Arizona, Laboratory of Isotope Geochemistry.

With the earlier radiocarbon date from the Floor 4 post confirmed, the most obvious, and likely, explanation is that this dating situation ran afoul of the "old wood" problem (Schiffer 1982): the juniper post chosen for dating was a substantial one, with an unknown number of outside rings missing. It may have been either reused from a much earlier structure, or obtained as an already dead, old tree. The durability of juniper posts is well known to ranchers, and was demonstrated repeatedly by finds on the ANAMAX-Rosemont Project. Unburned juniper posts and entryway sills were found in 14 pit houses from eight sites. Hindsight indicates that some other, smaller specimen, such as one of the burned wall or roof members from Floor 4, would have been a more prudent choice, given the possible reuse of large posts.

Dating concerns aside, the ceramic assemblage from AZ EE:2:76 was especially useful in its abundance of whole and partial vessels, from both cremation deposits and pit houses, and was notable for the breadth of types present. AZ EE:2:76 yielded all 20 of the decorated ceramic types or varieties recognized in the analysis of the project pottery, except Rincon Polychrome and Cerros Red-on-white.

Nonceramic Artifacts

Counts of all artifact types can be found in Table 3.4. Like the ceramic assemblage, the chipped stone, utilitarian and nonutilitarian ground stone, shell, and worked bone collections from AZ EE:2:76 show virtually the whole range of materials found for the project as a whole (Table 3.4). This is not surprising, as AZ EE:2:76 was occupied over a greater span of years than any other site in the exchange area. Interestingly, although the total number of artifacts collected from AZ EE:2:76 is less than that from AZ EE:2:105 or EE:2:113, nonutilitarian stone and shell items are relatively more common on AZ EE:2:76. Further, marine shell items at AZ EE:2:76 are most numerous in absolute numbers as well, due in part to the substantial mortuary assemblage at AZ EE:2:76.

Subsistence

Although animal bone from AZ EE:2:76 was relatively abundant and diverse in the species represented (Appendix A), it was not as common as at AZ EE:2:105 and AZ EE:2:113. This may be due in part to the fact that trash could more easily be discarded on off-site slopes at AZ EE:2:76 than at either of the other two sites. Regardless, while we can infer the regular hunting of deer and rabbits at AZ EE:2:76, the relative importance of hunting with respect to agriculture and the gathering of wild plant foods cannot be assessed.

Flotation samples (Miksicek 1984a; Appendix B) consistently yielded corn remains, chenopod seeds, acorns, pigweed seeds, and an unidentified columnar-celled shell, in that order of abundance, with sporadic occurrences of other wild plant foods. Pollen samples (Appendix C) are dominated by cheno-ams, suggesting the importance of these plants, second only to corn, in the vegetal diet of the Rosemont Hohokam. Again, it is clear that corn was a regular staple, but the relative ranking of meat, and wild and domesticated plant foods is impossible to assess.

Summary

This medium-sized site possesses features ranging in age from late Cañada del Oro to late Rincon/early Tanque Verde phase, spanning the known Hohokam occupation of the exchange area. The suggested ages for the structures (Table 3.6) imply that the population of AZ EE:2:76 was relatively large at its founding, remained stable through Rillito and early and possibly middle Rincon phase times, and decreased somewhat in size in the late Rincon phase. This reconstruction is based on the assumption that the occupation of the various structures was spread evenly through time, and is only one, possibly oversimplified, interpretation. Alternatively, the site might have been occupied on a short-term, intermittent basis. However, if any site in the exchange area can be said to have been stable, it would presumably be AZ EE:2:76, by merit of its lengthy occupation and desirable location. In any case, the initial population appears to have been relatively large, and at the final abandonment of the site, was noticeably smaller.

The specific plant and animal foods found at AZ EE:2:76 were noted above. At a more general level, it is of note that AZ EE:2:76 is located on the only sizeable area of relatively flat, elevated land at what is a particularly wide point along the Barrel Canyon channel. With Rosemont Springs less than 400 m to the northwest, and the mix of grassland and oak-juniper woodland in the immediate vicinity, the site seems to have been auspiciously located with respect to potential agricultural fields, wild plant and animal populations, and water. It is probably in large part because of this combination of desirable attributes that this site exhibits the longest overall life span of the investigated Hohokam sites.

Although the growth of the site cannot be discussed on a feature-by-feature basis, several interesting points can nevertheless be noted concerning site structure and the general patterns of growth.

All discernable entryway orientations are north, northeast or north-northeast. A northern orientation for pit houses is the preferred one for virtually all the habitation sites examined. Whether this is due to cultural preference or the dictates of topography is discussed in Chapter 10.

The eight house pits (presuming Feature 16 is indeed a structure) form two arcs of four houses each, as noted above. The upslope arc consists of Features 7, 8, 10, and 29, the downslope arc of Features 3, 16, 25, and 27. Contemporaneous occupation of any two structures cannot be demonstrated, and the actual number of structures occupied at any one time is impossible to assess. Granted this, Figure 3.9 presents one of many possible sequences of the growth at AZ EE:2:76, this one showing the most plausible sequence if the house occupations are distributed as evenly as possible through the five time periods. It must be stressed that this is only one possible sequence; a sequence in which more and finer time divisions were used, during each of which only two structures were occupied, is another possibility. The minimum number of contemporaneous structures at sites in the Rosemont area, even at presumed short-lived sites such as AZ EE:2:116, EE:2:117, and EE:2:122, appears to be two. Regardless, the important point here is the continuity exhibited in house locations and arrangement.

As suggested in Figure 3.9, occupation of AZ EE:2:76 apparently began on the toe of the ridge, with most or all of the downslope arc occupied either contemporaneously or in very rapid succession, possibly with extramural features located behind (upslope of) the houses (Fig. 3.9a). This area was subsequently abandoned and succeeded by the upslope arc, which consisted at various times of the houses in Features 7, 8, 10, and probably 29, possibly with extramural features behind them (Fig. 3.9b-d). The abandoned houses downslope were apparently rapidly filled and that whole area used both for additional extramural work areas and as a cemetery area. The suggested rapid house use, abandonment, and reuse as a cemetery is based on the absence of houses of earlier than Cañada del Oro phase age, and the dating of most of the cremation deposits to the late Cañada del Oro (2) or Rillito phases (6).

In essence, AZ EE:2:76 exhibits patterned groupings of houses, which are clearly different from the common entryway focus of houses surrounding courtyards repeatedly identified at sites in the Phoenix Basin since their initial recognition by Wilcox (Wilcox and others 1981) at Snaketown. This and related issues are discussed more fully in Chapter 10.

AZ EE:2:84

This moderate artifact density, small area site is located on a small ridge terminus north of, and directly overlooking, middle Barrel Canyon (Fig. 3.1). The habitation area is estimated to be 30 m long and 20 m wide, to the west of the linear rock outcrop (Fig. 3.10). All areas east and upslope of this outcrop lack topsoil, with the cobble to boulder gravel substrate exposed on the surface; three 2-m-by-4-m test pits confirmed these areas to be culturally sterile. The site contains four structures and at least 22 extramural features (Table 3.8). All artifacts recovered are tabulated in Table 3.9.

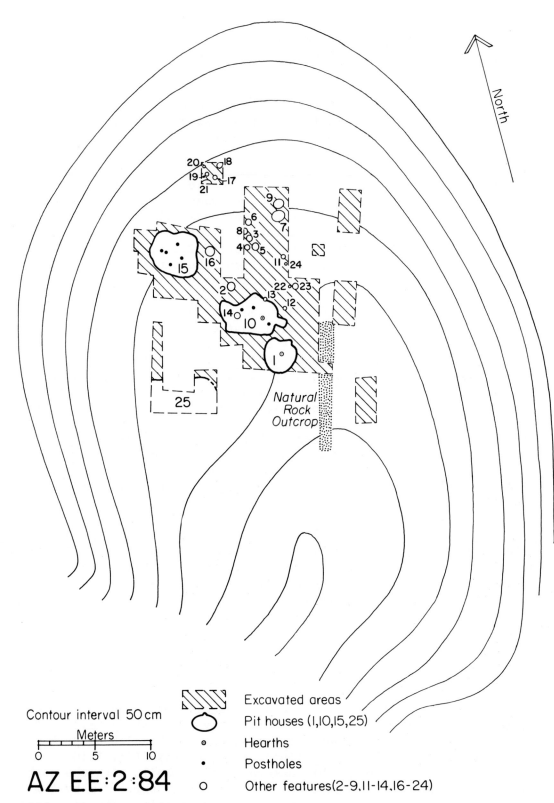

Figure 3.10 Site map, AZ EE:2:84.

Structures

Three pit houses (Features 10, 15, and 25) and one limited-use structure (Feature 1) were partially or completely excavated (Table 3.10). No other structures are thought to be present on this site.

Table 3.8

TYPES AND NUMBERS OF FEATURES, EXCAVATED
AND UNEXCAVATED, AT AZ EE:2:84

Feature Type	Excavated	Unexcavated	Total
Pit houses	3		3
Limited-use structures	1		1
Pits	6	3	9
Roasting pit-hearths	2		2
Pits with rocks	4	2	6
Rock clusters	2		2
Rock-lined pits	1		1
Slab-lined pits	1		1
Cremation deposits	1		1
Total	21	5	26

Feature 1

Feature 1 was a subcircular limited-use structure 3 m in maximum
dimension, with rodent disturbance at its southern edge. It had a
single floor pit, a probable hearth, a possible entryway on its
flattened, northeastern side, and at least six small postholes, most
around its perimeter. A whole basin metate was found inverted in the
fill just above the floor and behind the "entryway." There were also
seven unmodified rocks on the floor, three on the northwest edge of the
hearth.

Features 10, 15, and 25

Both Features 10 and 15 were large, irregularly shaped
structures (6.15 m and 4.5 m in maximim witdth, respectively) which
exhibited a good deal of rodent disturbance. The entryway and eastern
two-thirds of the floor of Feature 10 were fairly well defined; however,
the western one-third of this structure is so badly disturbed that the

Table 3.9

ARTIFACT TOTALS BY CLASS FOR AZ EE:2:84

Artifact Type	Count	Category Total	Percent of Assemblage
Ceramics		619	45.7
Decorated sherds	305		
Plain ware sherds	314		
Chipped Stone		700	51.7
Debitage	627		
Retouched pieces	51		
Cores	16		
Hammerstones	6		
Utilitarian Ground Stone		23	1.7
Metates	7		
Mano-handstones	10		
Polishing stones	1		
Other	1		
Nonutilitarian Stone		5	0.4
Palettes	1		
Bowls	1		
Crystals or minerals	3		
Shell		6	0.4
Bracelets	1		
Other	5		
Worked Bone		1	0.1
Awls-hairpins	1		
Total		1,354	100.0

location of the walls could not be determined. Bulges on the western and southern sides of the Feature 15 house pit could conceivably have been entryways, but were rodent-riddled beyond definition.

The eastern end of Feature 25 was easily followed, but the western end and floor were not, and the full outline of this feature was never exposed. If all of this area was a single structure, it was over 6 m long.

Table 3.10

STRUCTURE DATING AND CONTENT SUMMARY, AZ EE:2:84

Feature Number	Age Assignment	Basis for Dating					Burned	Trash Filled	Floor Assemblage	Intrudes Features	Intruded by Features
		Site Ceramics	Floor Ceramics	Fill Ceramics	Superimposition	Other					
001000	Rillito or early Rincon	x									
010000	Rillito or early Rincon			x							?
015000	Rillito or early Rincon			x							
025000	Rillito or early Rincon			x				u		u	u

Slope Trash

Slope trash was thinly but evenly distributed on the west, north, and east slopes of the ridge terminus.

Extramural Features

Twenty-one extramural features were found, including nine pits (Features 6, 8, 9, 16, 19, 20, and 22 through 24), six pits with rocks (Features 3, 4, 5, 14, 18, and 21), two roasting pit-hearths (Features 7 and 17), two rock clusters (Features 2 and 11), and two stone-lined pits (Features 12 and 13). A visual inspection of the site map (Fig. 3.10) strongly suggests that were the north central part of the habitation area excavated further, many more such features would be found.

Flotation samples from three adjacent pits with rocks (Features 3, 4, and 5), and a roasting pit-hearth nearby (Feature 17) produced relatively abundant corn remains (Miksicek 1984a; Appendix B).

Burials

Cremation Deposits

In the middle of Feature 7, a roasting pit, was a small plain ware jar tilted slightly to the southeast, with a partial Rincon Red-on-brown, Style A bowl beneath it, on the northwest. A few bones of a child no more than one and a half years old were recovered from the jar fill (Appendix D).

Ceramics and Dating

The ceramics from the site indicate an occupation which probably occurred during the end of the Rillito phase and beginning of the Rincon phase (Table 3.11). The relative abundance of Rincon Red-on-brown, Style A and other Rincon Red-on-brown sherds of indeterminate style show the bulk of the occupation was probably in early Rincon times. A single sherd of Rio Rico Polychrome from the upper fill of a pit house, Feature 15, appears to be a later intrusive.

Nonceramic Artifacts

Counts of all artifact types can be found in Table 3.9. The artifact assemblage at this site is notable for an extremely high percentage of chipped stone items in comparison to sherds; chipped stone actually outnumbers sherds. The only other site where this occurred was AZ EE:2:129, across Barrel Canyon to the west. At AZ EE:2:129, this situation may be attributed to an artifact assemblage associated with an extramural work area and roasting pits rather than a habitation area, as well as admixture from an Archaic component. To an extent, the same may be true at AZ EE:2:84, where extramural features are unusually numerous; however, there is no suggestion of Archaic admixture at AZ EE:2:84.

Subsistence

Thirty-five pieces of animal bone, representing at least three rabbits and a turtle, were recovered (Appendix A). Most of the fragments (24) were unidentified large mammal bone.

Corn was the only commonly occurring plant in the flotation samples, present in several extramural features and one pit house, Feature 15 (Miksicek 1984a; Appendix B). Acorns, walnuts, pinyon cone scales, and pigweed and chenopod seeds all occurred in limited numbers. Interestingly, most of these were recovered from the Feature 10 pit house, and corn was absent from these samples.

Table 3.11

DECORATED POTTERY TYPES FROM AZ EE:2:84

Provenience	Rillito Red-on-brown	Unidentified Colonial	Rincon Red-on-brown Style A	Rincon Red-on-brown Style ?	Rio Rico Polychrome	Sacaton Red-on-buff	Total
Stripping			9	5			14
Feature 10 (pit house)		1	18				19
Feature 15 (pit house)	2		4	3	1	3	13
Feature 25 (pit house)	2			2			4
Feature 6 (pit)			1				1
Feature 7 (cremation deposit)			PB				PB
Total	4	1	32	10	1	3	51

PB = partial bowl
Note: partial vessel not included in totals

Summary

Dating to Rillito and early Rincon phase times, AZ EE:2:84 is the only essentially single component, small, early site among those excavated in the exchange area. Other sites with components contemporaneous with AZ EE:2:84, and which may have resembled it in size at one time (AZ EE:2:76, EE:2:105, and EE:2:113), had other earlier or later components which obscured the late Rillito/early Rincon configuration of features. Even at AZ EE:2:84 all features may not have been absolutely contemporaneous, and any description of site structure is tentative. With none of the structures obviously trash filled, and only Feature 10 having a clear predominance of identifiable decorated sherds from a single time period (Table 3.11), no ordering of feature construction or abandonment can be inferred. In very general functional terms, it can be noted that the extramural features appear to cluster on the northern edge of the site. Unlike limited-use structures used for the ritual seclusion of "dangerous" individuals, which tend to be separated from permanent structures, the limited-use structure (Feature 1) is not isolated from the pit houses, suggesting it may have been used for temporary habitation or storage (this problem is further discussed in Chapter 10). The proportion of extramural features to structures is quite high, although the significance of this is unclear.

Subsistence data suggests some dependence on corn, with a variety of wild plant foods harvested as well. Animal bone is relatively more common at AZ EE:2:84, as compared to later small sites, suggesting a proportionately greater dependence on hunting at AZ EE:2:84.

AZ EE:2:105--The Ballcourt Site

AZ EE:2:105, the Ballcourt Site, was recorded as a high artifact density, large area site occupying a 300 m long segment of one of the largest flat-topped ridges in the exchange area, along upper South Canyon (Fig. 3.1). This ridge is almost 1000 m long, aligned on a roughly southwest-northeast axis, and slopes downhill towards the north. The southern end of the site area corresponds to a break in slope, the elevation of the ridge dropping abruptly from 1 m to 4 m in elevation at this point. The ridge then drops gradually some 10 m in elevation over the length of the site area (300 m), and another 10 m over the remainder of the ridgetop. The ridge is terminated by the convergence of two flanking washes, South Canyon on the east side, and an unnamed tributary on the northwest.

The entire 1000 m length of the ridge was tested with parallel backhoe trenches spaced 8 m apart and perpendicular to the long axis of the ridge when possible. Some areas required judgemental trench placement and orientation so as to accommodate the topography or to avoid cutting the water line which runs the length of this ridge. A map of the entire ridge showing elevation contours and trench locations is on file, with the rest of the project records, with the Cultural Resource Management Division, Arizona State Museum.

In width, the ridge ranges from 30 m to 60 m, with the habitation area occupying the widest segment (Fig. 3.11). This area contains at least 27 house pits and 112 known extramural features (Table 3.12). Collected artifacts are tabulated in Table 3.13, and Table 3.14 presents a list of the features and subfeatures.

Structures

Twenty-one house pits, representing 23 pit houses and 3 limited-use structures, were partially or completely excavated; an additional 6

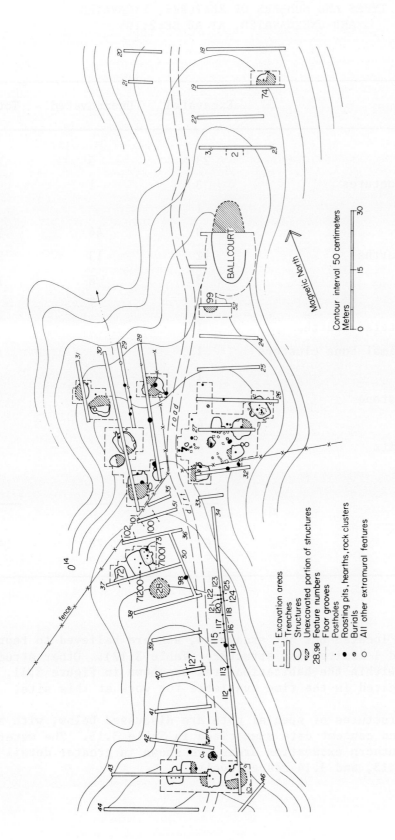

Figure 3.11 Site map, AZ EE:2:105 -- the Ballcourt Site.

Table 3.12

TYPES AND NUMBERS OF FEATURES, EXCAVATED
AND UNEXCAVATED, AT AZ EE:2:105

Feature Type	Excavated	Unexcavated	Total
Pit houses	23	5	28
Limited-use structures	3	1	4
Ballcourts	1		1
Pits	9	44	53
Roasting pit-hearths	12	13	25
Pits with rocks	3	8	11
Rock clusters		7	7
Extramural plastered hearths	1		1
Artifact and animal bone clusters	1		1
Borrow pits (?)	1		1
Caches: ground stone	4		4
Caches: pottery	4		4
Cremation deposits	4		4
Inhumations	1		1
Total	67	78	145

house pits were located but not excavated, and are believed to represent
5 pit houses and 1 limited-use structure (Table 3.12). Other structures
probably exist within the habitation area as shown in Figure 3.11, but
could not be located in the time available for work at this site.

Only structures of special note are discussed below, with basic
chronological and content data summarized in Table 3.15. The wstern,
eastern, and southern excavation areas are shown in greater detail in
Figures 3.12, 3.13, and 3.14 respectively.

Table 3.13

ARTIFACT TOTALS BY CLASS FOR AZ EE:2:105, THE BALLCOURT SITE

Artifact Type	Count	Category Total	Percent of Assemblage
Ceramics		15,673	61.6
Decorated sherds	2,694		
Red ware sherds	48		
Plain ware sherds	12,925		
Figurine fragments	6		
Chipped Stone		9,378	36.8
Debitage	8,314		
Retouched pieces	790		
Cores	184		
Hammerstones	90		
Utilitarian Ground Stone		238	0.9
Metates	53		
Mano-handstones	156		
Polishing stones	11		
Tabular knives	4		
3/4-grooved axes	3		
Other	11		
Nonutilitarian Stone		43	0.2
Palettes	13		
Worked slate	2		
Bowls	4		
Jewelry	6		
Crystals or minerals	16		
Other	2		
Shell		58	0.2
Bracelets	38		
Other	26		
Worked Bone		73	0.3
Awls-hairpins	43		
Antler flakers	4		
Other	26		
Total		25,463	100.0

Table 3.14

EXCAVATED FEATURE INFORMATION, AZ EE:2:105

Feature or Subfeature Number	Interpretation and Description
1	ballcourt
1001	posthole or pit in ballcourt floor
5	pit house
5001	intrusive roasting pit-hearth
5002	possible hearth (unlined pit with ash)
6	two superimposed pit houses ?
6001	intrusive roasting pit-hearth
6007	floor pit or posthole
7	two superimposed pit houses: upper (earlier) Floor 1 and lower (later) Floor 2
7007	floor pit in Floor 2
7009	floor pit in Floor 1
7022	floor pit in Floor 2, with infant inhumation
9	pit house with a later limited-use structure (Feature 60) within it
9001	intrusive pit in entryway
9002	floor pit
9003	floor pit
9004	intrusive pit
9005	hearth (burned area of floor plaster)
10	two superimposed pit houses ?

Table 3.14, continued

EXCAVATED FEATURE INFORMATION, AZ EE:2:105

Feature or Subfeature Number	Interpretation
10001	hearth (burned area of floor)
11	pit house
12	pit house (severely rodent disturbed)
13	collective designation for a corner of a pit house, an extramural pit, and an extramural roasting pit-hearth (contents of 5 subfeatures can no longer be separated)
14	ground stone cache on surface
15	pit with rocks
16	roasting pit-hearth
25	roasting pit-hearth
28	cremation deposit, Trench 26
29	pottery cache
30	limited-use structure
30001	intrusive (?) roasting pit-hearth
30002	pit (intrusive ?) in Feature 30 structure floor
30003	floor pit
34	roasting pit-hearth
35	borrow pit (?)
38	pit house
38008	probable hearth (unlined pit)

Table 3.14, continued

EXCAVATED FEATURE INFORMATION, AZ EE:2:105

Feature or Subfeature Number	Interpretation
41	pit house
41001	cluster of animal bone above floor
41002	intrusive roasting pit-hearth
41013	intrusive cremation deposit
44	pottery cache
46	pit
50	two superimposed pit houses: upper (earlier) Floor 1 and lower (later) Floor 2
50001	intrusive roasting pit-hearth
51	cremation deposit
52	pit with rocks
53	pottery cache
56	pit
57	ground stone cache (?)
60	limited-use structure within the Feature 9 house pit
60001	probable hearth
60002	probable hearth, cut by 60003
60003	probable hearth, cuts 60002
62	roasting pit-hearth
63	rock-lined roasting pit-hearth

Table 3.14, continued

EXCAVATED FEATURE INFORMATION, AZ EE:2:105

Feature or Subfeature Number	Interpretation
65	two superimposed pits
71	two superimposed pit houses: later (71001) house and earlier (71200) house
71001	pit house, intrudes 71200 pit house
71007	hearth (unlined pit)
71200	pit house, intruded by 71001 pit house
71201	hearth (unlined pit)
71202	floor pit
71205	floor pit
71208	main roof support posthole (1 of 2)
71209	floor pit
71214	main roof support posthole (1 of 2)
71215	floor pit
71216	posthole
72	pit house
74	pit house located north of ballcourt, Trench 19
76	ground stone cache
78	pit
80	cremation deposit
81	pit house

Table 3.14, continued

EXCAVATED FEATURE INFORMATION, AZ EE:2:105

Feature or Subfeature Number	Interpretation
81001	hearth (plastered)
81009	hearth (plastered)
82	pit
87	pit house
87001	shallow depression in corner of pit house, ringed with postholes (may be intrusive)
87006	hearth (unlined, rodent-disturbed pit)
88	pit house, intrudes Feature 91 pit house
90	limited-use structure intruded by two roasting pit-hearths
90001	intrusive (?) roasting pit-hearth (may be rock lined)
90002	intrusive (?) roasting pit-hearth
91	pit house, intruded by Feature 88 pit house
98	roasting pit-hearth, Trench 50
103	roasting pit-hearth
110	pit with rocks, intrudes Feature 81 pit house
126	extramural hearth (plastered)

Table 3.15

STRUCTURE DATING AND CONTENT SUMMARY, AZ EE:2:105

Feature Number	Age Assignment	Basis for Dating									
		Site Ceramics	Floor Ceramics	Fill Ceramics	Superimposition	Other	Burned	Trash Filled	Floor Assemblage	Intrudes Features	Intruded by Features
005000	Colonial ?			x			+				+
006000 (Floor 1)	Colonial			x	x						+
006000 (Floor 2)	early Rincon	x			x		+	+		+	+
007000 (Floor 1)	Colonial			x	x		?				+
007000 (Floor 2)	early Rincon			x	x		+			+	
009000	Colonial			x	x		+				+
010000 (Floor 1)	Cañada del Oro			x	x		?				+
010000 (Floor 2)	Colonial			x	x		?			+	
011000	?						?				
012000	early Rincon			x			+	?			
013000	?						?				
030000	Colonial ?			x							+
038000	Colonial			x			?				

Table 3.15, continued

STRUCTURE DATING AND CONTENT SUMMARY, AZ EE:2:105

Feature Number	Age Assignment	Basis for Dating						Burned	Trash Filled	Floor Assemblage	Intrudes Features	Intruded by Features
		Site Ceramics	Floor Ceramics	Fill Ceramics	Superimposition	Other						
041000	Colonial			x					?			+
050000 (Floor 1)	Colonial			x	x				?			+
050000 (Floor 2)	early Rincon	x		x	x				+		+	+
060000	early Rincon			x	x						+	
071001	early Rincon			x	x				+		+	
071200	Rillito		x	x	x			+	?	+		+
072000	Rillito ?			x					?			
074000	early Rincon	x		x				+				
081000	early/middle Rincon			x		x						
087000	early Rincon			x								?
088000	Rillito/ early Rincon			x	x						+	
090000	early Rincon			x		x						+
091000	Rillito/ early Rincon			x	x							+

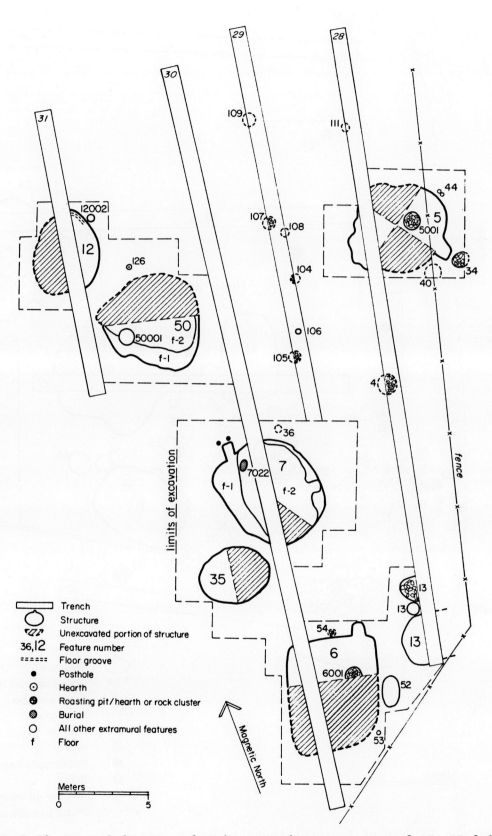

Figure 3.12   Map of features found at northwestern part of AZ. EE:2:105.

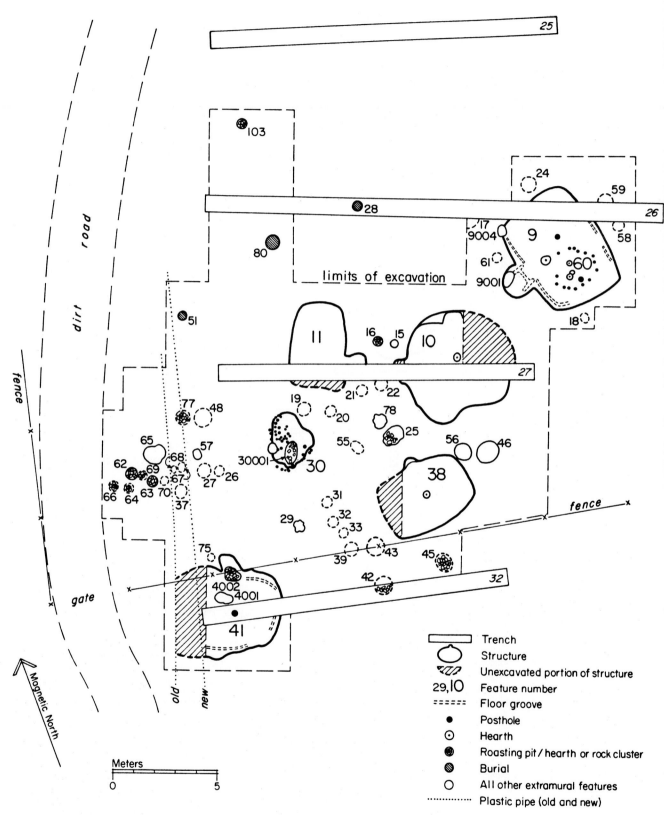

Figure 3.13 Map of features found at northeastern part of AZ EE:2:105.

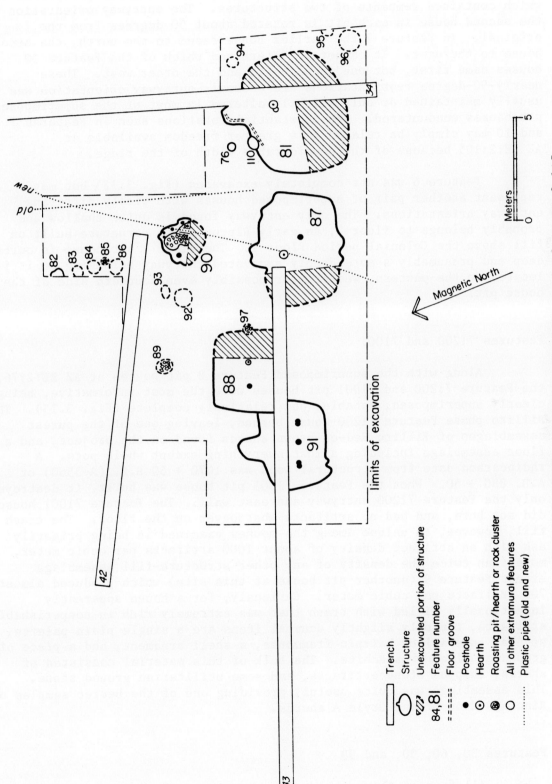

Figure 3.14 Map of features found at southern end of AZ EE:2:105.

Features 6, 7, and 10

Features 7 and 10 (Figs. 3.12 and 3.13) are house pits, each of which contained remnants of two structures. The entryway orientation of the second house in each pit is rotated about 90 degrees from the original. In Feature 7 the earlier house faced to the north, the second house to the east. It cannot be determined which of the Feature 10 houses came first, but one faced north and the other west. These nearly-90-degree reorientations are unusual; entryway orientation was usually maintained or only slightly altered in most of the superimposed pit houses encountered. The substantial rotations seen in Features 7 and 10 may simply be related to a greater freedom available at AZ EE:2:105 because of the considerable width of the ridge.

Feature 6 was not completely excavated (Fig. 3.12) but may represent another pair of superimposed houses with widely differing entryway orientations. The only entryway found is quite shallow and probably belongs to Floor 2, an early Rincon phase structure built on fill above the Colonial period Floor 1. The Floor 1 pit house is quite deep and presumably a more deeply excavated entryway belonging to it is located on the eastern, western, or possibly even southern side of the house pit.

Features 71200 and 71001

Along with the superimposed Feature 8 pit houses at AZ EE:2:76, the Feature 71200 and 71001 pit houses were the most informative, being clearly superimposed, datable, and relatively complete (Fig. 3.15). The Rillito phase Feature 71200 house burned, leaving one of the purest assemblages of Rillito Red-on-brown sherds found on the project, and a floor assemblage including almost everything except whole pots. A radiocarbon date from structural wood was 1070 ± 50 B.P. (A-3560) or A.D. 880 ± 50. When the Feature 71001 pit house was built, it destroyed only the Feature 71200 entryway and east wall. The Feature 71001 house did not burn, and had no artifacts whatsoever on the floor. The trash fill, however, is unique among the houses examined in being primarily ash with an artifact density of about 1000 artifacts per cubic meter, more than twice the density of any other structure-fill assemblage except Feature 9 (another pit house at this site) which produced almost 700 artifacts per cubic meter. Curiously, for a house apparently intentionally filled with trash that was extremely rich in nonperishable artifacts, the only slightly unusual items are a single plain palette, several bone awl or hairpin fragments, a shell ornament, and a piece of ground azurite and malachite. The bulk of this material consisted of sherds, chipped stone artifacts, and some utilitarian ground stone. This assemblage was quite useful, providing one of the better samples of Rincon Red-on-brown, Style A sherds.

Features 30, 60, 90, and 99

All four of these structures, by virtue of their small size or lack of internal features, are classed here as limited-use structures.

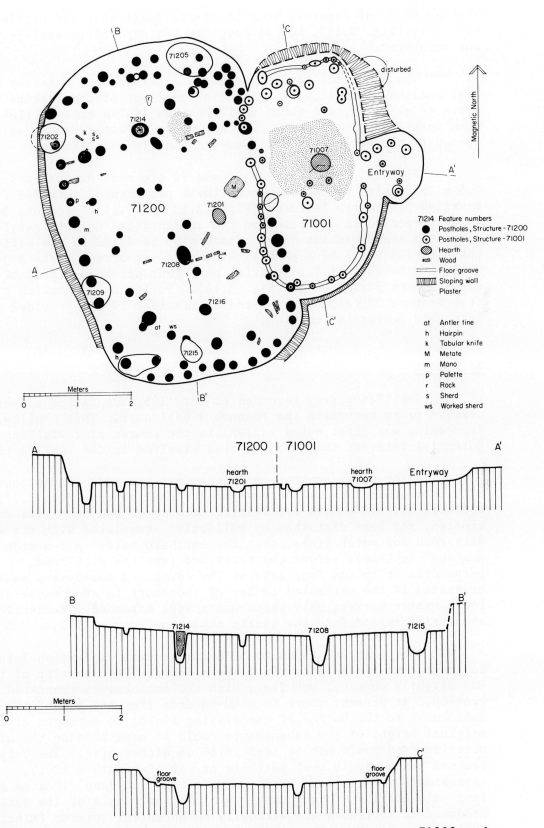

Figure 3.15 Plan view and cross sections of the Feature 71200 and 71001 pit houses at AZ EE:2:105.

Feature 99 is of interest because of its small size and proximity to the ballcourt (Fig. 3.11), but although it was exposed in profile, it was not excavated.

The existence of Feature 60 is inferred from a fairly distinct oval outline of shallow postholes in the floor of the Feature 9 pit house (Fig. 3.16), and three small hearths inside this outline, which seem unrelated to the layout of that house. Feature 60 appears to have opened to the northwest, and possessed no floor artifacts.

Finally, both Features 30 and 90 are oval excavations less than 2.5 m long, with postholes around their perimeters, intruded (?) by roasting pit-hearth features (Figs. 3.13 and 3.14). Feature 30 may be Colonial period in age based on two unidentified Colonial style decorated sherds in its fill. Feature 90 is dated to the early Rincon phase on the basis of a partial Rincon Red-on-brown, Style A jar in its fill, and because of its location near four pit houses probably also early Rincon phase in age (Fig. 3.14). Pollen and flotation samples from Feature 30 (Appendixes B and C; Miksicek 1984a) provided no insight into this feature's function.

Ballcourt

The 1976 survey recorded AZ EE:2:105, but failed either to observe or to recognize the Feature 1 ballcourt. This shallow, oval depression was first noted in 1981 in the course of revisiting sites of potential interest that had not been examined in the testing phase.

Prior to excavation, a contour map was made of the court, using a 10-cm contour interval because of its shallowness (Fig. 3.17). The southern end was chosen for testing because it had been less damaged by erosion, and less disturbed by bulldozing associated with the adjacent dirt road and water lines, than the northern half. A 1-m-wide trench was dug completely across the court and into the dirt road, by hand, perpendicular to the long axis of the court. A 4-m-by-4-m square was excavated in the estimated center of the court in an unsuccessful hunt for a center marker; only these units were screened. Excavation was eventually expanded to the limits shown in Figure 3.17.

The court was found to be a simple oval excavation into sterile sediments; no plastered surfaces were found. The interior of the court was slightly concave, not flat, with the embankments truncated by erosion. At present there is a 40-cm drop from the top of the west embankment to the bottom of the playing field; no estimate of the original height of the embankments could be made because the original outer surface could not be identified on either side. The only internal feature was a single oval posthole or pit (Subfeature 1001), approximately 40 cm long by 30 cm wide by 35 cm deep, located along the long axis midline of the court. A flotation sample of its entire fill produced no artifacts and virtually no botanical remains (Miksicek 1984a; Appendix B). The Subfeature 1001 posthole-pit appears to be located somewhere between one-fourth and one-third of the length of the

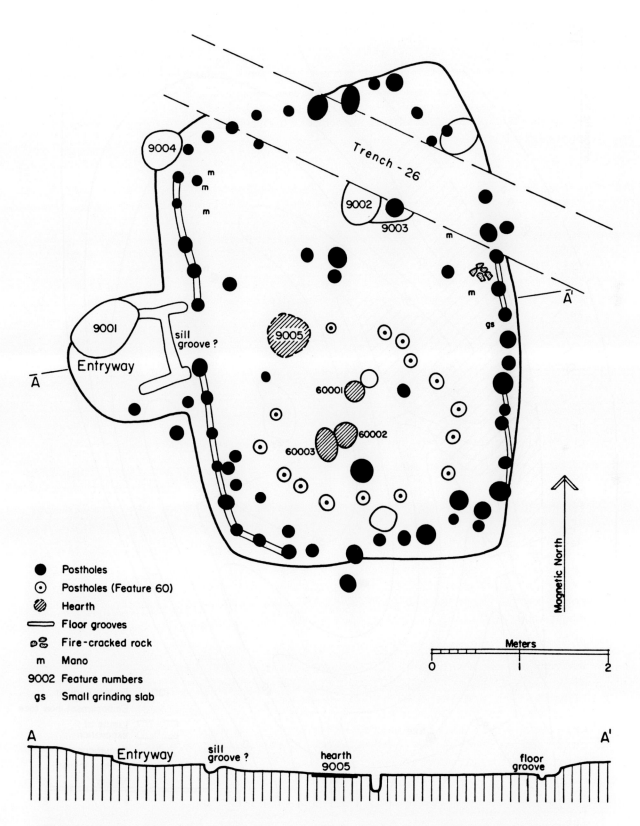

Figure 3.16 Plan view and cross section of the Colonial period Feature 9 pit house and intrusive postholes and hearths associated with the early Rincon phase limited-use structure, Feature 60, at AZ EE:2:105.

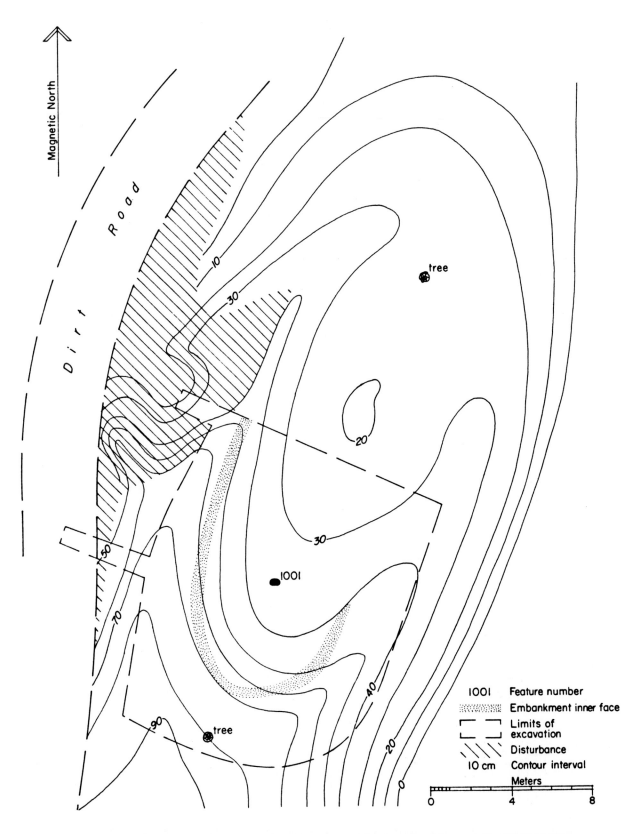

Figure 3.17 Contour map of the ballcourt (Feature 1) at AZ EE:2:105
prior to excavation. The inner face of the embankments and the location
of a pit or posthole in the playing field (Subfeature 1001) also shown.

court from the south end (Fig. 3.17). Although neither center nor end
markers were found, it would be of interest to know if a similar
posthole or pit exists along the long-axis midline in the northern one-
third of the court.

Wilcox and Sternberg (1983: 182) questioned whether there might
have been fences or palisades around ballcourts or perhaps along the
embankment tops. The area excavated around the AZ EE:2:105 ballcourt
was purposely extended outside the embankments to look for postholes
which might have been part of such features. None were found
immediately outside the court, and the erosion of the embankment tops
has been such that evidence of such features would probably have been
obliterated.

The extreme southern edge of the excavated embankment inner
surface was indistinct, and it is impossible to determine whether the
ends of the court were open or closed. This problem is largely
attributed to severe root disturbance from a large mesquite at this end
of the court (and a smaller tree not shown in Fig. 3.17); unfortunately,
the presence of another mesquite at the northern end offered little hope
for resolving this question. If present, the passage through the
southern end of the court was no more than 1 m in width.

Both red-on-brown and red-on-buff sherds were recovered from the
court fill; however none were identifiable as to type. The only
temporally diagnostic prehistoric artifact recovered was an Archaic
projectile point. The court contained relatively few artifacts and did
not appear trash filled.

Excavation of the ballcourt had just begun when Wilcox and
Sternberg (1983) was in press, and some modifications to the data they
present (1983: 102) on the AZ EE:2:105 court are now needed. Their
embankment-crest-to-embankment-crest length and width measurements of
24.8 m and 12.0 m, respectively, are accurate. However, their estimates
of interior dimensions of 17.5 m and 7.4 m are probably somewhat small.
An estimate of approximately 20.0 m long by 8.5 m wide for the court's
playing field or floor is suggested, based on the excavated area.
Wilcox and Sternberg estimated a depth of 50+ cm for the court which,
again, is probably as accurate as possible without the original height
of the embankments.

One problem of interest is the estimate of court orientation.
During a field inspection prior to excavation, Wilcox estimated the
AZ EE:1:105 court to be oriented 44 degrees east of true north (Wilcox
and Sternberg 1983: 102). Excavation showed the court to be oriented
somewhat more to the west than expected based on the configuration of
the pre-excavation contour lines (Fig. 3.17), at about 35 degrees east
of true north (22-23 degrees east of magnetic north). This suggests
that the accuracy of compass orientations for unexcavated ballcourts is
probably proportional to the size and absolute height of the embankments
and the degree of disturbance. The AZ EE:2:105 court is extremely
shallow and is located next to the edge of the ridge, causing greater
erosion of the eastern embankment. Drainage of water out of the

court to the northeast has caused the erosion to be lopsided, all of which contributed to the 10-degree error in the surface estimates.

The absence of rock construction, trash mounds, and platform mounds in association with the AZ EE:2:105 court noted by Wilcox and Sternberg (1983: 102) are correct; however, it is conceivable that a plaza area does exist between the ballcourt and the pit houses to the south, between Trenches 52 and 26 (Fig. 3.11). Additional testing of this area might support or refute this suggestion.

Finally, Wilcox and Sternberg classify the Rosemont court as their Type A, (short and narrow), presumably used by two teams of one or two members each (1983: 177-179). The area of the playing field for the Rosemont court (calculated using a compensating polar planimeter) would be about 112 square meters if Wilcox and Sternberg's estimates of 17.5 m and 7.4 m are used, 144 square meters using the measurements (20.0 m and 8.5 m) suggested here.

Slope Trash

Prior to trenching the site, a reconnaissance of the entire slope perimeter of the ridge was made. The probable location of the habitation area of the site was determined based on the distribution of slope trash, and was confirmed by the subsequent trenching and excavation. Trash was present on both the eastern and western slopes only in those areas where there were adjacent pit houses or features (not including the ballcourt). Trash was notably densest on the eastern slope, south of the fence, below Trench 34 (Fig. 3.11).

Extramural Features

A total of 107 extramural features was found, including 53 pits, 25 roasting pit-hearths, 11 pits with rocks, 1 extramural plastered hearth, 7 rock clusters, 1 artifact and animal bone cluster, 8 caches of pottery or ground stone, and 1 probable borrow pit. Upon excavation six of these ("Features" 8, 23, 47, 49, 79, and 119) were attributed to natural rather than cultural processes, and have been omitted from site maps and tables.

Pits and Hearths

Pits and roasting pit-hearths occur in all extramural feature areas. Those in Trench 34 (Fig. 3.11) may or may not be isolated from pit houses.

Flotation samples from 10 roasting pit-hearths, 3 pits, and 1 pit with rocks produced varied results. The amount of botanical materials recovered was generally low; corn, and to a lesser extent, chenopod seeds, were the only items recovered with any regularity (Miksicek 1984a; Appendix B). The roasting pit that intrudes into the

Feature 5 pit house (Subfeature 5001) was a notable exception to this, producing corn and chenopod remains in abundance, some agave fiber, and single occurrences of a variety of seeds including clammy weed, hedgehog cactus, juniper, Acalypha, and Argemone (Miksicek 1984a; Appendix B). Very little bone was recovered from extramural feature fill.

A single extramural, plastered hearth (Feature 126) was found just north of the Feature 50 house pit (Fig. 3.12). It was an irregularly shaped, flat area of burned plaster some 20 cm across resting on the prehistoric ground surface. Only one other plastered, extramural hearth was found on the project, Feature 46 at AZ EE:2:77. It too is of uncertain function, although it may be associated with a sherd-lined, sherd-filled pit.

Artifact and Animal Bone Clusters

Just above the floor of the Feature 41 pit house was a substantial, intrusive cluster of deer bone and a thoroughly fire-shattered, elongate slab metate (Subfeature 41001). While virtually all portions of the deer were represented, no antler fragments were found, and only the cranial material was burned. The entire animal might have been processed on the spot, with the head, shorn of its rack (to be used as tools ?), and promptly cooked for a meal of brains. Alternatively, as at AZ EE:2:76 and EE:2:113, this type of feature may represent trash disposal or may be a ritual deposit, not associated with food processing.

Possible Borrow Pit

Feature 35, located just southeast of the Feature 7 house pit, was the largest extramural pit found at the site (Fig. 3.12). Because of its size, it is presumed to have been used as a source of clay. Its fill included sherds, flaked stone artifacts, and hammerstones. This deposit apparently dates to the Colonial period, based on the decorated ceramics in the fill (Table 3.16). An elaborate shell bird pendant, also presumed to be of Colonial period age, was found in the upper fill of the pit.

Caches: Ground Stone and Pottery

Four caches of utilitarian ground stone items were found on AZ EE:2:105, and are discussed in detail in Chapter 6.

Four caches of pottery were also found. Feature 44 consisted of a whole plain ware jar and bowl inverted on the prehistoric ground surface immediately outside the Feature 5 pit house (Fig. 3.12). Feature 53 was a whole plain ware jar inverted on the prehistoric ground surface outside the Feature 6 house pit (Fig. 3.12). A red ware bowl, also apparently intact, was presumably upside down on the prehistoric ground surface just south of the Feature 50 house pit (Fig. 3.12);

Table 3.16

DECORATED POTTERY TYPES FROM AZ EE:2:105

Provenience	Cañada del Oro Red-on-brown	Rillito Red-on-brown	Unidentifiable Colonial	Rincon Red-on-brown, Style A	Rincon Red-on-brown, Style B	Rincon Red-on-brown, style ?	Snaketown Red-on-buff	Gila Butte Red-on-buff	Santa Cruz Red-on-buff	Sacaton Red-on-buff	Dos Cabezas Red-on-brown	Galiuro Red-on-brown	Cerros Red-on-white (early)	Trincheras Purple-on-red	Total
Stripping	20	45	24	69	2	70		3	9	5	3	1	1	2	254
Feature 5 pit house	3	6	3			7		1							20
Feature 6 pit houses	12	15	13	2PB,1WB 37		15		13	4		1	1			111
Feature 7 pit houses	4	16	15	14	2	61	2	3	6			1	1		125
Feature 9 pit house	2	2	4	7	1	5		5	4			1			31
Feature 10 pit houses	10	2	5			1		1	2						21
Feature 11 pit house						1									1
Feature 12 pit house		1	1	4		1		1							8
Feature 30 limited-use structure			2												2
Feature 38 pit house	1	1							1						3
Feature 41 pit house	1	1	4			3		1	3						13
Feature 50 pit houses	4	4	5			10			1	1					25
Feature 71001 pit house	1	9	3	26		126			2	1		1			169
Feature 71200 pit house	1	59	28	7	1	36			9	1	1				142
Feature 72 pit house		4	1		1	2									8
Feature 74 pit house						3									3
Feature 81 pit house	1	3	3	2	5	9								1	24
Feature 87 pit house	2		2	9		4			1					3	21
Feature 88 pit house		3	8	1		23									35
Feature 90 limited-use structure				PJ					2	1				3	6
Feature 91 pit house	2		4	2		11									19
Feature 5001 roasting pit-hearth						6									6
Feature 29 pottery cache				4BP,1PJ											4PB,1PJ
Feature 35 borrow pit	3	6	1	1		1									12
Feature 51 cremation deposit	PJ														PJ
Total*	67	177	126	179	11	395	2	28	44	9	5	5	2	9	1059

*Partial vessels not included in totals.

although not given a feature number, it is included in Table 3.12.
Given that all these vessels were inverted, apparently empty, and near
pit houses, they may simply be vessels not in use, placed in temporary
storage around their owner's homes, such as can be seen in many early
photographs of the homes or brush-kitchens of the Pima, Papago, and
various Yuman groups.

Feature 29 may be different from the three caches described
above. It was located equidistant from several structures (Fig. 3.13)
and consisted of a cluster of 36 miscellaneous plain ware sherds and 4
partial Rincon Red-on-brown, Style A vessels (3 small bowls, 1 small
jar). All had been thoroughly jumbled by the roots of a mesquite tree.
Whether these vessels were originally unbroken, or even complete, is
impossible to tell. This feature could have been a group of temporarily
stored pots, similar to Features 44 and 53, or a deposit of
intentionally smashed vessels.

Burials

Four cremation deposits (Features 28, 41013, 51, and 80) and one
inhumation (Feature 7022) were found. Considering the size of the
burial populations associated with partially contemporaneous occupations
at AZ EE:2:76 and EE:2:113, the sample from AZ EE:2:105 seems
anomalously small. Three were found north of Feature 11 (Fig. 3.13), on
the southern edge of what has already been mentioned as a possible open
area or plaza between the pit houses and the ballcourt. This might be a
cemetery area; if so, the burials are few and dispersed.

Cremation Deposits

Feature 28. This cremation deposit was removed by Trench 26 and
recovered by screening the backdirt. A small, unworked piece of
hematite may be associated with this deposit. No other cultural
materials were found.

Feature 41013. Feature 41013 designates a quantity of cremated
human bone recovered from various levels in the Feature 41 pit house,
both north and south of the backhoe trench. Whether it was originally
scattered through the fill of the Feature 41 pit house, or deposited in
a pit is unknown. It may have been disturbed when the Feature 41001
artifact and animal bone cluster was intruded into the pit house fill.

Feature 51. Although severely rodent disturbed, this deposit is
apparently the cremated bones of an adult and the unburned bones of a
fetus, placed in a pit in an upright jar of Cañada del Oro Red-on-brown.
Four rocks may have been placed around the southeastern edge of the pit.
A few fragments of a cremated Glycymeris bracelet were also found.

Feature 80.   This deposit consisted of cremated bone placed in a shallow pit.   Three flakes, 10 plain ware sherds and 1 unidentifiable red-on-buff sherd are presumably fortuitous inclusions in the pit fill.

Inhumations

Feature 7022.   The remains of a newborn infant were found in a pit within the Feature 7 house pit.   Whether this pit was dug specifically for this interment or was an extant floor pit in either Floor 1 or Floor 2 cannot be determined.   A rodent burrow damaged much of the burial, but it appears that the body was placed face down against the west side of the pit, head to the north, with about half a plain ware bowl placed over the torso and legs.

Ceramics and Dating

The dating of the structures on the basis of floor and fill ceramics is presented in Table 3.16; superpositions and radiocarbon dating (Feature 71200) have been summarized in Table 3.15. Archaeomagnetic samples taken from both superimposed hearths in the Feature 81 pit house (Subfeatures 81001 and 81009) were analyzed.   One produced a date somewhat later than anticipated based on the decorated ceramics; the other failed to yield a date (Appendix F).

Of all the extramural features at the site, only the Feature 29 pottery cache, Feature 35 borrow pit, and Feature 51 cremation deposit could be dated by their artifact contents.

The most informative aspects of the ceramic assemblage are the Rillito Red-on-brown and Rincon Red-on-brown, Style A sherd collections from the 71200 and 71001 pit houses.   AZ EE:2:105 also produced the largest assemblage of Cañada del Oro Red-on-brown found at any of the sites examined.

Nonceramic Artifacts

AZ EE:2:105, the largest site examined, possesses the most varied assemblage of stone, shell, and bone artifacts found on the project (Table 3.13).   Each of these assemblages is detailed in the corresponding section of this report.

Subsistence

Animal bone was abundant at AZ EE:2:105, surpassed in quantity only at AZ EE:2:113.   This may be due in part to a pattern of trash disposal different from that seen at smaller sites, on narrow ridges, where it is easier to throw trash over the side of the ridge. Regardless, it is clear that hunting was an integral part of

subsistence, although its importance relative to growing corn or
gathering wild plant foods cannot be assessed.

Many pollen samples from AZ EE:2:105 had very little preserved
pollen; others showed a complete dominance by cheno-ams, as did all the
analyzed samples from Hohokam sites (Appendix C).

Flotation samples, from extramural features and pit houses
alike, clearly indicate a heavy reliance on corn and chenopods,
supplemented liberally with a wide variety of gathered plants including
pigweed, purslane, clammy weed, prickly poppy, Acalypha, squaw-bush,
juniper berries, hedgehog cactus, prickly pear, mesquite, acorns,
walnuts, agave, and the unidentified seed or fruit represented by the
columnar-celled shell (Miksicek 1984a).

Summary

AZ EE:2:105 was the largest site examined in the Rosemont area,
and the only one believed to have a ballcourt. Throughout its
occupation, from Cañada del Oro through early Rincon phase times, it was
apparently as large as, or several times larger than contemporaneous
sites in the exchange area.

As at virtually all the sites examined, subsistence was based on
a combination, in unknown proportions, of corn agriculture, hunting of
large and small game, and gathering of wild plant foods. Heavy use of
chenopod seeds is also indicated, although whether this plant was a
field weed harvested with the corn, or a cultivated crop in its own
right, is unclear.

Because it includes a ballcourt, site structure at AZ EE:2:105
is obviously different from other sites examined. In the absence of
associated datable material, it was impossible to determine when the
court was built or abandoned, relative to the founding and abandonment
of the site. The ballcourt seems to have been physically isolated from
the habitation area, and may even have been set off from the houses to
the south by a "buffer zone," devoid of features. The exact nature of
this zone or space is unclear.

Only one structure was found north of the ballcourt. Although
only one-quarter of this pit house (Feature 74) was dug, it shows no
observable differences in size, shape, or content from any other pit
house; the reason for its isolated location, north of the ballcourt is
known. Unfortunately, this house could not be dated with any certainty,
but whether earlier than, later than, or contemporaneous with the
ballcourt, it still appears very much isolated from the rest of the
settlement.

The Feature 28, 51, and 80 cremation deposits are all located in
the northern portion of the habitation area as are all cemetery areas
that have been identified on Rosemont Hohokam sites including

AZ EE:2:76, EE:2:77, EE:2:113, and possibly EE:2:84, EE:2:107, and EE:2:120. The unusual aspect of the cemetery area at AZ EE:2:105 is the small number of burials relative to the size of the site. To judge by AZ EE:2:76, EE:2:113, and EE:2:77, one would expect several times the number of cremation deposits and inhumations that were actually found on the Ballcourt Site.

Pit house locations show some continuity through time, and although no obvious Phoenix Basin-type house clusters have been identified, a number of roughly contemporaneous structures in the central part of the site could be said to have entryways with a common focus. A more complete exposure of the main habitation area, and additional houses, might clarify this aspect of site organization.

Finally, in terms of site growth, the central portion of the site (Figs. 3.11, 3.12, 3.13) appears to have been the original, Colonial period, core. In early Rincon times the eastern part of this area (Fig. 3.13) appears to have fallen into disuse, except for the Feature 60 limited-use structure. The western area (Fig. 3.12, 3.15) shows continued use in early Rincon times, possibly expanding to the south; the latest excavated houses are the southern cluster of four structures (Fig. 3.14). Whether the isolation of the Feature 81, 87, 88, and 91 pit houses from the earlier core area is real, or merely a function of trench placement and spacing, is uncertain. Nevertheless, they would appear to be the last houses occupied at the site, and Feature 81 may have been the latest of the four.

AZ EE:2:113--Bumblebee Village

AZ EE:2:113 and EE:2:129 were originally recorded as two separate loci, but were combined in the research design (Gregory and Ferg 1982) as a single large site (comparable to AZ EE:2:105). Backhoe trenching, however, revealed that these two loci were spatially discrete, separated by about 180 m of unoccupied ridge and a small, narrow saddle (Fig. 3.18). AZ EE:2:113 itself is a high artifact density, medium area site on a ridge terminus directly overlooking the confluence of Barrel and McCleary canyons. The habitation area, a roughly circular area some 50 m in diameter, almost completely covers the ridge end (Fig. 3.19). Within this area are 14 structures, at least 211 extramural features, and 26 burials (23 humans and 3 dogs; Table 3.17). All artifacts recovered are tabulated in Table 3.18, and Table 3.19 presents a list of the features and subfeatures.

Structures

Seven house pits, representing 12 pit houses (6100, 6200, 6300, 8, 10100, 10200, 10300, 10400, 11, 12, 83, 154), were partially or completely excavated, as were two limited-use structures (Features 7, 86; Table 3.20). No other structures are thought to be present on the site.

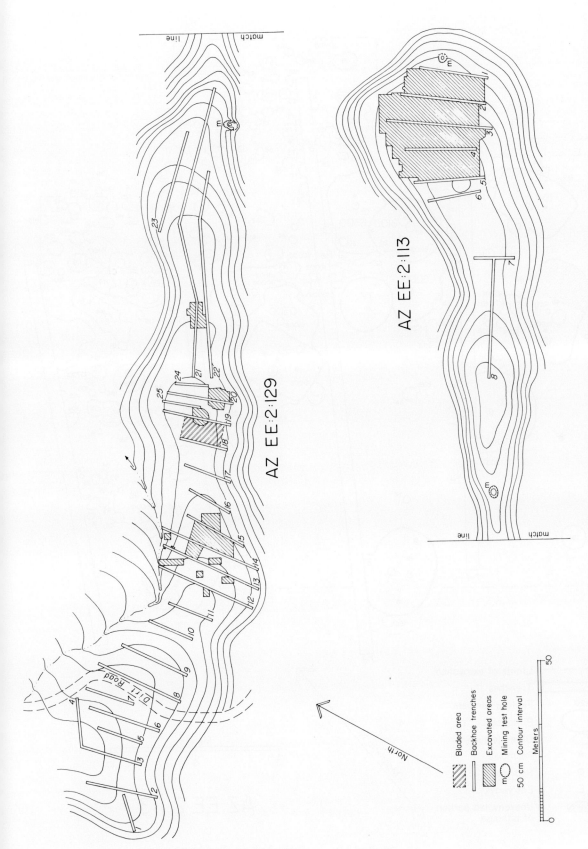

Figure 3.18 Map of ridge upon which AZ EE:2:113 and 129 are located, showing trenches and excavations.

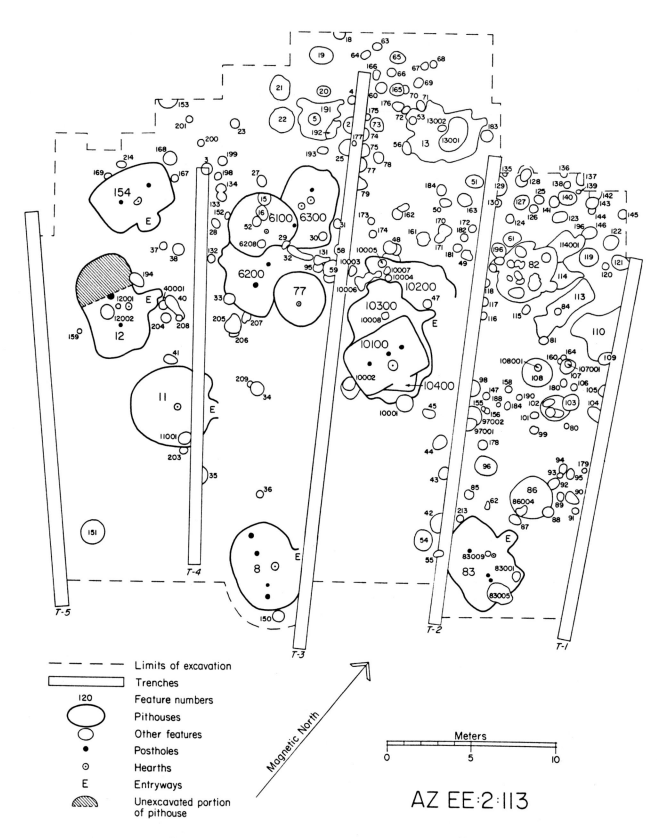

Limits of excavation
Trenches
120 Feature numbers
Pithouses
Other features
Postholes
Hearths
E Entryways
Unexcavated portion of pithouse

Magnetic North

Meters
0   5   10

AZ EE:2:113

Figure 3.19 Site map, AZ EE:2:113 -- Bumblebee Village.

Table 3.17

TYPES AND NUMBERS OF FEATURES, EXCAVATED
AND UNEXCAVATED, AT AZ EE:2:113

Feature Type	Excavated	Unexcavated	Total
Pit houses	12		12
Limited-use structures	2		2
Pits	49	56	105
Roasting pit-hearths	25	18	43
Pits with rocks	9	15	24
Rock clusters	11	17	28
Artifact and animal bone clusters	4		4
Stone platforms	1		1
Borrow pits	2	4	6
Cremation deposits	14		14
Human inhumations	9		9
Domestic dog inhumations	3		3
Total	141	110	251

Features 6100, 6300, 6200, 7

These four structures are notable primarily for the complexity
of their superpositions (Fig. 3.20). Feature 6100 is the earliest of
the four, and possibly the earliest structure on the site; its fill
yielded two sherds that are probably Cañada del Oro Red-on-brown.
Whether there were Cañada del Oro or Rillito phase occupations at
AZ EE:2:113 is difficult to evaluate, for decorated sherds representing
the former phase are extremely rare, and sherds from the latter phase
are invariably mixed with early Rincon materials (Table 3.21). Feature
6100 was intruded by three seated or slouched inhumations (Features 15,
16, 52) and was partially covered by the floors of later pit houses
(6200 and 6300).

Table 3.18

ARTIFACT TOTALS BY CLASS FOR AZ EE:2:113

Artifact Type	Count	Category Total	Percent of Assemblage
Ceramics		8,168	54.0
Decorated sherds	2,921		
Red ware sherds	21		
Plain ware sherds	5,225		
Figurine fragments	1		
Chipped Stone		6,637	43.8
Debitage	5,700		
Retouched pieces	389		
Cores	127		
Hammerstones	61		
Utilitarian Ground Stone		206	1.4
Metates	49		
Mano-handstones	130		
Polishing stones	6		
Tabular knives	3		
3/4-grooved axes	4		
Other	14		
Nonutilitarian Stone		35	0.2
Palettes	10		
Worked and unworked slate	6		
Bowls	1		
Jewelry	5		
Crystals or minerals	12		
Other	1		
Shell		35	0.2
Bracelets	23		
Other	12		
Worked Bone		57	0.4
Awls-hairpins	24		
Other	23		
Total		15,138	100.0

Table 3.19

EXCAVATED FEATURE INFORMATION, AZ EE:2:113

Feature or Subfeature Number	Interpretation and Description
1	probable cremation deposit
2	inhumation; Trench 3
3	inhumation; Trench 4
4	cremation deposit; Trench 3
5	rock-lined roasting pit-hearth
6	collective designation for three superimposed pit houses, all stratigraphically below the Feature 7 pit house; from earliest to most recent, they are: 6100, 6300, 6200
6100	earliest of the three superimposed pit houses that are collectively designated Feature 6; intruded by three inhumations, Features 15, 16 and 52
6102	plastered hearth
6300	pit house, occupied after 6100, and before 6200
6301	cluster of artifacts which intrudes 6300 pit house
6302	lens of ashy soil which intrudes 6300 pit house
6303	cluster of animal bone which intrudes 6300 pit house
6304	cluster of deer mandibles which intrudes 6300 pit house
6305	possible hearth (ash-filled, unlined pit in suitable location in 6300 house floor)
6306	possible hearth (ash-filled, unlined pit in suitable location in 6300 house floor)

Table 3.19, continued

EXCAVATED FEATURE INFORMATION, AZ EE:2:113

Feature or Subfeature Number	Interpretation and Description
6307	one of two main roof support postholes in 6300 pit house
6308	floor pit in 6300 pit house
6309	one of two main roof support postholes in 6300 pit house
6200	most recent of the three superimposed pit houses that are designated Feature 6
6202	floor pit in 6200 house floor
6203	floor pit in 6200 house floor
6204	posthole in 6200 house floor
6205	posthole in 6200 house floor
6206	one of two main roof support postholes in 6200 house floor
6207	posthole with burned post fragment in 6200 house floor
6208	floor pit in 6200 house floor
6209	one of two main roof support postholes in 6200 house floor
7	limited-use structure, stratigraphically above all the Feature 6 pit houses, and actually intrudes the 6200 pit house; Feature 7 is intruded by 7001 and 7002
7001	intrusive cremation deposit
7002	intrusive rock cluster

Table 3.19, continued

EXCAVATED FEATURE INFORMATION, AZ EE:2:113

Feature or Subfeature Number	Interpretation and Description
7003	floor pit
7004	probable hearth (ash-filled, unlined pit in suitable location in limited-use Structure 7)
7005	floor pit
7006	floor pit
8	pit house, entryway cut by Trench 3
8001	main roof support posthole in pit house 8
8002	main roof support posthole in pit house 8
8003	plastered hearth in pit house 8
8004	floor pit in pit house 8
8005	floor pit or possibly a major roof support posthole in pit house 8
8006	floor pit or posthole in pit house 8
8009	floor pit or possibly a major roof support posthole in pit house 8
8011	semicircular group of five small postholes south of hearth in pit house 8; each is round, 5-8 cm in diameter and 7-11 cm deep
8012	at least 15 small postholes in northern corner of floor in pit house 8; 12 form a patterned grouping of six sets of two; each posthole is round, 5-12 cm in diameter and 5-20 cm deep
10	collective designation for what appears to be four superimposd pit houses; from earliest to most recent, they are: 10200, 10300, 10400, 10100

Table 3.19, continued

EXCAVATED FEATURE INFORMATION, AZ EE:2:113

Feature or Subfeature Number	Interpretation and Description
10001	intrusive roasting pit-hearth
10002	intrusive roasting pit-hearth
10007	intrusive pit
10008	intrusive rock cluster
10200	pit house, earliest of the superimposed pit houses that are collectively designated Feature 10; 10200 cuts Feature 48003, was intruded by Feature 47, and was cut by the 10300 pit house
10300	pit house, cuts 10200 pit house, and is cut by 10100 and possibly by 10400 pit houses
10400	probable pit house that cut 10300 pit house and was later almost completely obliterated by 10100 pit house; evidence for 10400 is a corner formed by postholes, east of 10100
10100	pit house, most recent of the superimposed pit houses that are collectively designated Feature 10; 10100 cuts the 10400 and 10300 pit houses
10101	hearth (unlined pit)
11	pit house, intruded by Features 11001 and 203; cut by Trench 4
11001	pit intrusive into fill of Feature 11
11003	ash-filled floor pit
12	pit house, intruded by 12001 and 12002 and superimposed by Feature 194
12001	intrusive pit with rocks

Table 3.19, continued

EXCAVATED FEATURE INFORMATION, AZ EE:2:113

Feature or Subfeature Number	Interpretation and Description
12002	intrusive pit with rocks
12003	hearth (unlined pit)
13	borrow pit with Features 13001, 13002, 13004, 53, 56 and 183 in fill
13001	ash lens, with a possible hearth in it
13002	cluster of animal bone
13004	trenchlike excavation in the bottom of the Feature 13 borrow pit
22	roasting pit-hearth; rock-lined with whole fire-cracked metate sitting in it. Superimposes or is simply a remodeling of earler Feature 22001
22001	roasting pit-hearth under Feature 22
25	inhumation
29	cremation deposit
30	roasting pit-hearth, intruded into fill of Feature 6300 pit house
32	rock cluster
32001	pit partly covered by Feature 32
33	roasting pit-hearth partly atop the 6200 pit house
34	pit atop Feature 209
36	pit
40	pit, cuts or cut by Features 40001 and 208

Table 3.19, continued

EXCAVATED FEATURE INFORMATION, AZ EE:2:113

Feature or Subfeature Number	Interpretation and Description
40001	pit with rocks, cuts or cut by Feature 40
41	roasting pit-hearth
42	pit with rocks; Trench 2
47	roasting pit-hearth
48	collective designation for three superimposed roasting pit-hearths
48001	most recent roasting pit-hearth; cut 48002 and 48003
48002	remnant of a pit cut by 48001
48003	roasting pit-hearth cut by both 48001 and the Feature 10200 pit house
52	inhumation
53	inhumation
54	pit
55	pit
56	pit
60	domestic dog inhumation
61	roasting pit-hearth
62	cremation deposit
62001	pit or posthole adjacent to deposit
66	pit with rocks

Table 3.19, continued

EXCAVATED FEATURE INFORMATION, AZ EE:2:113

Feature or Subfeature Number	Interpretation and Description
70	cremation deposit intruded by the Feature 165 inhumation
72	inhumation
73	pit
75	pit; Trench 3
77	roasting pit-hearth; Trench 3
79	pit; Trench 3
80	cremation deposit; vandalized
81	cremation deposit in fill of Feature 113
82	borrow pit intruded by subfeatures 82001 thru 82011
82001	pit
82002	pit
82003	pit
82004	pit
82005	pit
82006	pit
82007	pit
82008	pit
82009	pit
82010	rock cluster

Table 3.19, continued

EXCAVATED FEATURE INFORMATION, AZ EE:2:113

Feature or Subfeature Number	Interpretation and Description
82011	pit
83	pit house, with Features 213 and 83001 in fill, and 83009 and possibly 83005 intrusive into the fill and floor
83001	intrusive rock cluster
83002	hearth (plastered)
83005	large intrusive pit
83009	intrusive floor pit
83015	cremation deposit in fill of Feature 83 pit house
84	cremation deposit in fill of Feature 113 borrow pit
86	limited-use structure, intruded by Features 87, 88 and 86004
86001	floor pit (?)
86004	intrusive roasting pit-hearth
87	rock cluster
97	collective designation for a roasting pit-hearth (97001) atop a pit (97002)
97001	roasting pit-hearth
97002	pit
99	pit
101	pit

Table 3.19, continued

EXCAVATED FEATURE INFORMATION, AZ EE:2:113

Feature or Subfeature Number	Interpretation and Description
102000	large pit, the floor of which appears to seal 102002 and 102003, and the fill of which is intruded by 102001 and 103000
102001	rock cluster
102002	roasting pit-hearth, probably rock-lined
102003	pit cut by 102002
103	pit; intrudes fill and floor of 102000
106	roasting pit-hearth, rock-lined bottom
107	pit with half bowl on top and another pit (107001) in bottom
107001	pit in bottom of Feature 107 pit; may be a cremation deposit
108	slab-lined shallow pit or platform
108001	intrusive roasting pit-hearth
118	pit with rocks; Trench 2
128	collective designation for two superimposed features
128001	pit with rocks (probable hearth)
128002	pit which apparently cuts 128001
131	rock-filled pit (cache of rocks ?)
147	possible cremation deposit
150	pit with rocks (roasting pit-hearth ?)

Table 3.19, continued

EXCAVATED FEATURE INFORMATION, AZ EE:2:113

Feature or Subfeature Number	Interpretation and Description
153	pit
154	pit house
154001	ash pit
154002	sherd-lined pit (hearth ?)
155	pit, superimposed with Feature 156
156	pit, superimposed with Feature 155
158	pit
159	domestic dog inhumation
160	cremation deposit; probably goes with Feature 164 to make up a single deposit
161	roasting pit-hearth
162	roasting pit-hearth
162001	pit superimposed with Feature 162
164	cremation deposit; see Feature 160
165	inhumation; intrudes Feature 70 cremation deposit
166	pit with rocks
167	pit
168	pit with rocks
169	domestic dog inhumation
175	pit; Trench 3

Table 3.19, continued

EXCAVATED FEATURE INFORMATION, AZ EE:2:113

Feature or Subfeature Number	Interpretation and Description
176	**pit**
177	**pit or posthole** in bottom of Trench 3 adjacent to **Feature 25** inhumation
192	**pit**
194	**roasting** pit-hearth superimposed on the Feature 12 **pit** house
204	bell-shaped pit
205	pit with rocks which intrudes Feature 206
206	pit, intruded by Feature 205
207	pit
208	pit
209	pit; superimposed by Feature 34
214	pit containing a human tibia

The Feature 6200 and 6300 pit houses may never have overlapped; however, the area where this might have occurred is disturbed to such an extent that this cannot be assessed. The suggested earlier age of Feature 6300 (Fig. 3.20 inset) is based on the fact that although the floors of Features 6200 and 6300 are indistinguishable (an orange or reddish brown clay of equal thickness in both), the Feature 6300 floor was more severely disturbed both by rodents and the intrusion of four cultural features. Only one intrusive feature was identified in the Feature 6200 house. Further, this ordering is supported by the relative proportions of Colonial period to Rincon phase pottery in the various structures at the site (see Ceramics and Dating section below).

Table 3.20

STRUCTURE DATING AND CONTENT SUMMARY, AZ EE:2:113

Feature Number	Age Assignement	Basis for Dating									
		Site Ceramics	Floor Ceramics	Fill Ceramics	Superimposition	Other	Burned	Trash Filled	Floor Assemblage	Intrudes Features	Intruded by Features
6100	Colonial			x	x						+
6200	late Rillito/ early Rincon			x	x	x	+			+	+
6300	late Rillito/ early Rincon			x	x	x		?		+	+
7	early Rincon ?	x			x					+	+
8	early Rincon		x	x			+		+		
10100	early Rincon		x	x	x		+	?	+	+	
10200	Colonial	x			x			?			+
10300	Colonial ?/ early Rincon ?	x			x			?		+	+
10400	late Rillito/ early Rincon	x			x		u	?	u	+	+
11	late Rillito/ early Rincon			x				?			+
12	late Rillito/ early Rincon			x							+
83	late Rillito/ early Rincon			x							+

Table 3.20, continued

STRUCTURE DATING AND CONTENT SUMMARY, AZ EE:2:113

Feature Number	Age Assignement	Basis for Dating									
		Site Ceramics	Floor Ceramics	Fill Ceramics	Superimposition	Other	Burned	Trash Filled	Floor Assemblage	Intrudes Features	Intruded by Features
86	Rillito or early Rincon	x						+			+
154	early Rincon	x	x				+	+			

Finally, Feature 7 intruded the Feature 6200 pit house, and was itself intruded by Subfeatures 7001 and 7002; none of these three had any associated identifiable decorated ceramics.

Features 8, 10100, 154

These three are almost certainly the last structures occupied on AZ EE:2:113, as indicated by several lines of evidence. None appear to be trash filled, and none have any features intrusive into their fill, although Feature 8 contained approximately 15 rocks and a number of sherds from a Rincon Red-on-brown, Style A jar, lying flat, in its fill, some 15 cm above the floor. Whether this represents material lying on a collapsed roof, trash thrown into the house pit after abandonment, or a reuse of the partially filled structure is unknown.

The fills of Features 8 and 10100 contained some of the very few Rincon Red-on-brown, Style B sherds found, suggesting they were occupied late in the life of the site. Although lacking Style B sherds, Feature 154 lacks Colonial period sherds, suggesting that it too is relatively late (Table 3.21).

All three houses burned, preserving floor assemblages which included partial vessels of Rincon Red-on-brown, Style A. The Feature 8

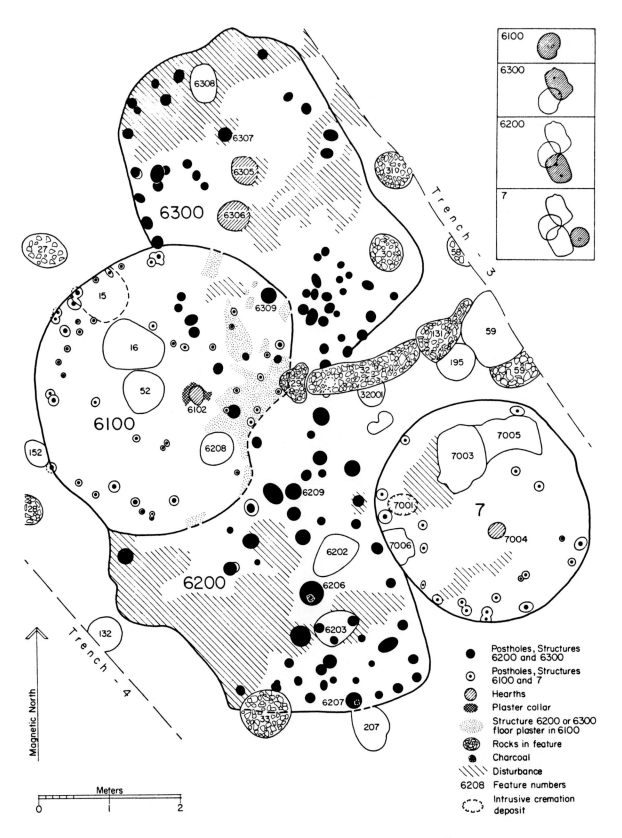

Figure 3.20   Plan view of the Feature 6100, 6300, 6200, and 7
structures with the suggested sequence of superposition (upper right).

Table 3.21

DECORATED POTTERY TYPES FROM AZ EE:2:113

Provenience	Rillito Red-on-brown	Unidentified Colonial	Rincon Red-on-brown Style A	Rincon Red-on-brown Style B	Rincon Red-on-brown Style ?	Santa Cruz Red-on-buff	Sacaton Red-on-buff	Galiuro Red-on-brown	Cerros Red-on-white	Trincheras Purple-on-red	Nogales Polychrome	TOTAL
Stripping	11	1	3PB 41		4	7				7		71
Feature 6 pit houses' fill			1									1
Feature 6100 first pit house		2			1							3
Feature 6300 second pit house	7	1	20		3		10	7		1		49
Feature 6200 third pit house	1		2		2					1		6
Feature 8 pit house	4	3	PB PJ 61	3	12		1	1	1	8		94
Feature 10 pit houses' fill	17	1	16		12		1	7	1	6		61
Feature 10100 pit house	10	6	35	1	24	2	1	8		3		90
Feature 11 pit house	19	1	40		4	3	6	8		4		85
Feature 12 pit house	3	4	24		7		1					39
Feature 83 pit house	15		26		6	3	6	2		2		60
Feature 86 limited-use structure								1			1	2
Feature 154 pit house			PJ 17		2	5				2		26
Feature 5 roasting pit-hearth			6									6
Feature 6301 artifact cluster	1		2									3
Feature 11001 pit								1		2		3
Feature 13 borrow pit	9	2	3		1		1			7		23
Feature 29 cremation deposit?							1					1
Feature 47 roasting pit-hearth			2									2

Table 3.21, continued

DECORATED POTTERY TYPES FROM AZ EE:2:113

Provenience	Rillito Red-on-brown	Unidentified Colonial	Rincon Red-on-brown Style A	Rincon Red-on-brown Style B	Rincon Red-on-brown Style ?	Santa Cruz Red-on-buff	Sacaton Red-on-buff	Galiuro Red-on-brown	Cerros Red-on-white	Trincheras Purple-on-red	Nogales Polychrome	TOTAL
Feature 53 inhumation	1											1
Feature 56 pit			1									1
Feature 62 cremation deposit							WB					WB
Feature 70 cremation deposit	PJ											PJ
Feature 77 roasting pit-hearth	1											1
Feature 80 cremation deposit			3					WB				3 WB
Feature 81 cremation deposit	PB									PB		2PB
Feature 82 borrow pit	3	5	5		1							14
Feature 84 cremation deposit			WJ									WJ
Feature 113 borrow (?) pit	1 / 1											1
Feature 160/164 cremation deposit			WB					WB				2WB
Feature 205 pit with rocks				2	1							3
Feature 206 pit					1			1				2
Feature 214 pit			3									3
TOTALS	103	26	308	6	81	20	28	36	2	43	1	654

PB = partial bowl
PJ = partial jar
WB = whole bowl
WJ = whole jar
Note: whole and partial vessels are not included in totals

assemblage is shown in Figure 3.21. Feature 10100 had half of a fire-warped plain ware jar, several sherds of a Rincon Red-on-brown, Style A bowl, three metates, four manos, two core-hammerstones, one tabular knife, and one palette blank on its floor. Feature 154 had sherds of a Rincon Red-on-brown, Style A jar scattered across the floor, as well as three manos, one plain palette, and a cluster of rabbit bones mixed with fire-shattered pieces of a second palette.

Finally, the late dating of Features 8 and 154 is supported by the proportions of Colonial period to Rincon phase pottery, a dating technique mentioned above, which will be discussed in the "Ceramics and Dating" section below.

Feature 86

This feature is classified as a limited-use structure based on its small size and lack of internal features. The only floor features consist of two floor pits or postholes, and a probable floor pit near one wall (86001). Neither this feature nor those which intrude it (86004, 87, 88) provided any datable material.

Slope Trash

Trash, primarily flaked and ground stone items, was abundant on all the ridge slopes. Material seemed most abundant on the eastern slope, but as this is also the gentlest slope it may simply be that less material deposited on the other, steeper slopes, was more rapidly carried away.

Extramural Features

Of the 211 extramural features found, 105 were pits, 24 were pits with rocks, 43 were roasting pit-hearths, 28 were rock clusters, 4 were artifact and animal bone clusters, 1 was a stone platform, and 6 were borrow pits. Upon excavation, 21 previously numbered "features" turned out to be natural or rodent in origin (Features 9, 12100, 14, 17, 24, 26, 39, 46, 57, 76, 100, 111, 112, 148, 149, 157, 185, 186, 187, 197,and 202), and do not appear in Figure 3.19 or Table 3.19.

Not all extramural features were excavated; instead, a representative sample was selected. All features were classified as pits, pits with rocks, or rock-filled pits prior to excavation, depending on how much rock was visible on their exposed surfaces, and half of each group was selected for excavation, using a nonrandom procedure designed to achieve a representative subset of the whole in terms of both size range and distribution within the site area.

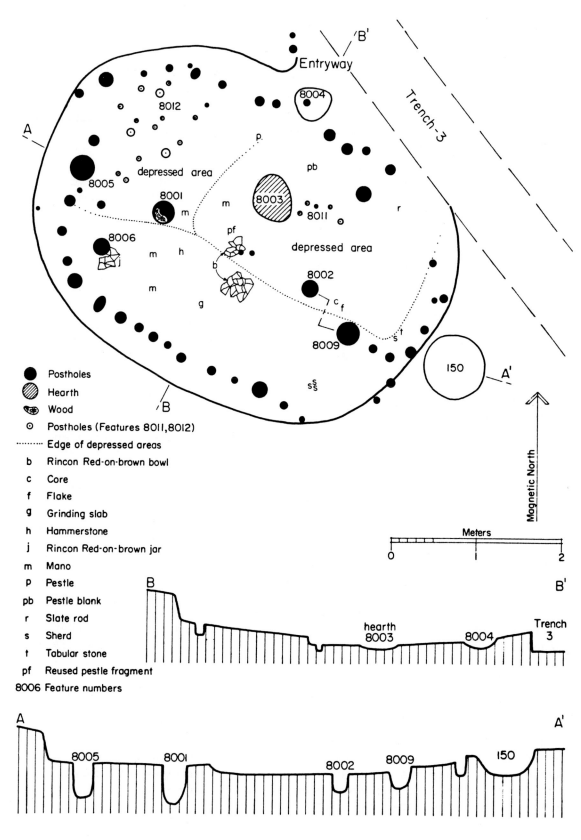

Figure 3.21 Plan view and cross sections
of the Feature 8 pit house, AZ EE:2:113.

Pits and Rock Clusters

Considering the number of pits, pits with rocks, rock clusters, and roasting pit-hearths that were excavated at AZ EE:2:113, information bearing on the functions, specific ages, and intrasite distribution of each group was scant. Morphology within each of these groups was highly variable (Figs. 3.22, 3.23). The various types of extramural features appeared fairly evenly distributed within extramural feature areas. Analyzed flotation samples from 1 pit and 14 roasting pit-hearths produced very limited botanical materials; only corn and chenopod remains were consistently recovered. Walnuts, mesquite seeds, acorns, the unidentified, columnar-celled seed, and one domestic bean were rare constituents (Miksicek 1984a; Appendix B). Animal bone was not common in extramural feature fill (Appendix A).

With such very general information on content and distribution, functional interpretations have been suggested based on gross feature morphology and comparative information from other sites. Roasting pit-hearths are primarily used for processing plant foods, mainly corn and chenopods. Rock clusters are rocks either cleaned out from, or intended for use in, roasting pit-hearths. At AZ EE:2:77, pits with rocks were so few in number that it may be suggested they are simply partially cleaned out roasting pit-hearths; the same may be argued at AZ EE:2:113, where this variable group makes up less than 10 percent of excavated extramural features. Finally, pits are undoubtedly multifunctional, although no evidence of their specific functions was found.

Perhaps the most important point concerning extramural features at AZ EE:2:113 is their abundance. Including all types of extramural features, except burials, there are 15 for every structure at the site, a ratio three times larger than that for any other site. Ratios of 5:1 and 4.4:1 were calculated for the number of extramurals per structure at AZ EE:2:84, and AZ EE:2:76, respectively. The significance of these data will be discussd in Chapter 10.

Artifact and Animal Bone Clusters

Four clusters of animal bone or animal bone and artifacts were found, three in the fill of the Feature 6300 pit house (6301, 6303, 6304), and one in the fill of the Feature 13 borrow pit (13002). All consisted of varying numbers of large mammal bones; associated artifacts (when present) included fragments of ground stone implements, hammerstones, and flakes. All may simply represent individual trash dumpings. The Feature 6304 cluster of five deer mandibles representing at least three individuals (Fig. 3.24), might be suggestive of a less mundane activity, although the associated plain ware sherds, flakes, and core-hammerstones are simple utilitarian items, and resemble the contents of the other artifact and bone clusters.

Figure 3.22 (upper left) Rock-filled, rock-outlined hearth with a flat slab bottom. Pile of small rocks at tip are from the fill of the hearth; Feature 5, AZ EE:2:113.

Figure 3.23 (upper right) Large roasting pit incorporating metate fragments in the lining and a fire-cracked basin metate in place on the top; Feature 22, AZ EE:2:113.

Figure 3.24 (lower left) Artifact and animal bone cluster of deer mandibles in the fill of the Feature 6300 pit house; Subfeature 6304, AZ EE:2:113.

Figure 3.25 (lower right) Large slab-lined pit or platform with a small intrusive roasting pit-hearth atop it (arrow); Features 108 and 108001, respectively, AZ EE:2:113.

Stone Platform

Feature 108 was a large, circular, shallow, slab-lined pit or platform about 175 cm in diameter (Fig. 3.25). Slabs in the center were flat-lying, while those around the perimeter were somewhat tilted. Some of the center slabs and those near the northern edge were missing, perhaps removed when a small, intrusive roasting pit-hearth was built in the fill (Feature 108001; Fig. 3.25). None of the original Feature 108 slabs showed any signs of burning. Results of analysis of both flotation and pollen samples from the Feature 108 platform were similar to those taken throughout the site (Appendixes B and C; Miksicek 1984a).

Similar stone platforms have been reported from a variety of prehistoric sites including Texas Canyon (Fulton 1934b: 11), Paloparado (Di Peso 1956: 144), the Swarts Ruin and two other southwestern New Mexico sites (Cosgroves 1932: 20-22), and at three sites in the Chiricahua Mountains of southeastern Arizona (Sauer and Brand 1930: 435, 439-440). Doyel (1977a: 117-118, Fig. 67) noted such a feature in the middle Santa Cruz area which may be protohistoric in age. Most are about 2 m in diameter, but smaller examples are reported as well. Most are flat, although the Cosgroves refer to "saucer-shaped" examples seemingly identical to that at AZ EE:2:113. Finally, most show no evidence of burning; fire-cracked rock and ashy fill are generally absent. Only Fulton (1934b: 11) noted that some of the rocks were burned, but not heavily, and there was no ash or charcoal in the fill. Functions as roasting pits or as platforms for large grain storage baskets are suggested by the various authors, with all acknowledging they had no clear evidence as to the use of these features. Feature 108 at AZ EE:2:113 expands the known distribution of this feature type, but provides no new insight into its use.

Borrow Pits

Six borrow pits (Features 13, 82, 110, 113, 114, and 114001) were located, of which two were excavated: Feature 13, with six individual extramural features discernible in its fill, and Feature 82, with thirteen. These two pits were each 3 m to 5 m in diameter and 60 cm deep. Borrow pits and probable borrow pits were found only at AZ EE:2:113, EE:2:107, EE:1:104, EE:2:105, and EE:2:129. The greatest number occurred at AZ EE:2:113, perhaps because of the relatively clean clay pockets that apparently exist between four parallel gravel bars at the northeastern edge of the site (Fig. 3.19). All the borrow pits except Feature 13 are located between these gravel bars. Whether the clay was used for building or as potter's clay is unknown.

Burials

Burials at AZ EE:2:113 included 14 cremation deposits (Features 1, 4, 701, 29, 62, 70, 80, 81, 84, 107001, 147, 160, and 164), 9 human inhumations (Features 2, 3, 15, 16, 25, 52, 53, 72, and 165), and 3 domestic dog inhumations (Features 60, 159 and 169).

In addition to the 14 cremation deposits noted above, a partial
Rincon Red-on-brown, Style A bowl from the northern end of Trench 1
might represent another cremation deposit, as might a partial knobbed
plain ware jar recovered in stripping above the Feature 82 borrow pit.
Knobbed vessels are rare in Hohokam assemblages, but of these, several
are known to have served as urns or offerings in Sedentary period
cremation deposits (two from Las Colinas, one from La Ciudad, one from
the West Bank sites and one from the Henderson Site), and a single sherd
of a knobbed vessel was found in a Snaketown phase cremation deposit at
the Hodges Ruin (Kelly 1978: 74).

Cremation Deposits

Feature 1. Feature 1 consisted of five plain ware bowl sherds
and a complete palette eroding out of the west bank of a mining test pit
on the extreme northeastern edge of the site, east of Trench 1 (Fig.
3.18). It is classified as a cremation deposit based on the burned
condition of all the artifacts; burned bone was absent.

Feature 4. This deposit was a small amount of bone in a pit
covered by a layer of rocks, apparently without grave goods.

Feature 7001. This cremation deposit had been placed in a pit
which was dug into the fill of the Feature 7 limited-use structure.

Feature 29. This was a jumble of rocks and burned bone,
possibly in a pit in the fill of the Feature 6300 pit house. A lump of
gypsum, possibly burned, may have been associated with it.

Feature 62. This deposit consisted of a Sacaton Red-on-buff
bowl inverted over a bone-filled pit; a nearby quartz crystal with a
spalled tip may have been associated.

Feature 70. This cremation deposit was apparently disturbed
when the Feature 165 inhumation was interred. A partial Rillito Red-on
brown jar was definitely associated with Feature 70, and a partial plain
ware bowl appears to have been removed by Feature 165 and then thrown
back in its fill.

Feature 80. This feature was vandalized during the excavation
of the site, but although its contents were thoroughly disturbed,
apparently nothing was taken. This multiple cremation deposit consisted
of an adult (probably female) and an infant. Grave goods included a
plain ware seed jar, a small plain ware jar, a large Galiuro Red-on-
brown bowl, a burned fragment of a Glycymeris bracelet, and a burned,

cut-off, proximal fragment of a bighorn humerus (Fig. 3.26b); a single flake is probably a fortuitous inclusion in the pit fill. It appears that the seed jar was inverted in the bottom of the pit, but whether it had held the bone could not be determined. Next to the seed jar was the small plain ware jar, with both covered by the inverted Galiuro Red-on-brown bowl.

Feature 81. This feature had a large Trincheras Purple-on-red bowl placed upright in the pit bottom, holding the bone, part of a small, micaceous plain ware jar and a fragment of a second such jar. Inverted over those fragments was a Rillito Red-on-brown flare-rimmed bowl. All four vessels were intentionally broken.

Feature 84. This deposit consisted of burned bone and a burned Glycymeris bracelet fragment, placed in a Rincon Red-on-brown, Style A jar which was inverted in a pit. The mouth of the jar rested on a rock placed in the bottom of the pit.

a   b   c   d

Figure 3.26 Bone tube and cut-off long bone ends from AZ EE:2:113. a, complete tube with poorly done groove-and-snap removal of the articular end at top; b, calcined proximal bighorn humerus from Feature 80 cremation deposit; c-d, two distal left femora from Feature 10103 pit house floor pit. Length of a is 9.3 cm.

Feature 107001. This appears to be a pit cremation deposit, with bone in the bottom of the pit and at least half of a small, unidentified red-on-brown bowl at the top. Part of the bowl may have been removed during stripping of this area.

Feature 147. This inverted, plain ware jar was presumably a cremation deposit, although no bone was found. While this vessel could be simply a cached pot, such as those described for AZ EE:2:105, its distance from any pit house and its proximity to other known cremation deposits suggests that it, too, probably represents a cremation. Only the rim and neck were found in place; the body of the jar, which apparently would have protruded above the prehistoric ground surface, was lost during stripping of the area.

Features 160 and 164. These two features are located adjacent to one another, each consisting of a pit with the sherds of a smashed bowl placed horizontally above the bone. Feature 160 contained only two bone fragments, a burned, whole-valve Aequipecten pendant, and sherds of a Galiuro Red-on-brown bowl. Feature 164 contained a great deal of bone covered by pieces of a Rincon Red-on-brown, Style A bowl. A projectile point was found above the sherds. Of the two bones from Feature 160, one is a large fragment of a left talus. Feature 164, also contains a similarly burned, left talus fragment, and it seems probable that the two features are in fact a single cremation deposit. Whether the two bones in the Feature 160 pit were placed there intentionally, or arrived there through rodent disturbance is uncertain.

Inhumations

Feature 2. Disturbed extensively by rodents and hit by Trench 3, this burial of an aged male was placed in a pit, seated, with the knees drawn up to the chest, the head down and facing northwest. The whole body had slumped forward somewhat and the positions of the arms are unknown. Several large rocks had been placed at the top of the burial pit.

Feature 3. Because it was completely removed by the backhoe, the orientation and position of this adult inhumation are unknown. In-place rocks suggest that either the burial was placed in an abandoned roasting pit, or that rocks were positioned in or above the burial pit fill, as seen in most of the other inhumations on the site.

Features 15, 16, and 52. All three of these are inhumations of older individuals placed in pits dug into the fill and floor of the Feature 6100 pit house (Fig 3.20). All three were apparently seated, none had any grave goods, and apparently all had rocks packed down

around the bodies and atop them. Soil samples from inside or below the
pelvis of each burial were examined for parasites, with negative results
(Appendix E).

The Feature 15 burial was seated on the floor of the pit house,
knees drawn up to the chest and together, head down, facing northeast.
The left arm was between the legs and the right was bent under the legs.

The Feature 16 burial had been heavily disturbed, possibly when
the other two burials were interred. What remained of it was an
articulated body from the lumbar vertebrae down, showing a seated or
slightly slouched position with knees flexed, body facing east. The
burial pit was slightly excavated into the floor of the Feature 6100 pit
house.

The Feature 52 burial was seated, knees drawn up and apart, left
arm flexed, hand in lap, right arm by the side. The body was facing
northeast. The burial pit was dug down some 70 cm below floor level in
the Feature 6100 pit house, and even so, the cranium extended above the
top of the pit.

The relative ordering of the Feature 15, 16, and 52 burials is
unknown; however, the excavation of a burial pit for Feature 15 is
presumed to have truncated the Feature 16 burial.

Features 25 and 72. Because of its unusual position, Feature 25
was one of the most interesting inhumations found. The body was placed
in a kneeling position facing east with the legs folded underneath,
buttocks on heels. Both arms had been displaced by rodents, but the
right may have been flexed, hand in lap. This is the only inhumation on
AZ EE:2:113 that lacked rocks around or above the body.

The Feature 72 burial appears to have been partially removed by
the blading done at the site, but may have been in a similar kneeling
position. Only the pelvis and legs remained in place, and were badly
crushed. Rocks had been placed around the body.

Feature 53. This individual was tightly flexed on its back with
the knees drawn up around the shoulders. The position of the arms could
not be determined but the head was oriented to the south. Rocks were
placed around and atop the body.

Feature 165. This inhumation may have been partially disturbed
by the blading, but appears never to have been complete. The partial
skull of an adult, a humerus and one tooth from a child, and several
rocks, were placed in a pit, disturbing part of the Feature 70 cremation
deposit.

Domestic Dog Inhumations

Three domestic dog inhumations (Features 60, 159, and 169) were
found at AZ EE:2:113; skeletal data is presented in Appendix A.

Feature 60. This dog was buried on its left side, possibly
slightly curled, and the head may have been bent back over the body.
The head was at the north end of the pit, and blading had crushed or
removed much of the upper body and skull. A turquoise pendant blank was
found in the pit, but because of the disturbed condition of the feature,
it is uncertain whether or not this association is fortuitous. Heavy
chop marks were found on the pelvis, right tibia and left femur, but do
not appear to be butchering marks (Appendix A); they may have
contributed to the death of the animal or may represent postmortem
damage.

Feature 159. This inhumation was also placed on its left side,
again possibly slightly curled, and disturbed during excavation. The
head would have been at the south end of the pit. No grave goods were
present, and pollen analysis produced no unusual results (Appendix C).

Feature 169. This dog was interred on its right side with the
head bent back over the body and at the southwest end of the pit. The
only aparent grave good was a piece of a large mammal long bone found
under the right tibia. Packed down around and on top of the dog were
aproximately ten rocks. Although the right side of the skull was intact,
the left side was crushed inward suggesting that the cause of the dog's
death may have been a blow to the head.

Ceramics and Dating

Dating of the Feature 6100, 6300, 6200, 7, 8, 10100, 86, and 154
structures has been discussed, and was based on fill and floor ceramics
(Table 3.21) and superposition (Table 3.20). Because the occupation of
AZ EE:2:113 was relatively short lived, and only two local decorated
pottery types (Rillito Red-on-brown and Rincon Red-on-brown, Style A)
were represented, a seriation of structures based on the percentage of
Rillito Red-on-brown sherds in their assemblages was attempted.
Specifically, it was hoped that this might help to date Features 11, 12,
and 83, which could not be dated by their stratigraphic position. This
technique was also applied to assemblages from houses that were dated by
their relative stratigraphic position, with largely successful results,
correctly ordering the superimposed Features 6100, 6300, and 6200 from
early to late, in that order (Table 3.22). It also correctly placed
superimposed Features 8 and 154 as the final structures in the sequence.
Feature 10100, believed to be roughly contemporaneous with Features 8
and 154, was placed near the early end of the seriation, perhaps because
of early sherds washing into it from an earlier pit house, Feature

Table 3.22

SUGGESTED TEMPORAL SERIATION OF STRUCTURES AT AZ EE:2:113,
BASED ON THE PROPORTIONS OF COLONIAL PERIOD AND
EARLY RINCON PHASE SHERDS IN THEIR FILL AND FLOOR ASSEMBLAGES

Feature Number	N of Rillito Red-on-brown Sherds[1]	N of Rincon A Red-on-brown Sherds[2]	Percent Colonial	Agrees with Stratigraphic Sequence ?
154	0	19	0	yes
8	7	73	9	yes
12	7	31	18	no data
6200	1	4	20	yes
10100	16	59	21	no
6300	8	23	26	yes
11	20	44	31	no data
83	15	32	32	no data
6100	2	1	66	yes

[1] includes unidentified Colonial red-on-brown
[2] includes rincon Red-on-brown, unidentified style

10300. Overall, this seriation agreed with the dating of the houses of
known age or ordering based on other lines of evidence. The collections
from the Feature 11 and 83 pit houses fall nearer the early end of the
series, and may well be of Rillito phase age; the Feature 12 pit house
dates later, probably to early Rincon times. Features 7, 10200, 10300,
10400, and 86 could not be assessed with this technique, since all of
them lacked identifiable red-on-brown sherds.

Archaeomagnetic samples were collected from hearths in the
Feature 6100 and 8 pit houses (Subfeatures 6102 and 8003), but were not
analyzed, due to the failure of most of the other Rosemont samples to
produce dates.

The ceramic assemblage from AZ EE:2:113, as a whole, is of
special interest in that it produced several times more San Simon series

and Trincheras series sherds and whole vessels that any other site. The
large numbers of these intrusives, when coupled with the high proportion
of inhumations at the site, has a number of implications regarding trade
and contact for AZ EE:2:113, in particular, and for the Rosemont area in
general. These are discussed in Chapter 10.

Nonceramic Artifacts

Counts of all artifact types are presented in Table 3.18. The
chipped stone assemblage is notable for its inclusion of three Mogollon
style projectile points. Nonutilitarian slate objects were abundant,
and include palettes, the only two slate rods from the project, and
several other worked and unworked slate pieces. Given such evidence of
substantial slate-working at the site, the absence of finger rings is
surprising. The only argillite artifact from the excavations also came
from AZ EE:2:113.

On the floor of the Feature 12 pit house were found two
Glycymeris bracelet band fragments, one reworked into a notched,
crescent-shaped pendant and the second presumably intended for the same
use.

Worked bone was more abundant at AZ EE:2:113 than at any other
site. In particular, a number of bone tubes (Fig. 3.26a) and cut-off
ends of long bones were found. The latter are often considered simply
waste produced in the manufacture of tubes or rings; however, the
recovery of several at AZ EE:2:113 in specific feature contexts suggests
they may have been finished artifacts in their own right. A thoroughly
burned fragment of a cut-off proximal fragment of a bighorn humerus was
found wth the Feature 80 cremation deposit (Fig. 3.26b), and two cut-off
distal fragments of left deer femora (from both white-tailed and mule
deer) were found together in a floor pit in the Feature 10100 pit house.
(Fig. 3.26c and d). It may be significant that all of the cut-off
fragments lacked the articular condyles; whether this was intentional or
an accident of preservation cannot be determined. If this is not
related to preservation, it would suggest that these bones too may have
been considered tubes by the Hohokam, perhaps of a variety distinct from
those cut from the middle of the long bone shaft.

Subsistence

AZ EE:2:113 produced more unworked animal bone than any other
investigated site. Both white-tailed and mule deer are well
represented, along with antelope jack rabbits, and large numbers of
cottontails and black-tailed jack rabbits. Exploitation of elevations
both higher and lower than that of the site are suggested by the bighorn
sheep and antelope jackrabbits, respectively. In short, of all the
Rosemont sites examined, hunting appears to have had the greatest
relative importance in the economy of AZ EE:2:113; however, it is still
impossible to determine the importance of hunting, agriculture, and wild
plant gathering relative to one another in the economy of this site.

The 13 prehistoric pollen samples examined corroborate the
overall picture gained from other sites: extensive use of Cheno-Ams
(probably chenopods), presumably as a food item. Of the 12 samples
which produced sufficient pollen for analysis, Cheno-Ams account for
75.9 to 95.2 percent of the total (Appendix C). One other interesting
occurrence is the presence of agave pollen on one of the manos from the
floor of the Feature 8 pit house.

Finally, flotation samples consistently yielded corn kernels and
cob fragments, and chenopod seeds. They also indicated use of agave,
acorns, and walnuts, and occasionally, a variety of other plants,
including mesquite, hackberry, juniper, yucca, prickly pear, and wild
cotton. One bean and one probable squash seed were recovered
(Appendix B; Miksicek 1984a).

Summary

This medium-sized site was occupied intensively for a relatively
short amount of time, possibly beginning in the Cañada del Oro phase,
with the primary occupation probably almost equally divided between
Rillito and early Rincon phase times. Dating of individual features was
based on the presence and relative proportions of decorated ceramics and
the superposition of features.

Subsistence data suggest relatively heavy use of a very broad
spectrum of wild plant and animal species as foods and presumably for
other uses, as indicated by the presence of wild cotton and worked bone.
The abundance of animal bone suggests that hunting was relatively more
important here than at the other Rosemont sites.

Site content and structure present several aspects unique to,
or best expressed at, this site. Conspicuous at AZ EE:2:113 is the
abundance of extramural features. Of greater interest, perhaps, is an
area between the Feature 83, 8, 11, 67, and 10 pit houses which was
essentially devoid of extramural features (Fig. 3.27). To have kept
this area free of pits, on a site where extramural features blanket
all other areas, implies an intentional avoidance of this area which
began early and was continued throughout the life of the site. The
maintenance of this open area may be analogous to the continuity through
time in location and size of house clusters seen in the Phoenix Basin.

Pit house orientation at AZ EE:2:113 is more variable than at
any other site except AZ EE:2:105 (Fig. 3.27). This is probably related
to cultural preferences for pit house orientation as constrained by the
size and slope of the ridge. The possible significance of pit house
orientation is discussed in Chapter 10.

AZ EE:2:113 had the most numerous and the largest borrow pits of
any site examined. This is undoubtedly related to the on-site presence
of clay pockets between the gravel bars on the ridge itself (Fig. 3.27),
a geologic feature unique to AZ EE:2:113. The presence of these gravel
bars may have doubly influenced the site structure by discouraging

154   Alan Ferg

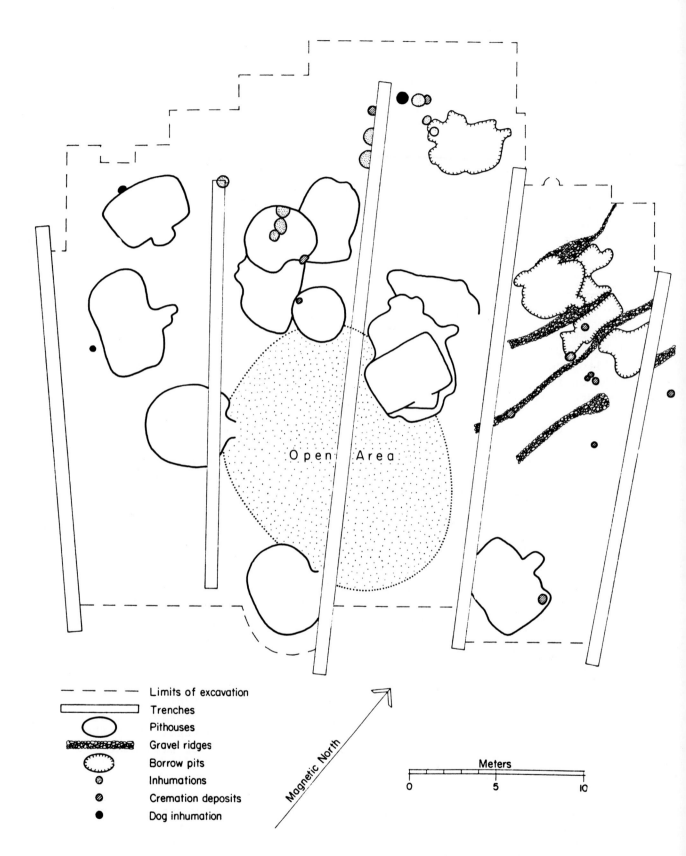

Figure 3.27 Site map of AZ EE:2:113
showing distributions of certain feature types.

placement of the earliest houses at the extreme downslope edge of the site, as apparently occurred at AZ EE:2:76.

Burials at AZ EE:2:113 differ from those found on other sites in both the types present and their distribution. These points will be taken up more fully in Chapter 10, but here it can simply be noted that AZ EE:2:113 possesses a larger proportion of inhumations which, combined with the high percentage of San Simon series red-on-brown pottery present, suggests substantial Mogollon influence at the site. The seated posture of many of these burials strengthens such an inference. Also of note is the largely discrete distribution of inhumations and cremation deposits, all of the former occurring on the northwestern edge of the habitation area, with most of the cremation deposits placed on the northeastern edge (Fig. 3.27).

Finally, three domestic dog inhumations occur on AZ EE:2:113, one near human burials, and each of the others directly outside the back wall of a pit house (Fig. 3.27). The presence of dog inhumations is unique to this site among the investigated Rosemont area Hohokam sites. Further, there were apparently certain constraints or mores governing the location of dog burials, as was the case with human burials.

AZ EE:2:129

As already noted, AZ EE:2:129 and AZ EE:2:113, once considered a single "large" site, are in fact two well-separated sites (Fig. 3.18). AZ EE:2:129 itself apparently consists of two discrete areas, separated from one another by a 20-m segment of the ridgetop which lacks features (Fig. 3.28). The western area consists of a thick cultural deposit peppered with extramural roasting pits, including at least one work area, while the eastern area consists of two house pits and additional roasting pits (Table 3.23). All artifacts recovered are tabulated in Table 3.24, and Table 3.25 presents a list of the features and subfeatures.

Structures

Two house pits (Features 1 and 2) representing four pit houses were partially excavated (Table 3.26). No other structures are thought to be present on this site.

Feature 1

This house pit contained three superimposed pit houses (Fig. 3.28). The earliest (Floor 1) is a floor remnant on the north side of the house pit, with numerous extramural postholes. The second house (Floor 2) is preserved as an L-shaped piece of floor on the east and northeast, exhibiting a floor groove, interior postholes and numerous rocks probably used to buttress the wall poles. The third house has

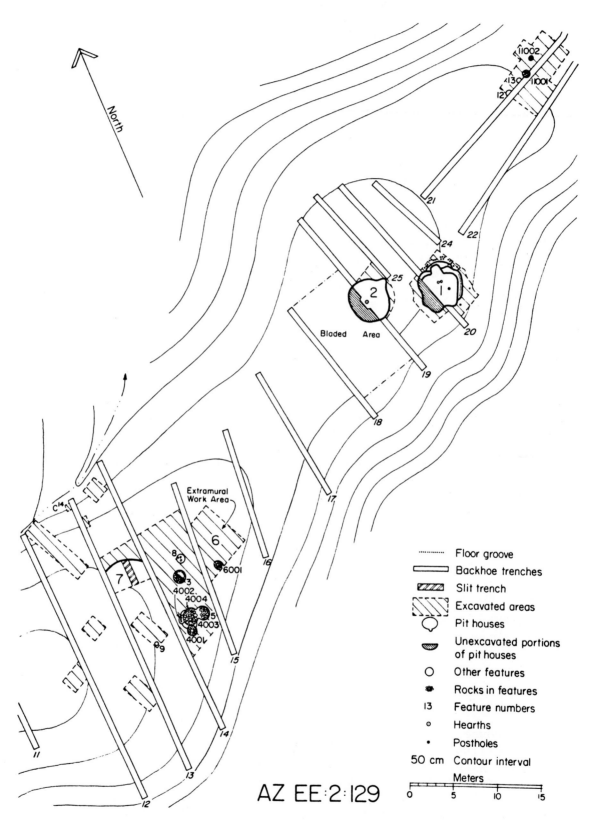

Figure 3.28   Site map, AZ EE:2:129.

Table 3.23

TYPES AND NUMBERS OF FEATURES, EXCAVATED
AND UNEXCAVATED, AT AZ EE:2:129

Feature Type	Excavated	Unexcavated	Total
Western area			
Pits	1	-	1
Roasting pit-hearths	7	-	7
Pits with rocks	1	-	1
Borrow pits (?)	1	-	1
Eastern area			
Pit houses	4	-	4
Pits	1	-	1
Roasting pit-hearths	3	-	3
Total	18	0	18

interior wall postholes, no floor groove and an entryway oriented
roughly to the north. The superpositioning of a house with outside wall
posts, a house with a floor groove and interior wall posts, and a final
house with interior wall support of the same type, is very similar to
the Feature 1 house pit at AZ EE:2:77; Floors 1 and 2 of these houses
are probably roughly contemporaneous.

The presence of a mixture of temporally distinct red-on-brown
types in the fill of Feature 1, combined with the superpositions, is the
basis of assigning Floors 1, 2, and 3 to the Rillito or early Rincon,
middle Rincon, and late Rincon phases, respectively (Table 3.26).

Feature 2

This pit house was notable for the presence of a well-preserved
hearth (Subfeature 2005), which produced a set of archaeomagnetic dates
not completely in accordance with the age suggested by the Rincon Red-
on-brown, Style A ceramics in its fill. The best fit interval was

Table 3.24

ARTIFACT TOTALS BY CLASS FOR AZ EE:2:129

Artifact Type	Count	Category Total	Percent of Assemblage
Ceramics		1,069	41.3
Decorated sherds	408		
Red ware sherds	1		
Plain ware sherds	660		
Chipped Stone		1,459	56.3
Debitage	1,342		
Retouched pieces	84		
Cores	27		
Hammerstones	6		
Utilitarian Ground Stone		47	1.8
Metates	11		
Mano-handstones	31		
Other	5		
Nonutilitarian Stone		4	0.2
Worked slate	2		
Bowls	1		
Minerals	1		
Shell		5	0.2
Bracelets	3		
Other	2		
Worked Bone		6	0.2
Awls-hairpins	3		
Antler flakers	1		
Other	2		
Total		2,590	100.0

A.D. 1200-1250, the 63 percent confidence level date, A.D. 1000-1340, and the 95 percent confidence level date, A.D. 940-1410 (Appendix F). The latter range covers a period representing over one-half the length of the Hohokam occupation in the project area, and is of little use.

Table 3.25

EXCAVATED FEATURE INFORMATION, AZ EE:2:129

Feature or Subfeature Number	Interpretation and Description
1	collective designation for three superimposed pit houses (Floor 1 is the earliest, Floor 3 the most recent)
1001	rock and sherd cluster in the fill, at approximately the Floor 2 floor level
1002	floor pit in Floor 3
1003	floor pit in Floor 3
1004	floor pit in Floor 3
1006	possible hearth in Floor 3
1008	probable posthole in Floor 3
1009	two adjacent pits, possibly two hearths in Floor 3
2	pit house
2001	floor pit containing two manos
2002	floor pit
2005	plastered hearth
3	roasting pit with rock-lined base
4	collective designation for four superimposed roasting pit-hearths
4001	next-to-oldest of four pits
4002	youngest of four pits

Table 3.25, continued

EXCAVATED FEATURE INFORMATION, AZ EE:2:129

Feature or Subfeature Number	Interpretation and Description
4003	next-to-youngest of four pits
4004	oldest of four pits
5	roasting pit-hearth
6	probable extramural work surface associated with subfeature 6001
6001	roasting pit-hearth
7	borrow pit(?)
8	pit with rocks
9	pit
11	natural depression which contained two roasting pit-hearths, 11001 and 11002
11001	roasting pit-hearth
11002	roasting pit-hearth
12	roasting pit-hearth
13	pit

Slope Trash

The eastern component of AZ EE:2:129, with the two houses, lacked substantial associated trash deposits, either on the ridgetop or the northern or southern slopes. Feature 2 was not trash filled, but the artifact density in the fill of the Feature 1 house pit was three times greater, suggesting that at least one of the three pit houses represented may have been trash filled.

Table 3.26

STRUCTURE DATING AND CONTENT SUMMARY, AZ EE:2:129

Feature Number	Age Assignment	Basis for Dating									
		Site Ceramics	Floor Ceramics	Fill Ceramics	Superimposition	Other	Burned	Trash Filled	Floor Assemblage	Intrudes Features	Intruded by Features
001000 (Floor 1)	Rillito or early Rincon			x	x			u			+
001000 (Floor 2)	middle Rincon			x	x			u		+	+
001000 (Floor 3)	late Rincon			x	x			?			+
002000	early Rincon			x		x					

The western component of AZ EE:2:129 was unique among investigated sites, with up to 60-70 cm of cultural fill on its gentle northern slope. Throughout this area, chipped stone artifact densities were high and sherd densities low, comprising 92.9 percent and 6.7 percent of recovered artifacts from the northwest units (Fig. 3.28), respectively. The pit house fills, on the other hand, were dominated by sherds. Features 1 and 2 produced considerably more sherds (72.2%) than chipped stone artifacts (26.4%).

The high percentage of chipped stone present in the northern slope deposit appears to be due to a combination of two factors, the relative importance of each being uncertain. First, the western component of AZ EE:2:129 may be a specialized site in its own right, and not part of a habitation site. As such, artifact proportions would be expected to differ from the eastern component, and from the other habitation sites examined, and in fact, they do. With the exception of AZ EE:2:84, all habitation assemblages are dominated by sherds. Chipped stone artifacts account for more than 50 percent of the assemblage from

AZ EE:2:84, similar to the western component of AZ EE:2:129. The common cultural denominator may be that both these loci are largely devoted to extramural activities involving roasting pits, suggesting that flaking may have been done in association with extramural work areas or was related to the processing of plant foods in roasting pit-hearths.

The second contributing factor to the high frequency of chipped stone in the western-component slope trash at AZ EE:2:129 is that the ceramic component appears superimposed upon and, to a degree, mixed with an earlier Archaic component. This earlier material is most clearly seen in the form of bifaces, and secondarily in the soft-hammer, biface-thinning flakes which are quite abundant when compared with any other ceramic period assemblage from the project area (see Chapter 5). Because no diagnostic Archaic projectile points were present, a single lump of charcoal was collected from the lowest level of trash exposed in the west wall of Trench 13 (Fig. 3.28), and submitted for radiocarbon dating. The date obtained was 1550 $\pm$ 190 B.P. (A-3558), A.D. 400 $\pm$ 190, earlier than any of the other analyzed samples from ceramic sites, which compares closely with radiocarbon dates obtained from AZ EE:2:50, a Late Archaic site exposed in the banks of Pantano Wash (Huckell 1984b).

Extramural Features

Fourteen extramural features were found at AZ EE:2:129, including 2 pits, 1 pit with rocks, 10 roasting pit hearths, and a possible borrow pit. Analyzed flotation samples from 9 of the 10 roasting pits consistently produced small quantities of corn, chenopod seeds, and the unidentified columnar-celled shell (Miksicek 1984a). In fact, AZ EE:2:129 had a greater proportion of samples producing the columnar-celled shells (over half) than any other site. Flotation samples from the two pits and the single pit with rocks produced almost no botanical remains. A pollen sample from Feature 8 (a pit with rocks) produced no pollen whatsoever (Appendix C).

The four superimposed roasting pits designated Feature 4 illustrate the repeated use of the western area of AZ EE:2:129 (Fig. 3.29), and Feature 3 shows the volume of rock (Fig. 3.30) which such features can potentially produce. Fire-cracked rock was abundant in the slope trash of the western component. Plant processing is the presumed function of these pits, particularly since virtually no animal bone was recovered from any of the roasting pits except Feature 6001. The bone in the latter feature is part of a concentration of fox bones in this part of the larger Feature 6 extramural work area. This occurrence of 150 spottily burned and unburned fox bones is unique among the sites examined, and is presumed to be an atypical use of a roasting pit.

The Feature 6 extramural work area was discernible as a large, slightly depressed area, east of Trench 15 (Fig. 3.28). This area contained the concentration of fox bones in and around the Feature 6001 roasting pit, as well as a mano, a slab metate, a bone awl fragment, an unidentified slate object, and a partial Rillito Red-on-brown jar, all lying on the sterile horizon. This area presumably extends to the north, east, and southeast, beyond the limits of excavation.

Figure 3.29 (left) Four superimposed roasting pit-hearths which make up Feature 4. Numbers in photo correspond to subfeature designations.

Figure 3.30 (right) Feature 3 roasting pit showing the quantity of burned rock removed from half of it. The feature is 1.5 m in diameter.

Burials

A number of cremated human skull fragments were found in the fill above the Feature 6 work area, suggesting that at least one cremation deposit had been present in this area at one time, but had been disturbed and scattered.

Ceramics and Dating

The western area of AZ EE:2:129 includes both an Archaic component, documented by the chipped stone assemblage and a radiocarbon date, and a Rillito and early Rincon phase component, as shown by the ceramics recovered. The partial Rillito Red-on-brown jar from the Feature 6 extramural work area and Rincon Red-on-brown sherds from Features 4004, 7, and 9 suggest repeated use of the area over a span of years (Table 3.27).

The eastern area more clearly shows repeated use in both the superimposed floors and ceramic assemblage of Feature 1. The age assignments of the various floors (Table 3.26) were derived from a simple correlation of pit house floors with the phases represented by the Rillito through Rincon Red-on-brown, Style C pottery found in the feature fill. Feature 2 with its predominance of Rincon Red-on-brown, Style A sherds appears to be of early Rincon age, despite the archaeomagnetic date obtained.

Table 3.27

DECORATED POTTERY TYPES FROM AZ EE:2:129

Provenience	Rillito Red-on-brown	Unidentified Colonial	Rincon Red-on-brown Style A	Rincon Red-on-brown Style B	Rincon Red-on-brown Style C	Rincon Red-on-brown Style ?	Total
Stripping	4	4	2	1		40	51
Feature 1 (pit house)	3		7	1	5	51	67
Feature 2 (pit house)		1	14			4	19
Feature 4004 (roasting pit)						1	1
Feature 6 (extramural work area)	PJ						PJ
Feature 7 (borrow pit)						2	2
Feature 9 (pit)						2	2
Feature 11002 (roasting pit-hearth)			1				1
Total	7	5	24	2	5	100	143

PJ = partial jar; not included in totals

Nonceramic Artifacts

A finely crafted pair of "flying bird" earrings (or possibly pendants) was recovered from the lower fill of, or possibly the Floor 3 assemblage of the Feature 1 house pit (illustrated in Appendix A). They are noteworthy both because they are made of bone, and because they may represent some type of ritual deposit. This type of pendant occurs almost exclusively in shell and argillite, but a few other specimens in bone and wood are known (Jernigan 1978: 111, Fig. 46a). The possible ritual significance of these items and a pair of phyllite earrings from AZ EE:2:76 is discussed in Chapter 7.

Subsistence

The discussion of extramural features summarized most of the
subsistence data collected. Corn, chenopods, and the unidentified,
columnar-celled shell were also the most commonly recovered plant
remains from the pit houses (Miksicek 1984a). Animal bone represents a
variety of large and small game, and includes the unusual occurrence of
three adult grey foxes (Appendix A).

Also of note are two cotton seeds. The only other recovery of
wild cotton in the project area came from nearby AZ EE:2:113.

Summary

Overall, AZ EE:2:129 appears to be made up of two discrete
areas, both used repeatedly but sporadically. Use of the western area
apparently began in late Archaic times and continued into the Rincon
phase. During the ceramic period, it apears to have functioned as a
specialized activity site where plant foods, including corn, chenopods,
and perhaps the seeds represented by the unidentified columnar-celled
shell, were processed in roasting pits. Site structure is not complex;
all features present appear related to the same task, and are in close
proximity to one another, often intruding earlier features. Unlike
habitation sites, trash, such as plant remains and rocks from roasting
pits, appears simply to have been left near at hand, rather than
discarded down the steep southern slope of the ridge. If, as suggested
here, use of the western area was intermittent, such trash build-up
would not have been an inconvenience, and would have led to the deep,
essentially on-site cultural deposit which distinguishes this area from
the other sites examined.

The eastern area, including Features 1, 2, 11002, 12, and 13, is
analogous to some of the other small habitation sites examined.
Although the eastern area produced Rillito through late Rincon phase
pottery, as did the western area, it may never have actually been
occupied at the times the western-area pits were in use. The completely
sterile appearance of the modern ground surface between Trenches 16 and
18, the absence of features in these trenches and the bladed area (Fig.
3.28), and the fact that the pit houses apparently have their own
associated extramural features, all suggest that the eastern and western
areas of AZ EE:2:129 were largely or completely independent of one
another. Site structure in the eastern area resembles, in the most
general terms, that found on other habitation sites, with extramural
features located northward and downslope of the houses on the ridgetop.
However, the apparent distance between the pit houses and the extramural
features is somewhat surprising; other extramural features may be
located closer to the pit houses, but none were located in Trenches 19
through 22, 24, or 25.

Middle Rincon Habitation Sites

Four sites were investigated that were either purely or largely middle Rincon phase settlements.

AZ EE:2:107, EE:2:109, and EE:2:120 all appear to have been in existence only during middle Rincon phase times. AZ EE:2:77 clearly began early in the Rincon phase and was abandoned by the end of the middle Rincon phase; given the physical proximity of this site to AZ EE:2:105, and their overlap in time (Fig. 3.3), they may have been related. Finally, it should be remembered that AZ EE:2:76 and AZ EE:2:129, although possessing earlier components, had middle Rincon phase features as well.

AZ EE:2:77--Lightning Camp

Lightning Camp was recorded as a high artifact density, moderate area site, located on a ridge, with an abundance of artifactual material on the slopes below. The site occupies the end of a ridge which projects northward into the eastern floodplain of upper South Canyon (Fig. 3.1). AZ EE:2:77 is higher in elevation than AZ EE:2:105, the Ballcourt Site, which is located just across South Canyon to the northwest. The habitation area of AZ EE:2:77 is approximately 50 m long and 25 m in width (Fig. 3.31), and contains 7 house pits and approximately 50 extramural features (Table 3.28). All artifacts recovered are tabulated in Table 3.29, and Table 3.30 presents a list of the features and subfeatures. Features 2 and 5, a house and a roasting pit, were excavated and backfilled during the 1979 testing phase.

Structures

Seven house pits (Features 1 through 4, 31, and 44) representing eight pit houses, and one limited-use structure (Feature 56) were completely excavated (Table 3.31). No other structures are thought to be present on the site.

Feature 1

This feature consists of three superimposed pit houses (Fig. 3.31). All that remains of the earliest (Floor 1) is a sliver of floor at the back wall, and about 40 postholes dug into the prehistoric ground surface. The second house (Floor 2) was dug deeper than, and slightly to the north of Floor 1, obliterating most of it. Floor 2 has a series of postholes inside the house pit, all apparently connected by a floor groove. Finally, a third house (Floor 3) was dug through the second; it has a bigger floor groove but no wall postholes. This last house may have burned and then been remodeled; there is evidence of two superimposed hearths, and the two main, upright roof support postholes

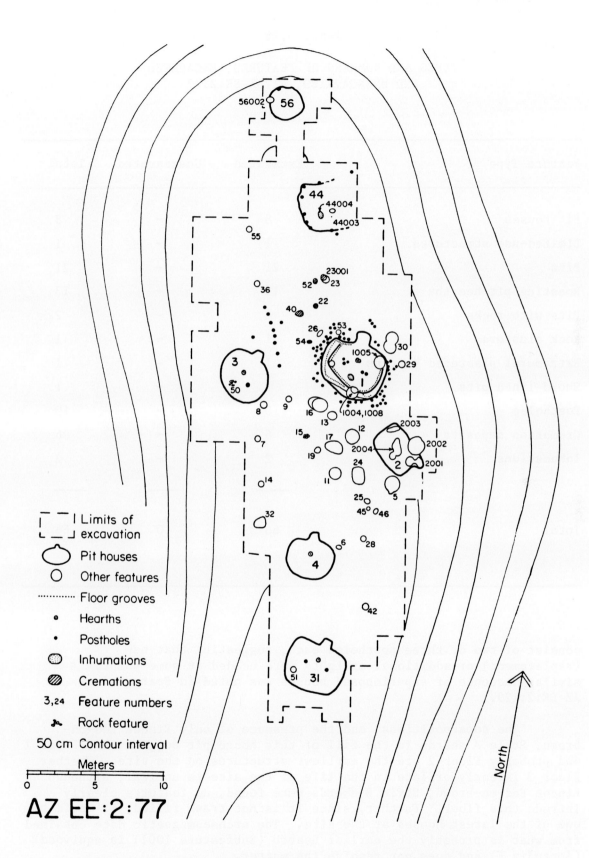

Figure 3.31   Site map, AZ EE:2:77 -- Lightning Camp.

Table 3.28

TYPES AND NUMBERS OF FEATURES, EXCAVATED
AND UNEXCAVATED, AT AZ EE:2:77

Feature Type	Excavated	Unexcavated	Total
Pit houses	8	–	8
Limited-use structures	1	–	1
Pits	21	–	21
Roasting pit-hearths	13	–	13
Pits with rocks	2	–	2
Rock clusters	1	–	1
Extramural plastered hearths	1	–	1
Sherd-lined pits	1	–	1
Postholes	10	–	10
Cremation deposits	6	–	6
Inhumations	2	–	2
Total	66	0	66

consist of two or three postholes each, suggesting that new
(replacement) or additional uprights were needed at some point. A
similar sequence of superimposed houses was noted in Feature 1 at
AZ EE:2:129.

The superpositions, and the presence of only Rincon Red-on-
brown, Style A sherds in the fill of this house pit suggest that Floor 1
and probably Floor 2 are the earliest structures on the site. Whether
Floor 3 is early or late in the life of the site is unclear; although no
Rincon Red-on-brown, Style B sherds were found, no features clearly
intrude this floor. Further, since it is not trash filled, it could be
one of the latest houses at the site. The archaeomagnetic date obtained
from what is probably the earlier hearth (Subfeature 1001) is equivocal
(Appendix F) and does not resolve the matter.

Table 3.29

ARTIFACT TOTALS BY CLASS FOR AZ EE:2:77

Artifact Type	Count	Category Total	Percent of Assemblage
Ceramics		2,558	73.0
Decorated sherds	1,218		
Red ware sherds	125		
Plain ware sherds	1,214		
Figurine fragments	1		
Chipped Stone		804	23.0
Debitage	687		
Retouched pieces	63		
Cores	27		
Hammerstones	27		
Utilitarian Ground Stone		108	3.1
Metates	17		
Mano-handstones	72		
Polishing stones	8		
Tabular knives	1		
3/4-grooved axes	1		
Other	9		
Nonutilitarian Stone		21	0.6
Worked slate	6		
Bowls	2		
Jewelry	7		
Bead lots (actual number = 30)	1		
Minerals	5		
Worked Bone		4	0.1
Awls-hairpins	2		
Other	2		
Total		3,504	99.8

Features 2, 3, and 31

All three of these pit houses were intruded by later features, indicating that probably none of them was the latest-occupied house on the site. The fill of Feature 2 was overlain by burned rock apparently cleaned out of the Feature 5 roasting pit; Subfeatures 2001 through 2004

Table 3.30

EXCAVATED FEATURE INFORMATION, AZ EE:2:77

Feature or Subfeature Number	Interpretation and Description
1	collective designation for three superimposed, pit houses; the upper (Floor 1) was the earliest and the deepest (Floor 3) was the latest
1001	hearth (plastered), Floor 3; see also 1009
1003	floor pit with infant inhumation, Floor 3
1004	roasting pit-hearth which either predates or postdates Floor 1; 1004 is intruded by a posthole that is part of Floor 2, and both 1004 and this posthole are cut by pit 1008; see also 1008
1005	pit which predates Floor 2, but could predate, be contemporaneous with, or postdate Floor 1; 1005 is intruded by a posthole that is part of Floor 2
1007	pit which cuts through both Floor 2 and 3, and could be associated with either floor
1008	pit which cuts through a Floor 2 posthole; 1008 therefore postdates Floor 2, but could predate, be contemporaneous with or postdate Floor 3
1009	hearth (unlined pit); Floor 3; construction of 1009 may postdate that of hearth 1001, and may be responsible for the partial destruction of the latter
2	pit house
2001	floor pit (intrusive ?)
2002	roasting pit-hearth (?) with rock-lined base; could either predate or postdate pit house

Table 3.30, continued

EXCAVATED FEATURE INFORMATION, AZ EE:2:77

Feature or Subfeature Number	Interpretation and Description
2003	floor pit (intrusive ?)
2004	three adjacent floor pits (intrusive ?)
3	pit house; see also Feature 50
3001	hearth (unlined pit)
3002	single main roof support posthole
4	pit house
4001	posthole
4002	floor pit or ash pit adjacent to hearth
4004	rodent-enlarged posthole (?)
4005	hearth (unlined pit)
5	roasting pit with a rock-lined base
6	pit
7	pit
8	pit
9	pit
11	roasting pit-hearth
12	pit with rocks, with a rock-lined (?) bottom, possibly a roasting pit
13	pit
14	roasting pit-hearth

Table 3.30, continued

EXCAVATED FEATURE INFORMATION, AZ EE:2:77

Feature or Subfeature Number	Interpretation and Description
15	rock cluster
16	collective designation for an earlier pit (16001) intruded by a later, deeper pit (16002)
16001	pit
16002	pit
17	roasting pit-hearth
17001	hearth intrusive into fill of Feature 17
19	pit with rocks
22	cremation deposit ?
23	roasting pit-hearth which cuts 23001, cremation deposit
23001	cremation deposit cut by Feature 23 roasting pit-hearth
24	pit
25	pit containing a smaller intrusive pit
26	roasting pit-hearth
28	pit (rodent disturbed)
29	pit (rodent disturbed)
30	collective designation for two superimposed features, 30001 and 30002
30001	pit

Table 3.30, continued

EXCAVATED FEATURE INFORMATION, AZ EE:2:77

Feature or Subfeature Number	Interpretation and Description
30002	roasting pit-hearth, cuts Subfeature 30001
31	pit house; intruded by Feature 51 roasting pit-hearth
31002	hearth (unlined pit)
32	pit
33	possible posthole; definitely rodent enlarged
36	pit ? (possibly rodent burrow)
37	rodent enlarged extramural posthole ?
38	rodent enlarged extramural posthole ?
39	rodent enlarged extramural posthole ?
40	cremation deposit
42	pit ? (possibly rodent burrow)
44	pit house (heavily eroded)
44001	floor pit
44002	hearth (unlined pit)
44003	floor pit (?) with cremation deposit
44004	floor pit (?) with infant inhumation
45	sherd-lined and filled pit
46	extramural hearth (plastered)
50	roasting pit-hearth intrusive into the fill of Feature 3 pit house

Table 3.30, continued

EXCAVATED FEATURE INFORMATION, AZ EE:2:77

Feature or Subfeature Number	Interpretation and Description
51	roasting pit-hearth intrusive into the fill and floor of Feature 31 pit house
52	cremation deposit (?)
53	roasting pit-hearth
54	pit (possibly a cremation deposit)
55	pit or posthole
56	limited-use structure
56002	intrusive (?) pit

may all be intrusive as well, but this could not be conclusively demonstrated. The fills of Features 3 and 31 were both intruded by roasting pit-hearths, Features 50 and 51, respectively.

Feature 3 is probably the only trash-filled pit house on the site. The only items found on its floor were two sherds from the large Sacaton Red-on-buff bowl that was part of the Feature 23001 cremation deposit, establishing a rough contemporaneity between the disturbance of the cremation by the Feature 23 roasting pit and either the occupation or, more likely, the postabandonment filling of the Feature 3 pit house.

Feature 56

This feature is classed as a limited-use structure because of its small size and lack of internal features. Subfeature 56002, a pit, may be intrusive. Flotation and pollen samples from both the structure floor and pit (Appendixes B and C; Miksicek 1984a) were unenlightening.

Table 3.31

STRUCTURE DATING AND CONTENT SUMMARY, AZ EE:2:77

Feature Number	Age Assignment	Basis for Dating									
		Site Ceramics	Floor Ceramics	Fill Ceramics	Superposition	Other	Burned	Trash Filled	Floor Assemblage	Intrudes Features	Intruded by Features
001000 (Floor 1)	early Rincon			x	x			?		?	+
001000 (Floor 2)	early Rincon			x	x			?		+	+
001000 (Floor 3)	early or middle Rincon	x		x	x	x	?	?		+	?
002000	early/middle Rincon			x						?	+
003000	early/middle Rincon	x			x				+		+
004000	early/middle Rincon	x			x						
031000	early/middle Rincon			x							+
044000	early or middle Rincon	x			x						?
056000	early or middle Rincon	x			x						?

Slope Trash

Trash, in the form of sherds, chipped stone, and utilitarian and nonutilitarian ground stone was abundant on the ridge slopes. It was less common on the northern and northwestern extremes, and most dense along the eastern side of the ridge.

Extramural Features

A total of 57 extramural features was found and excavated, as well as another 12 "features" which were assigned numbers but were later determined to be of natural or rodent origin (Features 10, 18, 20, 21, 27, 34, 35, 41, 43, 47, 48, and 49). The extramural features included 21 pits, 2 pits with rocks, 13 roasting pit-hearths, 1 plastered hearth, 1 rock cluster, 10 postholes not directly associated with a structure, and 1 sherd-lined pit.

Pits and Hearths

With the large sample of extramurals dug at AZ EE:2:77, it was hoped that analysis of flotation samples would help define functional classes of pits. Samples from both pits with rocks, nine roasting pit-hearths, and five pits were analyzed. The results showed that corn and agave remains were commonly present in all of these feature types (Miksicek 1984a). From the fire-reddened walls of Feature 11, and the thoroughly fire-cracked condition of the rock in many of the "roasting pit-hearths," it is clear that the functional name given these features is correct; the flotation samples suggest corn and agave were the most commonly roasted foods. For the pits without rocks, function is unclear. Flotation revealed contents similar to roasting pit-hearths, but this would be expected if their final use was as a receptacle for trash or roasting pit debris.

Pits are often called "storage pits." In order to see if such may have been the case at this site, pollen samples from three pits and one pit with rocks were analyzed. The pit samples produced almost no pollen, but the pit with rocks produced a high percentage of Cheno-Am pollen (Appendix C). The latter results are not necessarily significant, however, in that Cheno-Am pollen is dominant or extremely abundant in virtually all of the project samples with preserved pollen.

Animal bone was recovered from two roasting pit-hearths (Features 5 and 17) and three pits (Features 16, 28, and 30001), and consisted primarily of deer bone. Very little of the bone showed any signs of burning, and its presence in these features may well not relate to their primary function.

The majority of extramural pit features are of two types: either pits with no rock in their fills (21); or roasting pit-hearths (13), which are predominantly rock filled. The presence of only two pits with rocks (less than 50% rock filled) suggests that the latter

type is a spurious category, which was probably not recognized
prehistorically.

Finally, only two plastered extramural hearths were found on the
whole project: Feature 46 on AZ EE:2:77 and Feature 126 on AZ EE:2:105.
Feature 46 was in close proximity to Feature 45, a pit which was lined
and filled with sherds. Whether extramural plastered hearths have some
special significance or function is unknown. Neither example was
preserved well enough to take flotation samples.

Postholes

Ten extramural postholes were found just north of the Feature 3
pit house, eight of them forming what appears to be a short, linear
palisade or wall (Fig. 3.31). Whether this presumed wall or fence was
purely functional, or served to divide social space within the
habitation area, is unknown. No other such feature was found on the
project.

Although such features, along with palisades which completely
surround a site, are occassionally encountered in Anasazi sites (Hammack
and others 1983: 109-111), the only similar occurrence known to the
author from a Hohokam site is at the Bidegain Ruin. This site consists
of three small structures surrounded by a row of postholes (Di Peso
1958: 7-11, Fig. 1.1) atop a small knoll overlooking the San Pedro
River. The ceramic assemblage from the site suggests a late
Rincon-early Tanque Verde phase occupation (Di Peso 1958: 146). A
very extensive system of ramadas or jacal structures was found at the
Colonial period Henderson Site, on the Agua Fria River north of Phoenix
(Weed and Ward 1970). All of these posthole arrangements, however,
clearly enclosed particular areas, and no surrounding palisade was
found.

Sherd-Lined Pits

The possible association of Feature 45 with the Feature 46
extramural plastered hearth was noted above. Feature 45 itself
consisted of a 20 cm deep, 25 cm diameter pit. About 8 cm above the pit
bottom and an equal distance below the pit mouth were 31 sherds, some
placed with their interiors against the walls, the remainder arranged in
four or five horizontal layers. The sherds came from three vessels, a
Rincon Red-on-brown, Stype B bowl, an unidentified red-on-brown jar, and
a plain ware vessel of unknown form.

Burials

Six cremation deposits (Features 22, 23001, 40, 44003, 52, and
54) and two infant inhumations (Features 1003 and 44004) were found at
AZ EE:2:77.

Cremation Deposits

Features 22, 23001, and 52. The Subfeature 23001 pit deposit
was cut almost in half by the Feature 23 roasting pit-hearth. Part of a
Rincon Red-on-brown, Style A jar was found near the flattish bottom of
the pit. Above it were the nested sherds of a large Sacaton Red-on-buff
bowl.

Feature 52, just southwest of Subfeature 23001, consisted of a
jumble of sherds and bone in the top of what may have been at the time a
partially filled pit. Eight sherds from this feature are part of the
partial Rincon Red-on-brown, Style A jar found in Subfeature 23001, and
two others are part of the Sacaton Red-on-buff bowl from the same
subfeature.

It was noted already that two other sherds of the Sacaton bowl
were found on the floor of the Feature 3 pit house, and another sherd
almost certainly from this same vessel was found during stripping of the
area west of Feature 36. Finally, two sherds of the Rincon jar came
from the upper fill of the Feature 1 house pit. These do not, however,
indicate whether the disturbance of Subfeature 23001 predates or
postdates the abandonment of Feature 1; these two sherds could have been
either in the abandoned house pit, or incorporated into the soil
covering of a still-standing pit house.

These data indicate that when the occupants of AZ EE:2:77
inadvertently disturbed the Feature 23001 cremation deposit, they were
concerned enough to redeposit the disturbed material nearby (Feature
52), but not so carefully that sherds did not become scattered in
different parts of the site. Presumably some of the bone was also
displaced. Nearby Feature 22 also contained only a small amount of
bone, burned to a degree similar to the bone from Features 23001 and 52.
Bone from all three features is so scant and fragmentary that no
matching of pieces is possible, even though at least those from 23001
and 52 are almost certainly the same individual.

Feature 40. This deposit was placed in a round, flat-bottomed
pit. A flare-rimmed, Sacaton Red-on-buff bowl was sitting on its side
against the western edge of the pit and a flare-rimmed, Rincon Red-on-
brown, Style B bowl was sitting essentially upright next to the south
wall of the pit. The Rincon bowl was full of ash and bone. Both
vessels are extensively broken, but the sherds are not scattered, and
the breakage is probably the result of compaction when the pit was
filled prehistorically. Whether the Sacaton bowl served as a cover bowl
that slipped off is unclear. The inclusion of two bowls with life forms
is notable, especially in that the Sacaton vessel shows birds and the
Rincon vessel snakes, two creatures often combined in Hohokam shell work
(Jernigan 1978, Fig. 24).

Charcoal from the ash in the Rincon bowl included four pieces of
oak and one of Ceanothus greggii (Miksicek 1984a). A pollen sample from
the bottom of the pit below the Rincon bowl did not produce sufficient
pollen for analysis (Appendix C).

Feature 44003. This pit cremation deposit was found during the excavation of the Feature 44 pit house. It cannot be determined whether this deposit predates, postdates, or was contemporaneous with the house, or whether the pit was originally a floor pit, or was dug specifically to receive the cremation deposit. The 24-cm-deep pit had about 4 cm of fill in the bottom, above which was a 5-cm-thick layer of bone mixed with the sherds of a small San Simon series red-on-brown bowl, probably Galiuro Red-on-brown. Overlying the bone and sherd layer was 15 cm of fill which lacked artifacts.

Inhumations

Feature 1003. This infant inhumation was placed directly on sterile ground at the bottom of a round, flat-bottomed pit near the back wall of Floor 3 in the Feature 1 house pit (Fig. 3.31). This pit probably does not predate Floor 3 unless it was originally extremely deep. Whether this pit was originally a floor pit, or was dug specifically to receive this inhumation cannot be determined; the fill of the pit, however, suggests that the house could have continued in use after the burial was placed in it. The infant was covered with some 10 cm of cultural soil topped with a layer of five or six rocks, in turn capped with about 15 cm of a light-colored, compact, calichelike fill. This pit appears to have been intentionally caped and probably was indistinguishable from the floor when new. The infant was apparently supine, head to the east-northeast. No artifacts were recovered from the pit.

Feature 44004. As with the Feature 44003 cremation deposit, it cannot be determined whether the Feature 44004 infant inhumation predates, postdates, or is contemporaneous with the Feature 44 pit house, or whether the pit was originally a floor pit, or was dug specifically to receive the inhumation. The contents of this pit were jumbled by rodent action, but it appears that the infant was supine, head to the south, and was accompanied by 14 shell disk beads, 38 steatite disk beads, a rectangular piece of steatite or slate overlay(?), a turquoise pendant and pendant blank, and four chips of worked turquoise (Fig. 7.6a). Additional items and bone may have been lost in the rodent holes.

Ceramics and Dating

AZ EE:2:77 was occupied in early and middle Rincon phase times, and appears to squarely straddle the shift in popularity of Rincon Red-on-brown from Style A to Style B. Both styles are present in roughly equal amounts from the site as a whole, and consistently show up in varying proportions within individual features as well, including the Feature 2, 3, 4, and 31 pit houses and 2001 and 2002 pits (Table 3.32). Sacaton Red-on-buff is essentially the only buff ware type present, and occurs with both Style A and B, separately (Features 23001 and 40) and together (Feature 3). These proportions, combined with the complete absence of Rincon Red-on-brown, Style C, and the presence of only three identifiable sherds of Rillito Red-on-brown, clearly limit the occupation of AZ EE:2:77 to the early and middle Rincon phases exclusively.

Archaeomagnetic samples were collected from the Feature 1 pit house hearth (Subfeature 1001) and the Feature 46 extramural plastered hearth. The former was analyzed, but produced poor clustering and an equivocal set of dates (Appendix F).

Nonceramic Artifacts

AZ EE:2:77 produced a relatively diverse nonutilitarian assemblage of worked stone, shell, and bone. The most notable occurrences are five pieces of slate believed related to finger ring manufacture (out of a total of nine pieces from the project as a whole) and the turquoise, steatite, and shell items from the Feature 44004 infant inhumation (Fig. 7.6a). Oddities include what may be a phallic stone bowl (Fig. 7.5c) and a piece of worked slate (Fig. 7.4k). Palettes are conspicuously absent.

Subsistence

As already noted, corn and agave remains showed up with some consistency in extramural features, as did chenopod seeds in smaller quantities. Interestingly, mesquite seeds and acorns also occurred, primarily in pit house contexts (Miksicek 1984a). Animal bone occurred in pit houses and extramural features with no apparent patterning. Processing of corn, agave, and chenopods in roasting pit-hearths is indicated, perhaps as a substantial portion of the diet, with other wild plant and animal foods making up the remainder in unknown proportions.

Summary

This middle-sized site was occupied for apparently roughly equal periods during the early and middle Rincon phases. With the exception of AZ EE:2:76, it is the only site of any size that witnessed a substantial occupation during both of these phases; most sites in the exchange area were either founded or abandoned during the transition between early and middle Rincon times. The contemporaneity of features, and the construction and abandonment sequences for the pit houses and extramural features at the site can be discussed in only a limited way. Floors 1 and 2 in the Feature 1 house pit are probably among the earliest at the site, while the Feature 2, 3, and 31 pit houses are all superimposed by other features, indicating that they are not among the latest structures at the site.

Subsistence can best be summarized as heavily dependent on corn agriculture, followed by wild plant food gathering and hunting.

Table 3.32

DECORATED POTTERY TYPES FROM AZ EE:2:77

Provenience	Rillito Red-on-brown	Rincon Red-on-brown Style A	Rincon Red-on-brown Style B	Rincon Red-on-brown Style ?	Santa Cruz Red-on-buff	Sacaton Red-on-buff	Galiuro Red-on-brown	TOTAL
Stripping	1	16	14	56		1		88
Feature 1 pit house		7		29		4		40
Feature 2 pit house		1	2	8				11
Feature 3 pit house		6	3	17		3		29
Feature 4 pit house		1	9	17				27
Feature 31 pit house	2	4	3	29			7	45
Feature 44 pit house			1	1				2
Feature 56 limited-use structure				2				2
Feature 2001 pit		12	14	3				29
Feature 2002 roasting pit-hearth		12	PJ 4	24				PJ 40
Feature 2003 pit				1				1
Feature 2004 pit				4				4
Feature 5 roasting pit			1	2				3
Feature 12 rock-lined pit		6		1				7
Feature 13 pit		1						1
Feature 16 two pits				4				4
Feature 17 two roasting pits				10				10
Feature 23001 cremation deposit		PJ				PB		PJ PB
Feature 30 roasting pit			1	3	1			5
Feature 32 pit	1							1
Feature 40 cremation deposit			WB			WB		2WB
Feature 45 sherd-lined pit		PB						PB
Feature 50 roasting pit-hearth				1				1

Table 3.32, continued

DECORATED POTTERY TYPES FROM AZ EE:2:77

Provenience	Rillito Red-on-brown	Rincon Red-on-brown Style A	Rincon Red-on-brown Style B	Rincon Red-on-brown Style ?	Santa Cruz Red-on-buff	Sacaton Red-on-buff	Galiuro Red-on-brown	TOTAL
Feature 51 roasting pit-hearth		2				1		3
Feature 52 cremation deposit		8				2		10
TOTAL	3	77	52	212	1	11	7	363

PJ = Partial jar
PB = Partial bowl
WB = Whole bowl

Note: Whole and partial vessels are not included in totals.

Site structure, as usual, cannot be discussed in diachronic terms, but several observations can be made concerning the pattern displayed by all the features. All entryways are oriented north or slightly northeast. Spatially, Features 2 and 31, 1 and 4, and 3 and 44 form three pairs of structures, the members of each pair being approximately 15 m apart (from center to center); the significance (if any) of this relationship is unknown. Extramural features clustered near the middle of the site, in front of some pit houses, but behind Feature 1 and some distance from Feature 31. Burials are clustered towards the northern end of the site, and all the extramural cremation deposits occur together in an area less than 6 m long. The extreme end of the ridge is occupied by the Feature 56 limited-use structure, somewhat isolated from the other structures. Finally, the row of postholes in front of the Feature 3 pit house suggests a wall or fence, which may indicate some sort of social division of site space.

AZ EE:2:107

This site was recorded as a moderate artifact density, small area site on a ridge overlooking upper Barrel Canyon (Fig. 3.1). The habitation area is approximately 20 m wide and 45 m long (Fig. 3.32), containing 5 structures and at least 11 extramural features (Table 3.33). All artifacts recovered are tabulated in Table 3.34.

Structures
=====

Four pit houses (Features 1, 2, 3, and 5) and what may have been a pit house or ramada, or both (Feature 4), were partially or completely excavated (Table 3.35). These are believed to be the only structures on the site.

Feature 1

This pit house had a large, in-place, wooden sill at the outer end of the entryway. Three sherds, making up a partial Rincon Red-on-brown, Style B scoop, were found immediately behind the hearth.

Feature 2

This pit house was dated on the basis of Rincon Red-on-brown and Sacaton Red-on-buff sherds from both structure fill and the fill of floor features 2001, 2004, 2006 and 2010. Rincon Red-on-brown, Style B is dominant.

The depositional history of this house is unclear. Sherds of a single plain ware jar were found in all fill proveniences, as well as the floor assemblage and three floor pits. Burned chenopod seeds were recovered in huge numbers from the floor and three floor pits; no fill flotation samples were taken (Miksicek 1984a). Artifact densities within the house fill do not suggest that this structure was trash filled; however, a floor pit (Subfeature 2001) was apparently intentionally filled with burned metate fragments, sherds, and other worked stone. Finally, both the hearth (Subfeature 2005) and Subfeature 2001 were intruded by pits or postholes. All of this suggests either some major disturbance to the house after it was already filled in, thereby homogenizing the artifact distribution in the fill, or perhaps that the house was intentionally filled with earth which contained occasional discarded items.

Feature 3

This is one of the few houses investigated in the project area which had both clearly burned and had an intact floor assemblage of artifacts. Even so, the floor assemblage was of no help in dating the house; it consisted of three partial plain ware jars, one whole and one partial plain ware scoop, several additional sherds and flakes, and a fire-shattered mano (Fig. 3.33). Also of interest in this house is its three-step entryway.

Feature 4

This feature may represent either a pit house later intruded by a substantial ramada or the reverse. The house pit may have had an

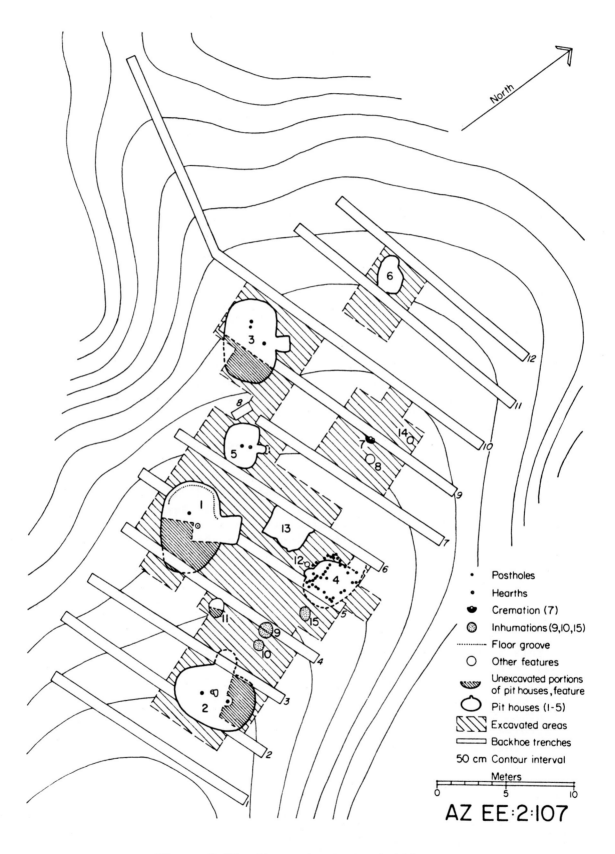

Figure 3.32 Site map, AZ EE:2:107.

Table 3.33

TYPES AND NUMBERS OF FEATURES, EXCAVATED
AND UNEXCAVATED, AT AZ EE:2:107

Feature Type	Excavated	Unexcavated	Total
Pit houses	5	-	5
Pits	2	-	2
Roasting pit-hearths	1	-	1
Borrow pits (?)	3	-	3
Cremation deposits	2	-	2
Inhumations	3	-	3
Total	16	0	16

entryway on the southwest or northwest or both, and the numerous
postholes outline a vaguely square or rectangular area (Fig. 3.32).

Feature 5

This is a pit house with a single central roof support and a
northeast-facing entryway. The floor asemblage included red wares,
Rincon Red-on-brown, Style B and Rio Rico Polychrome sherds.

Slope Trash

Trash was quite dense along the whole eastern slope, and on the
southwestern slope behind Feature 1, less dense behind Features 3 and 5,
and almost nonexistant on the northwestern spur and the northern end of
the ridge.

Extramural Features

Six extramural features were found, including two pits (Features
8 and 12), one roasting pit-hearth (Feature 14) and three possible

Table 3.34

ARTIFACT TOTALS BY CLASS FOR AZ EE:2:107

Artifact Type	Count	Category Total	Percent of Assemblage
Ceramics		1,811	85.4
Decorated sherds	345		
Red ware sherds	45		
Plain ware sherds	1,421		
Chipped Stone		246	11.6
Debitage	219		
Retouched pieces	12		
Cores	4		
Hammerstones	11		
Utilitarian Ground Stone		49	2.3
Metates	12		
Mano-handstones	30		
Polishing stones	2		
3/4-grooved axes	1		
Other	4		
Nonutilitarian Stone		1	0.1
Worked slate	1		
Shell		9	0.4
Bracelets	5		
Other	4		
Worked Bone		4	0.2
Awls-hairpins	4		
Total		2,120	100.0

borrow pits (Features 6, 11, and 13). None of these features produced temporally diagnostic materials, and analyses of flotation samples from Features 6, 8, 11, and 14 were uninformative (Miksicek 1984a). Features 6, 11, and 13 were extremely rodent or root disturbed and their identification as borrow pits is tentative. None of these possible borrow pits appeared trash filled.

Table 3.35

STRUCTURE DATING AND CONTENT SUMMARY, AZ EE:2:107

| Feature Number | Age Assignment | Basis for Dating | | | | | Burned | Trash Filled | Floor Assemblage | Intrudes Features | Intruded by Features |
		Site Ceramics	Floor Ceramics	Fill Ceramics	Superimposition	Other					
001000	middle Rincon		x				+				
002000	middle Rincon		x	x			+				?
003000	middle Rincon	x		x			+				
004000	middle Rincon	x					+			?	?
005000	middle Rincon	x	x	x			+	+	+		

Burials

Two cremation deposits (Subfeatures 7001 and 7002) and three flexed inhumations in pits (Features 9, 10, and 15) were found at AZ EE:2:107.

Cremation Deposits

Subfeatures 7001 and 7002. Trench 9 cut through two adjacent cremation pits, Subfeatures 7001 and 7002. The two pits overlap each other, but whether one intruded the other, or both are contemporaneous is impossible to determine. The Feature 7002 pit also has a low "bench" of unknown function on its southwestern side. Feature 7001 consists of an upright Rincon Red-on-brown, Style B jar which contained the bone of an adult of undetermined sex and an incinerated bone awl or hairpin. It was covered by a red-on-brown bowl, and next to it was a plain ware jar lying sideways on a partial red-on-brown bowl. Feature 7002 consisted

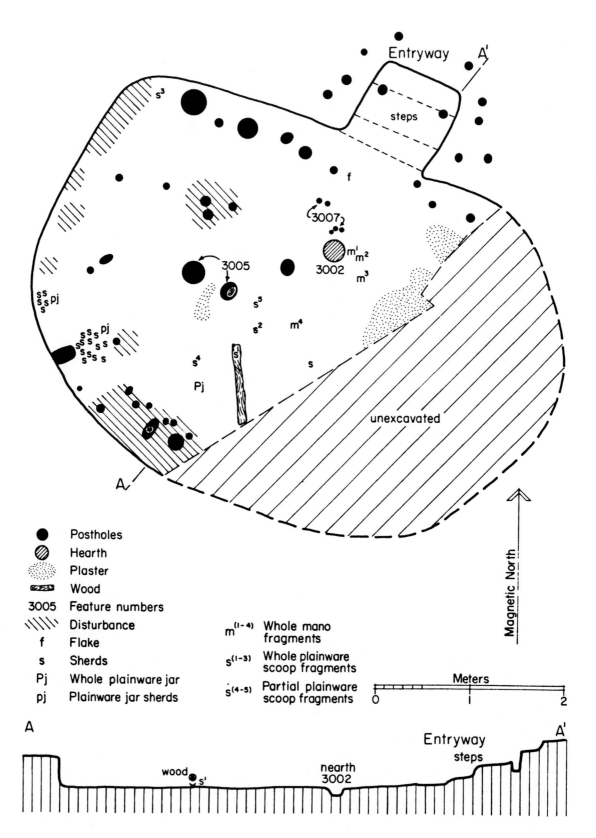

Figure 3.33 Plan view and cross section, Feature 3 pit house, AZ EE:2:107.

of an upright, bilobed Rincon Red-on-brown, Style B jar, containing bone
from a second adult, fragments of an incinerated bone awl or hairpin,
and burned shell representing at least five Glycymeris bracelets, one
small diameter Glycymeris "bracelet" or pendant, and one or possibly two
unidentifiable, centrally perforated, tabular pendants.

Inhumations

Feature 9. This inhumation was tightly flexed on its left side,
with the right arm extended by the pelvis, and the left arm flexed below
the skull. The cranium itself is turned downward and to the left, due
to settling or possibly rodent disturbance of the cervical area, and is
oriented to the east. Above the left knee and arm was a bone hairpin,
and a handstone was found at the right knee. Covering the body was a
layer of 11 large rocks and 4 metate fragments. One metate fragment was
found, grinding surface down, above the chest; the grinding surface and
the bone hairpin showed traces of red ochre.

Feature 10. This individual was in a slouched sitting position,
knees up and together, arms at its sides, with both hands palm down.
The skull was resting chin on chest, and was oriented to the southwest.
Immediately above the right innominate were two small Glycymeris whole
valve pendants. A whole boulder trough metate was found directly above
the skull, trough up. This metate might have been used in this
position, but its location immediately above the skull suggests it might
have served as a grave marker.

Feature 15. This inhumation was tightly flexed, lying on its
left side with the head curled in, face down and cradled in the hands.
The head was at the north-northwest end of the pit. There were no grave
goods, but six large rocks covered the body.

Ceramics and Dating

The dominant decorated type at AZ EE:2:107 is Rincon Red-on-
brown, Style B (Table 3.36), although a fair showing of Style A sherds
in the fill of the Features 2 and 3 pit houses indicates at least some
occupation in early Rincon phase times. The presence of Rincon and Rio
Rico Polychrome and Sacaton Red-on-buff sherds supports the idea of a
primarily middle Rincon phase occupation. Archaeomagnetic samples were
taken from the hearths in the Feature 1 and 3 pit houses (Subfeatures
1002 and 3002), but were not analyzed after the poor results obtained
from the initial batch of project samples.

A notable inclusion in the ceramic assemblage is a rare bilobed
jar form. Unfortunately, the discovery is dampened by the poor
condition of the decoration; it is obscured by a tenacious covering of

Table 3.36

DECORATED POTTERY TYPES FROM AZ EE:2:107

Provenience	Rincon Red-on-brown Style A	Rincon Red-on-brown Style B	Rincon Red-on-brown Style ?	Rincon Polychrome	Rio Rico Polychrome	Sacaton Red-on-buff	Total
Stripping		1	6				7
Feature 1 (pit house)		PS	3				3*
Feature 2 (pit house)	8	26	15			2	51
Feature 3 (pit house)	PB	1	10	1	1		13*
Feature 5 (pit house)		1	1		3		5
Feature 6 (borrow pit)			2				2
Feature 7001 (cremation deposit)		WJ					WJ
Feature 7002 (cremation deposit)		WJ					WJ
Total	8*	29*	37	1	4	2	81*

PS = partial scoop
PB = partial bowl
WJ = whole jar
Note: whole and partial vessels are not included in totals

what is apparently a fine clay, naturally deposited on exposed surfaces of all the Feature 7 vessels.

Nonceramic Artifacts

The chipped stone assemblage includes a Type 3 projectile point from the Feature 1 pit house. This occurrence supports the inferred

Rincon phase age of this site, given the probable middle Rincon phase popularity of this point style. The nonutilitarian ground stone assemblage consists of a partially drilled slate disk (Fig. 7.4e), probably a finger ring in manufacture. Shell jewelry was restricted to mortuary contexts as described above. Four bone awls or hairpins were recovered. Two of these, from the Feature 9 inhumation and the Feature 7001 cremation deposit, are illustrated in Appendix A.

Subsistence

Animal bone was not abundant at AZ EE:2:107; only two jack rabbits are represented by unworked bone, although the bone awls or hairpins are made of artiodactyl bone.

Flotation samples (Appendix B) produced consistently low frequencies of corn, huge numbers of chenopod seeds, and a wide variety of other plants, usually represented by single specimens. This latter group included seeds from hedgehog cactus, juniper, mesquite, pigweed, spiderling, and portulaca, agave remains, one domestic bean, and one squash seed. A pollen sample from Subfeature 2001 produced high frequencies of Cheno-Am pollen (Appendix C) .

Summary

This small site appears to have first seen use in the early Rincon phase, but the primary occupation clearly occurred during the middle Rincon phase and apparently did not continue into late Rincon times.

Subsistence data, like those from virtually all of the other small sites, indicate corn agriculture supplemented by hunting and gathering of wild plant foods in unknown quantities. The abundance of chenopod seeds at AZ EE:2:107 tempts one to overemphasize the role of plant gathering at this site, but its abundance may be due to the vagaries of preservation. The variety of plants present, however, compares well with that found at some of the larger sites with extended occupations, suggesting AZ EE:2:107 may have been a relatively well extablished village.

Site structure, unfortunately, cannot be discussed at length. Although it is probable that the site witnessed new constructions, at least one abandonment of a house (trash-filled Feature 5), and the burial of at least 5 people, the sequence of these events cannot be reconstructed. Feature 5 may have been abandoned first; Features 2 and 3 have some early Rincon sherds in their fills, but this information is equivocal, especially in light of the apparently disturbed condition of Feature 2. Only Feature 4 shows clear evidence of superposition. In general, the houses are all on the upslope and southern edges of the available ridgetop space, with cremations and inhumations on the northern and eastern edges of the site, apparently segregated from one another and from the houses. Trash is predominatly in "front" of most of the structures, on the eastern ridge slope.

AZ EE:2:109

This site was recorded as a moderate artifact density, small area site on a "false terminus" ridge segment near the head of Barrel Canyon (Fig. 3.1). At 5245 feet in elevation, it is the highest ceramic period habitation site investigated. The habitation area of the site is some 60 m long and from 8 m to 18 m wide (Fig. 3.34), and contains five structures and at least five extramural pits (Table 3.37). Artifacts recovered are listed in Table 3.38.

Structures

Four pit houses (Features 1, 2, 3, and 5) and one limited-use structure (Feature 4) were partially or completely excavated (Table 3.39). No other structures are thought to be present on this site.

Feature 2

In addition to the single Rincon Red-on-brown, Style B sherd from the fill of this structure, archaeomagnetic samples were collected from the hearth (Subfeature 2001) and analyzed. The best fit interval was A.D. 1040-1090; the date at the 63 percent confidence level was A.D. 1040-1140, and at the 95 percent confidence level, A.D. 1000-1180 (Appendix F). A flaked stone tool, the most elaborate carved stone bowl from the project, and an unworked quartzite slab were found on the floor.

Feature 3

This house was tentatively dated by three Rincon Red-on-brown, Style B sherds found in the fill. Although the actual artifact density of this fill was low, it is twice that of any other structure at this site, suggesting that this house may be trash filled. A map of this feature, and a series of photographs taken during its excavation, are shown in Figure 3.2.

Slope Trash

Although some items were found on the western slope of the ridge, the vast majority of trash was found on the eastern slope.

Extramural Features

Five extramural pits were found (Features 6 through 10), and except Feature 10, all were excavated. Features 6 and 7 were deep and

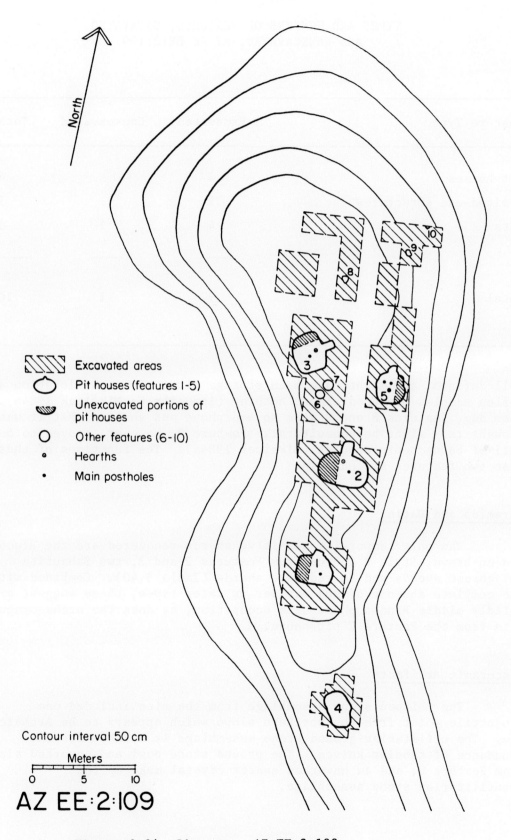

North

Excavated areas

Pit houses (features 1-5)

Unexcavated portions of pit houses

Other features (6-10)

Hearths

Main postholes

Contour interval 50 cm

Meters

0   5   10

AZ EE:2:109

Figure 3.34   Site map, AZ EE:2:109.

Table 3.37

TYPES AND NUMBERS OF FEATURES, EXCAVATED
AND UNEXCAVATED, AT AZ EE:2:109

Feature Type	Excavated	Unexcavated	Total
Pit houses	4		4
Limited-use structures	1		1
Pits	4	1	5
	——	——	——
Total	9	1	10

well defined, and might have been storage pits, although flotation and
pollen samples produced almost nothing (Appendix C; Miksicek 1984a).
When dug, Features 8 and 9 were so amorphous and shallow that it was
thought they might be noncultural. Feature 9, however, proved to be
full of burned corn cupules (Miksicek 1984a). The functions of these
last two features are unknown.

Ceramics and Dating

The only temporally sensitive sherds recovered are the Rincon
Red-on-brown, Style B sherds from Features 2 and 3, two Sahaurita
Polychrome sherds and 18 red ware sherds (Table 3.40). Combined with
the complete absence of any earlier or later types, these suggest a
solidly middle Rincon phase site occupation, as does the archaeomagnetic
date from the Feature 2 pit house.

Nonceramic Artifacts

The chipped stone assemblage from the site included one
projectile point from the northern slope which appears to be Archaic in
age. The utilitarian ground stone assemblage is notable for the
abundance of tabular knives. The ground stone bowl and unworked slab
from Feature 2, and an unworked quartz crystal make up the
nonutilitarian stone assemblage.

Table 3.38

ARTIFACT TOTALS BY CLASS FOR AZ EE:2:109

Artifact Type	Count	Category Total	Percent of Assemblage
Ceramics		142	59.4
Decorated sherds	50		
Red ware sherds	18		
Plain ware sherds	74		
Chipped Stone		80	33.5
Debitage	67		
Retouched pieces	8		
Cores	2		
Hammerstones	3		
Utilitarian Ground Stone		14	5.9
Metates	2		
Mano-handstones	7		
Tabular knives	3		
Other	2		
Nonutilitarian Stone		3	1.2
Bowls	1		
Crystals	1		
Other	1		
Total		239	100.0

Subsistence

The only animal bone recovered from AZ EE:2:109 was a pronghorn mandible from the fill of the Feature 1 pit house. Thin-sectioning of a first molar suggested a late winter or early spring time of death for this 4 or 5 year old animal (Appendix A).

Pollen samples were largely unproductive (Appendix C). Flotation samples produced small quantities of a variety of plant

Table 3.39

STRUCTURE DATING AND CONTENT SUMMARY, AZ EE:2:109

Feature Number	Age Assignment	Basis for Dating									
		Site Ceramics	Floor Ceramics	Fill Ceramics	Superimposition	Other	Burned	Trash Filled	Floor Assemblage	Intrudes Features	Intruded by Features
001000	middle Rincon	x		x			+				
002000	middle Rincon	x		x	x		+				
003000	middle Rincon	x		x			+	+			
004000	middle Rincon	x									
005000	middle Rincon	x					+				

remains. Corn, a tepary bean, walnut shell fragments, agave, and chenopod, pigweed, panic grass and prickly pear seeds were all recovered from a pit house and extramural contexts (Miksicek 1984a).

Summary

This small site appears to date solely to the middle of the Rincon phase. With an occupation of fairly limited duration, it seems likely that two or more of the structures on this site were occupied contemporaneously, but this is not certain. In the absence of superimposed features and more, or different, decorated ceramics, no demonstration of either simultaneous or sequential occupation can be made. Concomitantly, it is unclear whether the great variety of floral remains is the result of a diverse subsistence regimen during one occupation, or of several occupations during which the site served several different purposes. And, as with so many of the small sites, the small amount of bone recovered makes the importance of hunting at this site virtually impossible to assess.

Table 3.40

DECORATED POTTERY TYPES FROM AZ EE:2:109

| Provenience | Rincon Red-on-brown | | Sahuarita | |
	Style B	Style ?	Polychrome	Total
Stripping		6	1	7
Feature 1 (pit house)		2	1	3
Feature 2 (pit house)	1			1
Feature 3 (pit house)	3	2		5
Feature 5 (pit house)		14		14
Total	4	24	2	30

Site structure cannot be addressed in any detail. Pit houses are oriented north and northeast, with the few extramural features "in front" of the structures. The limited-use structure (Feature 4) appears somewhat isolated from the other structures, as far upslope on this ridge as was feasible. The areas up and downslope of Feature 4 and the northwestern edge of the ridgetop were not tested, because surface exposure of the cobble and gravel substrate in these areas clearly indicated that no buried features were present.

AZ EE:2:120

This site was recorded as a moderate artifact density, small area site, on a bench immediately above the drainage bottom, in upper Barrel Canyon (Fig. 3.1). The habitation area is about 45 m long and varies in width from 8 m to 20 m (Fig. 3.35), and contains seven structures and at least six extramural features (Table 3.41). All artifacts recovered are tabulated in Table 3.42.

Structures

Seven structures were partially or completely excavated (Table 3.43). Only Features 1 and 6 resemble "standard" pit houses in size and character, and even so, both apparently lack hearths. Feature 11 could

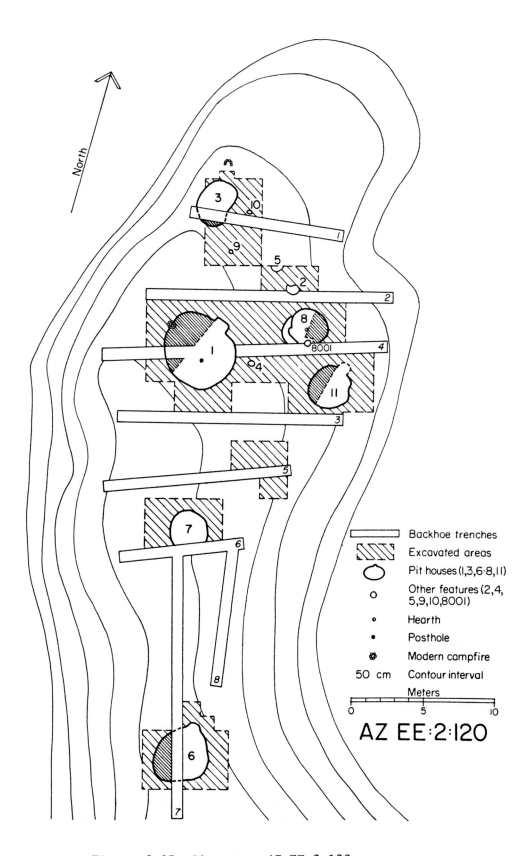

Figure 3.35   Site map, AZ EE:2:120.

Table 3.41

TYPES AND NUMBERS OF FEATURES, EXCAVATED
AND UNEXCAVATED, AT AZ EE:2:120

Feature Type	Excavated	Unexcavated	Total
Pit houses	3	-	3
Limited-use structures	4	-	4
Roasting pit-hearths	1	-	1
Pits with rocks	2	-	2
Artifact and animal bone clusters	1	-	1
Cremation deposits	2	-	2
Total	13	0	13

be classed as either a limited-use structure or a pit house with a single central roof-support post, depending on whether it actually possesses an entryway, and whether it has main roof support postholes. Rodent disturbance has effectively precluded a definitive statement about either; it is tentatively classed as a pit house. Features 3, 7, and 8 (both Floor 1 and Floor 2) are all classified as limited-use structures based on their small size or their lack of hearths, entryways or postholes. For Features 3 and 8, however, these classifications are tentative in that both are at the larger end of the "small" size range (see Chapter 10), do have postholes, and Feature 8 may have a hearth (Subfeature 8002). In sum, the structures on AZ EE:2:120, individually and as a group, are rather equivocal morphologically, and do not fall clearly into even the fairly gross groupings of "pit houses," and "limited-use structures."

Slope Trash

The northwestern ridge slope is extremely steep, a distinct "cliff" whose foot is washed by the Barrel Canyon stream bottom; any trash thrown over this edge would have been washed away eventually. The southwestern slope is less steep but shows little trash. The whole eastern side of this bench is a gentle slope and the main deposition of trash seems to have been here, essentially east and northeast of the structures.

Table 3.42

ARTIFACT TOTALS BY CLASS FOR AZ EE:2:120

Artifact Type	Count	Category Total	Percent of Assemblage
Ceramics		775	75.8
Decorated sherds	107		
Red ware sherds	18		
Plain ware sherds	650		
Chipped Stone		230	22.5
Debitage	186		
Retouched pieces	25		
Cores	12		
Hammerstones	1		
Utilitarian Ground Stone		13	1.3
Mano-handstones	8		
Polishing stones	1		
Tabular knives	1		
3/4-grooved axes	1		
Other	2		
Nonutilitarian Stone		4	0.4
Crystals or minerals	4		
Total		1,022	100.0

Extramural Features

Four extramural features were found, including two pits with rocks (Features 2 and 5), one roasting pit-hearth (Feature 10), and one deposit of sherds (Feature 4).

Pits with Rocks and Roasting Pit-Hearths

Features 2 and 5, both pits with rocks, contained pockets of ashy fill and a few rocks, but no definite signs of in situ burning. Flotation and pollen samples were largely unproductive, and the function of these pits is unclear. The Feature 10 roasting pit-hearth was quite shallow but contained numerous rocks and abundant oak charcoal. A

Table 3.43

STRUCTURE DATING AND CONTENT SUMMARY, AZ EE:2:120

Feature Number	Age Assignment	Site Ceramics	Floor Ceramics	Fill Ceramics	Superimposition	Other	Burned	Trash Filled	Floor Assemblage	Intrudes Featues	Intruded by Features
001000	middle Rincon	x				x	+				
003000	middle Rincon	x									
006000	middle Rincon	x					+				
007000	middle Rincon	x									
008000 (Floor 1)	middle Rincon	x									+
008000 (Floor 2)	middle Rincon	x								+	
011000	middle Rincon	x	x				+				

flotation sample produced only burned grass stems (Miksicek 1984a), giving no indication of what might have been prepared in it.

Artifact Cluster

Feature 4 consisted of a three-layered pile of sherds apparently placed on the prehistoric ground surface. Three are unidentifiable red-on-brown sherds, probably from a single bowl, the other ten are plain ware sherds from a single vessel of unidentified form. All sherds were placed concave side down. The apparently intentional arrangement of the sherds representing two vessels argues against this being a simple potbreak, and the absence of bone argues against it being a burial.

Unfortunately, there was considerable rodent and root disturbance around this feature. Flotation and pollen samples were analyzed but produced no decisive results.

Burials

Cremation Deposits

Features 8001 and 9. A pit cremation was found in Trench 4, inside the Feature 8 house pit. Although the cremation materials were intact, it cannot be ascertained whether this pit deposit intrudes or predates either of the superimposed Feature 8 structures. Feature 9, an extramural cremation deposit in a pit, was found in the same general area. Neither Feature 8001 nor the Feature 9 cremation deposit had associated temporally diagnostic artifacts.

Ceramics and Dating

Few identifiable decorated sherds were recovered from AZ EE:2:120 (Table 3.44), but the 2 sherds of Rincon Red-on-brown Style B, 1 sherd of Rio Rico Polychrome, and the 18 red ware sherds suggest a middle Rincon phase occupation.

A Type 3 projectile point from the fill of the Feature 1 pit house indicates a Rincon phase assignment for AZ EE:2:120, based on this point style's ceramic associations at AZ EE:2:76, EE:2:105, and EE:2:107.

Table 3.44

DECORATED POTTERY TYPES FROM AZ EE:2:120

Provenience	Rincon Red-on-brown Style B	Style ?	Rio Rico Polychrome	Total
Stripping		2	1	3
Feature 11 (pit house)	2	3		5
Total	2	5	1	8

Nonceramic Artifacts

Table 3.42 presents the types and quantities of flaked and ground stone artifacts from this site. Nothing is particularly remarkable about the assemblage, aside from the projectile point noted above. Nonutilitarian stone included one modified quartz crystal, one piece of unworked limonite, and two pieces of unworked azurite or malachite.

Subsistence

Only six animal bones were recovered from this site, representing a minimum of two rabbits and one deer (Appendix A). The flotation samples (Appendix B; Miksicek 1984a) produced only scant remains of corn, walnuts, and agave, as well as chenopod and pigweed seeds.

The limited recovery of both bone and plant remains make interpretation of subsistence strategies at AZ EE:2:120 a difficult task. As usual, one can infer a mixed regimen of corn agriculture with hunting and wild plant collection in unknown proportions relative to one another.

Summary

This small site appears to date to the middle of the Rincon phase, but this assessment is based on very limited data. The superposition of the Feature 8 structures, and the fact that Feature 11 is probably trash filled indicate some time depth to the site. This also suggests that Feature 8, Floor 1 and Feature 11 may be the earliest structures at the site. However, the lack of temporally diagnostic materials from the various features makes their seriation impossible, as are reconstructions of site growth or structure.

The limited recovery of faunal and floral materials at this site is not unexpected in light of the results from other small sites; however, the extremely low number of grinding implements, combined with the number of rather unusual structures, is interesting. The location of the site on a low ridge above the canyon is also unusual. AZ EE:2:120 seems to differ slightly, either functionally or structurally, or both, from other sites in the area, although it is not readily interpretable in its own right.

Late Rincon Habitation Sites

A group of five small habitation sites seem to be predominantly late Rincon phase settlements. Of these five sites, AZ EE:1:104, EE:2:106, EE:2:116, EE:2:117 and EE:2:122, only EE:2:106 appears to have been occupied at length, and its occupation may well have begun during the middle of the Rincon phase. AZ EE:2:106, EE:2:116, and EE:2:117 have some early Tanque Verde Red-on-brown pottery, making them the latest prehistoric sites known in the exchange area. It should also be remembered that AZ EE:2:76 and AZ EE:2:129, which have early components, both have late Rincon phase components as well.

AZ EE:1:104

This site was recorded as a moderate artifact density, small area site, on an east-west trending ridge segment relatively high in the foothills (Fig. 3.1). The habitation area of the site is estimated to be 40 m long by 20 m wide (Fig. 3.36), and contains two pit houses and at least two extramural features (Table 3.45). It was tested in 1979 and one feature was identified then. All artifacts recovered are tabulated in Table 3.46.

Structures

Two pit houses (Features 1 and 2) were partially or completely excavated (Table 3.47). No other structures are thought to be present on this site.

Feature 1

This small pit house with a single, central roof support burned down. The floor assemblage included a complete flake, 8 plain ware sherds, and 14 red-on-brown sherds. One of the latter is Rincon Red-on-brown, Style B, which, along with a partial Rincon Red-on-brown, Style C jar from the fill and the Sacaton Red-on-buff and Rio Rico Polychrome sherds from Feature 4, suggests a late Rincon phase age assignment for this structure in particular, and the site in general.

Feature 2

This house also burned and in so doing, preserved a fairly complete assemblage of architectural wood, including a sill at the outer end of the entryway. The only item on the floor aside from wood was a large (95 g) chunk of chrysocolla near its northwest corner. Archaeomagnetic samples were collected from the hearth (Subfeature 2001) but not analyzed.

Slope Trash

Trash was present on both the northern and southern ridge slopes primarily in the form of chipped stone and utilitarian ground stone

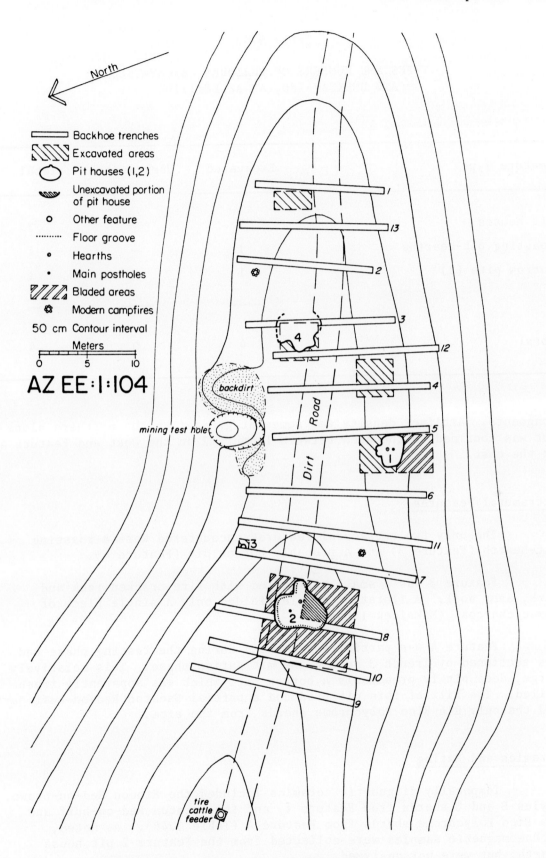

North

Backhoe trenches
Excavated areas
Pit houses (1,2)
Unexcavated portion of pit house
○ Other feature
········· Floor groove
⊛ Hearths
· Main postholes
Bladed areas
⊛ Modern campfires
50 cm Contour interval

Meters
0   5   10

AZ EE:1:104

backdirt

mining test hole

Dirt Road

1
13
2
3
12
4
5
6
11
7
13
4
8
10
9

2

tire
cattle
feeder

Figure 3.36   Site map, AZ EE:1:104.

Table 3.45

TYPES AND NUMBERS OF FEATURES, EXCAVATED
AND UNEXCAVATED, AT AZ EE:1:104

Feature Type	Excavated	Unexcavated	Total
Pit houses	2	–	2
Roasting pit-hearths	1	–	1
Borrow pits (?)	1	–	1
Total	4	0	4

fragments. Artifact density was somewhat greater on the northern slope but was confined to the area between Feature 2 on the west and Feature 4 on the east.

Extramural Features

The only two extramural features encountered were a roasting pit-hearth (Feature 3) and a probable borrow pit (Feature 4).

Feature 3 was a small pit filled with fire-cracked rock and dark, ashy soil. A flotation sample yielded only a single piece of sumac charcoal (Miksicek 1984a).

Feature 4 was partially excavated during the testing phase and was sectioned by Trench 3 during the mitigation phase. This relatively large, deep pit is presumably a borrow pit, which was apparently trash filled. The fill of this pit produced a partial Sacaton Red-on-buff jar and the only Rio Rico Polychrome sherds from the site.

Ceramics and Dating

Temporally diagnostic ceramics included the Rincon Red-on-brown, Styles B and C sherds from Feature 1, and the Sacaton Red-on-buff and Rio Rico Polychrome sherds from Feature 4 (Table 3.48). As noted, archaeomagnetic samples were collected from the Feature 2 pit house hearth, but were not analyzed.

Table 3.46

ARTIFACT TOTALS BY CLASS FOR AZ EE:1:104

Artifact Type	Count	Category Total	Percent of Assemblage
Ceramics		214	76.4
Decorated sherds	97		
Red ware sherds	6		
Plain ware sherds	111		
Chipped Stone		51	18.2
Debitage	44		
Retouched pieces	5		
Cores	2		
Utilitarian Ground Stone		14	5.0
Metates	4		
Mano-handstones	8		
Tabular knives	1		
3/4-grooved axes	1		
Nonutilitarian Stone		1	0.4
Crystals or minerals	1		
Total		280	100.0

Other ceramics of interest include red ware bowl sherds from the fill of Feature 2, and a miniature plain ware jar from the fill of Feature 1.

Nonceramic Artifacts

The relatively small utilitarian ground stone assemblage from AZ EE:1:104 is remarkably diverse. Further, this is the only late habitation site to yield a stone axe.

Subsistence

A single burned long bone, of a small mammal, came from the fill of Feature 2 (Appendix A). Flotation and pollen samples (Appendixes B and C) produced little of interest other than the very limited corn remains.

Table 3.47

STRUCTURE DATING AND CONTENT SUMMARY, AZ EE:1:104

		Basis for Dating									
Feature Number	Age Assignment	Site Ceramics	Floor Ceramics	Fill Ceramics	Superimposition	Other	Burned	Trash Filled	Floor Assemblage	Intrudes Features	Intruded by Features
001000	late Rincon	x	x	x			+		+		
002000	late Rincon	x					+				

Summary

This small site dates to late Rincon phase times. The trash-filled Feature 4 suggests at least a moderate length of occupation for the site, but whether or not both pit houses were occupied simultaneously cannot be determined.

The subsistence data are very limited, but corn remains are present, and grinding implements suggest domesticated or wild plant food processing. The importance of hunting at AZ EE:1:104 cannot be assessed.

Site structure is obviously fairly simple, but without knowing whether the pit houses were occupied simultaneously or sequentially, its history is unclear. This is the only site located on a ridge that is not oriented roughly north-south; however, because there are only two houses, it is impossible to determine how this might have affected pit house orientation and site layout.

AZ EE:2:106

This site was recorded as a moderate artifact density, small area site with sherds, chipped stone, ground stone and a slate palette present on the surface. The habitation area is roughly 50 m long by

Table 3.48

DECORATED POTTERY TYPES FROM AZ EE:1:104

Provenience	Rincon Red-on-brown Stype B	Rincon Red-on-brown Style C	Rincon Red-on-brown Style ?	Rio Rico Polychrome	Sacaton Red-on-buff	Total
Stripping			2			2
Feature 1 (pit house)	1	6	13			20
Feature 4 (borrow pit)			7	6	6	19
Total	1	6	22	6	6	41

25 m wide, and is located on a false ridge terminus (Fig. 3.37) in upper Barrel Canyon. Trenching was begun well back on the ridge, but as expected, all of the 11 features found (Table 3.49) were located on the wider portion of the ridgetop. Artifacts recovered are shown in Table 3.50.

Structures

Four pit houses (Features 2, 3, 6, and 7) and one limited-use structure (Feature 1) were partially or completely excavated (Table 3.51). No other structures are thought to be present on this site.

Feature 1

This tiny structure might have had no upper walls or roof, although a complete metate found on the floor was fire-cracked in place, suggesting some sort of flammable superstructure. The rest of the floor assemblage included a core-hammerstone sitting next to the metate, a Rincon Red-on-brown, Style B jar sherd, about 50 plain ware sherds, and a single flake.

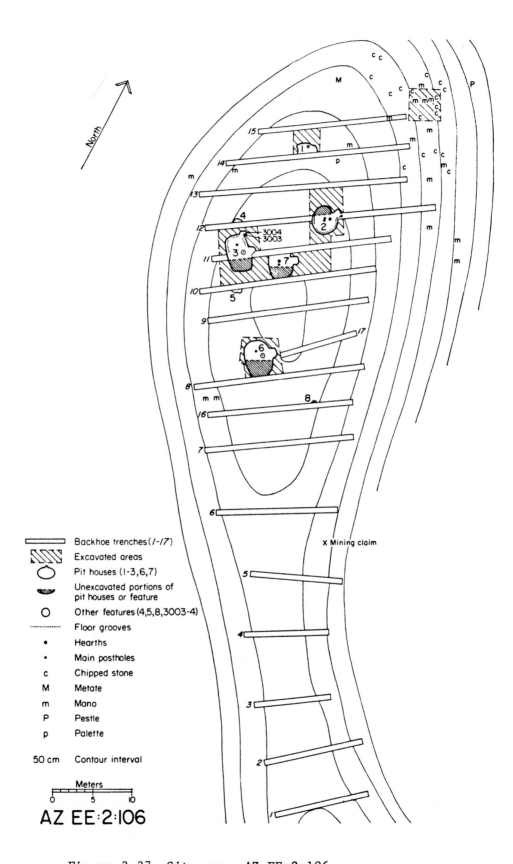

Figure 3.37　Site map, AZ EE:2:106.

Table 3.49

TYPES AND NUMBERS OF FEATURES, EXCAVATED
AND UNEXCAVATED, AT AZ EE:2:106

Feature Type	Excavated	Unexcavated	Total
Pit houses	4		4
Limited-use structures	1		1
Pits	2		2
Roasting pit-hearths	1	1	2
Rock-lined pit	1		1
Slab-lined pit	1		1
Total	10	1	11

Feature 2

     This pit house with a single central roof-support burned,
leaving numerous pieces of structural wood on the floor (Fig. 3.38).
It may be the latest of the structures excavated on the project, for
a partial Tanque Verde Red-on-brown bowl was found on the floor. The
remainder of the floor assemblage consisted of 40 plain ware sherds
(mostly part of a single bowl), one flake, and a large unmodified rock
which could have served as a seat. Archaeomagnetic samples collected
from the hearth (Subfeature 2001) were analyzed but did not produce a
date (Appendix F). A radiocarbon date of 870 $\pm$ 50 B.P. (A-3561),
A.D. 1080 $\pm$ 50 was obtained from one of the burned wall or roof members
and seems somewhat too early for the house.

Feature 3

     This is the only structure at the site which was trash filled,
suggesting it may be the earliest on the site; it may also have been
intruded by Subfeatures 3003 and 3004, both lined extramural pits. The
trash in this house included a partial Rincon Red-on-brown, Style C jar.

Table 3.50

ARTIFACT TOTALS BY CLASS FOR AZ EE:2:106

Artifact Type	Count	Category Total	Percent of Assemblage
Ceramics		356	77.6
Decorated sherds	91		
Red ware sherds	9		
Plain ware sherds	256		
Chipped Stone		79	17.2
Debitage	70		
Retouched pieces	5		
Cores	3		
Hammerstones	1		
Utilitarian Ground Stone		22	4.8
Metates	3		
Mano-handstones	17		
Tabular knives	2		
Nonutilitarian Stone		1	0.2
Crystals or minerals	1		
Worked Bone		1	0.2
Bone tubes	1		
Total		459	100.0

Feature 6

Archaeomagnetic samples were collected from the hearth (Subfeature 6002) of this oval pit house; unfortunately they did not produce a date (Appendix F). The weathered appearance of the plastered hearth suggests that the house or house pit may have stood open for some period of time after abandonment.

Slope Trash

Trash, in the form of abundant ground and chipped stone, and smaller quantities of sherds, was concentrated on the northeastern edge of the "false terminus" (Fig. 3.37). Although relatively dense on the surface, a 4-m-by-4-m unit excavated in this area showed that materials

Table 3.51

STRUCTURE DATING AND CONTENT SUMMARY, AZ EE:2:106

Feature Number	Age Assignment	Basis for Dating					Burned	Trash Filled	Floor Assemblage	Intrudes Features	Intruded by Features
		Site Ceramics	Floor Ceramics	Fill Ceramics	Superimposition	Other					
001000	late Rincon	x	x				+		+		
002000	late Rincon/ early Tanque Verde		x			x	+		+		
003000	late Rincon			x			+	+		?	?
006000	late Rincon	x									
007000	late Rincon	x									

were not found more than a few centimeters below it. This area appears to have been the main, and perhaps only area for trash discard, and is located more or less in front of all the pit houses.

Extramural Features

Six extramural features were found: two pits (Features 4 and 5), one slab-lined pit (Subfeature 3003), one rock-lined pit (Subfeature 3004), and two roasting pit-hearths (Feature 8 and an unnumbered feature intrusive into Subfeature 3003). Extramural stripping was not extensive, and other extramural features may well exist on this site.

Pits

Features 4 and 5 were found on either side of the Feature 3 pit house (Fig. 3.37), and upon excavation, both proved to be shallow, amorphous pits with brown earth fill. No artifacts were recovered, and

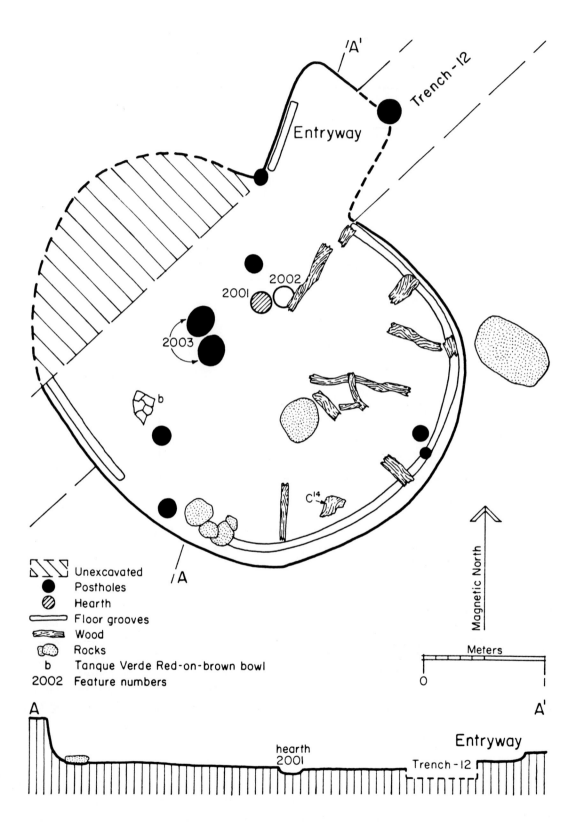

Figure 3.38 Plan view and cross section of the Feature 2 pit house, AZ EE:2:106. Note: Subfeature 2002 is an ash pit.

flotation and pollen samples were virtually devoid of remains
(Appendix C; Miksicek 1984a).

Roasting Pit-Hearths

        Feature 8 was found late in the excavation in Trench 16, and was
not excavated. Fire-cracked rock, none of which appeared artifactual,
made up about half of the pit fill. The second roasting pit-hearth (not
assigned a feature number) was found within the fill of Subfeature 3004,
as described below.

Lined Pits

        Subfeatures 3003 and 3004 have been called extramural features
although it is possible that they were actually built as part of the
Feature 3 pit house (Fig. 3.37). The bottom of Feature 3003 was lined
with tabular rocks (slab-lined) while the bottom of Feature 3004 was
lined with irregular stones and a mano. Feature 3004 adjoins 3003 which
in turn adjoins the northwest corner of the Feature 3 pit house; the
fill of all three features was uniform and gave no indication of
intrusion or superposition. Within the lower fill of Feature 3003 was a
small deposit of fire-cracked rock which, as noted above, appears to be
an intrusive hearth. Although the pit house wall appeared to continue
smoothly into the wall of Feature 3003, a corner post presumably blocked
access to it from within the house. So, although Subfeatures 3003 and
3004 could be part of the pit house, they probably were not. Their
relative ages are unknown and all could be contemporaneous. Feature
3003 yielded two Rincon Red-on-brown sherds.

        In terms of function, both Features 3003 and 3004 may have been
lined storage pits or cleaned roasting pit-hearths. Neither shows any
sign of burning, aside from the small hearth intrusive into 3003.
Flotation samples from both pits produced little to aid in their
interpretation (Miksicek 1984a), and a pollen sample from Feature 3004
produced only a few identifiable grains (Appendix C).

Ceramics and Dating

        The decorated ceramics at AZ EE:2:106 are notable for the
presence of a single sherd of Sahuarita Polychrome from Feature 3, and
the Tanque Verde Red-on-brown bowl from Feature 2. Temporally
identifiable materials include the Tanque Verde bowl, and the limited
amount of Rincon Red-on-brown, Styles B and C (Table 3.52). Occupation
of the site probably began in the middle or, more probably, late Rincon
phase, and extended through the end of that phase and into the Tanque
Verde phase. The early Tanque Verde Red-on-brown bowl on the floor of
Feature 2 makes it (and by extension, the whole site) one of the latest
in the exchange area.

Two archaeomagnetic samples failed to produce dates (Appendix F), and the radiocarbon sample from structural wood in Feature 2 dated earlier than would have been predicted by its Tanque Verde Red-on-brown ceramic association (Chapter 10).

Nonceramic Artifacts

The chipped stone assemblage is quite small, but resembles the other, larger sites in the proportions of artifact types. Numerous gray green quartzite fragments from the fill of the Feature 2 pit house can be refitted to form the remains of an extensively reduced core, suggesting that someone was flint-knapping into the naturally filling depression of the burned pit house.

Table 3.52

DECORATED POTTERY TYPES FROM AZ EE:2:106

Provenience	Rillito or Rincon Red-on-brown	Rincon Red-on-brown Style B	Rincon Red-on-brown Style C	Rincon Red-on-brown Style ?	Sahuarita Polychrome	Tanque Verde Red-on-brown	Unidentified Red-on-brown	Total
Stripping							1	1
Feature 1 (structure)		1						1
Feature 2 (pit house)						PB	8	8
Feature 3 (pit house)		2	4 PJ	14	1		8	29
Feature 6 (pit house)							3	3
Feature 7 (pit house)				1			8	9
Feature 3003 (lined pit)	1			2				3
Total	1	3	4	17	1	PB	28	54

PB = partial bowl; not included in totals
PJ = partial jar; not included in totals

Nonutilitarian ground stone at the site was represented by a single complete palette of local slate (Fig. 7.3g).

One worked fragment of large mammal bone was found in the fill of the Feature 1 limited-use structure. It is partially burned, and when complete was probably a finished tube.

Subsistence

Animal bone from AZ EE:2:106 consisted of only 18 bones, from a minimum of 1 artiodactyl and 1 rabbit (Appendix A).

Flotation samples (Appendix B; Miksicek 1984a) produced small quantities of a variety of plants; only corn appeared in any amount, from a floor pit (3002) in the Feature 3 pit house. Abundant grass stems and ocotillo charcoal from the floor of the Feature 2 pit house probably represent structural components. Pollen samples (Appendix C) were unenlightening.

Summary

This medium-sized habitation site appears to have been occupied primarily during late Rincon phase times, with at least Feature 2 occupied early in the Tanque Verde phase. The contemporaneity of any or all of the structures is difficult to assess, but three points may be noted. First, only the Feature 3 pit house appears trash filled, and therefore _may_ be the earliest construction. Second, although the exact temporal relationships of Features 3, 3003, 3004, and the hearth intrusive into 3003 are unclear, they are the only features showing evidence of superposition, perhaps again indicating an early position in the life of the site. Finally, although the Feature 2 pit house contains the latest ceramics at the site, and was not trash filled, the reconstructable core from its fill indicates that its destruction by fire was not the final event at the site. As such, the Features 6 and 7 pit houses, although they could not be dated, _could_ have been occupied after Feature 2.

Subsistence data are meager, but the presence of both corn and grinding implements suggests that agriculture played some role in the site activities, perhaps a dominant one. Animal bone is quite scarce, and the role of hunting is consequently difficult to assess with respect to either farming or the gathering of wild plant foods.

Finally, while several elements of site structure are obvious, how they were integrated is not. The four pit houses all face toward the northeast, and the main trash area is approximately in front of them. A limited-use structure is somewhat isolated from the pit houses at the extreme end of the ridge terminus. General aspects of site structure are discussed at greater length in Chapter 10.

AZ EE:2:116

This site was recorded as a moderate artifact density, small area site located in upper Barrel Canyon (Fig. 3.1), with a large, oval scatter of rock on the surface, indicating some type of structure. The habitation area of the site is difficult to estimate with only two house pits present; while the houses are only 5 m apart (thus defining a small area), the relatively flat portion of this ridgetop is about 50 m long (Fig. 3.39). The house pits noted above were the only features identified (Table 3.53), although a substantial portion of th ridgetop was stripped. All artifacts recovered are tabulated in Table 3.54.

Structures

Two house pits (Features 1 and 2) representing three pit houses were partially or completely excavated (Table 3.55). No other structures are thought to be present on this site.

Feature 1

This pit house was unusual in that its presence was indicated on the modern ground surface by a dense oval scatter of rock whose outline corresponded roughly with the subsurface limits of the house pit. There is no evidence to suggest that the rocks were part of the structure, rather, it appears they were simply thrown out of the house pit during its excavation, and never cleared away. Only one other example of this phenomenon was noted in the exchange area, at an uninvestigated site east of AZ EE:2:109 and just outside the Barrel Canyon drainage network. At that site the surface rocks outlined three walls and an entryway, all relatively straight and meeting at right angles (Debowski 1980, Fig. 17), suggesting that these rocks may actually have been part of the structure's foundation or walls. Its shape may also suggest a Tanque Verde or Tucson phase age.

The late Rincon or early Tanque Verde phase age assignment of Feature 1 is based on the recovery of eight Rincon Red-on-brown, Style C and three Tanque Verde Red-on-brown sherds from the fill. Archaeomagnetic samples were collected from the hearth (Subfeature 1001) and processed, but did not produce a date (Appendix F).

Feature 2

Although the hearth and two main roof support postholes show no signs of modification, a second, more complete, inner floor groove (Fig. 3.40) presumably represents either a second pit house within the Feature 2 house pit, or a major remodeling of the first house. This second house (Floor 2) may have burned, judging by the charcoal in Subfeature 2009, and the presence of a floor assemblage. This assemblage consists

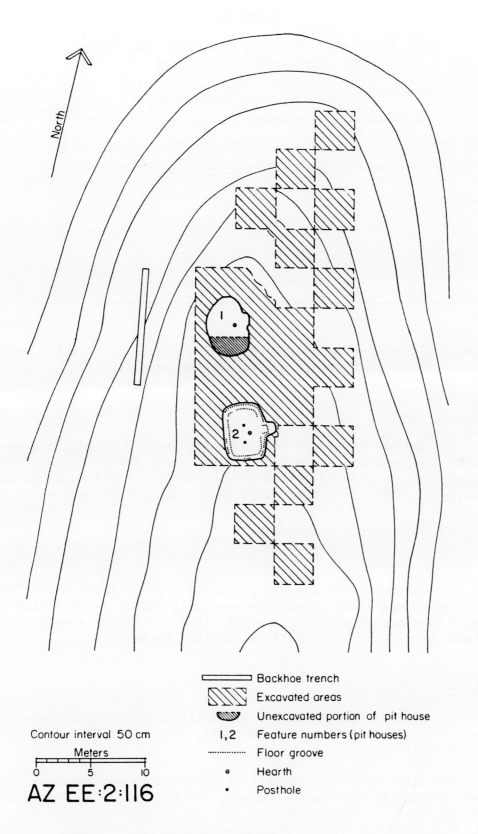

Backhoe trench
Excavated areas
Unexcavated portion of pit house
1,2   Feature numbers (pit houses)
Floor groove
Hearth
Posthole

Contour interval 50 cm

Meters
0   5   10

AZ EE:2:116

Figure 3.39   Site map, AZ EE:2:116.

Table 3.53

TYPES AND NUMBERS OF FEATURES, EXCAVATED
AND UNEXCAVATED, AT AZ EE:2:116

Feature Type	Excavated	Unexcavated	Total
Pit houses	3	–	3
Total	3	0	3

of sherds, flakes, two manos, and several rocks, some of which were clustered around the hearth, perhaps serving as a trivet.

Ceramics and Dating

The absence of Rincon Red-on-brown, Style B sherds, the presence of Rincon Red-on-brown, Style C and Tanque Verde Red-on-brown (Table 3.56), and the presence of only a single red ware sherd, suggest an occupation of AZ EE:2:116 restricted to the late Rincon and early Tanque Verde phases.

Nonceramic Artifacts

The chipped stone assemblage lacked projectile points. The utilitarian ground stone assemblage was small and included a slab metate, a form more typical of earlier sites. A single mineral specimen of calcite was the only nonutilitarian stone found.

Subsistence

Animal bone from AZ EE:2:116 consisted of only eight bones representing a minimum of one artiodactyl, one jack rabbit, and a lizard (Appendix A).

Flotation samples (Appendix B; Miksicek 1984a) produced corn and chenopod remains in very small numbers, and wood charcoal dominated by juniper and oak.

Table 3.54

ARTIFACT TOTALS BY CLASS FOR AZ EE:2:116

Artifact Type	Count	Category Total	Percent of Assemblage
Ceramics		647	86.6
Decorated sherds	115		
Red ware sherds	1		
Plain ware sherds	530		
Figurine fragments	1		
Chipped Stone		88	11.8
Debitage	78		
Retouched pieces	4		
Cores	3		
Hammerstones	3		
Utilitarian Ground Stone		11	1.5
Metates	4		
Mano-handstones	6		
Other	1		
Nonutilitarian Stone		1	0.1
Minerals	1		
Total		747	100.0

Summary

This small habitation site was probably occupied exclusively during the late Rincon and early Tanque Verde phases. Extramural features and prominent extramural trash deposits on the ridgetop or slopes are lacking. The Feature 1 pit house was trash filled, but the second house in Feature 2 apparently was not, suggesting that Feature 1 predated one or both of the Feature 2 pit houses.

Subsistence data are almost nonexistant, but faintly echo the dependence (in unknown proportions) seen at all the other habitation sites, on corn agriculture, hunting, and wild plant gathering.

With only two house pits, site structure is easily described but difficult to interpret. The two house pits face east-northeast and are

Table 3.55

STRUCTURE DATING AND CONTENT SUMMARY, AZ EE:2:116

Feature Number	Age Assignment	Basis for Dating									
		Site Ceramics	Floor Ceramics	Fill Ceramics	Superimposition	Other	Burned	Trash Filled	Floor Assemblage	Intrudes Features	Intruded by Features
001000	late Rincon/ early Tanque verde			x				+			
002000 (Floor 1)	late Rincon	x				x	u	u	u		+
002000	late Rincon/ early Tanque Verde	x				x	+		+	+	

situated side-by-side. Although no extramural features were found, the trough metate outside the Feature 2 entry way (Fig. 3.40) suggests that some activities took place immediately in front of the houses.

AZ EE:2:117

This site was recorded as a moderate artifact density, small area site with sherds, chipped stone, and three caches of groundstone on its surface. The habitation area of the site is approximately 35 m long and 25 m wide, on a hump in the ridge (Fig. 3.41) which separates Barrel Canyon from South Canyon (Fig. 3.1). Seventeen features were found (Table 3.57), and all artifacts recovered are tabulated in Table 3.58.

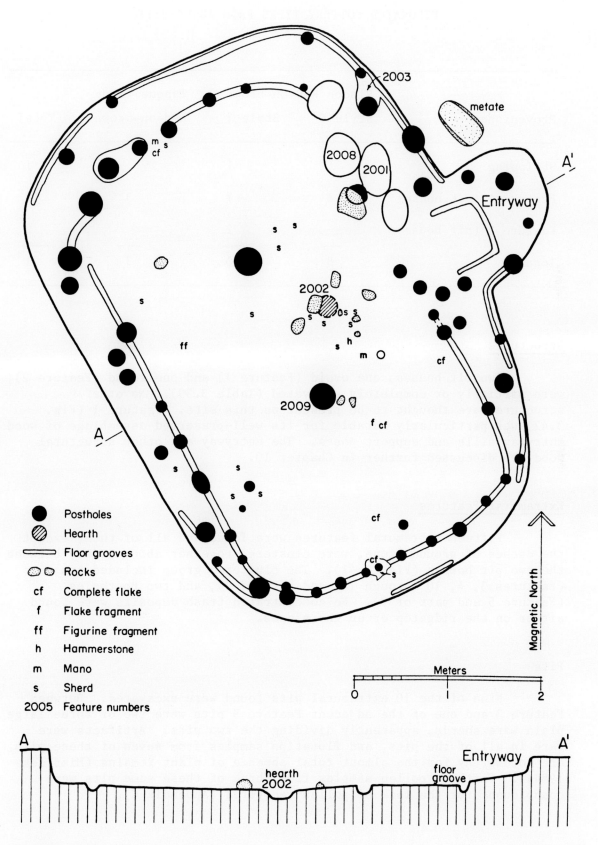

Figure 3.40 Plan view and cross section, Feature 2 pit house, AZ EE:2:116.

Table 3.56

DECORATED POTTERY TYPES FROM AZ EE:2:116

Provenience	Rincon Red—on—brown Style C	Style ?	Tanque Verde Red—on—brown	Total
Stripping		1		1
Feature 1 (pit house)	8	7	3	18
Feature 2 (pit house)		2		2
Total	8	10	3	21

Structures

Two pit houses, one ovoid (Feature 1) and one round (Feature 2), were partially or completely excavated (Table 3.59). No other structures are thought to be present on this site. Feature 1 (Fig. 3.42) was particularly notable for its well-preserved assemblage of wood entryway sills and support posts. The entryway and other structural wood are discussed further in Chapter 10.

Extramural Features

Fifteen extramural features were found and all of them, except the caches of ground stone, were clustered together about midway between the two pit houses (Fig. 3.41). The clustered group included ten pits (Features 3, 4, 10 through 14, and part of 9), and two postholes (Feature 5 and part of 9). No concentrated trash deposits were found either on the ridgetop or on the slopes.

Pits

Nine of the 10 extramural pits found were excavated. Between Feature 3 and one of the adjacent Feature 9 pits were two or three large plain ware sherds, apparently dividing the two pits. Artifacts were rare in all of the pits, and flotation samples from seven of these pits are noteworthy for the almost total absence of plant remains (Miksicek 1984a). Further, pollen samples from three of these same pits were conspicuous for the lack of pollen recovered (Appendix C).

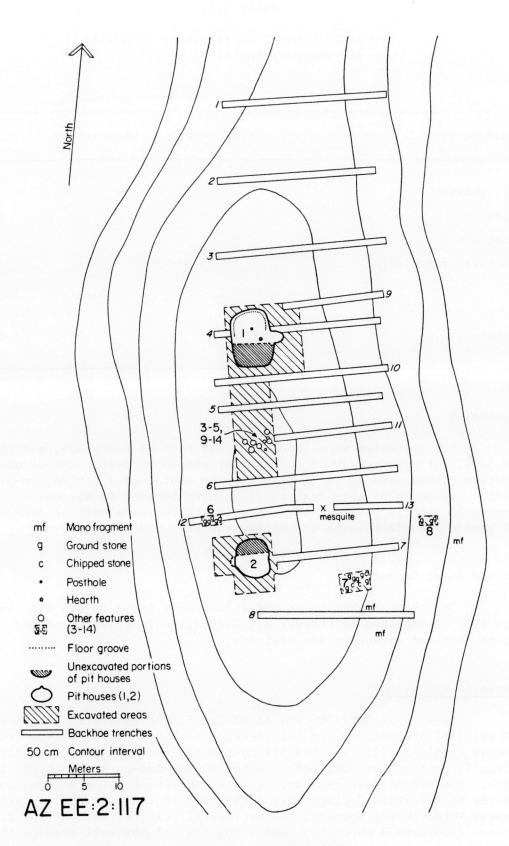

North

1

2

3

9

4   1

10

5

3-5,
9-14

11

6

6   x   13
12   mesquite
8

2   7

mf   Mano fragment
g   Ground stone
c   Chipped stone
•   Posthole
◦   Hearth
○   Other features
      (3-14)
.... Floor groove
      Unexcavated portions
      of pit houses
      Pit houses (1,2)
      Excavated areas
      Backhoe trenches
50 cm Contour interval

7
8   mf

Meters
0   5   10

AZ EE:2:117

Figure 3.41   Site map, AZ EE:2:117.

226 Alan Ferg

Table 3.57

TYPES AND NUMBERS OF FEATURES, EXCAVATED
AND UNEXCAVATED, AT AZ EE:2:117

Feature Type	Excavated	Unexcavated	Total
Pit houses	2		2
Pits	9	1	10
Postholes	1	1	2
Caches: ground stone	3		3
Total	15	2	17

Postholes

Two postholes were found; one was part of Feature 9, a cluster
of pits. It measured 20 cm in diameter and 55 cm deep. The second,
Feature 5, was also 20 cm in diameter and contained a rotted, in-place
post. The depth of this feature is unknown because it was not
excavated. It is possible that these postholes were part of some sort
of ramada associated with the extramural pits described above.

Ground Stone Caches

The three caches of ground stone tools found on the site surface
are fully enumerated in Chapter 6. Excavation immediately around these
items revealed no subsurface features.

Ceramics and Dating

As with AZ EE:2:106 and AZ EE:2:116, the decorated ceramics at
AZ EE:2:117 are notable for the presence of Tanque Verde Red-on-brown
sherds (Table 3.60). The two pit houses are presumed to be roughly or
actually contemparaneous, based on the Rincon Red-on-brown sherds in
both. The Rincon Red-on-brown, Style C and Tanque Verde Red-on-brown
sherds from Feature 2 place this occupation in the late Rincon/early
Tanque Verde phase; however, the extramural features between the pit
houses (Features 3 through 5, and 9 through 14) may well predate the pit

Table 3.58

ARTIFACT TOTALS BY CLASS FOR AZ EE:2:117

Artifact Type	Count	Category Total	Percent of Assemblage
Ceramics		160	62.3
Decorated sherds	105		
Plain ware sherds	53		
Chipped Stone		78	30.4
Debitage	68		
Retouched pieces	5		
Cores	2		
Hammerstones	3		
Utilitarian Ground Stone		18	7.0
Metates	1		
Mano-handstones	14		
Other	3		
Nonutilitarian Stone		1	0.3
Minerals	1		
Total		257	100.0

houses. No diagnostic sherds came from these features themselves, but all the Colonial period and Rincon Red-on-brown, Style A sherds (Table 3.67) came from stripping between these pits and Trench 6 (Fig. 3.41).

Similarly, it is conceivable that the three ground stone caches (Features 6 through 8) also predate the pit houses. As Tagg (Chapter 6) notes, these caches are not in close proximity to other features on the site, and the only other extramural caches of ground stone from the project area, at AZ EE:2:105 and AZ EE:2:113, date to the early Rincon phase or perhaps earlier. Feature 7 at AZ EE:2:117 and Feature 14 at AZ EE:2:105 are also similar in that both contain quartz monzonite mano "blanks" (for a fuller discussion of this artifact and material type, see "Manos" in Chapter 6).

Nonceramic Artifacts

The chipped stone assemblage contained no projectile points, and the substantial utilitarian ground stone assemblage came largely from

Table 3.59

STRUCTURE DATING AND CONTENT SUMMARY, AZ EE:2:117

Feature Number	Age Assignment	Basis for Dating						Burned	Trash Filled	Floor assemblage	Intrudes Features	Intruded by Features
		Site Ceramics	Floor Ceramics	Fill Ceramics	Superimposition	Other						
001000	late Rincon/ early Tanque Verde	x						+				
002000	late Rincon/ early Tanque Verde			x								

the three caches, which contained 13 of the 18 ground stone implements from the site. Finally, the nonutilitarian ground stone assemblage from this site consists of a large fragment of what was probably a plain slate palette.

Subsistence

No animal bone was recovered from AZ EE:2:117. Flotation samples (Appendix B) from pit houses and extramural features produced corn cupules and chenopod seeds in very small numbers. The abundant grass stems in most of the Feature 1 samples are doubtless part of the walls or roofing material of this burned structure. Pollen samples (Appendix C) were largely uninformative.

Summary

This small site appears to have at least two temporally discrete components. The earlier component consisted of at least one extramural work area with pits and perhaps a ramada, and ground stone caches that

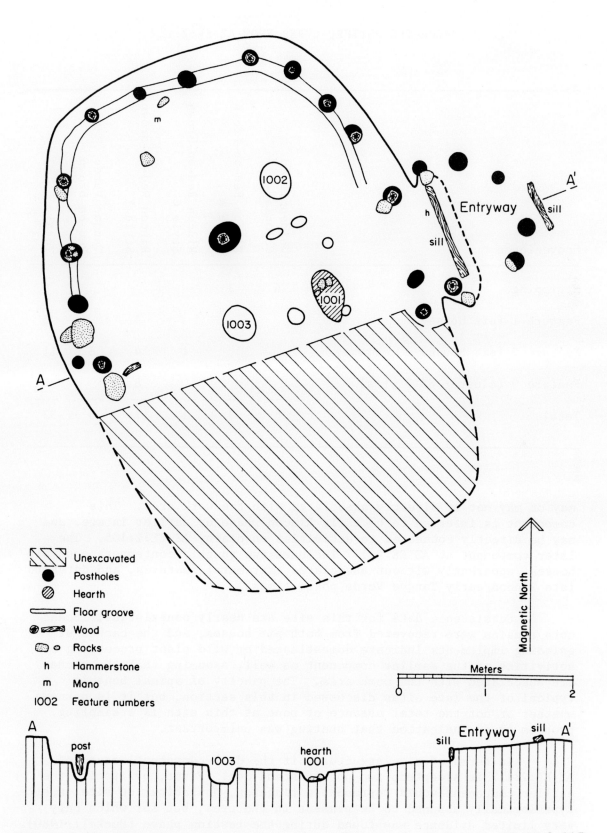

Figure 3.42   Plan view and cross section, Feature 1 pit house, AZ EE:2:117.

Legend:

- Unexcavated
- Postholes
- Hearth
- Floor groove
- Wood
- Rocks
- h   Hammerstone
- m   Mano
- 1002   Feature numbers

Magnetic North

Meters
0   1   2

Table 3.60

DECORATED POTTERY TYPES FROM AZ EE:2:117

Provenience	Unidentified Colonial	Rincon Red-on-brown Style A	Rincon Red-on-brown Style C	Rincon Red-on-brown Style ?	Tanque Verde Red-on-brown	Total
Stripping	6	3				9
Feature 1 (pit house)				5		5
Feature 2 (pit house)			1	4	6	11
Feature 9 (cluster of 3 pits)				8		8
Total	6	3	1	17	6	33

may or may not be directly associated with the work area. This component is inferred to be early Rincon phase or earlier in age, and may be directly connected to activities on nearby AZ EE:2:105. The later component at AZ EE:2:117 includes two roughly contemporaneous pit houses, apparently without associated extramural features, and dates to late Rincon/early Tanque Verde phase times.

Subsistence data for this site are nearly nonexistant. Scant corn remains were recovered from both pit houses, and the caches of grinding implements indicate domesticated or wild plant processing activities at the earlier component as well, assuming that the caches are associated with the work area. The paucity of animal bone is typical of the late sites discussed in this section, but it is unknown whether or not the total absence of bone at this site is a sampling problem or an indication that hunting was unimportant.

In terms of site structure, if the dual-component nature of AZ EE:2:117 is accepted, two points stand out. First, by itself, the earlier component would represent a ridgetop, nonhabitation site, a site type logically assumed to be present in the area, but for which only very limited evidence was found during the testing phase (Huckell 1980).

Second, the later, pit house component of AZ EE:2:117, which lacks extramural features, has a striking resemblance to AZ EE:2:116. Each has two pit houses positioned side-by-side, with entryways definitely or probably facing eastward. Each lacks or has very few extramural features and each lacks concentrated trash discard areas. On both sites one pit house is "standard" with a full complement of floor features such as a hearth, two main uprights, floor groove and wall postholes, while the second pit house lacks all of these, except for the hearth in Feature 1 at AZ EE:2:116. The significance of these similarities is taken up in Chapter 10.

AZ EE:2:122

This site was recorded as a moderate artifact density, small area site on a flat-topped ridge segment overlooking middle Barrel Canyon (Fig. 3.1). The habitation area of the site is difficult to assess given the tightly clustered nature of the subsurface features and the thin surface scatter of artifacts. The two pit houses that were found are only 2 m apart (Fig. 3.43), and only 6 features were found (Table 3.61). All artifacts recovered are tabulated in Table 3.62.

Structures

Two pit houses (Features 1 and 2) were partially or completely excavated (Table 3.63). No other structures are thought to be present on this site.

Feature 1

Feature 1 was partially excavated but produced no datable materials. It has two extramural rock clusters (Subfeatures 1002 and 1003) positioned atop its fill, but these features, too, were undatable. Feature 1 is tentatively assigned to the late Rincon or early Tanque Verde phase, assuming that it is roughly contemporaneous with Feature 2.

Feature 2

The assignment of Feature 2 to the late Rincon or early Tanque Verde phase is based on a radiocarbon date on charcoal associated with a primary cremation (Subfeature 2001) found on its floor. This date was 720 $\pm$ 50 B.P. (A-3300), A.D. 1230 $\pm$ 50. Much, but not all, of the pit house floor was burned, although it is uncertain whether the house was burned down over the body, or whether a cremation pyre was simply built in a recently abandoned house.

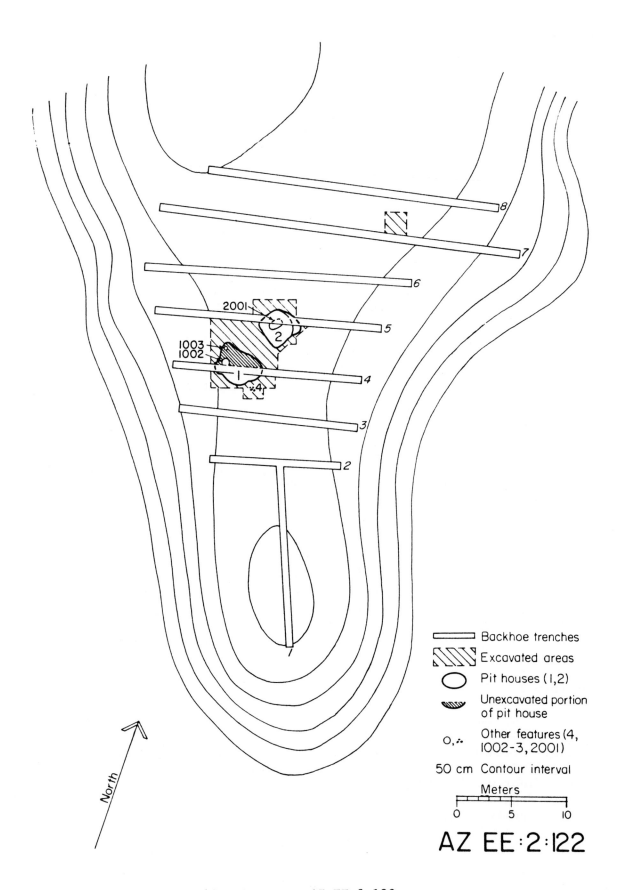

Figure 3.43 Site map, AZ EE:2:122.

Table 3.61

TYPES AND NUMBERS OF FEATURES, EXCAVATED
AND UNEXCAVATED, AT AZ EE:2:122

Feature Type	Excavated	Unexcavated	Total
Pit houses	2	-	2
Rock clusters	3	-	3
Primary cremations	1	-	1
Total	6	0	6

Table 3.62

ARTIFACT TOTALS BY CLASS FOR AZ EE:2:122

Artifact Type	Count	Category Total	Percent of Assemblage
Ceramics		58	49.6
Decorated sherds	1		
Plain ware sherds	57		
Chipped Stone		53	45.3
Debitage	47		
Retouched pieces	3		
Cores	3		
Utilitarian Ground Stone		6	5.1
Mano-handstones	5		
Other	1		
Total		117	100.0

Table 3.63

STRUCTURE DATING AND CONTENT SUMMARY, AZ EE:2:122

| Feature Number | Age Assignment | Basis for Dating | | | | | | | | | |
		Site Ceramics	Floor Ceramics	Fill Ceramics	Superposition	Other	Burned	Trash Filled	Floor Assemblage	Intrudes Features	Intruded by Features
001000	late Rincon/ early Tanque Verde					x					+
002000	late Rincon/ early Tanque Verde				x	x	?				+

Extramural Features

Rock Clusters

All three extramural features found were rock clusters. Subfeatures 1002 and 1003 both contained fire-cracked rock and were sitting atop the fill of the Feature 1 pit house. There was no evidence of in-place burning, suggesting both features may be debris from a nearby roasting pit-hearth that was not located.

Feature 4 was a pile of unfractured rock located just southeast of the Feature 1 pit house. This feature might be rock intentionally piled near or dug out of the pit house, or may be of natural origin.

Burials

Primary Cremation

Subfeature 2001 is the only primary cremation recovered from any of the sites in the exchange area. Trench 5 removed the body from the

hips up; the body was supine with rocks at either knee, and at the left
side of the hips. Three burned rocks from the trench backdirt are
presumed to have come from the right side of the hips and either side of
the torso or shoulders. Those rocks may have supported some sort of low
bier on which the body was laid.

Ceramics and Dating

Only a single decorated sherd was recovered from this site; it
is an unidentifiable red-on-brown vessel body sherd recovered from
stripping. The late Rincon or early Tanque Verde phase dating of the
site, as noted above, is based on a radiocarbon date of A.D. 1230 $\pm$ 50
on the Subfeature 2001 primary cremation.

Subsistence

No animal bone was recovered from AZ EE:2:122. The three
flotation samples and two pollen samples (Appendixes B and C) produced
virtually no plant remains or interpretable pollen.

Summary

This small site dates late in the Rincon phase or early in the
Tanque Verde phase, and appears to have been occupied either very
briefly, or perhaps sporadically, judging by the small artifact
assemblage. Subsistence data are negligible. The occupation sequence
for the identified features appears to include the early abandonment of
the Feature 1 pit house and its superimpostion by Subfeatures 1002 and
1003, which were possibly used by occupants of the Feature 2 pit house.
The burning of the Subfeature 2001 cremation may have been the final
event on the site, either coinciding with or following close on the
abandonment of the Feature 2 pit house.

Chapter 4

POTTERY

William L. Deaver

The importance of pottery in the interpretation and reconstruction of Tucson Basin prehistory cannot be overemphasized. Dating of the archaeological record often hinges upon the ability to identify and recognize a succession of changes in pottery decoration and shape, and chronology is the core of all interpretations. Also, the recognition of nonindigenous pottery enables documentation of trade with neighboring regions. The Tucson Basin ceramic sequence was originally defined with the intent to use pottery as a tool for chronology building and as a way to perceive intercultural relationships, particularly with the Phoenix Basin Hohokam to the north and the Mogollon to the east. These issues were the primary research interests in the 1930s. While these two issues are still unquestionably important in understanding Tucson Basin prehistory, the continued focus of pottery studies solely upon these issues has limited the information obtained. Since the development of the original pottery sequence, research interests have expanded and are no longer concerned simply with dating the archaeological record or documenting regional patterns of exchange, but also with defining settlement and subsistence patterns, community and village organization, and intraregional patterns of exchange and redistribution. Pottery has the potential to provide important information toward these and other research objectives but it cannot be realized within the traditional analytical framework. These newer research areas require different kinds of data, and different analytical frameworks to gather these data, but the development of new analytical approaches has lagged behind.

Traditionally, studies of Tucson Basin pottery have applied a typological classification using the Tucson Basin pottery type sequence defined by Kelly (1978), Greenleaf (1975), and Doyel (1977a). These studies usually consist of no more than classifying and tabulating potsherds into the type categories. This approach can be an efficient way to collect chronological information, but its utility is limited by biases built into the type categories when the Tucson Basin ceramic sequence was originally defined.

At the time the Tucson Basin ceramic sequence was defined, typological classification in Hohokam ceramics served as a tool for chronology building and for perceiving intercultural patterns of

exchange; chronology building was most important (Haury 1976: 254;
Masse 1982: 75). The pottery types were defined in such a way as to be
temporal and cultural indicators. Consequently there is a one-to-one
correspondence between the pottery types and the cultural phases, a
feature unique in the Southwest to Hohokam pottery (Masse 1982: 75).
The Tucson Basin ceramic sequence was built upon stylistic parallels
with the Gila Basin Hohokam pottery types (Kelly 1978: 3). Because of
this bias in the definition of the ceramic types, classifications
employing these typological constructs can effectively collect data
useful for dating the archaeological record and identifying cultural
authorship. The same type categories are not, however, appropriate for
obtaining other kinds of information such as that needed to interpret
vessel use, nor does this approach provide a means to improve our
knowledge and understanding of pottery technology and variability.
Built into a simple typological classification is the assumption that
the type categories are well defined. Clearly this is not the case.
The range of stylistic, technological, and formal variability and the
causes of this variability are not well understood. Recent revivals of
the Cortaro issue (Reinhard 1982; Wallace 1983) demonstrate that the
decorative tradition is not completely understood. Neither are the
technological and formal aspects of the pottery completely defined. The
typical characteristics and the range of variability for the Tucson
Basin types are still largely unknown.

A final consequence of the classificatory approach is that the
focus upon pottery as a dating tool has biased studies toward decorated
pottery at the expense of detailed investigation of plain and red-
slipped pottery, due to the perceived relationship between changes in
decoration and time. Kelly (1978: 69) notes that differences in the
plain pottery from phase to phase were not sufficiently marked to
justify type groupings. This clearly demonstrates the focus upon
pottery types as phase indicators. Because plain pottery could not be
equated with the phases on a one-to-one basis, no types were defined,
yet in her description of plain pottery Kelly (1978: 69-76) indicates
that there are observable differences within the plain ware as well as
significant changes through time. Nevertheless, the prevailing opinion
is that plain pottery cannot be classified (Greenleaf 1975: 56; Doyel
1977a: 26). Attempts have been made to sort plain pottery into
taxonomic classes, but because of the focus upon the phase-type
parallels of the decorated pottery, attempts to use the same approach
have met with discouraging results. Consequently plain pottery has been
less intensively studied, and there is still no accepted typology for
plain pottery.

Not all pottery studies have relied solely upon a classificatory
analysis using the Tucson Basin ceramic types. Most notable is the work
of Di Peso (1956) and Grebinger (1971a; Grebinger and Adam 1974, 1978).
In his treatment of the pottery from San Cayetano del Tumacacori,
Di Peso conducted what should be called a functional classification of
the whole vessels recovered in addition to a traditional type
classification. He placed vessels into categories based upon their
inferred use, such as water storage jars or cooking vessels. This
treatment departed from the traditional view of pottery because many of

the use-categories crosscut the traditional pottery types. This study approached the ceramic vessels within the context of how they may have functioned in the day-to-day lives of the people that made and used the pottery rather than simply as phase indicators.

Grebinger's (1971a; Grebinger and Adam 1974, 1978) studies, although working within the framework of Tucson Basin pottery types, also departed from the traditional approach. This study was based upon a stylistic approach attempting to identify local pottery styles that could be used to trace the interaction between people from different areas within the Tucson Basin. Both Di Peso's and Grebinger's studies are important models, because they attempted to determine how pottery was used, manufactured, and distributed, rather than simply using pottery as a chronological indicator. More importantly, because the information needed to address these research issues could not have been obtained using the traditional pottery type series, these researchers adopted different theoretical and methodological approaches to collect the necessary information.

The basic underlying premise that determined the form and detail of this pottery study is that pottery must be viewed within different analytical contexts depending upon the research objectives. Pottery possesses attributes that can provide insights into many research areas, not only dating archaeological remains, but also defining the structure of the ceramic tradition--how and why different types of vessels were made--and identifying regional variations within a larger, broader cultural pattern. There is a wealth of potential information in ceramics that can provide insights into the past, but one standard analytical approach can tap only a small portion of this information (Abbott 1984). The present study employs a traditional classification using the pottery type sequence (as it is now known) to collect chronological and regional information, plus a broader analytical approach which will examine the pottery from a variety of theoretical and practical perspectives as required by the research objectives outlined below.

Research Objectives

Three principle goals structured the theoretical approach to pottery. They are: (1) to provide data pertinent to the project research goals, (2) to document and interpret the variability seen in the pottery, and (3) to develop a broader, more rigorous analytical approach toward pottery studies. The project research objectives are: (1) to identify functional site types, (2) to reconstruct economic and subsistence strategies, (3) to determine the distribution of sites and population and define intersite organization, and (4) to identify areal and regional relationships (Chapter 2). Pottery analysis may yield three major classes of information that pertain to project research objectives. By far the most direct contribution lies in providing chronological control for the archaeological remains. By virtue of its frequency, painted pottery provides the most practical dating tool, augmenting and in many cases, replacing other means of dating, such as radiocarbon and archaeomagnetic techniques. Because of the scarcity of materials datable by these means, dating, at the site and intrasite levels, is based largely upon decorated pottery. Radiocarbon and archaeomagnetic dating techniques have been used as a check for the pottery sequence.

Another important contribution pottery can make toward the project research objectives lies in identifying classes of pottery relevant toward assessing site function. Recognizing functional classes within the pottery could aid making functional distinctions between sites. To do this an assumption must be made that sites that served similar functions in the settlement and subsistence system would be characterized by similar sets of activities and consequently would have similar artifact inventories. Conversely, sites performing different functions in the settlement-subsistence system should produce different (McAllister and Plog 1978: 19; Pilles 1978: 124) artifact assemblages. While it is possible that functionally different sites within a community could contain similar artifact assemblages, it is unlikely that sites serving the same purpose would contain dissimilar artifactual records. Thus the discovery of functionally meaningful classes within the pottery will be attempted.

Function can be assessed at two levels. At the site level, noted above, the role of the site in the settlement-subsistence system should affect the presence and frequency of artifact types. At the artifact level function should affect the formal and technological aspects of the pottery vessels (DeGarmo 1975; S. Plog 1980; Crown 1981; Abbott 1984; Crown 1984a). Function includes both day-to-day and ritual and economic uses (Crown 1984a). This study is concerned with identifying the effects of the intended use of the vessel on its technological and formal characteristics.

While previous pottery studies have focussed on dating (Crown 1984a; Masse 1982), functional studies are not yet standard components of pottery analyses in the Tucson Basin. With the exception of Di Peso's (1956) work, other references to pottery's uses are limited to casual statements that some vessels were used for cooking and others for storage without attempting to associate particular vessels with functions. Not surprisingly, these studies provide little insight into those characteristics of pottery which are most useful in addressing such questions. The information needed to interpret vessel use is different from that required to assess its age, and cannot be collected in the same manner. Use-related classes of pottery may crosscut traditional wares and types (Di Peso 1956: 272-291), and must be collected in a different analytical fashion. The evidence needed to interpret use can be found in aspects of shape, technology, and even use-caused wear. Due to time constraints this study has focused upon the formal and technological aspects that should be indicative of vessel use; it was not possible to conduct a use-wear study.

Finally, pottery analysis can contribute to project research objectives by identifying patterns of regional exchange. This can be accomplished by identifying nonindigenous pottery imported into the project area from other regions in southern Arizona. Such examples are the most obvious evidence of contacts and relationships between different cultural groups. In addition, it may be possible to identify evidence of intraregional exchange of pottery.

The second and third goals of this pottery study are closely related. Little is known about the specific technological and formal aspects of the pottery because of the past emphasis upon decoration as a temporal indicator. Kelly's (1978) description of Tucson Basin pottery still serves as the standard for all pottery classifications; however, this work lacks some basic information about the pottery. For example, ceramic technology is poorly discussed in that work, with no clear references to tempering agents or construction techniques. Even in reports where this information is presented (Greenleaf 1975; Doyel 1977a) it is inconsistent and unquantified. A major concern of this study has been to quantifiably and objectively document the ceramic technology of the ANAMAX-Rosemont assemblage, using rigorous, and replicable analytical techniques. Balanced against this was a desire to maintain the flexibility necessary to interpret chronology, use, and region of manufacture. While acknowledging the utility of the Tucson Basin pottery type sequence, this study also focused upon documenting the range of variability within type categories, modifying them when necessary, or in some cases identifying new types.

In addition to these major research objectives, two special issues were targeted for study. The first was the need to clarify the differences between Rillito Red-on-brown and Rincon Red-on-brown. These types, traditionally, are notoriously difficult to separate (Doyel 1977a: 30). The second issue was to determine if the plain ware could be sorted into definitive, mutually exclusive type categories. Typological classification of Tucson Basin plain ware has been considered practically impossible (Greenleaf 1975: 55; Doyel 1977a: 26).

Methods

The methods used in the study have been shaped by the analytical approach and research questions set forth in the previous section, as well as the physical characteristics of the pottery collection. Predictably, five different types of ceramic artifacts might be found, including: (1) wholly, or partially restorable vessels, (2) rim sherds, (3) body sherds, (4) reworked vessels or worked sherds, and (5) figurines and other nonvessel clay artifacts. Additionally, it was also possible to predict that three general classes of pottery would be recovered: (1) painted (both local and nonlocal), (2) plain (undecorated), and (3) red-slipped. Once the analysis began, a fourth and smaller lot of pottery decorated with punched, incised, or appliqued decoration was recognized and is referred to as textured pottery. This class does not, however, include the painted pottery of the Pioneer and early Colonial periods whose exteriors are sometimes decorated with incised lines. Hence four major classes of pottery--painted, plain, red-slipped, and textured--have been identified in the ANAMAX Project area.

The pottery analysis was carried out in six successive stages, each with one or more phases dictated largely by the nature of the sample. Because the recorded variables are different for painted, plain, red-slipped, and textured pottery, the collection was initially subdivided along those lines. For example, providing chronological control for the sites within the study area required the typological classification of painted pottery, whereas plain, red-slipped, and textured pottery had little value for dating. However, painted, plain, red-slipped, and textured pottery were equally valuable in studying vessel function. After the initial sorting of the ceramics into the above defined ware classes, ware-specific analyses were conducted. This was followed by the study of worked sherds, a category which crosscuts ware classes. Figurines and nonvessel ceramic artifacts were extremely rare; these artifacts were simply described. The ware-specific analyses were subdivided according to the following artifact classes: restorable or semirestorable vessels, rim sherds, and body sherds.

Three aspects of the pottery--decoration, technology, and shape--are essential to fulfill the research objectives, and each constitutes a major part of this study. In addition to these three aspects, the manner of rim finish is also a prime concern. Although this attribute is poorly understood, there may be changes through time in the manner of rim finish which could have some temporally diagnostic value. The particular attributes of each aspect studied and the methods used are described below.

Decorative Study: A Stylistic Model

In Southwestern pottery studies, ceramic type categories have traditionally been defined with respect to aspects of technology, shape, and painted decoration. The Tucson Basin ceramic sequence is somewhat unique in the sense that the ceramic types are defined with respect to aspects of vessel shape and painted decoration exclusively; to date, no reported study presents a comprehensive discussion of the typical technological attributes of pottery types in the sequence. Diagnostic aspects of vessel shape are not always observable on sherds, and in such cases classification is based entirely upon the painted decoration. Another characteristic of the Tucson ceramic sequence is its one-to-one equivalency between types and cultural phases, a feature it shares only with the Phoenix ceramic sequence (Masse 1982: 75). As noted earlier the principle function of the pottery types has been as phase (time) markers. Because painted decoration seems to be the most commonly observable attribute on which type determinations can be made, and the types are primarily chronological markers, an enormous amount of information is dependent upon interpretation of changes in the decorative tradition.

In this study the identification of types relies solely on painted decoration. In this way it has been possible to independently compare changes in technological and formal aspects of the pottery to changes in time as inferred from the style of painted decoration. Using decoration as a temporal indicator requires identification of a progression of decorative changes. This study follows a stylistic approach, defining a model of decorative changes which focuses on identifying a sequence of decorative styles rather than a sequence of pottery types.

The principle difference between a stylistic and a typological approach is that in the latter changes in pottery are represented by pottery types, while in the former changes in the pottery tradition are traced by a succession of changes in the decorative tradition. The connective units of a decorative tradition are not pottery types but design styles. Such a stylistic approach is not new, and the two approaches are not mutually exclusive; in fact painted ceramic types are defined in part upon styles of decoration. The Tucson Basin ceramic sequence is based upon stylistic concepts. It seems that every archaeologist familiar with Tucson pottery has an implicit stylistic model, as witnessed by "early," "middle," and "late" qualifiers appended to type names (for example Greenleaf 1975). Such assessments of "earlyness" and "lateness" necessitate some conceptual model of a continuous stream of decorative development, whether implicit or explicit. In all likelihood, no two people view this progression in exactly the same way. All models are based upon the work of Kelly (1978), however, each researcher's interpretation varies. What is referred to here as late Rincon Red-on-brown may not be completely synonymous with Greenleaf's (1975) usage, nor is the model presented below the definitive model of stylistic development. Rather, it is an interpretation of the stylistic changes used to guide the identification of types.

The concept of style can be abstracted at any number of levels and is by no means an absolute. It might be possible to discuss a Hohokam style, a Tucson Basin style, or even particular village, guild, or individual potter's styles. This model focuses upon defining temporal pottery styles for the Tucson Basin. The mainstay of this model is the concept of "decorative style," which is a particular decorative configuration in design structure, decorative units, and execution, that can be recognized independently of archaeological context or association. This is much the same as Wasley's (1959: 227) definition:

> A style of design is a particular manner of ceramic decoration with characteristics which distinguish it from all other manners of ceramic decoration, even though content may be very similar.

This definition is particularly useful because it stresses that a style is defined on more than decorative components. Experience with Tucson

Basin pottery has taught that few decorative units are restricted to any one type. Wasley's definition indicates that the spatial relationship between two decorative units may be as important as the decorative units themselves, if not more so, for identifying the style. Thus, the definition of decorative styles must take into account the location and arrangement of decorative units. In this model, design styles are not defined on the use of particular decorative units but are based on the way these units are combined and arranged to form a whole design.

In dealing with prehistoric pottery it is not possible to ask the potter for the rules of decoration as has been done for some modern Pueblo pottery types (Guthe 1925; Bunzel 1929). Instead the underlying common features of the decoration that make up the style must be recognized on finished products. Recognizing the common decorative theme is the first step toward defining a style. The next step is to identify the shared characteristics, whether in the organization of the decorative units, the handling and execution of line work, the particular combinations of design features, or a focus upon a particular theme. These shared characteristics, whatever they may be, are the embodiment of style.

To fully comprehend the particulars of the styles, they must be defined from complete designs where the inherent contextual relationships between decorative units can be observed, in such a manner that they can be recognized on sherds (Wasley 1959: 226). Most pottery analyses have focused, not on whole designs but on design elements and motifs as seen on sherds. This perspective tends to treat whole designs, and consequently styles, as agglomerations of the pieces. I do not believe this approach can truly define a style. It is not always possible to determine from fragments how the various decorative units function together. In addition, when working with sherds, the sharing of certain decorative elements and motifs among several styles or types is another problem. However, if the spatial relationships between these and other elements within the context of the design differs from type to type, or from style to style, this provides an additional analytical tool.

This stylistic approach has important implications for any interpretation of Tucson Basin pottery development. By focusing on the concept of decorative style it is theoretically possible to provide better chronological resolution by recognizing early, middle, and late developments. Specifically, this study identifies 3 styles within Rincon Red-on-brown. The stylistic model also shows that the decorative tradition may have an internally consistent development, less affected by outside influences than previously assumed. For example, Classic period Tucson Basin pottery seems to develop smoothly from Sedentary period pottery, and does not represent an intrusive Mogollon style as suggested by Kelly (1978: 59). The major changes seen in Tanque Verde Red-on-brown are in fact established in the Sedentary period.

Another important asset of the stylistic approach is that it provides a mechanism whereby issues of similarities or differences in the pottery can be addressed (Wasley 1959), as exemplified by Grebinger's study of Classic period decoration (Grebinger 1971a;

Grebinger and Adam 1974, 1978). In these studies, Grebinger attempted
to define pottery styles unique to villages or localized centers of
production and then trace the movement of these styles across space and
through time. These were the first attempts to identify socially
meaningful groupings of pottery and infer from their observed spatial
and temporal distributions the movement of people. If it is possible to
identify regional, local, or village styles it may then be possible to
look at the exchange of pottery at regional, local, or even village
levels. Such an approach, once developed, when combined with
technological studies like those of Abbott (1984) and Crown (1984a)
could revolutionize the interpretive potential of archaeological
ceramics.

Finally a stylistic study can identify designs that are not
typical of a particular place or time. Traditionally, contact between
prehistoric peoples has been documented by finding pieces of intrusive
pottery traded from other regions; however, there may be evidence of
contact and exchange that can be seen, not in actual intrusive ceramics,
but in locally made ceramics that imitate or incorporate designs more
typical of another region. Some designs on Tucson Basin pottery, while
clearly of Hohokam authorship, seem more typically Puebloan or Mogollon
in the elements used and the organization of the design. With this type
of analysis it may be possible to demonstrate contact and exchange even
when actual pieces of pottery did not change hands, but notions of
pottery decoration were borrowed.

Design Structures

Previous classifications of Tucson Basin pottery designs have
used Amsden's (1936) study of Hohokam decoration as a guide. In his
scheme of pottery decoration a decorative layout is the painting of
lines by the prehistoric potter to subdivide the decorative field into
smaller more manageable units:

The lines which close scrutiny reveals as laid down first
(because they are overlapped by others) usually are lines of
division, not of decoration (Amsden 1936: 7).

The phrase "design structure" will be used in this study to refer to the
spatial arrangement inherent in the painted design. Every design, no
matter how simple or elaborate, has a structure; it may be a haphazard
arrangement of design units or highly structured about geometric,
anthropomorphic, or zoomorphic shapes. In some respects this is
synonymous with Amsden's decorative layout; however, the structure of a
design need not be physically painted on the pot, and it may be an
organizational scheme rather than a divisional one.

This distinction between design layout and design structure
makes classifying Hohokam pottery designs easier, particulary for
Colonial period pottery. Most Colonial pottery, and some Sedentary and
Classic period pottery as well, is decorated with horizontal, vertical,

or diagonal rows of decorative units in a banded fashion but because it lacks upper and lower boundary lines this material cannot be classified as banded in Amsden's scheme (Amsden 1936: 9).

Kelley's use of Amsden's notion of a band has restricted the classification of banded designs largely to jar decorations and exterior-decorated bowls where the design field is delimited by upper and lower framing lines. Decorations on bowl interiors have not been as readily classified as banded though the inherent structure of the design within the field may be identical to that of jar and exterior bowl designs (Kelly 1978). In this study, designs are classified as banded when the decorative units are structurally arranged in linear rows within the decorative field, whether or not these bands (or rows) of decorative units are delimited by upper or lower boundaries.

Figure 4.1 illustrates the design structures observed on Tucson Basin pottery and their proposed temporal positions. Only the Colonial and Sedentary periods are included in this figure. At present, too little is known about Pioneer pottery to define the decorative structures. Classic period material is a logical continuation of Sedentary period design structures, but because it is absent in the ANAMAX-Rosemont Project area, it has not been included.

The decorative structures fall into three general headings: (1) banded, (2) sectored, and (3) allover. Banded designs are those in which the inherent structure between the decorative units is linear, whether horizontal, vertical, or oblique with respect to the vertical axis of the pot. Sectored designs are those in which the field of decoration is subdivided into geometric units. The final category, allover, applies to vessels on which a single decorative unit appears. Preferences for horizontally banded and sectored designs changed significantly through time, therefore the discussion of styles focuses upon the relationships of these types of decorative structures to one another. Allover designs are largely problematical and rarely carry diagnostic information: consequently there will be little discussion of this type of decorative structure. The various types of banded and sectored designs are described below, relying heavily on illustrations to depict design and stylistic concepts.

Banded Designs

As discussed above, banded decorations are those in which the decorative units are arranged in linear rows with or without upper and lower framing lines. The figured and circling design layouts of Amsden (1936) and Kelly (1978) are included in this category. Banded designs of one form or another occur throughout the ceramic sequence, but reach their greatest diversity and complexity in the Colonial period. Five different types of bands are defined, based on the relationships between the direction of the banding and the axes of the vessel: horizontal, oblique, combined horizontal-oblique, spiral, and cross banded.

Horizontal Band

Horizontally banded designs are those in which the decorative units are arranged in parallel rows perpendicular to and encircling the vertical axis of the vessel and parallel to the rim. These bands need not be strictly linear arrangements, and in the Colonial period there is a preference for banded arrangements using zigzagging lines that form bands of hachure. Horizontally banded designs are visually static, lacking the appearance of motion inherent in oblique or combined horizontal-oblique bands. This type of banding is present through all phases of the prehistoric sequence.

Oblique Band

In this decorative structure the rows of decorative units are arranged diagonally to the vertical axis of the pot. Oblique designs are visually dynamic with a strong sense of motion, giving the appearance of spiraling upward on jars and bowl exteriors and swirling on bowl interiors. The representation shown in Figure 4.1 depicts bands running from lower left to upper right on jars and radiating outward in a clockwise direction on bowls. Not all designs follow these patterns; numerous examples exist that flow in the opposite directions. Obliquely banded designs appear to be restricted to the Colonial and early Sedentary periods.

Combined Horizontal-Oblique Band

As the name implies, these designs combine features of the two previous design structures. While the physical structure of the design is usually horizontal (determined from running scroll designs where each scroll connects to another at the same vertical level) the placement of the main decorative units is controlled with respect to the other bands so that the eye follows the pattern upward and to the right or left, depending upon the direction of the oblique structure. In the illustration of this design structure in Figure 4.1, the principal decorative units would occur at the intersections of the horizontal and oblique lines. This representation has been simplified to more clearly illustrate the structure; in actual designs the pattern is more complex. Although this type of design structure occurs in both the Colonial and early Sedentary periods, it is most common in the Colonial period and appears to be the dominant decorative treatment at that time.

Spiral Band

Only a single example of a spiral band is known from the Tucson Basin (Greenleaf 1975, Fig. 3.2). This decoration might be considered an allover pattern, since the spiral is a representation of a snake; however, the snake forms the ground line for a row of birds pecking at the snake. Significantly, this unique example is typologically

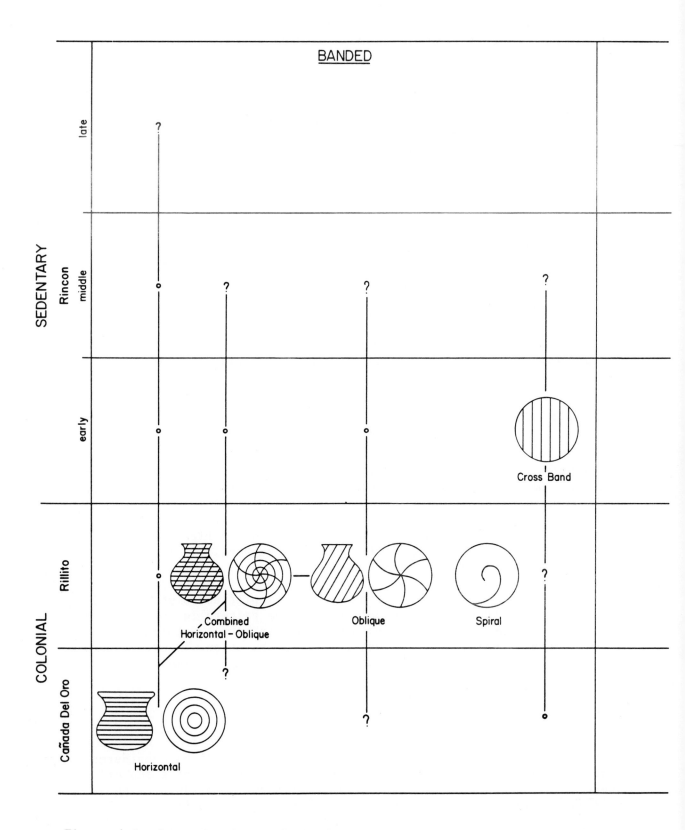

Figure 4.1   Synoptic chart of the decorative structures on Tucson Basin
pottery of the Colonial and Sedentary period.

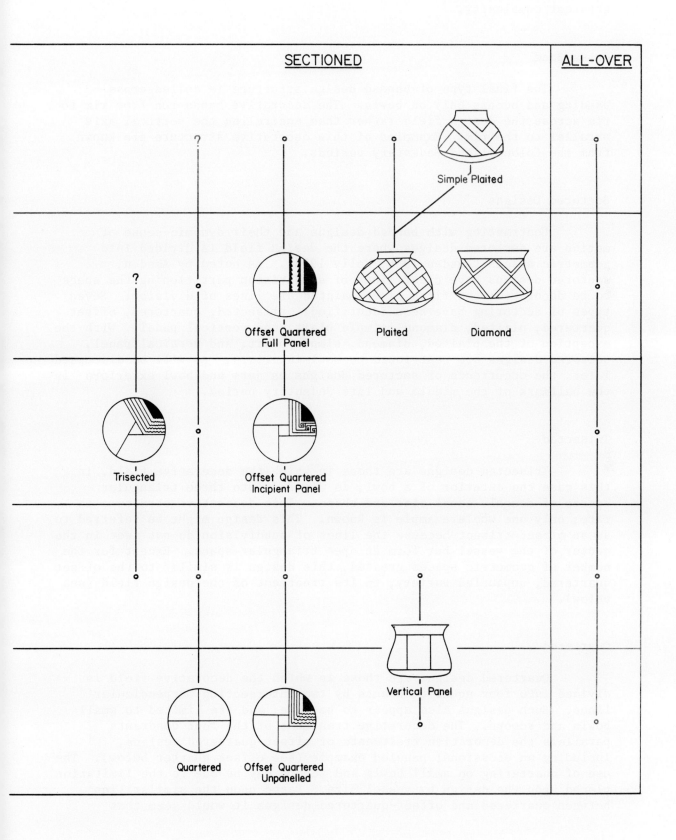

attributable to the Colonial period where banded designs reach their greatest complexity.

Cross Band

The final type of banded design structure is called cross banding and occurs only on bowls. The decorative bands run from rim to rim across the design field rather than encircling the vertical axis parallel to the rim. Examples of this decorative structure are known from the Colonial and Sedentary periods.

Sectored Designs

Contrasting with banded designs and their dynamic sense of motion are sectored designs where the design field is divided into geometric spaces (Amsden 1936; Kelly 1978). As noted by Amsden, sectored designs have clear lines of subdivision partitioning the space to be decorated; the first lines painted are lines of division. Seven types of sectoring have been identified: trisected, quartered, offset quartered, plaited, diamond, simple plait, and vertical panel. With the exception of the plaited, diamond, simple plait, and vertical panel, sectored designs are restricted to bowl interiors. As will be discussed later, the occurrence of sectored designs on jars and bowl exteriors is the hallmark of the middle and late Sedentary period.

Trisected

Trisected designs are those in which the decorative field, in this case the interior of a bowl, is divided into three triangular spaces of roughly equal size and shape. This decorative structure is rare; only one whole example is known. This design might be referred to as an offset trisect because the lines of subdivision do not meet in the center of the vessel but form an open triangular space. Except for the number of geometric spaces created, this design is similar to the offset quartered, unpaneled variety, in its treatment of the design field (see below).

Quartered

Quartered designs are those in which the decorative field is divided into four equal quadrants by two intersecting perpendicular lines. Such designs also appear to be rare, and are limited to small bowls and scoops. The decorative treatment of the four quadrants parallels the decorative treatments of offset-quartered designs, including an occasional paneled example (see offset quarter below). The use of quartering on small bowls and scoops may be due to the limitation placed upon the design by vessel size. Based upon the similarities between quartered and offset-quartered designs it would seem that quartered designs were used when the size of the vessel and decorative field made execution of an offset quarter impractical.

Offset-Quartered

The most common type of sectoring is the offset quarter. The four lines of subdivision are offset from the center of the vessel, creating four triangularly shaped spaces surrounding a square space at the bottom center of the design field. There are three varieties of the offset quarter: unpaneled, incipient paneled, and paneled. These are distinguished by the development of a rectangular panel within the triangular space.

In unpaneled, offset quartered designs the four triangular spaces are usually decorated with a triangular motif which depends from the rim, framed with combined straight and squiggly line chevron hatch. This treatment is the same used for the trisected and quartered design structures, with accommodations for the shape of the partitioned spaces. In the early Sedentary or possibly the late Colonial periods, the potters began to alter the character of the chevron hatch and create rectangular rows of design. These rows of decorative units appear to further divide the triangular space into two spaces—a rectangular space and a triangular space—but a true rectangular area is not delimited. The decorative treatment of creating a rectangular panel within the triangular space seems to stem from this "incipient" panel. By the middle Sedentary the use of a separate rectangular unit has developed to the point that it is defined during the initial layout of the decoration.

In the Colonial period and the early and middle Sedentary period the square space at the center of the offset is decorated with either a single scroll, or a double, interlocking scroll. However, by the late Sedentary this central square is rarely if ever filled with decoration.

Plaited

Plaited designs occur on bowls, but are most common on jars (Kelly 1978: 41). The design field is decorated in a basketweavelike pattern of panels. This treatment creates three different types of space within the decoration: triangular areas between the panels and the upper and lower framing lines, rectangular panels, and square spaces surrounded by the panels. Each of these spaces is handled differently by the potter and receives a different array of decorative features, largely dependent upon the shape of the spaces.

This design structure appears at first to be a radical departure from the banded and even sectored designs, but it does not appear without precedent. Kelly (1978: 41) notes that this design structure is the structural equivalent of the offset-quartered bowl designs. Note in Figure 4.1 that the arrangement of panels around the center square unit is similar to the offset-quartered, paneled designs. The plaited decoration may be an adaptation of the offset quarter design structure to the demands of an exterior design field.

Simple Plait

A variation of the plaited design can be recognized and is referred to as the simple plait. It is similar to the plaited structure, except that the scale is increased and the number of panels in the decorative field therefore decreases. The illustration of this structure in Figure 4.1 represents an extreme simplification of the plaited design, much as it is seen on Classic period pottery. The relationship between the simple plait and the plaited design can be clearly seen if a rule is laid across the center of the squares in the plaited design. The structural division between the rule and the upper framing line is identical to the simple plait.

Diamond

Another design structure possibly derived from plaited designs is the diamond pattern (Kelly 1978: 43). This design structure is characterized by large, diamond-shaped areas set apart by smaller triangular areas. It is probably related to the plaited design, although the focus has shifted from the panels, to the square spaces within the plaiting.

Vertical Panel

Finally, Kelly (1978: 24) noted the occurrence of vertical paneling on jars in the Cañada del Oro phase and examples dating to the Rillito phase have since been documented (Doyel 1977a; Greenleaf 1975). This decorative treatment appears to occur only on exterior design fields, and may be associated with particular vessel forms (Doyel 1977a: 34, Fig. 14; Greenleaf 1975: 46, Fig. 3.1a). The design field is segmented into a series of wide vertical panels.

Styles

Seven decorative styles are recognized within the prehistoric Tucson Basin decorative tradition. These styles are based upon design structure, style of linework, and draftsmanhip within the principal fields of decoration (the interior of bowls and jar exteriors) with the intent to identify horizon markers within the decorative development. This model has been defined to identify those pottery styles that are indicative of time. Controlling for time, not only for the purpose of dating the sites, but for documenting the technological and formal traditions of the pottery was a major concern. This model is purely seriational, based upon observations of whole and restorable vessels in published accounts and those housed at the Arizona State Museum.

Because the model is not based upon chronometric, associational, or stratigraphic information, its validity must await confirmation from such detailed studies. This model may prove to be oversimplified in that it fails to account for all pieces of pottery, but future research in the Tucson Basin should be able to refine it as new information becomes available.

There is no one-to-one correspondence between decorative structures and styles. There are some decorative structures that are peculiar to a style or are so frequent as to be diagnostic of that style, yet few are actually restricted to any particular interval of time, and in some phases several decorative structures are in use simultaneously.

The following stylistic concepts serve as horizon markers, but there is not a direct correspondence between styles and the pottery type sequence as known from the works of Kelly (1978), Greenleaf (1975), and Doyel (1977a). While certain types represent the epitome of each style, other types have characteristics that are transitional between styles (Table 4.1). These styles are recognizable decorative configurations, but they are not static, and it can be seen that one style is clearly developed from another.

Table 4.1

TUCSON BASIN DECORATED POTTERY TYPES AND
CORRESPONDING DECORATIVE STYLES

Pottery Type	Decorative Style
Tanque Verde Red-on-Brown	Classic Style
Rincon Red-on-Brown	Rincon Style C Rincon Style B Rincon Style A
Rillito Red-on-Brown	Colonial Style
Cañada del oro Red-on-Brown	Transitional "late" Pioneer Style and Colonial Style
Snaketown Red-On-Buff	"Late" Pioneer Style
Sweetwater Red-on-Gray	Transitional "early and "late" Pioneer Styles
Estrella Red-on-Gray	"Early" Pioneer Style

Pioneer Period Styles

Pioneer period ceramics are characterized by two distinct styles referred to here as the "early" and "late" Pioneer styles. Little Pioneer period material has been recovered from the Tucson Basin, so the stylistic concepts are derived from Haury's descriptions of the Pioneer pottery from Snaketown (1976: 214-222). This reliance upon the Phoenix Basin sequence to set the stage for the Tucson Basin decorative developments is supported by Kelly's (1978: 3) observation that the pottery of the Tucson Basin Pioneer period is indistinguishable from its Phoenix Basin counterpart. Future work may challenge this assessment. The distinguishing characteristic between the Pioneer styles is the rendering of the decoration. The early Pioneer style is characterized by simple, broad-line renderings and is epitomized by Estrella Red-on-gray. The late Pioneer style, on the other hand, is defined by a preference for hachure-filled patterns and is typified by Snaketown Red-on-buff (Haury 1976: 214). Sweetwater Red-on-gray, therefore, is a type that occurs during the transition between these two styles, and shows both the use of broad-line designs and the initial appearance of hachure-filled patterns (Haury 1976: 217-219).

Colonial Period Style

The diagnostic characteristics of the Colonial style are an emphasis on small, tightly packed, well drafted patterns, the manipulation of decorative structures to create visually dynamic designs, and the repetition of only one or two design elements or motifs (Figs. 4.2 through 4.5). Rillito Red-on-brown is the epitome of the Colonial style. In those cases where late Colonial and Sedentary pottery share the same decorative structure, it is the weight and precision of the linework that sets them apart. Lines are thinner on Colonial pottery, more closely spaced, and exhibit better draftsmanship than the later Sedentary styles. The Colonial style more than any other shows the manipulation of the spatial arrangements of the decorative units to produce visually complex, and frequently dynamic designs. Although the designs are visually complex, the Colonial period potters did not use a large array of decorative units on any one vessel, but rather employed only one or two different decorative units in the design. The focus was instead upon repetition and arrangement of design motifs to achieve the design pattern.

Banding is the most common decorative treatment on the Colonial style. The types of banding reach their greatest diversity, in this style, including horizontal and oblique designs, and the combined horizonatal-oblique banding arrangement, with its dynamic "swirling" appearance. The spiraling design shown in Figure 4.5f is especially interesting in the animation of the design. The dynamism of the decorative structure is enhanced by the depiction of the birds' pecking and is a unique and masterful manifestation of the Colonial art style. This vessel also illustrates the Colonial potters' apparent "need" to fill the available decorative space. Beginning at the head of the

Figure 4.2 Colonial style exterior designs. a, Vertically paneled;
b-l, horizontal banded designs. (b and j, Cañada del Oro Red-on-brown;
all others Rillito Red-on-brown. l, Rim diameter is 24.0 cm.)

Figure 4.3   Colonial style exterior designs.   d, Oblique; a-c, e, f, combines horizontal-oblique banded designs.   (All Rillito Red-on-brown. f, Maximum diameter is 48.0 cm.)

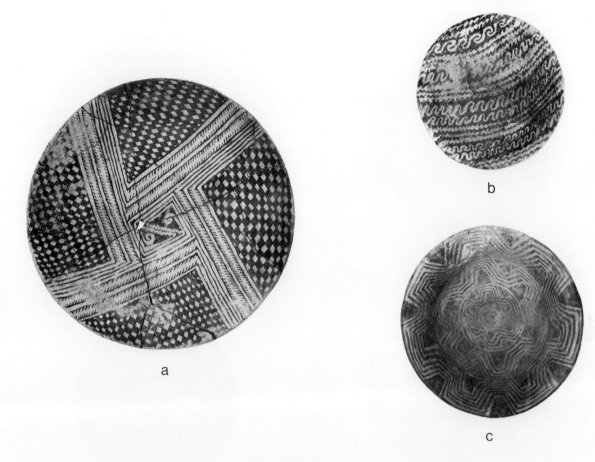

Figure 4.4 Colonial style bowl interior designs. a, Offset quartered; b, cross-banded; c, horizontal banded designs. (b, Cañada del Oro Red-on-brown; a and c, Rillito Red-on-brown. Diameter of a is 30.0 cm.)

snake, between each of the fourth, fifth, sixth, and seventh birds are small triangular motifs carrying negative snakes. Another negative snake occurs in the narrow triangle formed between the snake's body and the rim where the body emanates from the rim. These decorative units are not part of the action depicted in the design and appear merely to be fillers. Perhaps the empty spaces between the birds caused by the curve of the snake were too large to be left unadorned. Similar use of fillers is seen in other designs as well.

Sectored designs occur on Colonial style bowls; most frequently used is the unpaneled, offset quarter, but quartered and trisected examples are also known. The overall decorative treatment of the sectored designs is to fill the triangular spaces with a small triangular motif pendant from the rim, which is framed by combined straight and squiggly line hachure. The small triangular motif usually contains single or double-interlocking scrolls, and also frequently contains a lifeform in either positive or negative rendering (additional detail is provided in the description of Rillito Red-on-brown).

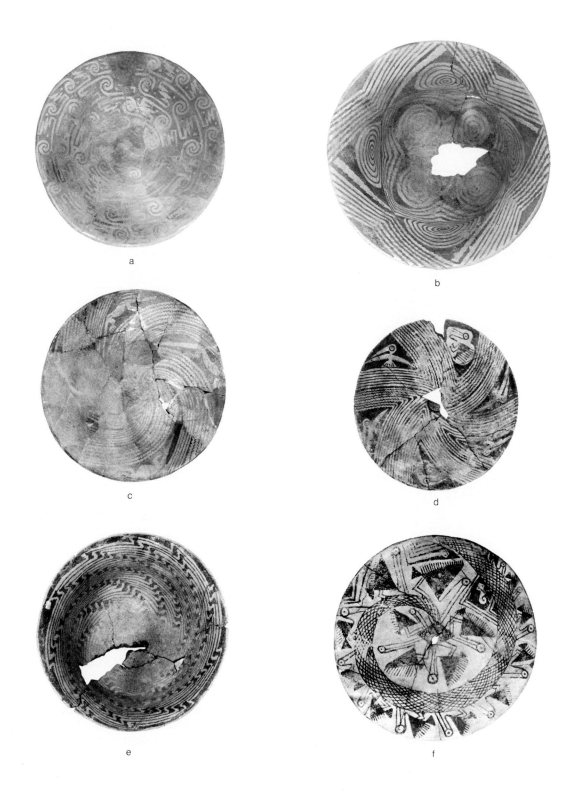

Figure 4.5   Colonial style bowl interior designs. a and b, Horizontal;
c and d, oblique; e, combined horizontal-oblique; f, spiral banded
designs. (a, Cañada del Oro Red-on-brown; b-f, Rillito Red-on-brown.
Diameter of b is 37.6 cm.)

Sedentary Period Styles

        It has long been recognized that the Sedentary period type,
Rincon Red-on-brown, is a heterogenous lot of material with a wide
variety of decorative treatments:

>   Rincon Red-on-brown is . . . a somewhat heterogenous assemblage.
>   It has not been possible to subdivide it into more than one
>   phase, because the various features which survive from the
>   Rillito phase and those which have just been noted as innovations
>   both occur associated in cremations. Three large sherd
>   cremations . . . were checked carefully for stylistic elements.
>   Ceramically, two of the cremations were predominantly a carry-
>   over from Rillito; the third lot showed similar heritage, but
>   at the same time there was a noticeable increase in what may be
>   called intrusive elements. It must be emphasized that here
>   these new elements do not occur in isolation but in association
>   with the essentially Rillito heritage of Rincon (Kelly 1978: 47).

Kelly did not subdivide the pottery into several styles because they did
not occur independently of one another. However, a decorative style is
a recognizable design configuration, not necessarily a temporally
distinct entity. Greenleaf has defined an early variant (Greenleaf
1975: 50) that retains Rillito-like designs as well as a "late" Rincon
Red-on-brown that shows remarkable rectilinearity and simplification of
design verging upon Tanque Verde Red-on-brown (Greenleaf 1975: 60-66).
I have divided the Rincon material into three stylistic subdivisions
referred to here as Rincon Style A, Style B, and Style C. While these
can be respectively equated with early, middle, and late subdivisions of
the Sedentary period, these styles are not strictly restricted to the
phases. For example, while Style A is the only style of pottery made in
the early Sedentary, it persists into the middle and late Sedentary as
well.

Rincon Style A

        This style is similar to the early Rincon described by Greenleaf
(1975: 50) and is clearly developed from the Colonial style. It shows
the same preference for banded designs and the repetition of only one or
two decorative units as the Colonial style (Figs. 4.6 and 4.7); however,
the decorative treatment is larger, heavier, and more "slap-dash" (Kelly
1978: 39). In short, it appears to be a decadent form of the Colonial
style. The imprecision and greater line width is the principal
difference between Rincon Style A and the Colonial style. Combined
horizontal-oblique bands are less frequent, and simple horizontal and
oblique bands are more common. In consequence, Rincon Style A is
frequently banded, but rarely exhibits the dynamism of the Colonial
style.

        The unpaneled, offset quartered design continues on bowl
interiors, but there is the beginning of a development toward the use of
paneled offset quarters. The first appearances of the panel are similar

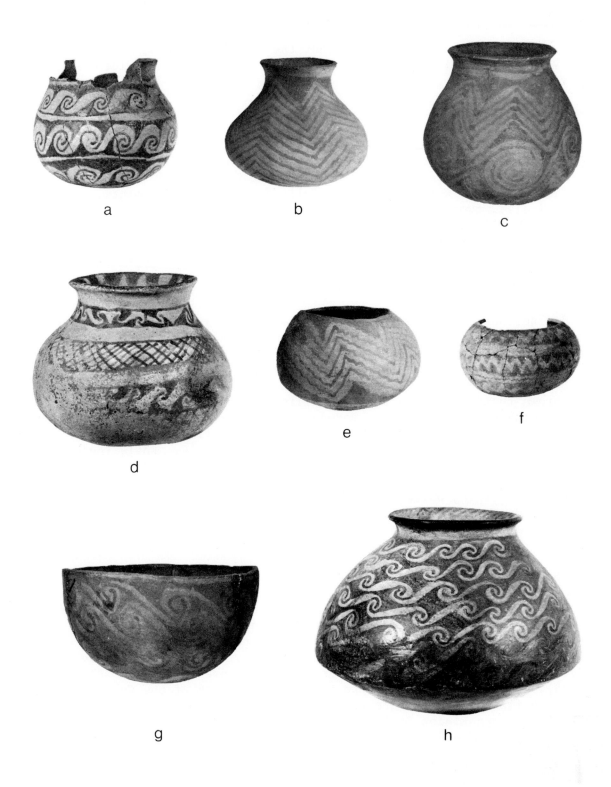

Figure 4.6 Rincon Style A exterior designs. a–f, Horizontal banded; g and h, combined horizontal-oblique banded. (All Rincon Red-on-brown. Maximum diameter of h is 30.6 cm.)

a   b

Figure 4.7 Rincon Style A interior designs: cross banded. (Rincon
Red-on-brown. Diameter of b is 25.3 cm.)

in construction to the unpaneled offset quarter, but incorporate a row of decorative units that give the impression of a panel.

Rincon Style B

Kelly (1978: 39) noted that Rincon Red-on-brown shows the same decadence that marks the change from Santa Cruz Red-on-buff to Sacaton Red-on-buff in the Phoenix Basin; however, the draftsmanhip of Style B, cannot be called decadent. While some of the material does exhibit a slap-dash approach, much of this style shows a well controlled use of line width. There appears in fact to be a recrystallization of the pottery craft with emphasis upon geometric design structure (Fig. 4.8 through 4.10). Its hallmark is a movement away from banded designs toward geometric, gridlike patterns in plaited and paneled designs for both bowls and jars. The geometric patterns on jars appear at odds with the Colonial heritage of the decorative tradition, and these may be what Kelly (1978: 47) referred to as intrusive elements. It is possible to show that the development of the paneled and plaited designs are local innovations with precedents in the offset-quartered bowl designs of the Colonial period. Thus the plaited jar designs are not necessarily intrusive elements, but a stylistic innovation adapting the offset-quartered structure to the demands of a jar's exterior surface.

The most typical design structure employed on jars is the plaited design, while bowls are exclusively decorated with the paneled variety of the offset quarter (Fig. 4.1). There appears to be a close relationship between these two designs, with the plaited jar patterns being an adaptation of the paneled offset-quartered structure to the surface area provided by jars. Another jar design typical of Style B is the diamond pattern which, although rarer than the plaited designs, is closely related to it.

Unlike the Colonial style and Rincon Style A, there is a concerted use of many different design units rather than the repetition of only one or two. There is still, however, a tight packing of these design units. Repetition is also still characteristic, but rather than repeating a single design element, entire panels are repeated. The interior, long borders of the panels are frequently adorned with some type of fringe motif, and the center of the panel is filled with a long, running motif or a longitudinal repetition of a single motif.

Rincon Style C

This style is essentially what most have referred to as late Rincon Red-on-brown (Greenleaf 1975: 60-66), or Cortaro Red-on-brown (Reinhard 1982), while it is defined as a stylistic development rather than a pottery type, it may be a potential horizon marker for the late Sedentary period. Rincon Style C represents the stylistic transition between Rincon Style B and the designs typical of the Classic period.

Figure 4.8 Rincon Style B exterior designs. a and b, Diamond; c-f, plaited design structures. (All Rincon Red-on-brown. Rim diameter of c is 39.0 cm.)

Figure 4.9 Rincon Style B (a and b) and Style C (c-e) exterior designs. a and e, Simple plait; b-d, plaited design structures. (All Rincon Red-on-brown. Maximum diameter of d is 30.5 cm.)

Though structurally similar to Style B, Style C has an openness about the decoration as more undecorated space is incorporated into the design (Figs. 4.9, 4.10, and 4.11). In Rincon Style B there is a tendency to fill all available space with decorative units possibly a carry-over from the Colonial period.

The most typical jar design is the simple plait, which, as mentioned above, is an enlargement and simplification of the plaited design. This increase in the scale may have caused the overall simplification of the design, or the simplification may have resulted in the increase in scale. Regardless, the designs are simpler and more open. Rather than fill the available decorative space there is a focus upon the fringing in the panels which also become larger and simpler. The frequent use of repeated design units in the center of the panels is lost.

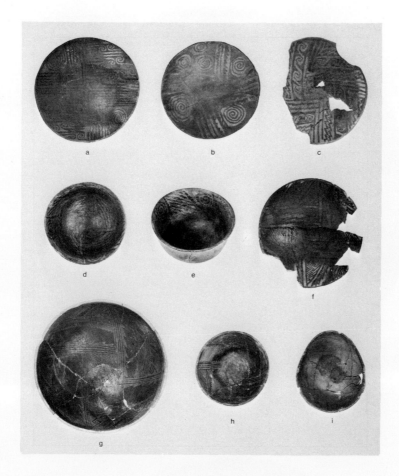

Figure 4.10 Rincon Styles A (a), B (b-f), and C (g-i) interior designs.
a, Quartered, b, offset quarter incipient panel, and c-i, offset quarter
paneled. (d and e, Two views of same vessel. Diameter of g is 28.7 cm).

This style is clearly intermediary between the more elaborate
Rincon Style B and the bolder, simpler, Classic style as represented by
Tanque Verde Red-on-brown (Kelly 1978: 48-59).

Technological Study

By using the stylistic model above to control for time, it is
possible to carry out detailed studies of ceramic technology and vessel
shape. Study of technological attributes is intended to determine
whether there are variations in the pottery that can be attributed to
differences in age, intended use, or geographic origin. Current
knowledge of Tucson Basin Hohokam pottery indicates that there is indeed
technological variation, but these aspects have yet to be fully studied
to discover whether patterns and modes exist within this variation.

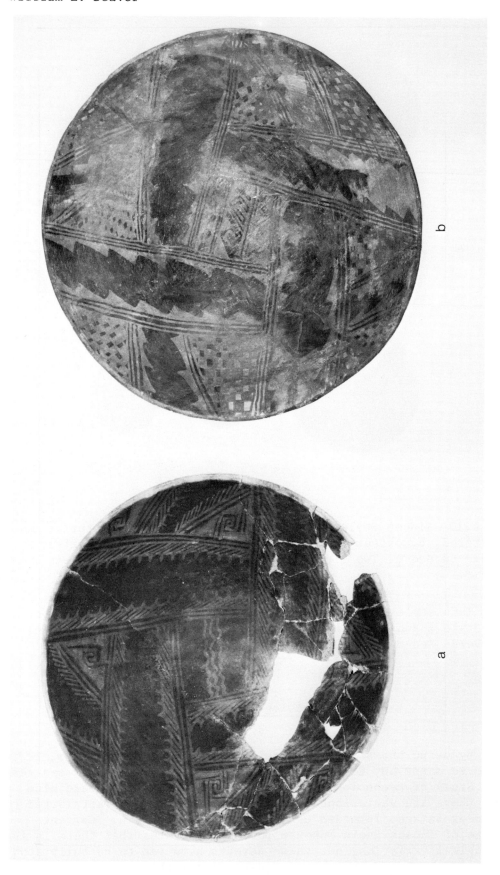

Figure 4.11 Rincon Style C bowl interior designs: offset-quartered, paneled. (All are Rincon Red-on-brown. Diameter of <u>b</u> is 40.0 cm.)

A number of technological attributes may be studied depending upon the kinds of research questions asked and the technological sophistication of the pottery. Several basic technological attributes were chosen for study including temper, amount and type of surface mica, quality and characteristics of polishing, and manufacturing technique. Slipping and smudging were examined on decorated and red-slipped pottery.

Technological attributes were not recorded for all pieces of pottery recovered from the Rosemont sites; the sheer quantity made sampling necessary. Rim sherds were selected as the sample for study for two reasons. First, they provided a simple, defined sample and contained all technological attributes selected for study. Second, rim sherds also carry attributes of vessel form, and because this is another important aspect of this pottery study, selecting rim sherds enabled technological and formal studies to be conducted concurrently.

Temper

All nonplastic inclusions in the pottery whether of natural origin or intentional addition to the clay are considered temper. A total of 19 temper classes were identified for the ANAMAX pottery (Table 4.2). Temper identifications were made using a binocular microscope at no less than 20 power magnification. The 19 temper categories are based primarily upon the use and mixture of two types of temper: sand and crushed rock. All nonplastic tempering material that was rounded and presumably stream rolled was classed as sand, regardless of particle size. It was easily distinguishable from the crushed rock, which exhibited sharp angular shapes. No detailed mineralogical assessment of the sand particles was undertaken. Petrographic or other mineralogical studies of sand temper may prove fruitful in future studies, in determining the probable manufacturing source of the pottery, but these could not be included in the present study. This study focuses on the more general issue of whether the potters gathered clay containing natural inclusions, gathered stream sand to add to the clay, or prepared crushed rock for tempering material.

A variety of crushed rock tempers have been identified, including micaceous schist, an unidentified micaceous rock (probably gneiss), phyllite, and other nonmicaceous rock. None of these rocks are available in the Rosemont area, and documenting their occurrence as temper may have some implications for identifying regional exchange.

Another component of the temper is free mica platelets, which never occur alone as temper, but with sand. Free-floating platelets are distinguished from those that occur embedded in a rock matrix. In pottery tempered with crushed micaceous rock the mica platelets are usually embedded in some type of matrix, although free-floating platelets also occur. Samples of wash sands collected near the excavated Rosemont sites were viewed under a binocular microscope at

Table 4.2

TEMPER CLASSES USED IN THE TECHNOLOGICAL STUDY
OF ANAMAX-ROSEMONT POTTERY

Temper Type	Description
Sand	(only)
Sand with mica	(variable quantities of mica)
Crushed schist	(only)
Crushed micaceous rock	(only)
Crushed phyllite	(only)
Other crushed rock	(only)
Sand and crushed schist	(approximately equal amounts)
Sand and crushed micaceous rock	(approximately equal amounts)
Sand and crushed phyllite	(approximately equal amounts)
Sand and other crushed rock	(approximately equal amounts)
Sand with crushed schist	(predominantly sand)
Sand with cruched micaceous rock	(predominantly sand)
Sand with crushed phyllite	(predominantly sand)
Sand with other crushed rock	(predominantly sand)
Crushed schist with sand	(predominantly crushed schist)
Crushed micaceous rock with sand	(predominantly crushed micaceous rock)
Crushed phyllite with sand	(predominantly crushed phyllite)
Other crushed rock with sand	(predominantly crushed rock)
Sand with mica with some crushed rock	(predominantly sand with mica containing varying amounts of schist)
Unknown	

20-power magnification and were found to contain free floating mica; mica frequently occurred in local clay samples as well. Therefore it seems likely that the free floating mica platelets are natural or accidental inclusions in the pottery. Conversely, no schist, phyllite, or other micaceous rocks were seen in any of the sand or clay samples.

The remainder of the 19 temper categories are based upon the presence and relative proportions of sand, mica, crushed schist, crushed micaceous rock, crushed phyllite, or other crushed rock to one another. The format of the temper category descriptions indicates the relative proprtions between tempering agents (Table 4.2). "With" indicates that the tempering material listed first is proportionately greater than that following, and "and" indicates that the two materials are of approximately equal proportion. Pottery with temper classed as "sand," "crushed schist," or "crushed micaceous rock" had exclusively these temper classes visible in cross section. The proportional relationship between the tempering materials is based upon visual impression, and is thus a relative, not absolute, proportion. Particle size also plays a role. Sand particles are generally smaller than particles of crushed rock and are visually more frequent, but might not be proportionately more frequent than schist if the the frequencies were determined by weight or volume of these components within the pottery.

Surface Mica

The relative amounts and types of surface mica were studied to determine whether there was a correlation between the type of temper used and the quantity and type of surface mica. It was also anticipated that some types of mica might be geographically restricted in distribution so that they could be useful as geographic indicators. Three types of mica were identified: muscovite (silver), phlogopite (gold), and biotite (black). In addition to the three mica types above four other categories indicated the occurrence of any combination of those types.

Polish

Surface polishing was recorded on a relative scale using four categories: no polish, lightly polished, moderately polished, and heavily polished. Although these are strictly subjective categories, their application within the study was consistent to ensure that differences represent observable characteristics.

Vessel Form Study

Vessel from is one of the most important aspects of pottery, as well as one of the least studied. Most studies of vessel form have consisted of no more than showing photographs or drawings of different forms; none has attempted to explicitly define the variables on which form classes are based; shape classes are apparently determined solely from visual perceptions. Admittedly, identifying differences in vessel shape is a matter of perception, but perception is based on definite characteristics, usually the proportions of various parts of the vessel to one another, and the comparison of these vessel parts to geometric figures. It is difficult to reliably reproduce the perception of an individual researcher, but if those attributes of the vessel that cause a researcher to perceive different forms can be identified explicitly, it may be possible to produce replicable results. The lack of detailed qualitative and quantitative data about vessel forms is due, in part, to the lack of explicit qualitative or quantitative values in the methods used to record vessel forms. However, the theoretical and methodological background for such a study does exist (Shepard 1976), though it has not been applied to Tucson Basin pottery, and has only recently been applied to Hohokam pottery of the Gila and Salt valleys (Crown 1984a). This study of vessel form is based upon Shepard's (1976) methods.

Anna Shepard (1976) has demonstrated that vessel shapes can be quantitatively recorded with respect to key points in the contour of the vessel profile. These points are the end point, inflection point, vertical tangent, and corner point (Shepard 1976: 226).

The various parts of a vessel such as the body, mouth, neck, rim, base, and shoulder, can be defined with respect to these reference points. These reference points are identifiable landmarks in the profile of a vessel and can provide comparability of results.

Initially ceramic vessels can be divided into two groups, one whose members are symmetrical with respect to the vertical axis of the vessel, and a second group of vessels that are asymmetical with respect to the vertical axis. The following discussion of methodology focuses on those vessels that are symmetrical around the vertical axis. Asymmetrical vessels are more difficult to treat in a systematic fashion and are best analyzed individually.

Three basic structural classes of symmetrical vessels can be identified based upon characteristics of the orifice and whether the form is necked; these are: (1) unrestricted, (2) simple and dependent restricted, and (3) independent restricted (Shepard 1976: 230). During the initial classification of the ANAMAX pottery, however, the only distinction of concern was whether the vessels were unrestricted or restricted. All unrestricted forms are referred to in this chapter as bowls, and all restricted forms are classed as jars.

In this study the characteristic points in the profile have been used to define the various parts of the vessel. Those referred to in this chapter are listed below with respect to the reference point or points that define them (Fig. 4.12).

1. Lip. The surface of the orifice is called the lip. In many cases it is synonymous with "rim," but the lip is actually a part of the rim. It is referred to only when discussing the practice of painting rims.

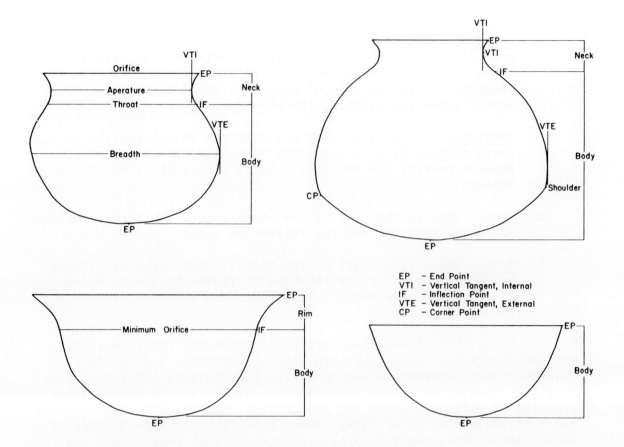

Figure 4.12 Various parts of vessels used in this study and the characteristic points used to define them.

2. <u>Orifice</u>. The orifice or mouth is the intial opening of the vessel and is defined by the upper end point.

3. <u>Aperture</u>. This is the narrowest constriction in the neck of the jar through which items must pass. It is the aperture more than the orifice that controls access to a vessel. The aperture can be defined by the existence of an interior vertical tangent. It is thus distinguished from the breadth, which is defined by an exterior vertical tangent. The aperture may not always exist as an independent point on the vessel profile. For example, jars whose necks curve upward and inward may never reach a point of vertical tangency or may obtain the vertical tangent at the rim. In these cases the orifice and aperture are the same.

4. <u>Minimum orifice</u>. Minimum orifice was recorded for flare-rim bowls. The minimum orifice is measured at the juncture between the flaring rim and the main body at the point of inflection.

5. <u>Throat</u>. The throat is the point where the neck of a vessel joins the body and is located at the point of inflection or a corner point.

6. Breadth. Breadth is the maximum diameter of the vessel body, and is generally also the maximum diameter of the vessel. The breadth is located either at the point of exterior vertical tangency or, in the case of some shouldered vessels, at the corner point representing the shoulder.

7. Shoulder. A sharp, angular point in the vessel profile characterized by a corner point is called the shoulder. On Hohokam pottery the shoulder usually occurs at or below the breadth.

8. Neck. This is the part of the vessel above the throat, between the upper endpoint and the inflection point.

9. Body. The largest part of the vessel, comprising everything below the throat or, in the case of flare-rim bowls, below the rim is called the body. The breadth and shoulder are parts of the body.

Using this streamlined version of Shepard's (1976) methods, orifice, minimum orifice, aperture, throat, breadth, and shoulder diameters were recorded as were neck and body height, and total vessel height. These measurements provided the data to record vessel shape profiles as well as compute the proportions used later in the temporal and functional studies of form. There were two principle sources of vessel shape data, completely or partly restorable vessels and rim sherds. Because of physical limitations present by these two different data sources, each was interpreted in a different manner. It was hoped at the outset that these two classes of information could be integrated together as one data set. However, due to the low incidence of whole vessels this goal could not be realized, except in the cases of direct rims where the rim sherds can be identified to vessel shape classes.

Restorable Vessels

Restorable vessels include those from which it is possible to reconstruct the entire profile and those with one-half or, in some cases, as little as one-third of the profile present. All restorable vessels, whether complete or partial, were photographed in silhouette on slide film with care taken to make certain the camera's line of sight was perpendicular to the vertical axis of the vessel. A scale was included in each photograph. The silhouette of the vessel was then projected on a flat surface at natural size, one-half natural size, or some convenient scale. Measurements of each vessel were taken from this two-dimensional projection of the vessel. This technique proved an extremely useful way of measuring vessels.

Measurements of the orifice, minimum orifice, aperture, and breadth, as well as the neck height, body height, and total vessl height were recorded on a standarized form for each vessel. From these measurements it was possible to compute the various proportions used to

determine special shape classes. Unfortunately, the collection of
restorable vessels was too small to enable identification of particular,
distinct shape classes; however, it was possible to use these data to
make some interpretations about vessel use and changes in shapes through
time.

Rim Sherds

Rim sherds were also important for the study of vessel shape
because they possess some attributes of shape and size. Some of the
vessel form traits that can be found on the rim sherds are: (1) orifice
diameter; (2) aperture diameter; (3) throat diameter; (4) neck height;
(5) shape of the neck; and (6) occasionally information concerning the
shape of the vessel body.

Many rim types appear in the literature, including: direct,
flared, everted, incurved, outcurved, and recurved. Some of these terms
refer not to the finishing technique of the rim but to characteristics
of vessel shape. A flare-rimmed bowl is a specific vessel shape and not
a type of rim finish or elaboration. In studying vessel shapes from rim
sherds, five categories have been distinguished: (1) direct, (2) flared,
(3) everted, (4) upcurved, and (5) recurved. These terms do not refer
to rim finish but to vessel shape, and have been used in a fashion
consistent with the existing literature.

These classes are important because they indicate the type of
information that can be obtained from the sherds. Direct rimmed
vessels, for example, are those where there is no visible or apparent
break between the vessel body and rim (Shepard 1976: 245). It is
therefore possible to infer the entire shape from a correctly oriented
rim sherd. On the other hand, from the remaining classes it is often
only possible to determine the shape of the rim or neck; the shape of
the body is rarely discernible.

Rim angle, or the direction of the rim, was recorded for all
types except direct rims. It is a relative measure of the severity of
the curvature (Fig. 4.13). There may be discernible differences in the
amount of flare or eversion of the rim. Three variations each of flared
and everted rims were recorded, and are referred to as slight, moderate,
and severe as the rim curves more toward the horizontal. Only two types
of uncurved rims were recorded: complete, if the tangent to the rim
reaches the vertical, and incomplete if it ends before reaching vertical
tangency.

Sidewall angle was measured for all rims: it is the direction
of the vessel body sidewall. On direct rims this is the vessel wall
leading directly into the finished edge; for all others this is the
direction of the body sidewall below the inflection or corner point that
defines the rim. The seven types of sidewall angles and the forms they
represent are shown in Figure 4.14.

Flare Rims

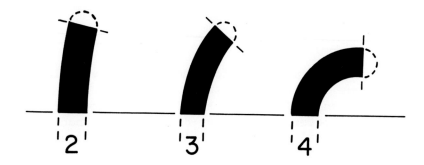

Everted Rims

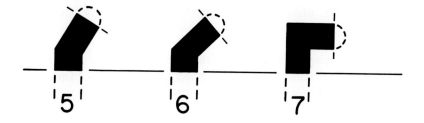

Upcurved Rims

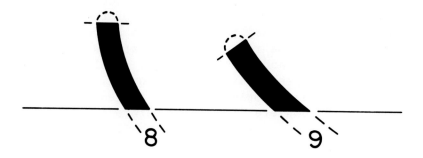

Rim Angles For Non-Direct Rims

Figure 4.13 Rim angles for nondirect rims: (2) slight flare; (3) moderate flare; (4) pronounced flare; (5) slightly everted; (6) moderately everted; (7) pronounced everted; (8) complete upcurve; and (9) incomplete upcurve.

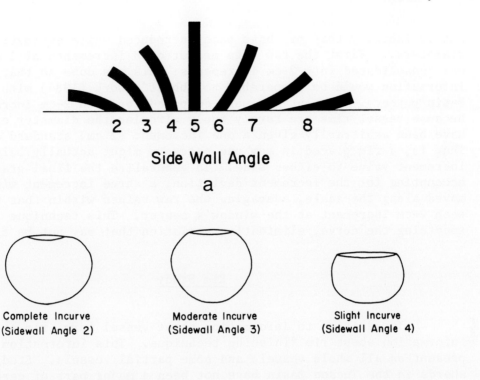

Side Wall Angle

a

Complete Incurve
(Sidewall Angle 2)

Moderate Incurve
(Sidewall Angle 3)

Slight Incurve
(Sidewall Angle 4)

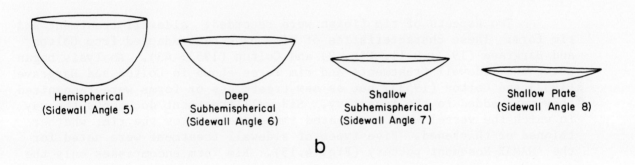

Hemispherical
(Sidewall Angle 5)

Deep
Subhemispherical
(Sidewall Angle 6)

Shallow
Subhemispherical
(Sidewall Angle 7)

Shallow Plate
(Sidewall Angle 8)

b

Figure 4.14 Side wall angles used to infer vessel shape from rim sherds
(a), and the idealized shapes that they may represent (b).

Measuring Orifice and Aperture Diameters

Orifice diameters were measured from rim sherds using a board of
concentric circles with diameters from 1 cm to 50 cm in increments of
1 cm and matching the curve of the rim to one of these circles. Few
rims are truly circular, therefore this technique can only provide
an approximation. The minimum orifice and aperture diameters were
estimated in the same manner. In presenting the diameter estimates
of the orifice, minimum orifice, and aperture a technique referred
to as "running averages" was utilized. This technique averages

out variability that may have been introduced while estimating the
diameters.   First the raw data measured in increments of 1 cm
was consolidated into 2-cm increments; this was done so that this
information would be comparable to Abbott's work (1984) with Phoenix
Basin pottery.   Percentages were computed for each 2-cm increment.
Because vessel rims are rarely truly circular the diameter estimates
have been arbitrarily given a one increment (2 cm) standard deviation.
That is, a rim placed in any one category might actually belong in the
increment value to either side.   To generalize the final graphs
accounting for the increment deviation, a three increment window was
moved along the scale, averaging the raw values within that window for
each 2-cm increment at the window's center.   This technique resulted in
smoothing the curve, eliminating variation that may not be significant.

Rim Study

In addition to information about vessel form, rim sherds carry
information about rim finishing technique.   This information is also
present on all whole vessels and some partial vessels.   Studies of rim
sherds in the Tucson Basin have not been a major part of ceramic studies
to date; no study has explored whether rim finishing may have some
important, temporally diagnostic value.

Two aspects of rim finish were recorded: sidewall treatment and
rim form.   These characteristics of rims have been adapted from Colton
and Hargrave (1937: 9-11, Fig. 2) and Colton (1953: 43).   Analysis began
using the sidewall treatments and rim forms shown in Colton and Hargrave
(1937) and Colton (1953), but as new treatments or forms were recognized
they were added to the inventory.   Sidewall treatment documents the way
in which the vessel wall is treated immediately below the rim, whether
thinned or thickened.   Five types of sidewall treatment were noted for
the ANAMAX-Rosemont pottery (Fig. 4.15).   Rim form encompasses only the

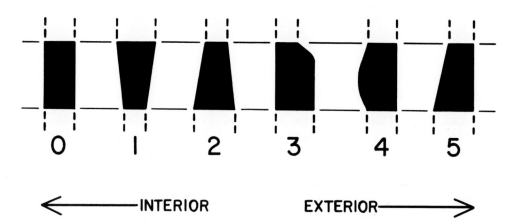

Figure 4.15 Variety of side wall treatments identified during this
pottery study: (0) straight; (1) thickened; (2) thinned; (3) exterior
thinned; (4) interior "bulge"; (5) interior thinned.

manipulation of clay at the orifice to create a finished edge.
Classification of the rim form was determined by vertically orienting
the sidewall immediately below the rim. During the analysis a total of
29 different rim forms were identified (Fig. 4.16), but two classes were
eventually combined with other forms, leaving 27 different rim forms.
This does not mean that there are 27 distinct elaborations of the rim;
rather, the overall manner of rim finish appears to be quite casual.
Many of the various rim forms appear to be closely related. For
example, Forms 1, 2, and 16 in Figure 4.15 are quite similar to each
other, as are Forms 3, 13, 22, and 24. Therefore in interpreting these
data, the various forms have been grouped into five classes: tapered

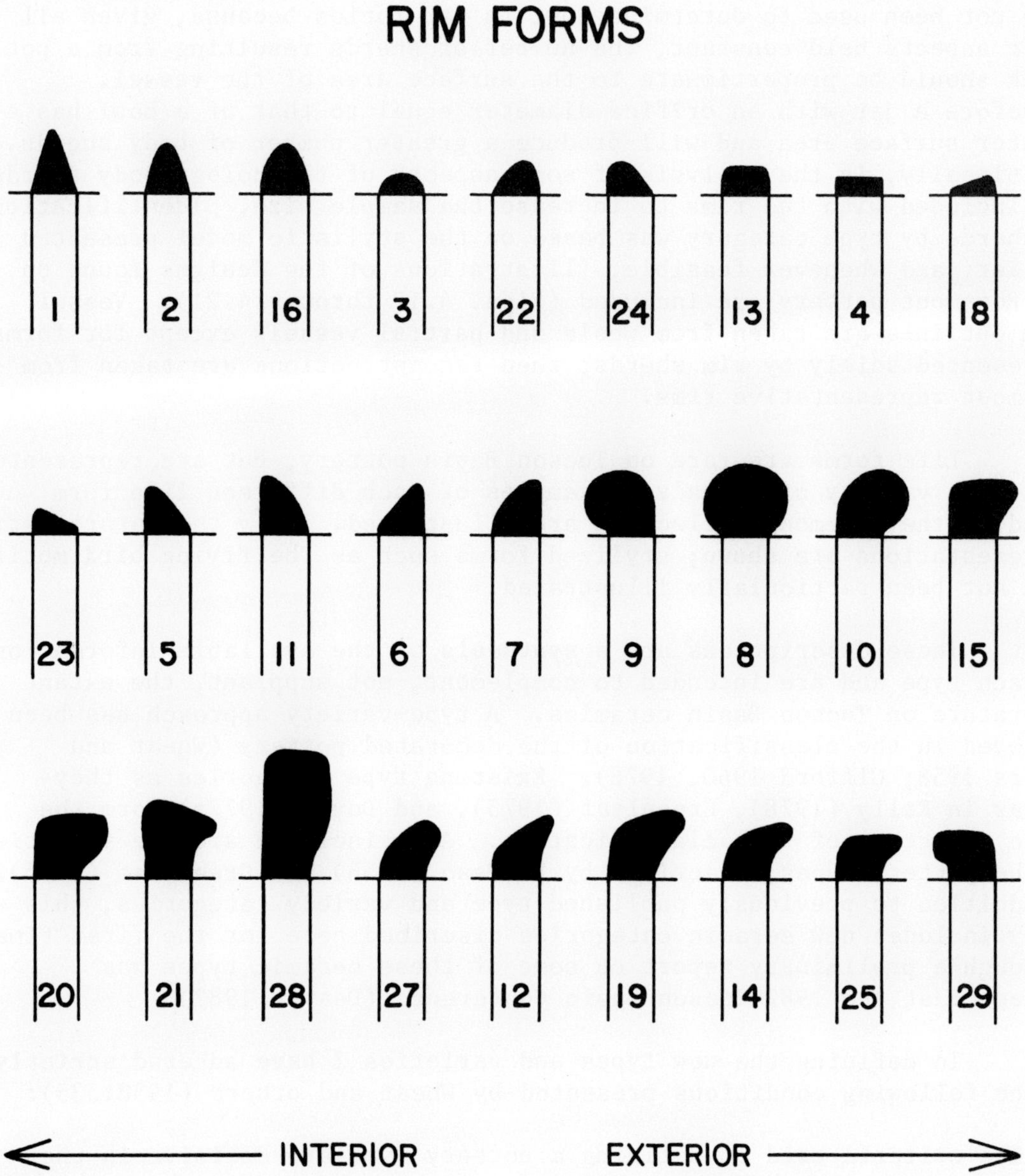

RIM FORMS

Figure 4.16 Variety of rim forms identified during this study: (1, 2, 16)
tapered; (3, 22, 24, 13) rounded; (4, 18, 23) squared; (6, 7) beveled; and
remainder miscellaneous forms.

(Forms 1, 2, 16); rounded (Forms 3, 13, 22, and 24); square (Forms 4, 18, and 23); beveled (Forms 5, 6, and 7); and miscellaneous (which includes the remaining forms).

Painted Pottery

The following pottery descriptions are based primarily upon the ANAMAX-Rosemont collection as summarized in Table 4.3, and concentrate upon aspects of technology, vessel form, and rim finish. Bowl to jar ratios have been computed using rim sherd counts. Body sherd counts have not been used to determine bowl to jar ratios because, given all other aspects held constant, the number of sherds resulting from a pot break should be proportionate to the surface area of the vessel. Therefore a jar with an orifice diameter equal to that of a bowl has a greater surface area and will produce a greater number of body sherds. Occasionally, in the analysis of some aspects of technology body sherds are included with the rims to increase the sample size. Identification of sherds by type category was based on the stylistic model presented earlier, and whenever feasible, illustrations of the designs found on the Rosemont pottery are included (Figs. 4.17 through 4.21). Vessel form outlines are taken from whole and partial vessels except for forms represented solely by rim sherds; then reconstructions are taken from the most representative rims.

Life forms are rare on Tucson Basin pottery, but are represented by a wide variety of animals. Examples of each different life form found in the Rosemont collection are illustrated. Only the naturalistic representations are shown; stylized forms such as the flying bird motif have not been particularly illustrated.

These descriptions are a synthesis of the available information on each type and are intended to complement, not supplant, the extant literature on Tucson Basin ceramics. A type-variety approach has been employed in the classification of the decorated pottery (Wheat and others 1958; Gifford 1960, 1976). Existing type categories as they appear in Kelly (1978), Greenleaf (1975), and Doyel (1977a) form the basic structure of this classification. Also included are the varieties of the pottery types, described by Di Peso (1956) and Greenleaf (1975). In addition to previously published type and variety categories, this study includes new ceramic categories discribed here for the first time, although a preliminary report on some of these ceramic types was presented at the 1982 Tucson Basin Conference (Deaver 1982).

In defining the new types and varieties I have adhered strictly to the following conditions presented by Wheat and others (1958: 35):

The criteria used in defining a pottery type are decisive in the designation of varieties and their relationship to established types. A variety differs from the type to which it is related only in one or more particulars. In terms of geographical

Table 4.3

SUMMARY OF PAINTED POTTERY FROM THE ANAMAX-ROSEMONT SITES

	EARLY			MIDDLE			LATE				MIXED			
	AZ EE:2:105	AZ EE:2:113	AZ EE:2:84	AZ EE:2:107	AZ EE:2:109	AZ EE:2:120	AZ EE:1:104	AZ EE:2:106	AZ EE:2:116	AZ EE:2:117	AZ EE:2:76	AZ EE:2:77	AZ EE:2:129	Total
Sweetwater Red-on-gray											1			1
Snaketown Red-on-buff	2										2			4
Cañada Del Oro Red-on-brown	67(1)*	10(2)	4								2	3	21	69(1)
Rillito Red-on-brown	177	26	1	11		11					28(6)			337(8)
Unidentified Colonial Red-on-brown	126		12				5			6	42(1)		5	206(1)
Indeterminate Red-on-brown	104	252						1			97	14	11	518
Rincon Red-on-brown, Style A	199(7)	292(5)	29(1)	8(1)							43(3)	62(1)	18	650(18)
Rincon Red-on-brown, Style B	8	3		8(2)	2			3			39(2)	45(4)	1	109(8)
Rincon Red-on-brown, Style C									1		42(1)		2	45(1)
Rincon Red-on-brown, Style ?	322	68	9	22	22	3	21	15	6	12	101(1)	162	77	840(1)
Rincon Red-on-brown (white slip variety), Style A	9	9(1)									8	3	2	25(1)
Rincon Red-on-brown (white slip variety), Style B	1			8		2	1				3	2	1	23
Rincon Red-on-brown (white slip variety), Style C								4(1)						7(1)
Rincon Red-on-brown (white slip variety), Style ?	17	1				1	1			2	17	15	13	74
Rincon Red-on-brown (smudged), Style A	17	1	1								17	5	4	35
Rincon Red-on-brown (smudged), Style B	2	6	3		2									26
Rincon Red-on-brown (smudged), Style C								7	7		19	5		29
Rincon Red-on-brown (smudged), Style ?	55	7		6	2	1				3	23	7	3	114
Rincon Black-on-brown, Style A														4(1)
Rincon Black-on-brown, Style B		1		12								(1)		12
Rincon Black-on-brown, Style C														6
Rincon Black-on-brown, Style ?				4			6	2	3	3	6	16	10	31
Rincon Black-on-brown (white slip variety), Style A		3									10			14
Rincon Black-on-brown (white slip variety), Style B		3		1						1				1
Rincon Black-on-brown (white slip variety), Style C														
Rincon Black-on-brown (white slip variety), Style ?		2		1							10	20		35
Indeterminate Black-on-brown		9		10					1		15	9		44
Rincon Polychrome				1										1
Rio Rico Polychrome			1	4							17			29
Sahuarita Polychrome						1					2			5
Tanque Verde Red-on-brown					2			1	3		7			16(1)
"Crude" Red-on-brown	3	44(1)					6	(1)		6	2			49(1)
Total Identified Types	1111(8)	830(9)	60(1)	100(3)	30	19	40	26(2)	21	33	554(14)	367(6)	168	3359(43)
Total Unidentifiable Red-on-brown	1268	1100	206	154(2)	20	75(1)	31	28	59(1)	72	1283	647	232	5176(4)
Total Tucson Basin Series	2379(8)	1930(9)	266(1)	254(5)	50	94(1)	71	54(2)	80(1)	105	1837(14)	1014(6)	400	8535(47)

*( ) Number of Restorable Vessels

279

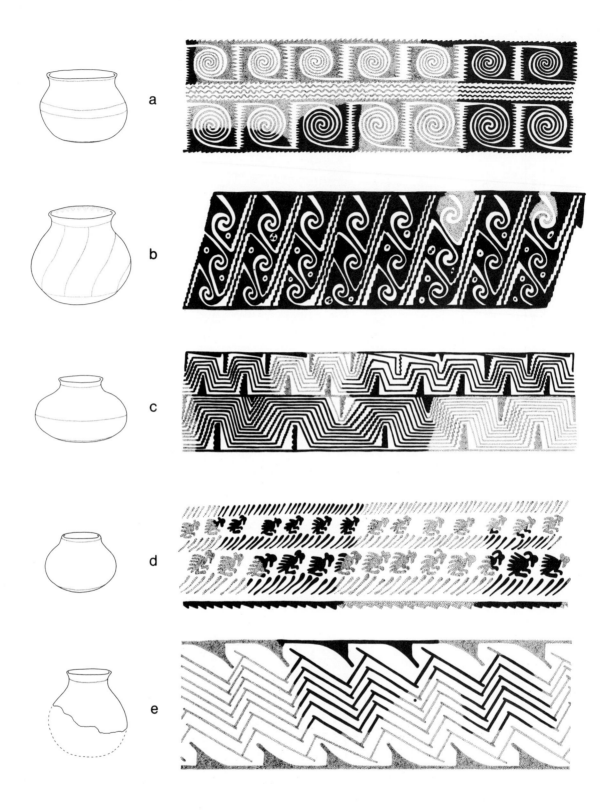

Figure 4.17 Exterior designs on the ANAMAX-Rosemont restorable vessels.
a, Cañada del Oro Red-on-brown; b-d, Rillito Red-on-brown; e, Rincon
Red-on-brown Style A. Designs shown at conventionalized scale, vessel
profiles are shown to scale. (b, Maximum diameter is 23.0 cm.)

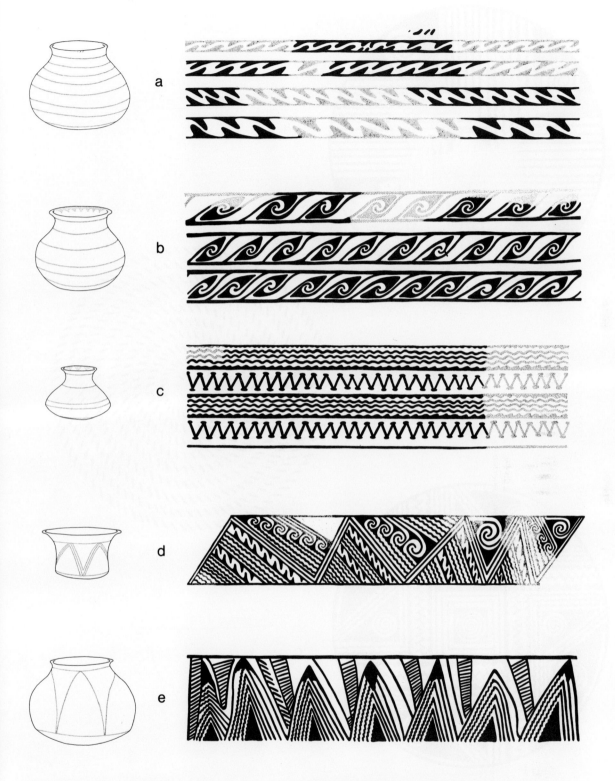

Figure 4.18   Exterior designs on the ANAMAX-Rosemont restorable vessels.
a–c, Rincon Red-on-brown Style A; d, Rincon Red-on-brown Style B; e,
Rincon Red-on-brown indeterminate style. Designs shown at conventionalized scale, vessel profiles are shown to scale. (b, Maximum diameter
is 20.5 cm.)

Figure 4.19   Interior bowl designs on the ANAMAX-Rosemont restorable vessels.   a, Rillito Red-on-brown; b, Rincon Red-on-brown Style A; c, Rincon Red-on-brown Style B.   Designs shown at conventionalized scale, vessel profiles are shown to scale.   (c, Diameter is 34.0 cm.)

Figure 4.20   Interior bowl designs on the ANAMAX-Rosemont restorable vessels. a-c, Rincon Red-on-brown Style A.   Designs shown at conventionalized scale, vessel profiles are shown to scale. (c, Diameter is 22.0 cm.)

Figure 4.21   Interior bowl designs on the ANAMAX-Rosemont restorable
vessels. a-x, Rincon Red-on-brown Style A. Designs shown at
conventionalized scale, vessel profiles are shown to scale.
(c, Diameter is 38.0 cm.)

distribution and time span it may be equal to that of the type,
although generally it is more restricted in one or both of these
elements. A variety cannot be temporally and areally distinct
from the type manner of design execution, surface finish, or
character of paint or paste utilized, else the variety warrants
designation as a type.

The new types presented here are based upon the use of a blackish paint
either alone in a bichrome color scheme or combined with the normal red
paint in a polychrome color scheme. In naming the new types I have
maintained the convention giving Hohokam ceramics names which are
equivalent to the phases in which the type occurs. However, when this
exhausted the available names, new ones were selected according to the
rules for naming pottery types outlined by Colton and Hargrave's (1935).
The varieties have been defined by technological or stylistic criteria
and are designated by appending the particular style or technological
attribute in question to the type name.

    Not all the sorting categories shown in Table 4.3 are described
in detail below. There are of course various indeterminate and
unidentified categories as well. There are three major indeterminate
categories: unidentified Colonial period, indeterminate Rillito or
Rincon Red-on-brown, and indeterminate Tucson Basin red-on-brown. These
three categories have been separated because each possesses some
interpretive value. The unidentified Colonial category includes sherds
that are probably of Colonial period age but could not be further
segregated as either Cañada del Oro or Rillito Red-on-brown. Likewise
the indeterminate Rillito or Rincon Red-on-brown category contained
sherds that for one reason or another could not be sorted definitely
into either Rillito or Rincon Red-on-brown. It should be stressed that
this is an indeterminate category and does not contain pottery
transitional between the Colonial and Sedentary periods. The final
category, indeterminate Tucson Basin red-on-brown, contains what are in
all likelihood, locally produced red-on-browns that are too small or
eroded to be classified further. On the average this category comprises
nearly 61 percent of all locally produced decorated pottery, ranging
from as little as 40 percent to as much as 79 percent at some sites.
The following descriptions concentrate on the pottery type categories
that form the Tucson Basin ceramic sequence.

Pioneer Period

    One sherd of Sweetwater Red-on-gray and four of Snaketown Red-
on-buff represent the entire collection of Pioneer period pottery
recovered. These came from only two sites: AZ EE:2:105 and AZ EE:2:76.
All pieces were too small or weathered to discern details of the
decoration so identification was based on the depth and precision of the
exterior incisions. These sherds fit the appropriate type descriptions
(Gladwin and others 1937: 189-198; Haury 1976: 214-219). The most
common tempering material in these few sherds is a mixture of crushed
schist and sand with the former dominant.

Colonial Period

Cañada Del Oro Red-on-brown

Cañada del Oro Red-on-brown was also recovered from all sites where Pioneer pottery was found. Cañada del Oro pottery may also be present at AZ EE:2:113; several sherds of unidentified Colonial period pottery were classified as Cañada del Oro Red-on-brown; although none were definitely assignable to this type. Two relatively pure deposits of Cañada del Oro phase trash and a single cremation of this phase were discovered at AZ EE:2:105.

Cañada del Oro Red-on-brown pottery has been identified principally by decoration. As stated in the stylistic model, the type has characteristics intermediate between the late Pioneer style typified by Snaketown Red-on-brown and the Colonial style typified by Rillito Red-on-brown. Attributes considered diagnostic of Cañada del Oro Red-on-brown are the use of serration on scrolls, double interlocking scrolls and lines (Fig. 4.17a, 4.22), the retention of hachure fill, and closely spaced exterior trailing lines (Fig. 4.22; Kelly 1978: 24-27). The present sample represents the third largest known collection following the collections from the Hodges Ruin (Kelly 1978) and the Hardy Site (Gregonis 1983). The following description is based primarily upon the Cañada del Oro pottery recovered from the ANAMAX-Rosemont sites; however, the Arizona State Museum type collection, the Hodges Ruin (AZ AA:12:18) type collection, and Hardy Site (AZ BB:9:14) type collection were also inspected. In the following tables and descriptions the data from these other collections are clearly segregated.

Color

Surface color varied widely in the Rosemont sample. The range is basically the same as noted by Kelly (1978: 23), varying from brown, to tan, to dark gray with common fire clouds. Still, approximately 57.1 percent of the bowl sherds and 60 percent of the jar sherds lack fire clouds on the decorated surface. The intent of the potters appears to have been to achieve a light-colored background. This is further evidenced by a significant percentage of sherds that bear a thin white or cream colored slip. This tendency parallels the same development in the Phoenix Basin that marks the change from Snaketown Red-on-buff to Gila Butte Red-on-buff. However, lightening of the background never reaches the consistency seen in the Phoenix Basin.

Shape

Vessel forms have been determined from a single vessel and 26 rim sherds. The range and frequency of vessel shapes, as determined from rim sherds is shown in Table 4.4, and the single whole vessel is shown in Figure 4.17a. Based on the rim counts, bowls outnumber jars by

Figure 4.22 Cañada del Oro Red-on-brown sherds showing decorative treatment. r-u, White-slipped variant. (c, Maximum dimension is 13.0 cm.)

Table 4.4

INVENTORY OF VESSEL SHAPES FOR CAÑADA DEL ORO
RED-ON-BROWN AS DETERMINED FROM RIM SHERDS

Vessel Shape	Count	Percent of Shape	Percent of Total
BOWLS	21		100.0
Direct Rim	(1)		(4.8)
Shallow subhemispherical	1	100.0	4.8
Flared Rim	(20)		(95.4)
Slight flare	1	5.3	4.8
Moderate flare	18	89.4	85.8
Indeterminate flare	1	5.3	4.8
JARS	5		100.0
Incurved neck	(1)		(20.0)
Slight	1	100.0	20.0
Flared neck	(4)		(80.0)
Moderate	2	50.0	40.0
Pronounced	2	50.0	40.0

( ) = Category total

a ratio of 4:1 with flare-rimmed bowls the dominant form. Of the 21
bowl rims all but 1 are from flare-rimmed bowls. The remaining one is
from a shallow, subhemispherical bowl. The sample of rims is too small
to determine the preferred bowl diameter, but estimates of orifice
diameters document a range of from 12 cm to 42 cm. Only five jar rim
sherds are present. One jar sherd is from an incurving form with an
estimated aperture diameter of 10 cm. The remaining four jar rims are
from vessels with flaring necks with estimated aperture diameters of
from 8 cm to 18 cm.

Paste

The paste is generally dense; however, Kelly (1978: 27) notes
that occasional pieces may equal the porosity of Phoenix ceramics. Some
of the Rosemont sherds are slightly porous, yet they never attain the
porosity of the Phoenix Basin types and there is little difficulty

distinguishing them from Gila Butte Red-on-buff. Paste color varies
from brown to tan to dark gray, and may grade into the surface color,
except in those pieces that have a white or cream-colored slip.

Previous descriptions have not mentioned the basic tempering
material for this pottery. Detailed study of 26 rim sherds and 59 body
sherds reveals that a large portion contain a mixture of crushed
micaceous schist and sand (Table 4.5). Crushed schist occurs as a
component of the temper in either equal or dominant proportion to the
sand in 91 percent of the pottery. Pure crushed schist temper occurs in
15.3 percent of the sherds. The Hodges, Hardy, and ASM type collections
reveal the same preference for crushed schist as the dominant tempering
material (Table 4.5).

Design

Figure 4.22 shows a synopsis of the typical decorative
characteristics as seen on the Rosemont sherds; a rollout reconstruction
of the single jar design is shown in Figure 4.17a. Generally, the
linework is slightly heavier than the later Rillito Red-on-brown while
execution is precise. Many sherds exhibit retention of the hachure-
filled designs as a holdover from the "late" Pioneer style. When
present, exterior trailing lines are closely spaced and take a variety
of patterns. The typical patterns are long, closely spaced trailing
lines, short, closely spaced trailing lines (Fig. 4.22i), and open-
hatched triangles (Fig. 4.23). Exterior trailing lines occurred on
62 percent of the bowl rim sherds.

One life form, a negatively rendered lizard, is present in the
collection (Figs. 4.22c and 4.24). The rendering is remarkably similar
to that of negative lizards on a Gila Butte Red-on-buff plate from
Snaketown (Haury 1976: 234, Fig. 12.79a), down to the body proportions
and the use of dots to layout the basic design format (Haury 1976: 235,
Fig. 12.80). This sherd best illustrates the close decorative parallels
between the Phoenix and Tucson Basins during this time.

Surface Finish

The most obvious departure of the Rosemont pottery from the
description by Kelly (1978) is that none of the Cañada del Oro pottery
has exterior scoring; this might imply that the collection was produced
late in the phase, verging upon Rillito Red-on-brown, by which time
scoring disappears completely. Greenleaf reached this same conclusion
about the Cañada del Oro Red-on-brown from the Punta de Agua sites based
upon a similar absence of exterior scoring (Greenleaf 1975: 45).
However, the retention of hachure-filled designs reminiscent of
Snaketown Red-on-brown in several examples from the Rosemont collection
(Fig. 4.22f, h, j, and l) indicates that some are early Cañada del Oro
phase, despite the lack of exterior scoring. Still, scoring of bowl and
jar exteriors does occur on Cañada del Oro Red-on-brown pottery in the
three comparative collections. It is possible that exterior scoring was

Table 4.5

FREQUENCY OF TEMPER CLASSES FOR CAÑADA DEL ORO RED-ON-BROWN FROM THE
ANAMAX-ROSEMONT, HODGES RUIN, HARDY SITE, AND ASM TYPE COLECTIONS

Temper Type	Type Collection				
	ANAMAX-Rosemont	Hodges Ruin	Hardy Site	ASM	Total
Sand and Sand with mica	5 (8.5)	16 (27.1)	36 (24.0)	1 (8.3)	58 (20.7)
Sand with schist	10 (16.9)	4 (6.8)	23 (15.3)	5 (41.7)	42 (15.0)
Sand and schist	4 (6.8)	3 (5.1)			7 (2.5)
Schist with sand	31 (52.5)	36 (61.0)			67 (23.9)
Schist	9 (15.3)		91 (60.7)	6 (50.0)	106 (37.9)
Total	59 (100)	59 (100)	150 (100)	12 (100)	280 (100)

( ) = percent

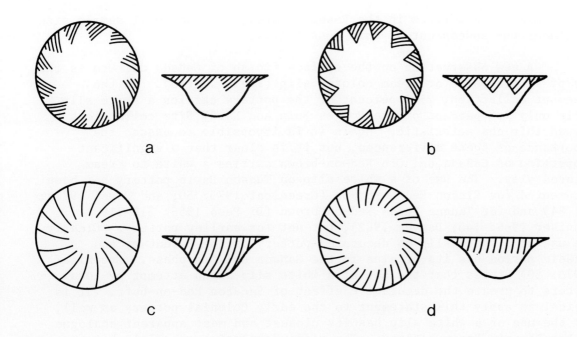

Figure 4.23 Exterior bowl design patterns noted on Cañada del Oro Red-on-brown in the ANAMAX-Rosemont and Hodges collections.

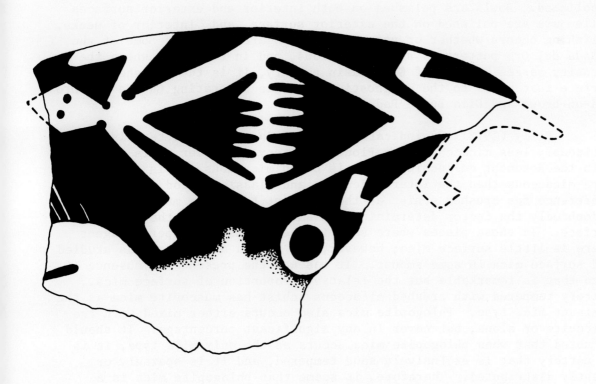

Figure 4.24 Cañada del Oro Red-on-brown life form (also shown in Fig. 4.22c).

not popular with potters in the Rosemont area, but the small sample size precludes the assessment of this possibility.

A new observation on the surface finish of Cañada del Oro is the use of a thin white or cream colored slip (Fig. 4.22r-u). In the Rosemont collection, 25.4 percent of the pottery carries a white slip while only 7.3 percent of the Hodges Ruin and Hardy Site collections showed this characteristic. Again it is impossible to assess the importance of these differences, but it is clear that a significant proportion of Cañada del Oro Red-on-brown carries a white to cream colored slip. The use of a white slip on Tucson Basin pottery has been documented for Rincon Red-on-brown (Greenleaf 1975: 50; and Doyel 1977a: 36, 84) and for Tanque Verde Red-on-brown (Di Peso 1956: 318-319; Zahniser 1966: 143; Deaver 1982), but not for earlier pottery. Clearly the use of a white slip on decorated pottery of the Sedentary and Classic period has its origins in the Cañada del Oro phase. Greenleaf (1975: 50) states that the use of a white slip is an attempt by local potters to create the decorative effect of Sacaton Red-on-buff. It is logical to apply this statement to the early Colonial pottery as well, for the use of a white slip has its closest and most apparent analogue in the Phoenix Basin pottery. The close decorative parallels between Gila Butte Red-on-buff and Cañada del Oro Red-on-brown further confirm this idea.

Vessel surfaces are usually moderately polished, although pieces exhibiting a light polish do occur. None of the examined sherds were unpolished. Bowls are polished on both interior and exterior surfaces while jars are polished on the exterior surface, and interior of necks. Polishing occurs whether or not the surfaces are slipped. Some of the Cañada del Oro pottery is slightly porous, and in the cases where the porosity verges on that of Gila Basin pottery, it is the polished surface that seems to the diagnostic attribute separating Cañada del Oro Red-on-brown and Gila Butte Red-on-buff.

Kelly (1978: 27) indicates that Cañada del Oro pottery is noticeably less micaceous than Pioneer pottery. However, this conflicts with the Rosemont collection which is often micaceous and is definitely more micaceous than the later Sedentary and Classic period pottery. The preference for crushed schist as the dominant tempering material is undoubtedly the factor determining the amount of mica on the vessel surface. In those pieces where sand is the exclusive tempering agent there is little surface mica; however, all Cañada del Oro sherds studied had surface mica in some amount. It was not the presence or absence of mica that is remarkable but the relative proportion of surface mica. Pottery tempered with crushed micaceous schist has muscovite mica as the dominant mica type. Phlogopite mica also occurs either mixed with the muscovite or alone, but never in any significant percentage. It should be noted that when phlogopite mica occurs as the only mica type, it is on pottery that is exclusively sand tempered, and it is sparsely or lightly distributed. Therefore, it seems that phlogopite mica is a natural inclusion in either the sand or the clay. Much of the sand tempered pottery also has muscovite mica; therefore it seems logical that some muscovite mica is also a natural inclusion in the sand or

clay. In fact, muscovite and phlogopite mica occur in some amount in
all the decorated pottery from all time periods in the Rosemont area,
although the use of crushed schist accounts for the abundance and
dominance of muscovite mica.

Rims

        Cañada del Oro rim finishes are generally quite simple, and the
range of rim forms is presented in Figure 4.25. Only four basic rim
finishes are present when the various related forms shown in the figure
are combined: (1) rounded (Numbers 3, 13, and 22); (2) tapered (Numbers
1, 2, and 16); (3) beveled (Numbers 6 and 7); and (4) squared (Numbers 4
and 18). Tapered (34.6%) and rounded (34.6%) rims are most common and
equally as frequent, while beveled (15.4%) and squared (15.4%) rims are
less common. Within this small sample there do not appear to be
differences between bowl and jar forms.

        Interestingly, of the 21 bowl rims none of the lips are painted
with a red line (Table 4.6). However, jar rims are painted red almost
as often as not. The presence or absence of a painted rim was recorded
for bowl and jar rim sherds in the Hodges Ruin, Hardy Site, and ASM type
collections. The results of this tabulation are also shown in Table
4.6. For these three collections 97 percent of the bowl rims lack a red
painted line, and slightly more than half of the jar rims are not
painted.

RIM FORM		BOWL	JAR	TOTALS	RIM FORM		BOWL	JAR	TOTALS
1		2	1	3	4		1	0	1
2		1	1	2	18		3	0	3
16		4	0	4	6		1	1	2
3		3	1	4	7		2	0	2
22		1	0	1					
13		3	1	4	TOTAL BOWL RIMS-21			TOTAL JAR RIMS-5	

Figure 4.25 Variety of rim forms noted on Cañada del Oro Red-on-brown
rim sherds in the ANAMAX-Rosemont collection.

Table 4.6

FREQUENCY OF CANADA DEL ORO RED-ON-BROWN RIMS WITH PAINTED LIPS FROM THE
ANAMAX-ROSEMONT, HODGES RUIN, HARDY SITE, AND ASM TYPE COLLECTIONS

Vessel Type	Lip Treatment	Type Collection									
		ANAMAX-Rosemont		Hodges Ruin		Hardy Site		ASM		Total	
		N	%	N	%	N	%	N	%	N	%
Bowls	Painted	0		1	2.5	2	5.7	0		3	2.7
	Unpainted	21	95.5	39	97.5	33	94.3	12	85.7	105	94.6
	Indeterminate	1	4.5	0		2	14.3	3	2.7
	Total	22	100.0	40	100.0	35	100.0	14	100.0	111	100.0
Jars	Painted	3	75.0	0		1	33.3	0		4	40.0
	Unpainted	1	25.0	3	100.0	2	67.7	0		6	60.0
	Indeterminate	0		0		0		0		0	
	Total	4	100.0	3	100.0	3	100.0	0		10	100.0
Total		26		43		38		14		121	

Further study indicated that Rillito Red-on-brown bowl rims were also generally unpainted, whereas Rincon Red-on-brown bowl rims were invariably painted red. Kelly noted this trait as one of the distinguishing characteristics between Rillito and Rincon Red-on-brown in a progress report to H. S. Gladwin dated May 31, 1937 (Kelly 1937: 28); however, this observation did not survive into the published report on the Hodges Ruin (Kelly 1978).

When Cañada de Oro Red-on-brown vessel rims are painted it is usually with a solid red line; however, one jar rim in the Rosemont collection and one bowl rim from the ASM type collection were decorated with ticks. The only other occurrences of this treatment were found on two Rincon Red-on-brown jar rims.

Varieties

It may be possible in the future to identify regional varieties based upon the presence, absence, or frequency of certain traits but at present the only known variety of this type is white slipped: Cañada del Oro Red-on-brown, white-slipped variety.

Remarks

Kelly (1978: 29) has pointed out the close similarities between Cañada del Oro Red-on-brown and Gila Butte Red-on-buff. It is almost impossible to distinguish between the two types by decoration alone, and the parallels are not limited to decoration and vessel shape, for this study shows that there are strong similarities in technology as well. Both pottery types are manufactured using a paddle and anvil construction technique, and both types are tempered with a crushed micaceous schist (Haury 1976: 212). Cañada del Oro phase potters seem to have attempted to achieve a light colored background, even using a white slip on the decorative surface. In almost every aspect the two types are identical. The major distinctions between the two are the use of a fine-grained brown ware clay and a polished surface finish for Cañada del Oro Red-on-brown and the use of a porous buff clay and the absence of polished surfaces for Gila Butte Red-on-buff. Doyel (1977a: 30) attributes the difference in pastes to exploitation of locally available clays; however, even given the differences in clays it is difficult to distinguish Cañada del Oro Red-on-brown from Gila Butte Red-on-buff based upon porosity and paste color. Kelly has noted that some examples of Cañada del Oro are porous, occasionally verging on the porosity of the Gila Basin examples, and this same tendency was seen on Cañada del Oro Red-on-brown in the ASM and Hardy Site type collections. Even though local clays may have been exploited, the gradation in porosity from the Tucson types into the Phoenix Basin types makes it difficult to use porosity as a distinguishing characteristic. Therefore, only the preference for polishing on Cañada del Oro Red-on-brown distinguishes it from Gila Butte Red-on-buff.

This preference for polish has been taken to suggest Mogollon affinities. Haury notes that a light stroke of the polishing tool is typical of Snaketown Red-on-buff (Haury 1976: 214), and even Kelly notes the presence of polishing on Snaketown Red-on-buff (Kelly 1978: 22), the progenitor of Cañada del Oro Red-on-brown. Therefore, rather than attribute the presence of polishing to the borrowing of the idea from the Mogollon or to a blending of Hohokam and Mogollon pottery traditions, the preference for polishing in the Rosemont examples can be explained as a continuation of an existing local tradition, which was not parallelled in the Phoenix Basin.

Rillito Red-on-Brown

Rillito Red-on-brown is clearly the technological and stylistic successor to Cañada del Oro Red-on-brown. Decoratively Rillito is the zenith of the Colonial style. Close stylistic and technological parallels are maintained with the Phoenix Basin equivalent, Santa Cruz Red-on-buff. The most obvious distinctions between Rillito Red-on-brown and Santa Cruz Red-on-buff are polished surfaces on the former and the greater use of a white-washed background on the latter. Rillito Red-on-brown was recovered from six of the Rosemont sites.

Color

Surface color shows the same variation as Cañada del Oro Red-on-brown ranging from light brown, to tan, to dark gray. Overall, though, a larger proportion of sherds display a light-colored background. While the Tucson potters never mastered control of the firing atmosphere as well as their Gila Basin neighbors, Rillito Red-on-brown represents the greatest degree of mastery among Preclassic Tucson Basin potters.

Shape

An apparently greater range in vessel shape than in the Cañada del Oro phase is due in large part to the increase in the number of Rillito vessels and rim sherds in the Rosemont collection. The range in shapes for Rillito Red-on-brown is shown in Figure 4.26, and the frequency of shapes as determined from rim sherds is listed in Table 4.7. Bowl rims outnumber jar rims by a ratio of 8:1; flare-rimmed bowls are the dominant form, comprising 92.3 percent of all bowls. Hemispherical and deep, subhemispherical shapes are also represented. Bowl rim diameters range from 12 cm to 44 cm.

Only a small number of jar rims were recovered, but they indicate that jars with flaring necks occur as well as incurved jars. The incurved shapes appear to be similar to some depicted by Kelly (1978, Fig. 4.13h, i), which she refers to as incurved bowls. A single jar with a short upcurved neck and an estimated aperture diameter of 18 cm was also found.

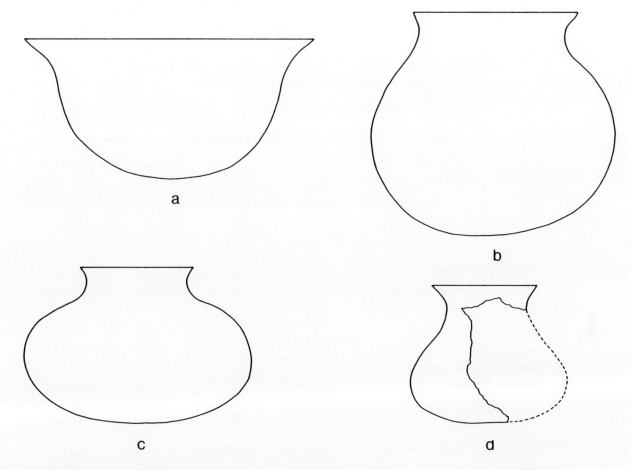

Figure 4.26   Rillito Red-on-brown vessel forms.   a, Flare-rimmed bowl;
b-d, jars.   (a, Rim diameter is 26.0 cm).

Paste

     The paste is generally fine-grained and ranges in color from an
orangish brown, to tan, to brown, to dark gray.   As with Cañada del Oro
Red-on-brown there is a preference for crushed schist as the main
tempering material, although there is a noticeable increase in the
percentage of sand-tempered examples (Table 4.8).   Schist occurs as
temper in 88 percent of the pottery, either alone or in combination with
other materials, and occurs in amounts equal to or greater than sand in
69 percent.   Sand occurs as the sole temper in approximately 12 percent
of the pottery.

Design

     Decoratively, Rillito Red-on-brown represents the climax of the
Colonial style.   The draftsmanship and intricacy of the decoration are
unsurpassed (Figs. 4.17b-d, 4.19a, 4.27, and 4.28).   The most common
feature of the decoration may be termed "simple complexity."   That is,
Rillito phase decoration exhibits the repetition of one or two
decorative units within a decorative structure to create a visually
complex design.   Dynamism is characteristic of Rillito vessels and many
Rillito decorations present the optical illusion of motion.

Table 4.7

INVENTORY OF RILLITO RED-ON-BROWN VESSEL SHAPES
AS DETERMINED FROM RIM SHERDS

Vessel Shape	Count	Percent of Shape	Percent of Total
BOWLS	65		100.0
Direct rim	(5)		(7.7)
Hemispherical	2	40.0	3.1
Deep subhemispherical	3	60.0	4.6
Flared rim	(60)		(92.3)
Slight	3	5.0	4.6
Moderate	47	78.3	72.3
Pronounced	3	5.0	4.6
Indeterminate	7	11.7	10.8
JARS	8		100.0
Incurved neck	(3)		(37.5)
Moderate	2	66.7	25.0
Slight	1	33.3	12.5
Flared neck	(4)		(50.0)
Slight	1	25.0	12.5
Moderate	2	50.0	25.0
Pronounced	1	25.0	12.5
Upcurved neck	(1)		(12.5)
Complete	1	100.0	12.5

( ) = Category total

Exterior trailing lines are still frequent, but the number of patterns in which they are used is greatly reduced from the Cañada del Oro phase. Even when there are many exterior trailing lines the general pattern is a series of parallel lines oblique to the rim around the vessel. No hatched triangles or hatched open triangles are seen. By the end of the Rillito phase the standardized pattern of trailing lines appears to be four opposing trailing lines, one at each quarter of the vessel. The paired trailing lines typical of the Rincon phase do not occur on Rillito Red-on-brown.

Table 4.8

FREQUENCY OF TEMPER TYPES FOR RILLITO RED-ON-BROWN

Temper Type	Count	Percent
Sand	1	1.4
Sand with Mica	8	10.8
Sand with Schist	14	18.9
Sand and Schist	9	12.2
Schist with Sand	42	56.8
TOTAL	74	100.1

According to Kelly (1978: 38), life forms are not as common on Tucson Basin pottery as they are for Phoenix Basin pottery. This may indeed be true, although it remains untested. Nevertheless, a wide variety of different life forms are present on the Rillito Red-on-brown from the Rosemont sites (Fig. 4.17d; 4.27n and o; and 4.29). Both avian and reptilian forms are present. Life forms occur within one of two contexts within the design, either repeated in bands (Fig. 4.29a and b) or as filler elements in the triangular areas of offset quartered designs (Fig. 4.29c-e).

Surface Finish

Exterior scoring of vessels has completely vanished from the pottery tradition by this time, but the use of a white slip continues. Twelve rim sherds (16.2%) carry a thin white to cream-colored slip. Bowls are typically slipped on the interior and exterior surfaces; jars are slipped primarily on the exterior, but the slip can be carried over onto the interior depending upon the shape of the jar. These slips are quite thin, allowing the temper particles to show through.

Most of the sherds exhibit a light to moderate polish, and only one sherd completely lacked polishing. In general the polish is as well done as on Cañada del Oro Red-on-brown, and is smoother and more consistent than on later Rincon phase pottery. Several sherds have a slightly dimpled surface resulting from the polishing. Bowls tend to be polished on both surfaces, though if only one surface is polished it is

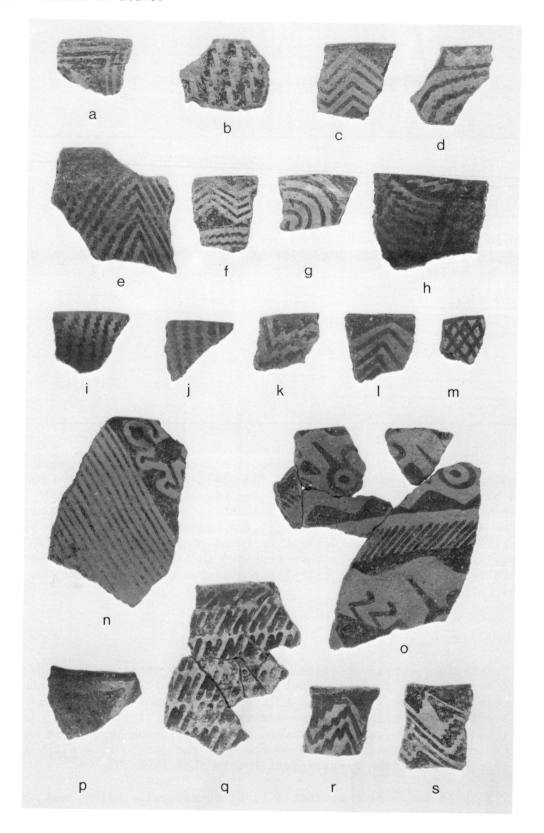

Figure 4.27   Rillito Red-on-brown rim sherds showing typical decorative treatment.   f, m, q, r, White-slipped variant.   (h, Maximum dimension is 6.0 cm.)

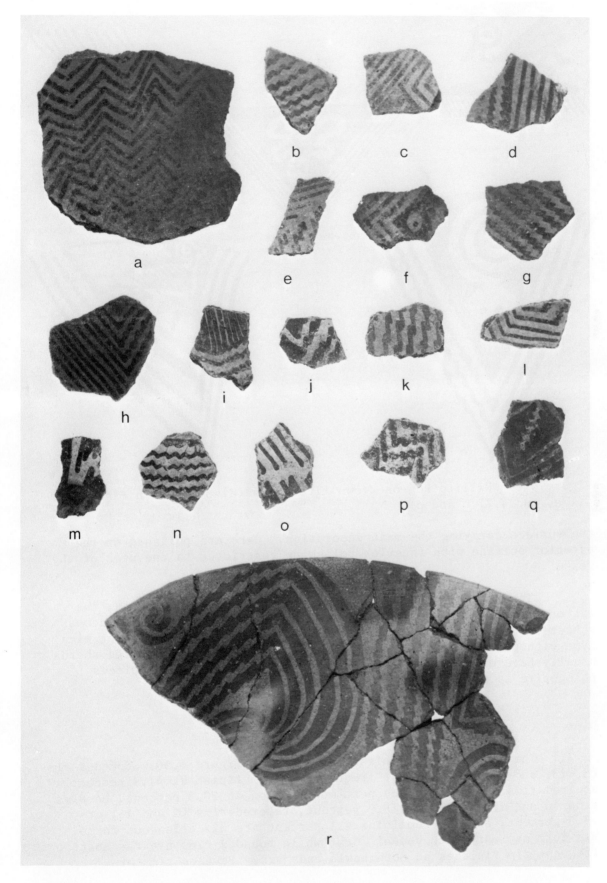

Figure 4.28   Rillito Red-on-brown body sherds showing typical decorative
treatment. p, White-slipped variant. (r, Maximum dimension is 21.0 cm.)

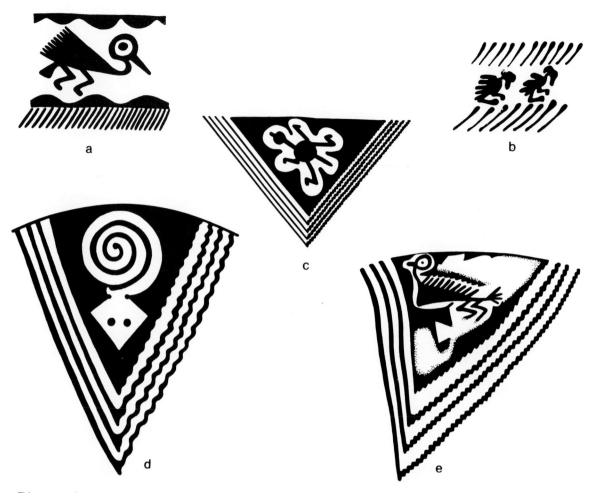

Figure 4.29 Rillito Red-on-brown life forms (also shown in Figs. 4.17d, 4.19a, and 4.27 n and o).

the surface carrying the main decoration. Jars are polished on the exterior surface with interior polishing restricted to the neck of the vessel.

The surfaces may display low to high densities of mica, the latter resulting from the continued preference for crushed micaceous schist as temper. Muscovite mica, consequently, is the dominant mica type with phlogopite occurring in minor amounts. Sand tempered sherds usually have only a light scattering of mica, and in these pieces phlogopite is more obvious.

Rims

The range of rim finishes is shown in Figure 4.30. Rounded rims (3, 13, and 22) are the most frequent form of finish at 41.9 percent, squared rims (4 and 18), the next most common at 20.3 percent, beveled rims (6 and 17) follow at 18.9 percent, tapered rims (2 and 16) at 13.5 percent, and the remaining 4.1 percent are miscellaneous forms. Rim form may vary with vessel form; while rounded rims are the most frequent rim finishes on both bowls and jars. Beveled rims are

RIM FORM		BOWL	JAR	TOTALS	RIM FORM		BOWL	JAR	TOTALS
2		2	0	2	11		0	1	1
16		7	1	8	6		9	0	9
3		14	2	16	7		5	0	5
22		7	2	9	10		1	0	1
13		6	0	6	15		2	0	2
4		4	2	6					
18		9	0	9	TOTAL BOWL RIMS-66			TOTAL JAR RIMS-8	

Figure 4.30 Variety of Rillito Red-on-brown rim forms.

noticeably more common on the former. This discrepancy can be partly attributed to the small number of jar rims recovered. An addition to the rim inventory is the thickening of the rim itself (Fig. 4.30, Form 10); this does not appear to be the result of the addition of a rim coil but the shaping of excess clay.

The preference for painting rims with a red line is more frequent than in Cañada del Oro, but is still not the dominant treatment (Table 4.9). Thirty-three percent of the bowl rims carry a red painted line. This increase in the frequency of painted bowl rims fits seriationally between the near absence of painted bowl rims for the early Colonial period and the dominance of this treatment on Sedentary period bowl rims. Rillito Red-on-brown jar rims were few in number, but were nearly evenly split between having a painted rim or not.

Varieties

At Paloparado, Di Peso identified two varieties of Rillito Red-on-brown: a micaceous variety and a nonmicaceous variety (Di Peso 1956: 355). The micaceous variety identified by Di Peso is probably equivalent to that portion of the Rosemont collection identified as schist tempered, while the nonmicaceous variety is probably equivalent to the sand tempered material. The dominance of the micaceous variety (95.9%) at Paloparado (Di Peso 1956: 355), does not precisely mirror its frequency in the Rosemont collection, but illustrates the same preferences by the potters. The distinction between schist and sand temper does not warrant varietal status, therefore these have not been retained as named varieties.

Table 4.9

FREQUENCY OF RILLITO RED-ON-BROWN RIMS
WITH PAINTED AND UNPAINTED LIPS

Lip Treatment	Bowls		Jars		Total
	N	%	N	%	
Painted	15	22.7	4	50.0	19
Unpainted	50	75.8	3	37.5	53
Indeterminate	1	1.5	1	12.5	2
Total	66	100.0	8	100.0	74

The only variety distinguished here is white slipped: Rillito Red-on-brown: white slipped variety. This material is distinguished to emphasize the continuation of the trait seen on Cañada del Oro Red-on-brown, and to emphasize the continued parallel with the Phoenix Basin pottery tradition.

Remarks

Rillito Red-on-brown represents the full crystallization of the Colonial style, and is intermediate between Cañada del Oro, and Rincon decorated pottery in attributes of technology as well as in time. Technologically Cañada del Oro and Rillito Red-on-brown are similar in the preference for crushed micaceous schist temper, occasional application of a thin white or cream colored slip, the consistent polishing of the vessel surfaces, and the dominance of unpainted bowl rims over painted bowl rims. Together Cañada del Oro and Rillito Red-on-brown contrast markedly with the later Sedentary period pottery with its sand temper, light, haphazard polishing, and the predominance of painted bowl rims. Still, there is a significant increase in the use of sand temper and painting of bowl rims in Rillito Red-on-brown that presages the change seen in the Sedentary period.

These contrasts between the Colonial and Sedentary period are also seen in aspects of vessel form and design. Flare-rimmed bowls occur for a brief period in the early Sedentary, but subhemispherical bowls, both deep and shallow, become the preferred types. In decoration Rillito and Rincon are markedly different. The distinction is not in the decorative motifs or design structure, but in a degeneration of the draftsmanship and an expansion of the scale of design. Rillito exhibits a much finer control of the linework, with an overall smallness about the decoration that contrasts with the bolder, larger, Rincon Style A. The change between these two styles seems to occur rather abruptly, but there are pieces that demonstrate the development of Rincon Style A from the Colonial style.

Rillito Red-on-brown maintains the same similarities to the Phoenix Basin exemplified in the earlier Cañada del Oro Red-on-brown pottery. In many instances, the Tucson type visually grades into its Phoenix Basin counterpart, Santa Cruz Red-on-buff. Both are tempered with a crushed micaceous schist. Santa Cruz Red-on-buff, however, tends to be a dark pinkish color (Haury 1976: 210), whereas Rillito Red-on-brown tends to be brown or orangish brown. As noted for Cañada del Oro Red-on-brown, surface polishing distinguishes Rillito Red-on-brown from Santa Cruz Red-on-buff.

Sedentary Period

In the Sedentary period there is a marked divergence from the Phoenix Basin decorated types. Beginning with the Sedentary period and continuing into the Classic period, Tucson Basin potters begin to experiment with a black as well as red paint on a variety of background field colors: white, black, brown, and red. The result of this experimentation is a virtual explosion of technological variants (Table 4.10), clearly indicating that in the Sedentary period, the Tucson Basin pottery tradition rapidly expands, a trend unparalleled in the Phoenix Basin. Contemporary with the various decorated pottery types of the Tucson Basin is Sacaton Red-on-buff, the only Phoenix Basin decorated type of the Sedentary period. This increase in the number of pottery varieties in the Sedentary period has seen limited recognition in previous studies; therefore, the following descriptions include several new types as well as new varieties. In addition to the technological variation in Rincon Red-on-brown there also appears to be a rapid change in the decorative styles. Three stylistic variants--Style A, Style B, and Style C--have been defined as a part of the decorative study and are not repeated here. They are simply treated as variants of Rincon Red-on-brown.

Rincon Red-on-Brown

The following description of Rincon Red-on-brown is based upon the collection of pottery from the Rosemont sites as summarized in Table 4.3. As a general rule, bowl-to-jar ratios and percentages of temper classes are based upon the study of rim sherds; however, in order to examine some of the changes through the Sedentary period small sample sizes were augmented by using body sherds.

Table 4.10

SYNOPSIS OF THE TUCSON BASIN PAINTED POTTERY SEQUENCE
SHOWING NAMED TYPES AND TECHNOLOGICAL VARIANTS

Period	Phase	Pottery Type	Variants
Colonial	Cañada del Oro	Cañada del Oro Red-on-brown	White-slipped
	Rillito	Rillito Red-on-brown	White-slipped
Sedentary	Rincon	Rincon Red-on-brown (Styles A, B, and C)	White-slipped Smudged Micaceous
		Rincon Black-on-brown (Styles A, B, and C)	White-slipped
		Rincon Polychrome	
		Rio Rico Polychrome	
		Sahuarita Polychrome	Red-on-brown Black-on-brown
Classic	Tanque Verde	Tanque Verde Red-on-brown	White-slipped Smudged
		Tanque Verde Black-on-brown	White-slipped Smudged
		Tanque Verde Polychrome	
		Saguaro Polychrome	

Color

Surface color ranges from orangish brown, to brown, to dark gray. Surfaces are frequently fire clouded, often obscuring the design. The predominance of fire clouding indicates a decline in control of the firing atmosphere, whether intentional or fortuitous. Smudging of bowl interiors becomes common and evidently intentional, ranging in color from a light gray to dark gray or black.

Shape

The array of shapes for Rincon Red-on-brown as known from
restorable vessels, is illustrated in Figure 4.31; the relative
frequency of each shape is given in Table 4.11. Not apparent in the
display of vessel shapes are the changes that seem to occur within the
Sedentary period. While flare-rimmed bowls still occur in low
frequency, most of the known examples seem to be from the early
Sedentary phase. In the middle Sedentary period there appears to be a
shift away from flare rimmed-bowls towards deep, subhemispherical and
hemispherical bowls. Flare-rimmed bowls comprise only 13.2 percent of
all Rincon phase bowls; deep and shallow subhemispherical bowls become
the dominant bowl form (86.8%), completely replacing flare-rimmed bowls
by the middle Sedentary. An apparently specialized shape appears by the
middle Sedentary period, seemingly developed from the flare-rimmed bowl;
this is the concave-sided, flare-rimmed bowl (Fig. 4.31g). The
cauldron, too, (Fig. 4.31i) may have its roots in the flare-rimmed bowl,
although it probably developed from the wide-mouthed jar form. A
shallow, platelike form is also represented by a single sherd.

Jar shape, too, seems to change during this period. Jars from
early Sedentary contexts clearly show their derivation from Rillito
shapes in their low rounded shoulders and gently curving necks.
However, the typical Sedentary jar forms with the sharp, angular
shoulder, short, abrupt neck, and more massive body appear with Rincon
Style B.

Bowls are still the dominant vessel form, outnumbering jars by a
ratio of 5:1 based upon rim counts. The collection of bowl rims is
large enough to document the preferred bowl sizes. Estimates of the
minimum orifice diameters (Fig. 4.32) show a clearly bimodal
distribution with one modal diameter at 25 cm to 26 cm and the other at
48 cm. Large bowls, with minimum orifice diameters greater than 40 cm,
were also present in the Colonial period pottery, but in small
quantities.

Paste

Unlike Colonial period pottery, Rincon Red-on-brown is
predominantly sand tempered (Table 4.12). Sixty-one percent of Rincon
Red-on-brown sherds are tempered exclusively with sand while the
remaining 39 percent contain a mixture of sand and schist. A comparison
of temper classes by design styles shows a shift toward sand temper
through time, that by the middle and late Sedentary, it is the only
tempering agent used (Table 4.12). It should be noted that Rincon Style
A may be produced throughout the Sedentary period. Nevertheless, by
middle Sedentary schist does not appear at all.

Figure 4.31 Rincon Red-on-brown vessel forms. a, Shallow subhemispherical bowl; b and d, deep sub-hemispherical bowls; c, hemispherical bowl; e-h, flare-rimmed bowls; i, cauldron; j-l, jars; m, bilobed jar. (m is 26.3 cm high.)

Table 4.11

INVENTORY OF RINCON RED-ON-BROWN VESSEL SHAPES
AS DETERMINED FROM RIM SHERDS

Vessel Shape	Count	Percent of Shape	Percent of Total
BOWLS	250		100.0
Direct rim	(217)		(86.8)
Hemispherical	21	9.7	8.4
Deep subhemispherical	116	53.4	46.4
Shallow subhemispherical	50	23.0	20.0
Plate	1	0.5	0.4
Indeterminate	29	13.4	11.6
Flared rim	(33)		(13.2)
Slight	1	3.0	0.4
Moderate	27	81.8	10.8
Pronounced	1	3.0	0.4
Indeterminate	4	12.1	1.6
JARS	45		99.8
Incurved neck	(4)		(8.8)
Complete	1	25.0	2.2
Moderate	2	50.0	4.4
Slight	1	25.0	2.2
Flared neck	(39)		(86.6)
Slight	5	12.8	11.1
Moderate	24	61.5	53.3
Pronounced	10	25.6	22.2
Upcurved neck	(2)		(4.4)
Complete	2	100.0	4.4

( ) = Category total

Design

    The previously described stylistic model details the changes in design seen in the Sedentary period, and will only be summarized here. Briefly, Style A is a continuation of the Colonial style with its banded designs (Figs. 4.17e, 4.18a-c, 4.19b, 4.20, 4.33, and 4.34). This style

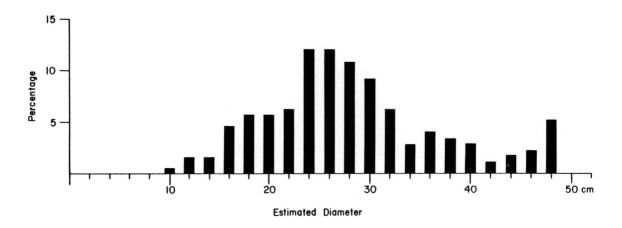

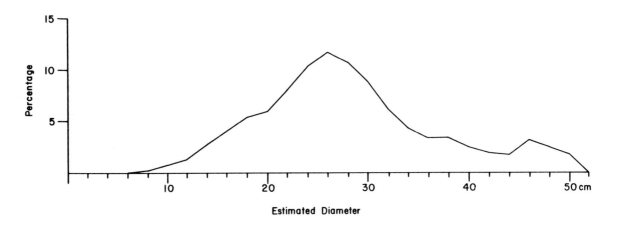

Figure 4.32 Size distribution of Rincon Red-on-brown bowls based on estimated minimum orifice diameter from rim sherds. Bar graph was constructed using raw percentages; lower graph depicts smoothed curve using the running average technique.

is characteristic of the early Sedentary though it continues to be manufactured in the middle and possibly late Sedentary periods as well. Brushwork is heavier than the Colonial style and much less precise. Style B shows a marked divergence from the banded designs, emphasizing instead a gridlike pattern using smaller geometric spaces such as rectangles, diamonds, or triangles to subdivide the decorative field (Figs. 4.18d, 4.19c, and 4.35). Brushwork becomes more refined, though it never equals that seen on Colonial pottery, and there is an improvement in the draftsmanship over Style A. Style B is also marked by the use of an overwhelming number of decorative units. While the Colonial style and Rincon Style A rely upon the repetition of one or two decorative units, Style B uses a variety of decorative units within a single design. This style is the horizon marker for the middle Sedentary period. By the late Sedentary, Style B has developed into Style C, which is similar in its basic decorative structure. What sets style C apart is a movement toward a simplification of the design and a greater incorporation of open space in the decoration (Fig. 4.35). Style C as used in this report is equivalent to the still undocumented Cortaro Red-on-brown (Kelly 1978: 47; Reinhard 1982).

Table 4.12

FREQUENCY OF TEMPER CLASSES FOR RINCON RED-ON-BROWN BY STYLE
FOR THE ANAMAX-ROSEMONT COLLECTION

Temper Type	Rincon Red-on-brown Style A		Rincon Red-on-brown Style B		Rincon Red-on-brown Style C		Rincon Red-on-brown Style ?		Total	
	N	%	N	%	N	%	N	%	N	%
Sand	3	2.7	1	7.1	7	53.8	23	14.7	34	11.6
Sand with mica	54	48.7	13	96.9	6	46.2	74	47.4	147	50.0
Sand with schist	54	48.6	0		0		57	36.5	111	37.8
Sand and schist	0		0		0		1	0.6	1	0.3
Schist with sand	0		0		0		1	0.6	1	0.3
Total	111	99.9	14	100.0	13	100.0	156	99.8	294	100.0

Figure 4.33   Rincon Red-on-brown Style A bowl sherds showing typical decorative treatment and trailing line treatments (a'-c').   (a, Maximum dimension is 11.5 cm.)

Figure 4.34 Rincon Red-on-brown Style A jar sherds showing typical decorative treatment. (c, Maximum dimension is 33.0 cm.)

Figure 4.35 Rincon Red-on-brown Style B (a-e) and Style C (f-k).
(f, Maximum dimension is 19.0 cm.)

Life forms occur on Rincon Red-on-brown bowls only, and given the number of sherds and vessels recovered, they are more rare than on Rillito Red-on-brown. Only reptilian respresentations were found, and these are shown in Figure 4.36. The location of life forms with respect to the main design appears to be less formal and consistent than for Rillito Red-on-brown. Rincon phase life forms occur as the principal unit of the design (Fig. 4.36b), as a unit at the bottom of an interior bowl design (Fig. 4.36c), and in a negative rendering at the top of triangular motifs (Fig. 4.36a). The first two examples each occur only once; however, three examples of the negative snake rendering were observed.

The use of exterior trailing lines is again emphasized in the early Sedentary (Figs. 4.33a-c and 4.37). The single trailing line is still most common, but paired and even tripled trailing lines occur frequently. Usually there are four single or paired trailing lines located at the quarters of the vessel circumference, though examples with three and five pairs are known. Treatment of the trailing lines themselves also becomes varied. The lines can be straight, squiggly, or zigzagged. This rapid expansion of the exterior trailing line patterns is short lived, and by middle Sedentary the use of trailing lines ceases.

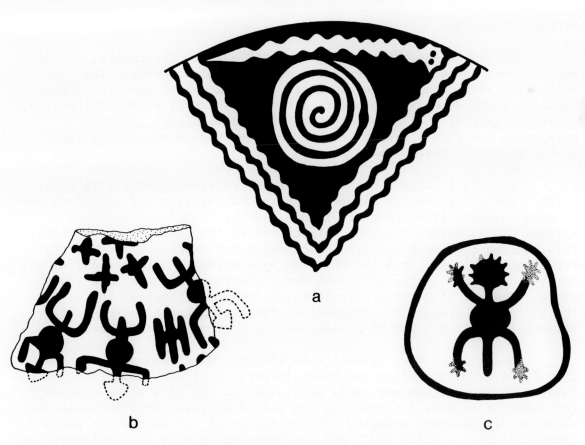

a

b

c

Figure 4.36 Rincon Red-on-brown life forms (also shown in Figs 4.19c and 4.34 t).

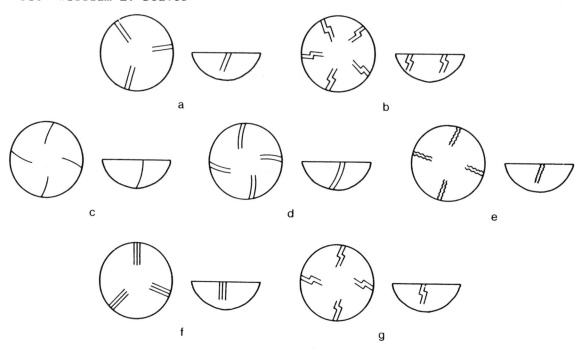

Figure 4.37 Exterior design patterns noted on Rincon Red-on-brown bowls.

Surface Finish

Rincon Red-on-brown has three basic surface treatments, all of which appear intended to alter the decorative color scheme. The decorative background can be the plain unaltered paste color (orangish brown to gray, depending upon fire clouds), can carry a thin white slip, or in the case of bowl interiors, may be smudged black. These background treatments result in red-on-brown, red-on-white, and red-on-black color schemes, respectively.

Roughly 6 percent of Rincon pottery carries a white slip (Fig. 4.38). Bowls are usually slipped on both the interior and exterior, but if only one side is slipped, it is usually the interior. Jars are slipped on the entire exterior surface and on the interior of the neck. This surface treatment was first documented for Sedentary pottery by Greenleaf (1975: 50) from the Punta de Agua sites, and Doyel (1977a: 36) further confirmed its existence in the collection from the Baca Float sites. The use of a white slip is apparently an attempt on the part of the potters to produce the decorative effect of Sacaton Red-on-buff (Greenleaf 1977: 50) and is a continuation of the Colonial practice.

Smudging of bowl interiors is slightly more common than the use of a white slip, occurring on almost 10 percent of all bowls (Fig. 4.39). While smudging obviously precludes the use of a white slip on the interior it does not preclude the use of an exterior white slip, as shown by one Rosemont example. The character of the smudge can range from dull gray to crisp black and can sometimes partly or completely obscure the design (Fig. 4.39). From the variability in the smudging it may be inferred that smudging was a new technique. Not until the late Sedentary is consistent control of the smudged background achieved.

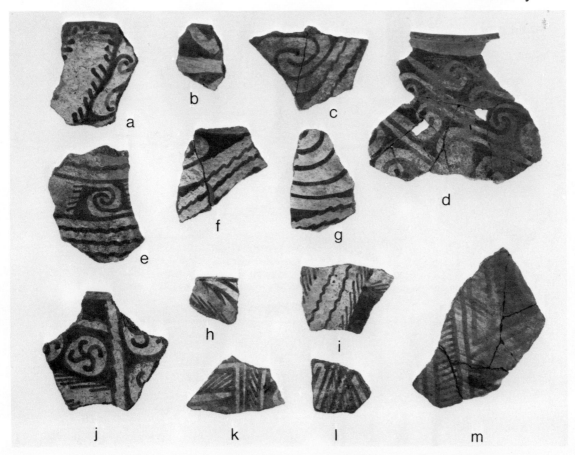

Figure 4.38 Rincon Red-on-brown, white-slipped variant. a-g, Style A;
h, Style C; i-m, Style B. (d, Maximum dimension is 13.5 cm.)

It has been suggested that smudging may be a trait borrowed from
the Mogollon, where it has been documented early in the cultural
sequence (Haury 1940: 87-90). However, in the Mogollon area smudging is
the sole interior decoration, if it is indeed intended as an aesthetic
technique, and is virtually never used with painted decoration. The
only exception to this is a rare type, Starkweather Smudged (Nesbitt
1938; Rinaldo and Bluhm 1956: 173; Chapman 1961: 216-217), and in this
case it is not the contrast between the color of the paint and the black
background that produces the decorative effect, but the contrast between
the black matte paint and a black gloss background (Chapman 1961: 217).
The use of a smudged background with a red painted design is unique to
the Tucson Basin.

Thus, smudging may be a trait copied from the Mogollon and
modified to fit the local potters whims, or may be the accidental result
of the lack of control over the firing atmosphere common in the
Sedentary period, which potters recognized and adopted as an aesthetic
treatment. There is at present no simple answer to this question.

Whether the surface is slipped, unslipped, or smudged, it is
invariably lightly polished, although Rincon phase pottery is generally
less well polished than Colonial period pottery. The most obvious shift
in the surface appearance is the decrease in the amount of mica visible.

Figure 4.39 Rincon Red-on-brown, smudged variant. a-l, Style A; m, Style B. (a, Maximum dimension is 9.0 cm.)

Generally, mica particles on Rincon phase pottery are sparse, undoubtedly due to the shift toward sand as the sole tempering material. Pieces that contain some schist tend to be more micaceous than those without schist. Due to the decrease in schist temper, there is an increase in the proportion of phlogopite mica, although muscovite mica still occurs.

Although Rincon Red-on-brown is generally less micaceous, some of this material is obviously heavily micaceous, with a resultant micaceous sheen. This variety of Rincon Red-on-brown has been noted by Greenleaf (1975: 50) and is not accidental. Unlike the earlier Colonial pottery the sheen does not result from the use of crushed micaceous schist, but instead appears to come from either selecting sand that is naturally rich in mica or by the addition of crushed mica. If the latter is the case, the potters must have used a pure mica, as no crushed rock matrix is present in the paste. This variety may be a conscious effort to duplicate the micaceousness of Colonial period pottery. Of the 21 rim sherds assigned to this variety, 12 are decorated in Rincon Style A and the remainder could not be positively identified to style, suggesting that this variety occurs primarily in the early Sedentary period.

Rims

Rim forms for Rincon Red-on-brown (Fig. 4.40) are quite simple overall. The majority, 65.2 percent, are rounded (3 and 13), 20.1 percent are squared rims (4 and 18), 7.5 percent are tapered (1, 2, and 16), 4.8 percent are beveled (7), and the remaining 2.4 percent of the rims (all bowls) have miscellaneous shaping of the excess clay.

RIM FORM		BOWL	JAR	TOTALS	RIM FORM		BOWL	JAR	TOTALS
1		1	0	1	7		11	3	14
2		6	1	7	8		1	0	1
16		7	7	14	10		2	0	2
3		78	23	101	15		2	0	2
22		24	2	26	20		1	0	1
13		58	6	64	28		1	0	1
4		17	0	17	INDETERMINATE		1	0	1
18		39	3	42	TOTAL BOWL RIMS-249			TOTAL JAR RIMS-45	

Figure 4.40   Variety of Rincon Red-on-brown rim forms.

Tapered rims occur more frequently on jars than bowls, possibly related to the use of the flared shape, but rounded rims are the most common form for both bowls and jars. Also, painting of the lip with a red line now becomes a preferred treatment. Approximately 96 percent of all Rincon Red-on-brown Style A bowl rims are painted red (Table 4.13); on Rincon Styles B and C all rims are painted red. Although this sample is small (these two styles are represented by 21 rims), it is suspected that this figure would be closely approximated in a larger sample. Rincon Red-on-brown jar rims are all painted red. Again, the number of jar rims is small, but this sample is larger than either the Cañada del Oro Red-on-brown or Rillito Red-on-brown jar rim samples, which exhibited approximately equal numbers of painted and unpainted jar rims.

Varieties

The number of varieties in the Tucson Basin pottery tradition increases dramatically in the Sedentary period. Four technological varieties and three stylistic varieties may be recognized. Since the stylistic and technological attributes can vary independently, 12 varieties have been defined. They are:

Rincon Red-on-brown: red-on-brown variety
    Style A
    Style B
    Style C

Rincon Red-on-brown: white slipped variety
    Style A
    Style B
    Style C

Rincon Red-on-brown: smudged variety
    Style A
    Style B
    Style C

Rincon Red-on-brown: micaceous variety
    Style A
    Style B
    Style C

Table 4.13

FREQUENCY OF PAINTED AND UNPAINTED LIPS ON
RINCON RED-ON-BROWN RIMS, BY STYLE

Style	Bowls			Jars			Total
	Painted	Unpainted	Indeterminate	Painted	Unpainted	Indeterminate	
A	88	4	6	12	0	1	111
B	9	0	0	4	0	1	14
C	12	0	0	1	0	0	13
?	104	6	18	20	0	7	155
Total	213	10	24	37	0	9	293

All but two of these varieties--Rincon Red-on-brown, micaceous variety, Styles B and C--were documented in the Rosemont collection. They are included, however, because this study did not conclusively show that they do not occur.

Remarks

Traditionally, it has been difficult to distinguish between Rillito and Rincon Red-on-brown (Doyel 1977a: 30). This difficulty stems from the fact that Rincon Red-on-brown develops out of Rillito Red-on-brown, so that changes between these types are gradual. These two types share many decorative motifs and design structures, at least until the appearance of the plaited and paneled designs (by the middle Sedentary period). The distinguishing characteristic between Rillito Red-on-brown and early Rincon Red-on-Brown is in the quality of the line work; Rillito Red-on-brown shows a lighter handling of line width than Rincon Red-on-brown with its sloppier, heavier treatment (Kelly 1978: 37).

This study has identified other attributes that distinguish these two types. Essentially, there appears to be an abrupt change in ceramic technology at the transition from the Colonial to the Sedentary period, with Rillito being part of the earlier Colonial tradition, and Rincon part of the later Sedentary tradition. Changes in several attributes--tempering agent, the frequency of red paint on the lips of bowl rims, the treatment of exterior trailing lines, and the preferred bowl shapes--are indicative of this shift.

The temper analysis of the decorated pottery revealed that Rillito Red-on-brown and earlier types were most often tempered with a crushed micaceous schist or a mixture of schist and sand. About 88 percent of Rillito Red-on-brown contains schist. In contrast, only 49 percent of the early Sedentary pottery contains crushed schist and by the middle and late Sedentary period schist temper is no longer used. The shift to sand temper is unparalleled in the Phoenix Basin (Haury 1976; Abbott 1984). Rincon Red-on-brown on the whole appears to have thicker vessel walls than Rillito Red-on-brown. This tendency may be due to an increase in the size of vessels, but may be attributed in part to the use of sand temper. In the plain ware collection it is apparent that schist tempered pottery is thinner than sand tempered pottery, and it may be that the shift to sand temper necessitated thicker vessel walls.

Correlating with the change in the tempering material is a change in the treatment of rims, most noticeably bowl rims. Colonial period bowl rims are almost never painted with a red line on the lip; 76 percent lack red painted lips. However, 96 percent of the early Sedentary bowl rims are painted red and by middle and late Sedentary periods all bowl rims are red painted. The treatment of jar rims is not as clear cut. Colonial period jar rims are painted red as often as not, but all Sedentary period jar rims are painted.

Another diagnostic attribute is the treatment of exterior trailing lines. Both Rillito Red-on-brown and the early Rincon material have trailing lines. However, the treatment of trailing lines is more varied on Rincon Red-on-brown than on Rillito Red-on-brown. Trailing lines are either straight, squiggle, or zigzag; and may occur either singly, paired, or tripled (Kelly 1978: 45; Greenleaf 1975: 49). Trailing lines on Rillito Red-on-brown are apparently always straight and occur singly.

The final distinction observed is the shift from the preference for flare-rimmed bowls to simpler, subhemispherical bowls. Although the sample of Rillito Red-on-brown bowl rims is small (N = 66) flare-rimmed bowls are overwhelmingly dominant (92.3%). However, flare-rimmed bowls are much less common (only 13.2%) in Rincon Red-on-brown.

Rincon Black-on-Brown (new type)

The use of a pigment which retains a blackish brown color in an oxidizing firing atmosphere appears in the Sedentary period. The use of a black pigment was first noted on Rincon Polychrome (Greenleaf 1975) and later on Rio Rico Polychrome (Doyel 1977a). Recent studies have noted the use of black paint in a bichrome color scheme, on either a brown or white-slipped background. Rincon Black-on-brown comprises 6.9 percent of all Sedentary period pottery in the Rosemont collection, and the type apparently has a wide distribution. References to this type first appear in Ervin (1982: 25-37) and in Huntington (1982: 110), where it is referred to as Rincon "Black-on-white." It has also been found at sites in the Rincon Mountains (Simpson and Wells 1983: 64), and in type collections from the Hodges Ruin, Los Morteros (AZ AA:12:57), and the Baca Float sites.

Color

The range in background color for Rincon Black-on-brown is basically the same as for Rincon Red-on-brown, though there is a greater use of white-slipped background. No smudging occurs in this type, probably bacause the black paint would be lost on a black background. However, when the surface is heavily fire clouded, it is impossible to distinguish Rincon Black-on-brown from misfired Rincon Red-on-brown. It is only on neutral or oxidized backgrounds that the black and red colors are readily separable. Only sherds that definitely carried black pigment were identified as Rincon Black-on-brown, therefore the relative proportion of this type to Rincon Red-on-brown may actually be slightly higher than that given here.

Shape

The range in vessel shapes is probably the same as for Rincon Red-on-brown, with deep, subhemispherical bowls and shouldered jars with short, flaring necks being the dominant forms. The known vessel shapes

are shown in Figure 4.41. Only one (Fig. 4.41b) is from the Rosemont
area; the others are included to show the known range for this type.

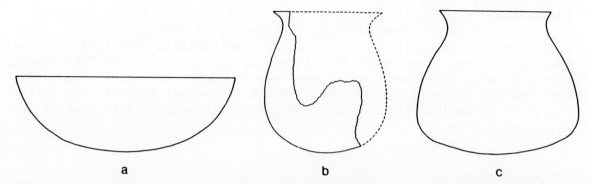

Figure 4.41   Rincon Black-on-brown vessel shapes.   c, In a private
collection. (a, Diameter is 28.0 cm.)

Paste

Paste is similar to that of Rincon Red-on-brown. The
frequencies of temper classes shown in Table 4.14 are derived from a
study of all available body sherds as well as the rims. Sand is the
preferred tempering material, although a small handful of sherds from
AZ EE:2:113, possibly from a single vessel, contained a mixture of sand
with schist.

Table 4.14

FREQUENCY OF TEMPER TYPES FOR RINCON BLACK-ON-BROWN

Temper Type	Count	Percent
Sand	13	12.6
Sand with mica	81	78.6
Sand with schist	9	8.7
Total	103	99.9

Design

Rincon Black-on-brown is decorated in Rincon Styles A, B (Fig. 4.42), and C. The pigment used on this type has not yet been identified. When first recognized as a black pigment, it was expected that it would be a manganese oxide (Shepard 1976: 40-42); however, preliminary tests indicate that it is an iron mineral. Chemical analysis of some examples of the Classic period equivalent of this type have indicated that the black pigment has a greater amount of manganese than the red paint (Brantley 1982). While the actual mineral from which the paint is derived has not been identified, it seems likely that it may be magnetite.

Surface Finish

Surfaces are usually lightly polished, and a thin white slip is applied to some 48.5 percent of this type. This percentage is nearly eight times greater than the proportion of white-slipped Rincon Red-on-brown, suggesting that this was the preferred surface treatment. Surface mica, as with Rincon Red-on-brown, is sparse, and includes both muscovite and phlogopite mica. No equivalent of the highly micaceous variety of Rincon Red-on-brown has been identified for this type.

Rims

Due to the paucity of rim sherds, little can be said about rim forms; it is expected that the range will be similar to Rincon Red-on-brown. On those rims that are known, the lip is invariably painted with a black line.

Varieties

The only observed variety of this type is the high percentage with a white slip: Rincon Black-on-brown, white-slipped variety.

Remarks

Stylistically and technologically Rincon Black-on-brown is indistinguishable from its red-on-brown counterpart, supporting the inference that this type is produced in the Tucson Basin. The only distinguishing attribute is the use of a blackish pigment.

The known geographic extent of this type mirrors that of Rincon Red-on-brown. Besides the occurrences documented by Ervin (1982), Huntington (1982), Simpson and Wells (1983), and this report, this type has been recognized in the pottery collections from the Hodges Ruin, the Punta de Agua sites, Los Morteros (AZ AA:12:57), and the Baca Float sites.

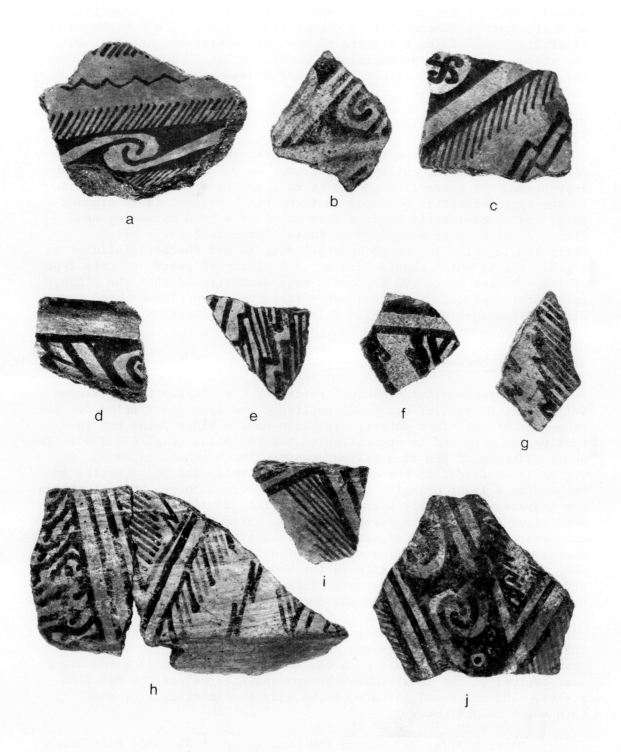

Figure 4.42   Rincon Black-on-brown sherds.   a, Style A; b-j, Style B.
b, d-h, j, White-slipped variant.   (h, Maximum dimension is 13.0 cm.)

This type is apparently associated with the middle to late Sedentary periods, as suggested by the preference for jars with the Gila shoulder and the use of sand temper. It is most commonly associated with sites where Rincon Style B occurs (Table 4.3). The few sherds from AZ EE:2:113 containing a mixture of sand and schist suggest that while the temporal range is predominantly middle to late Sedentary, the type may make its first appearance in the early Sedentary.

Rincon Polychrome

This pottery type is defined in Greenleaf (1975: 67-73). Although the Rosemont collection includes only a single sherd of Rincon Polychrome, one correction should be made to Greenleaf's description. In the type definition he noted that the black pigment is an organic paint that occasionally turns a dark brown or maroon depending upon firing conditions or secondary oxidation (Greenleaf 1975: 67). Variation in color due to secondary firing is not characteristic of an organic paint, which should burn out. Refiring of sherds of this type at temperatures up to 700 degrees C have demonstrated that the pigment is mineral, not organic. Presumably it is the same pigment used for Rincon Black-on-brown, Rio Rico Polychrome, and Sahuarita Polychrome.

Rio Rico Polychrome

Two years after Greenleaf published the description of Rincon Polychrome, Doyel (1977a: 36-40) published the type description for Rio Rico Polychrome. This pottery type also uses a black paint but in combination with and in opposition to the red paint (Fig. 4.43a-e). The small quantity of Rio Rico Polychrome from the Rosemont sites is virtually identical to the description by Doyel. The paste varies in color from a light orangish red to a tan or cream color, and all sherds are tempered exclusively with sand. Specific details about the decorative style and the design structures used for this type are unknown. Only two partial vessels of this type are in the Arizona State Museum collections; one from the Baca Float sites (Doyel 1977a, Fig. 44a) and the other from a site in the Whetstone Mountains. A paneled offset quartered design structure (like that typical of Rincon Red-on-brown Style B) is employed in the decoration of both vesels.

A small number of sherds of Rio Rico Polychrome stand out from the rest and by appearances may not be local products. These sherds have a finer textured paste of a tan to cream color and lack the orange cast typical of the local red-on-browns and the rest of the Rio Rico pieces. The color and texture of the clay is reminiscent of some Chihuahuan polychromes.

Doyel (1977a: 37) placed the time range of Rio Rico Polychrome from A.D. 850 to 1000 based upon its association with late Rillito and early Rincon material. At the Rosemont sites this pottery type is

Figure 4.43 Polychromes and unidentified decorated wares. a-e, Rio
Rico polychrome; f, Sahuarita polychrome, black-on-brown variant; g,
unidentified decorated. (c, Maximum dimension is 11.0 cm.)

predominantly associated with Rincon Styles B and C which would place it
within the middle and late Sedentary, approximately A.D. 1000 to 1200.
Only one sherd was found on a site that did not produce middle or late
Sedentary pottery. Further, the absence of Rio Rico Polychrome from
AZ EE:2:105 and AZ EE:2:113, the two largest early sites, is significant, especially in light of the occurrence of this type at sites where
decorated pottery is less abundant. It seems therefore that Rio Rico is
most popular in the middle Sedentary, or after approximately A.D. 1000.
The use of a paneled, offset quartered design structure on the two
existing partial vessels further corroborates this age estimate.

Based on evidence from other areas, the later end of the time
frame should probably be extended beyond A.D. 1000 to 1200. At
Paloparado, Di Peso identified a type he referred to as Tanque Verde-
Rincon Transition polychrome (Di Peso 1956: 334). This pottery is
stylistically intermediate between Rincon Red-on-brown and Tanque Verde
Red-on-brown but is decorated in a red and black-on-brown color scheme.
Tanque Verde Polychrome (Di Peso 1956: 319; Danson 1957: 223; Deaver
1982) is the Classic period equivalent of Rio Rico Polychrome. Given
these circumstances it seems likely that Rio Rico Polychrome is the
first in a series of polychrome pottery that develops into Tanque Verde
Polychrome and possibly even Santa Cruz and Babocomari Polychrome (Doyel
1977a: 37).

<u>Sahuarita Polychrome</u> (new type)

This new pottery type is apparently a hybrid of Rincon Polychrome and Rio Rico Polychrome and occurs only in bowl form. An exterior decoration similar to Rio Rico Polychrome is combined with the polished red-slipped interior of Rincon Polychrome or Rincon Red. The exterior decoration can occur in three varieties: a red-on-brown color scheme; a black-on-brown color scheme (Fig. 4.43f); and a red and black-on-brown polychrome color scheme, similar to Rio Rico Polychrome. Frick was the first to mention the existence of this type:

> Nine bowl sherds with red-slipped interiors and red-on-brown painted exteriors were found on sites along the river . . . The ware appears to be a local combination of the unnamed red ware [Rincon Red] and the red-on-brown wares (Frick 1954: 54).

This type has recently been observed at an as yet unrecorded site near the town of Sahuarita and at two sites within the Tucson city limits (Ervin 1982: 41; Huntington 1982: 114). At the latter sites, this pottery has been referred to as a variant of Rincon Polychrome.

Only five sherds of this type were found in the Rosemont area. The following description therefore relies upon these few sherds as well as those from the other sites previously mentioned. The small number of examples may argue against the designation of a new type, but because attributes of both Rio Rico and Rincon polychromes are incorporated, a new type name is proposed rather than refer to it as a variant of either Rincon or Rio Rico polychromes. The name is taken from the town of Sahuarita.

Color

The exterior color ranges from a brown to a reddish brown, and none of the sherds in this small sample exhibit fire clouding. The interiors are slipped a bright red, identical in color to Rincon Red and the red-slipped interiors of Rincon Polychrome.

Paste

All known sherds of this type are exclusively sand tempered. The paste ranges in color from brown to reddish brown.

Shape

This type occurs only as bowls. Two Rosemont examples are from straight-sided, shouldered bowls, possibly similar in shape to the small shouldered, flare-rimmed bowl shown in Figure 4.31g.

Design

Because of the small size of these sherds detailed assessments
of the designs are impossible, but when both red and black paint are
used together it is in an opposed, balanced fashion, like the decorative
color scheme of Rio Rico Polychrome. Stylistically the bichrome color
schemes are decorated in Rincon Style B, using a tightly packed,
geometric design structure.

Rims

The few examples of rims are invariably painted with a red line
on the red-on-brown variety and black on the other two varieties. No
definite assessment of rim forms can be presented.

Varieties

The varieties of this type correspond to each of the decorative
color schemes: Sahuarita Polychrome, red-and-black-on-brown variety;
Sahuarita Polychrome, red-on-brown variety; and Sahuarita Polychrome,
black-on-brown variety.

Remarks

The fact that this type is a hybrid of two other polychrome
types further illustrates that the Tucson Sedentary period potters were
experimenting with the ceramic technology. Again, the decorative style
seen on these pieces is identical to Rincon Red-on-brown. This contrast
between experimentation in technology and conservatism in style of
decoration is an interesting paradox. Apparently, as long as the
decorative style conformed to tradition, the color scheme rendering was
almost unlimited. It is possible to infer, from the low incidence of
this and other polychromes, they were produced for specific purposes;
however, to date, none have been found in cremations or caches.
Alternately, these types may be the product of individual experimentation, yet the geographic range of this type indicates a possibly
widespread, if infrequent production, or at least a broad exchange
network within the basin. As yet, it is impossible to assess the
significance of this or the other polychrome types.

Miscellaneous Painted Pottery

Many sherds of crude red-on-brown decorated type were recovered
from three sites at AZ EE:2:113, EE:2:105, and EE:2:76. All these
pieces are technologically crude with simple, poorly executed designs,
and are essentially identical to Plain Type I except for the presence of
crudely painted red decorations. Surface color is highly variable,
ranging from nearly black to an orangish red, with fire clouding common.
This type occurs primarily as small, usually hemispherical bowls with

rim diameters ranging from 6 cm to 27 cm. A single partial bowl of this type was found. No jar rims or large sherds were found, so it is not possible to infer anything about jar shapes.

The clay from which this pottery was made was evidently high in organic content, for the paste is consistently black. It is similar to the dark organic paste of historic Papago pottery, but the pottery contains sand as well. The sand is poorly sorted, ranging from small grains to pebbles, sometimes equal to the thickness of the sherd.

Decorative structures and design motifs are rarely discernible, but where visible, the design consists of simple geometric figures or parallel lines. The single partial vessel found appears to be decorated with human and animal figures. Both are done in simple lines as stick-figures. The human figures are arranged in a row holding hands; the animal figures are apparently quadrupeds. Exterior trailing lines are present on several examples, in one instance apparently paired. The surfaces are not smoothed or polished, and rims are usually rounded, although tapered, squared, and beveled rims also occur (Fig. 4.44). Three rims are definitely not painted red, but it is impossible to determine whether the remainder are painted or not. It is therefore impossible to determine whether the sanctions goverening rim painting on the normal red-on-brown types applied to this type.

The crude red-on-brown appears to be primarily associated with the Colonial and early Sedentary periods. The simplicity of the decoration and the crudeness of construction might suggest an earlier horizon, but the contextual information indicates otherwise. The type is absent from sites dating to the middle or late Sedentary periods. Another interpretation is that, like its plain counterpart, this type may be the handiwork of children, although its absence in later deposits may contradict this assessment. In sum it is impossible at present to assess the significance of this lot of painted pottery.

Another unusual sherd was recovered from AZ EE:2:107, a middle Sedentary period site. The sherd is from a straight-sided bowl with the remnants of a red slip on the interior. The exterior of the sherd is red-slipped and polished, but a narrow strip of the sherd was left unslipped (Fig. 4.43g). Close inspection of this piece under a

RIM FORM		BOWL	JAR	TOTALS	RIM FORM		BOWL	JAR	TOTALS
2		3	0	3	23		1	0	1
3		16	0	16	11		1	0	1
13		4	0	4	TOTAL BOWL RIMS-27			TOTAL JAR RIMS-0	
4		2	0	2					

Figure 4.44 Variety of crude red-on-brown rim forms.

binocular microscope confirms that this strip was never slipped. The
crispness of the edges indicated that the slip had been carefully
applied, possibly with a brush. After the slip was applied, both the
slipped and unslipped portions were polished.

Classic Period

Tanque Verde Red-on-brown

The low incidence of this type in the project area suggests that
the occupation ended before the Classic period fully developed. Several
sherds were found that typologically fit the description of Tanque Verde
Red-on-brown, with the characteristic use of triangular-barbed lines,
and bowls with exterior decoration. All the Tanque Verde Red-on-brown
from the Rosemont sites appears to be stylistically early. A partial
bowl, recovered from a pit house floor at AZ EE:2:106, is a deep,
subhemispherical form with exterior decorated and interior smudging.
Unfortunately, the piece had been burned, obliterating a large portion
of the design, but it clearly lacks the interior band of decoration
typical of Tanque Verde Red-on-brown. Further, that portion of the
exterior decoration still visible resembles Rincon Style C, and if it
were on the interior of a bowl, the vessel could have been assigned to
that type. Other sherds of Tanque Verde also show these early
attributes, so it seems evident that this material is stylistically
early in the Classic period.

Plain Pottery

Undecorated, unslipped pottery comprises the bulk of the
Rosemont ceramics. Analysis of this class of pottery was most difficult
because there is no accepted taxonomy for the classification of plain
pottery. Some researchers have said that plain pottery cannot be
classified and defies the typologist (Greenleaf 1975: 55; Doyel 1977a:
26). However, this assessment is biased by the traditional view that
pottery types should have value in defining chronological phases or
identifying cultural groups. This is evident in the following statement
by Kelly (1978: 69):

We have preferred not to designate the local plain ware by any
partiular name, comparable to the Gila Plain of the Gila Basin.
The series is too diverse to be included under one caption, and
differences from phase to phase are not sufficiently mapped to
justify separate type groupings.

Although the differences may not be marked from phase to phase, there
may still be distinct classes, or types, of plain ware that are
otherwise meaningful.

Despite the traditional belief that plain pottery cannot be classified, most studies have attempted to classify the plain pottery according to attributes of surface finish and temper. The ability of these studies to sort this material into groups demonstrates that patterned variation in these attributes does exist. It now seems appropriate to refine the taxonomy and its classificatory units to form categories useful for posing and answering questions about Tucson Basin prehistory. Although many studies have sorted the plain pottery into classificatory units, few have taken the additional steps necessary to define the significance or meaning of these units.

This study of the plain ware is based on the premise that it may be possible to identify temporal, regional, or functional patterns in the plain pottery. In her overview of the plain pottery from the Hodges Ruin, Kelly (1978: 74-75) notes that Colonial period plain ware is noticeably more micaceous than the preceeding Pioneer or the succeeding Sedentary period plain wares. This indicates that there may be significant variation in plain ware that correlates with time, although not at the phase level. In addition, it may be possible to record attributes of the plain ware that are relevant to the identification of patterns of regional exchange or site function. For example, the micaceous plain ware noted by Kelly (1978) for the Colonial period is essentially identical to Gila Plain (Gladwin and others 1937; Haury 1976). Franklin (1980: 102-103) and Masse (1982: 82) have suggested that its presence in areas such as the San Pedro Valley and the Papaguería is due to regional exchange with the core area, and that it is therefore an indicator of regional exchange. On the otherhand, Goodyear (1975) and Raab (1973, 1974) have interpreted the differences between Gila Plain and other plain wares as relating to different intended uses.

Thus, the goals of this study were: (1) to document observed variation in plain ware, and (2) to determine whether that variation might be indicative of temporal, regional or functional differences. First, several plain ware types were developed by defining and refining rough sorting categories. These types, of necessity, are defined using technological and formal attributes of the plain pottery. Because of the volume of plain pottery recovered only a sample was examined. This sample was designed to: (1) ensure adequate representation of each site, and (2) include sufficient rim sherds and restorable vessels for formal studies. Two samples were selected for various studies. All collections from trash-filled features, including pit houses and trash-filled extramural features, were selected to provide information about the sites themselves. Additionally, all rim sherds and restorable vessels were segregated for the technological and formal analyses.

The preliminary sort created two categories: micaceous and nonmicaceous plain ware. These categories were based on Kelly's (1978) outline of plain ware and preliminary observations of pottery from the Rosemont sites. The distinguishing criterion was the absence or presence of visible surface mica, nonmicaceous pottery lacked visible mica, whereas micaceous pottery was liberally covered with mica, resulting in a surface sheen. This approach proved to be futile, for

virtually all pottery from the Rosemont sites had some surface mica. It
became apparent that the distinction between the micaceous and
nonmicaceous groups was not simply presence or absence, but the relative
proportion of surface mica, and the presence or absence of a micaceous
sheen.

Accordingly, the original sorting categories were scrapped, and
new ones devised, although the classification was still based on the
relative amount of surface mica. By examining bags of sherds from
several sites, three distinct groups were identified: Group 1, with
little or no visible mica; Group 2, with light to moderate mica, but
lacking a micaceous sheen; and Group 3, heavily micaceous with an
obvious micaceous sheen. These groups were readily distinguished.
Later, a fourth group was created to accommodate sherds with large,
platey chunks of what appeared to be phyllite visible on the surface.
These four groups formed the foundation of the initial sort.

After completing the initial sort of the plain pottery into the
four groups above, these categories were further refined. Group 1
appeared to contain two subgroups: Group 1A which was crudely finished,
unpolished, and often had a black paste; and Group 1B which was
consistently smoothed, and lightly polished, and had a light brown to
gray colored paste. Group 3 also contained two subgroups: Group 3A,
with fine micaceous particles; and Group 3B, with large, obvious
platelets. A detailed technological study was then carried out on a
sample of sherds from each of the four main groups and the identified
subgroups.

The final step in defining the plain ware typology was
synthesizing the results of the technological analysis with observations
made during the plain ware sort, in order to develop a plain ware
typology. Four types were defined: Type I, which corresponds to Group
1A; Type II which is composed of Groups 1B and 2; Type III, which is
composed of Groups 3A and 3B; and, finally, Type IV which corresponds to
Group 4. Groups 1B and 2 were combined to form a single type because
the technological study indicated that, with the exception of the
quantity of surface mica, they were identical. Further, 1B was distinct
from Subgroup 1A in all major aspects of technology, construction, and
surface finish.

The pottery descriptions are based upon the plain ware pottery
from the ANAMAX-Rosemont Project as summarized in Table 4.15. Note that
the types have been referred to by numerical headings rather than names.
Some of these type categories correspond to existing named plain ware
types and should be considered synonyms for those type names. Although
the following type descriptions refer only to the pottery from the
excavated sites in the Rosemont area of the Santa Rita Mountains, I
believe that these types also occur at most sites in the Tucson Basin.

Table 4.15

SUMMARY OF PLAIN WARE FROM THE ANAMAX-ROSEMONT SITES

	EARLY			MIDDLE			LATE					MIXED			UNPLACED	
	AZ EE:2:105	AZ EE:2:113	AZ EE:2:84	AZ EE:2:107	AZ EE:2:109	AZ EE:2:120	AZ EE:1:104	AZ EE:2:106	AZ EE:2:116	AZ EE:2:117	AZ EE:2:122	AZ EE:2:76	AZ EE:2:77	AZ EE:2:129	AZ EE:2:52	Total
Type I	628* 4**	349 4	24	44 2	4 1	10 1	 1	7 1	5	2		134 6	30	11 2	13	1261 21
Type II	3653 1	2686 3	141	759 1	97	357	89	152	238 3	35	9	2610	774	373	6	11979 8
Type III	3527	491 2	28 1	70 1	11	34	20	19	5	5	2	540 4	154	25		4931 8
Type IV	133	3										18 1	4			158 1
Total Identified Plain wares	7941 5	3529 9	193 1	873 4	112 1	401 1	109 1	178	248 3	42	11	3302 11	962	409 2	19	18329 38
Total Eroded or Unidentified	1700	613	36	161	10	138	27	48	159	5		1225	211	75		4408
Total	9641 5	4142 9	229 1	1034 4	122 1	539 1	136 1	226	407 3	47	11	4527 11	1173	484 2	19	22737 38

* Count
** Number of restorable vessels

Type I

One small, but readily identified lot of sherds is crudely made, with coil joints and finger indentations clearly visible. It is distinct from the other defined types in almost every respect, including the clay that was used, the construction technique, and the surface finish. There is no clear equivalent to this type in previous work except possibly a crude, sand-tempered plain ware found at the Punta de Agua sites (Greenleaf 1975: 56-57). Although similar plain ware had not been reported from other locations, it is undoubtedly present in most ceramic collections.

Color

The exterior and interior color varies from an orangish red, to brown, to black, depending on fire clouding. Both interior and exterior surfaces are frequently mottled. There is no evidence that smudging was intentional.

Shape

Bowls, jars, and scoops comprise the range of vessel forms. One outstanding characteristic of this type is the predominance of bowls. Based upon rim counts, bowls outnumber jars by a ratio of two to one, the opposite of the trend observed in the other plain ware types. Another outstanding characteristic is the small vessel size. Estimated minimum orifice diameters for bowls, and aperture diameters for jars, are shown in Figure 4.45. Although the size distributions overlap with Types II and III, the Type I modal class is distinctly smaller. All but one of the complete or partial miniature vessels recovered have been assigned to this type. This has clearly affected the assessment of vessel size, but even the largest vessels of this type do not excede 24 cm in orifice diameter, placing the entire range for this type below the modes for Types II and III.

The array of vessel shapes known from restorable vessels is shown in Figure 4.46; miniature vessels are illustrated in Figure 4.47. The frequency of shapes, as determined from rim sherds, is presented in Table 4.16. Subhemispherical bowls (Fig. 4.46c and d) are the most common bowl shape, followed closely by hemispherical bowls. Shallow plates (Fig. 4.46b), and bowls with flared (Fig. 4.46e) and everted rims also occur. Observations on rim sherds suggest that jars with short, upcurved necks are most common, followed by those with flaring necks. Incurved jars (seed jars) are also common. Moderately incurved and slightly incurved (Fig. 4.46f) shapes are more common in this type than in Types II or III. Scoops (Fig. 4.46a) occur only in this type. In general, except for the greater proportion of incurved jar forms and the occurrence of scoops, there are few differences in shape frequencies between Types I, II, and III.

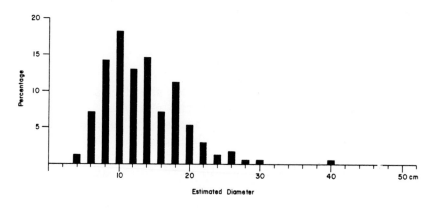

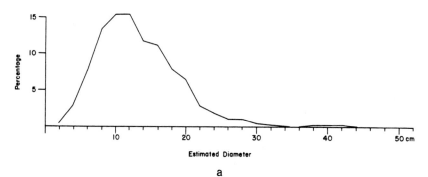

a

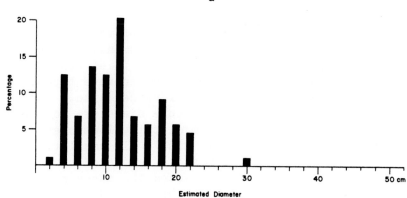

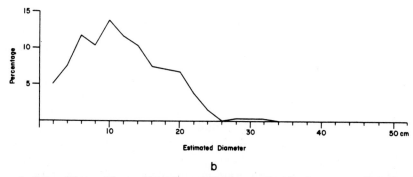

b

Figure 4.45 Size distribution of Type I plain ware bowls based on minimum orifice diameter (a) and the range of jar aperture diameters (b) as estimated from rim sherds. Bar graphs were constructed using raw percentages; the lower graphs depict smoothed curves using the running average technique.

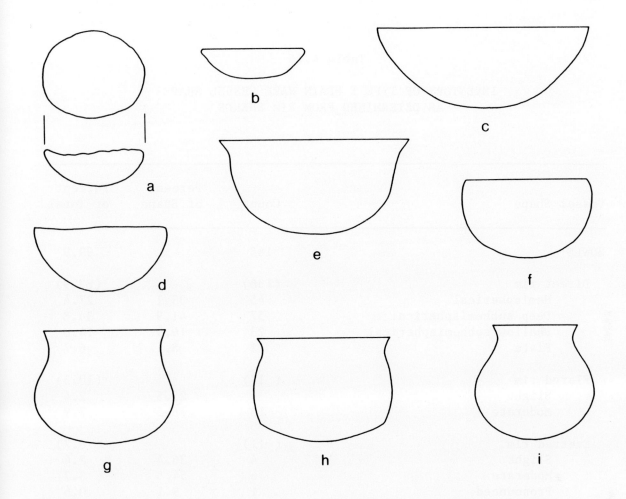

Figure 4.46   Type I plain ware vessel shapes.   a, Scoop; b, shallow plate; c and d, deep subhemispherical bowls; e, flare-rimmed bowl; f, slightly incurved jar; g-i, jars.   (c, Diameter is 23.0 cm.)

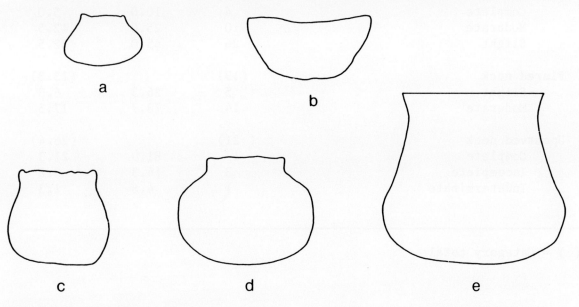

Figure 4.47   Type I plain ware minature vessels.   (e, Maximum diameter is 8.4 cm.)

Table 4.16

INVENTORY OF TYPE I PLAIN WARE VESSEL SHAPES
AS DETERMINED FROM RIM SHERDS

Vessel Shape	Count	Percent of Shape	Percent of Total
BOWLS	165		99.9
Direct rim	(136)		(82.9)
Hemispherical	45	33.1	27.4
Deep subhemispherical	57	41.9	34.8
Shallow subhemispherical	23	16.9	14.0
Plate	11	8.1	6.7
Flared rim	(17)		(10.3)
Slight	4	23.5	2.4
Moderate	13	76.5	7.9
Everted rim	(11)		(6.7)
Slight	4	36.4	2.4
Moderate	6	54.5	3.7
Pronounced	1	9.1	0.6
JARS	80		100.2
Incurved neck	(40)		(50.0)
Complete	4	10.0	5.0
Moderate	10	25.0	12.5
Slight	26	65.0	32.5
Flared neck	(19)		(23.8)
Slight	5	26.3	6.3
Moderate	14	73.7	17.5
Upcurved neck	(21)		(26.4)
Complete	17	81.0	21.3
Incomplete	3	14.3	3.8
Indeterminate	1	4.8	1.3

( ) = Category total

Paste

Apparently made from a highly organic clay, the paste color is consistently dark brown to black. All pieces contain poorly sorted sand as temper (Table 4.17), with frequent pebbles, often equaling or exceeding the thickness of the vessel wall.

Table 4.17

FREQUENCY OF TEMPER TYPES FOR TYPE I PLAIN WARE

Temper Type	Count	Percent
Sand	302	97.4
Sand with mica	8	2.6
Total	310	100.0

Surface Finish

Surfaces are generally unsmoothed and unpolished, but occasional pieces exhibit a light to moderate polish. These pieces, too, are unsmoothed and the polish is applied over the finger indentations or coil joints. Only one partial bowl and a single sherd exhibit scraping marks, yet neither of these pieces was subsequently polished.

Surface mica is sparse to nonexistent. Approximately 66 percent of the sherds have no visible surface mica and only 0.3 percent were classified as having moderate to abudandant surface mica. When mica is present it is almost invariably phlogopite, with muscovite occurring rarely.

Rims

This type exhibits a wide range of rim finishes (Fig. 4.48). In general, little care was taken in shaping the rim and most of the different finishes apparently represent a haphazard redistribution of excess clay.

RIM FORM	BOWL	JAR	TOTALS	RIM FORM	BOWL	JAR	TOTALS
1	1	0	1	11	2	0	2
2	19	4	23	6	1	0	1
16	17	6	23	7	1	6	7
3	103	30	133	8	1	2	3
22	7	1	8	10	1	2	3
24	7	5	12	15	1	0	1
13	38	19	57	20	0	1	1
4	5	7	12	27	1	0	1
18	2	1	3	14	0	1	1
23	4	6	10	INDETERMINATE	2	0	2
5	0	2	2	TOTAL BOWL RIMS-213		TOTAL JAR RIMS-93	

Figure 4.48   Variety of Type I plain ware rim forms.

Remarks

Type I can be readily distinguished from the other plain ware types by its dark paste, irregular unsmoothed surfaces, and the presence of large pebble inclusions. In some cases, the color and texture of the paste approaches the range of variability seen in Type II, but these pieces can be distinguished by their uneven surfaces. This type was consistently constructed by hand modeling or a combination of coiling and hand modeling, creating vessels significantly smaller than Types II or III. This plain ware is closely related to the unknown red-on-brown decorated type previously described, differing only in the absence of crudely painted, red designs.

Plain Type I is present in Cañada del Oro phase through late Sedentary period deposits. Although its frequency varies, it comprises a small but consistent percentage of the plain sherds. Although no obviously equivalent plain ware type is described in the existing

literature on Tucson Basin pottery, the description of a crudely made
plain ware found in Rillito and Rincon phase contexts at the Punta de
Agua sites (Greenleaf 1975: 56-57) is similar. At Paloparado (San
Cayetano de Tumacacori), Di Peso (1956: 298-305) noted that some pieces
of Paloparado Plain and Ramanote Plain were hand modeled, but it is
unclear whether these tended to be small or miniature vessels, or the
surfaces tended to be rough and undulating. Di Peso (1956: 303) notes
the presence of tool polishing on Paloparado Plain; suggesting that Type
I may be partly synonymous with the unpolished Ramanote Plain. Similiar
plain ware pottery was also recovered from the Baca Float sites near Rio
Rico, where Doyel (1977a: 26) noted some extremely crude pieces. After
inspection of the whole vessels from those sites, several were
classified as Type I, although they are generally larger than those from
the Rosemont sites.

The significance of this pottery type is not easily determined.
The manner of construction, heavy carbon content of the clay, and crude
finish set it apart from all other plain ware types. Greenleaf (1975:
57) has suggested that it may be no more than child's play. Such an
explanation could account for the differences in clay used, vessel size,
and the overall crudeness of the pottery. However, it is also possible
that it was made for a specific purpose. The fact that all but one of
the miniature vessels fall into this category, and that several
miniatures were recovered from cremation deposits suggests that some of
this pottery may have served a ritual function. On the other hand, a
good deal of this type was recovered from refuse deposits as well; so it
is unlikely that this type is strictly ritual. Another possibility is
that these small bowls and jar were simply expediently produced by hand
modeling a lump of clay rather than using a paddle and anvil technique.
The size disparity between Type I and Types II and III supports this
inference, but this does not account for the differences in the clays
used nor the lack of smoothing on vessel surfaces. It is not yet
possible to interpret the significance of this type, and all
possibilities need further evaluation.

Type II

Type II is a paddle-and-anvil constructed, sand-tempered pottery
occurring throughout the occupation of the Rosemont area from the Cañada
del Oro through late Rincon phases. Although no sites in the Rosemont
area date to the Classic period, most plain pottery from Classic period
sites in the Tucson Basin would fall within the description of this type
(Danson 1954: 230; Kelly 1978: 73-76). Sand-tempered plain ware appears
to be the most frequent plain pottery found in Tucson Basin Hohokam
sites, and has been described in most previous studies. In the Rosemont
collection, Type II is numerically the dominant plain ware in all phases
except Rillito.

As noted above, two of the initial plain ware sorting categories
(Groups 1B and 2) were combined to form Type II. Both are paddle-and-
anvil constructed, sand tempered, and well smoothed and polished. The

only discernible difference is the absence of surface mica on the
Group 1B sherds. It is probable that Group 1B represents the extreme,
nonmicaceous, end of the variation found in Type II plain ware.
Characteristics of construction technique, surface finish, and technology were given more weight than the quantity and type of surface mica.

Color

Surface color varies from orangish brown to dark gray, with dark
brown to gray most common. Fire clouding is common, and smudging may or
may not be intentional.

Shape

Only bowl and jar forms were assigned to this type; no scoops
were found. Based upon rim sherd counts, jars outnumber bowls by a
ratio of approximately three to one, the reverse of the trend seen in
Type I. The average vessel size is also larger for Type II than Type I
as shown by the frequency distribution of the estimated minimum orifice
diameters for bowls and the aperture diameters for jars (Fig. 4.49).

The known vessel shapes are illustrated in Figure 4.50, and the
relative frequency of particular forms based upon rim sherds is detailed
in Table 4.18. Bowls are most frequently either deep, subhemispherical
or hemispherical forms, although shallow, subhemispherical bowls and
plates also occur. Bowls with flared and everted rims occur rarely
(only 12 percent of the collection, combined).

Flaring-necked jars are most common, followed by those with
short upcurved necks; incurved jars also occur, though not in any
abundance. Moderate and slightly incurved shapes are less common than
in Type I.

One unusual form is the trough-shaped or elongated vessel (Fig.
4.50a) recovered from AZ EE:2:79 during the testing phase (Huckell 1980:
83). The known distribution of this shape is restricted to southern
Arizona. Similar examples are known from sites in Texas Canyon (Fulton
1934b, Plate VIII; Fulton 1938, Plate XII), Gleeson (Fulton and Tuthill
1940, Plate XIV), Tres Alamos (Tuthill 1947: 56), the Hardy Site
(Gregonis 1983), the Hodges Ruin (Kelly 1978), the Baca Float sites
(Doyel 1977a: 27), Snaketown (Haury 1976: 227), and Paloparado (Di Peso
1956, Plates 84 and 86). The examples from Snaketown have roughened
bottoms, suggesting that they may have been molcajetes (Haury 1976: 227)
but the Rosemont example lacks this feature. The known examples span
the Pioneer through Sedentary periods; however, the Rosemont specimen
cannot be reliably placed in time.

Paste

Paste color varies from reddish brown to dark gray and is rarely
uniform throughout the cross section of a sherd; however, a carbon

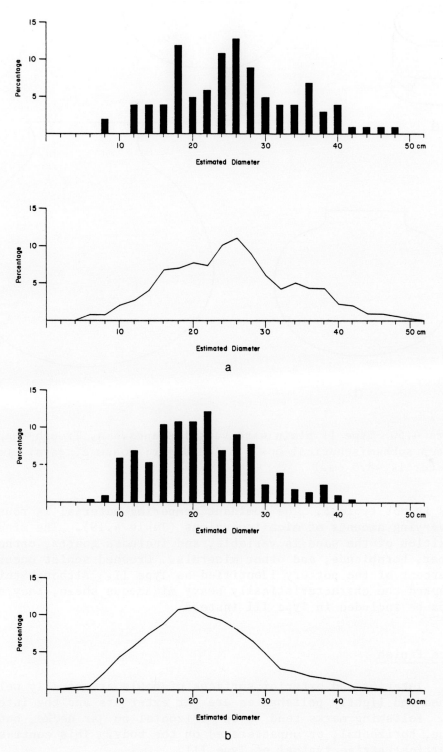

Figure 4.49 Size distribution of Type II plain ware bowls based on minimum orifice diameter (a) and the range of jar aperture diameters (b) as estimated from rim sherds. The solid bar graphs depict the raw percentages and the lower graphs depict the smoothed curves using the running averages technique.

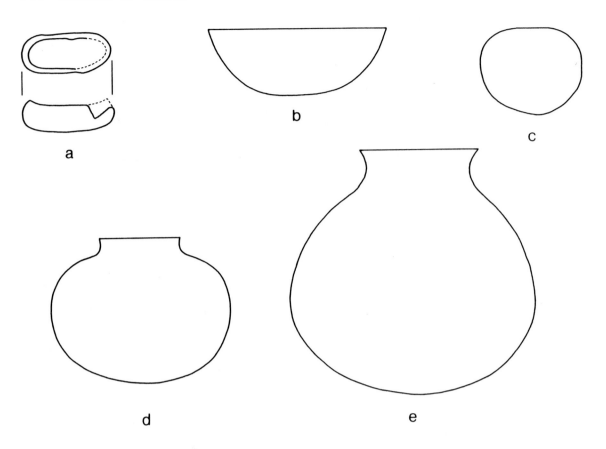

Figure 4.50 Type II plain ware vessel shapes. a, Trough-shaped vessel; b, deep subhemispherical bowl; c, seed jar; d and e, jars. (e, Maximum diameter is 48.0 cm.)

streak is not typical. The dominant tempering material is rounded sand with varying amounts of mica inclusions (Table 4.19). The mineralogical composition of the sand is variable, and includes quartz, orthoclase feldspar, hornblende, and other minerals. Crushed schist occurs in only 1.5 percent of the pottery identified as Type II. Although this small lot lacked the characteristically heavy micaceous sheen, they could perhaps be included in Type III instead.

Surface Finish

Interior and exterior surfaces of bowls are usually well smoothed and lightly polished as are jar exteriors and the interior of necks. Polishing marks tend to be horizontal on jar necks, but can be oblique, horizontal, or unpatterened on the body. This contrasts with the vertical striae typical of Type III.

The quantity of mica particles on the surface can range from none (21%) to dense (only 6%), but the majority (73%) have variable quantities of mica in the light to moderate range. Both muscovite and phlogopite mica are common. A few of the pieces with dense mica attain a micaceous sheen like that typical of Type III, but can be distinguished by the absence of crushed schist or micaceous rock as temper.

Table 4.18

INVENTORY OF TYPE II PLAIN WARE VESSEL SHAPES
AS DETERMINED FROM RIM SHERDS

Vessel Shape	Count	Percent of Shape	Percent of Total
BOWLS	100		100.0
Direct rim	(88)		(88.0)
Hemispherical	28	31.8	28.0
Deep subhemispherical	52	59.1	52.0
Shallow subhemispherical	5	5.7	5.0
Plate	2	2.3	2.0
Indeterminate	1	1.1	1.0
Flared rim	(10)		(10.0)
Slight	4	40.0	4.0
Moderate	6	60.0	6.0
Everted rim	(2)		(2.0)
Moderate	2	100.0	2.0
JARS	298		99.9
Incurved neck	(31)		(10.3)
Complete	23	74.2	7.7
Moderate	4	12.9	1.3
Slight	4	12.9	1.3
Flared neck	(172)		(57.7)
Slight	53	30.8	17.8
Moderate	118	68.6	39.6
Indeterminate	1	0.6	0.3
Upcurved neck	(95)		(31.9)
Complete	87	91.6	29.2
Incomplete	8	8.4	2.7

( ) = Category total

Table 4.19

FREQUENCY OF TEMPER TYPES FOR TYPE II PLAIN WARE

Temper Type	Count	Percent
Sand	268	45.4
Sand with mica	313	53.1
Sand with schist	7	1.2
Sand and schist	2	0.3
Total	590	100.0

Rims

The inventory of rim finishes for this type is shown in Figure 4.51. Unlike Type I, there appears to have been a greater degree of care taken in shaping the rim, although rim finish still seems casual. Rounded rims (3 and 13) are by far the most common, comprising 67.5 percent of the examples, and are followed by squared rims (4 and 18), which account for 16.4 percent. Tapered rims (1, 2, and 16) comprise only 6.3 percent of the collection, and beveled rims comprise 4.9 percent. The remaining 4.9 percent consists of miscellaneous rim finishes.

On the whole there does not appear to be significant variation in the type of rim finish by vessel form. The only appreciable difference is that squared rims are more common on bowls than jars, and conversely rounded rims are more common on jars than bowls. Miscellaneous rim finishes occur on both vessel forms.

Remarks

Type II is easily distinguishable from Type I by its smooth, even surface, and more uniform temper size; it also lacks the large pebble inclusions and dark, often black paste of Type I. Vessels are larger and the number of jars far exceeds the number of bowls, opposite the trend in Type I. Types II and III are more similar to each other than either is to Type I, especially in terms of vessel shapes and

RIM FORM		BOWL	JAR	TOTALS	RIM FORM		BOWL	JAR	TOTALS
1		2	0	2	11		0	4	4
2		0	6	6	6		1	5	6
16		7	22	29	7		8	10	18
3		49	148	197	8		1	1	2
22		15	34	49	10		0	3	3
24		0	3	3	15		4	4	8
13		35	98	133	20		0	1	1
4		7	17	34	28		0	1	1
18		29	37	66	25		0	2	2
23		1	3	4	TOTAL BOWL RIMS-159			TOTAL JAR RIMS-399	

Figure 4.51 Variety of Type II plain ware rim forms.

sizes. The primary differences between Types II and III are the tempering material and surface finish.   Type II displays rounded sand particles as temper while crushed schist or crushed micaceous rock temper gives Type III its characteristic micaceous sheen. Although Type II may also have abundant surface mica, the micaceous sheen occurs on only 6 percent. Finally, the exterior surfaces of Type III jars are given a light polishing, resulting in vertical striations; no examples of Type II exhibited this pattern.

Type II is probably the same as the Pioneer, Sedentary, and Classic period plain wares described by Kelly (1978). Because Kelly does not describe the tempering material, it is assumed that what she refers to as "nonmicaceous" plain ware is synonymous with Type II. Type II is more clearly synonymous with what Danson (1954: 230) refers to as Gila Plain, Tucson variety. He also notes that it is a local plain ware variety which can be distinguished from Gila Plain by the profusion of evenly spaced mica platelets and surface sheen on the latter (Danson 1954: 230). Although that collection is from a late Classic period site, Danson noted that it is "difficult, if not impossible to differentiate the Classic plain ware from that of the Sedentary period"

(Danson 1954: 230), and his description can, therefore, include the earlier nonmicaceous plain pottery.

Evidence from the ANAMAX-Rosemont Project indicates that the sand-tempered, nonmicaceous plain ware (Type II) should be considered a separate type, rather than a variant of Gila Plain. Type II plain ware has a longer history in the Tucson Basin than the micaceous Gila Plain, and may represent a local plain ware tradition. Micaceous plain ware appears during the Colonial period and becomes a companion type. In Cañada del Oro through late Rincon phase deposits in the Rosemont area, Gila Plain (called Type III in this study) occurs with Type II, but, except in the Rillito phase, Type II is the dominant plain ware. There is no evidence to indicate that Type II develops out of Gila Plain. Kelly (1978) notes that the plain ware of the Pioneer period is nonmicaceous, and that in the Colonial period there is a vast increase in the mica content; in the succeeding Sedentary and Classic periods there is a decrease in the micaceousness of the pottery. Thus, it appears that Type II may be the dominant, if not exclusive, plain ware pottery in the Pioneer period, and that Gila Plain becomes a companion type in the Colonial period, reaching its greatest popularity during the Rillito phase and then decreasing during the Sedentary period.

Type III

This pottery type was originally distinguished by its characteristically heavy micaceous sheen. In all attributes this type is indistinguishable from Gila Plain (Gladwin and Gladwin 1933: 26-27; Gladwin and others 1937: 174-175; Haury 1976: 223-225), and the designation "Type III" given here should be considered a synonym for Gila Plain. Other designations that have been used for this type of plain ware in the Tucson Basin include: Rillito phase micaceous plain ware (Kelly 1978: 74; Greenleaf 1975: 56); mica schist-tempered plain ware (Doyel 1977a: 27; Huckell 1978: 15); finely crushed mica schist plain ware (Gregonis 1983), micaceous plain (Deaver 1984); and, possibly, sand and mica tempered plain ware (Ervin 1982: 24). Two subtypes have been defined based upon the principal tempering agents and their effects on the surface appearance.

Color

Surface color on bowl interiors and exteriors and jar exteriors typically ranges from tan, to gray, to nearly black, but is most commonly dark brown to gray. Some jar interiors have the same slight rose-colored cast noted by Kelly (1978: 73-74).

Shape

An inventory of the typical vessel forms is shown in Figure 4.52, and the frequency of vessel shapes as determined from rim sherds

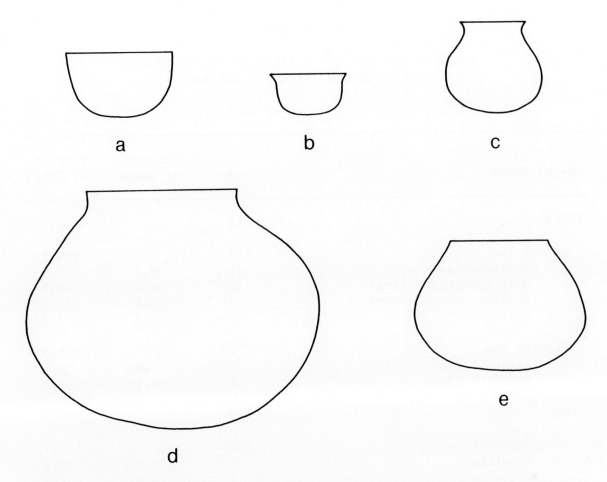

Figure 4.52 Type III plain ware vessel shapes. a, Hemispherical bowl;
b, flare-rimmed bowl; c-e, jars. (d, Maximum diameter is 45.0 cm.)

is summarized in Table 4.20. Vessel shapes and estimates of minimum
orifice (bowls) and aperture (jars) diameters for Type III (Fig. 4.53)
are quite similar to Type II. Based upon rim counts, jars outnumber
bowls by a ratio of about three to one, virtually the same as for Type
II. Also, scoops are lacking and incurved jars are infrequent.

    The deep, subhemispherical bowl is the most common shape,
followed by hemispherical bowls and shallow subhemispherical bowls.
Together hemispherical and subhemispherical bowls comprise 84.1 percent
of the bowl shapes represented. Both slightly and moderately flared
rims occur as well, and together make up the remaining 15.9 percent of
the bowls represented.

    Jars with slightly to moderately flaring necks are
overwhelmingly the typical shape, followed by those with upcurved necks.
Incurved jars comprise only a small percentage of the collection. Two
recurved rim sherds are particularly interesting and appear to be from
double-flared bowls or bilobed jars.

Table 4.20

INVENTORY OF TYPE III PLAIN WARE VESSEL SHAPES
AS DETERMINED FROM RIM SHERDS

Vessel Shape	Count	Percent of Shape	Percent of Total
BOWLS	44		100.0
Direct rim	(37)		(84.1)
Hemispherical	11	29.7	25.0
Deep subhemispherical	18	48.6	40.9
Shallow subhemispherical	7	18.9	15.9
Plate	1	2.7	2.3
Flaring rim	(7)		(15.9)
Slight flare	3	42.9	6.8
Moderate flare	4	57.1	9.1
JARS	149		100.0
Incurved neck	(10)		(6.7)
Complete	2	20.0	1.3
Moderate	7	70.0	4.7
Slight	1	10.0	0.7
Flaring neck	(96)		(64.5)
Slight	43	44.8	28.9
Moderate	52	54.2	34.9
Pronounced	1	1.0	0.7
Upcurved neck	(41)		(27.5)
Complete	38	92.7	25.5
Incomplete	3	7.3	2.0
Recurved rim	(2)		(1.3)

( ) = Category total

Paste

The color of the paste ranges from tan to dark gray and is often not uniform in a sherd cross section. This plain ware type is typically tempered with abundant, angular, mica-bearing rock sometimes in conjunction with sand (Table 4.21). The size and angularity of the particles

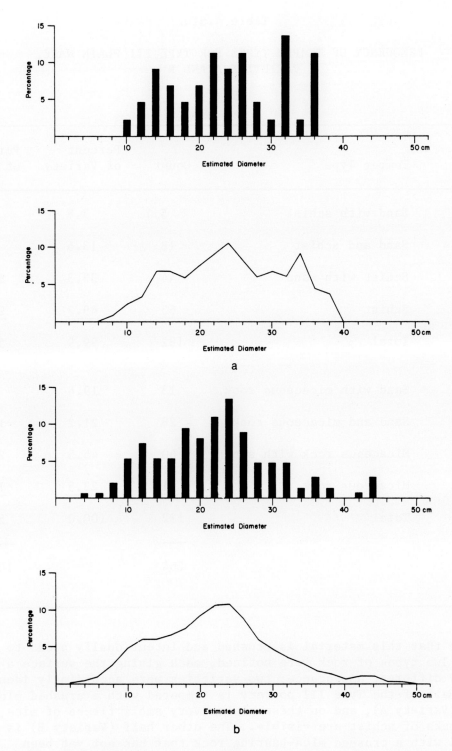

Figure 4.53 Size distribution of Type III plain ware bowls based upon minimum orifice diameter (a) and range of jar aperture diameters (b) as estimated from rim sherds. The solid bar graphs depict raw percentages and the lower graphs depict the smoothed curves produced with the running averages technique.

Table 4.21

FREQUENCY OF TEMPER TYPES FOR TYPE III PLAIN WARE,
VARIETIES A AND B

Variety	Temper Type	Count	Percent of Variety	Percent of Total
A	Sand with schist	5	3.8	1.9
	Sand and schist	18	13.6	6.8
	Schist with sand	44	33.3	16.7
	Schist	65	49.2	24.6
	Total	132	99.9	50.0
B	Sand with micaceous rock	13	19.8	4.9
	Sand and micaceous rock	28	21.2	10.6
	Micaceous rock with sand	60	45.5	22.7
	Micaceous rock	31	23.5	11.7
	Total	132	100.0	50.0
Total		264		100.0

indicate that this material is crushed and intentionally added to the paste. Two types of rock were noticed, each giving the surface a slightly different appearance; two varieties were accordingly identified. Half of the Type III pottery is tempered with a crushed micaceous schist (Variety A), and on these pieces very small flecks of mica, and many chunks of schist are visible. The other half (Variety B) is tempered with a crushed mica-bearing rock that has not yet been positively identified, but it characteristically has large chunks of quartz with large platelets of mica, and may be gneiss. Platelets of mica on the surface of sherds containing the unidentified crushed micaceous rock often range up to 1 mm in diameter, and it is easy to distinguish individual platelets. Sand also occurs frequently but is not the principle tempering material. Variety A, with schist temper, contains very little sand; however, when other micaceous rock is used (Variety B), sand is more common.

Surface Finish

The exteriors of jar bodies and the interiors of jar necks, and bowl interiors and exteriors are generally well smoothed and lightly polished. The polishing strokes on jar exteriors commonly form vertical striae which occasionally reach onto the neck of the vessel, but commonly stop at the throat. The patterning of the polishing strokes does not seem to be as consistent on bowls; however, the sample size is too small to make conclusive statements. Both the interior and exterior surfaces of bowls and jars have a micaceous sheen resulting from the use of mica bearing rocks as temper.

Rims

The various rim finishes for this type (Fig. 4.54) differ from the pattern typical of Type II. Rounded rims (3, 13, and 22) are still the most common rim finish (54.5%) followed by squared (4, 18, and 23) rims at 18.9 percent. The remaining miscellaneous rim forms account for 13.3 percent of the collection; greater than in any other pottery type. Beveled (9.1%) and tapered rims (4.2%) comprise the remainder of the rims. There are no obvious differences in rim form by vessel form, except that miscellaneous rim sherds are nearly twice as common on bowls than jars.

Remarks

Type III vessels are similar in shape, size, and frequency of distribution to Type II, but can still be distinguished from Type II by presence of crushed micaceous rock temper, the resulting micaceous sheen, and by the vertical polishing striae. Two distinct varieties of this plain ware have been identified, one with crushed schist and minute flecks of mica, the second with other crushed, mica-bearing rock and larger platelets. These two varieties have also been observed in the plain ware from the Punta de Agua sites (Greenleaf 1975: 56). Type III can be separated from Type IV not by the mineralolgy of the tempering material, but by the size of the temper particles. The potters selected larger chunks of schist for temper in Type IV, which also lacks the micaceous sheen typical of Type III.

It has been noted that Type III is identical to and synonymous with Gila Plain as defined by Gladwin and Gladwin (1933), Gladwin and others (1937), and Haury (1976). Although Masse (1982) and Franklin (1980) have indicated that Gila Plain may be present in southern Arizona as a result of trade with the Phoenix Basin, I believe that Type III was locally made. Masse (1982: 82) has projected that the trade of Gila Plain was "down the line," with the frequency decreasing with increased

RIM FORM	BOWL	JAR	TOTALS	RIM FORM	BOWL	JAR	TOTALS
1	0	1	1	8	0	1	1
2	1	3	4	10	0	8	8
16	0	5	5	15	6	2	8
3	3	35	38	20	0	2	2
22	8	23	31	21	1	0	1
24	1	0	1	27	0	1	1
13	13	47	60	12	1	0	1
4	1	10	11	19	1	1	2
18	8	24	32	14	1	2	3
23	0	1	1	25	1	5	6
6	1	5	6	TOTAL BOWL RIMS-61		TOTAL JAR RIMS-176	
7	4	10	14				

Figure 4.54 Variety of Type III plain ware rim forms.

distance from the Gila Basin. However, at the Rosemont sites Gila Plain
(Type III) has been found to comprise from to 44 to 49 percent of the
total Colonial period plain ware sherd assemblage. It seems
inconceivable that nearly half of all plain ware vessels would be
imported into the project area. These values are much too high to fit
Masse's "down the line" model, considering the location of the project
area, on the Hohokam periphery.

Interestingly, the micaceous rocks used to temper this pottery
are not available in the Santa Rita Mountains. The nearest recorded
schist outcrops occur at the southeast edge of the Rincon Mountains, on
the east flanks of the Whetstone Mountains (Arizona Bureau of Mines

1959a), and on the Tanque Verde Ridge (Arizona Bureau of Mines 1960). Presuming that the other crushed micaceous rock used as temper is indeed gneiss, the nearest sources are the Catalina, Tanque Verde, and Rincon mountains (Arizona Bureau of Mines 1960). If the Gila Plain from the Rosemont sites is indeed locally produced, the potters obtained the tempering materials outside the project area.

Type IV

The designation Type IV has been applied to material similar to what has been called Wingfield Plain (Colton 1941: 46). This type, distinguished by the presence of large, coarse chunks of crushed schistose rock as temper, is the rarest plain ware, comprising only 0.86 percent of the total plain ware assemblage and never amounting to more than 4 percent in any single deposit. Like Type III, Type IV reaches its greatest frequency during the Rillito phase. Because of the low incidence of this type it is not possible to present a detailed description.

When first observed it was suspected that this pottery was tempered with a coarsely ground phyllite. However, microscopic examination revealed that it is principally crushed micaceous schist, although phyllite and other unidentified rock fragments do occur (Table 4.22). The schist is similar, if not identical to the schist in Type III, variety A. The distinguishing characteristic is not the tempering material, but the size of the temper particles; large chunks used in Type IV, and smaller, often minute, particles selected for Type III.

Table 4.22

FREQUENCY OF TEMPER TYPES FOR TYPE IV PLAIN WARE

Temper Type	Count	Percent
Schist with sand	1	1.2
Schist	74	88.1
Phyllite	3	3.6
Other crushed rock	6	7.1
Total	84	100.0

Possibly as a consequence of the selection of the larger particles, Type IV does not attain the micaceous sheen seen on Type III.

Only six rim sherds, all from jars, were recovered. While this precludes detailed examination of rim form, rounded, squared, and beveled rims were noted (Fig. 4.55).

RIM FORM		BOWL	JAR	TOTALS	RIM FORM		BOWL	JAR	TOTALS
13		O	2	2	6		O	1	1
4		O	1	1					
18		O	2	2	TOTAL BOWL RIMS-O TOTAL JAR RIMS-6				

Figure 4.55 Variety of Type IV plain ware rim forms.

As with Type III it was assumed this type was locally produced, although the tempering material must have been imported; the low incidence of this type might suggest that it is intrusive. Unfortunately, it is not possible to further evaluate either possibility at this time.

Red Ware

The red ware from the Rosemont sites was difficult to analyze. While red ware types have been defined for the Tucson Basin and the San Pedro Valley, the descriptions are difficult to use and often overlap with one another. Therefore, instead of using a typological classification, a multivariate analysis of the red ware was conducted looking at technological aspects such as temper, slip color, slip location, polish, type and quality of surface mica, paste color, and smudging. The results of this analysis reveal that the red ware from the Rosemont area is a largely undifferentiated assemblage. It has, however, been possible to define four distinct variations based upon certain technological aspects. These are not intended as types but are referred to as Groups 1 through 4. The following description of the entire red-slipped collection is summarized in Table 4.23.

Color

Surface color varies depending on whether or not the surface is slipped and the amount of fire clouding present. Bowl interiors are

Table 4.23

DISTRIBUTION OF RED WARE BY SITE

Site Number	Red Ware Group 1	2	3	4	Total
AZ EE:1:104	6				6
AZ EE:2:76	145 (2)	1			155
AZ EE:2:77	119 (1)		3	3	125
AZ EE:2:78	64				64
AZ EE:2:79	6			1	7
AZ EE:2:80	12				12
AZ EE:2:94	11				94
AZ EE:2:105	38 (1)	1	2	7	48
AZ EE:2:106	9				9
AZ EE:2:107	44		1		45
AZ EE:2:109	18				18
AZ EE:2:113	16			5	21
AZ EE:2:116	1				1
AZ EE:2:120	17			1	18
AZ EE:2:129	1				1
Total	507	2	6	26	541

( ) = Number of restorable vessels; not included in totals

almost always slipped with a uniform red to deep maroonish red color.
Six bowl sherds exhibit interior smudging and consequently have black
interiors. The exterior color of bowls is rarely uniform, even when
slipped, and is commonly mottled from fire clouding. Exterior colors
vary from orangish red, to dark maroonish red, to yellowish brown, and
to gray.

Shape

Bowls are overwhelmingly the dominant vessel form, outnumbering
jars by a ratio of 82:1 based on rim sherd counts. All identifiable
bowl shapes are deep, subhemispherical forms (Fig. 4.14). The size and
condition of the jar sherds preclude any assessment of shape.

Paste

The paste is typically uniform in color, although some examples
show variation in color through the cross section. Color varies from
red to dark gray. Sand and sand with mica are the most common tempering
materials, although a small percentage contains both sand and crushed
schist, and two sherds contain crushed micaceous rock (Table 4.24). The
latter examples are identical to Type III plain ware with the addition
of a thin, fugitive red slip.

Table 4.24

FREQUENCY OF TEMPER TYPES FOR RED WARE

Temper Type	Bowls		Jars		Total
	N	%	N	%	
Sand	125	26.2	13	27.1	138
Sand with mica	331	69.4	33	68.7	364
Sand with schist	18	3.8	2	4.2	20
Sand and schist	1	0.2	0		1
Crushed micaceous rock	2	0.4	0		2
Total	477	100.0	48	100.0	525

Surface Finish

        Bowls are almost always slipped on the interior, the only
exception being six sherds with smudged black interiors. Exteriors of
bowls are also commonly slipped, and 86.7 percent of all bowl sherds are
slipped on both surfaces. Jars are slipped only on the exterior
surface.

        The slip is usually thin with temper particles from the
underlying paste protruding through it, but some examples have slips
thick enough to completely cover the temper particles. The hardness of
the slip and the quality of bonding to the paste varies. Some slips are
hard and well bonded, others exfoliate, and still others are well bonded
but chalky to the touch. Only the two sherds with crushed micaceous
rock temper exhibited what would be classified as a fugitive slip. Bowl
interiors and exteriors and jar exteriors are moderately to well
polished whether slipped or not. One partial bowl exhibits evidence of
patterned polishing, with striae radiating outward from the center of
the bowl.

Rims

        Rounded and squared forms are the most common rim finish (Fig.
4.56), and beveled and tapered rims are rare. A few miscellaneous rim
finishes are also present.

Remarks

        The results of the technological analysis indicates that there
are no significant divisions in the red-slipped pottery. Despite a
great deal of variation in surface treatment, temper, and slip color,
none of this variability clusters into definite categories.

        The bulk of the red-slipped pottery would fall within the
description of Rincon Red (Kelly 1978; Greenleaf 1975; Doyel 1977a:
44-46), but it also fits the description for Dragoon Red (Fulton and
Tuthill 1940: 45; Tuthill 1947: 55). It is difficult to distinguish
Rincon Red and Dragoon Red based upon the existing descriptions; both
types have interior and exterior red slips, are sand tempered, and occur
predominantly in bowl forms. The only definite difference is the
presence of iron pyrite inclusions in Dragoon Red (Fulton and Tuthill
1940: 45). Dragoon Red is associated with the Cascabel phase in the San
Pedro River Valley, which is coeval with the Rillito phase in the Tucson
Basin (Franklin 1980: 73), and would therefore be earlier than Rincon
Red, which occurs as part of the Sedentary period ceramic assemblage.
Red-slipped pottery was found in Colonial period deposits in the ANAMAX-
Rosemont Project sites, and it may be that some of these are Dragoon
Red. However, although they are temporally equivalent to Dragoon Red,

RIM FORM	BOWL	JAR	TOTALS	RIM FORM	BOWL	JAR	TOTALS
1	1	0	1	11	1	0	1
3	37	1	38	7	3	0	3
22	3	0	3	10	2	0	2
13	17	0	17	14	1	0	1
4	5	0	5	25	1	0	1
18	10	0	10	TOTAL BOWL RIMS—82		TOTAL JAR RIMS—1	
23	1	0	1				

Figure 4.56 Variety of red ware rim forms.

no iron pyrite inclusions were noted and the red-slipped pottery from the Colonial deposits is not distinct in any way from red-slipped pottery in later deposits. It would seem, therefore, that Dragoon Red and Rincon Red may be local expressions of a broader red ware tradition inspired by San Francisco Red (Fulton and Tuthill 1940: 45).

Some pieces exhibit a highly polished and somewhat dimpled surface, and are thus similar to San Francisco Red, Peppersauce variety (Masse 1979a). Many sherds exhibit exterior fire clouding and colors also similar to San Fransisco Red, Peppersauce variety. This type has been found at several sites in the middle and lower San Pedro River Valley, and occurs in the Sedentary and early Classic periods. As with Dragoon Red, it has not been possible to classify any of the sherds in the Rosemont collection as San Francisco Red, Peppersauce variety. Those pieces that exhibit a high polish and dimpled surface are not distinct in any other respect.

Even though the red-slipped pottery cannot be differentiated
into distinct types, there are some notable technological distinctions
that have been used to identify four groups of red wares. Group 1 is
the largest and is composed of the sherds which are tempered with sand
or sand and schist, have an interior or interior and exterior red slip,
and are lightly to well polished. Group 2 consists of six sherds that
possess an interior smudge and exterior red slip. It is not possible to
place all of these sherds precisely in time, but four are from Rincon
phase contexts and the other two are definitely of Preclassic age.
Smudged red wares are normally considered a component of Classic period
assemblages, and their occurrence in Preclassic contexts was
unanticipated. In all other technological aspects these six sherds are
like the bulk of the red ware and may, therefore, represent no more than
localized experiments within the red ware traditon. By the Rincon
phase, smudging becomes frequent on decorated bowls, and considering the
range of innovation and elaboration seen in Sedentary period decorated
pottery, it is quite possible that the smudged red wares are no more
than experiments.

Two other groups are worth special note. Group 3 contains two
sherds tempered with crushed micaceous rock identical in all aspects to
Type III plain ware except that these sherds bear a fugitive red slip on
the interior and exterior. Finally, Group 4 consists of 23 sherds with
a deep maroonish red slip. Similar to San Francisco Red in color, these
sherds lack the dimpled, well-polished surfaces typical of San Francisco
Red (Haury 1936: 28-31; Martin 1943: 240; Tuthill 1947: 54-55). In all
other respects they are identical to Group 1.

Although red-slipped pottery is present in Cañada del Oro
through late Rincon phase deposits in the Rosemont area, it occurs most
frequently during the middle Rincon phase, in association with Rincon
Red-on-brown, Style B. It would seem that red ware pottery is firmly
established shortly after A.D. 1000 and is a component of the expanding
pottery tradition. Its popularity is short lived, and by the late
Rincon phase it rapidly decreases in frequency.

Textured Pottery

Three sherds and a partial jar were found during the ANAMAX-
Rosemont excavations on which the sole decoration had been achieved
through texturing of the surface, either by appliqué or incision. The
jar and one of the sherds exhibited small appliquéd lumps of clay and
are probably fragments of hobnail vessels (Haury 1976: 206-210; Kelly
1978: 74). One other sherd has a rectangular piece of clay applied to
the surface, resembling the butt of a strap handle or perhaps a wing, as
on a bird effigy (Di Peso 1956). However, the piece is too small to
determine if it is indeed a piece of either a handled vessel or an
effigy pot. All pieces of pottery exhibiting appliquéd decoration are
similar to Type III plain ware in paste, being tempered with a mixture
of crushed schist and sand, and having a slight micaceous sheen. The

last sherd exhibits three parallel rows of closely spaced fingernail indentations. The physical properties of this sherd are similar to Type I plain ware with the only distinction being the occurrence of the exterior indentations.

The significance of the textured pottery is difficult to assess from this collection. The fact that only three sherds and a single partial vessel were recovered indicates that such treatments of the pottery were rare and may have been produced to serve specific uses. Hobnail vessels have been found at other Hohokam sites (Haury 1976; Kelly 1978), and seem to be typically associated with cremations. The partial jar recovered from the Rosemont excavations was found in the general vicinity of several cremations, but was not specifically associated with any of them. Other examples of hobnail vessels have been found with cremations at the Hodges Ruin (Kelly 1978: 74), and recent excavations at the West Bank sites recovered a knobbed vessel, coated with red ochre, and containing cremated bone.

A single sherd exhibits an appliquéd appendage suggestive of either a strap handle or the wing of a bird effigy, although the sherd is too small to be certain. Nevertheless, Haury (1976) illustrates examples of decorated red-on-buff pottery and plain buff pottery possessing strap handles. In the case of the Santa Cruz Buff vessels with strap handles, these are most commonly found associated with cremations (Haury 1976: 212). Bird effigy pots, although decorated, have also been recovered from Hohokam sites and may also have been produced as funerary or ceremonial objects.

The fingernail indented sherd most closely resembles Alma Punched of the Mogollon pottery tradition (Haury 1936: 39) in the manner of decoration. However, the similarity may be only superficial and except for the fingernail indentations, the sherd is identical to Type I plain ware which bears no resemblances to the Mogollon plain ware, Alma Plain (Haury 1976: 32-34).

Intrusive Pottery

Recognition of nonlocal pottery in the Rosemont area documents contact with the Phoenix Basin Hohokam, San Simon Mogollon, the Trincheras culture, and the Anasazi. It has been possible to use the intrusive pottery to document the scale of the exchange network but not as an aid for absolute dating. Nevertheless, associations of San Simon and Tincheras pottery with Tucson Basin pottery types provide additional information regarding the time(s) these types were introduced. The intrusive pottery recovered from the ANAMAX-Rosemont sites is summarized in Table 4.25.

Phoenix Basin Hohokam Types

Red-on-buff pottery was the most common intrusive ware recovered
(77.4% of all intrusives and varying from 57 to 100% of the intrusives
by site), yet it comprises only 6.9 percent of the total pottery
assemblage, in contrast to sites in the Tucson Basin proper, where it
may comprise, as at Hodges, as much as 40 percent of the decorated
pottery in some test cuts (Kelly 1978: 77). The lower frequency of buff
wares is probably due to the Rosemont area's location on the periphery
of the Tucson Basin and the Hohokam culture area.

The red-on-buff types present include Gila Butte, Santa Cruz,
and Sacaton Red-on-buffs (Figs. 4.57, 4.58, 4.59a). As mentioned in the
description of the local red-on-browns, the Pioneer period types have
been treated as local, or at least Tucson Basin, products (Kelly 1978).
Only two instances of direct association of red-on-buff vessels with
red-on-brown vessels were encountered. Sacaton Red-on-buff bowls were
associated in one instance with a Rincon Black-on-brown Style A jar and
in another case with a Rincon Red-on-brown Style B bowl. Comparing the
sherd counts by the three main periods of occupation--early (Cañada del
Oro, Rillito, and early Rincon phases), middle (middle Rincon phase),
and late (late Rincon phase)--it was found that red-on-buff pottery
occurs in all three periods. Further, Colonial period types occur only
in the early period, whereas Sacaton Red-on-buff occurs in all three
(Table 4.25). Specifically in the few stratified deposits Gila Butte
Red-on-buff was found in Cañada del Oro phase deposits, Santa Cruz Red-
on-buff was found in both Cañada del Oro and Rillito phase deposits,
and Sacaton Red-on-buff was found with Rincon Red-on-brown (Table 4.26).

San Simon Mogollon Types

In recent years there have been discussions of the relationships
between the San Simon branch of the Mogollon culture and the Dragoon
culture (Franklin 1980: 110-114; Masse 1979a: 88-89), indicating close
parallels between these cultural phenomena. Masse (1979a: 88, 1982) has
used "Dragoon culture" to refer to the cultural manifestations described
by Fulton and Tuthill in Texas Canyon and the Upper San Pedro River
Valley (Fulton 1934a, 1934b, 1938; Fulton and Tuthill 1940; Tuthill
1947) as well as those described by Sayles (1945) at San Simon Village.
At present this issue remains unsettled; however, the San Simon and
Dragoon pottery series are not identical. The San Simon Series seems to
be a regional expression of the Mogollon tradition, distinct from the
Dragoon phenomenon. There are strong stylistic relationships between
the pottery of the San Simon Valley and Mimbres Valley to support the
inference that the San Simon pottery is ultimately derived from the
Mimbres Series (Sayles 1945: 46-48; Franklin 1980: 110). The Dragoon
Series appears to be a distinct manifestation of the Mogollon tradition
which is localized in the San Pedro River Valley.

Table 4.25

SUMMARY OF INTRUSIVE POTTERY FROM THE ANAMAX-ROSEMONT SITES BY OCCUPATION PERIOD

Occupation Period	Site Number	Gila Butte Red-on-buff	Santa Cruz Red-on-buff	Sacaton Red-on-buff	Unidentified Red-on-buff	Total Red-on-buff	Dos Cabezas Red-on-brown	Galiuro Red-on-brown	Cerros Red-on-white (early)	Cerros Red-on-white	Unidentified San Simon Series	Total San Simon Series	Trincheras Purple-on-red	Nogales Polychrome	Total Trincheras	Indeterminate Black-on-white	Total Intrusive Ceramics
Early	AZ EE:2:105	28	44	9	105	186	5	5	2	2	13	27	9		9	1	223
	AZ EE:2:113		20	28[1]	96	144		36[2]	2	3	27	68	43[1]	1	44		256
	AZ EE:2:84			6	20	26											26
	Total	28	64	43	221	356	5	41	4	5	38	95	52	1	53		504
Middle	AZ EE:2:107			2	12	14					2	2					16
	AZ EE:2:120				6	6											6
	Total			2	18	20					2	2					22
Late	AZ EE:1:104			6	20	26											26
	AZ EE:2:116										2	2					2
	Total			6	20	26					2	2					28
Mixed	AZ EE:2:76 (early, middle, late)	1	31[1]	8	146	186	1	7		1	19[1]	28	3	8	11		225
	AZ EE:2:77 (early, middle)		1	11[2]	41	53		7			0[1]	7					60
	AZ EE:2:129 (middle, late)				8	8											8
	Total	1	32	19	195	247	1	14		1	19	35	3	8	11		293
Grand Total		29	96	70	454	649	6	55	4	6	54	134	55	9	64	1	848

Note: Superscript number is number of restorable vessels.
Restorable vessels not included in totals.

Figure 4.57 Phoenix Basin intrusives. a-h, Gila Butte Red-on-buff;
i-s, Santa Cruz Red-on-buff. (k, Maximum dimension is 8.5 cm.)

Figure 4.58   Phoenix Basin intrusives: Sacaton Red-on-buff.   (k, Maximum dimension is 15.0 cm.)

Figure 4.59 Restored intrusive vessels from the ANAMAX-Rosemont sites. a, Sacaton Red-on-buff; b, Trincheras Purple-on-red; c-e, Galiuro Red-on-brown; f and g, unidentified San Simon Series intrusive miniature vessels. (a-e to same scale, diameter of c is 35.5 cm; f and g are shown at larger scale. Diameter of g is 13.5 cm.)

Table 4.26

ASSOCIATION OF INTRUSIVE TYPES AND TUCSON BASIN RED-ON-BROWN TYPES
IN SPECIFIC STRATIFIED DEPOSITS

Provenience	Age of Deposit	Tucson Series			Intrusives							
		Cañada del Oro Red-on-brown	Rillito Red-on-brown	Rincon Red-on-brown*	Gila Butte Red-on-buff	Santa Cruz Red-on-buff	Sacaton Red-on-buff	Dos Cabezas Red-on-brown	Galiuro Red-on-brown	Cerros Red-on-white	Trincheras Purple-on-red	Nogales Polychrome
AZ EE:2:105-6	Cañada del Oro	7		1	4			1				
AZ EE:2:105-10	Cañada del Oro	10	2	1	1	2						
AZ EE:2:105-71200	Rillito	1	59	44		9		1		1		
AZ EE:2:105-71001	early Rincon	1	9	152		2	1		1			

* All styles

The principle pottery types of the Dragoon Series, from early to late, are: Cascabel Red-on-brown; Dragoon Red-on-brown; and Tres Alamos Red-on-brown. Dragoon pottery has been interpreted as a blending or hybridization of Mogollon and Hohokam pottery techniques and decoration (Fulton and Tuthill 1940: 58; Tuthill 1947; Masse 1982). However, others have pointed out that there is no distinguishable Hohokam influence on Cascabel Red-on-brown (Franklin 1980: 110), and that it is stylistically similar to San Lorenzo and Mogollon Red-on-brown of the Mimbres Series (Tuthill 1947: 50). Similarly, Galiuro Red-on-brown is closely allied to Mogollon Red-on-brown (Franklin 1980: 111; Masse 1982: 89). In fact, Galiuro and Cascabel Red-on-brown are stylistically identical and seem to be regional variations of Mogollon Red-on-brown with foci in the San Simon and San Pedro River valleys respectively (Franklin 1980: 55, 111). Therefore, this early horizon of the San Simon and San Pedro pottery is viewed as part of the Mogollon tradition.

Hohokam traits first clearly appear on Mogollon pottery coeval with the Sacaton phase at around A.D. 900. This suggests that Dragoon pottery, or even the Dragoon culture as presently defined, does not exist until after the appearance of Hohokam traits. Inspection of Dragoon Red-on-brown in the Arizona State Museum collections and close scrutiny of published illustrations indicate that Dragoon Red-on-brown does not represent a distinct type, but appears to be a mixture of several types. Consequently, Dragoon Red-on-brown does not represent a single pottery type, but a "catch-all" of several types (Masse 1979a, 1982). There may very well be pottery manufactured in the upper San Pedro River Valley that represents a hybridization with both Hohokam and Mogollon characteristics upon a single vessel, but the vessels illustrated as Dragoon Red-on-brown by Fulton (1934a, 1934b, 1938), Fulton and Tuthill (1940), and Tuthill (1945) seem stylistically to be either Galiuro Red-on-brown, Encinas Red-on-brown, and even Rincon Red-on-brown with few showing mixed characteristics on a single vessel.

Without further excavations in the San Simon and San Pedro River valleys it is premature to consider the San Simon Series anything other than a regional expression of the Mogollon. The strong stylistic parallels between the San Simon Series and the Mimbres Series are clearly evident for the early red-on-browns (compare Sayles 1945 with Haury 1936), the principle difference being the lack of finger-dented exteriors on San Simon pottery. It is only with the advent of Encinas Red-on-brown in the San Simon Series and Mangus Black-on-white in the Mimbres Series that the two series diverge. Further, Encinas Red-on-brown shows the first clear Hohokam influences in its use of paneled, offset-quartered and plaited bowl designs. Due to these considerations, this study does not follow Masse (1979a, 1982) who considered San Simon and Dragoon pottery traditions as one, but instead relies on Sayles' (1945) definitions and descriptions of the San Simon Series red-on-browns.

San Simon pottery is the second most frequent intrusive ware, comprising 14.9 percent of the total intrusives. The relatively high frequency may be due to the proximity of the Rosemont sites to the source of San Simon pottery; sites in the Tucson Basin proper rarely yield similarly high quantities.

San Simon pottery recovered from the Rosemont sites includes Dos Cabezas Red-on-brown, Galiuro Red-on-brown, and Cerros Red-on-white (Figs. 4.59c-g, 4.60). No Encinas Red-on-brown was identified, although some unidentified San Simon Series pottery is from contexts coeval with the manufacture of Encinas Red-on-brown. Also, all of the Cerros Red-on-white appears to be stylistically early, essentially Galiuro Red-on-brown with the addition of a white slip.

The majority of the sherds are from subhemispherical bowls, although a few jar sherds are also present. The exteriors of all bowl sherds bear the remnants of a red slip, and the decoration on both bowls and jars is consistently polished over. During the sorting and classification of decorated pottery, it was noticed that the color and consistency of the paste was sufficiently different from the Tucson Basin red-on-browns that many of the intrusive San Simon types could be sorted by these paste characteristics alone. The clay used in the intrusives fires to a light cream or tan color and the paste is soft and crumbly.

Temporally, the strongest correlation between the San Simon and Tucson Series is with the Cañada del Oro through early Rincon phases (Table 4.25). The majority of the San Simon wares (70.9%) are from the early time period and only a small percentage (3.0%) occur in the middle and late Sedentary combined. The remaining 26.1 percent is from mixed sites. The few sherds from the late time period are those that might be Encinas Red-on-brown, though they are too small to be positively identified. They do, however, bear polish over the paint, a characteristic not present on Rincon Red-on-brown. Inspection of Table 4.25 shows that Dos Cabezas Red-on-brown was recovered only from those sites that also yielded Gila Butte Red-on-buff, Cañada del Oro Red-on-brown, and Pioneer period pottery. In a similar fashion, Galiuro Red-on-brown and Cerros Red-on-white occur at sites with Santa Cruz Red-on-buff, Rillito Red-on-brown, and earlier pottery, but it also occurs at two sites lacking pottery earlier than the Rillito phase. Although this evidence is not conclusive, the occurrence of Dos Cabezas Red-on-brown seems to correlate with Gila Butte Red-on-buff and Cañada del Oro Red-on-brown, and Galiuro Red-on-brown and Cerros Red-on-white correlate similarly with Santa Cruz Red-on-buff and Rillito Red-on-brown. The data in Table 4.26 show a similar correspondence. However, one whole vessel of Galiuro Red-on-brown was found in association with a bowl of Rincon Red-on-brown, Style A, white slipped variety, suggesting that the type may persist beyond the Rillito phase. Nevertheless, this evidence suggests that the strongest temporal association of the San Simon wares is with the Colonial and early Sedentary periods.

Trincheras Types

Trincheras Purple-on-red and Nogales Polychrome have consistently been found at Hohokam sites in the Tucson Basin (Kelly 1978; Di Peso 1956; Doyel 1977a) and the Papaguería (Withers 1941; Haury and others 1950; Masse 1980a) although never in any abundance. Like the

Figure 4.60   San Simon intrusives.   a, Dos Cabezas Red-on-brown; b, Cerros Red-on-white; c, Galiuro Red-on-brown.

San Simon pottery, the Trincheras pottery appears in relatively large quantities in the Rosemont area, comprising 7.6 percent of the total intrusives and 9.1 percent of the intrusives at sites where it occurs, again perhaps as a result of the area's proximity to the Trincheras culture area. Both Trincheras Purple-on-red (Sauer and Brand 1931: 108-109; Withers 1941: 36-40; Di Peso 1956; Johnson 1960: 62-66) and Nogales Polychrome (Di Peso 1956) were recovered (Figs. 4.59b, 4.61a-h). Excavations at Potrero Creek (Grebinger 1971a), southwest of the project area recovered large quantities of Trincheras pottery, 8 percent of the total decorated with the remainder mainly Rincon Red-on-brown.

Trincheras pottery has not been well dated. Though first discovered in stratified Pioneer period deposits at Snaketown (Gladwin and others 1937: 218), later work at Ventana Cave (Haury and others 1950) demonstrated that this association was much too early and should be revised to include only the Colonial and Sedentary periods. The associations of Trincheras pottery from the Rosemont sites confirms this temporal placement, but further indicate that Trincheras Purple-on-red probably does not occur after the early Rincon phase. Inspection of Table 4.26 reveals that all Trincheras pottery is from the early or mixed period sites, and one bowl of Trincheras Purple-on-red (Fig. 4.59b) was found in a cremation associated with a Rillito Red-on-brown bowl (Fig. 4.19a).

Anasazi Types

Two white ware sherds, probably from a single vessel, were recovered at the Ballcourt Site (AZ EE:2:105), documenting trade with peoples to the north (Fig. 4.61i). These sherds are from the neck of a jar or pitcher of an unidentified Cibola white ware type.

Miscellaneous Intrusives

One sherd of a red-on-brown pottery type was recovered that could not be placed. In decoration, surface finish, and vessel form it is most similar to the Trincheras Purple-on-Red pottery, but it is decorated with rust red hematite pigment rather than the more typical purplish paint.

Discussion

Tables 4.25 and 4.26 document the association of intrusive pottery types with the Tucson Basin pottery types. This information has been used above to infer the period of manufacture or importation of the intrusive pottery. The absence of Trincheras pottery, and the decrease in frequency of San Simon pottery after the early Rincon phase may indicate that these types were no longer being manufactured, but the

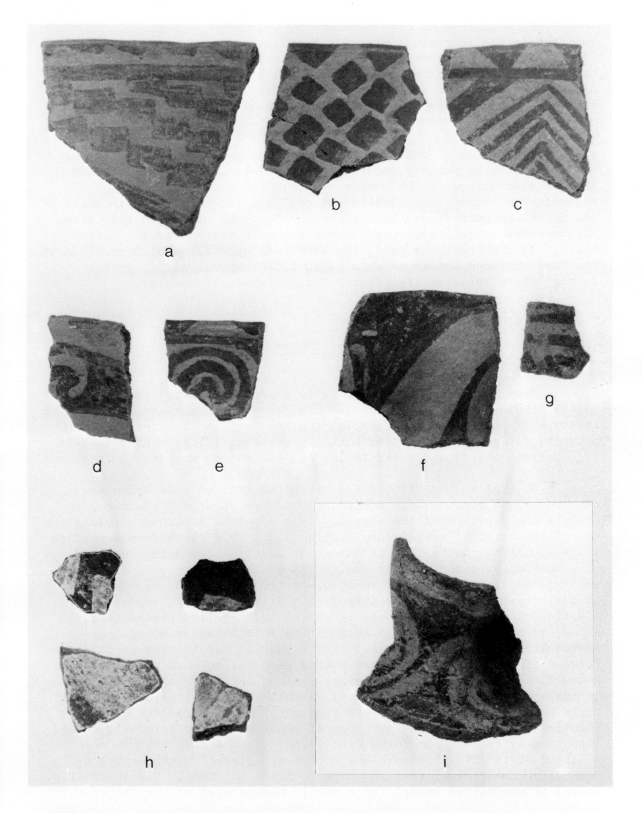

Figure 4.61 Trincheras and Anasazi intrusives. a-d, Trincheras Purple-on-red, specular paint variety; e-g, Trincheras Purple on-red, nonspecular paint variety; h, Nogales polychrome; i, unidentified black-on-white. (a, Maximum dimension is 9.0 cm.)

decrease in the intrusives may also be related to changes in the Rosemont settlement system or in the exchange network. The shift from the early to middle time periods is marked by a noticeable shift in population to new and smaller sites (Chapter 10), and accompanying this shift may be a cultural realignment or loss of the ability to acquire nonlocal items.

Finally, 50.7 percent of all San Simon pottery and 68.8 percent of all Trincheras pottery occur at a single site, AZ EE:2:113. This site is also unique in the number of human inhumations present, suggestive of strong Mogollon influence. The frequency of Trincheras and San Simon pottery may be affected by features unique to this site, and not representative of the general exchange system for the Tucson Basin. In the final analysis, the kinds and quantities of intrusives in the Rosemont area appear to be a product of temporal and geographic factors whose relative significance is difficult to specify.

Worked Sherds

Many sherds and some restorable vessels exhibited postfiring modifications. These sherds can be divided into four classes based upon the type of postfiring modification and the form of the finished product: (1) repair or refurbishment of vessels; (2) secondary vessels; (3) utilized sherds and sherd tools; and (4) shaped sherds.

Several restorable vessels exhibited drilled mend holes and cut-and-ground rims. These modifications were apparently intended to prolong the use-life of the vessel. This apparent desire to prolong the use of the original vessel form distinguishes this class from secondary vessels. Although the type of damage or imperfection being repaired may have necessitated a change in use, bowls could still be used as bowls and jars as jars. Secondary vessels, on the other hand, are large sherds or parts of vessels reshaped to a different form, and used for a different purpose. Bowls may be worked into shallow plates (Fig. 4.62a, b) or scoops; jars may be modified into bowls or scoops, or sherds of either bowls or jars, often reshaped, can be used as palettes (Fig. 4.62c-i) or scoops. These sherds need not be modified--several house floors from the Rosemont sites yielded large jar sherds in contexts suggestive of use, yet few exhibited intentional alteration of their shape. Several sherds were apparently used as palettes and are considered secondary vessels. Some of these have been carefully shaped into roughly rectangular forms (Fig. 4.62c-e), but only one has a hematite stain (Fig. 4.62d). The others are placed in this category because of their similarity in shape to stone palettes. One sherd (Fig. 4.62g) is unmodified except for a small, square area at the center which is defined by scratched lines. The remaining sherds are unmodified but are covered with thick concentrations of hematite, suggesting that they too had been used as palettes (Fig. 4.62f, h, i).

Figure 4.62 Worked sherds: secondary vessels. a and b, large sherds shaped into plates; c-e, rectangularly shaped sherds palettes; g, possible sherd palette with incised square area; f, h-i, unmodified sherds with hematite stains. (c, Maximum dimension is 18.0 cm.)

A large number of sherds exhibited no evidence of modification other than a smoothing, rounding, or beveling of an edge, probably the result of use (Fig. 4.63a, b). The edges of these sherds can be straight, concave, convex, or irregular. Another group of worked sherds has been shaped into roughly elliptical or rectangular pieces with a flange or tab (Fig. 4.63c-f). These sherds exhibit a beveling of the edge opposite the tab and appear to have been intended as scraping tools.

The final group consists of sherds which were modified to produce disks or other geometric shapes (Fig. 4.64). By far the most common form in this group is the sherd disk. The sherd disks recovered range in size from 16 mm to 123 mm. Two kinds of sherd disks were identified: perforated (21) and unperforated (23). Perforated disks were rarely found whole (14.3%), whereas the unperforated sherd disks were commonly found whole (93.9%). Although the size range of all sherd disks varied from 16 mm to 123 mm, perforated disks displayed a range of only 27 mm to 70 mm. This more restricted range might indicate that most perforated disks were intended for a single use, while the greater variability in the size of unperforated disks might indicate a number of

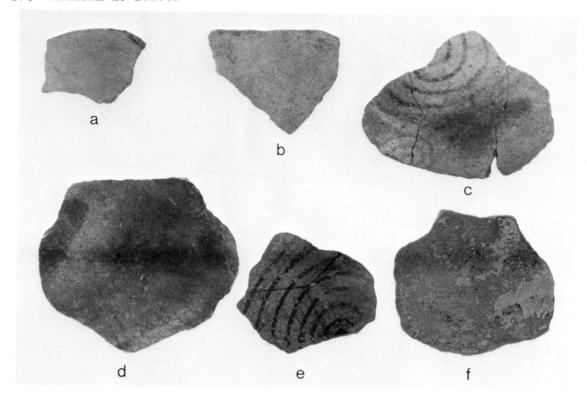

Figure 4.63 Worked sherds: tools. a and b, Use-modified edges; c-f, sherd tools with "tabs." (d, Width is 13.0 cm.)

uses. Various functional labels have been assigned to unperforated sherd disks, including practical (pot lids, gaming pieces, and small secondary vessels) and ceremonial uses. It is unlikely that any of the disks in this collection were used as pot lids. The largest disk measures only 12.3 cm in diameter, whereas the average aperture diameter for Type II and Type III plain ware jars is around 26 cm. Painted pottery jars also had average aperture diameters greater than the largest sherd disk. It is possible that some could have been used to seal small vessel openings, and the range of aperture diameters of all pottery types does overlap with the size of unperforated sherd disks. There is also some evidence of ceremonial use. Two unperforated sherd disks (Fig. 4.64w and x) were recovered together in a probable mortuary cache at AZ EE:2:76 (Feature 16002). Bundles of sherd disks, apparently offerings, were found at Winchester Cave (Fulton 1941: 24-25).

The remaining shaped sherds are a variety of geometric shapes (Fig. 4.64y-ff); several have serrated edges (Fig. 4.64hh-ii), one appears to have been scalloped (Fig. 4.64jj), and one red ware sherd was clearly used as a pendant (Fig. 4.64kk). The functions of miscellaneous geometric forms, serrated, and scalloped sherds are uncertain.

Figurines

The collection of figurines from sites in the study area is small. Only 12 ceramic items were identified as figurine fragments; of

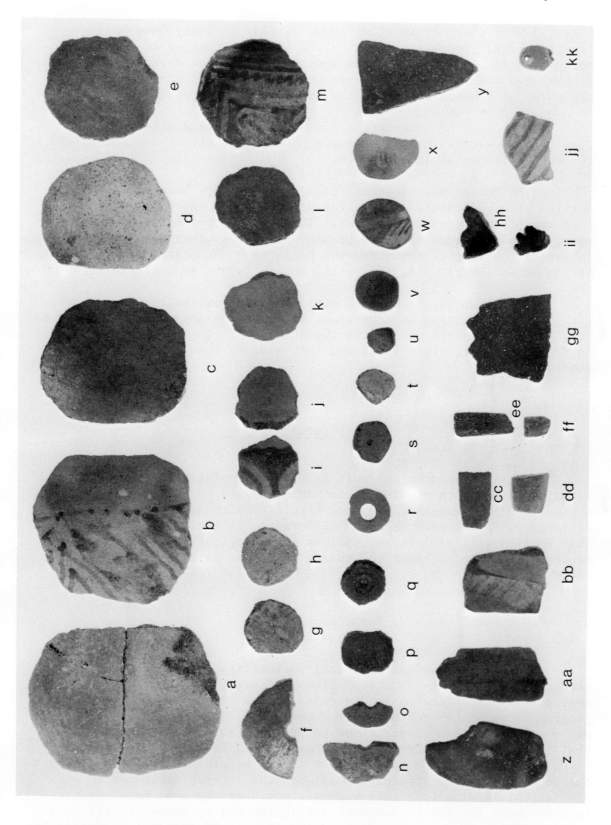

Figure 4.64   Worked sherds.   a-x, Sherd disks; u-jj, miscellaneous shapes; kk, sherd pendant.   (a, Maximum dimension is 12.0 cm.)

these, 5 were short cylindrical lumps of clay that may have been
figurine legs. One has a small hollow in the center as if it had been
molded around a twig, all others were solid. Of the seven remaining
pieces, two are fragments of quadruped figurines and one appears to be
the torso of a human figurine; the remainder (4) were unidentifiable.

All figurine fragments are made from a clay similar to the
Type I plain wares. Some pieces are untempered, others are moderately
tempered, with occasional pebbles.

The two animal figurine fragments include a head and the rear
portion of a quadruped. The latter piece has two short legs and a tail
that was probably nearly vertical. The head is complete except the
ears, which are represented by breaks, but lacks other facial features.
In general outline it resembles the heads of quadrupeds found in a cache
at Snaketown (Haury 1976, Fig. 11.6) though is not as well finished.

The human figurine (Fig. 4.65) consists of the torso and arms,
with breaks indicating attachment of the head and legs. The arms are no
more than small protrusions from the shoulders. The torso is decorated
on the left front, right back, and left side by rows of crescentic
punctations.

Pottery Variability

Having presented the results of the typological, technological,
formal, and rim form studies it is now necessary to attempt to determine
whether the patterns in these data result from changes through time,
differences in intended uses, or differences in region of manufacture.
This section will explore the various technological and formal aspects
of the pottery and attempt to explain patterned variation in terms of
these factors.

Temporal Variation

In order to define patterned variability that correlates with
time, it is important to control other potential causes of variation,
most notably those due to the intended use of the vessel, or to the
geographic region where the pottery was made. Abbott (1984) has pointed
out yet another form of variation referred to as residual variation;
that is, variability that cannot be attributed to changes in either
time, geography, or function. While it may be statistically factored
out to eliminate the effects it has upon the interpretation of
statistical information, this approach could not be used here because
in many cases the entire Rosemont collection had to be considered as a
single sample. However, at this scale of analysis residual variation is
not believed to create a significant problem.

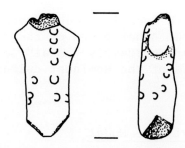

Figure 4.65 Human torso figurine fragment showing pattern of crescentic
punctations. (Height is 2.9 cm.)

It has been possible in most cases to control for functional
variation. Function can be viewed at either the site or vessel level.
The function of sites in the broader settlement and subsistence system
should dictate the range of activities that were performed at the site
and, consequently, structure the resulting artifact assemblage. At
present, it is assumed that the Rosemont sites which procuced this
collection of pottery are functionally the same; that is, they are all
primarily habitation sites. The results of Phillips' settlement pattern
study (Chapter 9) indicate that site location may be directly related to
farming activities, further supporting the assumption of functional
uniformity. Therefore, variability among site assemblages should not be
caused by differing site function.

Just as site function will determine the nature of the artifact
assemblage, the intended use of a ceramic container will affect the
technological and formal aspects of that vessel. Function includes not
only the intended menial use of a vessel, but ritual and economic uses
as well (Crown 1984a). This study focused on the menial use of vessels;
ritual and economic uses, and their effects on pottery are matters for
further study. Eight gross classes were used to describe intended
vessel use. Clearly bowls, jars, and scoops were intended to serve
different purposes, and therefore represent use-determined categories.
In some cases painted, plain, and red-slipped pottery may be better
suited to one use than another. Theoretically then, it is possible to
create nine functional classes based upon the combination of form and
ware; however, because no red-slipped scoops were recovered, only eight
functional categories were used to examine temporal changes in the
pottery: painted bowls, jars, and scoops; plain bowls, jars, and
scoops; and red-slipped bowls and jars.

Controlling for possible geographic or regional variation is
simpler. Obviously intrusive pottery such as the Phoenix Basin Hohokam
buff wares, San Simon Mogollon red-on-browns, and Trincheras painted
pottery have been excluded. For the purpose of this study, it is
assumed that the remaining Tucson Basin Series painted types, plain
ware, and red-slipped pottery were manufactured at the Rosemont sites,
although it is highly probable that some of the decorated pottery was
manufactured outside the project area. It is also possible that some of
the plain pottery, or more likely their raw materials, were imported;
however, without detailed physical and chemical analyses of the pottery
and potential clay sources in the vicinity of the sites, it is not

possible to distinguish locally produced vessels from those that may
have been imported from other parts of the Tucson Basin. The Tucson
Basin pottery types are certainly "local" in the sense that they
represent the products of the dominant cultural tradition in the
Rosemont area.

Evaluation of the Stylistic Model

All of the age assessments have relied on the stylistic model
of painted pottery development presented in the methods section. If
this model is essentially correct in its chronological sequence, then
the various styles should occur in that order in stratified deposits.
Few such stratified deposits were present in the Rosemont sites, but
they do provide some confirmation, of the relative sequence of styles.

There are only three instances of stratigraphic superpositioning
where the deposits were relatively pure. In two of these cases, Rincon
Red-on-brown, Style A overlies Colonial material: several Rincon Style
A vessels were recovered on and above a house floor which sealed a thin
deposit of Cañada del Oro trash (Feature 6, AZ EE:2:105); in another
instance a trash-filled house containing Rincon Style A is superimposed
on a house filled with predominantly Rillito Red-on-brown and which had
a partial, reworked Rillito bowl on the floor (Features 71001 and 71200,
AZ EE:2:105). In the latter case, rodent activity had mixed some of the
material, but it was possible to sort out the disturbance. The third
case demonstrates that Rincon Red-on-brown, Styles A and B are
stratigraphically later than the Colonial Style. A Rillito Red-on-brown
jar was found on a floor that had been intruded by a later house that
yielded both Rincon Style B and Style A vessels on the floor (Feature 8,
AZ EE:2:76). From these cases of superpositioning it has been possible
to document that both Rincon Style A and Rincon Style B are later than
the Colonial Style.

None of these cases illustrates the proposed sequential
relationship between Rincon Styles A, B, and C. In the last example
mentioned above, both Style A and B were found on the same house floor.
This evidence suggests that the two styles are at least partly
contemporaneous, and in fact this relationship between Styles A and B
was noted at all sites where Style B occurred. Although it has not been
possible to identify specific cases where the two styles occur in the
correct stratigraphic order, there is indirect evidence supporting the
inference that Style A occurs alone for a brief period of time before
the appearance of Style B. The two largest sites, AZ EE:2:105 and
AZ EE:2:113, yielded predominantly Colonial style and Rincon Style A
pottery; Style B occurred only in small quantities. The paucity of
Style B at these sites suggests that they were abandoned prior to the
large-scale production and popularity of this style. A third site,
AZ EE:2:84, has exclusively Rillito and Rincon Style A pottery. If
Styles A and B were contemporaneous throughout their entire span,
Style B should occur more frequently at these three sites. It would
seem then, that there is a length of time following the Colonial style,

when only Rincon Style A is produced, but that it is still manufactured as Style B develops and becomes more popular.

Just as there are no cases of superposition of Style B over Style A, there are no occurrences of Styles B and C in the anticipated order. It has been stated that Style C developed from Style B by a simplification and expansion of the design incorporating a greater amount of open space. There are examples that clearly typify either end of this developmental continuum; however, there are also many examples that grade between the two styles and are difficult to distinguish. Although it is possible in some cases to separate Styles B and C, it is consistently easier to distinguish Style A from either Styles B and C. It is clear that there are two distinct decorative styles in the Sedentary period, an "early" Sedentary style, Style A, that represents a continuation of the Colonial preference for banded designs, and a "late" style consisting of Styles B and C with their emphasis upon geometric, paneled designs that foreshadows the development of the Classic period decorative style. The exact relationship between Styles B and C requires investigation at sites where adequate stratigraphic superpositioning is present.

In addition to the stratigraphic evidence discussed above, archaeomagnetic and radiocarbon evidence was used to evaluate the estimated chronological ages of the styles. The results of archaeomagnetic dating efforts (Appendix F) were disappointing. Four samples yielded some form of interpretable results, but only one sample has a resolution tight enough to be of use in dating the pottery styles. This sample was taken from a hearth in a structure at AZ EE:2:109, dated ceramically as middle Rincon. The expected age was approximately A.D. 1000 to 1100; in fact, the sample dated between A.D. 1000 and 1180 at the 95 percent confidence interval. Although the resolution of this sample is larger than the estimated range, it tends to confirm the development of Style B after A.D. 1000.

The results of the radiocarbon dating were only slightly more useful. Originally, three charcoal samples and one wood sample found in association with stylistically uniform pottery assemblages were submitted for radiocarbon analysis (Table 4.27). These samples were taken from architectural timbers in burned structures whose floor assemblages included restorable or semirestorable vessels. Two of the samples, A-3562 and A-3891, are from houses that were mentioned in the discussion of stratigraphic evidence.

Architectural members were selected in an attempt to control for the old wood problem (Schiffer 1982: 324-326), assuming that the builders would have used freshly cut timbers in construction rather than dead wood (this pattern of wood use has yet to be demonstrated). To control for the disparity between when a tree begins its growth and when it is felled (Dean 1978), only the outermost rings were taken. In all but one case it was possible to obtain 10 g of material without removing more than one-quarter inch of the outer surface. Due to the condition of the samples it was not possible to count the exact number of rings removed. In one instance, due to the size and nature of the sample it

Table 4.27

CALIBRATED RADIOCARBON DATES FROM CERAMICALLY DATED CONTEXTS

Lab #	Provenience and Feature Description	Associated Pottery And Estimated Date	Date (B.P.)	Date (A.D.)	Calibrated Date (A.D.)
A-3561	Feature 2, AZ EE:2:106; carbonized wall or roof member found on pit house floor	late Rincon/early Tanque Verde; A.D. 1175-1225	870 + 50	1080 + 50	1035-1225
A-3562	Feature 71200, AZ EE:2:105; carbonized structural member found on pit house floor	Rillito; A.D. 700-900	1070 + 50	880 + 50	870-1050
A-3559	Feature 8, AZ EE:2:76, Floor 1; carbonized wall post fragment (found in place)	Rillito or earlier; A.D. 700-900 or earlier	1070 + 70	880 + 70	770-1190
A-3560	Feature 8, AZ EE:2:76, Floor 4; outermost preserved rings of uncarbonized roof support post butt	middle Rincon; A.D. 1000-1100	1360 + 60	590 + 60	465 - 870
A-3891	Second sample from roof support post from Feature 8, AZ EE:2:76, Floor 4 (taken immediately below A-3560)	middle Rincon; A.D. 1000-1100	1250 + 60	700 + 60	600 - 910

was impossible to obtain the outermost rings, so the entire specimen was submitted for dating. Finally, the samples were subjected to long counting times in order to maximize confidence in the accuracy of the date.

The samples submitted for radiocarbon dating were chosen from ceramically dated contexts: one from a burned Rillito phase house, one from a burned middle Rincon phase house, and one from a late Rincon or Tanque Verde phase house. A fourth sample was taken from a house floor which lacked associated decorated vessels, but had been intruded by a Rillito phase house. In only one instance does the date range not correspond at least grossly to the expected age based on the ceramic sequence. Sample A-3560 from Feature 8 at AZ EE:2:76 was expected to date in the A.D. 1000 to 1100 range. It was taken from a post in a house floor (Floor 4) which yielded Rincon Styles A and B vessels, and was stratigraphically later than a floor (Floor 2) on which a Rillito Red-on-brown jar was found (no sample was taken from this floor). Further, this sample should be younger than Sample A-3559, which comes from a floor (Floor 1) stratigraphically earlier than Floor 2. In fact, the dates obtained are the reverse of the expected sequence. A second sample (A-3891) taken from the post which produced the apparently anomalous date (A-3560) was analyzed, and yielded a similar result. The only conclusion that can be drawn is that these specimens yielded anomolous dates or may have been taken from an old post which was reused.

Three of the radiocarbon dates, A-3559, A-3562, and A-3561, provide relevant data on the pottery styles. Two of these are associated with the Colonial style. Sample A-3559 dates a house floor which was intruded by a floor on which a partial Rillito Red-on-brown jar was found, and should therefore be Rillito phase or earlier. Sample A-3562 was taken from a charred post in a house with a partial Rillito Red-on-brown bowl on the floor (Feature 71200, AZ EE:2:105), and should, therefore, date between A.D. 700 to 900. This house had been intruded by a house containing Rincon Style A trash fill. The date of sample A-3562 should therefore predate the appearance of Rincon Style A. Sample A-3561 is from a beam in a burned house whose floor assemblage included an early Tanque Verde Red-on-brown bowl (Feature 2, AZ EE:2:106). Ceramically, an estimated age of A.D. 1100 to 1250 was predicted.

None of the radiocarbon samples yielded results with a resolution tighter than the estimated age. In the case of sample A-3561 the estimated age of A.D. 1175 to 1225 lies well within the tree-ring-calibrated radiocarbon date of A.D. 1035-1255. The radiocarbon dates for A-3562 and A-3559 overlap with the estimated ages, but are generally later. To date, these are the only Rillito phase or earlier ceramic period radiocarbon dates from the Tucson Basin. It is therefore impossible to evaluate the correlation between calendric dates and the ages assigned to the pottery types and named phases. The archaeological contexts from which these samples were taken seem to be reliable and undisturbed. The precision of the A-3559 date is less than the currently accepted, 200-year-long phases; the A-3562 is slightly better.

While it is too early to propose revision of the chronology, it is clear that additional dates are badly needed. The late Rincon-early Tanque Verde date matches the anticipated range, supporting the stylistic inference that the development of the simple plaited designs occurs during the last half of the Sedentary period.

Ratios of Plain, Painted, and Red-Slipped Wares

Using the stylistic model as a chronological tool, the next level of temporal variation that may be examined is the change in the relative proportions of painted to plain to red-slipped pottery, through time. It has been suggested that the percentage of painted pottery increased through time; however, this trend has not been quantifiably demonstrated, probably because few pure deposits of trash from all phases have been isolated. Even at the Hodges Ruin, where the original sequence and chronolgy was defined, Kelly (1978: 1) noted the paucity of unmixed trash deposits. In the Rosemont area, at least one deposit of refuse has been identified representing each of the chronological subdivisions, and several sites can be assigned to a single phase or subphase. In many instances the deposits are free of mixture, but one or two earlier or later sherds always seem to occur. When computing the number of decorated sherds assignable to any one unit of time, those sherds that were definitely attributable to either an earlier or later time frame were deleted; the unidentifiable red-on-browns were assumed to be from the time frame in question and were added to the painted pottery total for the phase in question. Unfortunately, because this reconstruction is based upon a limited number of provenience units, it is not possible to determine whether the relative frequencies of bowls, jars, and scoops also vary; the number of rim sherds is too small to be reliable. Vessel form is examined using less specific temporal units, resulting in larger sample sizes.

The relative proportions of painted to plain to red-slipped pottery are shown in Figure 4.66. From the Cañada del Oro through early Rincon phases there is a significant increase in the proportion of painted pottery. Interestingly, red-slipped pottery occurs in all phases in low frequencies, contradicting the notion that the Pioneer period red ware tradition dies out prior to the Colonial period and that locally produced red wares do not appear again until the Sedentary period. The red wares from these early proveniences are no different than the red-slipped pottery in later deposits.

A puzzling phenomenon is the decrease in the proportion of painted pottery from the early to middle Rincon. The increase in the red-slipped pottery at this time was expected, and the decrease in the relative quantity of painted pottery may be due in part to the expenditure of more effort on the production of red-slipped pottery. However, the increase in the percentage of red-slipped pottery does not offset the decrease in the painted pottery. Sampling error may account for this discrepancy, since the early Sedentary period (the early Rincon phase) is represented by a single deposit.

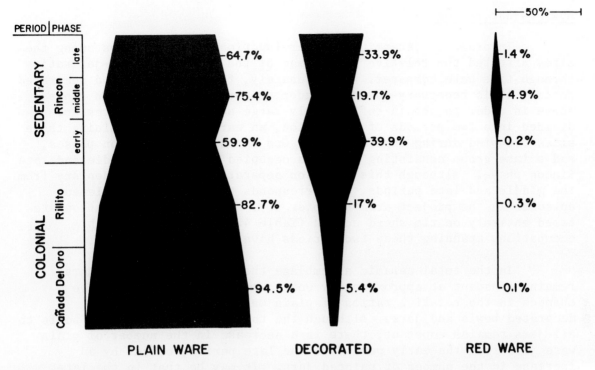

Figure 4.66 Relative proportion of plain to decorated to red wares by phase.

The increase in the percentage of red-slipped pottery from 0.2 percent in the early Sedentary to 4.9 percent in the middle Rincon is significant. These data indicate that the local production of red-slipped pottery reaches its peak during the middle Sedentary, or inferentially, between A.D. 1000 and 1100. As expected, the percentage of red ware declines in the late Sedentary and by the Classic period, there are apparently no locally produced red wares (Kelly 1978: 67). There is again an increase in the percentage of painted pottery in the late Sedentary period, but it does not achieve the prominance it had in the early Sedentary period.

Overall it appears that the relative percentages of painted and red ware pottery do change significantly through time. Painted and red-slipped pottery increase in proportion from the Colonial to the Sedentary period, and presumably, the percentage of painted pottery continues to increase into the Classic period. Red-slipped pottery has a brief florescence during the middle Sedentary, then dies out altogether. The fluctuations in the relative percentages of painted pottery cannot be easily explained; they may be due to small sample size, sampling error, or may be truly representative of the trends in the Rosemont area. However, if the assumptions that the pottery is locally made, or that all the sites are functionally identical prove false, then the patterns noted above may be due to factors other than the passage of time.

Bowl-to-Jar Ratios

In order to determine whether functional distinctions among the sites affected the relative percentage of the wares, bowl-to-jar ratios through time were compared. Unfortunately, for both plain and decorated pottery it is necessary to use broader temporal groupings than those above in order to obtain sufficiently large samples. The sites are divided into two periods of occupation, an early group containing those sites occupied during the Cañada del Oro through early Rincon phases, and a late group consisting of sites occupied during the middle and late Rincon phase. Although this division separates the early Sedentary from the middle and late periods, it corresponds to two major settlement episodes in the project area (Chapter 10). The bowl-to-jar ratios are based entirely on rim sherd counts (Table 4.28), and sites with occupations spanning these two periods have been deleted.

In the total ceramic assemblage the ratio of bowls to jars remains constant at approximately one to one. However, there are changes in the relative ratios of plain ware bowls and jars and decorated bowls and jars. Although the total proportion of all bowls to all jars remains constant, there is a decrease in the number of plain ware jars from the early period to the late period, offset by an increase in the number of painted jars. It may be that in the late period, painted jars are assuming uses that were served principally by plain ware jars in the early period, but these data do not suggest functional differences between the early and late sites. In both groups the proportions of bowls and jars are roughly equal.

Changes in Decorated Pottery

The most pronounced temporal changes in the decorated pottery are the evolution of the decorative designs, as detailed in the stylistic model and partially confirmed by data from the Rosemont sites. Not only do the decorative features change, but there are correlated changes in technology and vessel shape.

Two of the most obvious technological attributes that change significantly through time are the preferred tempering material and the painting of the lips of bowl rims. Figure 4.67 illustrates the frequencies of schist versus sand-tempered pottery and painted versus unpainted bowl rims. These two traits are inversely related; as the presence of schist temper declines, the number of painted bowl rims increases. The abruptness of these changes indicate that it is possible to sort the pottery using these attributes. Colonial period and earlier pottery is schist tempered and lacks painted bowl rims; in the Sedentary period, and later, the most pottery is sand tempered, and bowl rims are painted.

The abruptness of these shifts is suprising. The practice of painting bowl rims can only be attributed to aesthetic values. As noted with the plain wares below, the shift from schist or mixed schist and sand to sand temper may result from a decline in the availability of

Table 4.28

BOWL-TO-JAR RATIOS BY TIME

Period	Ware	Number of Bowls	Number of Jars	Bowl-to-Jar Ratio
Early[1]	Decorated	188	26	7:1
	Plain	251	419	1:2
	Total	439	445	1:1
Late[2]	Decorated	21	6	4:1
	Plain	60	68	1:1
	Total	81	74	1:1

[1] includes Colonial period and early Rincon phase sites
[2] includes middle and late Rincon phase sites

schist.   Another possible explanation for the second phenomenon is that the decorated pottery that contains schist is imported into the Rosemont area, while the sand-tempered vessels are locally produced. If this were the case, it seems likely that the pottery would be imported from the Tucson Basin proper, where the technological shift from schist to sand temper should not be present. While this has yet to be systematically tested, an examination of Sedentary period pottery from the Hodges Ruin, the Hardy Site, and other sites in the basin proper, reveals a corresponding change during this period. It seems that, for whatever reasons, the change in tempering material occurs throughout the Tucson Basin.

A final technological characteristic that seems to have increased significance through time is the use of a black paint in both bichromatic and polychromatic color schemes. The temporal distribution of the black paint has been assessed in two ways: by its association with red-on-brown pottery and by the decorative style in which the black paint is used.

All black painted pottery is attributed to the Sedentary period based on its association with Rincon Red-on-brown and by its stylistic

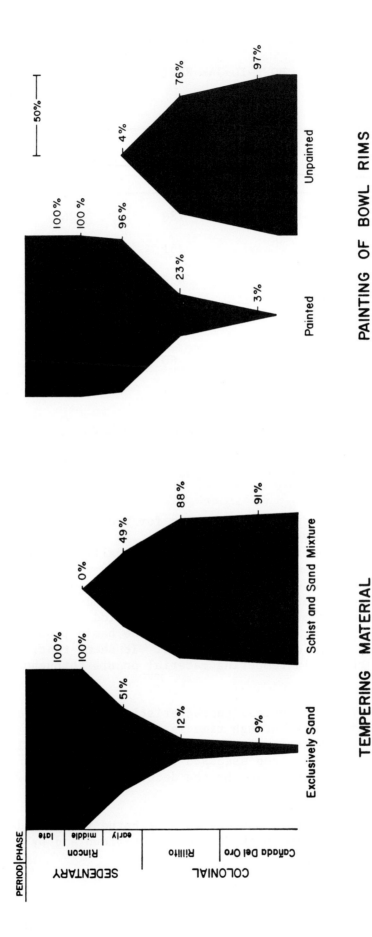

TEMPERING MATERIAL

PAINTING OF BOWL RIMS

Figure 4.67 Seriation of temper and bowl rim painting showing the decrease in occurrence of schist as a temper component and the increase in the practice of painting bowl rims through time.

rendering.   Further, the use of black paints is most common during the middle and late Sedentary (Table 4.29).   Although over half of all black-painted bichromes and polychromes occur at two Rosemont sites which are occupied during both time periods, over two-thirds of the remaining black-painted sherds are from late period sites.   When the frequency of the decorative style is computed (Table 4.30), the majority of stylistically identifiable sherds are Style B (middle Sedentary). The low frequency classified as Rincon Black-on-brown, Style C might imply that the popularity of black paint is waning; however, two Classic period sites in the Tucson Basin, Los Morteros (AZ AA:12:57) and Whiptail (AZ BB:10:3), have yielded significant quantities of a new black-painted type, Tanque Verde Black-on-brown (Deaver 1982), suggesting continued use of the black paint.

The technological traits examined support the stylistic model. The decrease in the preference for schist-tempered pottery and the increase in the practice of painting bowl lips with a red line accentuate the break between the Colonial style and Rincon Style A. Further, the use of black paint correlates to the break between Rincon Style A and Rincon Style B.   These attributes support the stylistic concepts, as well as providing tangible markers for the shifts from the Colonial period to the early Sedentary period, and between the early and middle Sedentary period.

Pronounced changes in preferred bowl shapes occur between the Colonial and Sedentary periods (Table 4.31).   Colonial potters preferred the flare-rimmed bowl, whereas Sedentary potters favored direct-rimmed bowls, primarily the deep, subhemispherical shape.   The sample of jar sherds is too small to be conclusive, but jars with flaring necks are apparently preferred throughout the sequence.   However, the sharp, angular Gila shoulder and the short, flaring neck are apparently associated with Rincon Style B.

Another type of form change centers around the increase in decorated vessel size through time.   Raab (1974) has explained this tendency as an increased need for storage jars, but few other researchers have addressed this point.   Raab (1974) used rim diameter as a measure of vessel size; however, this is a poor index of vessel size.   Only for direct rim bowls does the orifice diameter reflect vessel size.   The orifice diameter of jars is probably affected most by changes in the vessel's aperture, and the aperture size is affected by the intended use and frequency of access to the vessel (S. Plog 1980; Crown 1981, 1984a). Vessels of equal height and width, with nearly equal volume, may have significantly different aperture diameters depending upon whether the vessel is intended for a high- or low-access-frequency use.   For example, cooking jars and storage jars should display markedly different aperture diameters.   Therefore, if intended use controls aperture size, it should not be used as a measure of vessel size, and since orifice is related to aperture size, it also is a poor indicator of vessel size.

The most logical index of absolute vessel size would be volume; this unfortunately requires a large collection of whole or restorable vessels.   In the absence of such a collection two indices of vessel size

Table 4.29

DISTRIBUTION OF BLACK PAINT IN BICHROME AND
POLYCHROME COLOR SCHEMES BY TIME

Period	Rincon Black-on-brown N	%	Polychrome Types N	%
Early[1]	10	9.4	1	2.9
Late[2]	33	31.2	15	42.9
Mixed	63	59.4	19	54.3
Total	106	100.0	35	100.1

[1] includes Colonial and early Rincon sites
[2] includes middle and late Rincon sites

Table 4.30

DISTRIBUTION OF BLACK PAINT BY DECORATIVE STYLE,
RINCON BLACK-ON-BROWN

Style	Count	Percent
A	7	6.6
B	26	24.5
C	7	6.6
Indeterminate	66	62.3
Total	106	100.0

Table 4.31

INVENTORY OF BOWL AND JAR SHAPES* FOR CAÑADA DEL ORO, RILLITO, AND RINCON RED-ON-BROWN

Vessel Shape	Cañada del Oro		Rillito		Rincon	
	N	%	N	%	N	%
BOWLS						
Direct rim	21		65		250	
Hemispherical	(1)	(4.8)	(5)	(7.7)	(217)	(86.8)
Deep outcurved			2	3.1	21	8.4
Shallow outcurved	1	4.8	3	4.6	116	46.4
Plate					50	20.0
Indeterminate					1	0.4
					29	11.6
Flared rim	20		60		33	
Slight	1	95.3	3	92.3	1	13.2
Moderate	18	4.8	47	4.6	27	0.4
Pronounced		85.7	3	72.3	1	10.8
Indeterminate	1	4.8	7	4.6	4	0.4
				10.8		1.6
JARS	5		8		45	
Incurved neck	(1)	(20.0)	(3)	(37.5)	(4)	(6.6)
Slight	1	20.0	1	12.5	1	2.2
Moderate			2	25.0	2	4.4
Complete					1	2.2
Flared neck	(4)	(80.0)	(4)	(50.0)	(39)	(86.6)
Slight			1	12.5	5	11.1
Moderate	2	40.0	2	25.0	24	53.3
Pronounced	2	40.0	1	12.5	10	22.2
Upcurved neck			(1)	(12.5)	(2)	(4.4)
Complete			1	12.5	2	4.4

* as determined from rim sherds

( ) = category total

were computed for the ANAMAX-Rosemont collection of whole and partial
vessels. One is based on total vessel height and breadth, while the
second, computed from body height and breadth, was designed to measure
those partial vessels which lacked rims. The index of vessel size is
obtained by multiplying the body height by the breadth. This index is a
representation of size, but is neither an estimate of volume nor an
index of vessel shape.

The values of this index for decorated bowls and jars are shown
in Tables 4.32 and 4.33 respectively. The sample size is too small to
determine whether the average jar size increases through time; however,
as discussed below, this can be demonstrated for bowls. Because most
restorable vessels are from cremation contexts and may be preselected
for size, it is possible that only a special size range is present. In
addition all of the largest jars were recovered from house floors, again
suggesting that this sample is not representative of the full size
range. Although it is impossible to determine if the average size of
the vessels increases through time, the data in these tables show that
the Sedentary period vessels overlap in size with the earlier Colonial
period vessels.

As mentioned above, orifice diameter is probably a reliable
index of vessel size for direct rim bowls; the minimum orifice of all
bowls should also be a reliable indicator of bowl body size. To
evaluate this, minimum orifice diameter for restorable vessels was
plotted against the vessel size index; the results demonstrated a linear
relationship between minimum orifice and vessel size. Minimum orifice
appears to be an accurate measure of overall bowl size, and may be used
to examine changes in bowl size through time. Rim sherds are combined
in two groups—Colonial and Sedentary—to obtain as large a sample size
as possible. The size distribution of bowls, based on minimum orifice
diameter, has been drawn using the running average technique discussed
in the methods section (Fig. 4.68).

Both Colonial and Sedentary period bowls exhibit a bimodal
distribution. The distribution of Colonial period bowls peaks at 22 cm
and 32 cm, whereas the Sedentary period bowl modes are 26 cm and 44 cm.
It would seem that while there are both large and small bowls in both
periods, there is indeed an increase in bowl size through time. Another
feature of the chart is that the two Colonial period modes are
approximately equally abundant, whereas the larger bowls in the
Sedentary period are distinctly less common than the small bowls.

Changes in Plain Pottery

There are interesting technological and formal changes in the
plain pottery as well. The collection of restorable vessels is
unfortunately too small and from insufficiently specific temporal
context to permit assessments of changes in vessel shape through time.
There are nevertheless noticeable differences in the relative frequency
of shapes among the plain ware types that are best treated as functional
differences. This discussion focuses upon changes in the technological
aspects.

Table 4.32

TYPOLOGICAL, CONTEXTUAL, AND METRIC DATA ON RESTORABLE PAINTED, PLAIN, AND RED WARE BOWLS
FROM THE ANAMAX-ROSEMONT COLLECTION

Provenience[+]	Type	Context	Orifice Diameter (O)	Minimum Orifice (MO)	Rim Height (RH)	Body Height (BH)	Vessel Height (VH)	Vessel Size Index (VSI:MOxBH)	BH/MO	RH/VH
Painted										
AZ EE:2:76, 1-1	Rillito Red-on-brown	Cremation	(26.0)	(21.0)	4.4	(8.4)	(12.8)	176.4	0.40	0.34
AZ EE:2:113, 81-11	Rillito Red-on-brown	Cremation	26.0	21.0	4.8	8.7	13.5	182.7	0.41	0.36
AZ EE:2:76, 5-1	Rincon Red-on-brown, Style A	Cremation (?)	(20.0)	(17.0)	4.0	(11.8)	(15.8)	200.6	0.69	0.25
AZ EE:2:77, 2-3	Rincon Red-on-brown, Style A	Pit house fill	(45.0)	(45.0)	0.0	(12.9)	(12.9)	580.5	0.29	0
AZ EE:2:84, 7-4	Rincon Red-on-brown, Style A	Cremation	(15.0)	(15.0)	0.0	7.3	7.3	109.5	0.49	0
AZ EE:2:105, 6-13	Rincon Red-on-brown, Style A	Pit house fill or floor	13.4	10.6	4.0	6.3	10.3	66.8	0.59	0.39
AZ EE:2:105, 6-14	Rincon Red-on-brown, Style A	Pit house fill or floor	(22.0)	(22.0)	0.0	10.2	10.2	224.4	0.46	0
AZ EE:2:105, 6-34	Rincon Red-on-brown, Style A	Pit house fill or floor	24.0	24.0	0.0	10.0	10.0	240.0	0.42	0
AZ EE:2:105, 24-5a	Rincon Red-on-brown, Style A	Cache	(23.0)	(23.0)	0.0	(9.0)	(9.0)	207.0	0.39	0
AZ EE:2:105, 29-5b	Rincon Red-on-brown, Style A	Cache	(22.0)	(22.0)	0.0	(10.0)	(10.0)	220.0	0.45	0
AZ EE:2:105, 29-6	Rincon Red-on-brown, Style A	Cache	15.0	15.0	0.0	7.2	7.2	108.0	0.48	0
AZ EE:2:107, 3-1	Rincon Red-on-brown, Style A	Pit house fill or floor	16.0	16.0	0.0	7.6	7.6	121.6	0.48	0.42
AZ EE:2:113, 0-28	Rincon Red-on-brown, Style A	Trench	(22.0)	(16.0)	5.5	(7.6)	(13.1)	121.6	0.48	0
AZ EE:2:113, N100 E128-2	Rincon Red-on-brown, Style A	Stripping	(39.0)	(39.0)	0.0	(14.7)	(14.7)	573.3	0.38	0
AZ EE:2:113, N104 E128-1	Rincon Red-on-brown, Style A	Stripping	(28.0)	(28.0)	0.0	13.8	13.8	386.4	0.49	0
AZ EE:2:113, 8-35	Rincon Red-on-brown, Style A	Pit house floor	38.0	38.0	0.0	13.0	13.0	494.0	0.34	0
AZ EE:2:113, 164-2	Rincon Red-on-brown, * Style A	Cremation	24.5	19.5	4.1	8.9	13.0	173.5	0.46	0.32
AZ EE:2:76, 8-109	Rincon Red-on-brown, Style B	Pit house floor	(28.0)	(28.0)	0.0	16.6	16.6	464.8	0.59	0
AZ EE:2:76, 44-3	Rincon Red-on-brown, Style B	Cremation	18.0	12.0	4.2	7.2	11.4	86.4	0.60	0.37
AZ EE:2:77, 2-6	Rincon Red-on-brown, Style B	Pit house fill	(36.0)	(36.0)	0.0	(17.0)	(17.0)	612.0	0.47	0
AZ EE:2:77, 40-7	Rincon Red-on-brown, STyle B	Cremation	34.0	25.0	4.9	11.0	15.9	275.0	0.44	0.31
AZ EE:2:77, 45-1	Rincon Red-on-brown, Style B	Sherd-lined Pit	(42.0)	(40.0)	9.0	19.4	28.4	776.0	0.49	0.32
AZ EE:2:80, 6-7	Rincon Red-on-brown, Style B	Cache	(28.0)	(28.0)	0.0	(10.0)	(10.0)	280.0	0.36	0
AZ EE:2:76, 27-13	Rincon Red-on-brown, Style C	Pit house fill	(28.0)	(28.0)	0.0	(17.5)	(17.5)	490.0	0.63	0
AZ EE:2:106, 2-2	Tanque Verde Red-on-brown	Pit house floor	(31.0)	(31.0)	0.0	15.2	15.2	471.2	0.49	0
AZ EE:2:113, 107	Crude Red-on-brown	Cremation (?)	11.0	11.0	0.0	5.2	5.2	57.2	0.47	0
AZ EE:2:107, 7001-3	Unid. Red-on-brown (Rincon?)	Cremation	(14.0)	(13.0)	2.3	(5.3)	(7.6)	68.9	0.41	0.30
AZ EE:2:107, 7001-6	Unid. Red-on-brown (Rincon?)	Cremation	16.5	16.5	0.0	10.0	10.0	165.0	0.61	0
AZ EE:2:116, 1-16	Unid. Red-on-brown (Rincon?)	Pit house fill	(21.0)	(21.0)	0.0	-	-	-	-	-
AZ EE:2:120, 11-6	Unid. Red-on-brown (Rincon?)	Pit house fill	16.0	16.0	0.0	6.0	6.0	96.0	0.38	0

* White slip variety
+ Intrasite provenience follows site number, either
  Feature - Field number or
  Grid unit - Field number
( ) = estimated size

Table 4.32, continued

TYPOLOGICAL, CONTEXTUAL, AND METRIC DATA FOR RESTORABLE DECORATED BOWLS FROM THE ANAMAX-ROSEMONT PROJECT

Provenience[+]	Type	Context	Orifice Diameter (O)	Minimum Orifice (MO)	Rim Height (RH)	Body Height (BH)	Vessel Height (VH)	Vessel Size Index (VSI:MOxBH)	BH/MO	RH/VH
Plain Ware										
AZ EE:2:76, 56-12	Type I (Miniature)	Cremation	5.5	5.5	0.0	3.2	3.2	17.6	0.58	0
AZ EE:2:105, 44-1	Type I	Cache	19.0	16.0	4.2	5.6	9.8	89.6	0.35	0.43
AZ EE:2:109, N14 E10-8	Type I	Stripping	23.0	23.0	0.0	8.4	8.4	193.2	0.37	0
AZ EE:2:113, 1-2	Type I	Cremation	15.0	13.0	1.6	-	-	-	-	-
AZ EE:2:113, 10-198	Type I	Pit house fill	13.0	13.0	0.0	6.8	6.8	88.4	0.52	0
AZ EE:2:113, 83-42	Type I	Pit house fill	10.0	10.0	0.0	3.0	3.0	30.0	0.30	0
AZ EE:2:116, 2-19	Type II	Pit house floor	38.0	38.0	0.0	14.4	14.4	547.2	0.38	0
AZ EE:2:76, TP3-16	Type III	Test Pit	18.0	18.0	0.0	11.2	11.2	201.6	0.62	0
AZ EE:2:80, 6-6	Type III	Cache	12.0	10.8	1.9	5.2	7.1	56.2	0.48	0.27
Red Ware										
AZ EE:2:76, 8-109	Rincon Red?	Pit house floor	30.0	30.0	0.0	12.8	12.8	384.0	0.43	0
AZ EE:2:76, 9-1	Rincon Red?	Artifact cluster	29.0	29.0	0.0	9.6	9.6	278.4	0.33	0
AZ EE:2:77, 31-18	Rincon Red?	Pit house fill	20.0	20.0	0.0	8.2	8.2	164.0	0.41	0
AZ EE:2:105, N144 E40-45	San Francisco Red?*	Cache (?)	27.0	27.0	0.0	9.6	9.6	259.2	0.36	0

* Peppersauce variety
+ Intrasite provenience follows site number, either
  Feature - Field number or
  Grid unit - Field number

Table 4.33

TYPOLOGICAL, CONTEXTUAL, AND METRIC DATA ON RESTORABLE PAINTED AND PLAIN WARE JARS FROM THE ANAMAX-ROSEMONT COLLECTION

Provenience [+]	Type	Context	Orifice Diameter (O)	Aperture Diameter (A)	Breadth Diameter (B)	Neck Height (NH)	Body Height (BH)	Vessel Height (VH)	Vessel Size Index (VSI=BxBH)	A/B Ratio	VH/B Ratio	NH/VH Ratio
Painted												
AZ EE:2:105, 51-2	Cañada Del Oro Red-on-brown	Cremation	(16.0)	(15.0)	20.0	3.6	13.1	16.7	262.0	0.75	0.84	0.22
AZ EE:2:76, 32-2	Unidentified Colonial (CDO?)	Cremation	19.0	19.0	21.0	2.4	(15.6)	(18.0)	327.6	0.90	0.86	0.13
AZ EE:2:76, 4-2	Rillito Red-on-brown	Cremation	10.0	9.0	21.0	3.1	11.9	15.0	249.9	0.43	0.71	0.21
AZ EE:2:76, 8-73	Rillito Red-on-brown	Pit house floor	UNMEASURABLE									
AZ EE:2:76, 56-1	Rillito Red-on-brown	Cremation	15.2	14.0	23.0	5.4	19.1	22.1	439.3	0.61	0.96	0.24
AZ EE:2:57001, 7	Rillito Red-on-brown	Cremation	(9.0)	(7.0)	(15.0)	5.9	7.4	13.3	111.0	0.47	0.89	0.44
AZ EE:2:76, 45-1	Rillito Red-on-brown	Cremation	-	-	(16.5)	5.0	9.8	-	161.7	-	-	-
AZ EE:2:113, 70-1	Rillito Red-on-brown	Cremation	11.0	8.2	(18.2)	5.2	-	-	-	0.45	-	-
AZ EE:2:76, 5-1	Rincon Red-on-brown, Style A	Cremation (?)	10.0	11.0	20.5	5.5	12.8	18.3	262.4	0.54	0.89	0.30
AZ EE:2:76, 51-3	Rincon Red-on-brown, Style A	Cremation	(14.0)	(10.0)	(14.3)	4.1	(13.7)	(17.8)	195.9	0.70	1.24	0.23
AZ EE:2:77, 23001-9	Rincon Black-on-brown, Style A	Cremation	(12.0)	5.0	15.0	4.2	8.2	12.4	123.0	0.33	0.83	0.34
AZ EE:2:105, 29-7	Rincon Red-on-brown, Style A	Cache	7.0	12.0	25.2	-	16.1	-	405.7	0.48	-	-
AZ EE:2:113, 84-4	Rincon Red-on-brown, Style A	Cremation	-	(17.0)	(33.0)	3.4	(20.6)	(24.0)	679.8	0.52	0.73	0.14
AZ EE:2:77, 2002-6	Rincon Red-on-brown, Style B	Floor Pit	(19.0)	10.8	25.6	3.6	18.6	22	476.2	0.42	0.87	0.16
AZ EE:2:107, 7001-5	Rincon Red-on-brown, Style B	Cremation	12.2	9.4	26.4	2.6	23.7	26.3	625.7	0.36	1.00	0.10
AZ EE:2:107, 7002-7	Rincon Red-on-brown, Style B	Cremation	11.0	(15.0)	(38.0)	3.0	(26.0)	(29.0)	988.0	0.39	0.76	0.10
AZ EE:2:106, 3-4	Rincon Red-on-brown, Style C *	Pit house fill	(15.0)	(15.0)	-	-	-	-	-	-	-	-
AZ EE:2:76, 44-2	Rincon Red-on-brown, ?Style	Cremation	14.4	13.0	24.8	3.9	16.5	20.4	409.2	0.52	0.82	0.19
Plain												
AZ EE:2:76, N52 E26-4	Type I (Miniature)	Stripping	6.0	5.5	8.4	4.9	3.5	8.4	29.4	0.46	1.00	0.58
AZ EE:2:76, 5-1	Type I (Miniature)	Cremation (?)	3.5	3.4	4.7	1.2	3.4	4.6	16.0	0.72	0.98	0.26
AZ EE:2:76, 56-13	Type I (Miniature)	Cremation	3.3	3.3	6.2	0.8	4.4	5.2	27.3	0.53	0.84	0.15
AZ EE:11:104, 1-6	Type I (Miniature)	Pit house fill	-	(18.2)	(25.0)	-	20.0	0	500.0	0.73	-	-
AZ EE:2:76, 8-113	Type I	Pit house floor	-	-	-	-	-	-	-	-	-	-
AZ EE:2:76, 65-2	Type I	Cremation	-	-	-	-	-	-	-	-	-	-

* White slip variety

+ Intrasite provenience follows site number, either
  Feature - Field number of
  Grid unit - Field number

( ) Estimated size

Table 4.33, continued

TYPOLOGICAL, CONTEXTUAL, AND METRIC DATA ON RESTORABLE PAINTED AND PLAIN WARE JARS FROM THE ANAMAX-ROSEMONT COLLECTION

Provenience[+]	Type	Context	Orifice Diameter (O)	Aperature Diameter (A)	Breadth Diameter (B)	Neck Height (NH)	Body Height (BH)	Vessel Height (VH)	Vessel Size Index (VSI=BxBH)	A/B Ratio	VH/B Ratio	NH/VH
Plain (continued)												
AZ EE:2:78, 1-1	Type I	Extramural Pit	(12.0)	(12.0)	(13.0)	0.0	8.0	8.0	104.0	0.92	0.62	0
AZ EE:2:105, 6-64	Type I	Pit house fill/floor	(12.0)	(10.0)	(12.0)	3.4	9.4	12.8	112.8	0.83	1.10	0.27
AZ EE:2:105, 44-2	Type I	Cache	(10.0)	( )	14.0	( )	–	–	–	–	–	–
AZ EE:2:105, 53-1	Type I	Cache	12.0	11.0	14.0	5.0	6.6	11.6	92.4	0.79	0.83	0.43
AZ EE:2:107, 3-29	Type I	Pit house fill/floor	9.4	8.6	14.5	4.0	(8.6)	(12.6)	124.7	0.59	0.87	0.32
AZ EE:2:107, 7001-4	Type I	Cremation	7.5	7.2	12.0	2.9	9.1	12.0	109.2	0.60	1.00	0.24
AZ EE:2:113, 80-8	Type I	Cremation	13.2	12.2	17.2	4.3	9.5	13.8	163.4	0.71	0.80	0.31
AZ EE:2:120, 11-1	Type I	Pit house fill	(10.0)	(10.0)	(11.0)	0.0	7.0	7.0	77.0	0.91	0.64	0
AZ EE:2:129, 1-24	Type I	Pit house fill/floor	(13.0)	(12.6)	(16.0)	2.0	11.6	13.6	185.6	0.79	0.85	0.15
AZ EE:2:129, 1-25	Type I	Pit house fill/floor	(13.0)	(12.0)	(14.0)	2.2	8.8	11.0	123.2	0.86	0.79	0.20
AZ EE:1:91, 1-15	Type II	Pit house floor	(13.0)	(13.0)	(35.0)	3.8	25.8	29.6	903.0	0.37	0.85	0.15
AZ EE:2:105, 6-32	Type II	Pit house fill/floor	(22.0)	(20.0)	(48.0)	9.6	(38.0)	(47.6)	1,824.0	0.42	0.99	0.20
AZ EE:2:107, 3-31	Type II	Pit house fill/floor	(23.0)	(22.0)	(53.0)	3.6	–	–	–	0.42	–	–
AZ EE:2:113, 10100-148	Type II	Pit house floor	BURNED AND WARPED, UNMEASURABLE									
AZ EE:2:113, 80-9	Type II	Cremation	10.0	10.0	22.0	0.0	8.2	8.2	180.4	0.45	0.37	0
AZ EE:2:113, 147-5	Type II	Cremation (?)	10.8	9.7	–	4.4	–	–	–	–	–	–
AZ EE:2:116, 2-61	Type II	Pit house fill/floor	(23.0)	(22.0)	(50.0)	5.4	–	–	–	0.44	–	–
AZ EE:2:116, 1-85	Type II	Pit house fill/floor	(17.0)	(17.0)	(39.0)	3.8	27.2	31.0	1,060.8	0.44	0.79	0.12
AZ EE:2:76, 8-111	Type III	Pit house floor	17.0	17.0	29.6	2.5	20.0	22.5	592.0	0.57	0.76	0.11
AZ EE:2:76, 10-81	Type III	Pit house fill	(18.0)	(18.0)	(38.0)	6.6	27.4	34.0	1,041.2	0.47	0.89	0.19
AZ EE:2:76, 21-5	Type III	Cremation	–	–	(31.0)	–	18.7	–	579.7	–	–	–
AZ EE:2:84, 7-4	Type III	Cremation	11.0	9.6	16.6	4.3	11.7	16.0	194.2	0.58	0.96	0.27
AZ EE:2:107, 2001-34	Type III	Floor Pit	22.6	22.6	(45.0)	5.2	(32.0)	(37.2)	1,440.0	0.50	0.83	0.14
AZ EE:2:113, 81-8a	Type III	Cremation	9.0	8.6	16.0	4.0	–	–	–	–	–	–
AZ EE:2:113, 81-8b	Type III	Cremation	–	–	16.0	–	10.6	–	169.6	–	–	–
AZ EE:2:76, 47-2	Type IV	Cremation	–	–	22.0	–	12.6	–	277.2	–	–	–

[+] Intrasite provenience follows site number, either
Feature - Field number or
Grid unit - Field number

( ) Estimated size

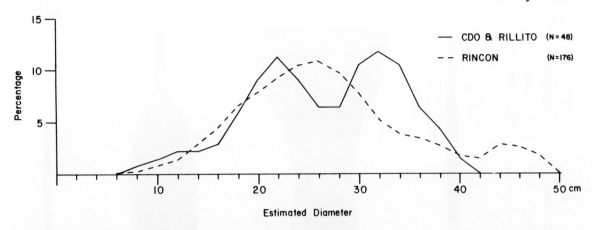

Figure 4.68 Comparison of Colonial and Sedentary period bowl size based on estimates of minimum origice diameter. (Curves produced using the running average technique.)

Kelly (1978: 72-76) has outlined the progression of plain ware from nonmicaceous in the Pioneer period, to micaceous in the Colonial period and back to nonmicaceous in the Sedentary and Classic periods. If accurate, this model of plain ware development may be duplicated in the Rosemont collection. To test this, it was necessary to select specific proveniences that could be assigned to single phases. Fortunately, there was at least one phase-specific trash deposit attributable to the Cañada del Oro and Rillito phases, and early, middle, and late Rincon phase. Although the number of sherds used to calculate the percentages is sufficient, the number of individual deposits and sites is low, restricted to single deposits or sites in many cases.

The relative percentages of each of the plain ware types is shown in Figure 4.69, and it is clear that sand-tempered Type II is made in all phases in large quantities. However, Types III and IV, those that are tempered with crushed schist or other crushed micaceous rock, occur most frequently in the Colonial period, reaching a peak during the Rillito phase. In fact, during the Rillito phase Type III is proportionately more frequent than Type II, reflecting the trend noted by Kelly (1978). The actual relative percentages of the types may be expected to vary depending upon a site's location with respect to the main flow of cultural development. The Rosemont sites are located on the periphery of the Tucson Basin culture area, perhaps explaining the continued use of sand tempered pottery. Ongoing excavations by the Arizona State Museum at a site in the Tucson Basin occupied in the late Pioneer and Colonial phases (AZ AA:12:149) reveal an overwhelming presence of Type III pottery, supporting the observation that Type III is most frequent in the Colonial period. However, while sand-tempered, nonmicaceous pottery (Type II) is present in this site collection, it is not as numerous as in the Rosemont collection. This latter point suggests that the percentage values may differ between sites or areas, even though the pattern is the same.

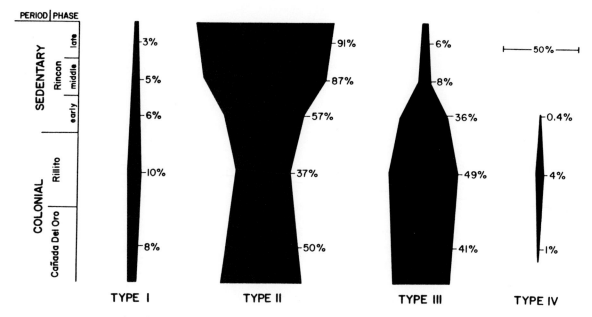

Figure 4.69 Relative proportion of plain ware types by phase.

One explanation of this pattern is that Colonial potters preferred micaceous rock tempers because of the micaceous sheen imparted to the vessel surface, and that the increases and decreases represent changes in aesthetic values. The micaceous sheen of Type III plain pottery is by far its most striking physical characteristic and may have been a form of decoration. It is also possible that the temper distinctions are not strictly dependent upon the passage of time, but are perhaps related to differences in the intended use of the vessels (Goodyear 1973; Raab 1973). However, the above correlation between the frequencies of each plain type and time, supports Doyel's (1976, 1977a: 29) argument that, if each temper type is related to a specific function, then either the function that necessitated crushed micaceous rock temper becomes less important through time, or this function can be served equally as well by sand-tempered pottery. This issue of different intended use is explored later.

Another possible explanation that involves the passage of time without changes in aesthetic values, is access to raw materials. The micaceous rocks used for temper in Types III and IV are not available in the Rosemont area, and must therefore have been obtained through trade or gathering excursions. The increases and decreases seen in Figure 4.69 may thus reflect fluctuations of supply in the exchange systems. The greatest incidence of Type III plain ware corresponds roughly to the last preference for crushed schist in the decorated pottery, and the abrupt shift from micaceous rocks to sand temper seen in the decorated pottery may also be explained by changes in the exchange network. When it became economically impractical to import schist in quantity, the use of sand may have increased. The persistence of micaceous rock temper in plain pottery may indicate that the imported schist and micaceous rocks continued to be used in plain ware. Regardless of the reasons, these are significant changes in the plain ware pottery that correlate with time.

Changes in Red Ware

In the collection of red wares from the ANAMAX-Rosemont Project, no technological or formal differences can be attributed to the passage of time.

Functional Variation

Intended use should affect the basic form of the vessel and the manufacturing technology. Painted vessels were probably not intended to be used as cooking vessels, as exposure over a wood fire would destroy or obscure the decoration. Also, clays and tempering materials may have been specifically selected for certain uses because of desirable physical properties. Various formal and technological aspects of the pottery have been explored, in an attempt to define patterns in the variability which relate to intended use. Time and geography have been controlled insofar as possible.

Vessel Shape

The adage that form follows function seems to have some importance in pottery studies; intended vessel use is equal to style in determining shape (Sackett 1977: 370). Clearly bowls and jars served different purposes and represent gross functional classes of pottery. Different pottery wares, plain, decorated, and red-slipped, were also intended for different uses. On the other hand, not all plain ware jars served the same purpose; some were undoubtedly cooking vessels and others were storage vessels. It may be possible, through the study of vessel form, to further distinguish particular kinds of bowls or jars intended for different uses. The most difficult aspect of functional studies is distinguishing between those attributes of form that are determined by intended use and those determined by style (Crown 1981).

Two important aspects of form are known to be affected by intended use: aperture diameter and volume (DeGarmo 1975; S. Plog 1980; Crown 1981). These then are the aspects of the pottery that should be studied to determine if there are finer distinctions within plain, painted, and red-slipped bowls and jars. This study of vessel shapes relies on the methods and theoretical position presented in Crown's (1984a) study of Classic period Phoenix Basin Hohokam pottery.

In this analysis, vessel proportions have been used to separate possible functional classes. These functional classes are then compared with Di Peso's (1956) use-study of Tucson Basin pottery and with Crown's (1984a) vessel form classes. These comparisons are necessarily general, as Di Peso does not clearly present his methods (thus the means to duplicate his results are lacking). Because Crown's study of Hohokam vessels encompasses the late Classic period in the Gila Basin it might be argued that it is inappropriate to use her form classes to describe the Preclassic Tucson Basin pottery at the Rosemont

sites; however vessel proportion data amassed by Crown (using vessels of
known use from ethnographic reports) illustrated an amazing consistency
in aperture-to-width and height-to-width proportions for vessels of
similar uses among different cultures with vastly different manufacturing traditions. Thus it may be proposed that the characteristics
which suit a vessel for a particular use are relatively consistent and
may differ little from region to region or through time.

Crown (1984a) uses two proportions, vessel height to breadth and
aperture to breadth, to define classes of bowls. For jars, vessel-
height-to-breadth, neck-height-to-vessel-height, aperture-to-breadth,
and neck-height-to-aperture ratios were used. These ratios were
computed for vessels in the Rosemont collection and are included in
Tables 4.32 and 4.33.

Bowls

Initially, bowls can be separated into two gross morphological
classes (those with direct rims and those with flaring rims); however,
these two classes are probably stylistic variations rather than
functionally distinct classes. As discussed above, flare-rimmed bowls
are the dominant bowl form during the Colonial period, with a shift
toward direct-rimmed bowls in the Sedentary period. It is unlikely that
this change represents a shift in the use(s) of bowls; it probably
indicates changing stylistic preferences. Therefore, flare-rimmed and
direct-rimmed bowls are not distinguished in this analysis.

If rim shape does not affect use, it seems likely that size and
overall shape may be functional indicators. Bowl size is determined by
multiplying minimum orifice diameter by body height, producing a "vessel
size index" (Table 4.32). By using minimum orifice diameter rather than
maximum orifice diameter, the distortion of actual vessel proportions
resulting from flared rims can be eliminated. In this analysis, only
the shape and size of the body is considered indicative of intended use.

Shape is also largely determined by the ratio of depth to width,
and can be quantified by computing the ratio of height to diameter.
Again, this ratio is based on height and minimum orifice, to eliminate
the distorting affects of flared rims. The ratio of body height to
minimum orifice diameter is also presented in Table 4.32.

Preliminary inspection of the vessel size index and body-height-
to-minimum-orifice-diameter ratio for the Rosemont collection indicates
that both measures have bimodal distributions. The vessel size index
ranges from 30.0 to 776.0, but two distinct clusters are present, one
ranging from 30.0 to 280.0, the other from 384.0 to 776.0. Based on
these data, the Rosemont collection contains two classes of bowls, small
and large, which may represent functional classes. Decorated, plain,
and red wares are present in each group; thus, although size may have
some impact on use, it is clear that there are a variety of functional
categories within each size cluster.

The ratio of body height to minimum orifice ranges from 0.29 to 0.69. Again, two clusters were identified, one ranging from 0.29 to 0.52 (shallow bowls, averaging 0.411) and the other from 0.59 to 0.69 (deep bowls, averaging 0.627). Again, both of these vessel shape classes contain bowls of all wares, and probably do not represent clearly use-related classes.

To examine the relationship between size and shape, the ratio of minimum orifice to body height was graphed against the vessel size index (Fig 4.70). Two groups are readily apparent in this scattergram, clustering by size rather than the height-to-breadth ratio; however, there are indications that both of these clusters may be subdivided into groups based on this ratio. These data suggest that the Rosemont collection might be divided into four classes: small, shallow bowls; small, deep bowls; large, shallow bowls; and large, deep bowls.

Even at this level, these classes do not seem to be use-specific, since each contains more than one ware. By dividing each of the size and shape classes by ware, 12 bowl types are possible, and it seems likely that each of these categories may be use-specific.

Crown's (1984a) study of Classic period pottery in the Phoenix Basin and Di Peso's (1956) classification of pottery from San Cayetano provide information on intended vessel use. Crown defines two bowl form classes based on the ratio of height to breadth (roughly equivalent to the ratio of body height to minimum orifice used here). Her Group 1 bowls have an average height-to-breadth ratio of 0.493, close to the 0.411 average of the shallow bowls in the Rosemont collection. Likewise her Group 2 bowls have an average height-to-breadth ratio of 0.617, very close to the 0.627 average of deep bowls in this study. Based on ethnographic comparisons, Crown determined that her Group 1 bowls could have been used as parching trays (probably plain wares, perhaps some decorated), griddles (plain wares), or serving and eating dishes (plain, painted, or red wares). She also inferred that her Group 2 bowls (deep bowls in the present study) could have been used as cooking vessels (plain and some painted wares), mixing bowls, cups, or serving and eating dishes (plain, painted, or red wares). With the exception of cups, the Rosemont vessels could have served any of these functions.

While it has been possible to define bowl shape classes which correspond to Crown's (1984a) Groups 1 and 2, no equivalents of her Groups 3 and 4 have been discussed. This is not because they are absent from the assemblage, but because vessels with incurved and recurved rims have been classified as restricted vessels, or jars.

Crown's use-categories are based on vessel shape and do not consider size; thus, they cannot explain the distinct size classes seen in the Rosemont bowls. It may be that size is not a function of intended use, but simply reflects the volume required. For example, a serving dish may be small or large, depending on whether it is intended for a single individual or an entire household. Di Peso (1956) makes such a distinction in the pottery of San Cayetano, identifying personal as well as family cooking vessels. The functional categories defined by

Di Peso are based on both size and shape; however he apparently relied on visual assessment of shape rather than height-to-breadth ratios, and comparisons to his use-categories are necessarily general. Of those, only what he calls stew bowls, Type 3a (Di Peso 1956: 280-281), and shallow and deep eating dishes are of concern here. His stew bowls are deep bowls with a capacity of 1 to 4.5 gallons, and are polished, painted and red-slipped wares (Di Peso 1956: 181). These may be roughly equivalent to two specimens in the Rosemont collection which are large, deep, decorated bowls (Fig. 4.70, Group 1). The eating dishes from San Cayetano are primarily red wares, with some painted and plain wares (Di Peso 1956, Fig. 42). There is no clear analogue in his study to the large, shallow bowls, but these may be included in his shallow eating dish category.

In sum, it is possible to define 12 bowl categories in the Rosemont collection, based on size, shape, and ceramic ware. Comparisons with the works of Crown (1984a) and Di Peso (1956) provide a means of postulating the intended uses of these vessels. The results of these efforts indicate that these bowl categories may represent specific use-related classes; however, the ANAMAX-Rosemong data are weak, given the lack of temporal control and the small sample size. Studies of vessel function are essential to identifying pottery variability and its potential causes.

Jars

Once again, the sample size is not large enough to explore phase by phase distinctions in jar shapes; however, the limited amount of information available suggests that there are no apparent differences in the vessel proportions and inferentially, their intended use. Those vessel proportions have been computed for all decorated and plain jars, and are shown in Table 4.33. Crown's (1984) study has shown that it is possible to identify shape classes based upon these proportions. One proportion, neck height to aperture diameter, is especially interesting because if it can be shown that vessels belonging to specific classes have consistent neck height-to-aperture ratios, these vessel classes can be identified from large rim sherds as well as restorable vessels.

In Figure 4.71, the ratio of vessel height to breadth is plotted against the aperture diameter-to-breadth ratio: Figure 4.72 illustrates the variation in those measurements on ethnographic examples (Crown 1984a). While there were no obvious clusters in the Rosemont collection (Fig. 4.71), if the values given by Crown (1984a) for ethnographically known water carrying, water storage, dry storage, and cooking vessels are imposed on this distribution (Fig. 4.73), all but four of the vessels fall within these partitions. Based upon this fit it would seem that the majority of the vessels are either cooking vessels or water storage or carrying jars. Of the four outlying vessels, three are located near the limits of the ethnographic data, and should probably be included with that material. The fourth vessel, however, is distinct; it is a seed jar, and no ethnographic vessels of this type were recorded by Crown (1984a).

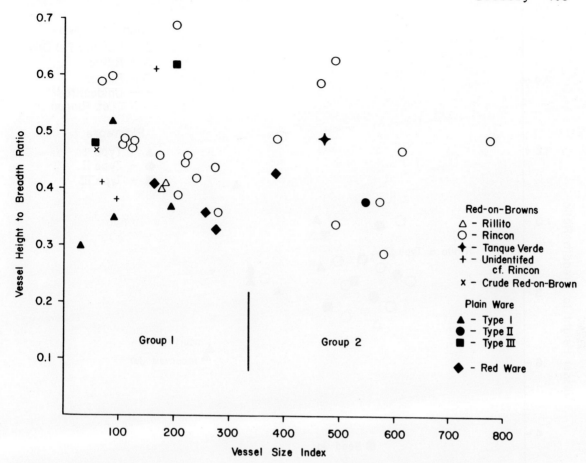

Figure 4.70   Vessel size index plotted against vessel height-to-breadth ratio for bowls.   Two distinct groups are visible based on size: Group 1 (small) and Group 2 (large).

Although these data correspond with the ethnographic information, there is no correlation with the jar shape classes defined by Crown. Most of the jars that could be called water storage jars according to the ethnographic data fall within Crown's Groups 1, 3, 4, and 5, which for the most part, are varieties of liquid storage containers (Crown 1984a). Group 1 is posited to include dry storage jars as well. Crown's Group 2, with large apertures and squat bodies, is inferred to represent cooking and mixing vessels; however, some of the ANAMAX vessels that correspond to ethnographic cooking vessels fall outside Crown's Group 2. Given the range of variation in the ethnographic cooking vessels it may be that there are regional or cultural variations. The posited cooking vessels in the Rosemont collection have much larger apertures with respect to vessels width, than do Crown's Group 2 jars.

Based on these comparisons it is possible to infer that those vessels with aperture-to-breadth ratios between 0.70 and 0.92 and heigth-to-breadth ratios between 0.60 and 1.24 are cooking vessels; however, this group contains both plain and painted vessels. It is unlikely that the painted vessels were intended to be used for cooking, because sooting would have obscured the decoration. It seems more

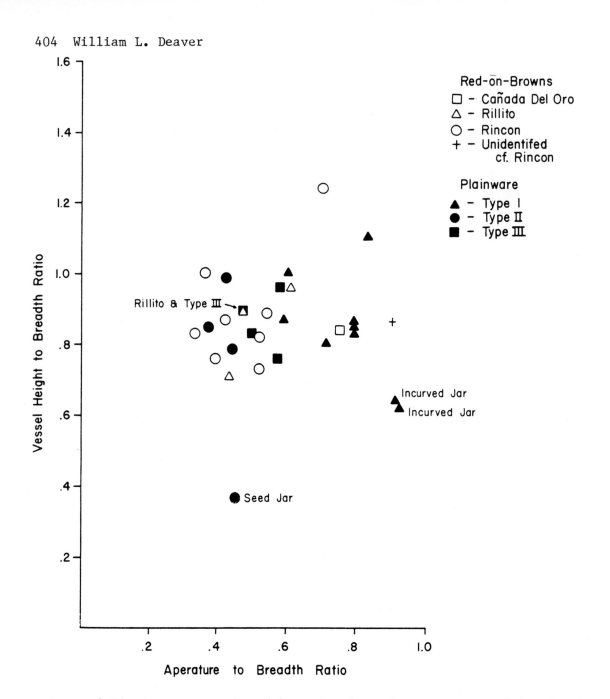

Figure 4.71 Aperture-to-breadth ratio plotted against vessel height-to-breadth ratio for jars.

likely that these vessels may have been mixing dishes. The remaining jars, with the exception of the example with a height-to-breadth ratio of 0.37, probably include water or liquid carrying and storage vessels and perhaps dry storage vessels as well.

The ratio of neck height to vessel height was computed for those jars with all vertical points present. Crown (1984a) presents these ratios for Groups 1 through 5. Generally, only Groups 1 and 2 stand out, with tall and short necks, respectively. There was virtually no correspondence between the Rosemont vessels and Crown's collection, based on the neck-height-to-vessel-height ratio. Her cooking vessels (Group 2) had an average neck-height-to-vessel-height proportion of

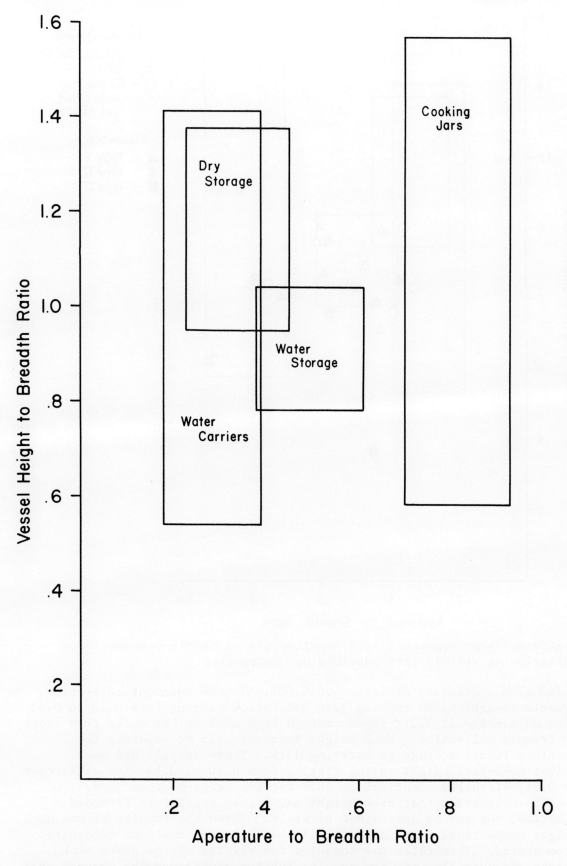

Figure 4.72 Limits of variation in vessel-height-to-breadth ratio and aperture-to-breadth ratio for historic vessels of known use (values taken from Crown 1984).

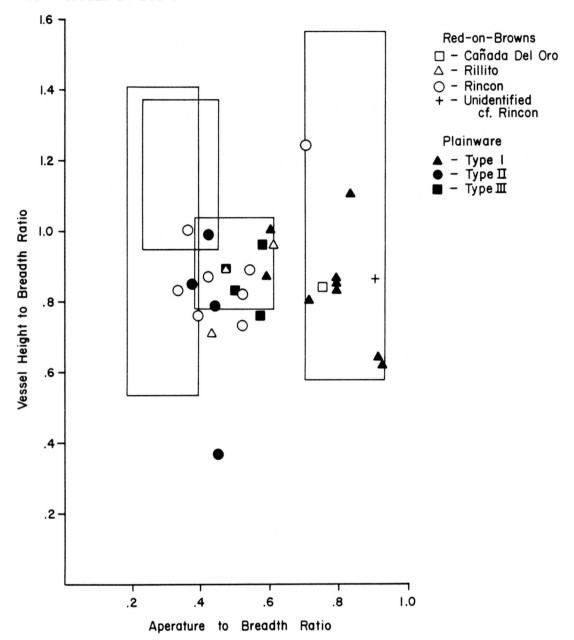

Figure 4.73 Ethnographic data superimposed on ANAMAX-Rosemont data,
partitioning vessels into possible use categories.

0.142 with a standard deviation of 0.068. In the Rosemont collection,
vessels thought to be cooking jars had ratios ranging from 0.15 to 0.43
with an average of 0.21; these vessels have much taller necks than those
in Crown's collection. Neck height does not help to separate the
possible liquid storage or carrying jars. These vessels had neck
height-to-vessel height ratios ranging from 0.10 to 0.44 with an average
of 0.21, virtually identical to that for the large-mouthed jars.
Therefore it seems that neck height may not be crucial to intended
function, but may be determined by style. Given the results of the neck
height comparisons it is doubtful if shape classes could be recognized
from sherds. This ratio was computed for all rim sherds where neck
height was possible, and the results further emphasized the absence of

major distinctions. In the Rosemont material, only one group is
distinct. Type I plain ware (the hand-made ware) has the smallest
average aperture and neck height.

Technology

It was anticipated that some technological differences in the
pottery would be related to function. It has already been demonstrated
that there are differences in the tempering materials for plain and
painted pottery; however, these differences are clearly related to time.
For each painted type and the red-slipped pottery, comparisons of temper
type by vessel form were made using the tighest chronological unit
possible, and no major distinctions were found. Comparing temper and
vessel form for the plain wares did reveal marked differences, however.
Although the shift from crushed micaceous rock to sand temper has been
correlated with the passage of time, there may also be functional
differences among the plain ware pottery types.

Comparisons of Plain Ware Types

Comparisons of functional differences in the plain ware types is
based upon the notion that temper selection is functionally related. If
there are indeed functional differences between the plain ware types
that necessitated the use of different tempers, there may be other
formal and technological distinctions as well.

Vessel Size

One of the most obvious differences in the plain pottery is the
small size of Type I. Figure 4.74 displays estimated minimum orifice
diameter for bowls, and aperture diameters for jars using the running
average technique. For both bowls and jars, Types II and III are more
similar to one another than either is to Type I.

These graphs, however, combine all time periods, and because it
has been shown that they have different temporal ranges, it may be that
at any one point in time there may be differences between Types II and
III. Type III is much more common in the early period (Cañada del Oro
through early Rincon), and if functional differences exist between it
and Type II, these should be more readily identified during this time.
However, the results (Fig. 4.75) do not demonstrate significant
differences between Types II and III.

Vessel Shape

Another test for possible functional differences among the plain
pottery types is based upon the premise that if vessel shape and temper
are determined to whatever extent, by intended use, then there should be
differences in either the range of forms present, or their relative

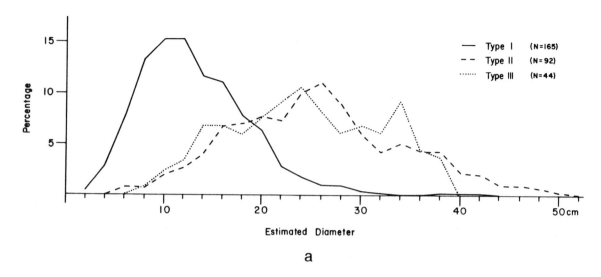

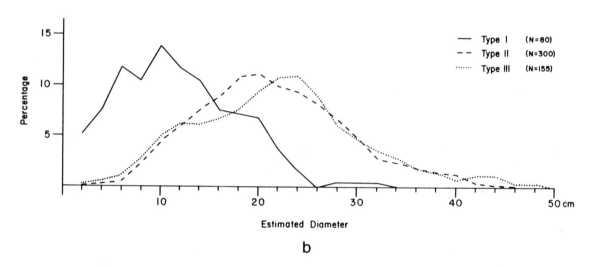

Figure 4.74 Comparison of Types I, II, and III plain ware bowls (a) based on minimum orifice, and jars (b) based on aperture diameter for all time periods. Curves are smoothed using the running average technique.

proportions, among types. As determined from rim sherds, there are three classes of bowl forms: direct rimmed, flaring rimmed, and everted rim.

Five form classes were identified for jars: incurved, flared neck, straight, recurved, and upcurved; within these several subclasses were identified. The frequencies for each type were computed by shape (Table 4.34), and are presented graphically in Figures 4.76 and 4.77.

It is clear that there is no major distinction among Types I, II, or III in bowl shapes. While the absolute values vary, the overall shape of the graphs are quite similar. However, Types II and III jars are most similar to one another, and both are distinct from Type I, principally due to the greater porportion of slightly and moderately incurved jars in Type I.

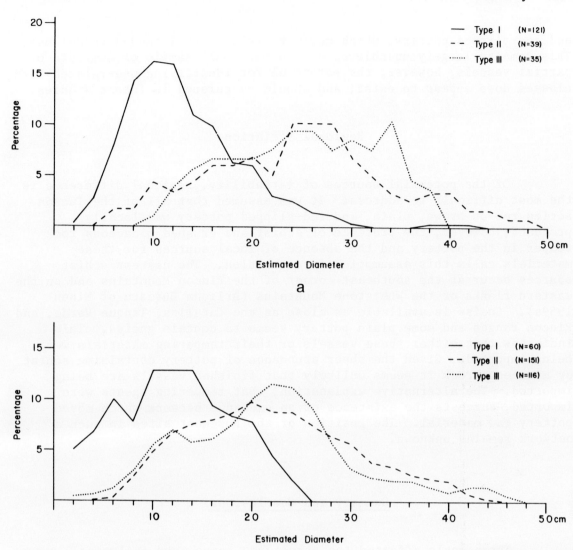

Figure 4.75   Comparison of Types I, II, and III plain ware bowls (a) based on minimum orifice, and jars (b) based on aperture during the "early" occupation (includes Cañada del Oro, Rillito, and early Rincon phases).   Curves are smoothed using the running average technique.

These comparisons indicate that there are few differences between Type II and III plain ware. Type I is distinct on all counts and therefore probably represents a functionally distinct type. The only significant difference between Types II and III is temper; if temper type was dictated by intended vessel use, apparently aperture size and vessel shape were not.

Summary of Function

At the outset of the ANAMAX pottery study it was hoped that specific formal classes could be defined within the plain, decorated,

and red-slipped pottery, which could be related to intended vessel use.
This remains largely unachieved due to the small sample of complete or
partial vessels; however, the potential for identifying use-related form
classes does appear to exist, and should be pursued in future studies.

Regional Variation

Of the potential sources of variability, regional difference is
the most difficult to address. It was assumed that all of the Tucson
series red-on-brown, plain, and red-slipped pottery was locally
produced; however, the presence of schist and crushed micaceous rock
temper in the pottery and the absence of local sources for these
materials calls this assumption into question. The nearest schist
sources occur at the southeast corner of the Rincon Mountains and on the
eastern flanks of the Whetstone Mountains (Arizona Burearu of Mines
1959a). Gneiss is available as close as the Catalina, Tanque Verde, and
Rincon ranges and some plain pottery seems to contain gneiss. This
indicates that either these vessels or their tempering materials were
being imported. Given the sheer abundance of pottery containing schist
or micaceous rock it seems unlikely that finished vessels are being
imported. The alternative explanation, that tempering agents were
imported, suggests the existence of an exchange network which moved
pottery raw material. The position of the Rosemont sites in such a
network remains unknown.

Summary and Conclusions

Three goals affected the structure, focus, and analytical
techniques employed in this study. The first goal was to attempt to
identify temporally, functionally, and regionally diagnostic classes of
pottery to provide the information needed to evaluate the project
research objectives (Chapter 2). The second goal was to describe the
variability in the painted, plain, and red ware pottery. Although
decorated pottery received the greatest amount of attention by virtue of
its ability to yield chronological information, the study of plain ware
was given special emphasis because previous studies and reports have
provided so little information concerning variability in this class of
pottery. The final goal was to emphasis the need to approach the
pottery from a variety of analytical perspectives, using analytical
approaches and techniques designed to collect the kind of data needed to
identify temporal, functional, and regional classes of pottery. The
intent of this study was not to create a listing of taxonomic headings,
but to document the variability in the pottery, and to understand how it
might provide information about the prehistoric people that produced,
exchanged, used, and ultimately discarded the pottery.

Identifying pottery classes and attributes that can be used as
horizon markers has been the most successful endeavor of this study.

Table 4.34

INVENTORY OF BOWL AND JAR SHAPES*
FOR TYPE I, II, AND III PLAIN WARES

Vessel Shape	Type I			Type II			Type III		
	N	Percent of Shape	Percent of Total	N	Percent of Shape	Percent of Total	N	Percent of Shape	Percent of Total
BOWLS									
Direct rim	(136)**		(82.9)	(88)		(88.0)	(37)		(84.1)
Hemispherical	45	33.1	27.4	28	31.8	28.0	11	29.7	25.0
Deep subhemispherical	57	41.9	34.8	52	59.1	52.0	18	48.6	40.9
Shallow subhemispherical	23	16.9	14.0	5	5.7	5.0	7	18.9	15.9
Plate	11	8.1	6.7	2	2.3	2.0	1	2.7	2.3
Indeterminate				1	1.1	1.0			
Flared rim	(17)		(10.3)	(10)		(10.0)	(7)		(15.9)
Slight	4	23.5	2.4	4	40.0	4.0	3	42.9	6.8
Moderate	13	76.5	7.9	6	60.0	6.0	4	57.1	9.1
Everted rim	(11)		(6.7)	(2)		(2.0)			
Slight	4	36.4	2.4						
Moderate	6	54.5	3.7	2	100.0	2.0			
Pronounced	1	9.1	0.6						
Total Bowls	164		100.0	100		100.0	44		100.0
JARS									
Incurved neck	(40)		(50.0)	(31)		(10.3)	(10)		(6.7)
Complete	4	10.0	5.0	23	74.2	7.7	2	20.0	1.3
Moderate	10	25.0	12.5	4	12.9	1.3	7	70.0	4.7
Slight	26	65.0	32.5	4	12.9	1.3	1	10.0	0.7
Flared neck	(19)		(23.8)	(172)		(57.7)	(96)		(64.5)
Slight	5	26.3	6.3	53	30.8	17.8	43	44.8	28.9
Moderate	14	73.7	17.5	118	68.6	39.6	52	54.2	34.9
Pronounced							1	1.0	0.7
Indeterminate				1	0.6	0.3			
Upcurved neck	(21)		(26.4)	(94)		(31.6)	(41)		(27.5)
Complete	17	81.0	21.3	86	91.5	28.9	38	92.7	25.5
Incomplete	3	14.3	3.8	8	8.5	2.7	3	7.3	2.0
Indeterminate	1	4.8	1.3						
Straight neck				(1)		(0.3)			
Recurved neck							(2)		(1.3)
Total Jars	80			298			149		

* As determined from rim sherds
** ( ) = Category total

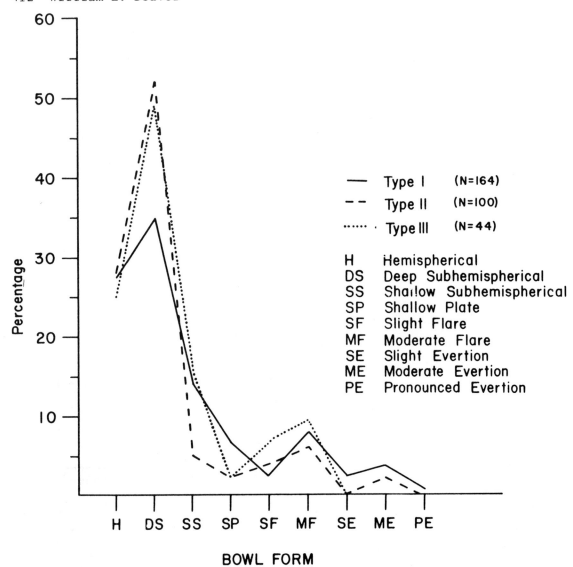

Figure 4.76 Comparison of Types I, II, and III plain ware bowl forms.

Decorated pottery has long been recognized as a good chronological tool (Kelly 1978; Haury 1976: 254). Changes in vessel shapes, manner of finish, and decorative style have been emphasized in defining typological constructs representing particular periods of time. Because Tucson Basin ceramic technology is poorly known, and because temporally sensitive changes in vessel shape are not often identifiable from sherds, decoration remains the principle attribute from which changes through time may be inferred. Changes in decoration have been studied within the framework of a sequential model of stylistic development which recognizes several particular design styles as horizon markers.

The model of stylistic development presented emphasizes those aspects of decoration that are most frequently used to assign phase affiliation. Although preliminary, it nevertheless documents significant, temporally diagnostic changes in decoration. The sequence of decorative styles has been at least partially supported by stratigraphic and chronometric evidence, as well as by the results of technological

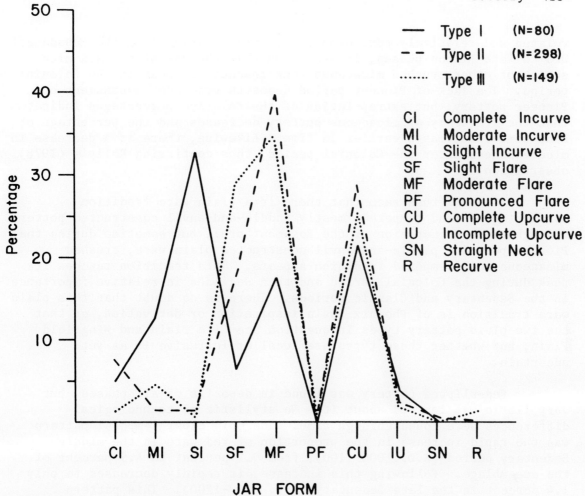

Figure 4.77 Comparison of Types I, II, and III plainware jar forms.

and formal analyses. Differences in pottery technology and shape have
been correlated with design styles, further enhancing the utility and
value of these stylistic concepts. The correlation of those technological and formal attributes with particular decorative configurations
provides additional means of separating the pottery into time-specific
types.

In addition to further clarifying changes in the decorated
pottery through time, patterned variation in the plain ware confirmed
Kelly's (1978: 69-77) assessment of plain ware development in the Tucson
Basin. She stated that Pioneer period plain ware was nonmicaceous
(presumably sand tempered), becoming noticeably more micaceous
(presumably crushed mica schist), in the Colonial period. The plain
ware of the Sedentary and Classic periods was again nonmicaceous (sand
tempered). Four distinct plain ware types were defined from the
Rosemont sites, based upon construction techniques, temper, and surface
finish. Two types contain sand temper, one manufactured using a coil
and hand modeling technique, the other constructed using paddle and
anvil. The two others contain crushed mica schist or some other
micaceous rock temper and are paddle-and-anvil constructed; they differ
only in the size of the temper particles. Using stratigraphically

related and relatively pure deposits of trash dating from the Cañada del Oro to late Rincon phases, it was shown that the use of crushed mica schist or other crushed micaceous rock reached its peak in the Colonial period. The lack of Pioneer period deposits precludes assessment of Pioneer pottery, but extrapolation of the relative percentages indicates that the frequency of micaceous pottery decreases and the percentage of sand temper increases earlier in time. Likewise, there is a decrease in micaceousness after the Colonial period, thus confirming Kelly's (1978) observation.

It would then seem that there is a plain ware tradition consisting of sand tempered, mostly paddle-and-anvil constructed pottery throughout the occupation of the Rosemont area, but sometime during the Pioneer period a paddle-and-anvil constructed plain ware, crushed micaceous rock-tempered tradition appears. This tradition reaches its peak during the Colonial period and then declines in relative importance in the Sedentary and Classic periods. There is no doubt that this plain ware tradition is of Phoenix Basin inspiration or derivation, or that the two plain pottery types in question are Gila Plain and Wingfield Plain, but whether these types are local or intrusive is as yet uncertain.

Red-slipped pottery was found in deposits of all phases, but very little was learned about it. No stylistic or technological differences were found through time. The only clear temporal pattern was the rapid increase in the proportion of red ware in the middle Sedentary period (A.D. 1000-1100), from 0.2 percent to 4.9 percent of the assemblage. Following this increase, it rapidly decreases to only 1.4 percent in the late Sedentary (A.D. 1100-1200). This pattern supports the inference that Tucson Basin red wares are produced only in the Sedentary, and not in the Colonial or Classic periods (Kelly 1978: 67-69; Greenleaf 1975: 58-60). The pre-Sedentary period red wares may be intrusive from the San Pedro or San Simon areas to the east where San Francisco Red is contemporaneous with the Colonial period (Fulton and Tuthill 1940: 45; Tuthill 1947: 57; Franklin 1980: 73); however, because the pre-Sedentary red wares in the Rosemont sites were not technologically distinct from the later ones, the pre-Sedentary red wares cannot clearly be attributed to trade.

While this study has succeeded in identifying temporal patterning in the painted and plain pottery, it failed to find patterned variation in the red-slipped pottery. It has been largely unsuccessful in identifying functionally related patterns in the pottery. It was initially expected that intended vessel use might affect formal and technological attributes, and that detailed studies identify these effects. Logically, shape can only be observed on whole or nearly whole vessels, but because of the scarcity of recovered vessels the vessel shape study relied on aspects of shape that can be observed on sherds. Technological variation in decorated and plain pottery was found to correlate with time. The use of decorated vessels probably did <u>not</u> change from the Colonial to the Sedentary period so function does not explain the shift from crushed mica schist to sand temper. Likewise, changes in bowl shapes from flared rims early in time to simple subhemispherical shapes, do not seem to represent functional distinctions. The only difference found in the painted pottery that might indirectly be related to use is the increase in the relative frequency of jars through time. Evidence from Snaketown indicates that both plain and painted jars were used for storage (Gladwin and others 1937: Plate XVII; Haury 1976: 207). The observed increase in the frequency of painted jars in the local sequence may represent an increase in the use of painted jars in conjunction with plain jars, as storage facilities. This does not represent a change in the use of decorated jars, which may have been used for storage prior to the Sedentary Period, but instead a change in the preference for the type of jars used for storage.

It has not been possible to demonstrate that painted, plain, or red wares were intended for different uses. Logically, plain ware was probably the preferred type for uses such as cooking, and there might likewise be specific uses for painted and red-slipped pottery. Measurements of jar apertures and bowl orifices (from rim sherds) indicated that if functional differences exist, they are not reflected in absolute aperture diameter. This does not preclude the possibility that there are overall differences in shape or in relative proportions of aperture to height or aperture to maximum vessel diameter. Comparison of these proportions on the few whole or partial vessels recovered with values obtained from ethnographic vessels of known use indicates that the uses of plain and painted vessels may have overlapped.

Neither was it possible to determine if the plain ware types were manufactured to serve different uses. It was thought that the selection of sand or crushed mica schist for temper might be related to different uses. Comparisons of jar aperture and bowl orifice diameters, and the inventory of vessel shapes indicates that there are no clear-cut, use-related differences in shapes between sand and schist tempered pottery. The only conclusion that can be drawn is that if there are functional distinctions between sand and crushed mica schist-tempered plain ware, they do not affect the shape or aperture size. Also, if crushed schist tempered pottery is intended for different uses, the schist is probably not crucial to the vessel's performance. The decrease in mica schist tempered pottery after the Colonial period and its apparent replacement by sand-tempered pottery indicates that sand tempered pottery could fulfill the same function(s).

The only apparently use-related plain ware type is a sand-tempered, hand-modeled pottery. This type differed from all other plain types in the size of the vessels (notably smaller) and in the array of vessel shapes. It was impossible to determine its particular function(s).

The final interpretive focus of this pottery study was to identify regionally specific classes indicative of exchange patterns. Pottery from four areas other than the Tucson Basin was identified: the Phoenix Basin (Hohokam); southeastern Arizona (San Simon Mogollon); Sonora (Trincheras); and the Colorado Plateau (Anasazi). It was also hoped that exchange between the ANAMAX-Rosemont study area and the Tucson Basin proper might be recognized; however, there is as yet no definite evidence of such exchange, although it probably occurred.

Further evidence of exchange was found in the plain pottery, but whether it was at the local or regional level cannot be determined; neither is it possible to determine exactly what was being exchanged. The micaceous rocks used for temper in the Gila and Wingfield plain pottery are not available within the project area; the nearest sources are in the Rincon Mountains to the north. At the very least the raw materials had to be brought into the project area and it is possible that finished vessels were imported. I prefer the interpretation that raw materials were being exchanged; it is difficult to believe that over one-half of the plain pottery of the Rillito phase was imported.

Until now, this discussion has summarized the findings of this pottery study and describes the variability seen in the Rosemont pottery assemblage. At a more general level, the relationships between Tucson Basin pottery and Phoenix Basin Hohokam and Mogollon pottery should be considered.

The relationship of Tucson Basin pottery to the ceramic traditions of southern Arizona has been a matter of confusion. The first work with Tucson Basin pottery classified it as red-on-buff (Gladwin and Gladwin 1929: 119; Gabel 1931; Fraps 1931). In 1935 Kelly (1978) identified it as red-on-brown, and stressed its similarities with the Mogollon red-on-browns to the east. Colton (1955) assigned the Tucson ceramics to the Mogollon brown ware, Santa Cruz series. Further confusion has been added by Ezell's assignment of Tanque Verde Red-on-brown to the Sonoran brown wares; a tradition which includes the Trincheras material and Papago Red-on-brown (Ezell 1954, 1955). Colton's assignment of the Tucson pottery to the Mogollon brown wares, and Ezell's assignment to the Sonoran brown wares are both erroneous; the first because it places the paddle-and-anvil Tucson ceramics in a tradition characterized by coil-and-scrape pottery. Ezell's assignment emphasizes the clay and ignores other attributes which may be culturally more significant. In fact, even the notion of Tucson pottery as intermediate between the Phoenix Basin buff wares and Mogollon red-on-browns is based upon superficial attributes.

Studies of Tucson Basin pottery, including Kelly's (1978) work at Hodges, have pointed out the similarities to Hohokam and Mogollon pottery. The following statement has often been used to introduce discussions of Tucson Basin pottery:

> Tucson Basin pottery appears to be intermediate between Hohokam red-on-buff and Mogollon red-on-brown, an ambivalence entirely expectable from its intermediate location. On the one hand, it has pronounced Mogollon affinities in its close grained paste, its polish, its relative absence of slip, its utilization of smudging; and, in certain vessel forms, a preference for geometric ornament. The Gila Basin rose-colored paste with its excessive porosity, its chalky slip, its fugitive pigment, and

its matte surface seems generally foreign to Tucson. On the
other hand, shape and ornamentation adhere closely to the Gila
Basin pattern (Kelly 1978: 3).

I agree that there are similarities with Mogollon red-on-brown pottery,
and some Mogollon ideas may have been incorporated into the local
pottery tradition, but these similarities have been overemphasized. It
is clear that Tucson Basin pottery is manufactured in the Hohokam mold.
A trait-by-trait comparison shows that Tucson pottery shares more
features with the Hohokam pottery tradition than the Mogollon,
especially if particular design configurations are considered (compare
illustrations in this chapter with Gladwin and others 1937 and Haury
1976, and contrast with Haury 1936a and Sayles 1945). Specifically
examinimg the "Mogollon" characteristics cited in Kelly's statement
shows that precedents for many of these attributes can be found in the
Phoenix Basin pottery tradition, or may be viewed as regional variation
within a single tradition.

The close-grained paste of Tucson Basin pottery is a trait that
can be explained by the use of locally available clays (Doyel 1977a: 31)
or even, again, as a continuation of Pioneer period ideas. Haury
attributes the porosity of the Gila Basin buff wares to some efferves-
cant impurities in the clay that disappear during firing or later (Haury
1976: 205). Clearly this is not a culturally significant characteristic
but one due to characteristics of the locally available clays. Phoenix
Basin potters probably did not select buff clays for their porosity, but
rather for the light buff color obtained when properly fired. Tucson
Basin potters obtained a light-colored background through the use of
slips, but the buff-colored clays of the Phoenix Basin may have been
unavailable. Instead, the Tucson potters used local (darker) clay
deposits. Some of these do approach the Phoenix Basin clays in color
and porosity so that in some cases it is difficult to distinguish the
local red-on-browns from the intrusive red-on-buffs by color and
porosity. This indicates that similar, though not identical clays may
have been selected.

The preference for polishing on the local Tucson pottery and the
general absence of slip can also be attributed to regional variation or
a continuance of earlier traditions. Kelly (1978) and Haury (1976, in
Gladwin and others 1937) note that Pioneer pottery is tool polished, and
the plain wares always exhibit tool polishing. Therefore it seems
possible that polishing of decorated pottery in the Tucson Basin may be
a local continuation of the Pioneer period surface treatment. This
style declines in popularity in the Phoenix Basin after the Pioneer
periods, possibly as a result of the shift to buff clays and the use of
a buff-colored wash. Polishing over the paint, which is typical of
Mogollon red-on-browns, does not appear on Tucson pottery.

Tucson Basin pottery does exhibit the use of a white or
buff-colored slip as early as the Cañada del Oro phase, but this is not
the dominant surface treatment at any time. The inception of this
treatment appears in the Snaketown phase in the Phoenix Basin (Haury
1976: 214); the earlier pottery lacking a slip. Again, Tucson Basin

pottery appears to retain the preference for unslipped surfaces, but whether this is indeed cultural conservatism is unknown.

Kelly's statement that geometric ornamentation was preferred by Tucson Basin potters apparently reflects the weak development of life forms on Tucson pottery (Kelly 1978: 38). No doubt this assessment was based on comparisons of the Hodges Ruin material and the material from Snaketown (Gladwin and others 1937). Life forms on Tucson Basin pottery do appear to be less frequent than at Snaketown, but the frequency of life forms on Snaketown pottery may not be truly typical of the Phoenix Basin at large. In fact, Snaketown is probably not a typical Phoenix Basin Hohokam site, but one of an important, specialized nature. The finding of a pottery workshop with pottery kilns at Snaketown (Haury 1976: 194-197) has been interpreted as evidence of the development of craft guilds and possibly of large scale production (Masse 1982: 79), and it may not be prudent to use Snaketown pottery to represent the area as a whole. It is therefore difficult to say for certain that life forms are more rare on Tucson Basin pottery than Phoenix Basin pottery. Even if such were shown to be the case, the Tucson Basin pottery still exhibits a great variety of life forms. If life forms are less common at sites other than Snaketown, geometric ornament may be relatively more abundant. In any case, the suggested similarity of the Tucson Basin and Mogollon pottery traditions based on the preference for geometric ornament seems unfounded at present.

Not only do these trait comparisons indicate close Gila Basin ties, but other attributes support this inference. The Pioneer and Colonial pottery from the Tucson Basin utilizes crushed mica schist, either alone or in conjunction with sand, and a paddle-and-anvil construction technique that is closely analogous to the use of schist temper and paddle-and-anvil construction in the Phoenix Basin (Gladwin and others 1937; Haury 1976). These traditions diverge at the interface of the Colonial and Sedentary periods, when Tucson Basin pottery technology shifts to the use of sand temper. The Phoenix Basin continues to use crushed mica schist (Haury 1976; Abbott 1982). Smudging and the use of a black pigment in bichrome and polychrome color schemes also appear in the Tucson Basin during the Sedentary period. These developments are unparalleled in the Phoenix Basin pottery tradition; however, there are still close parallels in vessel shape and design.

Taken as a whole, Tucson Basin pottery reflects the Phoenix Basin pattern. The differences in the array of vessel shapes, with the Tucson Basin having only a subset of the shapes present in the Gila Basin, and the lesser frequency of exterior scoring on early Colonial period Tucson pottery can be interpreted as no more than regional variation within a common pottery tradition. On the other hand the differences in surface finish and clay can be viewed as the local persistence of typical Pioneer period traditions, with the innovations seen in the Phoenix Basin only slightly reflected in the Tucson Basin. From its inception Tucson Basin pottery is produced in the Hohokam manner. Its Mogollon similarities are superficial, and are not evidence of a hybrid technology or culture. The Mogollon pottery tradition, with its coil and scrape construction technology, nonschist tempering, red exterior slip, and polishing over the painted decoration is foreign to the Tucson Basin. Tucson Basin pottery maintains its close ties to the Phoenix Basin throughout its history in vessel shapes and decorative styles. The development of a local identity does not appear until the Sedentary period when there is a shift in pottery technology and Tucson Basin potters began to experiment with variations of the red-on-brown color scheme, producing red-on-black, black-on-brown, black-on-white, and several polychrome color combinations.

There is, unfortunately, a limit to broad scale interpretation of the information from the Rosemont pottery study, namely the lack of comparative data. This can be attributed to the focus of pottery studies on type categories and the use of a classificatory approach. Classification of a pot sherd by type acknowledges the validity of the type category and confirms the definition, eliminating the need to further study or describe the sherd. New categories were defined, creating new temporal markers within the existing system, whenever sherds that did not fit existing type definitions were encountered.

Obviously, it was not possible to carry out all potential analyses. For example, petrographic studies and X-ray flouresence examinations of the pottery were not undertaken. Without a large scale sampling procedure, involving many other collections, which was beyond the project resources, the results of such studies would have been largely uninterpretable. Therefore, throughout the course of this study it was assumed that the Tucson series pottery from the Rosemont sites were locally made.

Chapter 5

FLAKED STONE

Kenneth C. Rozen

Introduction

Project Background

Fourteen Hohokam sites, located in the eastern foothills of the
Santa Rita Mountains, were excavated during the mitigation phase of the
ANAMAX-Rosemont project. Ceramic evidence indicates that these sites
are associated with a continuous, though temporally restricted
occupation of the study area which began during the Cañada del Oro phase
around A.D. 600, and ended at the close of the Rincon phase, sometime
around A.D. 1200. Although all of the sites yielded evidence of pit
houses, and can therefore be broadly classified as "habitation sites,"
they exhibit a great deal of variation with respect to a number of
nonassemblage characteristics. For example, the number of structures
present ranges from 2 to about 30. Artifact densities, calculated for
each site on the basis of the number of sherds and flaked stone items
recovered from pit house fill, vary from about 20 to 340 artifacts per
cubic meter. Numbers of extramural features range from none to nearly
200, and site areas range from approximately 600 to 7000 square meters.
These observations suggest that there may be substantial differences
among sites in terms of occupation duration, intensity, and possibly
periodicity. This chapter presents the results of the analysis of the
23,529 chipped stone artifacts collected during the mitigation phase.
Flaked stone artifacts recovered during the testing phase of the ANAMAX-
Rosemont project have been described and analyzed elsewhere by Huckell
(1980).

Research Objectives

Five problem domains which guided research at the ANAMAX-
Rosemont Hohokam sites have been identified in Chapter 2. The first of
these concerns definition of functional site types and intrasite
organization, and served as the principal research focus of the chipped
stone analysis. The goal of the analysis was to determine the extent to

421

which assemblage variation could be attributed to differences in site function.

In formulating specific research questions, it is important to consider two aspects of the notion of "site function"; flaked stone assemblage variation may be a product of either, or possibly an interaction of both of these factors. First, assemblage variation may result directly from different activities involving lithic reduction and tool use. For example, the technological characteristics of collections resulting from core reduction (primary reduction) may differ from those produced as a result of tool manufacture (secondary reduction). Relative frequencies of various tool types may differ according to varying emphases on activities such as woodworking, butchering, hide preparation, plant fiber processing, and so forth.

Second, variation in chipped stone assemblages may result indirectly from occupational differences, even though the range of tasks for which stone tools were used was the same. For example, lithic materials may have been repeatedly used and modified before discard, and therefore more exhaustively reduced, on sites which were permanently occupied by large groups of people for long periods. In contrast, on sites which were occupied by small groups of people for only short periods, lithic materials may have been subjected to relatively less reuse and modification before discard or abandonment, and therefore may not have been as intensively reduced. Strictly speaking, assemblage variation that reflects differences in the nature of site occupations is not "functional" variation in the sense that it results directly from different activities. Assuming, however, that occupational factors may be closely tied to site function, variation resulting from these factors may be considered "functional" to the extent that it reflects different roles or functions of sites within the broader settlement and subsistence system.

Another aspect of site function defined in Chapter 2 pertains to intrasite organization. From the standpoint of chipped stone variability, assemblages from various contexts within sites may differ according to the activities and associated behaviors that produced them. For example, some contexts, such as structure floors and extramural work areas may yield collections which consist primarily of the selected products of tool manufacture, while others, such as pit house fill, may contain mostly trash such as broken or exhausted tools and manufacturing debris.

In view of the general functional problems outlined above, specific research questions to be addressed by the chipped stone analysis may be stated as follows:

1. To what extent can variation in tool form and frequency be demonstrated among sites, and how does this variation relate to differences in the tasks for which those tool assemblages were used?

2. Can variation in the technological characteristics of debitage
    be demonstrated among sites, and if so, how does it reflect
    differences in lithic reduction?

3. What differences exist among assemblages from various intrasite
    contexts, and what does this variation indicate about the
    spatial distribution of activities involving lithic reduction
    and tool use and discard?

4. Can correlations between assemblage characteristics and
    occupational factors be demonstrated, and if so, what do these
    correlations indicate about site function?

In addition to functional studies, the remaining four research
problem domains identified in Chapter 2 deal with: (1) economy and
subsistence, (2) site distribution, population distribution, and
intersite organization, (3) areal and regional relationships, and (4)
temporal concerns. The chipped stone analysis was not designed to
address questions pertaining to the first two of these problem domains
because such questions can be answered with greater specificity using
other kinds of data. Similarly, the ANAMAX-Rosemont Hohokam chipped
stone assemblages have little potential for resolving matters of areal
and regional relationships because there is very little, if any,
evidence for artifacts of either nonlocal style or raw material.
Systematic investigation of chipped stone variability through time was
not selected as the major research focus of the analysis because many of
the assemblages were from mixed temporal contexts. Also, it seems
unlikely that any major technological change would have occurred during
the relatively short period during which the assemblages were produced.

Previous Research

Archaeological investigations of Hohokam prehistory have been
going on since the early decades of this century. Until recently, much
of this effort has been aimed at resolving culture history problems. As
is the case throughout the Southwest, Hohokam material culture studies
have traditionally focused on pottery. In comparison, there has been
little systematic description, analysis, and interpretation of flaked
stone variability. Huckell (1981b: 172) suggests that the greater
emphasis on ceramic studies is at least partially attributable to the
greater abundance of potsherds in relation to flaked stone on most
sites. In view of the culture-historical orientation of traditional
Hohokam archaeology, it also seems likely that pottery has been the
major focus of material culture studies because it is a more sensitive
indicator of age and cultural affiliation than is flaked stone.

Excavations at Snaketown (Gladwin and others 1937) and Los
Muertos (Haury 1945) in the Gila and Salt river valleys in south-central
Arizona, and at the Hodges Ruin (Kelly 1978) and University Indian Ruin
(Hayden 1957) in the Tucson Basin, represent pioneering efforts to

define the Hohokam culture sequence. These studies are typical of early Hohokam research in that they deal with large, permanently occupied habitation sites. Treatment of flaked stone assemblages is commonly limited to descriptive tool type inventories, often with a strong emphasis on the temporal placement of various projectile point styles.

Because many early works deal only with large habitation sites, and usually contain only very limited information about flaked stone assemblages, they are of little comparative value for investigating relationships between site function and assemblage variation. Nevertheless, some of these early reports contain useful generalizations about Hohokam chipped stone industries based on qualitative observations. With regard to tools from University Indian Ruin, for example, Hayden (1957: 151-152) suggests that the Hohokam were skilled at pressure flaking, but that simple percussion-flaked implements used for basic cutting, chopping, and scraping tasks were made with no investment of time or effort. Hayden also suggests that the simpler percussion-flaked forms had their origins in preceramic industries, and are of little value as indicators of culture change.

More recently, similar observations about chipped stone tools recovered from Snaketown during the 1964-1965 excavations have been made by Haury, who states that, with the exception of finely pressure-flaked projectile points, "heavy work tools were given not one bit more attention than was needed to make them effective" (1976: 298), and that ". . . simple tasks of cutting, scraping, crushing, and the like were done with the nearest rock at hand, modified as needed, and then discarded" (1976: 293).

With the advent of contract archaeology, and growing industrial and urban development in southern Arizona, there has been a vast increase in research on Hohokam sites. In contrast to earlier efforts which focused on large habitation sites, usually located along major drainages, contract projects have provided archaeologists with the opportunity to investigate a wide range of different kinds of sites located in more diverse physiographic settings. Concurrently, there has been a growing interest in research problems pertaining to site function and the development of regional settlement and subsistence systems.

Amidst the profusion of recent literature dealing with Hohokam archaeology, chipped stone assemblages have received highly variable analytic treatment. At one extreme, for example, some reports present little more than projectile point descriptions (Greenleaf 1975). At the opposite end of the spectrum, other studies are based on the quantitative description of assemblages, including debitage, and make use of various statistical techniques to determine the significance of variation (Bayham 1976a; Rice 1979). Because of its great quantity, the recent literature will not be exhaustively reviewed here; however, several of the more useful works dealing with Hohokam lithic technology and relationships between site function and assemblage variation will be examined briefly.

The first of these is Huckell's (1981b) study of the flaked
stone from Las Colinas, a large Classic period habitation site in the
Phoenix Basin. Based on a reexamination of the tool assemblage and
previously recorded debitage data, Huckell presents a model describing
lithic reduction sequences. This model indicates that the dominant
technology at Las Colinas involved simple hard-hammer percussion flaking
of locally available river cobbles of medium- to coarse-textured
materials. The resulting flakes were either used as is, or were
themselves modified by direct percussion. Smaller nodules of chert and
obsidian were also reduced by hard-hammer percussion, and the resulting
flakes shaped into more specialized tools, including projectile points,
by pressure flaking. The general absence of biface-thinning flakes
suggests that soft-hammer percussion thinning was not common. In
conclusion, Huckell (1981b: 199) states that:

> Perhaps the most remarkable aspect of Classic period Hohokam
> flaked stone assemblages is the technological continuity that
> completely overshadows any variation that could be attributed to
> culture change.

Rice's technological study of flaked stone assemblages from 13
Hohokam sites in the Gila Butte-Santan area (Rice 1979: 127-144) is
characteristic of recent attempts at defining assemblage variation that
is attributable to differences in site function. Variation among three
kinds of sites with respect to proportions of eight technologically
defined artifact classes was analyzed by means of multivariate
statistical techniques. The results of this analysis indicated that two
of those site types--large habitation sites with mounds, and small
sites, probably representing small habitation units with refuse
accumulations--were technologically very similar to each other, and were
contained in the same cluster. Sites of the third type, low density
sherd and lithic scatters with no evidence of structures, were
distinguished as a separate cluster. The basis of this distinction
appears to be that assemblages contained within the first cluster (large
habitation sites and small sites with trash deposits) are consistently
dominated by secondary and tertiary flakes. In contrast, assemblages
from low density sherd and lithic scatters tend to be more diverse as a
group, are dominated by shatter, and generally appear to be more
cortical. Although no interpretation of the differences between the two
clusters is advanced, it seems reasonable to assume that assemblages
from low density scatters are more strongly representative of core
reduction. In contrast, the higher proportions of partially cortical
and noncortical debitage at sites with trash accumulations may indicate
that there was a greater emphasis on secondary reduction (tool
manufacture) at habitation sites than at sherd and lithic scatters, or
that partially cortical flakes resulting from off-site core reduction
were brought to habitation sites for use or further reduction, or both.

Also relevant to the purposes of the present study is Antieau
and Greenwald's comparison between assemblages from the Cashion Ruin, a
large Hohokam habitation site along the Gila River, and those from two
upland "secondary resource zones" located a short distance downstream
from Cashion (Antieau 1981: 213-217). This analysis indicated that in

comparison to the Cashion assemblage, collections from the secondary resource zones tended to have relatively more cores and choppers, and less debitage. In addition, comparisons of the proportions of primary, secondary, and internal flakes suggested that debitage from the secondary resource zones tends to be more cortical than that from the habitation site. On the basis of these observations, Antieau (1981: 216) suggests that, in comparison to Cashion, there was "less need for further reduction of flakes and less time in the manufacture of the flakes and flake tools" in secondary resource zones. Therefore, it appears that core reduction may be the dominant technological activity in secondary resource zones, while more intensive kinds of reduction, such as secondary reduction, may have been more prevalent at habitation sites.

Further evidence that simple core reduction was the predominant technological activity in natural resource procurement areas can be found in Bayham's study of the flaked stone from the CONOCO survey area located along the Gila River, near Florence, Arizona (Bayham 1976a: 195-217). The flaked stone assemblage from this area is composed of items from low density surface scatters and isolated artifacts. Bayham (1976a: 216) states that it is technologically very simple, consisting primarily of flakes and cores, and interprets it as representing a localized pattern of procurement, modification, utilization, and discard. The fact that only an extremely small percentage of the artifacts showed any evidence of purposeful retouch (Bayham 1976a: 201) indicates that core reduction, rather than secondary reduction was the principal activity. Further, the fact that 79 percent of the debitage was cortical (Bayham 1976a: 204) suggests that core reduction was not especially exhaustive.

Finally, Bernard-Shaw (1984) has recently completed a functional analysis of stone tool assemblages, including ground stone, from 31 Hohokam sites located along the proposed Salt-Gila Aqueduct, Central Arizona Project. Of particular relevance to the present study is her analysis of variation among four kinds of sites with respect to proportions of 31 functionally defined artifact classes. A cumulative frequency distribution of these artifact classes (Bernard-Shaw 1984, Fig. II.1.7) for each of the four site types shows that the assemblages from three of the site types (hamlets, farmsteads, and field houses) are essentially the same. However, assemblages from plant processing sites, the third site type, are noticeably different in having higher frequencies of cores and lower frequencies of debitage. This suggests that core reduction may have been less exhaustive at plant processing sites than at sites with structures.

To summarize, previous research indicates that Hohokam chipped stone assemblages are the result of a simple technology focusing on the direct hard-hammer percussion flaking of locally available materials. The resulting flakes were either used as is, or were themselves modified by hard-hammer percussion. In general, the formal characteristics of Hohokam tool assemblages suggest little concern for the production of implements of any elaborate or preconceived form. Projectile points, the major exception to this generalization, were shaped from thin flakes of fine-textured materials by means of well-controlled pressure flaking. With the exception of projectile point styles, there appears to be little variation in Hohokam flaked stone assemblages through time. Evidence presented by Antieau (1981), Bayham (1976a), Bernard-Shaw (1984), and Rice (1979) suggests that there may be significant variation between assemblages from sites with and without structures. However, the results of the Gila Butte-Santan (Rice 1979) and Salt-Gila Aqueduct (Bernard-Shaw 1984) studies seem to indicate that there is little variation among assemblages from various kinds of sites with structures, regardless of site size or the number of structures present.

Theoretical Orientation and Analytic Approach

As was suggested earlier, assemblage variation reflecting differences in site function may result directly from differences in the activities which occurred at particular sites, or indirectly from differences in the nature of site occupations. The purpose of this section, which is based largely on Jelinek (1976) and Rozen (1979, 1981), is to present major assumptions concerning the ways both of these factors are expected to contribute to variation among chipped stone assemblages. This discussion provides the basis on which artifact attributes were chosen for analysis, and will serve as the theoretical framework in which the analysis results will be interpreted. As in any discussion of a theoretical nature, the assumptions presented below should not be viewed as immutable facts, nor are they offered as such. Rather, they are more profitably viewed as a series of related hypotheses whose validity must ultimately be judged in terms of their usefulness in explaining variation in the data.

Technological Considerations

Theoretically, two kinds of reduction--primary and secondary reduction--can be distinguished. Primary reduction (core reduction) is the reduction of a naturally occurring piece of material that has not previously been detached from another piece of material by intentional reduction. It is assumed that primary reduction was done to produce quantities of usable flakes or to shape a core tool, or possibly both. In any case, primary reduction yields cores or core tools, complete flakes, various kinds of flake fragments, and irregular, angular fragments often called "chunks" or "shatter." Secondary reduction is the reduction of any of the products of primary reduction except cores or core tools. Like primary reduction, secondary reduction yields flakes, flake fragments, and shatter. Unlike primary reduction, however, retouched pieces are produced instead of cores or core tools. It is assumed that the purpose of secondary reduction was to shape tools, refurbish implements after use, or to produce more flakes for use (the resulting retouched pieces are sometimes called "flake cores" or "secondary cores"). Because secondary reduction involves further reduction of an item which was itself removed from a core, secondary reduction is generally viewed here as representing a more intensive use of lithic material than is primary reduction alone.

With these definitions in mind, the problem of how to distinguish primary and secondary reduction in archaeological contexts can now be addressed. To do this, it will be useful to first consider how varying emphases on primary and secondary reduction may be recognized on the basis of assemblage characteristics, assuming that these characteristics have not been altered by either the removal of selected items, or the introduction of items produced elsewhere. Once the theoretical basis for distinguishing primary and secondary reduction in such "closed systems" has been established, it will be necessary to consider how assemblage characteristics may be affected by the introduction of items produced elsewhere, and the removal of selected items for use or disposal elsewhere. Because the ANAMAX-Rosemont Hohokam sites obviously represent such "open systems," consideration of the ways reduction, selection, relocation, and discard patterns may contribute to assemblage variation will be important in assessing the roles of various kinds of reduction at the site level. In addition, it seems likely that various contexts within sites may themselves represent open systems. Therefore, assumptions about the ways postreduction selective factors may have influenced assemblage characteristics will also be crucial to the correct interpretation of intrasite variation.

Assuming that assemblage compositions have not been altered by postreduction selective factors, varying emphases on primary and secondary reduction should be readily discernible from the relative abundance of cores and retouched pieces because, by definition, primary and secondary reduction yield cores and retouched pieces, respectively. In addition to ratios of cores to retouched pieces, debitage characteristics may also provide information concerning the kind of reduction represented. For example, in industries where secondary reduction focused on the production and refurbishing of very specific, formally consistent kinds of tools such as bifaces or certain kinds of scrapers, the resulting flakes will exhibit distinctive combinations of particular attributes. To the extent that they reflect the form of the items from which flakes were struck, these recurrent attribute combinations may be used to define flake types such as "biface-thinning flakes," "scraper retouch flakes," "scraper renewal flakes," "burin spalls," and so forth. The abundance of these flake types in relation to other flake types which presumably derive from core reduction (that is, "primary flakes" and "decortication flakes") may therefore provide some indication of the extent to which various kinds of reduction are represented in a given assemblage.

Preliminary examination of the ANAMAX-Rosemont collections indicated that intentionally retouched flakes were extremely diverse in many aspects of form, including size, shape, retouch location, and edge angle, regularity, and configuration. Further, with the exception of a relatively small number of items, such as projectile points and drills, this variation appeared to be largely unpatterned. Because of the general lack of standardization in tool form, it seemed unlikely that distinctive, recurrent combinations of attributes would be discernible in debitage resulting from tool reduction, and equally unlikely that attempts to separate flakes resulting from tool reduction from those resulting from core reduction on the basis of such attribute combinations would be very successful. Therefore, an alternative approach to debitage analysis was adopted.

This approach does not rely on inferences about the technological origins of individual artifacts, but instead, assumes that varying emphases on different kinds of reduction can be distinguished in more general terms on the basis of variation in debitage characteristics, at the assemblage level.

Again, assuming that postreduction selective factors have not altered assemblage characteristics, debitage resulting from primary reduction will exhibit a wider size range, tend to be larger, and have more cortex than that produced by secondary reduction. Thus, debitage size and the amount of cortex present may provide some indication of the extent to which primary and secondary reduction have contributed to assemblages. However, in situations where both kinds of reduction occurred in the same place, and where there is reason to suspect that primary reduction may have been especially thorough or exhaustive--for example in regions where raw material is scarce, or on sites that were intensively occupied for long periods--distinguishing primary and secondary reduction solely on the basis of debitage size and cortex may be difficult. Because exhaustive primary reduction yields more abundant, smaller, less cortical debitage than does less thorough, or nonintensive primary reduction, the range of variation in size and cortex for primary flakes and fragments will more completely overlap with that characteristic of secondary reduction. For this reason, it will be necessary to consider a number of characteristics of debitage assemblages besides size and cortex, for the purposes of distinguishing primary and secondary reduction.

Recent studies (Sullivan 1980, Rozen 1981) have indicated that strong inferences regarding the extent to which primary and secondary reduction are reflected in debitage assemblages can be made on the basis of differences in the proportions of certain types of debitage, especially when correlations between these differences and variation in debitage size and cortex can be demonstrated. Specifically, these studies suggest that, in addition to having larger and more cortical debitage, primary reduction assemblages are characterized by higher ratios of complete flakes to flake fragments, in comparison to secondary reduction debitage assemblages. In addition, nonflake fragments, such as chunks and shatter, tend to be more abundant in assemblages resulting from primary reduction than they are in secondary reduction debitage. While it therefore seems likely that proportions of complete flakes, flake fragments, and shatter may be relevant to distinguishing primary and secondary reduction in some cases, an important difference between one of the above mentioned studies and the present analysis should be mentioned.

The author's study of 23 assemblages from the vicinity of St. Johns, Arizona (Rozen 1981) not only showed differences between primary and secondary reduction with respect to debitage category proportions, but also demonstrated differences in striking platform characteristics, such as platform type and presence or absence of lipping. These differences indicated that secondary reduction focused on soft-hammer percussion biface reduction, while primary reduction (core reduction) was done by means of hard-hammer percussion. Assuming that flakes produced by soft-hammer percussion biface thinning, because of their relative thinness, are more likely to fragment under the force of the detaching blow than those resulting from hard-hammer percussion, differences in the ratios of complete flakes to various kinds of flake fragments seen in the St. John's data are probably more directly related to differences in reduction technique (that is, hard- vs. soft-hammer percussion) than to differences in the kinds of reduction (primary or secondary) represented. Nonetheless, because there were strong correlations between the use of soft-hammer percussion for secondary reduction, and the use of hard-hammer percussion for primary reduction, ratios of complete flakes to flake fragments proved very useful in distinguishing varying emphases on primary and secondary reduction, if only indirectly.

With regard to the ANAMAX-Rosemont collections, no such correlation between hammer type and kind of reduction can be assumed. Preliminary examination of the collections suggests that evidence of soft-hammer percussion is scant, and that both primary and secondary reduction were habitually done by hard-hammer techniques. Under these circumstances, the significance of varying ratios of complete flakes to flake fragments, with respect to differences in the extent to which primary and secondary reduction are represented in assemblages is as yet uncertain. Two alternative hypotheses regarding this question may be advanced. The first possibility is that secondary reduction tends to yield lower ratios of complete flakes to fragments than does primary reduction, even if both were accomplished by hard-hammer percussion. This could be true if, because of their smaller size, secondary flakes are more prone to breakage during detachment than are larger primary flakes. If this hypothesis is correct, variation in proportions of complete flakes, flake fragments, and shatter should be strongly correlated with variation in debitage size and cortex, as it was in the St. Johns study. Specifically, assemblages characterized by high ratios of complete flakes to flake fragments and high frequencies of shatter should also tend to have larger and more cortical debitage. Conversely, assemblages with lower ratios of whole flakes to flake fragments and less shatter should also have smaller and less cortical debitage.

The alternative, and intuitively more plausible hypothesis is that when hard-hammer percussion is used for both primary and secondary reduction, the resulting assemblages will be essentially the same with respect to proportions of complete flakes, flake fragments, and shatter. Under these circumstances, comparatively little variation in debitage category proportions should be apparent, though differences in debitage size and cortex should still be evident. If this second hypothesis proves correct, and if patterned associations among platform characteristics and other aspects of flake form cannot be identified and correlated with particular tool types, the theoretical distinction between primary and secondary reduction may be of limited use for the purposes of interpreting variation among the ANAMAX-Rosemont flaked stone assemblages. Instead, it may be more realistic to view differences in lithic reduction in terms of varying degrees of reduction intensity, rather than in terms of specific kinds of reduction.

Differences in reduction intensity (the extent to which lithic material was reduced) may be reflected in assemblage characteristics in several ways. First, and perhaps most obviously, debitage resulting from more thorough reduction should tend to be smaller and less cortical than that resulting from less exhaustive reduction. Second, if reduction intensity is defined in terms of: (1) the number of flakes struck per core, (2) the frequency with which these flakes were themselves subjected to further reduction, and (3) the amount of debitage produced per episode of flake reduction, variation in the proportions of cores, retouched pieces, and debitage may reflect differences in reduction intensity. For example, very nonintensive reduction should yield high ratios of cores to debitage, with no retouched pieces. However, as reduction becomes more thorough, ratios of cores to debitage should decrease, and secondary reduction should become more frequent, giving rise to increasing ratios of retouched pieces to cores. Third, cores subjected to more thorough reduction should be smaller, less cortical, and evidence the removal of flakes from a greater number of striking platforms than those subjected to less exhaustive reduction. Fourth, differences in the extent to which lithic materials were reduced may be reflected in a number of attributes of tool form. In contrast to retouched pieces which were not extensively reduced, those which were subjected to repeated cycles of modification and use before discard may tend to show more continuous retouch occupying a greater percentage of a given implement's periphery. In addition, where lithic materials were used to their fullest potential, retouched pieces may be more frequently bifacial, more often broken, and have steeper edge angles than those subjected to less extensive modification. Finally, variation in the proportions of certain striking platform types on flakes may also reflect differences in reduction intensity. It is possible, for example, that cortical platforms will be most common where core reduction is nonintensive, and where no flake reduction occurs. As core reduction becomes more thorough, and flake reduction more frequent, ratios of cortical platforms to noncortical plain platforms will decrease. Ultimately, as reduction becomes exhaustive, ratios of faceted platforms to noncortical plain platforms will increase.

So far, this discussion has shown how differences in the object, technique, and intensity of lithic reduction may be seen in a number of assemblage characteristics, assuming that these characteristics have not been altered by postreduction relocation of selected items. As previously mentioned, however, it is assumed that variation among the ANAMAX-Rosemont assemblages may reflect not only differences in on-site reduction, but differences in the extent to which selected items were either introduced to, or removed from particular spatial contexts. Therefore, it will be necessary to examine the ways selective factors may contribute to both intersite and intrasite assemblage variation.

Selective Factors

Because raw material suitable for stone tool production probably did not occur on habitation sites in sufficient quantities to meet the on-going needs of the inhabitants, it is assumed that, to some extent, material was obtained elsewhere, and brought to the sites. Therefore, one of the most important selective factors influencing the character of the assemblages at the site level concerns the form in which material was imported.

Two material procurement strategies can be hypothetically distinguished. First, material may have been transported to the sites in the form of cores which had undergone only limited reduction elsewhere to determine their suitability for further reduction at the sites. Second, raw material procurement may have involved more thorough core reduction at its source, and the subsequent transport of only selected products of this reduction to the site. Where it can be assumed that the former strategy prevailed, the characteristics of the resulting assemblages can be taken as a more accurate reflection of the full range of lithic reduction. In contrast, where the latter strategy prevailed, inferences concerning the kind of reduction responsible for the assemblages may be more difficult to make because the entire reduction sequence may not be represented. In addition, it is safe to assume that items brought to the sites were selected for this purpose on the basis of what was considered useful, and therefore were not "random samples" of the artifacts produced.

Potentially, the criteria used in selecting items for use elsewhere may not have been the same in all instances, and could have involved many of the same assemblage characteristics previously identified as being relevant to distinguishing differences in the object, technique, and intensity of on-site reduction. For example, variation in proportions of cores, retouched pieces and debitage, proportions of complete flakes, flake fragments and shatter, and debitage size and cortex distributions could all reflect differences in what was brought to the sites.

Undoubtedly, raw material procurement at the Rosemont Hohokam sites involved both of the strategies outlined above. The extent to which either of these strategies contributed to a particular assemblage may be difficult to determine because material brought to the sites as either tested cores or the selected products of reduction which occurred elsewhere, was itself subjected to further reduction. In general, however, it seems reasonable to assume that assemblages consisting mostly of material that was imported as tested cores should contain more evidence of on-site core reduction (more cores and larger, more cortical debitage) than those composed primarily of material which was imported in the form of selected products of off-site reduction.

In addition to influencing assemblage characteristics at the site level, selective factors may also be responsible for intrasite variation. While some contexts within sites may yield artifacts that were no longer considered useful, other contexts may produce items which

are more representative of fully functional assemblages. Here again,
the physical separation of artifacts on the basis of what was and was
not considered useful could potentially contribute to variation in many
of the assemblage characteristics previously discussed. For example, it
is possible that refuse assemblages will consist of broken or exhausted
tools, exhausted cores, and great quantities of manufacturing waste,
such as small flakes, flake fragments, and shatter. In contrast,
assemblages of more useful items, such as those recovered from the
floors of pit houses that were quickly abandoned, may consist of larger,
whole flakes, less extensively reduced cores, and retouched pieces, and
may contain less manufacturing debris. Therefore, variation in debitage
size, ratios of debitage to cores and retouched pieces, core and tool
form, and ratios of complete flakes to flake fragments may not only
reflect differences in the object, technique, and intensity of
reduction, but might be related as well to spatial patterns in
reduction, selection, relocation, use, and discard.

The preceding discussion has focused on the ways in which
different kinds of reduction and spatial patterning in reduction, use,
and discard may contribute to variation in the technological
characteristics of assemblages. While these issues are central to
analysis goals, the correct identification and interpretation of
variation attributable to these factors depends on the extent to which
other sources of variation can be controlled.

Raw Materials

Differences in raw material characteristics and availability are
potentially some of the most influential sources of such "incidental"
variation. The ways in which these factors may contribute to assemblage
variation have been treated in detail elsewhere (Jelinek 1976; Rozen
1979, 1981). A review of this topic with reference to the present
study's research objectives, and the kinds and distribution of raw
materials in the study area will be useful.

Many different materials suitable for stone tool manufacture are
widely and abundantly distributed throughout the Rosemont area. The
more common of these materials include a wide variety of quartzites,
metamorphosed mudstones and siltstones, silicified limestone, and in
lesser quantities, chert and chalcedony. These materials occur most
frequently as gravels in the drainages, and in the alluvial deposits
which make up the ridge systems of the area. Bedrock outcrops of
silicified limestone are also present. The relative abundance of
certain materials on particular ridges is highly variable, and reflects
localized differences in the petrological composition of alluvial
deposits. While it is safe to assume that the occupants of all the
sites in question had access to the same range of sources, differences
between sites with respect to proximity to particular sources could
result in variation in the raw material composition of assemblages.

Differences in the physical properties of raw materials, such as size, texture, elasticity, and structural homogeneity, could therefore contribute directly to intersite assemblage variation in several ways. The amount of cortex on flakes, as well as flake size, for example, will be functions of raw material size. Frequencies of flake fragments and nonflake fragments such as chunks and shatter, may vary according to the prevalence of structural flaws. Raw material variability may also contribute indirectly to assemblage characteristics in more subtle, but equally important ways. It is assumed, for example, that the physical properties of the materials outlined above operate collectively to influence the "suitability" of different materials for particular technological applications, and that "suitability" was an important factor governing the selection of materials for specific purposes. Thus, we may expect that where fine-textured, brittle, homogeneous rocks were available, soft-hammer percussion and pressure flaking may have been used more often than in areas where only more elastic, coarse-textured rocks were available, even though the advantages of soft-hammer percussion and pressure flaking were known in both instances. In more general terms, finer materials may have been subjected to more thorough reduction than coarser materials, simply because finer materials may have been considered more desirable.

Raw material variability may also contribute indirectly to assemblage characteristics by influencing the form in which materials were brought to the sites. Assuming that fine-textured materials tend to occur naturally in smaller pieces than do coarser materials, it may have been convenient to import finer materials as tested cores. In contrast, to avoid carrying large pieces of material even short distances, coarser materials may have been more frequently imported in the form of large flakes, or possibly more thoroughly reduced cores or core tools.

Yet another factor which could indirectly contribute to assemblage characteristics is raw material availability. In regions where raw material is scarce, for example, assemblage characteristics may reflect more intensive reduction than those from areas in which material is abundant. As previously noted, the Rosemont area does not suffer from a scarcity of workable materials. Therefore, it is assumed that raw material availability was not a significant factor influencing assemblage characteristics at the regional level. At the site level, however, differences in the distances at which particular materials could be obtained could affect the form in which materials were brought to the sites, and thus contribute to assemblage variation. More specifically, it is assumed that in comparison to materials which could only be obtained at greater distances, materials which occurred in close proximity to the sites, for example in the gravels on the slopes and in the drainages immediately below the sites, were more frequently imported as tested cores. Materials from more distant sources may have been more efficiently imported as the selected products of reduction which was accomplished at the source.

Occupational Factors

A major analysis objective was to determine the extent to which flaked stone assemblage variability reflects differences in the nature of site occupations. The most basic assumption regarding the relationship between occupational factors and assemblage variation is that the extent to which material was reduced is a function of occupation intensity. Before discussing in greater detail the ways in which occupational factors may influence assemblage characteristics, it will be useful to elaborate on what is meant by "occupation intensity," and how differences among sites with respect to this variable can be inferred from nonassemblage characteristics.

Theoretically at least, occupation intensity can be thought of as the product of the interaction of four independent variables: site size, occupation duration, the number of people involved, and the activities which occurred there. At one extreme, very nonintensive occupations are those involving few people operating in large areas, for short periods, conducting a limited range of activities which require little labor, such as food gathering. At the opposite end of the spectrum, very intensive occupations are those in which large numbers of people occupying small areas, over long periods, conduct a wider range of more labor-intensive activities, such as building pit houses, processing food, making and using stone tools and pottery, burying the dead, and so forth. Because the four factors which operate collectively to produce occupation intensity may vary independently of one another, a range of occupation intensities span the two extremes defined above.

The specificity with which varying degrees of occupation intensity can be inferred in archaeological contexts depends on how accurately differences in site size, the range of activities which occurred, occupation duration, and the number of occupants can be determined. With regard to the present study, the topographic situation of the sites on ridges makes replicable determinations of site size relatively easy. In addition, because all the sites in question had pit houses, and are thus "habitation sites," it is assumed that, in very broad terms, the range of activities which occurred was essentially very similar in all instances.

At first glance, inferences regarding occupation duration and numbers of inhabitants may also appear to be relatively easy to make on the basis of temporally diagnostic pottery styles and numbers of pit houses, respectively. On closer inspection, however, the accuracy of such inferences may be limited by the specificity with which the occupational histories of individual sites can be reconstructed. With regard to the Rosemont sites, for example, a particular range of pottery styles may reflect occupation span, but may not necessarily reflect occupation duration. That is, it may not be possible to distinguish sites which were intermittently occupied over a given period from those which were continuously occupied for the same period.

In a similar fashion, the number of occupants at a site at any given time cannot be directly inferred from the number of pit houses present when, as is often the case on many of the Rosemont sites, it is impossible to establish the temporal relationships between individual pit houses.

Because of these limitations in our understanding of occupation periodicity and intrasite occupation sequences, this analysis will not attempt to treat occupation intensity as a continuous variable. Instead, it will be more realistic to group the sites into broad classes on the basis of site size, occupation span, and numbers of pit houses and other features, and to assume that these classes are at least grossly representative of major differences in occupation intensity.

Hypothetically, differences in occupation intensity could indirectly contribute to assemblage variation in a number of ways. It seems reasonable to assume, for example, that the on-going demand for raw material resulting from a protracted occupation involving large numbers of people, in one place, may have depleted material sources close to the site. Although raw material is abundant throughout the study area in general, localized material shortages may therefore have developed in association with the more intensively occupied sites. In comparison, such shortages may not have occurred, or at least may not have been as severe, where less intensive occupations occurred in close proximity to material sources.

In cases where localized shortages developed as the result of intensive and extended occupations, the inhabitants may have had to travel farther afield, to more sources of different materials, to obtain sufficient quantities of material than did the occupants of less intensively occupied sites. If this were the case, assemblages from intensively occupied sites may tend to have more heterogeneous raw material compositions than those from less intensively occupied sites. In addition, differences in occupation intensity may have influenced the form in which material was imported. Assuming, for example, that the inhabitants of more intensively occupied sites had to import materials from greater distances than did the occupants of less intensively occupied sites, it may have been more efficient to import material to those intensively occupied sites in the form of selected products of reduction which was undertaken at or near the source. In contrast, at less intensively occupied sites located in close proximity to material sources, material may have been more commonly imported in the form of tested cores. Therefore, assemblages from more intensively occupied sites may tend to show less evidence of on-site core reduction than those from less intensively occupied sites.

In addition to influencing raw material composition and the form in which materials were imported, differences in occupation intensity could also contribute to differences in the nature of on-site reduction. For example, if localized material shortages developed at very intensively occupied sites, the inhabitants may have found it necessary to use available materials to their fullest potential before discarding them. Therefore, in comparison to less intensively occupied sites where

material demands may have been more easily satisfied, intensively
occupied sites may yield assemblages which are the result of more
exhaustive reduction and more repeated cycles of modification and use.
As noted earlier, such differences in reduction intensity may contribute
to variation in a number of assemblage characteristics, including
debitage size and cortex distributions, proportions of cores, retouched
pieces, and debitage, core and tool form, proportions of certain types
of striking platforms, and so forth. Also, because of the need to use
material to its fullest potential, ratios of used to unused debitage may
be higher in assemblages from more intensively occupied sites, and lower
in assemblages from less intensively occupied sites.

Tool Function

Another important analysis objective was to describe variation
in tool assemblages, and to relate this variation to differences in the
tasks for which tools were used. From a practical standpoint, the
classification of artifacts into tool and nontool categories was a
prerequisite to achieving this objective. Therefore, before discussing
various approaches to inferring tool function, some basic assumptions
concerning the distinctions between tools and other artifacts must be
examined.

Theoretically, tools can be defined as all items which were
used, and it is assumed that virtually any piece of stone that was large
enough to hold, and had a suitable edge could have been used. In
practice, tools may be recognized by the presence of physical evidence
of use, such as abrasion, striae, battering, and microflaking; however,
it is important to note several limitations of these edge alteration
attributes for the purposes of determining what was and was not used.
First, while the presence of abrasion, striae, and battering are
considered unmistakable evidence of use, the absence of these attributes
cannot be used to infer that a given artifact was not used. For
example, tools made of tough materials which were used for only very
short periods for certain tasks, such as slicing soft materials, may
have developed no readily observable wear. Second, while edge attrition
in the form of minute flake scars (microflaking) is undoubtedly the
result of use in some cases, this kind of edge damage may also result
from a myriad of sources other than use. For example, microflaking may
have occurred as flakes struck the ground during reduction, or when
artifacts were gathered together and dumped as trash. In addition,
archaeological recovery and processing methods may also be significant
causes of edge damage. Because factors unrelated to use are probably
responsible for a substantial, but unknown amount of edge damage in the
Rosemont assemblages, the criteria used to identify use-related
microflaking in this analysis were conservative. These criteria are
presented in the following section dealing with analysis terms and
procedures.

Regardless of the presence or absence of physical traces of use,
flakes which show evidence of intention modification (retouched pieces)

will be considered tools. It is assumed, for example, that in most
instances, retouch represents either a conscious attempt to enhance the
usefulness of a working edge for a particular task, or the modification
of an item to make it more convenient to hold during use. It is
therefore generally assumed that all retouched pieces are tools, with
one qualification. As mentioned earlier in the discussion of
technological considerations, some flakes may have been subjected to
reduction to obtain additional flakes, rather than to shape them into
tools. In such cases, the resulting retouched pieces may have served
only as secondary cores, and may never have been intended for use as
tools. In the absence of observable use-wear, the question of whether a
particular retouched piece represents either a unidirectionally reduced
"flake core" or a large, thick, coarsely flaked scraper is moot.
Finally, some cores may be recognized as tools when they exhibit
patterned associations of certain attributes which strongly suggest
intentional shaping for use, regardless of the presence or absence of
observable use-wear.

In view of these distinctions between tools and other artifacts,
ways of inferring tool function will now be briefly examined. For a
more thorough treatment of this topic, the reader is referred to
Jelinek's (1976) comprehensive evaluation of current approaches to
functional analysis.

Two major lines of evidence may be useful in determining the
tasks for which tools were used. First, recent studies such as those by
Semenov (1964), Tringham and others (1974), and Keely (1977) have
suggested that variation in use-related edge alteration attributes can
be correlated with the manner in which tools were physically applied to
specific materials. For example, tools used in slicing, scraping, and
rotary motions on materials of varying hardness, moisture content, and
organic composition may develop distinctive wear patterns in the form of
microflaking, abrasion, and striae.

No systematic use-wear analysis of the Rosemont tool assemblages
was attempted for several reasons. First, current understanding of
relationships between use-wear variation and tool function is based
primarily on experimental studies in which fine-textured rocks, usually
flint, are the only materials used. In contrast, the Rosemont
assemblages are composed of diverse materials, many of which undoubtedly
have flaking properties which are substantially different than those of
flint. Therefore, experimental studies using materials common in the
Rosemont assemblages would have been prerequisite to a use-wear
analysis. Such experimental studies were beyond the scope of the
project.

Second, as previously noted, it is assumed that a wide variety
of factors unrelated to use are responsible for some unknown amount of
edge damage in the assemblages. In the absence of a completely
satisfactory method of distinguishing microflaking resulting from use
from that caused by other factors, an analysis of this form of edge
alteration was unlikely to yield convincing results. Further,
frequencies of other forms of use-wear observable with a 10-power hand
lens were too low to warrant systematic analysis.

The second major line of evidence traditionally used in inferring tool function is gross form. This approach will be used here, and is based on the assumption that the tasks for which tools are used impose certain physical restrictions on the range of forms which will be effective. In very simple terms, for example, rounded cobbles cannot be used for slicing, and small flakes will be ineffective when used as hammers. Therefore, differences in the extent to which various tasks are reflected in assemblages may be indirectly inferred in very general terms by using typologies which describe variation in tool size, shape, edge angle, edge shape, and so forth.

Obviously, the major limitation of this kind of typological approach derives from the fact that, for any given task, there exists a range of forms which will function equally well, and that the use of a particular form for a given task is determined not only by the physical requirements imposed by the intended function, but is also the product of idiosyncratic choice (style). For some tasks, the range of effective forms may be so narrow that function may be confidently inferred in general terms directly from form. For many tasks, the range of effective forms may be very broad; that is, the same task could have been accomplished with many different kinds of implements. Similarly, a single tool may have served in a variety of functions. Therefore, a one-to-one relationship between tool form and function cannot be assumed, and inferences regarding the function of particular tool types must in many cases remain speculative.

Analysis Terms and Procedures

Basic Artifact Category Definitions

The basic artifact categories used in this analysis were defined as follows:

Complete flakes--Pieces of stone detached from other pieces of material, that show interior and exterior surfaces, the point of impact of the detaching blow, have both lateral edges and terminal edge, and that show no retouch were classified as complete flakes.

Split flakes--Pieces of stone struck from other pieces of material, that show interior and exterior surfaces, the point of impact of the detaching blow, which fractured through the point of impact, parallel to the axis of flaking, as a result of the detaching blow, and were not themselves intentionally modified were classified as split flakes.

Proximal flake fragments--Pieces of stone detached from other pieces of material that show interior and exterior surfaces, the point of impact of the detaching blow, but are missing through breakage either lateral edge, the terminal edge, or any combination of these edges, and are not split flakes, were classified as proximal flake fragments. These show no evidence of retouch.

Medial-distal flake fragments--Pieces of stone struck from other pieces of material that show interior and exterior surfaces, but that are missing through breakage the point of impact of the detaching blow and were not intentionally modified, were classified as other flake fragments.

Nonorientable fragments--Pieces of stone removed from other pieces of material, on which interior and exterior surfaces cannot be reliably distinguished were classified as nonorientable fragments. Nonorientable fragments are synonymous with "chunks" and "shatter."

Retouched pieces--Complete flakes, split flakes, proximal flake fragments, other flake fragments, and nonorientable fragments that show evidence of having been intentionally reduced, were classified as retouched pieces. Projectile points and bifaces are assumed to be retouched pieces even though these artifacts often show such extensive flake removal that it is not possible to determine if they were made on flakes or previously unaltered pieces of material. Retouched pieces were more specifically classified through the use of a tool typology described in a later section.

Cores--Artifacts showing one or more negative bulbs of percussion, which could be identified as not having been artificially detached from other pieces of material, which showed battering over less than 10 percent of their surface were classified as cores.

Core hammerstones--Cores showing battering over more than 10 percent of their surface were classified as core hammerstones. These items will be described in more detail in the section devoted to tool type descriptions.

Cobble hammerstones--Cobbles exhibiting battering but no intentional flake removal were classified as cobble hammerstones.

Thermal fragments--Pieces of chipped stone artifacts that were too extensively fragmented as a result of heat to be placed in any of the above categories were classified as thermal fragments.

Frequencies of the 10 basic artifact categories are given for each site in Table 5.1.

Table 5.1

BASIC CHIPPED STONE ARTIFACT CATEGORY FREQUENCIES BY SITE

Site	Missing Observations	Complete Flakes	Split Flakes	Proximal Flake Fragments	Medial-Distal Flake Fragments	Fragments	Retouched Pieces	Cores	Core Hammerstones	Cobble Hammerstones	Thermal Fragments	Total
AZ EE:2:76	0	1552	341	549	752	146	284	40	11	8	48	3741
AZ EE:2:77	0	420	53	67	12	35	63	27	22	5	5	809
AZ EE:2:84	1	323	52	52	155	45	51	16	6	0	6	707
AZ EE:1:104	1	30	1	4	5	4	5	2	0	0	0	52
AZ EE:2:105	1	3849	941	1372	1736	416	790	184	63	27	124	9503
AZ EE:2:106	0	38	4	10	8	10	5	3	1	0	0	79
AZ EE:2:107	0	128	14	33	35	9	12	4	9	2	2	248
AZ EE:2:109	0	40	4	11	9	3	8	2	3	0	0	80
AZ EE:2:113	2	2748	667	840	1089	356	389	127	55	6	93	6372
AZ EE:2:116	0	44	4	10	17	3	4	3	2	1	0	88
AZ EE:2:117	0	37	7	9	10	5	5	2	2	1	0	78
AZ EE:2:120	0	107	13	28	28	10	25	12	6	1	1	231
AZ EE:2:122	0	27	4	11	1	4	3	3	0	0	0	53
AZ EE:2:129	0	648	128	176	311	79	84	27	5	1	30	1489
Total	5	9991	2233	3172	4268	1135	1728	452	185	52	309	23530

Provenience Classes

In addition to the specific provenience information recorded in the field, all artifacts were assigned to 1 of 12 general provenience classes which were established during the analysis. These classes were designed to facilitate comparisons among various intrasite spatial contexts, and are described below:

Structure fill--All items recovered from pit houses and limited-use structures, excluding those found on the floor, in subfloor pits and postholes, and those from features which were obviously intrusive into the structure fill, were assigned to this class. All artifacts assigned to structure fill were collected by screening; not included are those items recovered without screening during excavation above structures to define their horizontal limits.

Floor--Artifacts found in contact with structure floors were assigned to this provenience class.

Floor pits--All artifacts found in floor features, including storage pits and hearths, and excluding postholes and features that were obviously intrusive into the floor from above, were assigned to this provenience class. All material from floor pits can safely be assumed to have been recovered with the use of screens.

Postholes--Artifacts found in subfloor features interpreted as postholes were assigned to this provenience class. In cases where the interpretation of a subfloor feature as being either a floor pit or posthole was uncertain, the artifacts were assigned to postholes. While posthole fill was not consistently screened, the excavation of these features with trowels suggests that the artifact recovery rate for postholes is probably comparable to that from other, screened, proveniences.

Extramural features--All artifacts from extramural features, including pits (extramural pit form and content is discussed by Ferg in Chapter 3), inhumations, cremations, and artifact caches, excluding the ballcourt at AZ EE:2:105 and large, trash-filled borrow pits, were assigned to this provenience class. Also included in extramural feature collections were artifacts from pits, inhumations, and cremations that were intrusive into structure fill. All extramural feature fill was screened.

Stripping--Artifacts found in the process of removing topsoil to locate feature outlines in the sterile substrate were assigned to this provenience class. At two sites (AZ EE:2:76 and EE:2:84) every other wheel barrow load of topsoil removed was screened. No screening was done during stripping at any of the other sites.

Borrow pits--This provenience class was established to account for three large, trash-filled depressions that were interpreted as borrow pits. One such feature occurs at AZ EE:2:105, and two were present at AZ EE:2:113. All excavated borrow pit fill was screened.

Ballcourt--Unique to AZ EE:2:105, this provenience class accounts for all artifacts that were recovered from the partial excavation of the ballcourt. Only a portion of the fill removed from the ballcourt was screened.

Trash--This provenience class is unique to AZ EE:2:129 and includes all artifacts recovered from the excavation of a sheet trash deposit suspected of being related to a preceramic occupation. Screening was done during all excavation of this deposit.

Feature 0--Artifacts of particular interest, most commonly tools, were collected from the surfaces of sites and the surrounding slopes and were assigned to this provenience class.

Backhoe backdirt--This provenience class was established to account for items that were collected from backhoe trench backdirt, none of which were recovered by screening.

Nonfeature--In several instances, extramural depressions containing artifacts were discovered, assigned feature numbers, and excavated. Full excavation indicated that the depressions were natural, rather than cultural in origin. This provenience class was created to account for the artifacts recovered from these excavations.

Artifact counts by provenience class are given for each site in Table 5.2. Counts by artifact type and provenience class, as well as individual structures, were also made. These data are too numerous to present here, and are on file at the Cultural Resource Management Division, Arizona State Museum.

Sampling Considerations

Because of the large number of artifacts recovered and the limited time available to conduct the analysis, it was necessary to sample the collections for the purposes of recording detailed observations of artifact attributes. The most important requirement of the sampling strategy was that it had to be flexible enough to permit broad descriptive statements pertaining to the entire project collection, as well as comparisons among major provenience classes within and between sites, and in some cases, comparisons among individual features. One sampling procedure considered was to draw random samples stratified by site, provenience class, and feature. This strategy would have required that each artifact from contexts to be

Table 5.2

NUMBERS OF CHIPPED STONE ARTIFACTS RECOVERED AND ANALYZED,
BY MAJOR PROVENIENCE CLASS, FOR EACH SITE

Site Number		Structure Fill	Floor	Floor Pits	Post Holes	Extramural Pits	Stripping	Borrow Pits	Ballcourt	Trash	Backhoe Backdirt	Feature 0	Nonfeature	Total
AZ EE:2:76	R	1,773	18	85	23	110	1,729	0	0	0	0	3	0	3,741
	A	957	16	85	23	110	271	0	0	0	0	0	0	1,462
AZ EE:2:77	R	441	3	14	2	84	260	0	0	0	0	3	2	809
	A	441	3	14	2	84	0	0	0	0	0	3	2	549
AZ EE:2:84	R	423	0	0	6	8	270	0	0	0	0	0	0	707
	A	423	0	0	6	8	192	0	0	0	0	0	0	629
AZ EE:1:104	R	47	1*	2	0	20	0	0	0	0	0	0	0	52
	A	0	0	0	0	0	0	0	0	0	0	0	0	0
AZ EE:2:105	R	6,687	7	110	44	60	2,089	221	125	0	149	11	0	9,503
	A	2,871	6	99	42	60	0	221	59	0	0	0	0	3,358
AZ EE:2:106	R	30	1	0	0	0	26	0	0	0	0	22	0	79
	A	30	1	0	0	0	26	0	0	0	0	22	0	79
AZ EE:2:107	R	180	19	4	0	12	33	0	0	0	0	0	0	248
	A	180	19	4	0	12	33	0	0	0	0	0	0	248
AZ EE:2:109	R	50	1	1	0	2	24	0	0	0	0	2	0	80
	A	50	1	1	0	2	24	0	0	0	0	2	0	80
AZ EE:2:113	R	4,989	15	101	39	478	246	459	0	0	0	1	44	6,372
	A	1,998	13	87	18	417	0	343	0	0	0	0	41	2,917
AZ EE:2:116	R	59	7	0	0	0	22	0	0	0	0	0	0	88
	A	59	7	0	0	0	22	0	0	0	0	0	0	88
AZ EE:2:117	R	49	1	5	1	13	9	0	0	0	0	0	0	78
	A	49	1	5	1	13	9	0	0	0	0	0	0	78
AZ EE:2:120	R	152	4	6	0	6	63	0	0	0	0	0	0	231
	A	152	4	6	0	6	63	0	0	0	0	0	0	231
AZ EE:2:122	R	13	0	2	0	1	27	0	0	0	0	3	7	53
	A	13	0	2	0	1	27	0	0	0	0	3	7	53
AZ EE:2:129	R	255	1	4	1	57	95	0	0	1,048	0	1	27	1,489
	A	255	1	4	1	57	0	0	00	861	0	0	27	1,206
Total Recovered		15,148	78	334	116	833	4,893	680	125	1,048	149	46	80	23,530
Total Analyzed		7,478	72	307	93	770	667	564	59	861	0	30	77	10,978

R = number of artifacts recovered
A = analyzed sample

sampled be given a unique number so that samples could be drawn using a table of random numbers. Because of the amount of time this would have taken and a number of logistic problems, this sampling method was rejected. Instead, collections from various proveniences were purposefully selected for attribute analysis on the basis of their applicability to the research objectives.

Two factors were considered in selecting collections for analysis. The first of these concerns sample sizes characteristic of the various provenience classes. Table 5.2 shows that collections from some provenience classes, such as structure fill and stripping, tend to be relatively large, while others, such as floor and extramural features, tend to be small. To help ensure that sample sizes adequate for statistical comparison were obtained from all provenience classes, and conversely, that unnecessarily large numbers of artifacts were not analyzed, the provenience classes were sampled proportionately. Therefore, collections from contexts with low sample sizes were generally more extensively analyzed than those with large sample sizes.

The second factor considered in choosing artifacts for attribute analysis pertains to artifact recovery techniques. As indicated in the provenience class definitions, not all artifacts were collected by screening, and it is assumed that screened and unscreened collections may differ with respect to both artifact size and percentages of artifact types. To avoid documenting variation that is potentially attributable to nothing more than differences in artifact recovery methods, collections selected for attribute analysis were generally confined to screened contexts. While considerations of provenience class sample size and recovery technique were the principal selection criteria, they were used as general guidelines rather than rules in choosing collections for analysis. Therefore, it will be useful to describe selection procedures in greater detail.

At sites with collections in excess of 300 items (AZ EE:2:76, EE:2:77, EE:2:84, EE:2:113 and EE:2:129) attribute observations were made on all, or nearly all, artifacts from extramural features, structure floors, and structure subfeatures, including floor pits and postholes. Attributes were generally not recorded on artifacts from unscreened surface stripping excavations, uncontrolled surface collections (Feature 0), or backhoe trench backdirt. To take full advantage of the potential for comparisons among individual structure fills, attributes were recorded on all artifacts in collections from these proveniences having less than 300 items. In cases where more than 300 artifacts were recovered from the fill of a single structure, material from arbitrary horizontal excavation units, usually including that from all levels in a particular one-quarter or one-half of the structure, was judgementally selected to yield between 100 and 300 items for attribute analysis.

Each of the remaining sites (AZ EE:1:104, EE:2:106, EE:2:107, EE:2:109, EE:2:116, EE:2:117, EE:2:120, and EE:2:122) yielded less than 300 items, and only two of these (AZ EE:2:107 and EE:2:120) produced 100 or more artifacts. In view of the small size of these collections, attributes were recorded on all artifacts regardless of recovery method, with one exception. Detailed attribute observations were not made on any artifacts from AZ EE:1:104.

The number of artifacts on which attributes were recorded are given for each site by provenience class in Table 5.2. The number of artifacts recovered from each structure, consisting of the combined counts for fill, floor, floor pits, and postholes, are given for each site in Table 5.3, followed by the number of those artifacts selected for attribute analysis. More specific definitions of the analyzed collections will be provided in sections devoted to particular aspects of the analysis as needed.

Attributes

In the preceding section dealing with theoretical considerations, assumptions regarding the ways in which a number of factors may contribute to assemblage variation were presented. Artifact attributes were chosen for analysis on the basis of those assumptions, and are summarized by artifact category in Table 5.4. Specific attribute definitions and the method by which those attributes were observed are presented below.

Material Type and Texture

Material type was recorded for all artifacts selected for analysis. Although 15 types were distinguished, 8 materials, when combined, account for approximately 99 percent of all analyzed artifacts. These materials are listed below in decreasing order of their relative abundance in the analyzed collection:

1. Quartzite
2. Metasediment
3. Silicified Limestone
4. Chert
5. Limestone
6. Rhyolite
7. Basalt
8. Chalcedony

Other recorded materials include: jasper, obsidian, crystalline quartz, andesite, unidentified igneous, unidentified metamorphic, and unidentified sedimentary rock.

Quartzite

Quartzite is ubiquitous throughout the project area in alluvial gravels on ridges and in drainages. Naturally occurring pieces are

Table 5.3

NUMBERS OF ARTIFACTS RECOVERED AND ANALYZED,
BY STRUCTURE, FOR EACH SITE

Site Number	Structure Number	N of Artifacts Recovered	N of Artifacts Analyzed
AZ EE:2:76	7	251	251
	8	545	268
	10	495	283
	25	52	52
	27	345	121
	29	211	106
Total		1899	1081
AZ EE:2:77	1	121	121
	3	142	142
	4	65	65
	31	92	92
	44	24	24
	56	16	16
Total		460	460
AZ EE:2:84	10	171	171
	15	258	258
Total		429	429
AZ EE:1:104	1	24	0
	2	26	0
Total		50	0
AZ EE:2:105	5	190	190
	6	945	279
	7	1144	265
	9	440	181
	10	467	248
	11	52	0
	12	55	0
	13	46	0
	30	39	39
	38	149	149
	41	304	162
	50	294	219

Table 5.3, continued

NUMBERS OF ARTIFACTS RECOVERED AND ANALYZED,
BY STRUCTURE, FOR EACH SITE

Site Number	Structure Number	N of Artifacts Recovered	N of Artifacts Analyzed
AZ EE:2:105, continued	71001	635	226
	71200	1236	249
	72	92	91
	74	16	0
	81	120	120
	87	218	218
	88	170	170
	90	24	0
	91	212	212
Total		6848	3018
AZ EE:2:106	1	2	2
	2	13	13
	3	8	8
	6	2	2
	7	6	6
Total		31	31
AZ EE:2:107	1	51	51
	2	67	67
	3	53	53
	4	11	11
	5	21	21
Total		203	
AZ EE:2:109	1	22	22
	2	7	7
	3	11	11
	4	5	5
	5	7	7
Total		52	52
AZ EE:2:113	6000	204	0
	6100	205	204
	6200	265	150
	6300	435	180

Table 5.3, continued

NUMBERS OF ARTIFACTS RECOVERED AND ANALYZED,
BY STRUCTURE, FOR EACH SITE

Site Number	Structure Number	N of Artifacts Recovered	N of Artifacts Analyzed
AZ EE:2:113, continued	7	210	208
	8	431	184
	10	1578	203
	11	756	304
	12	457	275
	83	356	166
	86	88	88
	154	159	154
Total		5144	2116
AZ EE:2:116	1	27	27
	2	39	39
Total		66	66
AZ EE:2:117	1	16	16
	2	40	40
Total		56	56
AZ EE:2:120	1	76	76
	3	18	18
	6	12	12
	7	5	5
	8	24	24
	11	27	27
Total		162	162
AZ EE:2:122	1	3	3
	2	12	12
Total		15	15
AZ EE:2:129	1	164	164
	2	97	97
Total		261	261

Table 5.4

RECORDED ATTRIBUTES FOR BASIC CHIPPED STONE ARTIFACT CATEGORIES

Artifact Category	Material Type	Material Texture	Size	Cortex	Platform Type	Platform Lipping	Flaking Direction	Microflaking	Abrasion
Complete flakes	+	+	+	+	+	+	-	+	+
Proximal flake fragments	+	+	+	+	+	+	-	+	+
Split flakes	+	+	+	+	-	+	-	+	+
Medial or distal flake fragments	+	+	+	+	-	-	-	+	+
Nonorientable fragments	+	+	+	+	-	-	-	+	+
Cores	+	+	+	-	-	-	+	+	+
Hammerstones	+	+	+	-	-	-	-	-	-
Retouched pieces	+	+	-	-	-	-	-	-	+
Thermal spalls	+	+	-	-	-	-	-	-	-

+ = recorded
- = not recorded

extremely variable with respect to size and shape, including boulder-sized blocks, tabular chunks, and well-rounded cobbles. Quartzite occurs in a wide variety of colors, but most artifacts are various shades of brown, purple, pink, gray, or greenish gray. Because this material tends to be medium to coarse in texture and relatively elastic, its suitability to reduction techniques other than direct hard-hammer percussion is very limited. Some quartzites, especially the greenish gray variety, tend to be flawed with numerous natural fracture planes. In view of its abundance in the study area, it is not surprising that quartzite accounts for about 44 percent of all analyzed artifacts.

Metasediment

This term was applied to a broad class of materials that consists of metamorphosed siltstones and mudstones. These materials are characteristically green, reddish brown, or tan, and frequently contain numerous white inclusions of about a millimeter in diameter. Metasediments exhibit a great deal of variation in texture, ranging from microcrystalline to quartzitic. While finer-textured pieces are amenable to soft-hammer percussion and pressure flaking, metasediments in general are frequently flawed with planes of natural fracture. Like quartzite, metasediments are abundant and widely distributed in gravels throughout the project area. Approximately 27 percent of the analyzed artifacts were made of metasediments.

Silicified Limestone

Cobbles of this dark gray or black, medium- to fine-textured, metamorphic material are common in drainages, and are locally abundant on some ridge systems. In addition, bedrock outcrops of a lighter, bluish gray, metamorphosed limestone are present in the study area at AZ EE:2:90, and were used prehistorically as raw material sources (Ervin and Tagg 1984). A discussion of that site is presented in Volume 4 of the ANAMAX-Rosemont report series. Finer examples of these materials respond reasonably well to soft-hammer percussion, and to a lesser extent, pressure flaking. As is the case with metasediments, natural bedding planes detract from the quality of silicified limestones. This is especially true with the material available at the bedrock quarries. Silicified limestones account for about 13 percent of the analyzed collection.

Chert

Naturally occurring chert suitable for chipped stone tool manufacture is nowhere abundant in the Rosemont area. However, two varieties, presumably derived from limestone formations to the west of the study area, are occasionally found in alluvial gravels in the Rosemont area. One of these is a very fine textured, black or bluish black material that occurs in small, tabular chunks rarely exceeding

10 cm in diameter. These chunks are almost invariably flawed by
extensive natural fractures, and as a result, are suitable for making
only the smallest tools. Also locally available is a mottled gray,
bluish gray or off-white, medium- to fine-textured chert most commonly
found in the form of well-rolled nodules, in major drainages. Pieces of
this material may sometimes exceed 20 cm in diameter, but they too tend
to be extensively fractured. In addition to the two varieties described
above, a number of other cherts are present in small numbers in the
artifact collections. In view of the geological diversity of the Santa
Rita Mountains, it seems likely that these materials either occur very
rarely within the project area, or were obtained from unknown nearby
sources. Approximately 10 percent of the analyzed artifacts were made
of chert.

Limestone

Limestone occurs throughout the project area in the form of
cobbles, tabular chunks, and bedrock outcrops. Typically, this material
is light gray or buff in color, develops a chalky white cortex, and is
sometimes banded. Although medium-textured limestones can be found in
relatively large, structurally homogeneous pieces, this material was
probably considered undesirable for tool manufacture because of its
softness. Nevertheless, some 3 percent of the analyzed artifact are
made of limestone.

Rhyolite

This is a broad term applied to a variety of aphanitic and
porphyritic siliceous igneous rocks which are plentiful throughout the
study area in bedrock outcrops and in gravels. These materials are
usually light gray, pink, or brown, tend to be coarse in texture, and in
general are poorly suited to tool manufacture. Rhyolite accounts for
about 1 percent of the analyzed artifacts.

Basalt

Dark-colored, mafic, medium- to coarse-textured, aphanitic
igneous rocks were classified as basalt. No known source of this
material exists in the study area, and basalt artifacts account for only
about 1 percent of the analyzed collection.

Chalcedony

Although chalcedony is essentially the same as chert with
respect to chemical composition, chalcedony is distinguished from chert
on the basis of its color, being transluscent white or colorless.
Within the project area, naturally occurring pieces of this material are
rare, but small, tabular chunks suitable for making small tools are
occasionally found in alluvial gravels. Approximately 1 percent of the
analyzed artifacts are made of chalcedony.

Other Materials

The remaining material types distinguished during the analysis, none of which accounted for more than one-half of 1 percent of the analyzed artifacts, include jasper, obsidian, crystalline quartz, andesite, and unidentified igneous, metamorphic, and sedimentary rocks. The term "jasper" was applied to a number of pink, red, or reddish brown, fine-textured, siliceous rocks. Some of these materials are probably sedimentary in origin, while others are probably very fine-grained, glassy rhyolite. While both jasper and crystalline quartz suitable for flaking occur naturally in the Rosemont area, both of these materials are scarce.

No source of obsidian is known to exist in the project area, and only five artifacts of this material, all from AZ EE:2:105, were recovered. Andesite and the unidentified igneous, sedimentary, and metamorphic materials area all almost certainly of local origin, and will be grouped under the term "other" for the remainder of this chapter.

Material Texture

Because texture may vary considerably within many petrologically defined material types, and because it is assumed that texture is a more important consideration in selecting materials for particular applications than is material type, material texture was recorded on all artifacts selected for analysis. A graduated series of eight rock specimens was established, encompassing the range of material textures present in the collections. At one end of this continuum, a piece of obsidian was used to represent the finest texture; at the other extreme a piece of quartzite, having a texture loosely comparable to 40-grit abrasive paper, was used to represent the coarsest texture. During attribute recording, each artifact was visually and sometimes tactually compared to the rock specimens and assigned to the one of eight texture classes represented by the specimen that best approximated the artifact's texture. In cases where artifacts were so extensively weathered or patinated that the texture of the stone could not be determined without breakage, texture was not recorded. This happened most frequently with limestone artifacts, and occasionally with those of silicified limestone and metasediment.

Artifact Size

Measures of artifact size were recorded on complete and split flakes, proximal and medial-distal flake fragments, nonorientable fragments, cores, and hammerstones. Length, width, and thickness were measured to the nearest millimeter on complete flakes. These attributes are defined as follows:

> Length is the distance between the point of impact of the detaching blow and the most distant point on the interior

surface. In cases where flakes terminated in hinge fractures, length was measured to the center of the distal edge.

Width is the distance between lateral edges, measured perpendicularly to length, at the midpoint of length.

Thickness is the distance between interior and exterior surfaces, measured perpendicularly to the plane common to length and width, at the midpoint of width.

A single size observation, maximum dimension, was recorded for split flakes, proximal and medial-distal flake fragments, nonorientable fragments, cores, and hammerstones. This attribute was measured to the nearest millimeter, and is defined as the greatest obtainable measurement on a given artifact. In addition, cores and hammerstones were weighed on a triple-beam balance, to the nearest whole gram.

Cortex

On all artifacts selected for analysis except retouched pieces, hammerstones, and thermal spalls, observations of the amounts of cortex present were recorded. For complete flakes, this was done by assigning the artifact to one of five classes, based on the percentage of the exterior surface, including the platform, estimated to be cortical. Initially, these classes were defined as follows: Class 1 (no cortex), Class 2 (some, but less than 10%), Class 3 (greater than 10% but less than 50%), Class 4 (greater than 50% but less than 90%), Class 5 (greater than 90%). Later in the analysis the cortex classes were simplified by combining Classes 2 and 3, and Classes 4 and 5.

Presence or absence of cortex was recorded for split flakes, proximal and medial-distal flake fragments, and nonorientable fragments. For cores, the percentage of the artifact's surface showing cortex was estimated using three classes: (1) no cortex, (2) some but less than 50 percent cortical, and (3) greater than 50 percent cortical.

Platform type

Observations of platform type were made on complete flakes and proximal flake fragments. Four platform types were distinguished, and are defined as follows:

Cortical--Platforms with any amount of cortex were classified as cortical.

Plain--Platforms showing no cortex, which consist of a single surface unbroken by the intersection of any flake scar margins, were classified as plain.

Faceted--Platforms consisting of two or more noncortical surfaces delineated by flake scar margins were classified as faceted.

Indeterminate--Complete flakes and proximal flake fragments retaining the points of impact of detaching blows, but which are missing major portions of their platforms as a result of shattering and crushing, were classified as having indeterminate platforms.

Platform Lipping

Platform lipping or "overhang" along the edge common to the platform and interior surface was recorded as either present or absent on complete flakes, proximal flake fragments, and split flakes.

Direction of Flaking

The observation was made only on cores, which were assigned to one of three classes on the basis of the number of platforms present. These classes are defined as follows:

Unidirectional cores are those having only one surface to which blows were delivered to remove flakes.

Bidirectional cores are those having two platforms.

Multidirectional cores show three or more surfaces to which blows were delivered to remove flakes.

Microflaking

Microflaking is comparable to what is sometimes referred to as "utilization," and consists of flake scars resulting from the unintentional removal of numerous minute flakes from artifact edges. Microflaking, observed with a 10-power hand lens was recorded as present or absent on all artifacts selected for analysis, except hammerstones, retouched pieces, and thermal spalls, to provide a measure of the extent to which unretouched debitage was used. Because microflaking often undoubtedly results from many factors other than use, the criteria used to determine its presence were conservative; that is, they were designed to identify edge damage that almost certainly resulted from use rather than other agencies. The presence of microflaking was identified by no less than four overlapping flake scars, usually considerably less than 3 mm in length, on one face of an artifact's edge.

Abrasion

Abrasion--the rounding of an edge or surface as the result of use--was observed with a 10-power hand lens. Its presence or absence

was recorded for all artifact types except hammerstones and thermal
spalls.

Tool Typology

The Approach

Tools include all retouched pieces, and cobble and core
hammerstones, all items showing microflaking or abrasion, and those
cores whose forms suggest intentional shaping for use. In the process
of sorting artifacts from all proveniences (including those not selected
for detailed attribute analysis) into the basic artifact categories, all
retouched pieces, hammerstones, and core tools were set aside for later
typological manipulation. Because it was not feasible to examine all
artifacts with a hand lens, all tools that could only be be identified
as such on the basis of microflaking or abrasion could not be separated
from the rest of the collection; however, all such artifacts encountered
in the collections selected for attribute analysis were set aside, and
are assumed to be representative of this class. By following this
procedure, the artifacts included in the typological study were isolated
from the rest of the collections, permitting the development of tool
types by physically grouping artifacts in view of the full range of
variation present in the tool collection. This approach to typology
formulation helped ensure that the criteria used to distinguish tool
types were more evenly applied than if the artifacts had been assigned
to predefined types on a bag-by-bag basis.

Preliminary examination of the collection indicated that the
tools, especially the retouched pieces, were extremely diverse in many
aspects of form, including size, shape, retouch extent and location,
edge shape and angle, and so forth. Within this great diversity, a
number of tool types, most notably projectile points, hammerstones, and
certain low-angled slicing implements made on large flakes ("mescal
knives"), were distinctive. In fact, these items are so distinctive
that we may reasonably assume that they represent types that were
functionally, and perhaps linguistically distinguished by the people
responsible for their manufacture and use. With the exception of these
classes, however, variation characteristic of the remainder of the
collection appeared to be largely unpatterned, and intuitively
discernible, recurrent attribute combinations on which tool types might
be based were not obvious. Further, when certain attribute combinations
were perceived and provisionally used to establish types, the resulting
types tended to gradually merge with one another through continuous
series of intermediate forms. Thus the first step in the tool analysis
was to determine how to partition the observed variation in a meaningful
and replicable way, if only for descriptive purposes.

To a great extent, consideration of the major research focus
provided a basis for designing a typology to solve this problem. As
previously discussed, an important goal of the analysis was to determine
the extent to which differences in the nature of site occupations may

have contributed to variation among the chipped stone assemblages. For
example, on sites that were occupied by relatively large groups of
people for long periods, tools may have been subjected to more repeated
use before discard than those at sites that were occupied by fewer
people for shorter periods. As a result, it is possible that tools from
more intensively occupied sites may show evidence of more extensive
modification or retouch, than those from less intensively occupied
sites.

       To test the validity of this notion, the typology was oriented
towards classifying the majority of tools according to retouch extent.
Figure 5.1, an outline of this typology, shows that two major tool
classes are distinguished. One of these consists of those tool types
which were intuitively discernible, and which are ostensibly
distinguished from each other, as well as other types, on the basis of
patterned, recurrent attribute combinations. The attributes which
distinguish these types will be discussed in the following section
devoted to specific type descriptions. The second major tool class
encompasses those items in which intuitively discernible types were not
obvious, and consists of arbitrarily defined types that were designed to
account for variation in retouch extent. Four variables pertaining to
the character of the retouch were considered in establishing these
types.

       For lack of a better term, the first of these variables is
referred to as retouch continuity or "continuousness." Retouch was
arbitrarily classified as continuous if it consisted of at least three
contiguous, intentionally produced flake scars, while retouched pieces
showing less than three adjoining flake scars were classified as having
discontinuous retouch. Continuous retouch presumably represents a more
intensive and extensive kind of edge modification than does
discontinuous retouch.

       The second variable considered in defining arbitrary tool types
was whether the retouch was unifacial or bifacial. Items showing
continuous retouch on one face, and those with continuous retouch on two
faces, distributed in such fashion that the retouch on one face was not
contiguous or overlapping with that on the other face, were classified
as unifacial. Artifacts with continuous retouch on two faces,
distributed so that the retouch on both faces originated from the same
portion of the artifact's edge, were classified as bifacial. It is
assumed that bifacial retouch represents a more intensive and extensive
form of edge modification than does unifacial retouch.

       The third variable used to define arbitrary tool types was
retouch depth, or the length to which retouch flake scars extended
inward from their origins at tool margins, across the artifact's
surface. If the length of the longest scar present was less than
10 percent of the artifact's maximum dimension, the retouch was
classified as "marginal." Retouched pieces having at least one flake
scar whose length exceeded 10 percent of the artifact's maximum
dimension were classified as having "invasive" retouch. Implements that
are characterized by invasive retouch are generally assumed to have

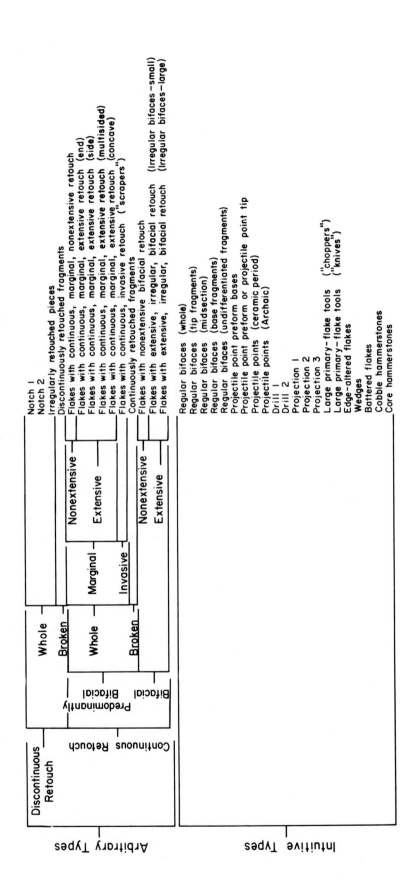

Figure 5.1 Tool typology outline.

undergone more extensive modification than those showing predominantly marginal retouch.

The percentage of an implement's peripheral edge that was modified by retouch was the fourth variable considered in establishing arbitrary types. Retouch that occupied less than 20 percent of an artifact's peripheral edge was classified as nonextensive, while retouch occurring along more than 20 percent of the artifact's circumference was classified as extensive. While all four of the variables discussed thus far can be thought of as measures of modification extent and intensity, it is important to emphasize that the terms "nonextensive" and "extensive" refer specifically to the percentage of an artifact's peripheral edge occupied by retouch, and that these distinctions are based on an arbitrary division of this continuous variable.

In addition to the four variables used as measures of retouch extent and intensity, a fifth variable, completeness, was also considered in establishing arbitrary tool types. This was necessary because it is not possible to determine the percentage of an artifact's peripheral edge occupied by retouch on broken tools. Similarly, reliable determinations of retouch depth cannot be made on broken pieces because such determinations are based on maximum retouch flake scar length relative to the implement's size (maximum dimension).

Given five variables, each of which independently assumes one of two possible states, 32 arbitrary tool types are theoretically possible. Figure 5.1 shows how the variables were applied in establishing arbitrary types, and indicates that only nine arbitrary types were distinguished. The large discrepancy between the number of types theoretically possible and the number actually distinguished is largely due to two factors. First, many theoretically possible types were not distinguished when they shared one attribute subjectively judged to be much more important in assessing retouch extent and intensity than other attributes. For example, discontinuously retouched artifacts were not further differentiated on the basis of marginal as opposed to invasive retouch, because the difference between the resulting types was considered to be relatively insignificant in view of the full range of variation in retouch extent present in the collection. Second, some types were essentially absent in the collection because they represent either improbable forms, such as items with discontinuous, bifacial, invasive, extensive retouch, or forms which were simply not commonly produced, such as flakes with continuous, bifacial, marginal retouch.

Figure 5.1 also shows that some arbitrary tool types were distinguished on the basis of attributes such as size and retouch location, that are not necessarily directly related to retouch extent or intensity. Thus, while attributes pertaining to retouch extent and intensity provided the underlying structure of the typology, other factors were considered in defining certain categories.

More specific descriptions of the arbitrary tool types are presented in the following section. Before proceeding with these descriptions, a few final observations about the typology should be made.

First, an attempt was made to arrange the arbitrary types in increasing order of retouch extent and intensity. In general, types characterized by discontinuous retouch are listed before those with continuous retouch, unifacial types are listed before bifacial types, items with marginal retouch are listed before those with invasive retouch, and so forth. However, because some types were distinguished on the basis of attributes which are not necessarily related to retouch extent or intensity, the ordering of some types is arbitrary.

Second, simple inspection of the tool collection indicated that material types tended to be evenly distributed across most tool categories. Therefore, no systematic attempt was made to seek correlations between material types and tool categories. Several exceptions to this observation were noted, and will be identified in the type descriptions. An apparent tendency for smaller tools to be made of finer-textured materials will be explored in greater detail in the following section.

Finally, it is reasonable to assume, at least in general terms, the functions of various intuitively derived types. There is little reason to doubt, for example, that hammerstones were used as hammers, that projectile points were hafted on arrows or darts, or that wedges were used for splitting. The functional significance of the arbitrarily defined types is by no means as clear. While it seems safe to assume that collectively, these implements were used for a wide variety of tasks involving slicing, scraping, gouging, piercing, shredding, whittling, and so forth, no assumptions about the functions of individual types are made.

Tool Type Descriptions

Notches

Flakes that were retouched by a single blow, resulting in the removal of one retouch flake were classified as notches. Two subtypes are distinguished: those in which the retouch resulted in a marked concavity along the flake's margin (Notch 1), and those in which the retouch resulted in only very slight concavities, or none at all (Notch 2). In both cases the location of the retouch appears to be unpatterned, both with respect to interior and exterior surfaces, and in relation to the artifact's major axis. Notches range from 22 mm to 101 mm in maximum dimension. On Type 1 notches, the concavities range from about 10 mm to 30 mm in width, and between 5 mm and 10 mm in depth; on Type 2 specimens they generally tend to be shallower in relation to width. All major material types are represented, including quartzite, metasediment, silicified limestone, and chert. In at least two cases, microflaking suggests that these tools were used as "spokeshaves" for whittling or scraping cylindrical wooden or possibly bone items. In

other cases, the placement of the notch in relation to a ridge on the
flake's exterior surface could be interpreted as an attempt to isolate
a projection. Other notches, especially those which do not show
pronounced concavities, may represent pieces which were tested, and
deemed unsuitable for further reduction.

Irregularly Retouched Pieces (IRP)

This is a formally diverse class encompassing all whole
artifacts showing discontinuous retouch. It includes pieces with two or
more noncontiguous retouch flake scars, flakes with only two contiguous
retouch flake scars (one or more noncontiguous flake scars may also be
present) and occasionally, pieces showing multiple, noncontiguous pairs
of contiguous retouch flake scars. In general, this retouch tends to be
predominantly unifacial, or alternately bifacial, and often results in a
jagged edge. Edge angle, retouch depth, and retouch location are all
highly variable, and appear to be independent of one another.
Irregularly retouched pieces range from 31 mm to 107 mm in maximum
dimension, and include all major material types.

Although in most instances the significance of this limited form
of edge modification is not clear, a number of possibilities may be
advanced. On some examples, the retouch location suggests an attempt to
remove a minor irregularity from an otherwise suitable working edge. In
other cases, jagged edges may have been intentionally produced for use
in some task involving sawing or shredding. In at least one instance,
the location of the retouch in relation to an edge showing no
modification except extensive microflaking suggests that the purpose of
the retouch was to make the implement more convenient to hold. Yet
another possibility is that some irregularly retouched flakes are tools
which were, for one reason or another, discarded during the very early
states of manufacture. Finally, some of the larger, thicker examples
may have been secondary cores which underwent only limited reduction.

Discontinuously Retouched Flake Fragments (DRF)

This class was established to account for flake fragments which
exhibit either notches or discontinuous retouch like that described for
the preceding type. Because it is impossible to determine the full
extent of retouch before breakage, distinctions between notches and
irregularly retouched pieces are unwarranted. Tool fragments showing
discontinuous retouch range from about 17 mm to 90 mm in maximum
dimension, and are made of all major material types, including
quartzite, metasediments, silicified limestone, chert, and limestone.

Flakes with Continuous, Marginal, Nonextensive Retouch (CMN)

By definition, this class of unifacially retouched pieces
includes all flakes which show at least three contiguous, intentionally
produced retouch flake scars, exceed 10 percent of the artifact's

maximum dimension in length, and which occupy no more than 20 percent of
the artifact's peripheral edge. As was the case with the other types
described thus far, retouch on these artifacts appears to be random with
regard to location, and results in edges of diverse angles and shapes.
Flakes with continuous, marginal, nonextensive retouch range from 33 mm
to 120 mm in maximum dimension, and possibly represent flakes which
required only minor modification prior to use.

Flakes with Continuous, Marginal, Extensive Retouch (CME)

These retouched pieces are essentially the same as those of the
preceding type, except that the retouch is more extensive, occupying
more than 20 percent of the artifact's peripheral edge. Three subtypes
(Fig. 5.2) are distinguished on the basis of retouch location in
relation to the artifact's major axis: end (a, b), side (c-g), and
multisided, or those with retouch along two or more edges (h-k). The
retouch occurs on flake exteriors (b-e, h-k), and less frequently on
interior surfaces (a, d, e), and commonly results in jagged,
"subdenticulate" edges, which are irregularly convex or straight. Most
examples appear to be the result of hard-hammer percussion, and could
have been useful in a variety of tasks involving light scraping. Those
with serrate edges may have been used as shredding implements or saws.
In some instances the retouch is steep, and is located opposite an
unmodified, low-angled edge that would have been well suited for
slicing. In these cases, we may speculate that the retouch served as
"backing" to prevent injury to the hand during use. On one example
(Fig. 5.2d) flake scar morphology and spacing suggest that the retouch
was accomplished by pressure flaking. This artifact may represent an
aborted attempt at projectile point manufacture.

A fourth subtype (Fig. 5.3) consists of flakes with continuous,
marginal extensive retouch which creates a concave working edge. Like
some notches, these tools were probably used as "spokeshaves" for
shaping cylindrical objects of bone or wood. They differ from notches
in that the concavity is formed by continuous retouch, rather than a
single flake scar; the resulting concavities tend to be wider and
shallower than those characteristic of notches. Flakes with continuous,
marginal, extensive retouch range from 20 mm to 112 mm in maximum
dimension, and are made of all major material types.

Flakes with Continuous, Invasive Retouch (CI)

This is by far the most abundant type of intentionally modified
tool in the collection, and includes all whole artifacts showing at
least three contiguous retouch flake scars whose lengths exceed
10 percent of the artifact's maximum dimension. The retouch is
predominantly unifacial, and often contributes to a plano-convex cross
section. These artifacts are loosely equivalent to what most
archaeologists recognize as "scrapers," and will be referred to as such
for the remainder of this chapter.

Figure 5.2. Flakes with continuous, marginal, extensive retouch (CME).

Figure 5.3 Flakes with continuous, marginal, extensive retouch (CME), resulting in a concave working edge.

Scrapers are very diverse in many aspects of form, and those shown in Figures 5.4, 5.5, 5.6, and 5.7 are representative of the range of variation characteristic of this class. Scrapers range in size from about 20 mm in length and width, and less than 10 mm in thickness to approximately 130 mm in length, 100 mm in width, and 70 mm in thickness. Some extremely large examples (Fig. 5.7m-o) would probably be classified as "choppers" or "planes" by many researchers; however, because variation in scraper size was obviously continuous throughout its range, typological distinctions based on size were not made. Scrapers of all sizes exhibit a wide variety of shapes, including discoids, and irregular ovoids and subrectangular forms of varying degrees of elongation. In the vast majority of cases, retouch was done by hard-hammer percussion, although at least two examples (Fig. 5.4, item 1, and Fig. 5.5, item j) appear to be the result of soft-hammer percussion. In general, the retouch is steep, and results in jagged edges suggesting little concern for the production of a regular working edge. On some scrapers (Fig. 5.5k) the character of the retouch suggests a deliberate attempt to produce a serrate edge. Examples showing very regular edges (Fig. 5.5, item 1) are rare. As was the case with the preceding type, retouch on scrapers occurs most often on flake exteriors, though scrapers having retouch on flake interiors (Fig. 5.6k) are not uncommon. Finally, scrapers vary considerably in retouch location with respect to the artifact's major axis, and in the percentage of the peripheral edge which was modified. Side and multisided scrapers tend to show the most extensive modification, while end scrapers are generally the result of less extensive retouch.

The great diversity of form characteristic of scrapers suggests equally diverse function. Many of the smaller examples were probably used in preparing hides or for light-duty woodworking. Those with distinctly serrate edges could have been used as saws or for shredding fibrous plant material. Abrasion on the planar surfaces of some of the larger, steeply retouched examples indicates that they were used as planes, possibly for heavy-duty woodworking tasks. It is also likely that some examples served as secondary cores, and were thus used only as a source of additional flakes. Finally, it is assumed that many scrapers, especially the more extensively modified examples, were subjected to repeated modifications for different tasks, and that they may not have been considered functional for any purpose when they were thrown away or abandoned.

Potentially, the diversity of scraper form opens many possibilities for defining subtypes on the basis of size, shape, retouch extent and location, edge regularity and angle, relative thickness, and so forth. However, variation in scraper form was found to parallel that typical of the tool collection in general. That is, intuitively discernible, recurrent, patterned associations among the above attributes, by which scraper subtypes might be defined, were not obvious. Therefore, no subtypes are distinguished.

Instead, a number of qualitative and quantitative attributes (material type, length, width, and thickness, and retouch extent) were recorded for all scrapers, providing basic descriptive information for

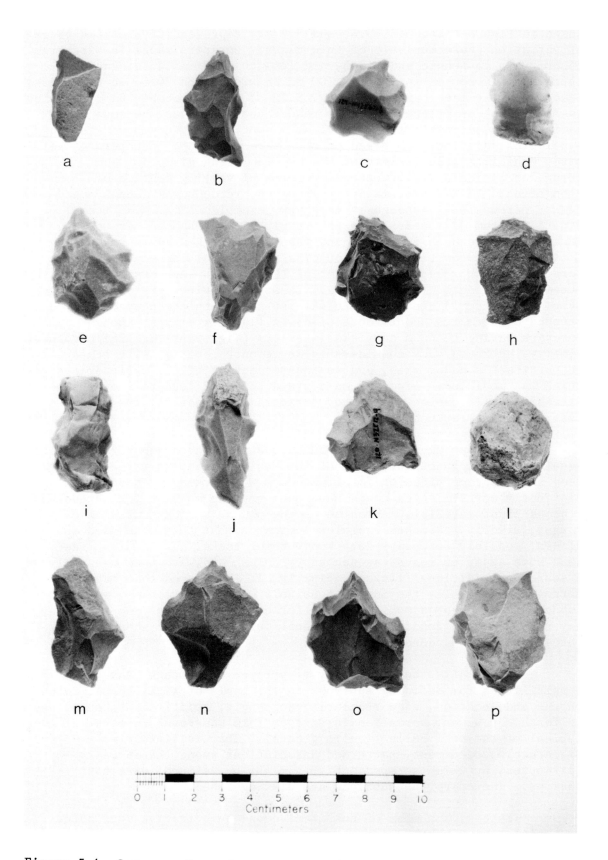

Figure 5.4   Scrapers from the Rosemont Hohokam sites.

Figure 5.5 Scrapers from the Rosemont Hohokam sites.

Figure 5.6   Scrapers from the Rosemont Hohokam sites.

Figure 5.7   Scrapers from the Rosemont Hohokam sites.

this broad artifact category. Length, width, and thickness were
measured to the nearest centimeter. Length and width were observed as
the dimensions of the smallest rectangle that would contain the artifact
when placed on its planar surface. Thickness was observed as the
maximum dimension between the planar surface and its opposite,
perpendicular to the plane common to length and width.

Retouch extent was observed as the percentage of the scraper's
peripheral edge modified by retouch. These values were computed from
measurements of the scraper's circumference and the length of the
retouched edge(s). Circumference was measured by rotating the
implement's peripheral edge 360 degrees along a line on a piece of graph
paper graduated in millimeters. Retouched edge length was measured in a
similar fashion. Data pertaining to attributes of scraper form will be
presented in sections dealing with specific analyses.

Continuously Retouched Fragments (CRF)

Broken implements showing continuous, unifacial retouch were
placed in this class. These items appear to be pieces of tools broken
in manufacture or during subsequent modification, and exhibit a range of
formal variation comparable to that seen in scrapers. Fragments showing
continuous, unifacial retouch range from 20 mm to 100 mm in maximum
dimension, and are made of all major materials.

Flakes with Nonextensive Bifacial Retouch (NBR)

This class includes a comparatively small number of flakes
showing bifacial retouch that tends to be nonextensive and marginal.
Some of the smaller examples made of fine-textured materials appear to
have been pressure flaked, and may be attempts at projectile point
manufacture that were abandoned because of difficulty in thinning.
Retouch on the other examples was accomplished by hard-hammer
percussion, and in some cases, was done only to remove the striking
platform and bulb of percussion. In one case, the retouch occurs
opposite a low-angled edge showing pronounced abrasion that resulted
from slicing. The purpose of such retouch was probably to make the
flake more convenient to hold. Flakes with nonextensive bifacial
retouch range from 17 mm to 71 mm in maximum dimension.

Irregular Bifaces

These bifacially worked implements (Fig. 5.8) are distinguished
from the preceding type in that the retouch tends to be more extensive
and invasive, although flake surfaces unmodified by retouch are still
evident in nearly all cases. In general, the retouch appears to be the
result of hard-hammer percussion, and creates a jagged edge. Most
examples are irregularly oval in outline, and tend to be thick in
relation to length and width. Two subtypes, small (items a-g) and large
(items h-j), were arbitrarily distinguished on the basis of size. Small

Figure 5.8   Irregular bifaces.   a-g, Type 1, small; h-k, Type 2, large.

and large irregular bifaces range from 20 mm to 65 mm, and from 70 mm to 110 mm in maximum dimension, respectively. Irregular bifaces are made of all major material types; chert and fine-textured metasediments are especially prevalent in the small subtype.

Many of the smaller examples and at least two of the larger ones are most reasonably interpreted as aborted attempts at bifacial thinning. Five of the larger variety have crushed and battered edges indicating their use as chopping tools. Other examples might be bifacially reduced secondary cores ("flake cores"). Yet another possibility is that some irregular bifaces are scrapers which were exhausted as a result of repeated bifacial refurbishing.

Regular Bifaces

In contrast to irregular bifaces, regular bifaces (Fig. 5.9) tend to be thinner in relation to length and width, and have edges that are more regular in both outline and profile. Regular bifaces have lenticular cross sections, and tend to be oval or subtriangular in outline. In most cases, the retouch extends around the artifact's entire periphery, and in many cases is so extensive that no traces of the original flake surface remain. In general, the retouch appears to be the result of soft-hammer percussion; a few examples show limited pressure flaking. Fine-textured materials, mainly chert and metasediments, were preferred, though a few examples are made of medium-textured quartzite and silicified limestone. Whole bifaces (Fig. 5.9i-t), tips (a-c), and midsections and base fragments (d-h) are distinguished within this category. Another fragment category, "undifferentiated," was established to account for edge fragments that could not be oriented. Whole examples range from 22 mm to 58 mm in length.

While the significance of the retouch on irregular bifaces is not always clear, there is little doubt that most regular bifaces represent attempts at projectile point manufacture that failed either because of breakage, or because problems such as numerous, nonrecoverable step terminations, were encountered in thinning. One well-thinned example (Fig. 5.9g) with very regular edges is probably a piece of a finished bifacial knife which broke during use or subsequent modification.

Projectile Point Preforms

These small bifaces (Fig. 5.10), all of which are broken, are distinguished from the preceding type by the presence of extensive pressure retouch. Preform bases (Fig. 5.10m-v) tend to be triangular in outline, have laterally expanding bases, and appear to be unfinished projectile points that were broken before final modifications to facilitate hafting were executed. Fragments classified as "preform tips" (Fig. 5.10a-l) also appear to be pieces of unfinished projectile points, though serrate edges on one example (f) suggest that this

Figure 5.9 Regular bifaces. a-c, tips; i-t, whole; d-h, midsections and bases.

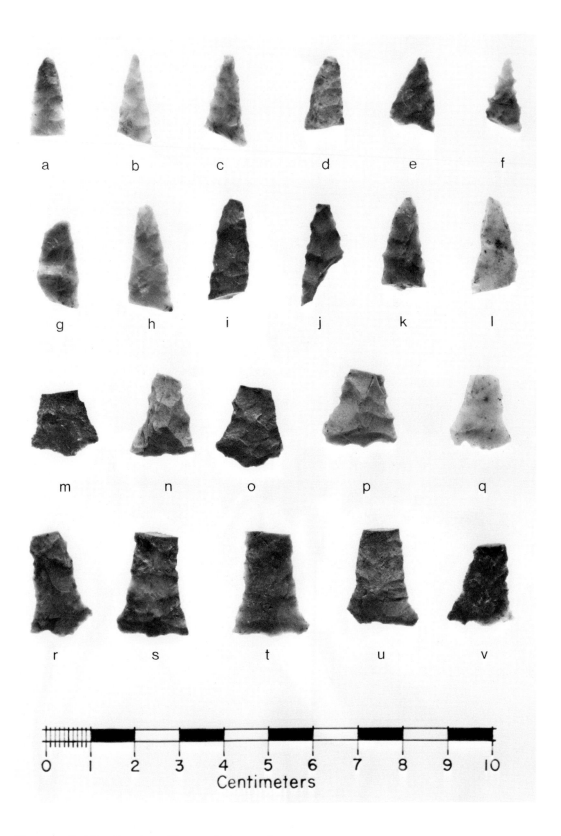

Figure 5.10 Projectile point preforms.

artifact was finished, or very nearly finished, when it was broken.
Preform tips and bases range from 13 mm to 23 mm, and from 15 mm to
22 mm in maximum dimension, respectively. Chert is the most common
material, but some examples are made of chalcedony, fine-textured
metasediment, and crystalline quartz.

Projectile Points

        Two broad classes of projectile points were distinguished on the
basis of size and manufacturing techniques. The first of these (Figs.
5.11, 5.12a-p) is attributed to the Hohokam, and consists of small,
light points that would have been suitable for hafting on arrows. These
points were made from thin flakes of fine-textured materials, and appear
to have been shaped exclusively by pressure retouch. Chert and
chalcedony are the most common materials, but silicified limestone,
fine-textured metasediment, and obsidian were also used.

        The second major group (Figs. 5.12q-u, 5.13, and 5.14) is
composed of larger, heavier points which were initially thinned by soft-
hammer percussion, followed by pressure retouch finishing. The
relatively large size of these points suggests that they were hafted on
darts, spears, or lances, rather than on arrows. Although they were
collected from Hohokam sites, these points have technological and
stylistic characteristics which are clearly preceramic, and bear a
strong resemblance to points recovered from sites of known preceramic
age elsewhere in the Rosemont area, which were described and illustrated
in the first volume of the ANAMAX-Rosemont report series (Huckell
1984a). Therefore, their manufacture and original use must be
ultimately attributed to the Archaic occupation of the study area. Like
their Hohokam counterparts, some Archaic projectile points are made of
chert, fine-textured metasediment, and obsidian. In addition, however,
fine-textured rhyolite is well represented among the Archaic points.

        Hohokam points, the first major class, have been further divided
into seven types; however, the majority of the Hohokam points can be
assigned to Types 1, 2, or 3. Types 4 through 7 were established to
account for a number of less numerous Hohokam point styles.

        Type 1. These are small, triangular points which are
distinguished by a very short, contracting stem (Fig. 5.11a-m). Blade
edges are concave or straight in outline, and often show pronounced
lateral expansion immediately above the stem. Only one example (c) has
distinctly serrate edges. The ratio of base width to blade length
varies considerably, resulting in forms ranging from nearly equilateral
triangles (d, e), to those which are markedly elongate and lanceolate
(h, i). Many of the chert examples show extensive, well-controlled
pressure retouch (g-k), but retouch on those of inferior materials such
as quartztite (l) is marginal, and results in steep-angled edges.
Type 1 points range from 13 mm to 32 mm in length.

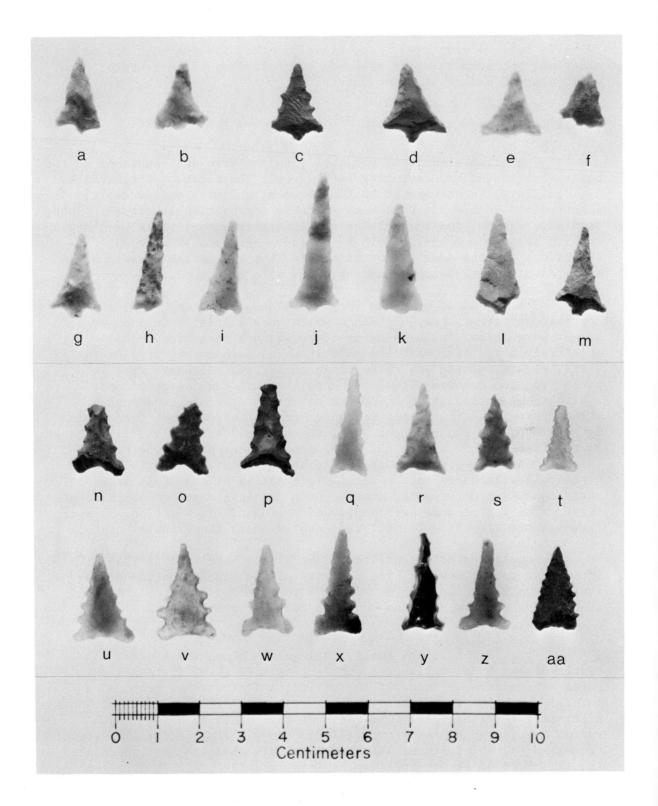

Figure 5.11 Hohokam projectile points. a-m, Type 1; n-aa, Type 2.

Figure 5.12 Projectile points. Hohokam styles: a–i, Type 3; j, Type 4; k–m, Type 5; n–o, Type 6; p, Type 7. Archaic style: q–u, Type 10.

Figure 5.13   Archaic projectile points.   a-g, Type 8; h-n, Type 9.

Figure 5.14. Archaic projectile points. a, Type 11; b, Type 12;
c-d, Type 13.

Points similar to those described above have been recovered from
the Hodges Ruin (Kelly 1978: 90, Fig. 6.7a-c) and the Hardy Site
(Reinhard 1981, Fig. 12a-e) in the Tucson Basin. Outside the Tucson
Basin, they have been reported from Snaketown (Gladwin and others 1937,
Plate XCI) and Gu Achi (Masse 1980b: 156, Fig. 69o-p). At the Hodges
Ruin, this style occurred in Cañada del Oro and Rillito phase contexts;
at Snaketown, it is most commonly associated with the Santa Cruz phase
(Gladwin and others 1937, Plate XCI), the Phoenix Basin equivalent of
the Rillito phase.

Type 2. Triangular points with serrate edges and concave bases
were assigned to this category (Fig. 5.11n-aa). Like Type 1, Type 2
points tend to have straight or slightly concave edges and show
considerable variation with respect to the ratio of base width to blade
length. Serration on some examples (n-p, s) tends to be coarse, while
others (q, t, aa) are much more finely serrated. Five specimens
(u-x, z) show a very noticeable increase in the coarseness of the
serrations, from tip to base. Most examples show well-executed pressure
retouch; however, the only recovered Hohokam point made of obsidian is
an exception to this observation. This artifact (y) is characterized by
extremely crude unifacial retouch producing edge angles of about

90 degrees. Thickness is approximately equal to blade width. The crudeness of this point is somewhat surprising as it is made of the finest material available to the Hohokam craftsman. Type 2 points range from 16 mm to 26 mm in length.

Small, triangular points with serrate edges and concave bases, similar to Type 2 points described above, have been recovered from Snaketown (Gladwin and others 1937, Plate LXXXV d-h), Los Muertos (Haury 1945, Plate 36i), the Hodges Ruin (Kelly 1978: 90, Fig. 6.6f-h), the Hardy Site (Reinhard 1981, Fig. 12f-o), and Gu Achi (Masse 1980b: 156, Fig. 69e-f). At Snaketown, these points are largely confined to Sacaton phase contexts (Gladwin and others 1937, Plate LXXXV); at Gu Achi, they are associated with late Santa Cruz/Sacaton phase contexts (Masse 1980b: 152). At the Hodges Ruin, this style dates to the Rincon phase (Kelly 1978: 90), the Tucson Basin counterpart of the Sacaton phase. In general, then, Type 2 points appear to postdate those with short, contracting stems (Type 1).

Type 3. These serrate points are similar to those of Type 2, but are distinguished by having straight or slightly convex, rather than concave bases (Fig. 5.12a-i). While there is considerable variation among Type 2 points with respect to serration width and depth, and regularity of spacing, Type 3 points consistently show fine, uniformly spaced serrations. As was the case with the preceding types, Type 3 points exhibit a great deal of variation in the ratio of base width to blade length. Cross sections through the long axes of the three most elongate examples (e-g) are concavo-convex, reflecting the curvature of the thin flakes from which these points were made. Some examples (a, b, d) have edges which are uniformly straight from tip to base, while others (c, e-g) show an abrupt lateral expansion immediately above the base. Type 3 points range from 18 mm to 39 mm in length.

Elongate, straight-sided, serrate points with convex or straight bases have been recovered from Snaketown (Gladwin and others 1937, Plate LXXXVc-h), Los Muertos (Haury 1945, Plate 36f-h), and Gu Achi (Masse 1980b, Fig. 69a, b, d). While none of these shows the same exaggerated basal flaring that is characteristic of some of the Rosemont examples, the points shown in the above cited illustrations are essentially the same as Type 3 points. At both Snaketown and Gu Achi, this style was most frequently encountered in Sacaton phase contexts, and to a lesser extent, in Santa Cruz phase associations (Gladwin and others 1937, Plate LXXXV; Masse 1980b: 152). It is therefore possible that the Rosemont examples date to the Rincon phase, and are roughly contemporaneous with Type 2 points.

Type 4. This class is composed of a single small, triangular, side-notched point with a straight base (Fig. 5.12j). It is made of chert, and is 19 mm long. The blade is not serrate, and the notches are located about one-third of the point's length above the base. Above the notches, both margins are heavily abraded, indicating use as a drill. Whether this artifact was made specifically for use as a drill, or served first as a projectile point is not clear.

In the Phoenix Basin, very similar points have been reported from Snaketown (Gladwin and others 1937, Plate LXXXIb), Los Muertos (Haury 1945, Plate 35f-i), and Las Colinas (Huckell 1981b, Fig. 111a-d). A small, triangular, side-notched point with a straight base was also recovered from University Indian Ruin in the Tucson Basin (Hayden 1957, Plate XLd). At Snaketown, this style occurs in Sacaton phase associations (Gladwin and others 1937, Plate LXXXVI), while it is attributed to the Classic period at both Las Colinas (Huckell 1981b: 173) and University Indian Ruin (Hayden 1957, Plate LXd). At the Hodges Ruin, small, triangular, side-notched points similar to the Rosemont specimen, but having concave rather than straight bases, first appear in Rincon phase contexts, and become dominant in the succeeding Tanque Verde phase (Kelly 1978: 90-91). In general then, small, triangular, side-notched styles appear to be characteristic of the Classic period.

Type 5. These three specimens are similar to Type 2 points in that they are small and triangular, and have slightly concave blades and markedly concave bases (Fig. 5.12k-m). Unlike Type 2 points, however, Type 5 points have plain, rather than serrate edges. All three Type 5 points are characterized by very steep, essentially unifacial pressure retouch which does not extensively alter the surfaces of the flakes from which these points were made. The character of the retouch on one example (k) may be related to the fact that it is made of quartzite. Although medium-textured, this material is not well-suited to extensive thinning and serration by pressure flaking. The other two examples (l, m) are made of fine-textured materials (metasediment and chert, respectively) that would have responded well to pressure flaking. Therefore, the quality of the retouch on these examples suggests that their makers were more concerned with the expedient production of small, sharp-pointed pieces of stone suitable for hafting, than they were with any particular stylistic convention. Type 5 points are not commonly reported in the literature, although Doyel illustrates two points (1977a, Fig. 39a, second and third from right) which appear to be very similar to the Rosemont examples. These were recovered from the Tinaja Canyon Site in the middle Santa Cruz Valley, and are associated with a Rillito/Rincon phase occupation.

Type 6. These are small, triangular, nonserrate points with slightly concave bases and slightly convex blade margins (Fig. 5.12n, o). Both are about 18 mm in length, are relatively thick, and were shaped by bifacial pressure retouch. One of the two specimens (n) is made of black chert, and the other (o) is of chalcedony. The latter example shows a small notch on one blade margin, directly above the base. The opposite edge was not notched, probably because of the point's thickness along this portion of the edge; this specimen may not be a finished implement. Small, triangular points with convex blade edges and concave bases have been attributed to the Papago at Ventana Cave (Haury and others 1950: 274) and to the Sobaipuri at the England Ranch Ruin in the middle Santa Cruz Valley (Doyel 1977a: 121). No evidence of Sobaipuri or Papago occupations was found at either of the Rosemont sites from which Type 6 points were recovered. Therefore, the similarity between the Rosemont specimens and those from Ventana Cave and the England Ranch Ruin is probably coincidental. Like Type 5, Type 6 is a very generalized, unembellished form that was expediently produced by the Hohokam.

Type 7. This category was established to account for a single large, triangular point of silicified limestone measuring 46 mm in length (Fig. 5.12p). This point is made on a thin flake and shows continuous, marginal, bifacial pressure retouch along both blade edges. The interior and exterior surfaces of the flake from which the point was made remain largely unaltered by retouch, and no basal modification to facilitate hafting was present. This specimen is unusually large in comparison to most of the Hohokam points from Rosemont, and bears a superficial resemblance to certain preceramic styles. However, the nature of the retouch, being limited to pressure flaking with no soft-hammer percussion shaping, is more typical of Hohokam than Archaic period technology. In view of this, and the point's recovery from the fill of a Hohokam pit house, there is little reason to doubt that the Type 7 point is of Hohokam origin.

Among the Archaic projectile points recovered from Hohokam sites in the Rosemont area, six types are distinguished. These are described below, and the temporal significance of each is briefly discussed. For a more detailed treatment of these styles, including their temporal and cultural relationship to the Archaic occupation of southeastern Arizona, the reader is again referred to Huckell's (1984a) study of the ANAMAX-Rosemont Archaic sites.

Type 8. These are large, lanceolate points with shallow, wide, side notches (Fig. 5.13a-g). Bases are convex (a ,b, d, g) or straight (c, e, f). On most examples, blade width exceeds base width, with maximum blade width occurring immediately above the notches. Blade edges are slightly convex or straight, and many specimens are serrate (a-c, e, f). Whole examples range from 40 mm to 70 mm in length. In general, Type 8 points are characteristic of the San Pedro stage of the Cochise culture (Sayles and Antevs 1941), the last Archaic phase before the appearance of pottery. The basal treatment of one example (f) suggests that this specimen may be an exception to the temporal placement of Type 8 points advanced above. This point might be viewed as having a short, broad, slightly expanding stem, rather than shallow, wide, side notches. As a result, this point bears some resemblance to Middle Archaic styles first described from the Pinto Basin in southern California (Campbell and Campbell 1935).

Type 9. These are large, triangular, unnotched, nonserrate points having concave or straight bases, and slightly convex or straight blade edges (Fig. 5.13h-n). Some examples (k-n) show a slight constriction of the blade margins immediately above the base. While some (m, n) are nicely thinned, others (i, j) are relatively thick in cross section, and show numerous, nonrecoverable, step-fracture flake

scar terminations. Whole examples range from 29 mm to 44 mm in length.
At Ventana Cave, large triangular and leaf-shaped points with concave
and straight bases were distributed throughout the deposits, but tended
to be concentrated in the upper levels (Haury and others 1950, Table
21). Other evidence from the study area suggesting that Type 9 points
represent a predominantly Late Archaic style is presented by Huckell
(1984a).

Type 10. Five nonserrate projectile points with corner notches
which create a stemmed base were assigned to this type (Fig. 5.12q-u).
Three of these (q-s) are essentially whole, and are from AZ EE:2:113.
The other two (t, u), both from AZ EE:2:105, are base fragments. Two of
the specimens from AZ EE:2:113 (v, s) have very wide notches resulting
in straight-sided to slightly expanding stems with straight or slightly
convex bases. Both are relatively thick in cross section, and their
blades appear to have been extensively reworked. The third example from
AZ EE:2:113 (q) is well thinned by soft-hammer percussion and pressure
flaking, and has deep, narrow, corner notches, which, in conjunction
with slightly concave blade margins, create downward-projecting tangs
above the notches. The stem is slightly expanding and has a convex
base. One of the base fragments from AZ EE:2:105 (u) consists of
nothing more than the stem of a point which was probably very similar to
Figure 5.12q. Little can be said of the remaining fragment (t); it
apparently had shallow, narrow notches forming a broad stem with a
convex base. On the basis of evidence from Ventana Cave, Haury and
others (1950: 292) suggested that a number of styles similar to Type 10
points tend to be relatively late in the preceramic sequence. In
addition, Huckell's recent unpublished investigations at AZ EE:2:30, an
intensively occupied preceramic village located 9 miles east of the
project area, have shown that nicely thinned, corner-notched points with
narrow expanding stems and convex bases were in common use around
A.D. 1. Because the study area is geographically transitional between
the Hohokam and San Simon branch Mogollon culture areas, it is worth
noting that corner-notched points similar to Type 10 persisted into
ceramic horizons in the Mogollon area (Wheat 1955: 127).

Type 11. This type accounts for a single large, chert point
having a parallel-sided stem which terminates in a convex base (Fig.
5.14a). The blade is triangular and coarsely serrate, and has a snapped
tip. This specimen has a relatively thick, plano-convex cross section,
and probably measured about 50 mm in length before it was broken. At
Ventana Cave, points similar to the Rosemont example described above
were characteristic of the Red Sand layer (Haury and others 1950: 203),
indicating that this style occurs relatively early in the preceramic
sequence.

Type 12. This is another large, stemmed projectile point which
differs from the preceding type in two respects (Fig. 5.14b). First,
the sides of the stem converge towards the base, rather than being
parallel to each other, resulting in a base which is more pointed than

that of the preceding type. Second, blade edges on the Type 12 point
are convex and plain, whereas those of the Type 11 example are straight
and serrate. The Type 12 specimen is made of chert and measures 46 mm
in length.

Haury and others (1950: 295) recovered points similar to the
Type 12 Rosemont example from Middle Archaic horizons of the midden at
Ventana Cave, and note their resemblance to points from Gypsum Cave,
Nevada (Harrington 1933).

Type 13. These are leaf-shaped forms which show no
modifications such as notches or stems, to facilitate hafting (Fig.
5.14c, d). They are classified as projectile points, instead of regular
bifaces, because they have been well thinned by extensive pressure
retouch. One example (c) is pointed at one end, convex at the opposite
end, and has plain edges. It is made of rhyolite, and is heavily
patinated. Although one end is broken, item d is more symmetrical
around its short axis, and was probably pointed at both ends. It is
made of obsidian, and has serrate edges. Leaf-shaped forms were widely
distributed throughout the midden at Ventana Cave, but tended to be most
abundant in the upper levels (Haury and others 1950, Table 21).

Drills

Two types of drills were distinguished. The first of these
(Fig. 5.15a-1) are small, elongate forms which may or may not have been
hafted. In general, these drills were shaped by extensive bifacial
pressure flaking, though two examples (a, i) are unifacially retouched
along both blade edges. Because the major manufacturing technique was
pressure flaking, it is not surprising that chert and fine-textured
metasediment are the dominant materials among these implements. Whole
specimens (a-f) exhibit varying degrees of basal flaring, have straight
or convex bases, and range from 26 mm to 31 mm in length. While some
examples (a-d) resemble Type 3 projectile points, the drills differ in
lacking serrations, and in having thicker, diamond-shaped blade cross
sections. Crushing and abrasion on the blades of at least two specimens
(c, f) clearly indicate that these items were used in a rotary fashion
to make holes in relatively hard materials, such as wood, bone, or
possibly potsherds.

Drills of the second type (Fig. 5.15m-q) were almost certainly
hand held, rather than hafted, and consist of flakes showing retouch
which creates a long, narrow, tapering drill blade. While the preceding
drill type is characterized by extensive, bifacial pressure flaking,
retouch on drills of the second type is predominately unifacial, and is
restricted to the blade, leaving a relatively large portion of the flake
unmodified. On most examples, the retouch appears to be the result of
direct percussion, and is located on both sides of a ridge on the
flake's exterior surface. Consequently, the blades tend to be
triangular in cross section. The unmodified portions of these tools are
commonly about four times wider than the blades, and undoubtedly served

Figure 5.15 Drills. a-l, Type 1; m-q, Type 2.

as "handles" during use. At least two specimens (n, o) have blades
showing crushing or abrasion, indicating their use in a rotary manner.
While fine-textured materials such as chert and metasediment are common
among the first drill type, drills of the second type are more
frequently made of coarser materials, including quartztite and
silicified limestone. Drills of the second type range from 30 mm
to 72 mm in length.

Projections

Projections (Fig. 5.16a-n) are flakes exhibiting retouch which
isolates a single, sharp point. Three subtypes are distinguished on the
basis of the formal characteristics of the projection. The first of
these (g-k) is composed of flakes having short, acutely pointed
projections created by essentially unifacial retouch. These implements
would have been useful for fine incising or engraving, and might be
classified as "gravers" or "perforators" by other researchers. The
second type (l-n) is essentially the same as the first, except the
working edge or bit is more robust, and is commonly the result of
bifacial, rather than unifacial retouch. These implements would have
been well suited to tasks involving gouging or heavy-duty boring. The
third type (a-f) consists of elongate triangular flakes whose ends have
been brought to a sharp point by unifacial retouch. This retouch
commonly extends from the tip downward along both edges, for about one-
third of the implement's length. Cross sections through the bits of
most examples are triangular. These projections would have been useful
for piercing soft materials, such as animal skins, though at least one
example (d) exhibits abrasion that indicates rotary use on some durable
material. Projections are made of most of the more common materials,
including quartzite, silicified limestone, metasediment, and chert; the
smaller examples tend to be made of the finer-textured materials.

Large Primary-Flake Tools

This type consists of a group of implements whose distinguishing
feature is that they are made on very large flakes (Fig. 5.17), usually
measuring over 100 mm in maximum dimension. They are most commonly made
of quartzite, are largely cortical, and show only limited retouch.
Huckell (1981b: 178-180) has described similar tools from Las Colinas,
noting that they have often been referred to as mescal knives, hoes, and
saws. Among the Rosemont specimens, two subtypes are recognized on the
basis of differences in working edge form, and in some cases,
differences in use-wear. The first of these (b-e, g, h) consists of
large flake tools having working edge angles of about 30 degrees or
less. These would have been very effective slicing implements, and at
least two examples (g, h) show striae paralleling the working edge on
both faces, confirming their use as knives. Large flake tools of the
second type (a, f, i) have edge angles in excess of 30 degrees, and
frequently show edge damage in the form of crushing and light battering.
These tools appear to have been used in a chopping manner.

Figure 5.16 Projections. a-f, Type 3; g-k, Type 1; l-m, Type 3.

Figure 5.17 Large primary flake tools. a, f, i, Type 2; b–e, g, h, Type 1.

Hammerstones

Two varieties of hammerstones are present in the Rosemont collections. By far the most common of these are cores showing battering over at least 10 percent of their surfaces. These core hammerstones (Fig. 5.18), as they are referred to here, are usually subspherical or polyhedral, though oblong and discoidal forms are occasionally encountered. Ninety-three core hammerstones were among the artifacts selected for attribute analysis. These range from 58 mm to 132 mm in maximum dimension, with a mean maximum dimension of 95 mm. Although quartzite is the most common material (78%), metasediment, silicified limestone, and limestone were also used. It seems reasonable to interpret these implements as cores that were unwanted or unsuited for further flake production, which were subsequently reused as hammers; however, the possibility that some may have been intentionally shaped by flaking to enhance their suitability as hammers cannot be discounted. With regard to function, core hammerstones probably represent very generalized implements that were used for a wide range of tasks involving hammering, pounding, pecking, and pulverizing. While these tasks undoubtedly included core reduction and ground stone shaping and refurbishing, we may also speculate that core hammerstones were used to make bark more pliable by pounding, for cracking walnuts, splintering animal bone, driving wedges, and so forth. Some core hammerstones exhibit well-developed use-polishes, in addition to battering. Such wear might have resulted from rubbing animal hides to make them more pliable.

The second type of hammerstone consists of unmodified, stream-rolled cobbles that show battering. Cobble hammerstones range from about 50 mm to 110 mm in maximum dimension, and are usually irregularly spherical or oblong in shape. Oblong examples commonly show battering only on one or both ends. Like core hammerstones, cobble hammerstones are most frequently made of quartzite, and it seems likely that they were used for very similar, if not the same purposes.

Battered Flakes

These are large, relatively thick flakes whose edges have been rounded by extensive battering (Fig. 5.19m-o). Most examples show no intentional retouch, and have battering which occupies more than one-quarter of the flake's peripheral edge. Battered flakes range from 65 mm to 112 mm in maximum dimension, and are most commonly made of quartzite and other medium- to coarse-textured materials. Huckell (1981b: 192) has described similar implements from Las Colinas, classifying them as "retouchers." He suggests that they served as light percussion hammers for retouching tools or reducing small cores.

Wedges

These are flakes or pieces of flakes with damage indicating that they were the object of repeated, powerful blows with a hard hammer

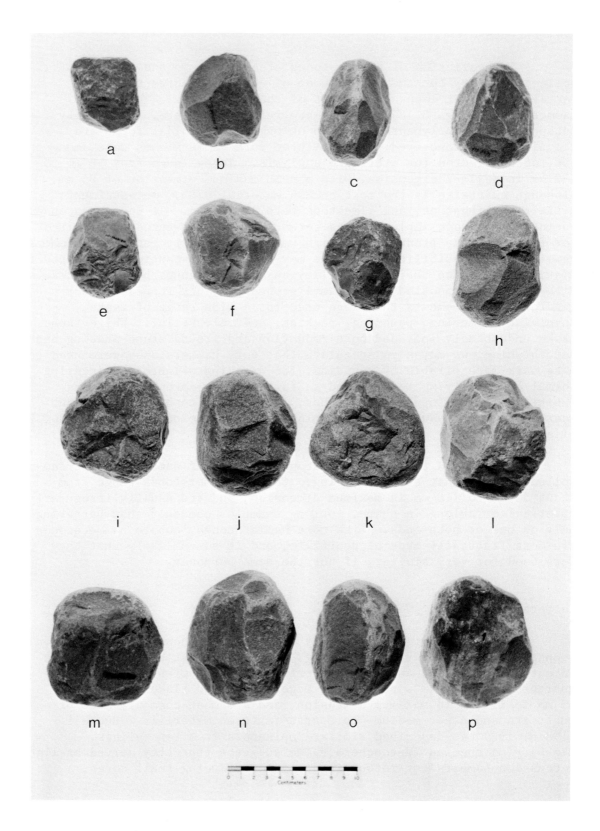

Figure 5.18   Core hammerstones.

Figure 5.19 Wedges (a-l) and battered flakes (m-o).

(Fig. 5.19a-1). In addition to extensive edge crushing, these artifacts commonly show very flat, negative percussion features which originate at the crushed edge, and extend down one or both faces of the flake. These features resulted from pieces of the flake shearing away during blows to the edge, and do not appear to represent purposeful retouch. Instead, these artifacts are more reasonably interpreted as flakes that were hammered into wood or bone to cause splitting. Wedges range from 21 mm to 71 mm in maximum dimension, and tend to be irregular in both outline and cross section. Flakes of all major materials were used as wedges, though fine- to medium-textured material predominate.

Edge-Altered Flakes

Flakes exhibiting microflaking, abrasion, or both of these kinds of use-wear, that lacked intentional retouch, were classified as edge-altered flakes. These are made of all major material types, and are extremely diverse with respect to size, and shape, and angle of the used edges. While it is assumed that unmodified flakes were used for a wide variety of tasks involving slicing, whittling, boring, and scraping, it is important to note that the criteria used to determine the presence of microflaking were deliberately designed to distinguish microflaking that could only have resulted from use, rather than a variety of postdepositional factors. Therefore, those flakes identifed as edge-altered on the basis of microflaking are undoubtedly biased in favor of activities such as scraping, which tend to produce continuous, extensive microflaking. In contrast, activities such as cutting durable materials, which tend to produce discontinuous, nonextensive microflaking, are probably underrepresented among the identified edge-altered flakes.

Though no systematic attempt was made to distinguish or record different kinds of use-polishes, four types were noted during attribute recording. The first consists of a slight rounding of a low-angled edge (less than 30 degrees), with striae running parallel to the edge. These flakes were obviously used as slicing implements. The second type of use-polish consists of a more pronounced rounding of the edge, and is associated with striae running perpendicular to the used edge. In some cases, this wear resulted in substantial edge attrition, and appears to be the result of scraping durable materials, or even intentional edge grinding. The third type of use-polish occurs on the tips and sides of pointed flakes and indicates use in a rotary manner. Finally, a few flakes of very coarse-textured materials show well-developed use-polishes on their bulbs of percussion, indicating that they were used as abraders or rasps, possibly in shaping wood.

Raw Material Variability and Assemblage Characteristics: Project-Wide Relationships

As noted in the discussion of theoretical considerations, differences in raw material characteristics may contribute to assemblage

variation by directly affecting artifact form, or by indirectly
influencing the kind of reduction which was applied. The purpose of
this section is to describe fundamental relationships between raw
material characteristics and assemblage variation, and to determine the
extent to which variation among assemblages of different materials
reflect either: (1) the uniform reduction of various materials having
different physical properties, or (2) differences in the object,
technique, and intensity of reduction as influenced by differences in
the flaking properties of various materials. More simply, the major
question addressed here is the extent to which the Rosemont Hohokam used
different kinds of material for different technological applications.

     To investigate this problem, the relationship between
petrologically defined material types and material texture will first be
defined. Because it is assumed that texture may have been more
important than material type as a factor governing the selection of
materials for particular uses, the remainder of this portion of the
analysis will focus primarily on bivariate relationships between texture
and a number of assemblage characteristics whose relevance to
distinguishing differences in reduction object, technique, and intensity
was established above. These characteristics include proportions of
debitage, cores, and retouched pieces, debitage size and cortex
distributions, platform type and lipping, and core size, direction of
flaking and cortex. In addition, scraper size and retouch extent will
each be examined in relation to raw material type. Once these
relationships have been defined, significant variation between
assemblages of different materials will be summarized and interpreted.

Raw Material Type by Texture Class

     To describe the relationships between petrologically defined
material types and material texture, all artifacts selected for
attribute analysis (Table 5.2) were treated as a single collection.
Frequencies and percentages of material types are given by texture
classes in Table 5.5. Comparison of the artifact totals given in Tables
5.2 and 5.5 indicates that 90 of the 10,978 selected for attribute
analysis are not accounted for in Table 5.5. This discrepancy reflects
the fact that texture was not recorded on some artifacts which were
heavily weathered. The data presented in Table 5.5 were used to
construct Figure 5.20, which shows relative frequency distributions of
major material types by texture class. As discussed above, material
texture becomes increasingly coarse as texture class number increases.
Although these distributions indicate that there is considerable
overlapping among materials with respect to texture, three broad
material classes may be distinguished on the basis of modal texture
class. Chert, jasper, and chalcedony, with a modal texture class of
three, form the first, and finest group of materials. The second group
consists of metasediments, silicified limestone, and limestone. These
materials all share a modal texture class of four, and therefore tend to
be somewhat coarser than materials of the preceding group. Quartzite
and basalt, with a modal texture class of five and six, respectively,

Table 5.5

FREQUENCIES AND PERCENTAGES OF MATERIAL TYPES BY TEXTURE CLASS

Texture Class		Quartzite	Metasediment	Silicified Limestone	Chert	Limestone	Rhyolite	Chalcedony	Basalt	Jasper	Obsidian	Quartz	Other	Total
fine 1	f	0	0	0	0	0	0	0	0	0	2	0	0	2
	%										100.0			
2	f	0	20	0	259	0	0	26	0	12	0	0	0	317
	%		0.7		24.1			27.1		27.3				
3	f	38	843	71	500	1	0	59	0	25	0	0	4	1,541
	%	0.8	28.3	5.1	46.5	0.3		61.5		56.8			9.1	
4	f	949	1,900	1,212	284	276	44	11	9	4	0	0	22	4,711
	%	19.8	63.7	87.3	26.4	95.2	44.9	11.5	12.9	9.1			50.0	
5	f	1,852	204	96	30	12	33	0	17	1	0	2	10	2,257
	%	38.6	6.8	6.9	2.8	4.1	33.7		24.3	2.3		66.7	22.7	
6	f	1,462	15	7	2	1	9	0	20	1	0	1	4	1,522
	%	30.5	0.5	0.5	0.2	0.3	9.2		28.6	2.3		33.3	9.1	
7	f	414	0	1	0	0	6	0	16	1	0	0	3	441
	%	8.6		0.1			6.1		22.9	2.3			6.8	
coarse 8	f	80	0	2	0	0	6	0	8	0	0	0	1	97
	%	1.7		0.1			6.1		11.4				2.3	

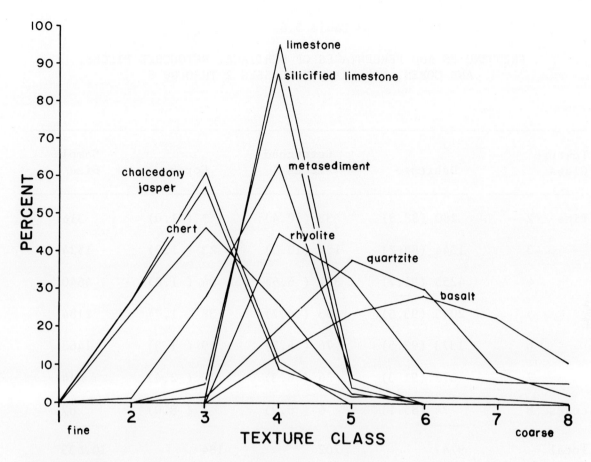

Figure 5.20. Frequency distributions for major material types by texture class.

form the third, and coarsest group of materials. The placement of rhyolite in either the intermediate or coarsest group is problematic. While this material has a modal texture class of three, it clearly tends to be coarser than the other materials of the intermediate group. The absence of rhyolite in Texture Classes 1, 2, and 3 probably reflects a tendency to classify fine rhyolites as jasper during attribute recording.

Bivariate Relationships between Material Texture
and Assemblage Characteristics

Proportions of Debitage, Retouched Pieces, and Cores, by Texture Class

Frequencies and percentages of debitage, retouched pieces, and cores are given for Texture Classes 2 through 8 in Table 5.6. These data include all artifacts selected for attribute analysis except hammerstones and thermal fragments. The debitage category includes complete flakes, all types of flake fragments, and nonorientable fragments. The finest texture class (Class 1) is omitted from this, and

Table 5.6

FREQUENCIES AND PERCENTAGES OF DEBITAGE, RETOUCHED PIECES,
AND CORES, FOR TEXTURE CLASSES 2 THROUGH 8

Texture Class		Debitage	Retouched Pieces	Cores	Sample Size
fine	2	280 (88.8)	33 (10.4)	3 (1.0)	316
	3	1344 (88.2)	157 (10.3)	23 (1.5)	1524
	4	4255 (91.7)	301 (6.5)	84 (1.8)	4640
	5	2043 (93.5)	103 (4.7)	38 (1.7)	2184
	6	1373 (93.5)	76 (5.2)	19 (1.3)	1468
	7	378 (91.3)	26 (6.3)	10 (2.4)	414
coarse	8	74 (85.1)	6 (6.9)	7 (8.0)	87
Total		9747	702	184	10,633

all subsequent manipulations involving texture, because of its extremely
small sample size.

The percentages given in Table 5.6 were used to construct Figure
5.21, which shows the relative frequencies of debitage, retouched
pieces, and cores plotted as a function of material texture. Inspection
of this figure indicates that there is little variation in proportions
of debitage, retouched pieces, and cores, by texture class. Debitage
makes up the great bulk of the collection, varying from about 85 to 94
percent by texture class. Retouched pieces and cores vary from about
5 to 10 percent, and from one to eight percent, respectively. Despite
the fact none of the three artifact categories varies by more than
10 percent across all texture classes, several minor trends are
apparent. For example, cores generally increase in frequency as texture
becomes more coarse. In contrast, there is some indication that
retouched pieces decrease in frequency with increasingly coarse texture.
Debitage percentages are greatest in the middle of the texture
continuum, gradually descreasing towards the ends of the distribution.

To further investigate the strength of these relationships,
Spearman's ranked correlation coefficient was calculated for comparisons

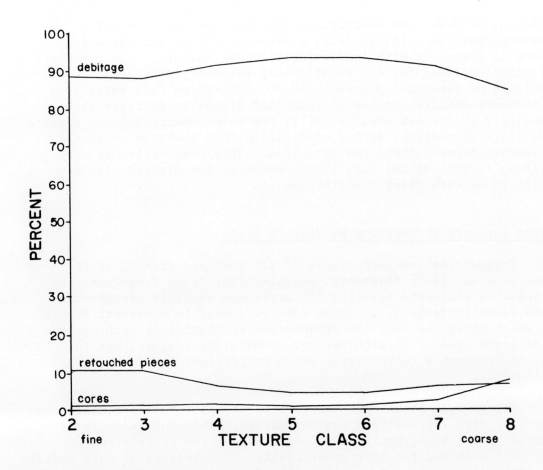

Figure 5.21. Relative frequency distributions of debitage, retouched pieces, and cores by texture class.

between texture class and each of the three artifact categories, using the formula:

$$r_s = 1 - \frac{6 \quad (R_1 - R_2)^2}{n(n^2 - 1)}$$

where r_s is the correlation coefficient, n is the sample size, in this case 7, and R_1 and R_2 are the ranks of each of the two variables being compared, in this case, material texture and artifact category percentages. Using this formula, a perfect positive correlation would yield a coefficient of 1.0, a perfect negative relationship would produce a value of -1.0, and no correlation would be indicated by a coefficient of 0.0. The coefficient obtained for cores is 0.75, suggesting that there is, in fact, a strong tendency for cores to increase in frequency with increasingly coarse texture. The correlation coefficient obtained for the relationship between texture and percentages of retouched pieces is −0.50, suggesting that there is a weak tendency for frequencies of retouched pieces to decrease with increasingly coarse texture. Finally, the relationship between texture and debitage percentages is 0.0, indicating that there is no linear relationship between these two variables. This observation is not surprising in view of the curvilinear shape of the distribution of debitage by texture class described above.

Debitage Category Proportions by Texture Class

Frequencies and percentages of all complete flakes, split flakes, proximal flake fragments, medial-distal flake fragments, and nonorientable fragments selected for attribute analysis are given by texture class in Table 5.7. These data were used to construct Figure 5.22, which shows the relative frequency distribution of each of the five debitage categories with respect to material texture, and to calculate Spearman's ranked correlation coefficient for each of the distributions.

Figure 5.22 shows that percentages of split flakes clearly tend to increase with increasingly coarse texture. This inference is supported by the high, positive value (0.87) of the correlation coefficient obtained for this relationship. Percentages of both medial-distal flake fragments and nonorientable fragments tend to decrease as texture becomes coarser, as indicated by correlation coefficients of −0.63 and −0.79, respectively. Figure 5.22 also suggests that, in general, percentages of complete flakes show some tendency to increase with increasingly coarse texture, but a low coefficient of 0.25 indicates that the correlation is very weak. Finally, the coefficient having the lowest absolute value (−0.12) was that obtained for the distribution of percentages of proximal flake fragments with respect to texture. This value indicates that no linear correlation between these two variables can be inferred.

Complete Flake Size by Texture Class

Complete flake size was recorded in terms of length, width and thickness. Means and standard deviations for these three variables are given in millimeters for each texture class in Table 5.8. These data are based on all complete flakes included in the collection selected for attribute analysis, and were used to construct Figure 5.23, showing mean length and width plotted for each texture class, and Figure 5.24, which shows complete flake thickness histograms for each texture class. Both figures clearly illustrate a strong correlation between texture and complete flake size; that is, size increases with increasingly coarse texture. Standard deviations for all three variables also tend to

Table 5.7

FREQUENCIES (f) AND PERCENTAGES (%) OF COMPLETE FLAKES,
SPLIT FLAKES, PROXIMAL FLAKE FRAGMENTS, MEDIAL-DISTAL FLAKE
FRAGMENTS, AND NONORIENTABLE FLAKE FRAGMENTS, BY TEXTURE CLASS

Texture Class			Complete Flakes	Split Flakes	Proximal Flake Fragments	Medial-Distal Flake Fragments	Nonorientable Flake Fragments	Total
fine	2	f	99	9	51	81	40	280
		%	35.4	3.2	18.2	28.9	14.3	
	3	f	670	89	194	315	76	1344
		%	49.9	6.6	14.4	23.4	5.7	
	4	f	2027	374	623	994	237	4255
		%	47.6	8.8	14.6	23.4	5.6	
	5	f	995	281	317	368	82	2043
		%	48.7	13.8	15.5	18.0	4.0	
	6	f	675	204	213	241	40	1373
		%	49.2	14.9	15.5	17.6	2.9	
	7	f	206	47	45	72	8	378
		%	54.5	12.4	11.9	19.0	2.1	
coarse	8	f	34	11	13	14	2	74
		%	45.9	14.9	17.6	18.9	2.7	
Total			4706	1015	1456	2085	485	9747

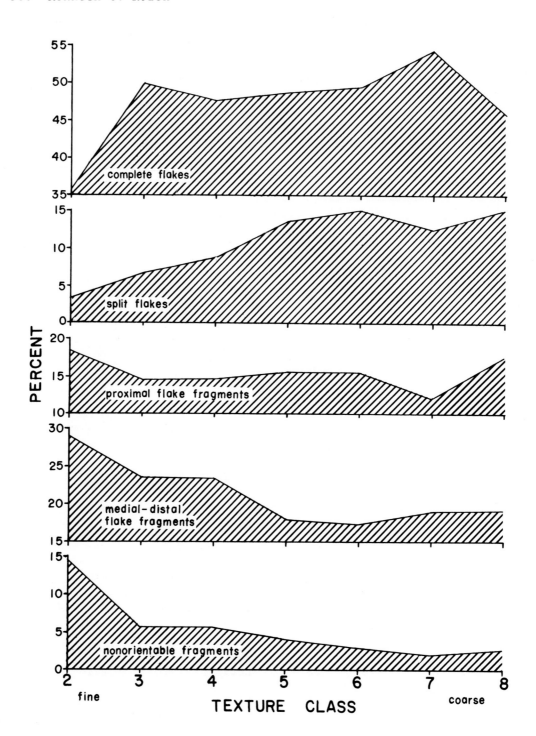

Figure 5.22 Relative frequency distributions of complete and split flakes, proximal and medial-distal fragments, and nonorientable fragments, by texture class

increase as texture becomes more coarse, suggesting that, in comparison to flakes of finer materials, those of coarser materials tend to be not only larger, but more variable with respect to size.

Table 5.8

MEAN, STANDARD DEVIATION, AND SAMPLE SIZE FOR COMPLETE FLAKE
LENGTH, WIDTH, AND THICKNESS BY TEXTURE CLASS

Texture Class		Length (mm)		Width (mm)		Thickness (mm)		Sample Size
		$\bar{x}$	sd	$\bar{x}$	sd	$\bar{x}$	sd	
fine	2	17.7	8.7	14.5	6.6	3.1	2.0	99
	3	25.0	11.3	18.7	8.3	4.5	2.9	670
	4	28.8	12.5	22.6	9.6	5.8	3.4	2025
	5	31.1	13.7	24.8	10.7	6.2	3.4	995
	6	36.1	15.9	30.0	13.0	7.2	4.1	674
	7	42.9	17.8	33.9	15.2	8.9	4.7	206
coarse	8	50.9	15.8	43.9	16.7	11.5	4.9	34

Complete Flake Cortex by Texture Class

Frequencies, percentages, and sample sizes of complete flakes,
by Cortex Classes 1 (no cortex), 2 (some, but less than 50% cortex),
and 3 (at least 50% cortex), are given for each texture class in
Table 5.9. These data are based on all complete flakes included in the
collection selected for attribute analysis, except those flakes which
were so heavily weathered that cortical and noncortical surfaces could
not be distinguished.

Figure 5.25, the relative frequency distribution of complete
flakes for each of the three cortex classes with respect to texture,
indicates that, for all texture classes, noncortical flakes are the most
abundant, ranging from about 44 to 82 percent. Flakes with some, but
less than 50 percent cortex, are the second most frequent type, varying
from about 14 to 33 percent, while flakes with 50 percent or more cortex
are the least abundant, ranging from about 4 to 22 percent.

Figure 5.25 also shows that, from fine to coarse along the
texture continuum, percentages of noncortical flakes decrease sharply
between the first three, and finest texture classes (Classes 2 through
4), are relatively constant in the middle of the distribution (Texture
Classes 4 and 5), and then decrease in progressively greater increments
toward the coarse end of the texture continuum, between Texture

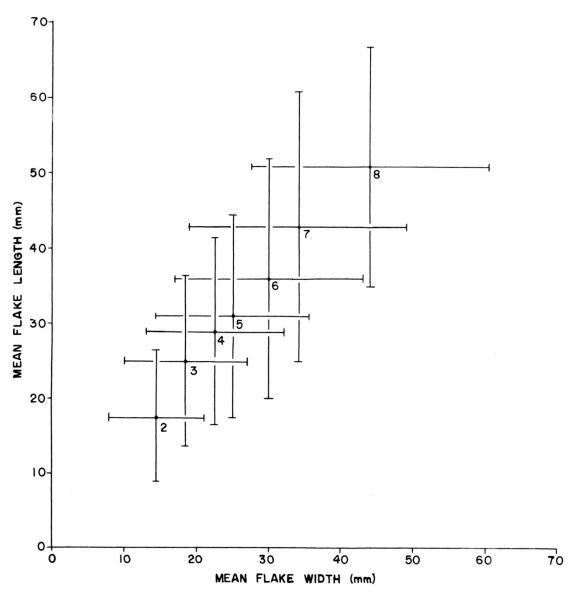

Figure 5.23.   Mean length and width of complete flakes by texture class.

Classes 5 and 8.   Spearman's ranked correlation coefficient for this relationship is -0.89, suggesting that there is a strong negative correlation between percentages of noncortical flakes and increasingly coarse texture.

The percentage of flakes having some, but less than 50 percent cortex (Class 2) increase sharply between Texture Classes 2, 3, and 4, as texture becomes coarser.   This increase almost entirely accounts for the corresponding sharp decrease in percentages of noncortical flakes for this texture range, as noted above.   Between Texture Classes 4 and 8, percentages of flakes with some, but less than 50 percent cortex, remain essentially the same, despite increasingly coarse texture.   The correlation coefficient obtained for this relationship is 0.45, suggesting that, in general, there is only a very slight tendency for

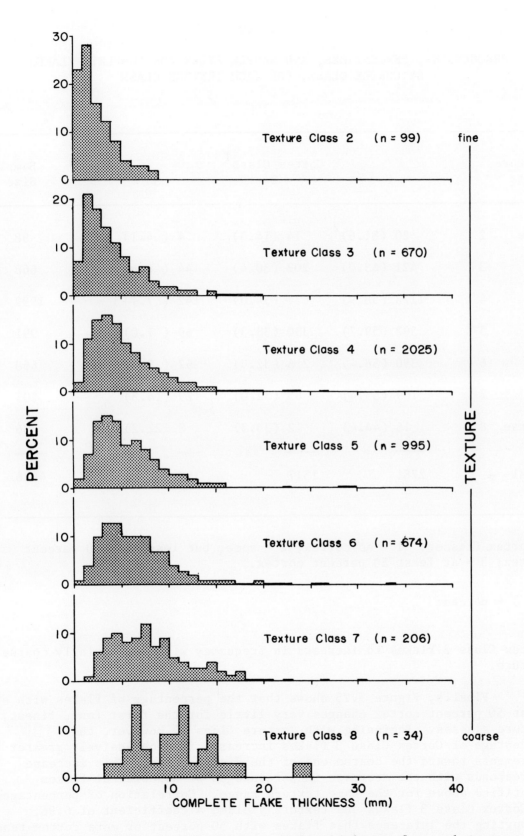

Figure 5.24. Histograms of complete flake thickness for each texture class.

Table 5.9

FREQUENCIES, PERCENTAGES, AND SAMPLE SIZES FOR COMPLETE FLAKES
BY CORTEX CLASS, FOR EACH TEXTURE CLASS

Texture Class		Cortex Class[1]			Sample Size
		1	2	3	
fine	2	80 (81.6)[2]	14 (14.3)	4 (4.1)	98
	3	421 (63.0)	203 (30.4)	44 (6.6)	668
	4	1173 (58.9)	677 (34.0)	142 (7.1)	1992
	5	592 (59.7)	330 (33.3)	69 (7.0)	991
	6	390 (58.4)	216 (32.3)	62 (9.3)	668
	7	109 (53.4)	65 (32.0)	29 (14.3)	203
coarse	8	16 (44.4)	12 (33.3)	8 (22.2)	36
Total		2781	1517	358	4656

[1] Cortex Classes: 1 = no cortex; 2 = some, but less than 50 percent cortex; 3 = at least 50 percent cortex.

[2] ( ) = percent

Cortex Class 2 flakes to increase in frequency with increasingly coarse texture.

Finally, Figure 5.25 shows that the percentage of flakes with at least 50 percent cortex changes very little for the first four, finest, texture classes. Beginning with Texture Class 5, however, the percentage of Cortex Class 3 flakes increases in progressively greater increments toward the coarse end of the distribution. This increase corresponds with the decrease in percentages of noncortical flakes identified above for the same texture range. Correlation of percentages of Cortex Class 3 flakes and texture yielded a coefficient of 0.96, supporting the inference that flakes with 50 percent or more cortex tend to become more abundant with increasingly coarse texture. Overall, the above defined shifts in proportions of flakes of the three cortex

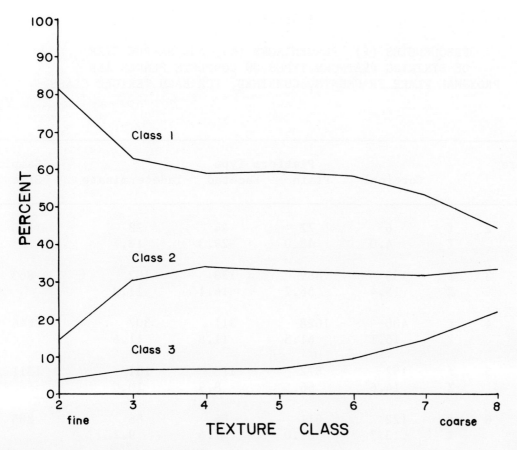

Figure 5.25. Relative frequency distributions of complete flake cortex classes by texture class.

classes with respect to texture suggest that flakes tend to become less cortical as texture becomes finer.

Proportions of Striking Platform Types by Texture Class

Frequencies and percentages of cortical, noncortical plain, faceted, and indeterminate striking platforms are given for each texture class in Table 5.10. The sample size for each texture class is based on the combined observations of platform type on all complete flakes and proximal flake fragments in the analyzed collection.

Figure 5.26, the relative frequency distribution of each of the platform types by texture, shows that for all texture classes, noncortical plain platforms are prevalent, varying from about 48 to 69 percent. From fine to coarse along the texture continuum, percentages of plain platforms clearly increase between Texture Classes 2 through 6, and then noticeably decrease between Classes 6 and 8, the coarsest texture classes. Spearman's ranked correlation coefficient for this relationship is 0.54, suggesting that while percentages of plain platforms tend to increase with increasingly coarse texture, these two

Table 5.10

FREQUENCIES (f), PERCENTAGES (%), AND SAMPLE SIZE
OF STRIKING PLATFORM TYPES ON COMPLETE FLAKES AND
PROXIMAL FLAKE FRAGMENTS, COMBINED, FOR EACH TEXTURE CLASS

Texture Class			Platform Type				Sample Size
			Cortical	Plain	Faceted	Indeterminate	
fine	2	f	6	72	44	28	150
		%	4.0	48.0	29.3	18.7	
	3	f	133	489	139	102	863
		%	15.4	56.7	16.1	11.8	
	4	f	400	1628	311	307	2646
		%	15.1	61.5	11.8	11.6	
	5	f	192	872	116	131	1311
		%	14.6	66.5	8.9	10.0	
	6	f	122	611	66	86	885
		%	13.7	69.0	7.4	9.7	
	7	f	48	161	17	25	251
		%	19.1	64.1	6.8	10.0	
coarse	8	f	13	27	4	3	47
		%	27.7	57.4	8.5	6.4	
Total			914	3860	697	682	6153

variables are not strongly associated. Like the distribution of
percentages of debitage by texture defined earlier, the distribution of
percentages of plain platforms by texture appears to be curvilinear,
rather than linear. Thus, a correlation coefficient intermediate
between 0.00 and 1.00 is not surprising.

Figure 5.26 also shows that percentages of cortical platforms
vary from about 4 to 28 percent across all texture classes. From fine
to coarse textures, percentages of cortical platforms increase sharply
between the first two, finest texture classes, and then remain
essentially the same throughout the middle of the texture distribution,
between Classes 3 through 6. The sharp rise in cortical platform
percentages towards the coarse end of the distribution, between Texture

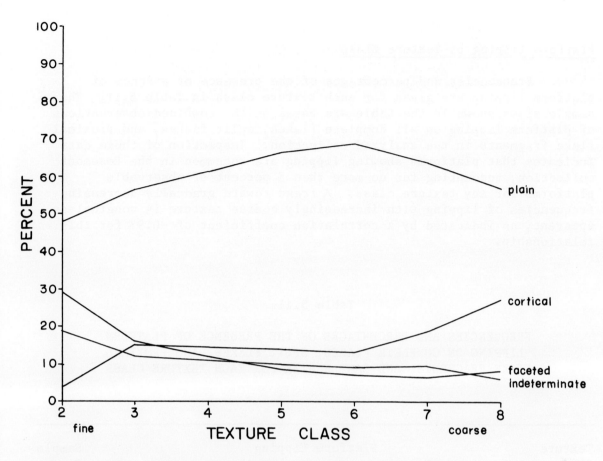

Figure 5.26. Relative frequency distributions of cortical, plain, faceted, and indeterminate platforms by texture class.

Classes 6, 7, 8, accounts almost entirely for the corresponding decrease in plain platform percentages noted above for this texture range. The coefficient obtained for the correlation between cortical platform percentages and texture class is 0.64, suggesting that there is a moderately strong, positive association between these two variables.

Finally, Figure 5.26 shows that percentages of both faceted and indeterminate platforms tend to decrease from about 20 to 30 percent of the finest texture class, to about 6 to 9 percent at the coarse end of the distribution. The coefficients obtained for the correlations between texture and percentages of faceted and indeterminate platforms are -0.73 and -0.92, respectively. The large absolute values of these coefficients support the inference that there is a strong, inverse relationship between increasingly coarse texture, and the relative frequencies of these platform types.

To summarize, cortical platforms generally become more abundant and faceted and indeterminate platforms become relatively less frequent, as texture becomes more coarse. Plain platform percentages first increase from the fine to intermediate texture range, and then decrease from the middle to coarse end of the texture continuum.

Platform Lipping by Texture Class

Frequencies and percentages of the presence or absence of platform lipping are given for each texture class in Table 5.11. The sample sizes shown in the table are based on the combined observations of platform lipping on all complete flakes, split flakes, and proximal flake fragments in the analyzed collection. Inspection of these data indicates that platforms showing lipping are uncommon in the Rosemont collection, accounting for no more than 5 percent of observable platforms for any texture class. A trend toward gradually decreasing frequencies of lipping with increasingly coarse texture is nonetheless apparent, as indicated by a correlation coefficient of -0.93 for this relationship.

Table 5.11

FREQUENCIES AND PERCENTAGES OF THE PRESENCE OF PLATFORM
LIPPING ON COMPLETE FLAKES, SPLIT FLAKES, AND PROXIMAL
FLAKE FRAGMENTS, AND SAMPLE SIZE FOR EACH TEXTURE CLASS

Texture Class		Platform Lipping		Sample Size
		Present	Absent	
fine	2	8 (5.0)	151 (95.0)	159
	3	49 (5.1)	904 (94.9)	953
	4	127 (4.2)	2897 (95.8)	3024
	5	69 (4.3)	1524 (95.7)	1593
	6	40 (3.7)	1052 (96.3)	1092
	7	8 (2.9)	290 (97.1)	298
coarse	8	0	58 (100.0)	58
Total		301	6876	7177

( ) = percent

Fragment Size by Texture Class

Fragment size was described in terms of maximum dimension. Mean and standard deviation for this measurement are given in millimeters for each texture class, with the sample size for each class, in Table 5.12. These data are based on observed maximum dimension of all split flakes, proximal and medial-distal flake fragments, and nonorientable fragments included in the attribute analysis.

These data indicate that fragments, like complete flakes, tend to become larger with increasingly coarse texture. Spearman's ranked correlation coefficient for this relationship is a perfect 1.0. Also like complete flakes, fragments not only become larger as texture becomes more coarse, but they also tend to become more variable with respect to size, as indicated by the standard deviations of fragment maximum dimension shown in the table.

Table 5.12

MEAN, STANDARD DEVIATION, AND SAMPLE SIZE FOR MAXIMUM
DIMENSION OF FRAGMENTS, BY TEXTURE CLASS

Texture Class		Maximum Dimension (mm) $\bar{x}$	sd	Sample Size
fine	2	21.7	8.8	181
	3	24.7	10.0	673
	4	28.5	12.0	2219
	5	30.1	12.3	1041
	6	34.2	13.9	698
	7	38.2	16.4	172
coarse	8	46.6	23.9	40

Cortex on Fragments by Texture Class

Frequencies and percentages of the presence or absence of cortex on fragments are given for each texture class, with the sample size of fragments for each class, in Table 5.13. These data were used to

Table 5.13

FREQUENCIES, PERCENTAGES, AND SAMPLE SIZES FOR THE PRESENCE
AND ABSENCE OF CORTEX ON FRAGMENTS, BY TEXTURE CLASS

Texture Class		Cortex Present		Absent		Sample Size
fine	2	27	(14.9)	154	(85.1)	181
	3	214	(31.8)	459	(68.2)	673
	4	651	(29.8)	1536	(70.2)	2187
	5	328	(31.5)	710	(68.4)	1038
	6	201	(28.7)	499	(71.3)	700
	7	48	(27.7)	125	(72.3)	173
coarse	8	15	(39.5)	23	(60.5)	38
Total		1484		3506		4990

( ) = percent

construct Figure 5.27, which shows the relative frequency distribution
of fragments having some cortex, by texture class. This figure
indicates that as texture becomes coarser, percentages of cortical
fragments increase sharply between the first two, finest texture
classes. These percentages remain essentially the same or decline
slightly, through the middle of the distribution (Classes 3 and 7), and
then rise sharply between the last two, coarsest texture classes. The
coefficient obtained for the correlation of texture and percentage of
cortical fragments is 0.32. Although a value greater than zero suggests
that, overall, cortex tends to become more common on fragments as
texture becomes more coarse, the low absolute value of this coefficient
indicates that the correlation between these two variable is weak.

Core Size by Texture Class

Maximum dimension was recorded on all cores in the analyzed
collection. Means and standard deviations for core maximum dimension

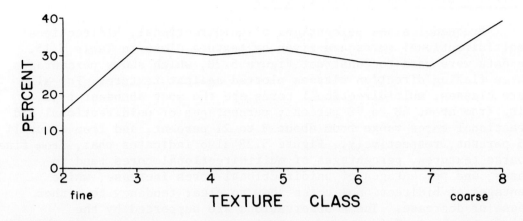

Figure 5.27. Relative frequency distribution of cortical fragments by texture class.

are given for Texture Classes 3 through 6, with counts by class, in Table 5.14. Data for Classes 2, 7, and 8 are omitted from this and all subsequent manipulations involving cores, because sample sizes for these classes are ten or less.

These data clearly indicate that, from fine to coarse textures, cores tend to increase in size. Spearman's ranked correlation coefficient for this relationship is a perfect 1.0, indicating a linear relationship between increasing core size and increasingly coarse material texture.

Table 5.14

MEAN AND STANDARD DEVIATION FOR MAXIMUM DIMENSION
FOR CORES BY TEXTURE CLASS

Texture Class		Maximum Dimension (mm) Mean	sd	Sample Size
fine	3	54.3	11.8	23
	4	67.4	17.4	82
	5	74.9	20.9	38
coarse	6	83.8	24.7	19

Core Flaking Direction by Texture Class

Frequencies and percentages of unidirectional, bidirectional, and multidirectional cores are given by texture class in Table 5.15. These data were used to construct Figure 5.28, which shows percentages of three flaking direction classes plotted against texture. For all texture classes, multidirectional cores are the most abundant type, varying from about 68 to 78 percent; percentages of unidirectional and bidirectional cores range from about 9 to 21 percent, and from about 11 to 15 percent, respectively. Figure 5.28 also indicates that, from fine to coarse textures, percentages of multidirectional cores tend to decrease, and percentages of unidirectional cores increase, while percentages of bidirectional cores show no clear tendency to either increase or decrease. These observations are supported by the coefficients obtained for the correlations between texture, and the three directional classes. These coefficients are -1.0, 1.0, and -0.4, respectively.

Cortex on Cores by Texture Class

Frequencies and percentages of cores by Cortex Classes 1 (0% cortex), 2 (some, but less than 50%), and 3 (at least 50% cortex) are given for Texture Classes 3 through 6 in Table 5.15. These data were used to construct Figure 5.29, which shows percentages of three cortex classes for cores plotted as a function of texture. This figure shows that, for all texture classes under consideration, cores having some, but less then 50 percent of their surface covered by cortex are the most common, noncortical cores are second most frequent, and that cores having at least 50 percent of their surface showing cortex are the least common. Figure 5.29 also provides some suggestion that percentages of noncortical cores tend to increase slightly with increasingly coarse texture. Though this increase is small, a correlation coefficient of 1.0 suggest that the relationship between these two variables is strong. When viewed individually, percentages of cores having up to 50 percent cortex, and percentages of cores showing 50 percent or more cortex show no clear trends with respect to texture (both relationships produce a correlation coefficient of -0.4). The combination of percentages of Cortex Classes 2 and 3—all cores with cortex on part of their surfaces—yields a trend toward slightly decreasing percentages of cores showing any cortex with increasingly coarse texture.

Scraper Size and Retouch Extent by Material Type

Due to logistic problems during attribute recording, texture data for scrapers are not available. Therefore, investigation of the relationships between certain aspects of scraper form and raw material characteristics relied on material type, rather than texture. Although the lack of texture data for scrapers is regrettable, a review of Figure 5.20, which shows the relative frequency distributions of material types with respect to texture, indicates that there are strong correlations between texture class and the four most common materials: quartzite,

Table 5.15

FREQUENCIES AND PERCENTAGES OF FLAKING DIRECTION CLASSES
AND CORTEX CLASSES FOR CORES, BY TEXTURE CLASS

Texture Class	Flaking Direction Class			Cortex Class			Total
	1	2	3	1	2	3	
fine 3	2 (8.7)*	3 (13.0)	18 (78.3)	3 (13.0)	18 (78.3)	2 (8.7)	23
4	10 (12.3)	12 (14.8)	59 (72.8)	20 (24.7)	57 (70.4)	4 (4.9)	81
5	6 (16.2)	5 (13.5)	26 (70.3)	10 (26.3)	24 (63.2)	4 (10.5)	37
coarse 6	4 (21.1)	2 (10.5)	13 (68.4)	5 (27.8)	13 (72.2)	0	19
Total	22	22	116	38	112	10	160

Flaking direction classes:
  1 -- unidirectional
  2 -- bidirectional
  3 -- multidirectional

Cortex classes:
  1 -- no cortex
  2 -- some, but less than 50 percent
  3 -- more than 50 percent

* ( ) = percent

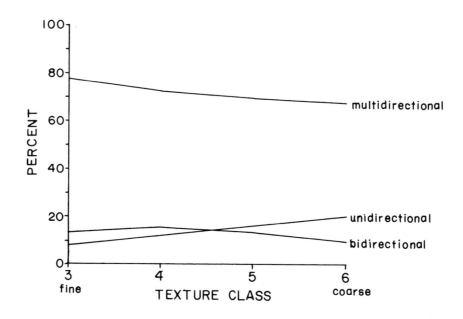

Figure 5.28. Percentages of multidirectional, bidirectional, and
unidirectional cores by Texture Classes 3 through 6.

metasediment, silicified limestone, and chert. For example, quartzite,
with a modal texture class of 5, tends to be the coarsest material,
while chert, with a modal texture class of 3, thus tends to be the
finest of the four major materials. Although both metasediment and
silicified limestone share a modal texture class of 4, intermediate
between quartzite and chert, Figure 5.20 shows that metasediment is more
strongly represented in Texture Classes 2 and 3, and therefore tends
to be somewhat finer, than is silicified limestone. In view of these
relationships between material type and texture, it is assumed here
that the four major material types, chert, metasediment, silicified
limestone, and quartzite, become increasingly coarse in that order.

Scraper size was described in terms of length, width, and
thickness, measured to the nearest whole centimeter. Means, standard
deviations, and sample sizes are given for scraper length, width, and
thickness for the four major material types in Table 5.16. These data
are based on 553 of the 580 whole scrapers contained in the collection.
Twenty-seven scrapers are not accounted for in Table 5.16 because of
random missing observations of length, width, thickness, or material
type, and because scrapers of some infrequent materials, most notably
limestone, are excluded. Jasper and chalcedony have been included under
the chert category. Simple inspection of the means for length, width,
and thickness shows that there is a clear trend toward increasing
scraper size with increasingly coarse materials. Standard deviations
also generally increase with increasingly coarse materials, indicating
that scrapers of coarse materials tend to be not only larger than those
of finer materials, but that they tend to be more variable in size.

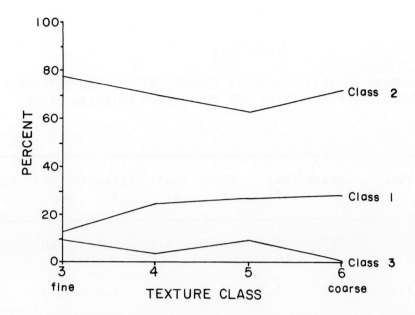

Figure 5.29. Percentages of core cortex classes by Texture Classes 3 through 6.

As described earlier, retouch extent on whole scrapers was recorded as the percentage of the implement's entire peripheral edge which showed intentional retouch. Percentage classes, based on the percent of a scraper's edge showing retouch, were used to make these data more amenable to descriptive display. These are: (1) 1-10 percent, (2) 11-20 percent, (3) 21-30 percent, (4) 31-40 percent, (5) 41-50 percent, (6) 51-60 percent, (7) 61-70 percent, (8) 71-80 percent, (9) 81-90 percent, and (10) 91-100 percent. For each of the four major materials, scraper frequencies and percentages by retouch extent percentage classes, means and standard deviations (calculated from class midpoints), and sample sizes are given in Table 5.17. These data are based on whole scrapers from all screened proveniences, including structure fill, floors, postholes, floor pits, extramural features, and portions of the sheet trash deposit at AZ EE:2:129. Scrapers from unscreened, or only partially screened contexts, including stripping, backhoe backdirt, and Feature 0, are excluded. Materials other than chert, metasediment, silicified limestone, and quartzite are also excluded, except jasper and chalcedony, which are included in the chert category.

The data presented in Table 5.17 were used to construct Figure 5.30, which shows the relative frequency distributions of chert, metasediment, silicified limestone, and quartzite scrapers, with respect to retouch extent percentage classes. Both the means given in Table 5.17 and the distributions shown in Figure 5.30 suggest that there is little, if any, significant variation in retouch extent among scrapers of different materials. Chert scrapers show the highest mean retouch percentage (46.9), but this value is only 1.7 percent greater than that for silicified limestone scrapers, which show the lowest mean retouch extent percentage (45.2). Following Thomas (1976: 235-238), the

Table 5.16

MEAN AND STANDARD DEVIATION SCRAPER LENGTH, WIDTH, AND THICKNESS
AND SAMPLE SIZE, FOR EACH OF THE FOUR MAJOR MATERIAL TYPES

Texture	Material Type	Length (cm) $\bar{x}$	sd	Width (cm) $\bar{x}$	sd	Thickness (cm) $\bar{x}$	sd	Sample Size
fine	Chert	7.7	8.7	4.5	6.6	3.1	2.0	199
	Metasediment	4.8	1.3	3.7	1.2	1.8	0.9	186
	Silicified Limestone	5.6	2.1	4.2	1.4	2.1	1.0	65
coarse	Quartzite	6.7	2.0	5.1	1.8	2.5	1.1	242
Total								553

Student's t-test for the differences of means was applied to the
distributions for chert and silicified limestone scrapers. With
70 degrees of freedom, the t-score obtained for this comparison was
0.331, well below the range of critical values of the Student's
t-distribution at the 0.4 through 0.001 probability levels (Thomas 1976:
497). Therefore, no difference between chert and silicified limestone
scrapers can be inferred with respect to mean retouch extent percentage.

Figure 5.30 also suggests that retouch extent percentage may be
polymodal. In the case of chert and silicified limestone scrapers, the
jagged appearance of the distributions is undoubtedly the result of
small sample sizes, rather than a real tendency towards polymodality;
however, sample sizes of quartzite and metasediment scrapers are both
well over 100. Thus, the increase in relative frequencies of scrapers
at the upper end of both of these distributions may represent a
secondary mode.

Table 5.17

FREQUENCIES(f) AND PERCENTAGES(%) OF SCRAPERS BY RETOUCH EXTENT PERCENTAGE CLASS
MEAN($\bar{x}$) AND STANDARD DEVIATION(sd) RETOUCH EXTENT PERCENTAGE, AND SAMPLE SIZE
FOR EACH OF THE FOUR MAJOR MATERIALS

Material		Retouch Extent Percentage Class										Sample Size	Mean*	sd*
		1	2	3	4	5	6	7	8	9	10			
Chert	f	1	4	5	3	8	5	2	5	0	2	35	46.9	23.2
	%	2.9	11.4	14.3	8.6	22.9	14.3	5.7	14.3		5.7			
Metasediment	f	0	12	21	20	27	13	6	5	9	7	120	46.6	22.7
	%		10.0	17.5	16.7	22.5	10.8	5.0	4.2	7.5	5.8			
Silicified	f	0	3	8	7	5	5	2	6	1	0	37	45.2	20.3
	%		8.1	21.6	18.9	13.5	13.5	5.4	16.2	2.7				
Quartzite	f	2	11	22	33	27	23	13	4	7	7	149	45.9	21.0
	%	1.3	7.3	14.8	22.1	18.1	15.4	8.7	2.7	4.7	4.7			
Total												341		

* calculated from class midpoints

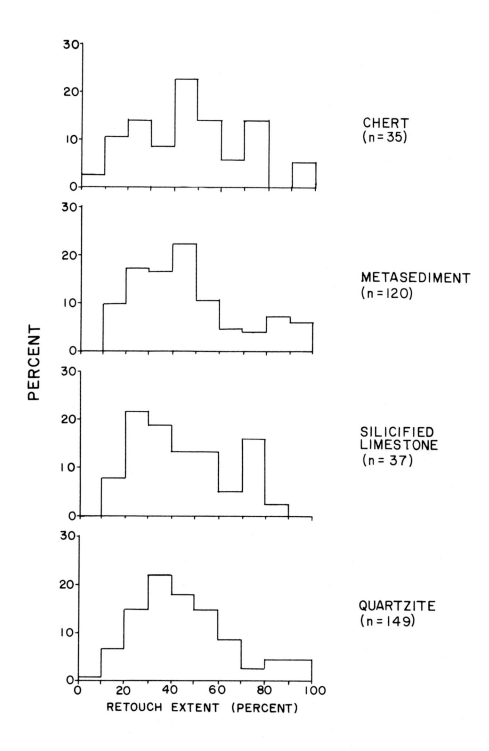

Figure 5.30. Relative frequency distributions of chert, metasediment, silicified limestone, and quartzite scrapers by retouch extent percentage class.

Summary and Interpretation of Project-Wide
Relationships Between Material Texture
and Assemblage Characteristics

The preceding discussion has defined the relationships between material texture and a variety of assemblage characteristics. These relationships are summarized by the following observations.

1. Proportions of debitage, retouched pieces and cores vary little by texture, although there appears to be some tendency for percentages of cores to increase slightly and for percentages of retouched pieces to decline slightly with increasingly coarse texture. Debitage percentages tend to be greatest in the middle of the texture range, and decline slightly towards either extreme.

2. Among the five debitage categories, percentages of both medial-distal flake fragments and nonorientable fragments clearly decrease with increasingly coarse texture, while split flakes become relatively more abundant as texture becomes more coarse. Complete flake percentages also generally increase with increasingly coarse texture, but the correlation is not strong. Percentages of proximal flake fragments do not vary in any clearly patterned way with texture.

3. Artifacts of all categories investigated, including all fragmentary debitage collectively, complete flakes, cores, and scrapers, clearly tend to become larger with increasingly coarse texture. Standard deviations for measures of size applied to these artifact classes also increase as texture becomes more coarse; artifacts of coarser materials therefore tend to be more variable in size than those of finer materials.

4. Both complete flakes and the various kinds of debitage fragments tend to be least cortical at the fine extreme of the texture continuum, and most cortical at the opposite extreme. Percentages of cortical flakes and fragments, as opposed to those showing no cortex, vary little throughout the middle range of the texture continuum. Although cortex data for cores are not available for either texture extreme due to poor sample sizes, occurrence of cortex on cores appears to decrease slightly with increasingly coarse texture, throughout the middle of the texture scale.

5. From fine to coarse textures, cortical striking platforms on complete flakes and proximal flake fragments tend to become relatively more common, while both faceted and indeterminate platforms become relatively less abundant. Percentages of noncortical plain platforms are greatest in the upper-middle of the texture continuum, and clearly decline towards either texture extreme.

6. From fine to coarse across the middle range of the texture scale, unidirectional cores increase in relative abundance, multidirectional cores become less common, and percentages of bidirectional cores remain essentially the same.

7. Although platform lipping is rare throughout the collection in general, relative frequencies of this attribute increase slightly with increasingly fine texture.

8. Retouch extent does not vary significantly among scrapers of different textured materials.

Of all the relationships summarized above, the one between texture and artifact size is unquestionably the clearest and most conspicuous. The strong tendency of artifacts of finer materials to be smaller than those of coarser materials could potentially be the result of two factors. As suggested earlier, it is assumed here that finer materials tend to occur naturally in smaller pieces than do coarser materials. While the validity of this assumption is readily confirmed by field observation, it is beyond the scope of this discussion to provide a detailed examination of the geologic factors responsible for the relationship between texture and raw material size. In general terms, however, we may suspect that this relationship results from an interaction between differences in the manner in which rocks were formed, their structural properties, and the processes by which rock formations are naturally broken down and redeposited. In any case, the strong correlation between texture and artifact size must to some extent, simply reflect the natural relationship between texture and raw material size.

The second factor which may contribute to the strong correlation between texture and artifact size is variation in the thoroughness or intensity with which different materials were reduced. It is possible, for example, that pieces of finer materials may have been more thoroughly reduced because they were both less abundant, and considered more desirable, than coarser materials. Further, the flaking properties of different-textured materials may have been considered in selecting materials for particular technological applications involving substantially different levels of reduction intensity. Large tools whose functions required durable edges, such as large scrapers and "choppers", may have been produced through nonintensive reduction of coarse materials. In contrast, other kinds of tools, such as small slicing implements, bifaces, drills, and projectile points may have been made through more intensive reduction of finer materials.

In all probability, both the natural relationship between raw material size and texture, and variation in the intensity with which different materials were reduced are responsible for the strong correlation between texture and artifact size seen in the Rosemont assemblage as a whole. The question therefore becomes one concerning the relative importance of these factors in contributing to the observed correlation.

Ideally, this question could be answered in very specific terms through an exhaustive refitting study involving measures of material size before reduction and the number of flakes produced by each reduction episode. This approach is grossly impractical for obvious reasons. Therefore, inferences regarding the extent to which raw material size and reduction intensity have each contributed to correlation between artifact size and material texture cannot be made in precise, quantitative terms. Instead, such inferences will be made here in more general terms by critically evaluating previously defined relationships between texture, and assemblage characteristics other than artifact size which may indirectly reflect either the natural correlation between raw material size and texture, or variation in reduction intensity.

Following assumptions presented in the theoretical discussion, a number of the patterned associations among texture and assemblage characteristics demonstrated above may be taken as evidence that finer materials were more intensively reduced than coarser materials. Assuming, for example, that coarser materials tend to occur naturally in larger pieces than finer materials, debitage resulting from the reduction of smaller pieces of finer material should tend to be more cortical than that produced by the reduction of larger pieces of coarser material, if both fine and coarse materials were reduced with approximately the same degree of intensity. This should be true because the ratio of surface area, in this case cortex, to volume increases with decreasing raw material size. In fact, the data indicate that there is some tendency for debitage of finer materials to be less cortical than that made of coarse materials, despite the fact that finer materials probably occur naturally in smaller pieces than coarser materials. This observation supports the inference that finer materials were more intensively reduced than coarser materials.

If fine-textured rocks were more thoroughly reduced than coarser materials, one would also expect that faceted striking platforms should be most common among debitage resulting from the reduction of finer materials, and that cortical platforms should be prevalent in the coarser texture classes. The relationship between texture and proportion of striking platform types demonstrated above conforms to this expectation. Further, indeterminate platforms (that is, platforms whose condition prior to detachment cannot be determined because they shattered as a result of the detaching blow) parallel faceted platforms by becoming increasingly common as texture becomes finer. This observation suggests that platform shattering may become more common as reduction becomes more thorough. Although the mechanical factors responsible for this relationship are not entirely clear, it seems likely that platform angles generally tend to increase as reduction advances, and that platform shattering may occur more often as platform angles increase.

Further evidence that finer materials may have been more intensively reduced than coarser materials can be seen in proportions of core flaking direction classes. As one would expect if reduction intensity varied by material texture, multidirectional cores become relatively more abundant as texture become increasingly fine, while unidirectional cores increase in relative frequency as texture becomes more coarse.

Still more evidence of differences in the thoroughness with which different textured materials were reduced may be found in proportions of cores, retouched pieces, and debitage, as these proportions vary with texture. Nonintensive reduction, as stated above, should yield higher ratios of cores to debitage. This analysis has shown that these ratios are, in fact, highest at the coarse texture extreme. It was also assumed that, as reduction intensity increases, the frequency with which flakes produced by core reduction are themselves selected for, and subjected to further reduction should increase. As a result, in comparison to less intensive reduction, intensive reduction should yield more retouched pieces and debitage, and fewer cores. Retouched pieces are most common at the fine texture extreme supporting the inference that finer materials were more exhaustively reduced that coarser materials; however, from coarse to fine texture, debitage percentages first increase toward the middle of the continuum, and then decline toward the fine texture extreme. At first glance, this decline may seem incompatible with the inference that reduction intensity increases as texture becomes finer, but consideration of debitage site may explain this apparent contradiction. It seems likely that much of the debitage resulting from reduction of flakes which were themselves quite small, would not have been recovered using one-quarter-inch mesh screens. Therefore, the decline in debitage percentages at the fine texture extreme probably reflects recovery techniques, rather than a shift in reduction intensity.

Finally, variation in proportions of some of the debitage categories may also be interpreted as evidence of the correlation between reduction intensity and material texture. For example, the relative frequency of nonorientable fragments gradually increases as texture becomes finer. This relationship parallels that which exists between texture and relative frequencies of both multidirectional cores and indeterminate striking platforms. Assuming that nonorientable fragments are often pieces of shattered platforms, and that platform shattering becomes more common as reduction advances, the fact that nonorientable fragments are most common at the fine texture extreme may therefore indicate that finer rocks were more intensively reduced than coarser materials.

Overall, percentages of whole flakes tend to decrease as texture becomes finer, while medial-distal flake fragments become relatively more abundant. As noted earlier, several recent studies (Rozen 1979, 1981; Sullivan 1980) have suggested that in some cases, ratios of whole flakes to flake fragments tend to be higher in assemblages reflecting a strong emphasis on core reduction, and lower in collections which consist primarily of secondary reduction debitage. Therefore, the trends in the percentages of whole flakes and medial-distal flake fragments seen here with respect to texture, may indicate that fine texture materials were more frequently subjected to secondary reduction than were coarse materials.

Thus far, this discussion has focused on evidence which supports the inference that variation in reduction intensity has contributed strongly to the correlation between material texture and artifact size. Although this evidence is abundant, relationships between texture and two of the attributes examined are clearly incompatible with the above stated inference, and therefore warrant careful consideration. The two relationships in question concern retouch extent on scrapers and cortex of cores. With regard to the former, one would expect that scrapers made of finer materials to show more extensive retouch than those of coarser materials, if reduction intensity varied by texture. This analysis has demonstrated that scrapers of different textured materials do not vary significantly with respect to retouch extent. Therefore, we must conclude that fine-textured scrapers are smaller than coarse-textured scrapers not because the former were subjected to more thorough reduction than the latter, but because the flakes from which fine-textured scrapers were made were smaller than those from which coarse-textured scrapers were made. Consequently, the correlation between texture and scraper size must reflect the natural relationship between raw material size and texture, and does not derive from variation in reduction intensity.

If fine-textured cores were more thoroughly reduced than those made of coarse materials, the former should tend to be not only smaller and more commonly multidirectional, but they should also be less cortical than coarse-textured cores. While core size and flaking direction conform to these expectations, the relationship between texture and cortex for cores is exactly the opposite of what one would expect. That is, there appears to be some tendency for cortex on cores to become more common with increasingly fine texture.

The observed relationships between texture and both scraper retouch extent and core cortex cannot be satisfactorily explained or accommodated within the interpretation as it has been developed thus far. Although they are few, these anomolous observations are nonetheless compelling evidence that the current interpretation must be modified, or at least refined. To do so, it will be necessary to reexamine the data, and determine the extent to which relationships previously interpreted as reflecting variation in reduction intensity may, in fact, be the result of other factors.

Review of Figures 5.25 and 5.28 will show that, as stated earlier, cortex on whole flakes and debitage fragments tends overall to become more common with increasingly coarse texture. These figures also show that most of the variation contributing to this trend occurs at either texture extreme, and that there is comparatively little cortical variation among whole flakes and debitage fragments throughout the middle of the texture range. This "leveling-off" of cortical variation may reflect the interaction of two factors, each one of which affects cortical variation in a manner opposite to that of the other. Assuming for example, that raw material size decreases with increasingly fine texture, and that ratios of cortical surface area to material volume increase with decreasing raw material size, the natural relationship between raw material size and texture may cause cortex levels to

increase with increasingly fine texture. Independently, cortex levels
may tend to be lowered as reduction advances with increasingly fine
texture, assuming that more thorough reduction yields more noncortical
debitage than does less exhaustive reduction. Raw material size and
reduction intensity may therefore operate simultaneously to cancel their
respective effects on cortical variation by texture.

While this explanation for the observed distributions of cortex
by texture has some merit, it is not completely satisfactory because it
does not account for the sharp fluctuations in cortex levels seen at the
texture extremes. More specifically, one would expect cortex to be
linearly distributed across the entire texture continuum, if reduction
intensity varied uniformly in a one-to-one relationship with texture,
regardless of the combined effects of raw material size and reduction
intensity on cortex levels.

An alternative, and somewhat simpler explanation for the shape
of the cortex distributions for whole flakes and debitage fragments by
texture is that reduction intensity did not vary uniformly with texture.
While extremely fine materials may have been very intensively reduced,
and extremely coarse rocks subjected to only very nonintensive
reduction, materials characteristic of the remainder of the texture
continuum may have been reduced with essentially the same intermediate
degree of intensity, or perhaps with only a slight tendency for finer
materials to be more thoroughly broken apart than coarser textured
rocks.

Evidence supporting the inference that reduction intensity did
not substantially vary throughout the middle of the texture continuum
can be found by returning to Figure 5.28. This figure shows that
percentages of cortical debitage fragments not only level off between
texture extremes, but that they may even increase slightly from coarse
to fine in the middle of the texture scale. This suggests that, for at
least this portion of the texture continuum, the natural relationship
between raw material size and texture contributes more strongly to the
correlation between texture and artifact size than does reduction
intensity.

Further evidence indicating that reduction intensity varied most
at the texture extremes, and least in the middle texture range can be
seen by reexamining proportions of striking platform types. A review of
Figure 5.26 shows that variation in percentages of cortical, faceted,
and indeterminate platforms supports the inference that reduction
intensity increases as texture becomes finer. Like cortical variation,
however, variation in percentages of platform types appears to be
greatest at the texture extremes.

Somewhat more subjective evidence that reduction intensity was
not a very strong factor contributing to the correlation between texture
and artifact size is apparent in proportions of debitage, retouched
pieces, and cores. While shifts in these proportions suggest that
reduction intensity increases with increasingly fine texture, Figure
5.21 indicates that this variation is by no means robust. Because this

variation is so slight, it seems intuitively unlikely that reduction intensity could have been a stronger contributor to the correlation between texture and artifact size, than was the natural relationship between raw material size and texture. The figure also suggests that, once again, variation in proportions of artifact categories, especially cores, tends to be most pronounced at the texture extremes.

The preceding discussion has reevaluated debitage cortex amounts, striking platform type, and proportions of debitage, retouched pieces, and cores, as these assemblage characteristics vary by texture. It suggests that, while there is some evidence that reduction intensity increases with increasingly fine texture, reduction intensity probably does not contribute to the correlation between artifact size and texture as strongly as does the natural relationship between raw material size and texture. Further, differences in reduction intensity are most noticeable at the texture extremes, and contribute little to variation in assemblage characteristics throughout the middle of the texture continuum. Before these inferences can be accepted, it will be necessary to examine the extent to which they are compatible with variation among those assemblage characteristics not yet reexamined, including proportions of debitage categories, flaking direction and cortex for cores, and scraper retouch extent.

With regard to debitage category proportions, review of Figure 5.22 shows that from coarse to fine texture, percentages of nonorientable fragments, proximal flake fragments, and medial-distal flake fragments all increase sharply at the fine extreme of the texture continuum, while percentages of whole flakes decrease sharply. As noted earlier, there is some reason to suspect that ratios of whole flakes to flake fragments decrease as reduction becomes more thorough, and that nonorientable fragments may become more abundant as reduction advances. Therefore, the above observations tend to support the inference that reduction of extremely fine materials was especially intensive. However, it is important to consider that factors other than reduction intensity may also contribute strongly to variation in debitage category proportions. While all of these factors may not be known, and others may be difficult to control, it is reasonable to assume that they are related to material flaking properties, reduction techniques, and postreduction destructive forces. For example, although the tendency for nonorientable fragments to become relatively more abundant as texture becomes finer may, to some extent, reflect variation in reduction intensity, it might equally reflect differences in the occurrence of structural flaws among different materials. More specifically, casual experiments involving hard-hammer percussion reduction of materials from the study area suggest that finer materials, including some of the cherts and metasediments, tend to be more frequently and more seriously flawed by natural fracture planes, than are coarser materials such as quartzite. As a result, finer materials may tend to be more prone to irregular fracturing and shattering than coarse materials. Reduction of finer materials may therefore yield more nonorientable fragments than coarser materials for reasons unrelated to reduction intensity.

Similarly, variation in proportions of whole flakes to flake fragments may have more to do with postreduction destructive forces, than it does with reduction intensity. It is possible, for example, that fine-textured flakes may be more susceptible to breakage during trampling or redeposition as trash because they are smaller, absolutely thinner, and possibly more brittle than flakes made of coarser materials.

Perhaps the most vivid example of how factors unrelated to reduction intensity may influence variation in debitage category proportions can be seen in the data pertaining to split flakes. Although the mechanical factors which cause flakes to split as a result of the detaching blow are not entirely clear, we may speculate that split flakes clearly tend to become increasingly common with increasingly coarse texture because coarse materials are inherently more prone to this kind of mechanical failure than are finer materials. It also seems likely that splitting is more prevalent among coarser materials because the blows needed to detach large flakes from big, coarse-textured rocks were more powerful, and probably less well controlled than those used to remove flakes from smaller pieces of finer material.

The preceding reconsideration of the debitage data suggests that variation in debitage category proportions is likely to be the product of differences in reduction intensity and a number of other factors, including material flaking characteristics, reduction techniques, and postreduction destructive forces. While these factors can be specified, they cannot be controlled with the available data. Therefore, no precise statement of the extent to which they are responsible for variation in debitage category proportions can be offered. In general, however, the recognition of these factors is consistent with, or at least does not contradict the inference that variation in reduction intensity with texture probably did not contribute as strongly to the correlation between texture and artifact size, as did the natural relationship between texture and raw material size.

Returning now to core attributes, this analysis has shown that, from coarse to fine throughout the middle of the texture continuum, the only portion of the texture scale for which core data are available, multidirectional cores become relatively more abundant, while percentages of unidirectional cores decrease. These trends have been interpreted as reflecting a tendency for finer-textured cores to be more thoroughly reduced than those made of coarser material. However, as was the case with proportions of debitage, retouched pieces, and cores, variation in percentages of multidirectional and unidirectional cores is very slight, differing by little more than ten percentage points in either case. In admittedly subjective terms, this variation is so slight that it is unlikely that the tendency for fine-textured cores to be more thoroughly reduced than ones made of coarser materials could have been very strong in these intermediate texture classes. One is also tempted to speculate that, if data were available for the texture extremes, they would show sharp increases in percentages of unidirectional and multidirectional cores at the coarse and fine texture extremes, respectively.

Another possibility which tends to diminish the role of reduction intensity in contributing to the correlation between texture and artifact size specifically concerns the relationship between core size and flaking direction. For example, instead of reflecting variation in reduction intensity, the observed trends in core flaking direction might indirectly reflect the natural relationship between texture and raw material size. While it may be possible to efficiently reduce larger pieces of material through a sequence of first unidirectional, then bidirectional, and ultimately multidirectional flake removal, it may be necessary to rotate smaller pieces of material more frequently, even during the initial stages of reduction, in order to obtain the maximum number of flakes possible. Therefore, in contrast to coarse materials, whose larger size may have permitted a wider choice of reduction strategies, the naturally small size of fine-textured materials may have necessitated multidirectional reduction from the beginning.

This possibility brings us back once again to the relationship between texture and cortex on cores, one of the "anomolous" relationships which prompted this reevaluation of the data. As originally interpreted, the tendency for cores to show slightly more cortex as texture becomes finer in the middle of the texture continuum was seen as contradicting the inference that reduction intensity increases as texture becomes finer. Because it now appears that reduction intensity varied to an appreciable extent only at the texture extremes, the relationship between core cortex and texture, like that between core flaking direction and texture, may be attributed to raw material size, rather than reduction intensity. For example, limitations imposed by the size of the human hand may dictate that fewer flakes can be removed from a small piece of raw material than can be detached from a large piece, before the core must be abandoned. Therefore, the chances of cortex surviving on small cores of fine-textured materials may be somewhat greater than for larger cores of coarse materials. In general, then, reconsideration of the core data supports the inference that reduction intensity did not vary substantially throughout the middle of the texture continuum, and that the relationships among core texture, flaking direction, cortex, and size are attributable to the natural correlation between raw material size and texture, rather than variation in reduction intensity.

Assuming that extremely fine materials were very intensively reduced, that extremely coarse materials were very nonintensively reduced, and that medium textured materials were reduced with essentially the same, intermediate degree of intensity, we may now seek an explanation for the lack of variation in retouch extent among scrapers of different material types. Probably the best explanation of this lack of variation concerns the selection of materials having particular qualities for the manufacture of certain kinds of tools. It seems reasonable to assume, for example, that extremely fine textured cherts and metasediments may have been reserved for tools such as projectile points, drills, and bifaces, whose manufacturing techniques included pressure flaking were intensively reductive, and demanded fine materials in order to be successful. In contrast, extremely coarse

materials may have been used only to manufacture, through very
nonintensive reduction, other implements whose function(s) demanded
great size and edge durability. Between these two extremes, scrapers
could have been made from a wide variety of materials characteristic of
the middle of the texture continuum, because the technique by which
scrapers were made (presumably hard-hammer percussion) does not require
extremely fine textured material, nor does their function require
extremely great size which is obtainable only through the nonintensive
reduction of large, coarse materials. This interpretation cannot be
confirmed with texture and material type data, because these data are
not available for all tool categories. However, as was noted earlier in
the tool type descriptions, raw material types appear to be evenly
distributed with respect to most tool categories. Tool types cited as
exceptions to this generalization include projectile points, bifaces,
and drills, which tend to be made most commonly of fine materials, and
large primary flake tools and hammerstones, which are made most often of
coarse materials.

The lack of variation in retouch extent among scrapers of
different petrologically defined material types may therefore indicate
that scrapers were typically made from materials contained within the
middle range of the texture continuum, and were thus not subjected to
substantially different degrees of reduction intensity. Review of
Figure 5.30 shows that the four petrologically defined material types
(quartzite, silicified limestone, metasediment, and chert) for which
scraper retouch extent was examined, overlap with each other to a
considerable degree throughout the middle of the texture continuum. In
subjective terms, then, there seems to be little reason to doubt that
cherts and metasediments of intermediate texture, for example Classes 4
and 5, would have been treated no differently than quartzite of the same
texture for the purposes of scraper manufacture. Extremely fine
materials were probably not wasted on scrapers, regardless of
petrologically defined material type.

The preceding discussion has shown that variation in debitage
category proportions, core attributes, and scraper retouch extent is at
least compatible with, if not clearly supportive of the inference that
the natural correlation between raw material size and texture
contributed more strongly to be relationship between artifact size and
texture than did variation in reduction intensity, and that variation in
reduction intensity is most pronounced at the texture extremes. Before
leaving this topic, one final line of evidence involving flake metrics
is worth noting. Assuming that the intervals between texture classes
established in the laboratory are approximately equal, and that texture
naturally varies in a uniform, linear relationship with raw material
size, one would expect that the magnitude of the difference in flake
size between adjacent texture classes should be constant, if reduction
intensity were constant. Similarly, the difference in flake size
between any two adjacent texture classes should be constant if reduction
intensity varied uniformly with texture, although the magnitude of this
difference should be greater than if reduction intensity did not vary at
all. However, if this were not a linear relationship, one would expect
that the difference in flake size between adjacent texture classes would

be greatest where reduction intensity varied most, and smallest where reduction intensity varied least. With regard to the Rosemont data, this means that the differences in flake size between adjacent texture classes should be greatest at the texture extremes, and smallest in the middle of texture continuum. Review of Figure 5.23 indicates that this is precisely the case; that is, differences in flake size between adjacent texture classes are smallest near the middle of the texture scale, between Classes 4 and 5, and become progressively greater towards either texture extreme. This observation is consistent with the inference that shifts in reduction intensity are most pronounced at the texture extremes.

Before summarizing the results of this analysis of project-wide relationships between assemblage characteristics and material variability, two observations which have been ignored to this point deserve mention. This analysis has shown that frequencies of platform lipping are very low in the Rosemont assemblage, and there is some tendency for lipping to become increasingly common as texture becomes finer. At first glance, this observation suggests that, while soft-hammer percussion was only rarely used, the Hohokam recognized the advantages of this technique when it was applied to fine texture materials. However, the validity of this inference is brought into question by the likelihood that some unknown percentage of the platforms identified as having lipping may have fortuitously resulted from hard-hammer percussion. Also, there is good evidence that at least two of the sites (AZ EE:2:105 and EE:2:129) saw substantial preceramic occupations. Because soft-hammer percussion seems to be more prevalent in preceramic flaked stone technology than in the ceramic period, some of the lipping seen in the Rosemont Hohokam assemblages may be the result of the mixture of Archaic and Hohokam artifacts. In view of these possibilities, we may seriously question whether the Rosemont Hohokam ever used soft-hammer percussion with any regularity.

Finally, retouch extent distributions for quartzite and metasediment scrapers appear to be bimodal. The secondary mode occurring at the high extreme of retouch extent continuum suggests that there may be some quantifiable basis for distinguishing multisided scrapers, such as ovoids, from all others.

Conclusions

So far, this analysis has shown that the Rosemont Hohokam relied almost entirely on locally available materials for the manufacture of their flaked stone tools. Quantitative description of the assemblage as a whole has demonstrated patterned associations between material texture and a number of assemblage characteristics, the most salient of which is the strong correlation between texture and artifact size. Although most of the variation contributing to these correlations must be attributed to nothing more than natural relationships between texture and raw material size and flaking properties, there is some evidence that the intensity or thoroughness with which materials were reduced varied by texture. Probably the strongest of this evidence can be seen in the distributions of debitage cortex and striking platform types by texture. These data suggest that extremely coarse materials were subjected to only very limited reduction, while very fine materials were exhaustively reduced. Between the texture extremes, the vast majority of artifacts were made from a wide variety of medium-textured materials which were reduced with about the same, intermediate, degree of intensity. The variation in reduction intensity seen at the texture extremes has been related to differences in tool form, manufacturing techniques, and material availability. Very fine materials were exhaustively reduced because they were both relatively scarce and highly desirable for making certain small, pressure-flaked tools, most notably projectile points, whose manufacturing techniques demanded fine material. Very coarse rocks were nonintensively reduced by hard-hammer percussion when the task at hand required a very large implement with durable edges. Medium-textured materials were used to make a formally diverse group of hard-hammer percussion-flaked tools, including scrapers, irregularly retouched pieces, and unmodified flake tools. Soft-hammer percussion was only very rarely used, if at all.

On the basis of this analysis, it now seems reasonable to propose that the Rosemont Hohokam recognized two kinds of rocks for the purposes of making chipped stone tools: extremely fine materials which were most commonly reserved for tools whose manufacture involved pressure flaking, and all other materials, with which the Hohokam did essentially the same thing. Within this latter group, very coarse materials may have been recognized as a separate class, useful only when large tools were needed.

Assemblage Variation Among Sites and Major Provenience Classes Within Sites

In the preceding section, fundamental relationships between material variability and assemblage characteristics were established by viewing the Rosemont Hohokam flaked stone assemblage as a whole. With this foundation in mind, we may now examine assemblage variation among sites and major provenience classes within sites. The goal of this portion of the analysis is to determine the extent to which such provenience-specific variation can be attributed to differences in material characteristics, the form in which material was brought to the sites, the object, technique, and intensity of reduction, spatial patterns of reduction, use, and discard, and ultimately, occupational factors and site function.

A review of the theoretical discussion will show that all of the assemblage characteristics examined in the preceding section are relevant to the objectives of the analysis presented here. These characteristics include material type and texture, proportions of the basic artifact categories, complete flake size and cortex, proportions of striking platform types, scraper size and retouch extent, debitage fragment size and cortex, and core attributes. All of these assemblage characteristics except the last two, will be examined here. Core attributes are excluded from this portion of the analysis because of poor sample sizes of this artifact type at all but two of the sites. Review of Table 5.1 shows that only AZ EE:2:105 and EE:2:113 yielded more than 100 cores, while all other sites produced less than 50. Debitage fragment size and cortex will not be investigated because it is assumed that these variables are strongly correlated with complete flake size and cortex. Therefore, to avoid redundancy, description of variation in debitage size and cortex will focus on whole flakes. Several assemblage characteristics which have not yet been investigated will also be introduced. These attributes include tool type proportions, and relative frequencies of microflaking and abrasion on debitage.

Definition of the Analyzed Collections

Twenty-five collections were treated as separate analytic units in this portion of the analysis. Twelve of these consist of the total artifacts from structure fills which were selected for attribute analysis, for each site. The numbers of artifacts contained within these "structure fill" collections are given by structure and site in Table 5.18. Each of these collections will be referred to using an abbreviation consisting of the two or three characters comprising the last field of the site number, and the suffix "SF". Because only 13 pieces of flaked stone were recovered by screening structure fill at AZ EE:2:122, this collection will not be analyzed.

Only three sites (AZ EE:2:76, EE:2:105, and EE:2:113) yielded large enough quantities of flaked stone artifacts from structure floor pits to justify individual treatment of this provenience class. These collections will be known as "76FP," "105FP," and "113FP," and contain 85, 99, and 87 artifacts, respectively. As Table 5.19 shows, each of the remaining sites produced less than 15 items from floor pits.

Table 5.19 also shows that five sites (AZ EE:2:76, EE:2:77, EE:2:105, EE:2:113, and EE:2:129) yielded sufficient quantities of material from extramural features to permit these collections to be analyzed separately. These extramural feature collections will be referred to as "76EX", "77EX", "105EX", "113EX", and "129EX". Extramural features at each of the remaining sites produced no more than 14 pieces of chipped stone, and were therefore not analyzed.

As noted earlier, two sites (AZ EE:2:105 and EE:2:113) had borrow pits. At AZ EE:2:105, the 221 artifacts recovered from Feature 35 were analyzed as a single collection, known here as "105BP." At AZ EE:2:113, 169 items from Feature 13 were combined with 174 artifacts from Feature 85 to yield a single collection of 343 pieces. This collection will be known as "113BP."

Table 5.18

STRUCTURE FILL COLLECTIONS BY SITE AND STRUCTURE NUMBER

Site Number	Collection Code	Sample Size	Structure Number	N of Artifacts per Structure
AZ EE:2:76	76SF	957	7	172
			8	252
			10	264
			25	48
			27	120
			29	101
AZ EE:2:77	77SF	441	1	114
			3	137
			4	63
			31	92
			44	20
			56	15
AZ EE:2:84	84SF	423	10	171
			15	252
AZ EE:2:105	105SF	2871	5	153
			6	279
			9	232
			10	248
			30	39
			38	148
			41	157
			50	215
			71001	223
			71200	238
			72	88
			81	96
			87	209
			88	159
			91	209
AZ EE:2:106	106SF	30	1	2
			2	12
			3	8
			6	2
			7	6

Table 5.18, continued

STRUCTURE FILL COLLECTIONS BY SITE AND STRUCTURE NUMBER

AZ EE:2:107	107SF	180	1	38
			2	63
			3	51
			4	11
			5	17
AZ EE:2:109	109SF	50	1	22
			2	6
			3	11
			4	5
			5	6
AZ EE:2:113	113SF	1998	6100	203
			6200	148
			6300	173
			7	201
			8	181
			10	203
			11	278
			12	228
			83	148
			86	87
			154	148
AZ EE:2:116	116SF	59	1	27
			2	32
AZ EE:2:117	117SF	49	1	14
			2	35
AZ EE:2:120	120SF	152	1	70
			3	16
			6	12
			7	5
			8	22
			11	27
AZ EE:2:129	129SF	225	1	160
			2	95

Table 5.19

ARTIFACT COUNTS BY PROVENIENCE CLASS AND SITE
FOR THE ANALYZED COLLECTIONS

Site Number	Structure Fill (SF)	Floor Pit (FP)	Extramural Feature (EX)	Stripping (S)	Borrow Pit (BP)	Trash (T)	Site Total
EE:2:76	957	85	110	271			1423
EE:2:77	441		84				525
EE:2:84	423						423
EE:2:105	2871	99	60		221		3251
EE:2:106	30						30
EE:2:107	180						180
EE:2:109	50						50
EE:2:113	1998	87	417		343		2845
EE:2:116	59						59
EE:2:117	49						49
EE:2:120	152						152
EE:2:122							0
EE:2:129	255		57			861	1173
EE:1:104							0
Site-specific Provenience Class Total	7465	271	728	271	564	861	10160
FLOOR							72
Total Analyzed Artifacts							10232

Overburden removed in surface stripping was screened at only two sites (AZ EE:2:76 and EE:2:84). None of the artifacts produced by surface stripping at AZ EE:2:84 was analyzed because most of this material appeared to be depositionally related to structure fill. That is, most of the area contained within screened surface stripping units was underlain by structures, and was therefore not representative of extramural areas. At AZ EE:2:76, 271 artifacts from screened, extramural stripping units were analyzed as a single collection known as "76ST." The artifacts contained within this collection were recovered from the units listed below:

> N28 E22 (eastern one-half)
> N28 E26 (entire 4-m-by-4-m unit)
> N28 E30 (western one-half)
> N32 E26 (southern one-half)
> N48 E22 (northeastern one-quarter)
> N48 E26 (northern one-half, southeastern one-quarter)
> N48 E34 (entire 4-m-by-4-m unit)

As previously mentioned, a portion of the sheet trash deposit at AZ EE:2:129 was suspected of being related to a preceramic occupation. A total of 1048 artifacts was recovered from this deposit, of which 861 were treated as a single collection known as "129T." These artifacts were recovered from the eastern one-half of N42 E62 and the southern one-quarter of N42 E70.

Finally, 72 pieces of chipped stone from structure floor contexts, combined for all sites, were treated as a single collection known as "FLOOR." The 25 analyzed collections are summarized by site and provenience class in Table 5.19.

Before proceeding with the analysis, several final observations concerning the analyzed collections should be made. Comparison of Tables 5.19 and 5.2 shows that the 25 analyzed collections account for only 10,232 (93%) of the 10,978 artifacts originally selected for attribute analysis. This discrepancy reflects the fact that some artifacts originally selected for analysis were later judged to be of only limited use in addressing the research objectives, and were thus excluded from the analysis. These artifacts include those from postholes and nonfeature contexts at all sites. At many of the sites with small assemblages, attributes were recorded on artifacts from stripping and uncontrolled surface collections (Feature 0). At first, this was done in an effort to increase sample sizes. These artifacts were later excluded from the analysis when it was decided that the uncertainty introduced by variation in recovery techniques outweighed the benefits of larger collections.

Attributes were recorded on 59 items from the ballcourt at AZ EE:2:105. These artifacts were later excluded from the analysis because it seemed unlikely that they were directly related to the primary function of this unique feature.

While none of the artifacts from AZ EE:2:122 were used in the analysis due to very small sample sizes, 52 pieces of chipped stone from AZ EE:1:104 were inadvertently omitted due to an oversight in the laboratory. Wherever feasible, however, an attempt will be made to describe the assemblage from this site in qualitative terms.

Although the 25 collections defined above served as the basic comparative units for this portion of the analysis, it was necessary to combine some of these collections for the purposes of describing certain assemblage characteristics. In particular, low sample sizes of tools necessitated that the collections be grouped to describe variation in tool type proportions, and scraper size and retouch extent. The manner in which the collections were combined will be described in the following section.

Finally, the provenience data presented here for the 25 analyzed collections are necessarily general due to space limitations. More specific provenience data for the collections are on file at the Cultural Resource Management Division, Arizona State Museum.

Data Presentation and Comparative Observations

Material Type

Frequencies and percentages of the various material types are given for all collections, except FLOOR, in Table 5.20. Material type percentages were used to construct a bar graph for each collection, showing the relative frequencies of material types. These bar graphs were then grouped on the basis of a subjective evaluation of similarity among the collections with respect to material type composition. Figure 5.31 shows the arrangement of those bar graphs, and indicates that two groups of collections were distinguished at the grossest level of comparison. Group 1 consists of a single collection (106SF) that differs from all others in that it has a homogeneous material composition, being composed of 90 percent quartzite. All other collections are contained within Group 2 because they have more heterogeneous material compositions in which no single material accounts for more than 70 percent of the artifacts. Group 2 is itself divided into two groups, Group 2.1 and Group 2.2. The first of these also contains only one collection (109SF) which is distinguished from Group 2.2 collections in that silicified limestone is the dominant material, accounting for 56 percent of the artifacts. Among Group 2.2, either quartzite or metasediment is the dominant material. The characteristic used to distinguish Groups 2.2.1 and 2.2.2 is that, among Group 2.2.1 collections, quartzite is about three or more times as abundant than is metasediment. In contrast, percentages of metasediment are only slightly less than, or greater than percentages of quartzite among Group 2.2.2 collections. Figure 5.31 also shows that in nearly all cases, Group 2.2.1 collections have substantially greater amounts of chert than do those of Group 2.2.2. Group 2.2.1 contains all collections from all provenience classes from AZ EE:2:76, EE:2:77, EE:2:105, EE:2:107,

Table 5.20

FREQUENCIES (f) AND PERCENTAGES (%) OF ARTIFACTS BY MATERIAL TYPE,
FOR ALL ANALYZED COLLECTIONS EXCEPT FLOOR

		Quartzite	Metasediment	Silicified Limestone	Chert	Limestone	Rhyolite	Chalcedony	Basalt	Jasper	Obsidian	Quartz	Other	Total
76SF	f	446	144	176	129	15	19	12	9	5	0	0	2	957
	%	46.6	15.0	18.4	13.5	1.6	2.0	1.3	0.9	0.5			0.2	
76FP	f	43	14	20	6	1	0	1	0	0	0	0	0	85
	%	50.6	16.5	23.5	7.1	1.2		1.2						
76EX	f	53	16	24	9	4	0	2	0	2	0	0	0	110
	%	48.2	14.5	21.8	8.2	3.6		1.8		1.8				
76STR	f	109	50	67	32	4	3	0	1	5	0	0	0	271
	%	40.2	18.5	24.7	11.8	1.5	1.1		0.4	1.8				
77SF	f	245	122	24	18	10	5	1	10	1	0	1	4	441
	%	55.6	27.7	5.4	4.1	2.3	1.1	0.2	2.3	0.2		0.2	0.9	
77EX	f	58	11	8	6	0	0	0	0	0	0	0	1	84
	%	69.0	13.1	9.5	7.1								1.2	
84SF	f	89	167	89	20	46	5	0	2	0	0	0	4	422
	%	21.1	39.6	21.1	4.7	10.9	1.2		0.5				0.9	
105SF	f	1,362	625	234	507	55	26	29	13	12	1	5	2	2,871
	%	47.4	21.8	8.2	17.7	1.9	0.9	1.0	0.5	0.4	–	0.2	0.1	
105FP	f	49	20	12	11	5	0	0	2	0	0	0	0	99
	%	49.5	20.2	12.1	11.1	5.1			2.0					
105EX	f	31	10	3	11	2	2	1	0	0	0	0	0	60
	%	51.7	16.7	5.0	18.3	3.3	3.3	1.7						
105BP	f	87	48	19	58	3	1	4	0	1	0	0	0	221
	%	39.4	21.7	8.6	26.2	1.4	0.5	1.8		0.5				
106SF	f	27	0	0	1	0	1	0	1	0	0	0	0	30
	%	90.0			3.3		3.3		3.3					
107SF	f	123	11	26	13	0	3	0	2	2	0	0	0	180
	%	68.3	6.1	14.4	7.2		1.7		1.1	1.1				
109SF	f	20	0	28	1	1	0	0	0	0	0	0	0	50
	%	40.0		56.0	2.0	2.0								
113SF	f	804	765	211	64	107	12	19	9	3	0	0	4	1,998
	%	40.2	38.3	10.6	3.2	5.4	0.6	1.0	0.5	0.2			0.2	
113FP	f	32	26	19	2	6	0	2	0	0	0	0	0	87
	%	36.8	29.9	21.8	2.3	6.9		2.3						
113EX	f	187	154	27	6	31	1	4	5	0	0	1	1	417
	%	44.8	36.9	6.5	1.4	7.4	0.2	1.0	1.2			0.2	0.2	
113BP	f	158	113	35	9	21	3	2	1	0	0	0	0	342
	%	46.2	33.0	10.2	2.6	6.1	0.9	0.6	0.3					
116SF	f	23	6	22	4	1	1	1	0	0	0	0	1	59
	%	39.0	10.2	37.3	6.8	1.7	1.7	1.7					1.7	
117SF	f	29	9	3	4	1	1	0	0	0	0	0	2	49
	%	59.2	18.4	6.1	8.2	2.0	2.0						4.1	
120SF	f	103	18	17	9	0	2	1	1	1	0	0	0	152
	%	67.8	11.8	11.2	5.9		1.3	0.7	0.7	0.7				
129SF	f	101	76	57	8	1	0	0	6	0	0	0	6	255
	%	39.6	29.8	22.4	3.1	0.4			2.4				2.4	
129EX	f	14	32	7	2	0	0	1	0	1	0	0	0	57
	%	24.6	56.1	12.3	3.5			1.8		1.8				
129T	f	256	354	138	83	3	2	8	1	9	1	0	6	861
	%	29.7	41.1	16.0	9.6	0.3	0.2	0.9	0.1	1.0	0.1		0.7	

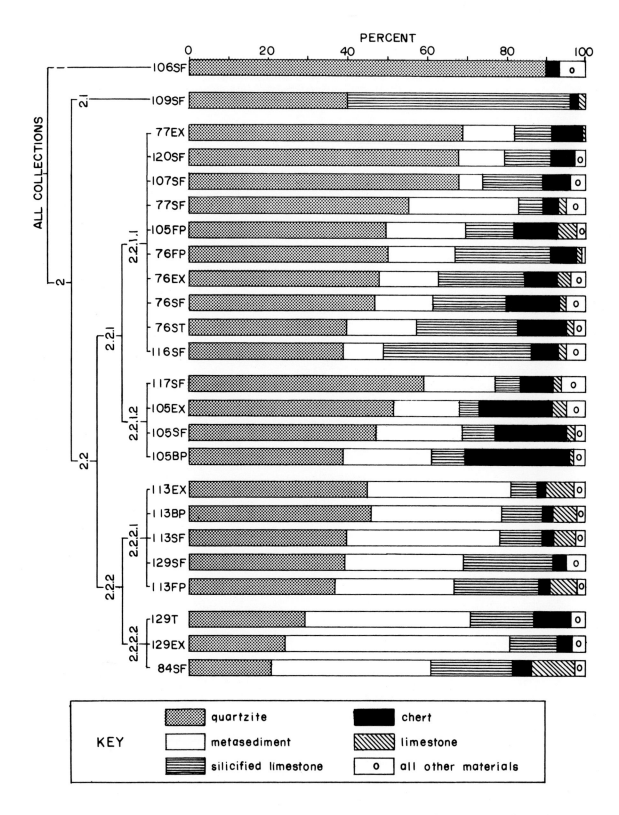

Figure 5.31. Material-type composition bar graphs for all analyzed collections.

EE:2:116, EE:2:117, and EE:2:120. Group 2.2.2 consists of all collections from AZ EE:2:84, EE:2:113, and EE:2:129.

At the level at which Groups 2.2.1 and 2.2.2 are distinguished, which is probably the most useful level of comparison for the purposes of this analysis, all collections from any one site are contained within the same group. This indicates that there is little variation in material type composition among collections from different provenience classes at the same site. However, Figure 5.31 also shows that Groups 2.2.1 and 2.2.2 may each be still further subdivided on the basis of relatively minor differences in proportions of certain materials. For example, among the Group 2.2.1 collections, all collections from AZ EE:2:76, EE:2:77, EE:2:107, and EE:2:120, and 105FP contain more silicified limestone than chert. These collections are distinguished as Group 2.2.1.1. In contrast, chert is relatively more abundant than silicified limestone in 105SF, 105EX, 105BP, and 117SF. These collections are members of Group 2.2.1.2.

Among Group 2.2.2 collections, 113EX, 113BP, 113SF, 113FP, and 129SF are distinguished as Group 2.2.2.1 because they all have slightly more quartzite than they do metasediment. In comparison, at 129T, 129EX, and 84SF (Group 2.2.2.2) metasediment is more abundant than quartzite.

Although detailed attribute observations were not made on the collection from AZ EE:1:104, simple inspection of this assemblage indicated that about 80 percent or more of the artifacts are made of quartzite. Therefore, the assemblage from AZ EE:2:104 is more similar to 106SF than it is to any other collection, and can be tentatively assigned to Group 1.

Material Texture

Frequencies and percentages of artifacts by texture class are given for all analyzed collections in Table 5.21. These data were used to construct Figure 5.32, which shows a histogram of texture class percentages for each collection. All of the histograms are quite similar, in that they all share the same modal texture class (Class 4). In all but one case, the coarser texture classes, to the right of the modal class, account for greater percentages of artifacts than do the finer classes. The exception to this pattern is 129T, where Classes 2 and 3, combined, are more strongly represented than are Classes 5 through 8, combined. Collection 129T therefore contains more artifacts of fine-textured materials than do the other collections. In general, however, the histograms suggest that the collections are very similar with respect to material texture, despite substantial differences in material type composition.

Table 5.21

FREQUENCIES (f) AND PERCENTAGES (%) OF ARTIFACTS
BY TEXTURE CLASS, FOR ALL ANALYZED COLLECTIONS

Collection Code		fine 1	2	3	4	Texture Class 5	6	coarse 7	8	Total
76SF	f	0	39	132	441	228	106	28	7	951
	%		4.1	13.9	43.2	24.0	11.1	2.9	0.7	
76FP	f	0	1	14	33	24	9	1	2	84
	%		1.2	16.7	39.3	28.6	10.7	1.2	2.4	
76EX	f	0	3	12	39	19	18	8	7	106
	%		2.8	11.3	36.8	17.9	17.0	7.5	6.6	
76STR	f	0	15	39	123	68	20	6	0	271
	%		5.5	14.4	45.4	25.1	7.4	2.2		
77SF	f	0	8	40	175	128	73	10	4	438
	%		1.8	9.1	40.0	29.2	16.7	2.3	0.9	
77EX	f	0	1	3	34	25	14	5	1	83
	%		1.2	3.6	41.0	30.1	16.9	6.0	1.2	
84SF	f	0	7	52	251	59	31	6	2	408
	%		1.7	12.7	61.5	14.5	7.6	1.5	0.5	
105SF	f	3	119	404	964	599	573	177	16	2855
	%	0.1	4.2	14.2	33.8	21.0	20.1	6.2	0.6	
105FP	f	0	3	7	35	30	17	7	0	99
	%		3.0	7.1	35.4	30.3	17.2	7.1		
105EX	f	0	5	7	17	12	14	3	2	60
	%		8.3	11.7	28.3	20.0	23.3	5.0	3.3	
105BP	f	0	20	44	65	37	37	18	0	221
	%		9.0	19.9	29.4	16.7	16.7	8.1		
106SF	f	0	0	4	12	7	2	2	3	30
	%			13.3	40.0	23.3	6.7	6.7	10.0	
107SF	f	0	1	26	103	33	11	3	2	179
	%		0.6	14.5	57.5	18.4	6.1	1.7	1.1	

Table 5.21, continued

FREQUENCIES (f) AND PERCENTAGES (%) OF ARTIFACTS
BY TEXTURE CLASS, FOR ALL ANALYZED COLLECTIONS

Collection Code		fine 1	2	Texture Class 3	4	5	6	coarse 7	8	Total
109SF	f	0	0	2	27	14	5	0	1	49
	%			4.1	55.1	28.6	10.2		2.0	
113SF	f	0	29	244	933	403	269	78	21	1977
	%		1.5	12.3	47.2	20.4	13.6	3.9	1.1	
113FP	f	0	2	9	44	21	9	1	1	87
	%		2.3	10.3	50.6	24.1	10.3	1.1	1.1	
113EX	f	0	4	57	197	66	51	33	9	417
	%		1.0	13.7	47.2	15.8	12.2	7.9	2.2	
113BP	f	0	3	32	150	59	72	17	7	340
	%		0.9	9.4	44.1	17.4	21.2	5.0	2.1	
116SF	f	0	1	11	27	9	9	1	1	59
	%		1.7	18.6	45.8	15.3	15.3	1.7	1.7	
117SF	f	0	2	5	18	8	15	0	1	49
	%		4.1	10.2	36.7	16.3	30.6		2.0	
120SF	f	0	1	19	78	34	14	5	1	152
	%		0.7	12.5	51.3	22.4	9.2	3.3	0.7	
129SF	f	0	1	36	124	62	28	4	0	255
	%		0.4	14.1	48.6	24.3	11.0	1.6		
129EX	f	0	0	11	32	12	1	0	1	859
	%			19.3	56.1	21.1	1.8		1.8	
129T	f	0	23	216	453	123	34	7	3	859
	%		2.7	25.1	52.7	14.3	4.0	0.8	0.3	
FLOOR	f	0	1	8	27	16	13	4	1	70
	%		1.4	11.4	38.6	22.9	18.6	5.7	1.4	

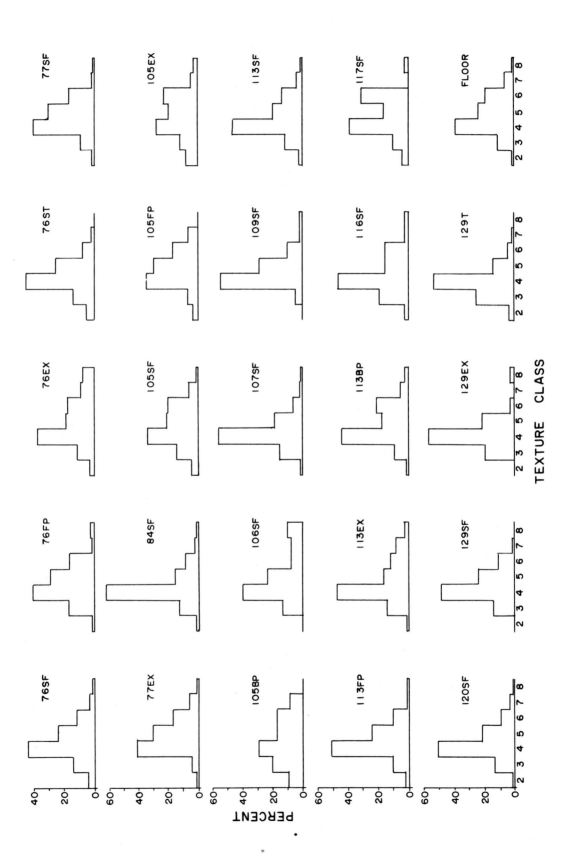

Figure 5.32 Texture class histograms for all analyzed collections.

Basic Artifact Categories
========================

Frequencies of the basic artifact categories are given for each collection in Table 5.22. Core and cobble hammerstones have been combined under "hammerstones". Category percentages calculated on the basis of all categories except thermal fragments are also presented. In order to assess variation among the collections with respect to artifact category proportions, the percentages given in Table 5.22 were analyzed using a multivariate statistical technique known as hierarchical clustering. This analysis was performed with a computer program which uses a clustering algorithm called Ward's method. Briefly, this program first produces a matrix of value based on the Euclidean distances between the collections, containing one value for each of all possible comparisons between two collections. Once the matrix has been established, the computer program groups the cases (collections) on the basis of relative similarity by taking each case and finding the other case that is most similar. The two cases are merged, and the next most similar case sought. Grouping continues, minimizing variability within groups, until all cases have been used. For a more thorough discussion of the Ward's method of hierarchical clustering, the reader is referred to Anderberg (1973).

The result of the cluster analysis is a dendrogram that graphically shows the relationships among collections in terms of similarities and differences in artifact category proportions. Figure 5.33 is adapted from the dendrogram obtained for the analysis of the Rosemont data. The horizontal scale in this diagram indicates "merge level", or the degree of similarity at which collections are grouped. The figure shows that two collection groups are clearly distinguished at a merge level of about 20. Group 1 consists of 77SF, 106SF, 107SF, 109SF, 116SF, 117SF, 120SF, 129SF, 76EX, 77EX, 105EX, and FLOOR. Group 2 contains 76SF, 84SF, 105SF, 113SF, 76FP, 76ST, 105FP, 105BP, 113FP, 113BP, 113EX, 129EX, and 129T.

In order to understand the basis on which the above-defined collection groups were distinguished by the cluster analysis, mean artifact category percentages were calculated for all groups under consideration, as well as for all collections combined. These data, given in Table 5.23, show that Groups 1 and 2 appear to be distinguished primarily on the basis of differences in proportions of complete flakes to flake fragments. Specifically, percentages of complete flakes tend to be greater among Group 1 collections, while percentages of all types of flake fragments, including split flakes, proximal flake fragments, and medial-distal flake fragments, tend to be greater among Group 2 assemblages. Differences between the groups with respect to flake fragments are most pronounced in percentages of medial-distal fragments, and least pronounced in percentages of split flakes. Group 1 collections also differ in that they tend to have more cores and hammerstones than Group 2 collection. Percentages of both nonorientable fragments and retouched pieces tend to be about the same in both groups.

Although the assemblage from AZ EE:1:104 was not included in the cluster analysis, comparison of the artifact category percentages given

Table 5.22

FREQUENCIES (f) AND PERCENTAGES (%) OF ARTIFACTS BY CATEGORY
FOR ALL ANALYZED COLLECTIONS

Collection Code		Complete Flakes	Split Flakes	Proximal Flake Fragments	Medial-Distal Flake Fragments	Nonorientable Fragments	Retouched Pieces	Cores	Hammerstones	Thermal Fragments	Total
76SF	f	411	76	135	199	43	67	7	6	13	957
	%	43.5	8.1	12.0	21.1	4.6	7.1	0.7	0.6		
76FP	f	33	10	13	20	2	3	0	2	2	85
	%	39.8	12.0	15.7	24.1	2.4	3.6		2.4		
76EX	f	51	8	14	13	0	7	8	4	5	110
	%	48.6	7.6	13.3	12.4		6.7	7.6	3.8		
76ST	f	95	25	47	56	10	33	2	0	3	271
	%	35.4	9.3	17.5	20.9	3.7	12.3	0.7			
77SF	f	240	29	35	75	16	28	9	5	4	441
	%	54.9	6.6	8.0	17.2	3.7	6.4	2.1	1.1		
77EX	f	34	7	6	13	5	3	7	9	0	84
	%	40.5	8.3	7.1	15.5	6.0	3.6	8.3	10.7		
84SF	f	197	33	34	89	26	27	8	4	5	423
	%	47.1	7.9	8.1	21.3	6.2	6.5	1.9	1.0		
105SF	f	1202	298	450	574	102	178	28	9	30	2871
	%	42,3	10.5	15.8	20.2	3.6	6.3	1.0	0.3		
105FP	f	40	9	11	26	4	4	2	1	2	99
	%	41.2	9.3	11.3	26.8	4.1	4.1	2.1	1.0		
105EX	f	21	2	7	8	2	7	7	6	0	60
	%	35.0	3.3	11.7	13.3	3.3	11.7	11.7	10.0		
105BP	f	98	16	28	47	11	8	1	8	4	221
	%	45.2	7.4	12.9	21.7	5.1	3.7	0.5	3.7		
106SF	f	13	4	2	3	3	1	3	1	0	30
	%	43.3	13.3	6.7	10.0	10.0	3.3	10.0	3.3		

Note: Percentages do not include thermal fragments. Cobble and core hammerstones are included under "Hammerstones"

Table 5.22, continued

FREQUENCIES (f) AND PERCENTAGES (%) OF ARTIFACTS BY CATEGORY
FOR ALL ANALYZED COLLECTIONS

Collection Code		Complete Flakes	Split Flakes	Proximal Flake Fragments	Medial–Distal Flake Fragments	Nonorientable Fragments	Retouched Pieces	Cores	Hammerstones	Thermal Fragments	Total
107SF	f	89	10	26	29	7	10	3	4	2	180
	%	50.0	5.6	14.6	16.3	3.9	5.6	1.7	2.2		
109SF	f	25	2	7	7	2	4	2	1	0	50
	%	50.0	4.0	14.0	14.0	4.0	8.0	4.0	2.0		
113SF	f	877	217	253	328	115	124	34	18	32	1998
	%	44.6	11.0	12.9	16.7	5.8	6.3	1.7	0.9		
113FP	f	26	8	11	24	5	10	1	1	1	87
	%	30.2	9.3	12.8	27.9	5.8	11.6	1.2	1.2		
113EX	f	155	47	63	88	16	21	12	9	6	417
	%	37.7	11.4	15.3	21.4	3.9	5.1	2.9	2.2		
113BP	f	144	46	40	65	12	27	4	1	4	343
	%	42.5	13.6	11.8	19.2	3.5	8.0	1.2	0.3		
116SF	f	31	4	8	12	2	1	0	1	0	59
	%	52.5	6.8	13.6	20.3	3.4	1.7		1.7		
117SF	f	26	5	4	8	4	1	0	1	0	49
	%	53.1	10.2	8.2	16.3	8.2	2.0		2.0		
120SF	f	77	9	16	22	9	12	3	3	1	152
	%	51.0	6.0	10.6	14.6	6.0	7.9	2.0	2.0		
129SF	f	29	18	22	44	2	15	6	4	15	225
	%	53.8	7.5	9.2	18.3	0.8	6.3	2.5	1.7		
129EX	f	21	4	12	13	1	4	2	0	0	57
	%	36.8	7.0	21.1	22.8	1.8	7.0	3.5			
129T	f	348	84	116	201	57	36	7	0	12	861
	%	41.0	10.0	13.7	23.7	6.7	4.2	0.8			
FLOOR	f	37	3	2	7	3	7	4	8	1	72
	%	52.1	4.2	2.8	9.9	4.2	9.9	5.6	11.3		

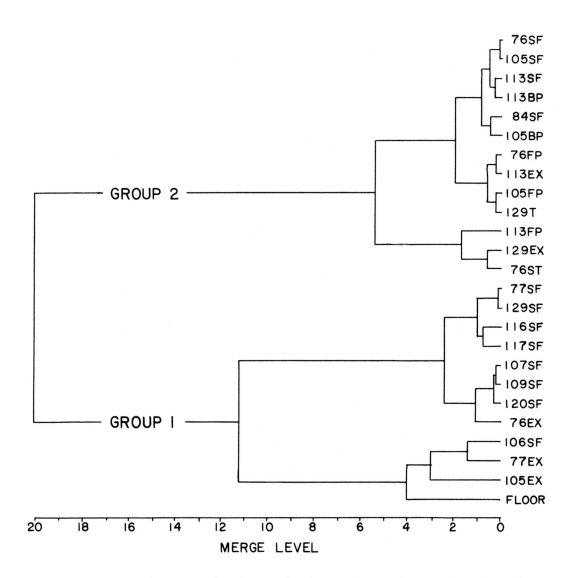

Figure 5.33. Dendrogram showing relations among the analyzed collections with respect to percentages of basic artifact categories.

for this collection in Table 5.1 with those in Table 5.23 suggests that the assemblage from AZ EE:1:104 can be tentatively assigned to Group 1.

Finally, its worth noting that collections from various intrasite provenience classes at AZ EE:2:76, EE:2:77, EE:2:105, and EE:2:129 are not always contained within the same dendrogram group (Fig. 5.23). This observation suggests that in some cases, substantial variation in artifact category proportions exists among collections from different provenience classes within the same site.

Complete Flake Size

Mean, standard deviation, and sample size for complete flake length, width, and thickness are given for all collections in Table 5.24. These data were used to construct Figure 5.34, a scattergram of

Table 5.23

MEAN ARTIFACT CATEGORY PERCENTAGES BY DENDROGRAM GROUPS

Artifact Category	All Collections	Dendrogram Groups	
		1	2
Complete Flakes	4.5	48.7	40.6
Split Flakes	8.4	7.0	9.8
Proximal Flake Fragments	12.1	10.0	14.1
Medial-Distal Flake Fragments	18.6	14.8	22.1
Nonorientable Fragments	4.5	4.5	4.4
Retouched Pieces	6.4	6.0	6.6
Cores	2.9	4.6	1.4
Hammerstones	2.6	4.3	1.0

mean flake length plotted against mean flake width. The scattergram shows that 22 of the 25 collections are very similar to each other with respect to flake size. Mean lengths for these collections vary by less than 8 mm, from about 25 mm to 33 mm. Mean widths vary even less, from about 20 mm to 26 mm. Three of the collections (106SF, 117SF, and FLOOR) appear to have somewhat larger flakes, with mean lengths and widths of about 39 mm and 30 mm, respectively. With the exception of these last three collections, it therefore appears that there is little variation among the collections with respect to flake size. However, because some of the collections, notably 76SF, 105SF, 113SF, and 129T, have very large sample sizes, it is possible that some of the variation described in the scattergram may be statistically significant, even though the magnitude of this variation is small.

To better evaluate the statistical significance of flake size variation, the 95 percent confidence interval for mean flake thickness was calculated for each collection. The confidence interval of each collection was then compared with that of every other collection to see if the intervals overlapped. This was done by constructing a 25-by-25-cell matrix containing 300 cells representing all possible, comparisons of collection pairs. This matrix showed that the confidence intervals overlapped in 266, or 89 percent, of the 300 pair-wise comparisons, further suggesting that there is little variation in flake size among the collections. However, in 34 of the individual, pair-wise comparisons (68 cells) the confidence intervals did not overlap,

Table 5.24

MEAN, STANDARD DEVIATION, AND SAMPLE SIZE
FOR COMPLETE FLAKE LENGTH, WIDTH, AND THICKNESS
FOR ALL ANALYZED COLLECTIONS

Collection Code	Length (mm)		Width (mm)		Thickness (mm)		Sample Size
	x̄	sd	x̄	sd	x̄	sd	
76SF	27.6	11.8	22.4	10.3	5.5	3.3	411
76FP	31.2	15.4	25.5	14.0	6.5	3.4	33
76EX	33.1	14.3	24.9	9.7	6.5	3.8	50
76ST	27.1	13.2	21.5	9.0	5.5	2.8	95
77SF	32.8	14.8	25.8	11.4	6.7	3.8	240
77EX	29.9	17.5	22.0	10.7	5.1	3.6	34
84SF	31.8	13.4	25.0	9.5	6.1	3.2	197
105SF	28.9	14.7	22.7	11.9	5.5	3.8	1202
105FP	27.0	14.7	22.7	11.9	5.3	3.4	40
105EX	33.2	16.7	23.2	10.0	6.9	3.9	21
105BP	27.2	15.3	20.2	10.8	5.0	3.9	98
106SF	38.6	11.8	30.4	20.2	7.6	3.9	13
107SF	31.6	14.5	24.8	10.3	6.5	3.2	89
109SF	32.6	12.6	25.5	10.4	7.0	4.2	25
113SF	31.8	13.9	25.0	10.8	6.4	3.7	867
113FP	32.6	14.8	26.1	11.4	6.7	3.6	26
113EX	32.0	13.4	23.9	11.2	6.5	4.0	155
113BP	30.9	12.2	25.5	11.0	6.6	3.8	144
116SF	28.6	7.6	24.5	11.5	5.9	2.8	31
117SF	38.4	15.5	30.7	13.9	8.0	3.2	26

Table 5.24, continued

MEAN, STANDARD DEVIATION, AND SAMPLE SIZE
FOR COMPLETE FLAKE LENGTH, WIDTH, AND THICKNESS
FOR ALL ANALYZED COLLECTIONS

Collection Code	Length (mm) x	Length (mm) sd	Width (mm) x	Width (mm) sd	Thickness (mm) x	Thickness (mm) sd	Sample Size
120SF	30.5	13.8	26.2	10.6	6.2	2.8	77
129SF	31.7	9.7	25.0	9.2	5.3	3.5	129
129EX	31.5	9.7	25.0	9.2	6.9	3.8	21
129T	25.7	11.7	20.5	9.5	5.3	3.5	348
FLOOR	39.2	19.5	28.6	13.9	6.5	2.9	37

suggesting that statistically significant differences in mean flake thickness can be inferred for these comparisons at the 0.05 probability level. These comparisons involved 16 different collections, usually those with either very large sample sizes, or extreme values for mean flake thickness. For example, 117SF, with the largest value (8.0), was involved in 10 of the 34 pairs. Table 5.25 lists mean flake thickness and a number of statistically significant statements which can be made about that collection (that is, the number of nonoverlapping confidence-interval pairs of which it is a member). Finally, a series of comparative statements presents the relationships which may be inferred from these data. The collections are arranged in order by absolute value of mean flake thickness; however, due to small sample sizes and large standard deviations, not all of these relationships can be expressed clearly. For example, 77EX, with a very small mean flake thickness (5.0)—only 105FP is smaller—has a very broad 95 percent confidence interval, thus the most powerful statement which can be made about flake size from this collection is that it is smaller than that of 117SF, the collection with the largest mean flake thickness.

These statements suggest that, in spite of the restricted range of flake size, we may distinguish three groups of collections with respect to flake thickness. Collections 76SF, 76ST, 77Ex, 105SF, 105BP, 105FP, and 129T have flakes which tend to be smaller than those of many of the other collections for which statistically significant differences can be shown. Collections 77SF, 107SF, 129SF, 113SF, 113EX, 113BP, 120SF, and 84SF have flakes which tend to be somewhat larger than those of the preceding collections. The third group contains only one collection (117SF) whose flakes tend to be larger than those of most of the other collections for which statistically significant differences

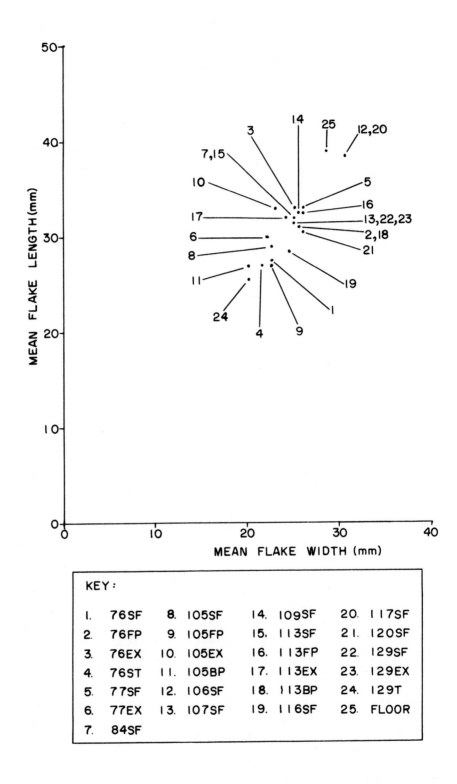

Figure 5.34. Mean-flake-length by mean-flake-width scattergram for all analyzed collections.

Table 5.25

COMPARATIVE FLAKE SIZE STATEMENTS BASED ON NONOVERLAPPING 95 PERCENT
CONFIDENCE INTERVALS FOR MEAN FLAKE THICKNESS

Collection Code	Mean Flake Thickness	Number of Pairs	Comparative Statement (These flakes tend to be . . .)
"Small"			
76SF	5.5	7	smaller than those in 77SF, 107SF, 113SF, 113EX, 113BP, 117SF, and 129SF
76ST	5.5	3	smaller than those in 77SF, 113SF, and 117SF
77EX	5.1	1	smaller than those in 117SF
105SF	5.5	7	smaller than those in 77SF, 107SF, 113SF, 113EX, 113BP, 117SF, and 129SF
105BP	5.0	4	smaller than those in 77SF, 107SF 113SF, and 117SF
105FP	5.3	1	smaller than those in 117SF
129T	5.3	8	smaller than those in 77SF, 84SF, 107SF, 113SF, 113EX, 113BP, 117SF, 129SF
"Medium"			
77SF	6.7	5	larger than those in 76SF, 76ST, 105SF, 105BP, and 129T
107SF	6.5	3	larger than those in 76SF, 105SF, and 129T
129SF	6.4	3	larger than those in 76SF, 105SF, and 129T
113SF	6.4	6	larger than those in 76SF, 76ST, 105SF, 105BP, and 129T, but are smaller than those in 117SF
113EX	6.5	3	larger than those in 76SF, 105SF, 105BP, and 129T

Table 5.25, continued

COMPARATIVE FLAKE SIZE STATEMENTS BASED ON NONOVERLAPPING 95 PERCENT
CONFIDENCE INTERVALS FOR MEAN FLAKE THICKNESS

Collection Code	Mean Flake Thickness	Number of Pairs	Comparative Statement (These flakes tend to be . . .)
113BP	6.6	4	larger than those in 76SF, 105SF, 105BP, and 129T
120SF	6.2	1	smaller than those in 117SF
84SF	6.1	2	larger than those in 129T, but smaller than those in 117SF
"Large"			
117SF	8.0	10	larger than those in 76SF, 76ST, 77EX, 84SF, 105SF, 105FP, 105BP, 113SF, 120SF, and 129T

can be inferred. The above-defined groups will be referred to as having
"small," "medium," and "large" flakes. Finally, the confidence
intervals for mean flake thickness from 76FP, 76EX, 105EX, 106SF, 109SF,
113FP, 116SF, 129EX, and FLOOR were so wide that they overlapped with
each other, and with the intervals for all other collections.
Therefore, meaningful comparative statements concerning flake size
tendencies in these collections cannot be made at the 0.05 probability
level.

It is also worth noting that in all but one case, collections
from different intrasite provenience classes at the same site are
contained within the same flake size group. The sole exception to this
observation occurs at AZ EE:2:77, where 77EX falls in the "small"
category, while 77SF is contained in the "medium" group.

Although flake metric data are not available for AZ EE:1:104, it
seems likely on the basis of visual inspection, that the flakes from
this site would probably be best assigned to the "medium" size category.

To summarize, this analysis of flake size variation has shown
that statistically significant differences can be demonstrated among
collections with very large sample sizes of complete flakes, even though
the range of variation is restricted. The archaeological significance
of this variation will be discussed in a following section. Data used
in this analysis, including the 95 percent confidence intervals for mean

flake thickness, and the 25-by-25-cell comparison matrix are on file at the Cultural Resource Management Division, Arizona State Museum.

Complete Flake Cortex

Frequencies and percentages of complete flakes are given by cortex class (1 = no cortex; 2 = some, but less than 50% cortex; 3 = at least 50% cortex) for all analyzed collections in Table 5.26. Simple inspection of these data will show that 21 of the 25 collections are similar to each other in that completely noncortical flakes are the most abundant type, flakes with some, but less than 50 percent cortex are the second most common, and flakes with 50 percent or more cortex are the least common. Four collections deviate from this cortex class ranking. In both 76EX and 117SF Cortex Class 2 flakes outnumber noncortical flakes (Class 1), while those of Class 3 are still the least abundant. In 106SF and 113FP, the cortex class ranking is similar to that of the majority of the collections in that noncortical flakes are the dominant type. However, Classes 2 and 3 are equally represented.

At first glance then, flakes in 76EX, 117SF, 106SF, and 113FP tend to be more cortical than those of all other collections. At a finer level of analysis, Table 5.26 also shows that there is considerable variation in percentages of noncortical flakes, even among the majority of collections in which Cortex Classes 1, 2, and 3 are ranked in decreasing order of abundance. At one extreme for example, only 41 percent of the flakes in 76EX are noncortical, while nearly 77 percent of the flakes in 120SF are noncortical.

To better assess variation in proportions of the cortex classes, the percentages given in Table 5.26 were used to construct Figure 5.35. This diagram shows percentages of the three cortex classes plotted on triangular-coordinate graph paper, for each collection. Two groups were arbitrarily distinguished on the basis of this plot. In Group 1 collections, including 76FP, 76EX, 77SF, 84SF, 106SF, 113SF, 117SF, and FLOOR, less than 56 percent of the flakes are noncortical; cortex is more common in these collections than it is in all other collections. Among Group 1, 76EX, 106SF, 113FP, and FLOOR can be further distinguished by their high percentages of flakes with 50 percent or more cortex (Class 3). Within Group 2 which includes all other collections, 120SF appears to represent an extreme case, with the highest percentage of noncortical flakes, and the lowest percentage of Class 3 flakes.

Both Figure 5.35 and Table 5.26 show that collections from intrasite provenience classes at AZ EE:2:76, EE:2:77, and EE:2:113 do not always fall in the same cortex group. This suggests that there is substantial variation in cortex levels at these sites. In contrast, all collections from AZ EE:2:105 and AZ EE:2:129, the only other sites for which intrasite collections were analyzed, are members of Cortex Group 2. No generalization concerning complete flake cortex can be advanced for the unanalyzed assemblage from AZ EE:2:104.

Table 5.26

FREQUENCIES (f), PERCENTAGES (%), AND SAMPLE SIZE
OF COMPLETE FLAKES BY CORTEX CLASS FOR ALL ANALYZED COLLECTIONS

Collection Code	Cortex Class						Sample Size
	1		2		3		
	f	%	f	%	f	%	
76SF	247	60.7	137	33.7	23	5.7	407
76FP	16	48.5	14	42.4	3	9.1	33
76EX	20	40.8	21	42.9	8	16.3	49
76ST	58	62.4	32	34.4	3	3.2	93
77SF	118	49.4	106	44.4	15	6.3	239
77EX	22	64.7	10	29.4	2	5.9	34
84SF	89	46.4	85	44.3	18	9.4	192
105SF	796	67.1	305	25.7	86	7.2	1,187
105FP	24	61.5	10	25.6	5	12.8	39
105EX	12	60.0	6	30.0	2	10.0	20
105BP	65	67.7	22	22.9	9	9.4	96
106SF	7	53.8	3	23.1	3	23.1	13
107SF	62	69.7	19	21.3	8	9.0	89
109SF	15	60.0	8	32.0	2	8.0	25
113SF	453	52.6	342	39.7	67	7.8	862
113FP	15	55.6	6	22.2	6	22.2	27
113EX	92	59.7	49	31.8	13	8.4	154
113BP	92	64.3	38	26.6	13	9.1	143
116SF	17	56.7	10	33.3	3	10.0	30
117SF	11	42.3	12	46.2	3	11.5	26
120SF	59	76.6	17	22.1	1	1.3	77
129SF	87	68.0	33	25.8	8	6.3	128
129EX	13	61.9	6	28.6	2	9.5	21
129T	225	65.4	93	27.0	26	7.6	344
Floor	18	48.6	12	32.4	7	18.9	37

Cortex Classes: 1 — no cortex
2 — some, but less than 50 percent cortex
3 — at least 50 percent cortex

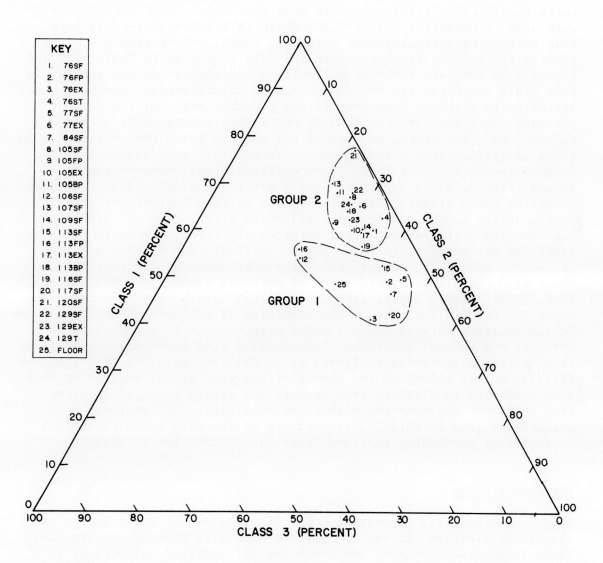

Figure 5.35 Triangular coordinate plot of percentages of complete flakes by cortex classes, for all analyzed collections.

Striking Platform Type

Frequencies of cortical, noncortical plain, faceted, and indeterminate striking platforms observed on complete flakes and proximal flake fragments combined, are given for each collection in Table 5.27. Platform type percentages, calculated on the basis of the three identifiable types only, are also provided. These percentages were used to construct Figure 5.36, which is a triangular-coordinate diagram showing percentages of cortical, plain, and faceted platforms plotted for each collection. Both the data presented in Table 5.27 and Figure 5.36 indicate that the collections are similar to one another in that plain platforms are the dominate type in all cases. However, some variation in platform type proportions is still evident; the three platform types vary by more than 20 percentage points each, across all collections. Therefore, an attempt was made to group the collections in terms of similarities and differences in platform type percentages. Because the collections do not form easily defined, nonoverlapping groups (Fig. 5.36), a number of purely arbitrary distinctions were used to define three groups. Group 1 consists of five collections (76FP, 105FP, 105EX, 120SF, 129EX, and 129T) which differ from all others in that faceted platforms outnumber cortical platforms. Among the remaining collections, in which plain, cortical, and faceted platforms are always the first, second, and third most abundant, respectively, those with the highest percentages of cortical platforms (76ST, 77SF, 84SF, 106SF, 107SF, 109SF, 116SF, and 117SF) have been designated as Group 2. Group 3 consists of the remaining 11 collections which tend to be intermediate between Group 1 and 2 with respect to proportions of cortical and faceted platforms. Figure 5.36 also shows that collections from intrasite provenience classes at AZ EE:2:76, EE:2:77, EE:2:105, and EE:2:129 do not belong to the same platform type group, suggesting that some variation in platform type proportions exists among collections from different proveniences within the same site. All analyzed collections from AZ EE:2:113 are members of the same group (Group 3). No statement concerning platform types can be made for AZ EE:1:104.

Platform Lipping

Frequencies, percentages, and sample sizes of the presence and absence of platform lipping on complete and split flakes, and proximal flake fragments, combined, are given for all analyzed collections in Table 5.28. These data indicate that percentages of the presence of platform lipping are very low in all cases; ranging from a maximum of about 10 percent in 106SF, to complete absence in 76EX. There is no reason to suspect that percentages of platform lipping are higher in the assemblage from AZ EE:1:104.

Edge Alteration Attributes

Frequencies, percentages, and sample sizes for the presence and absence of microflaking and abrasion on all deibitage categories (complete and split flakes, proximal and medial-distal flake fragments, and nonorientable fragments combined), are given for each analyzed collection in Table 5.29. These data indicate that there is extremely

Table 5.27

FREQUENCIES (f), PERCENTAGES (%), AND SAMPLE SIZES
OF CORTICAL, NONCORTICAL PLAIN, FACETED, AND INDETERMINATE STRIKING PLATFORMS
ON COMPLETE FLAKES AND PROXIMAL FLAKE FRAGMENTS,
COMBINED, FOR ALL ANALYZED COLLECTIONS

Collection Code	Cortical		Noncortical Plain		Faceted		Indeterminate	Total
	f	%	f	%	f	%	f	
76SF	89	18.7	322	67.8	64	13.5	71	546
76FP	5	12.8	27	69.2	7	17.9	7	46
76EX	10	17.2	42	72.4	6	10.3	6	64
76ST	31	24.4	74	58.3	22	17.3	15	142
77SF	56	22.9	161	65.7	28	11.4	30	275
77EX	5	13.2	31	81.6	2	5.3	2	40
84SF	56	38.0	122	61.0	22	11.0	30	230
105SF	195	13.4	1,085	74.8	170	11.7	202	1,652
105FP	3	6.0	38	76.0	9	18.0	1	51
105EX	4	16.0	15	60.0	6	24.0	3	28
105BP	19	17.6	71	65.7	18	16.7	17	125
106SF	4	28.6	10	71.4	0	.0	1	15
107SF	29	27.6	67	63.8	9	8.6	10	115
109SF	6	22.2	17	63.0	4	14.8	5	32
113SF	183	17.7	726	70.4	122	11.8	95	1,126
113FP	7	20.6	26	76.5	1	2.9	3	37
113EX	24	11.9	155	76.7	23	11.4	16	218
113BP	25	14.8	125	74.0	19	11.2	15	184
116SF	7	22.6	18	58.1	6	19.4	8	39
117SF	8	27.6	20	69.0	1	3.4	1	30
120SF	6	7.6	60	75.9	13	16.5	14	93
129SF	18	12.7	110	77.5	14	9.5	9	151
129EX	4	12.9	19	61.3	8	25.8	2	33
129T	56	14.1	258	65.2	82	20.7	68	464
Floor	7	18.4	29	76.3	2	5.3	1	39

Figure 5.27 Relative frequency distribution of cortical fragments by texture class.

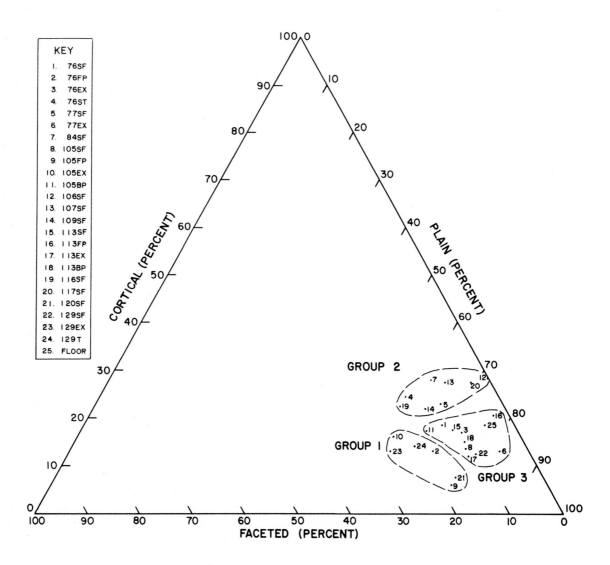

Figure 5.36   Triangular coordinate plot of cortical, plain, and faceted striking platforms.

Table 5.28

FREQUENCIES (f), PERCENTAGES (%), AND SAMPLE SIZES
OF THE PRESENCE AND ABSENCE OF PLATFORM LIPPING
ON COMPLETE FLAKES, SPLIT FLAKES, AND PROXIMAL FLAKE FRAGMENTS
COMBINED FOR ALL ANALYZED COLLECTIONS

| Collection Code | Platform Lipping | | | | | Sample Size |
| | Absent | | Present | | | |
	f	%	f	%		
76SF	601	96.6	21	3.4		622
76FP	54	96.4	2	3.6		56
76EX	72	100.0	0	.0		72
76ST	158	94.6	9	5.4		167
77SF	293	96.4	11	3.6		304
77EX	45	95.7	2	4.3		47
84SF	253	96.2	10	3.8		263
105SF	1,892	97.0	58	3.0		1,950
105FP	59	98.3	1	1.7		60
105EX	29	96.7	1	3.3		30
105BP	132	93.6	9	6.4		141
106SF	17	89.5	2	10.5		19
107SF	121	96.8	4	3.2		125
109SF	33	97.1	1	2.9		34
113SF	1,277	95.0	67	5.0		1,344
113FP	44	97.8	1	2.2		45
113EX	257	97.3	7	2.7		264
113BP	222	96.5	8	3.5		230
116SF	42	97.7	1	2.3		43
117SF	33	94.3	2	5.7		35
120SF	97	97.0	3	3.0		100
129SF	155	91.7	14	8.3		169
129EX	35	94.6	2	5.4		37
129T	501	91.4	47	8.6		548
Floor	40	95.2	2	4.8		42

Table 5.29

FREQUENCIES (f), PERCENTAGES (%), AND SAMPLE SIZES
OF THE PRESENCE AND ABSENCE OF MICROFLAKING AND ABRASION ON COMPLETE FLAKES, SPLIT FLAKES,
PROXIMAL FLAKE FRAGMENTS, MEDIAL–DISTAL FLAKE FRAGMENTS, AND NONOREINTABLE FRAGMENTS,
COMBINED FOR ALL ANALYZED COLLECTIONS

| Collection Code | Microflaking | | | | Abrasion | | | | Sample Size |
| | Absent | | Present | | Absent | | Present | | |
	f	%	f	%	f	%	f	%	
76SF	836	96.8	28	3.2	854	98.8	10	1.2	864
76FP	78	100.0	0	.0	78	100.0	0	.0	78
76EX	82	95.3	4	4.7	86	100.0	0	.0	86
76ST	220	94.4	13	5.6	228	97.9	5	2.1	233
77SF	378	95.7	17	4.3	392	99.2	3	.6	395
77EX	64	98.5	1	1.5	65	100.0	0	.0	65
84SF	355	93.7	24	6.3	378	99.7	1	.3	379
105SF	2,545	96.9	81	3.1	2,614	99.5	12	.5	2,626
105FP	88	97.8	2	2.2	90	100.0	0	.0	90
105EX	37	92.5	3	7.5	40	100.0	0	.0	40
105BP	191	96.0	8	4.0	198	99.5	1	.5	199
106SF	25	100.0	0	.0	25	100.0	0	.0	25
107SF	148	91.9	13	8.1	156	96.9	5	3.1	161
109SF	42	97.7	1	2.3	42	97.7	1	2.3	43
113SF	1,699	95.1	88	4.9	1,772	99.2	15	.8	1,787
113FP	73	98.6	1	1.4	74	100.0	0	.0	74
113EX	364	98.6	5	1.4	367	99.5	2	.5	369
113BP	299	97.4	8	2.6	300	97.7	7	2.3	307
116SF	54	94.7	3	5.3	57	100.0	0	.0	57
117SF	44	93.6	3	6.4	46	97.9	1	2.1	47
120SF	122	91.7	11	8.3	129	97.0	4	3.0	133
129SF	202	94.0	13	6.0	215	100.0	0	.0	215
129EX	49	96.1	2	3.9	51	100.0	0	.0	51
129T	756	93.8	50	6.2	802	99.5	4	.5	806
Floor	48	92.3	4	7.7	50	96.2	2	3.8	52

little variation among the collections with respect to the occurrence of
either edge alteration attribute. Like percentages of platform lipping,
percentages of both microflaking and abrasion are consistently very low,
never exceeding 10 percent in any collection. Although edge alteration
data are not available for AZ EE:1:104, it seems likely that
microflaking and abrasion are equally rare in this assemblage.

Tool Type Proportions

As noted at the beginning of this chapter, the tool typology was
developed on the basis of all tools recovered, and was not limited to
only those tools in the collections selected for detailed attribute
analysis. The exceptions to this generalization are utilized flakes
(flakes showing use-related edge alteration, but no intentional retouch)
which, because of practical limitations, were identified only during
attribute recording on the collections selected for detailed analysis.
The discussion of edge alteration above has demonstrated the relative
lack of variation in frequencies of utilized flakes among the analyzed
collections. Frequencies of all other tool types are given by
provenience class for each site in Tables 5.30 through 5.43. The
following tool type abbreviations and provenience class codes were
used to simplify presentation of those data:

Artifact Categories:
    IRP = Irregularly retouched piece
    DRF = Discontinuously retouched fragment
    CMN = Flake with continuous, marginal, nonextensive retouch
    CME = Flake with continuous marginal extensive retouch
    CRF = Continuously retouched fragment
    NBR = Nonextensive bifacial retouch
    LPFT = Large primary-flake tool

Provenience Classes:
    1   structure fill, including floor
    2   subfloor features, including floor pits and post holes
    3   extamural features, including borrow pits
    4   stripping, including nonfeature contexts
    5   surface collections (Feature 0)

In order to explore variation in tool type proportions, the data
presented in Tables 5.30-5.43 were simplified in two ways. First, the
number of tool types was reduced by combining some of the original
categories. This was done because tools of some categories were very
infrequent, even in some of the assemblages with large tool sample
sizes. The categories that were collapsed, and the resulting composite

Table 5.30

TOOL TYPE FREQUENCIES BY PROVENIENCE CLASS FOR AZ EE:2:76

Artifact Category	Provenience Class					Total
	1	2	3	4	5	
Notch 1	2			4		6
Notch 2	1		1	1		3
IRP	2			7		9
DRF	5			12		17
CMN	1			3		4
CME - side	2			3		5
CME - multisided	1					1
CME - concave	2			1		3
Scraper	31	1	4	41		77
CRF	19		2	19		40
NBR	1			2		3
Irregular biface - small	1			7		8
Irregular biface - large	1			1		2
Regular biface - whole	2			5	2	8
Regular biface - base	1			5		6
Regular biface - other	2			3		5
Preform - tip	2			1		3
Preform - base	1					1
Projectile Point - Hohokam	5	2		6	1	14
Drill 1	5			2		7
Drill 2	2					2
Projection 1	3			1		4
Projection 3	1					1
LPFT - knife	1					1
LPFT - chopper		1		1		2
Battered flake	1		1	1		3
Cobble hammerstone	2	2		2	1	7
Core hammerstone	5	1	5	1		12
Wedge	6		2	13		21
Total	108	7	15	142	3	275

Table 5.31

TOOL TYPE FREQUENCIES BY PROVENIENCE CLASS FOR AZ EE:2:77

Artifact Category	Provenience Class					Total
	1	2	3	4	5	
Notch 1				1		1
Notch 2				1		1
IRP	3			3	1	7
DRF	2			2		4
CMN	2					2
CME - side	1			2		3
Scraper	16	1	2	15		34
CRF	1			3		4
Irregular biface - small				1		1
Irregular biface - large	1			1		2
Regular biface - other	1					1
Drill 2	1					1
Projection 1	1			2		3
Projection 3					1	1
Battered flake	2					2
Cobble hammerstone	1		1	1		3
Core hammerstone	6	1	7	8		22
Wedge			1			1
Total	38	2	11	40	2	93

Table 5.32

TOOL TYPE FREQUENCIES BY PROVENIENCE CLASS FOR AZ EE:2:84

Artifact Category	Provenience Class					Total
	1	2	3	4	5	
Notch 1	1			1		2
Notch 2	2					2
IRP	4	1		3		8
DRF	2			1		3
CMN	1			2		3
CME - side				1		1
CME - multisided	1					1
Scraper	13			9		22
CRF	3	1		1		5
Irregular biface - large	2			1		3
Projectile Point - Archaic	1					1
Core hammerstone	4			1		5
Total	35	2	0	20	0	57

Table 5.33

TOOL TYPE FREQUENCIES BY PROVENIENCE CLASS FOR AZ EE:2:105

Artifact Category	Provenience Class					Total
	1	2	3	4	5	
Notch 1	7	1	3	4		15
Notch 2	4			4		8
IRP	20		1	19		40
DRF	21			10		31
CMN	5		1	7		13
CME - end	3			6		9
CME - side	14		1	15		30
CME - multisided	2			6		8
CME - concave	5			8		13
Scraper	102	2	5	121	1	231
CRF	55	2	1	37		95
NBR	9			5		14
Irregular biface - small	24		6	7		37
Irregular biface - large	1		2	8		11
Small biface - whole	17		2	6		25
Small biface - tip	1			1		2
Small biface - midsection	2			1		3
Small biface - base	6			3	2	11
Small biface - other	10		1	6		17
Preform - tip	13		2			15
Preform - base	6	1	2			9
Projectile Point - Hohokam	20	1	2	3	1	27
Projectile Point - Archaic	8		1	2	6	17
Drill 1	9	1				10
Drill 2	1			1		2
Projection 1	5			7		12
Projection 2	3			6	1	10
Projection 3	4		1	2		7
LPFT - knife	1			6		7
LPFT - chopper	2			2		4
Battered flake				2		2
Cobble hammerstone	9	1	1	13		24
Core hammerstone	19		14	37		70
Wedge	20		2	3		25
Total	428	9	48	358	11	854

Table 5.34

TOOL TYPE FREQUENCIES BY PROVENIENCE CLASS FOR AZ EE:2:106

| Artifact Category | Provenience Class | | | | | |
	1	2	3	4	5	Total
Scraper	2				1	3
CRF	1				1	2
Core hammerstone	1				1	2
Wedge						
Total	4				3	7

Table 5.35

TOOL TYPE FREQUENCIES BY PROVENIENCE CLASS FOR AZ EE:2:107

| Artifact Category | Provenience Class | | | | | |
	1	2	3	4	5	Total
CMN	1					1
Scraper	5			3		8
CRF	4					4
Projectile Point - Hohokam	1					1
Cobble hammerstone	2					2
Core hammerstone	5	2		2		9
Total	18	2		5		25

Table 5.36

TOOL TYPE FREQUENCIES BY PROVENIENCE CLASS FOR AZ EE:2:109

| Artifact Category | Provenience Class | | | | | |
	1	2	3	4	5	Total
Scraper	4				1	5
Projectile Point - Archaic					1	1
Core hammerstone	1			2		3
Wedge						
Total	5			2	2	9

Table 5.37

TOOL TYPE FREQUENCIES BY PROVENIENCE CLASS FOR AZ EE:2:113

Artifact Category	Provenience Class					Total
	1	2	3	4	5	
Notch 1	7	1	2			10
Notch 2	4		1	1		6
IRP	14	4	4	2		24
DRF	28	1	10	2		41
CMN	4	1	2	1		8
CME – end	3		1			4
CME – side	4	1	3			8
CME – multisided			3			3
CME – concave	2			1		3
Scraper	105	4	16	13		138
CRF	42	1	5	6		54
NBR	6					6
Irregular biface – small	5		1	1		7
Irregular biface – large	6	1	1	2		10
Preform – tip			1			1
Projectile Point – Hohokam	2		2			4
Projectile Point – Archaic	4		1			5
Drill 1	4					4
Drill 2	1		1			2
Projection 1	4	1		2		7
Projection 2	2					2
Projection 3	3					3
LPFT – knife	7	1	3			11
LPFT – chopper			2			2
Battered flake	3					3
Cobble hammerstone	4				1	5
Core hammerstone	43	5	6	1		55
Wedge	9					9
Total	317	21	65	32	1	436

Table 5.38

TOOL TYPE FREQUENCIES BY PROVENIENCE CLASS FOR AZ EE:2:116

Artifact Category	Provenience Class					Total
	1	2	3	4	5	
IRP				1		1
Scraper	1			3		4
Core hammerstone	1			1		2
Total	2			5		7

Table 5.39

TOOL TYPE FREQUENCIES BY PROVENIENCE CLASS FOR AZ EE:2:117

Artifact Category	Provenience Class					Total
	1	2	3	4	5	
Notch 1	1					1
DRF	1					1
Scraper		2	2	1		5
Cobble hammerstone			1			1
Core hammerstone	2					2
Total	4	2	3	1		10

Table 5.40

TOOL TYPE FREQUENCIES BY PROVENIENCE CLASS FOR AZ EE:2:120

Artifact Category	Provenience Class					Total
	1	2	3	4	5	
IRP	1			1		2
DRF	3					3
CMN	1					1
CME - side	3					3
Scraper	7			5		12
CRF	2					2
Irregular biface - large	1					1
Small biface base	1					1
Projectile Point - Hohokam	1					1
Drill 1	1					1
Cobble hammerstone	1					1
Core hammerstone	4	1		1		6
Wedge	1					1
Total	27	1		7		35

Table 5.41

TOOL TYPE FREQUENCIES BY PROVENIENCE CLASS FOR AZ EE:2:122

Artifact Category	Provenience Class					Total
	1	2	3	4	5	
DRF		1				1
Scraper	1			1		2
Total	1	1		1		3

Table 5.42

TOOL TYPE FREQUENCIES BY PROVENIENCE CLASS FOR AZ EE:2:129

| Artifact Category | Provenience Class | | | | | | Total |
	1	2	3	4	5	6	
Notch 1	1			1		3	5
Notch 2						1	1
IRP						3	3
DRF	2		2			2	6
CME – end	1						1
CME – side	1					1	2
CME – concave			1				1
Scraper	10	5	2			17	34
CRF	2		1			4	7
NBR						1	1
Irregular biface – small						1	1
Small biface – whole					1	5	6
Small biface – tip						2	2
Small biface – base						2	2
Small biface – other						2	2
Projection 1						1	1
LPFT – knife				1			1
Battered flake						1	1
Cobble hammerstone	1						1
Core hammerstone	3		1				4
Wedge	3					1	4
Total	24	6	8	1		47	86

Table 5.43

TOOL TYPE FREQUENCIES BY PROVENIENCE CLASS FOR AZ EE:1:104

| Artifact Category | Provenience Class | | | | | Total |
	1	2	3	4	5	
IRP			1			1
Scraper	5					5
Irregular biface – small			1			1
Total	5		2			7

tool types are summarized in Table 5.44. Second, even though the
frequencies given in Tables 5.30 through 5.43 are based on all recovered
tools except utilized flakes, tool sample sizes for some intrasite
provenience classes, and in some cases for entire sites, are often very
small. Therefore, some of the intrasite provenience classes were
collapsed, and in some cases, tool assemblages from different sites were
combined. For AZ EE:2:76, EE:2:77, EE:2:84, EE:2:105, EE:2:113, and
EE:2:120, the analysis of tool type proportions will be based on
assemblages consisting of tools from structure fill, subfloor features
(floor pits and post holes), floor contexts, and extramural features,
combined. Tools from stripping and backhoe backdirt are excluded
because these collections may be biased in favor of larger implements,
such as hammerstones, and against smaller artifacts types. Selective
surface collections, also excluded, may be biased in favor of "goodies,"
such as wedges, projectile points, and drills. At AZ EE:2:107, all
25 tools, including 20 from structure contexts, and 5 from stripping,
were treated as a single collection. Items recovered from nonscreened
stripping were included to increase the sample size from this site. The
possibility that this may have introduced certain biases will be
considered in the interpretation. At AZ EE:2:129, two tool assemblages
were treated separately. The first of these consists of all tools from
structure contexts and extramural features, combined. The second
collection contains all tools recovered by screening during excavation
of the sheet trash deposit. The former assemblage will be referred to
as "EE:2:129SF-EX," while the latter will be known as "EE:2:129T." Tool
sample sizes at the remaining sites (AZ EE:2:106, EE:2:109, EE:2:116,
EE:2:117, EE:2:122, and EE:1:104) are extremely small, never exceeding
10 in any case. Because one of the major research objectives is to
define the relationship between chipped stone artifact variability and
nonassemblage site characteristics, and because all of the sites
mentioned above are very similar to one another with respect to many
nonassemblage characteristics, tool assemblages form these sites were
combined to form a single collection. The resulting composite
assemblage includes all tools from these sites except those recovered
through selective surface collections (Feature 0). Here again, the
inclusion of tools from nonscreened stripping units and the resulting
biases will be considered in the interpretation. A more thorough
discussion of the basis on which these sites were grouped will be
presented below.

Frequencies, percentages, and sample sizes of tools by type,
for the above-defined assemblages are presented in Table 5.45. These
data were used to construct Figure 5.37, which shows the cumulative
percentage distribution of tool types for each assemblage. This diagram
shows that the assemblage from the sheet trash deposit at AZ EE:2:129
(129T) is distinguished from all other collections by a strikingly high
percentage of regular bifaces. Regular bifaces, both whole and broken,
account for more than 23 percent of the tools, and are outnumbered only
by scrapers (36%). Although the sample size for AZ EE:2:129T is only
47, the difference between this assemblage and all others with respect
to regular biface percentages is substantial. This tool type is
approximately three or more times more abundant in the assemblage from

Table 5.44

SUMMARY OF COLLAPSED TOOL TYPES

Composite Tool Type	Tool Type
Notches	Notch 1 Notch 2
IRF-CMN	Irregularly retouched pieces Flakes with continuous, marginal, nonextensive retouch
CME	Flakes with continuous, marginal, extensive retouch - end Flakes with continuous, marginal, extensive retouch - side Flakes with continuous, marginal, extensive retouch - multisided Flakes with continuous, marginal, extensive retouch - concave
Uniface Fragments	Discontinuously retouched fragments (DRF) Continuously retouched fragments (CRF)
Irregular Bifaces	Flakes with nonextensive, bifacial retouch (NBR) Small irregular bifaces (IBR - small) Large irregular bifaces (IBR - large)
Regular Bifaces	Small regular bifaces - whole Small regular bifaces - tip fragments Small regular bifaces - midsections Small regular bifaces - base fragments Small regular bifaces - other
Preforms	Preform - tip fragments Preform - base fragments
Projectile points	Projectile points - ceramic period Projectile points - Archaic period
Drills	Drill 1 Drill 2
Projections	Projection 1 Projection 2 Projection 3

Table 5.44, continued

SUMMARY OF COLLAPSED TOOL TYPES

Composite Tool Type	Tool Type
LPFT	Large primary-flake tool - knife
	Large primary-flake tool - chopper
Hammerstones	Core hammerstones
	Cobble hammerstones
	Battered flakes

Note: Scrapers and wedges are unchanged.

the sheet trash deposit at AZ EE:2:129 than in any other collection. Therefore, we can be reasonably certain that the high percentage of bifaces in this assemblage is not the product of chance.

Figure 5.37 also shows that the remaining collections are basically very similar to one another in that scrapers, uniface fragments, and hammerstones are usually the dominant categories, in varying proportions. Among these collections, those from AZ EE:2:76 and AZ EE:2:105 are very similar to each other, and all distinguished from the remaining assemblages on the basis of percentages of certain small tools. In particular, these two assemblages exhibit the highest percentages of regular bifaces, preforms, projectile points, and projections. In addition, percentages of drills and wedges are greater in these two collections than in most others. To a large extent, the comparatively high percentages of these small tools is off-set by relatively lower percentages of scrapers, uniface fragments, and hammerstones, which are less common at AZ EE:2:76 and AZ EE:2:105 than at most other sites. In general then, the tool assemblages from these two sites are the most diverse with respect to tool composition, and show the strongest representation of the widest range of types. The tool assemblages from AZ EE:2:76 and AZ EE:2:105 will be termed "heterogeneous."

In contrast, the assemblages from AZ EE:2:84, EE:2:107, EE:2:129SF-EX, and the composite assemblage from AZ EE:2:106, EE:2:109, EE:2:116, EE:2:117, EE:2:122, and EE:1:104 are recognized as a group because they are least diverse of all the collections. For example, most of the small tool categories, including regular bifaces, preforms, drills, projections, and wedges are not represented at all in these

Table 5.45

FREQUENCIES, PERCENTAGES, AND SAMPLE SIZES OF TOOLS BY TYPE FOR THE ANALYZED ASSEMBLAGES

Tool Type		AZ EE:2:76	AZ EE:2:77	AZ EE:2:84	AZ EE:2:105	AZ EE:2:107	AZ EE:2:113	AZ EE:2:120	AZ EE:2:129SF-EX	AZ EE:2:129T	Composite Assemblage+
Notches	f	4	0	3	15	0	15	0	1	4	1
	%	3.1	0	8.1	3.1	0	3.7	0	3.3	8.5	2.6
IRP-CMN	f	3	5	6	27	1	29	2	0	3	2
	%	2.3	9.8	16.2	5.6	4.0	7.2	7.1	0	6.4	5.3
CME	f	5	1	1	25	0	17	3	3	1	0
	%	3.8	2.0	2.7	5.2	0	4.2	10.7	10.0	2.1	0
Scrapers	f	36	19	13	109	8	125	7	15	17	22
	%	27.7	37.3	35.1	22.5	32.0	31.0	25.0	50.0	36.2	57.9
Uniface Fragments	f	26	3	6	79	4	87	5	4	6	3
	%	20.0	5.9	16.2	16.3	16.0	21.6	17.9	13.3	12.8	7.9
Irregular Bifaces	f	3	1	2	42	0	20	1	0	2	1
	%	2.3	2.0	5.4	8.7	0	5.0	3.6	0	4.3	2.6
Regular Bifaces	f	5	1	0	39	0	1	1	0	11	0
	%	3.8	2.0	0	8.0	0	0.2	3.6	0	23.4	0
Preforms	f	3	0	0	24	0	1	0	0	0	0
	%	2.3	0	0	4.9	0	0.2	0	0	0	0
Projectile Points	f	7	1	1	32	1	9	1	0	0	0
	%	5.4	2.0	2.7	6.6	4.0	2.2	3.6	0	0	0
Drills	f	7	1	0	11	0	6	1	0	0	0
	%	5.4	2.0	0	2.3	0	1.5	3.6	0	0	0
Projections	f	4	0	0	13	0	10	0	0	1	0
	%	3.1	0	0	2.7	0	2.5	0	0	2.1	0
LPFT	f	2	1	1	3	0	13	0	0	0	0
	%	1.5	2.0	2.7	0.6	0	3.2	0	0	0	0
Wedges	f	8	0	0	22	0	9	1	3	1	0
	%	6.2	0	0	4.5	0	2.2	3.6	10.0	2.1	0
Hammerstones	f	17	18	4	44	11	61	6	4	1	9
	%	13.1	35.3	10.8	9.1	44.0	15.1	21.4	13.3	2.1	23.7
Sample Size		130	51	37	485	25	403	28	30	47	38

+Combined tool assemblages from EE:2:106, EE:2:109, EE:2:116, EE:2:117, EE:2:122, and EE:1:104.

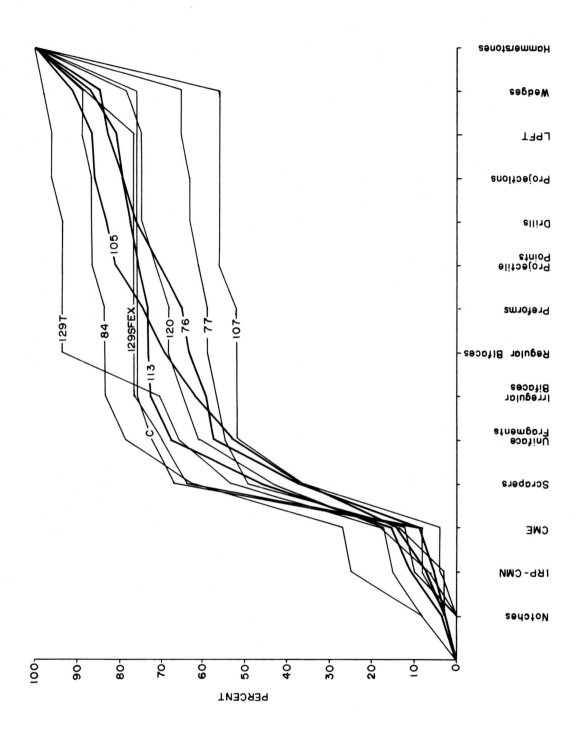

Figure 5.37   Cumulative percentage distributions of tool types for the analyzed assemblages.

assemblages.   At AZ EE:2:107, the absence of small tools is largely offset by a high percentage of hammerstones, while in the assemblages from
AZ EE:2:84, EE:2:129SF-EX, and the composite assemblage, the lack of
tool diversity is primarily the result of a high percentage of scrapers.
The assemblages from AZ EE:2:84, EE:2:107, EE:2:129SF-EX, and the
composite assemblage will be termed "homogeneous" with respect to tool
type composition.

Finally, the assemblages from the remaining three sites
(AZ EE:2:77, EE:2:113, and EE:2:120) appear to represent intermediate
cases with respect to tool diversity.   At AZ EE:2:113, for example,
projectile points, drills, projections, and wedges are present, but not
strongly represented, while regular bifaces and preforms are essentially
absent.   At AZ EE:2:120, percentages of regular bifaces, projectile
points, and drills are similar to those in the collections with
heterogeneous tool composition (AZ EE:2:76 and EE:2:105), but preforms
and projections are absent.   At AZ EE:2:77, wedges and preforms are
absent, but all other small tool categories are at least poorly
represented.   Therefore, the assemblages from AZ EE:2:77, EE:2:113, and
EE:2:120 will be referred to as being "intermediate" in diversity.

To summarize, four groups of assemblages have been distinguished.
The first of these consists of the single collection from the sheet
trash deposit at AZ EE:2:129 (129T).   This assemblage is unique in its
very high percentage of regular bifaces.   Although the remaining
collections are very similar to one another, three groups have been
distinguished primarily on the basis of proportions of scrapers,
hammerstones, and small tools.   The assemblages from AZ EE:2:76 and
EE:2:105 are heterogeneous, showing the strongest representation of the
widest range of tool types.   Assemblages from AZ EE:2:84, EE:2:107,
EE:2:129SF-EX, and the composite collection are dominated by either
scrapers or hammerstones, and are therefore homogeneous.   The remaining
assemblages, including AZ EE:2:77, EE:2:113, and EE:2:120 are
intermediate with respect to tool diversity.   Notches, irregularly
retouched pieces, flakes with continuous marginal retouch, uniface
fragments, irregular bifaces, and large primary flake tools were not
very useful in differentiating the above-defined groups.

Only three of the tool assemblages described above contain more
than 100 implements.   The implications of small tool sample sizes in the
remaining collections will be discussed in the interpretation of
variation in tool type proportions.

Projectile Point Types

Frequencies of the projectile point types defined under
"Analysis Terms and Procedures" are given by specific provenience in
Table 5.46.   These data indicate that three of the sites (AZ EE:2:76,
EE:2:105, and EE:2:113) combined, account for 67 (94 %) of the 71 points
recovered.   Of these three projectile point assemblages, the assemblage
of 14 points from AZ EE:2:76 is notable in several respects.   First, it
shows the widest range of Hohokam projectile point styles, including all

Table 5.46

PROJECTILE POINT TYPE FREQUENCIES BY PROVENIENCE

Provenience		Projectile Point Types													Total
		1	2	3	4	5	6	7	8	9	10	11	12	13	
AZ EE:2:76	Feature 7			4			1								5
	Feature 8				1										1
	Feature 27			1											1
	Stripping	1	2	2			1								6
	Feature 0					1									1
AZ EE:2:84	Stripping								1						1
AZ EE:2:105	Feature 6	2		1									1		4
	Feature 7	1	3								1				5
	Feature 9	1													1
	Feature 10	1							1						2
	Feature 11	1				1									2
	Feature 41	1													1
	Feature 50	2							1						3
	Feature 71001		1							1	1				3
	Feature 71200	1	3												4
	Feature 87		1							1					2
	Feature 88									1					1
	Feature 91		1												1
	Feature 4[1]		1												1
	Feature 57[1]	1													1
	Ballcourt									1					1
	Stripping	1	1			1			1					1	5
	Feature 0		1							3		1		2	7
AZ EE:2:107	Feature 1			1											1
AZ EE:2:109	Feature 0								1						1
AZ EE:2:113	Feature 10		1												1
	Feature 11										1				1
	Feature 6200								1						1
	Feature 6300										1				1
	Feature 83		1												1
	Feature 154								1						1
	Feature 13[2]		1								1				2
	Feature 164[1]							1							1
AZ EE:2:120	Feature 1			1											1
Total		13	17	10	1	3	2	1	7	7	5	1	1	3	71

Note: Feature numbers refers to structures, except extramural features ([1]), and borrow pit ([2]).

defined types (Types 1 through 7). In contrast, only three Hohokam
point types (Types 1, 2, and 5) are present at AZ EE:2:105, while only
Types 2 and 6 are known from AZ EE:2:113. Second, the assemblage from
AZ EE:2:76 differs from those from both AZ EE:2:105 and EE:2:113 in that
elongate points with serrate blades and laterally expanding, convex or
straight bases (Type 3) are the dominant type. Only one example was
recovered at AZ EE:2:105, and the type is completely absent at
AZ EE:2:113. Third, Archaic projectile points are absent at AZ EE:2:76.
In contrast, preceramic points are present at AZ EE:2:113, and are
especially well represented at AZ EE:2:105.

        Of the 44 points from AZ EE:2:105, 27 (61 %) can be attributed
to the Hohokam. All but three are either small triangular points with
short contracting stems (Type 1) or small triangular points with serrate
blades and concave bases (Type 2), represented by 24 examples in each
case. The remaining three Hohokam points from AZ EE:2:105 consist of
two nondescript triangular points with concave bases (Type 5), and the
above-mentioned Type 3 point. All six defined preceramic styles
(Types 8 through 13) are present at AZ EE:2:105. Of these, large,
triangular points with concave bases (Type 9) and San Pedro points
(Type 8) seem to be the dominant styles.

        Four of the nine points from AZ EE:2:113 are clearly
attributable to the Hohokam. Three of these are small triangular points
with serrate blades and concave bases (Type 2), while the fourth is a
small triangular point with convex blade edges and a concave base
(Type 6). The remaining five points from this site consist of three
corner-notched, stemmed points (Type 10), and two San Pedro points. In
comparison to AZ EE:2:105 then, the point assemblage from AZ EE:2:113
differs in two respects. First, while small triangular points with
short, contracting stems are strongly represented at AZ EE:2:105, this
style is absent at AZ EE:2:113. Second, AZ EE:2:113 shows a much more
restricted range of preceramic styles than does AZ EE:2:105.
AZ EE:2:113 yielded both absolutely and relatively fewer projectile
points than did either AZ EE:2:76 or AZ EE:2:105.

        The remainder of the points collected during mitigation
activities at Hohokam sites in the ANAMAX-Rosemont project area consists
of two Type 3 points, one each from AZ EE:2:107 and AZ EE:2:120, and two
San Pedro points, one each from AZ EE:2:84 and AZ EE:2:109.

Scraper Size

        In order to investigate intersite variation in scraper size,
eight scraper assemblages were analyzed. The analyzed assemblages from
AZ EE:2:76, EE:2:77, EE:2:84, and EE:2:129 included all recovered
specimens; from AZ EE:2:105 and EE:2:113, only scrapers from structure
contexts and extramural features are included. As was the case with
tool type proportions, scraper sample sizes at the remaining sites were
so low that assemblages from different sites were combined for this
analysis. All recovered scrapers from AZ EE:2:107 and AZ EE:2:120 were
treated as a single assemblage, as were all scrapers from AZ EE:2:106,

EE:2:109, EE:2:116, EE:2:117, and EE:2:122. Here again, these sites were grouped on the basis of similarities in certain nonassemblage site characteristics; a detailed justification for these groupings will be provided in a later section. No scraper data are available for AZ EE:1:104.

Means and standard deviations for scraper length, width, and thickness, and sample sizes are given for each of the eight analyzed assemblages in Table 5.47. These data indicate that scrapers from AZ EE:2:76, EE:2:84, EE:2:105, EE:2:113, and EE:2:129, and the composite assemblage from AZ EE:2:107 and EE:2:120 are essentially the same with respect to size. Among these collections, mean length varies by only 0.4 cm, mean width by 0.5 cm, and mean thickness by 0.2 cm. Mean lengths, widths, and thicknesses for scrapers from AZ EE:2:77, and for the composite assemblage from the rest of the sites are somewhat greater than they are for the above mentioned collections; however, because sample sizes for AZ EE:2:77 and the composite collection are only 34 and 18, respectively, the statistical significance of the differences in scraper size between these two collections, and all others, is open to serious question. In general then, it appears that there is little if any meaningful intersite variation in scraper size.

Table 5.47

MEAN, STANDARD DEVIATION, AND SAMPLE SIZE FOR WHOLE SCRAPER
LENGTH, WIDTH, AND THICKNESS BY TEXTURE CLASS
FOR ANALYZED SITES AND SITE GROUPS

Site Group	Length (cm) $\bar{x}$	Length (cm) sd	Width (cm) $\bar{x}$	Width (cm) sd	Thickness (cm) $\bar{x}$	Thickness (cm) sd	Sample Size
AZ EE:2:76	5.3	2.1	4.0	1.9	2.0	1.3	76
AZ EE:2:77	6.7	2.8	5.1	2.0	2.7	1.2	34
AZ EE:2:84	5.5	1.3	4.5	1.5	2.0	0.7	22
AZ EE:2:105	5.5	1.7	4.1	1.4	1.9	0.9	102
AZ EE:2:113	5.6	1.7	4.3	1.4	2.1	0.8	123
AZ EE:2:129	5.5	2.1	4.3	1.5	2.0	0.9	34
AZ EE:2:107, 120	5.7	2.1	4.3	1.2	2.0	1.0	20
AZ EE:2:106, 109, 116, 117, 122	7.5	3.3	6.2	2.9	2.9	2.0	18

Scraper Retouch Extent

The eight scraper assemblages defined in the preceding discussion were also described in terms of retouch extent. Frequencies and percentages of scrapers by retouch extent percentage classes (as defined earlier), mean and standard deviation retouch extent percentage (calculated using class midpoints), and sample sizes are given for each of the eight scraper assemblages in Table 5.48. These data show that, for the two sites with sample sizes greater than 100 (AZ EE:2:105 and AZ EE:2:113) mean retouch extent percentages are almost identical, 46.3 and 45.3, respectively. Among those assemblages with between 20 and 100 scrapers (AZ EE:2:76, EE:2:77, EE:2:84, and EE:2:129) mean retouch extent percentages range from 46.1 to 51.0. Although these values tend to be higher than those for AZ EE:2:105 and AZ EE:2:113, the difference is slight. The remaining two collections (the composite assemblages from AZ EE:2:107 and EE:2:120, and from AZ EE:2:106, EE:2:109, EE:2:116, EE:2:117, and EE:2:122) both show mean retouch extent percentages which differ markedly from those in all other collections. Once again, however, these differences are uninterpretable because of very small sample sizes.

Summary

So far, this analysis has examined variation in a number of assemblage characteristics among sites, and where sample sizes have permitted, among major provenience classes within sites. The results of these investigations are summarized below.

Substantial variation in material type proportions has been demonstrated among assemblages from different sites, but is not strongly evident among collections from different provenience classes within sites. The assemblages from AZ EE:2:106 and AZ EE:1:104 are unlike all others in that they are composed almost entirely of quartzite. All other collections are much more heterogeneous with respect to material composition. Of these, the assemblage from AZ EE:2:109 is the only one in which silicified limestone is the dominant material. Among the remaining sites, in which either quartzite or metasediment is the most common material, two groups have been distinguished on the basis of differences in the proportions of these two materials. All collections from AZ EE:2:113 and AZ EE:2:129, and the single collection from AZ EE:2:84 are essentially similar in that metasediment is only slightly less abundant, or more abundant than quartzite. At all remaining sites, including AZ EE:2:76, EE:2:77, EE:2:105, EE:2:107, EE:2:116, EE:2:117, and EE:2:120, quartzite is at least three times more abundant than is metasediment. Sites in the latter group also show higher percentages of chert than AZ EE:2:84, EE:2:113, and EE:2:129.

In comparison to material type composition, variation in other assemblage characteristics examined tends to be very limited; however, differences among assemblages with respect to some of these characteristics may be statistically significant. For example, the cluster analysis of artifact category proportions suggests that at least two

Table 5.48

FREQUENCIES(f) AND PERCENTAGES(%) OF SCRAPERS BY RETOUCH EXTENT PERCENTAGE CLASS MEAN(x̄) AND STANDARD DEVIATION(sd) RETOUCH EXTENT PERCENTAGE*, AND SAMPLE SIZES FOR AZ EE:2:76, 77, 84, 105, 113 AND 129, SEPARATELY, FOR AZ EE:2:107 AND 120 COMBINED, AND AZ EE:2:106, 109, 116, 117 AND 122 COMBINED

Site Number		1	2	3	4	5	6	7	8	9	10	Mean	sd	Sample Size
AZ EE:2:76	f	0	5	13	13	15	13	7	2	6	2	47.1	20.1	76
	%		6.6	17.1	17.1	19.7	17.1	9.2	2.6	7.9	2.6			
AZ EE:2:77	f	0	2	6	7	6	1	4	3	0	5	50.7	25.1	34
	%		5.9	17.6	20.6	17.6	2.9	11.8	8.8		14.7			
AZ EE:2:84	f	0	2	3	2	6	3	1	2	0	3	51.0	24.4	22
	%		9.1	13.6	9.1	27.3	13.6	4.5	9.1		13.6			
AZ EE:2:105	f	1	10	13	22	21	11	6	9	5	4	46.3	21.7	102
	%	1.0	9.8	12.7	21.6	20.6	10.8	5.9	8.8	4.9	3.9			
AZ EE:2:113	f	2	11	22	14	29	20	12	3	7	3	45.3	20.5	123
	%	1.6	8.9	17.9	11.4	23.6	16.3	9.8	2.4	5.7	2.4			
AZ EE:2:129	f	0	1	4	12	6	5	0	5	0	1	46.1	18.4	34
	%		2.9	11.8	35.3	17.6	14.7		14.7		2.9			
AZ EE:2:107, 120	f	0	2	4	6	4	3	0	0	1	0	39.0	16.3	20
	%		10.0	20.0	30.0	20.0	15.0			5.0				
AZ EE:2:106, 109,116,117, 122	f	0	0	2	4	2	2	3	3	1	1	55.5	21.4	18
	%			11.1	22.2	11.1	11.1	16.7	16.7	5.6	5.6			

Retouch Extent Percentage Class

*Calculated from class midpoints

groups of assemblages can be distinguished on the basis of differences in percentages of complete flakes, flake fragments, cores, and hammerstones. The first group (Group 1) consists of the structure fill assemblages from AZ EE:2:77, EE:2:106, EE:2:107, EE:2:109, EE:2:116, EE:2:117, EE:2:120, and EE:2:129, the extramural feature collections from EE:2:76, EE:2:77, and EE:2:105, and the composite collection from structure floors at all sites ("FLOOR"). The second group (Group 2) contains the structure fill assemblages from AZ EE:2:76, EE:2:84, and EE:2:105, all four collections from AZ EE:2:113, the floor pit collections from AZ EE:2:76 and EE:2:105, the surface stripping assemblage from AZ EE:2:76, the borrow pit collection from AZ EE:2:105, and both the extramural and sheet trash assemblages from AZ EE:2:129. In comparison to Group 2, Group 1 collections tend to show somewhat higher percentages of complete flakes, and lower percentages of flake fragments, especially medial-distal flake fragments. Group 1 collections also tend to have higher percentages of cores and hammerstones than do Group 2 collections. Percentages of retouched pieces and nonorientable fragments are approximately the same in both groups.

Although the analyzed collections are very similar to one another with respect to flake size, analysis of the 95 percent confidence intervals for mean flake thickness has shown that three groups of collections can be recognized. In comparison to flakes in many of the other collections, those from AZ EE:2:117 tend to be the largest. At the opposite extreme, the structure fill and stripping collections from AZ EE:2:76, all assemblages from AZ EE:2:105 except that from extramural features, the sheet trash assemblage from AZ EE:2:129, and the extramural feature collection from AZ EE:2:77 have flakes which tend to be smaller than those of most other assemblages. Between these two extremes, the structure fill assemblages from AZ EE:2:77, EE:2:84, EE:2:107, EE:2:113, EE:2:120, and EE:2:129, and both the extramural feature and borrow pit collections from AZ EE:2:113, tend to be intermediate with respect to flake size.

Two collection groups have been distinguished with respect to complete flake cortex. In comparison to all other collections, the structure fill assemblages from AZ EE:2:77, EE:2:84, EE:2:106, EE:2:113, and EE:2:117, the floor pit assemblages from AZ EE:2:76 and EE:2:113, and the composite floor assemblage tend to be more cortical.

All of the analyzed collections are similar to one another in that noncortical plain striking platforms are the most common platform type. However, the floor pit assemblages from AZ EE:2:76 and EE:2:105, the extramural feature collections from AZ EE:2:105 and EE:2:129, the structure fill assemblage from AZ EE:2:120, and the sheet trash collection from AZ EE:2:129 have been grouped because percentages of faceted platforms are greater than cortical platform percentages in these collections. In contrast, percentages of cortical striking platforms are highest in the structure fill assemblages from AZ EE:2:77, EE:2:84, EE:2:106, EE:2:107, EE:2:109, EE:2:116, and EE:2:117, and in the surface stripping assemblage from AZ EE:2:76. The remaining collections are intermediate with respect to proportions of cortical and faceted striking platforms.

The tool assemblage from the sheet trash deposit at AZ EE:2:129 differs from all other tool assemblages in its high percentage of regular bifaces. All other tool assemblages are similar to one another in that scrapers, uniface fragments, and hammerstones are the dominant tool types, although their proportions vary. Within these assemblages, however, three groups of sites have been distinguished in terms of tool diversity. The tool assemblages from AZ EE:2:76 and EE:2:105 are the most diverse, showing the highest percentages of the full range of tool forms, including small tools such as regular bifaces, preforms, projectile points, drills, projections, and wedges. At the opposite diversity extreme, the tool assemblages from AZ EE:2:84, EE:2:107, the composite structure fill-extramural feature assemblage from AZ EE:2:129, and the composite assemblage from AZ EE:2:106, EE:2:109, EE:2:116, EE:2:117, EE:2:122, and EE:1:104 are the least diverse in tool composition. Small bifacial tools are generally absent in these collections, while either scrapers or hammerstones are the dominant types. Tool assemblages identified as being intermediate with respect to diversity are those from AZ EE:2:77, EE:2:113, and EE:2:120.

Variation in material texture, scraper size and retouch extent, frequencies of striking platform lipping, and frequencies of micro-flaking and abrasion on debitage is so limited that, at the present level of analysis, the collections are essentially the same with respect to these characteristics.

Interpretation of Observed Variation

The purpose of this discussion is to evaluate the extent to which assemblage variation among sites and major provenience classes within sites can be attributed to differences in material character-istics, the object, technique, and intensity of reduction, spatial patterns of reduction, use, and discard, and most importantly, occupational factors and site function. Before proceeding with this evaluation, it will be necessary to group the sites into classes reflecting broad differences in occupation intensity and permanence. Toward this end, five nonassemblage site characteristics, presumably indicative of differences in the nature of site occupations, were considered. These characteristics include artifact density, numbers of structures, extramural features, and burials, and occupation span. The underlying assumption made here is that sites with higher artifact densities, greater numbers of structures, extramural features, and burials, and longer occupation spans were more intensively and permanently occupied than those with lower artifact densities, fewer features, and shorter occupation spans.

Artifact densities were calculated on the basis of the number of sherds and flaked stone artifacts per cubic meter of structure fill, for all structures (collectively) at each site. Numbers of structures were determined on the basis of the minimum known number of pit houses at each site. Note that no assumptions are made regarding structure contemporaneity; that is, the minimum number of structures at each site cannot be taken as the number of pit houses occupied at any given time. Further, the number of structures is in many cases greater than the number of house pits because single house pits were often used through time for more than one structure. Minimum numbers of extramural features, excluding burials, are based on the known number of such features. In most cases, these numbers may be taken as reasonably accurate, or at least as comparable estimates of the number of extramural features present at each site. The most obvious exception to this generalization is at AZ EE:2:84, where the spatial distribution of known extramural features in relation to nonexcavated areas suggests that a substantial number of pits remain unexposed. Minimum numbers of burials include known occurrences of both cremations and inhumations for each site. Occupation span was determined on the basis of ceramic evidence, and is expressed as being either "short" or "long." Sites with short occupation spans are those which yielded ceramic types that were produced within about 100 years. Sites with long occupation spans are those which produced ceramic assemblages representing 200 or more years. It is important to recall that occupation span is not synonymous with occupation duration because many of the sites were probably occupied intermittently.

Three classes of sites were distinguished on the basis of a subjective evaluation of similarities and differences with respect to the above-defined nonassemblage characteristics. These site groupings will be referred to as occupation classes. Artifact densities, minimum numbers of structures, extramural features, and burials, and occupation span are given for each site in Table 5.49. This table indicates that Class I sites, including AZ EE:2:105, EE:2:113, and EE:2:76, are distinguished from all other sites because they have the highest artifact densities (from 243 to 341 artifacts per cubic meter), the greatest numbers of structures (17 to 32), and the greatest numbers of extramural features (74 to 214). In addition, both AZ EE:2:76 and EE:2:113 yielded at least three times as many burials as any other site. The number of burials known from AZ EE:2:105 is unusually low in comparison to the other two Class I sites; an anomaly which will be discussed by Ferg in Chapter 10. Sites AZ EE:2:76, EE:2:105, and EE:2:113 are further distinguished from all but one of the other sites because they all have long occupation spans. AZ EE:2:129 is the only other site with an occupation span which exceeds 200 years. In general then, the nonassemblage characteristics of AZ EE:2:76, EE:2:105, and EE:2:113 clearly indicate that these sites represent the most substantial known Hohokam occupations in the study area.

At the opposite extreme of occupation intensity and permanence, Class III sites, including AZ EE:2:106, EE:2:109, EE:1:104, EE:2:116, EE:2:117, and EE:2:122, represent the least substantial occupations of all sites under consideration. These sites have short occupation spans, and are most clearly distinguished from all other sites by having the lowest artifact densities (from 18 to 58 artifacts per cubic meter), and, with the exception of AZ EE:2:122, no burials. Further, at most Class III sites, the numbers of both structures and extramural features tend to be lower than they are at most other sites.

Table 5.49

ARTIFACT DENSITY, NUMBERS OF STRUCTURES, EXTRAMURAL FEATURES, AND BURIALS,
AND OCCUPATION SPAN FOR ALL SITES, BY OCCUPATION CLASS

Occupation Class	Site Number	Artifact Density[1]	Minimum Number of Structures	Minimum Number of Extramural Features	Minimum Number of Burials[2]	Cañada del Oro	Rillito	Early Rincon	Middle Rincon	Late Rincon	Early Tanque Verde	Relative Lenght of Occupation
I	AZ EE:2:105	341	32	108	5	+	+	+				Long
	AZ EE:2:113	241	14	214	23	+	+	+				Long
	AZ EE:2:76	254	17	74	27	+	+	+	+	+	+	Long
II	AZ EE:2:77	164	9	49	8			+	+			Short
	AZ EE:2:129	133	4	14	1		+	+	+	+		Long
	AZ EE:2:84	93	4	21	1		+	+				Short
	AZ EE:2:107	103	5	6	5				+			Short
	AZ EE:2:120	108	7	4	2				+			Short
III	AZ EE:2:106	58	5	6	0					+	+	Short
	AZ EE:2:109	22	5	5	0				+			Short
	AZ EE:1:104	28	2	2	0				+	+		Short
	AZ EE:2:117	21	2	15	0					+	+	Short
	AZ EE:2:116	56	3	0	0					+	+	Short
	AZ EE:2:122	18	2	3	1					+	+	Short

Class II sites, AZ EE:2:77, EE:2:129, EE:2:84, EE:2:107, and EE:2:120, appear to be intermediate with respect to occupation intensity. These sites have artifact densities which are lower than those of Class I sites, but higher than those characteristic of Class III sites. In addition, burials are present at Class II sites, but tend to be fewer than at Class I sites. Class II sites can be further distinguished from Class I sites in having fewer structures and extramural features. Thus, although there is considerable overlap between Classes II and III with respect to numbers of structures and extramural features, Class II sites, collectively, tend to have more of both of these kinds of features than do Class III sites. Four of the five Class II sites have short occupations spans, and are in this sense more similar to Class III than Class I sites. As noted above, occupation span at AZ EE:2:129 is long, unlike other Class II sites.

Returning now to the interpretation of flaked stone assemblage variation, the analysis has shown that the most obvious and most easily demonstrated intersite assemblage variation is in material type composition. Two factors were identified in the theoretical discussions as potential contributors to differences in material type composition: source proximity and occupational factors. With regard to the latter, it was hypothesized that localized material shortages may have developed in association with extended occupations involving large numbers of people. As a result, the inhabitants of more intensively occupied sites may have had to travel farther afield to obtain sufficient quantities of material than did the inhabitants of sites which were nonintensively occupied for shorter periods. It was therefore suggested that assemblages from more intensively occupied sites should have more heterogeneous material compositions than those from less intensively occupied site. A comparison of Figure 5.31 and Table 5.49 will show that material type composition is not patterned by occupational site class. For example, although all three Class I sites (AZ EE:2:105, EE:2:113, and EE:2:76) have heterogeneous material compositions, all five Class II sites (AZ EE:2:77, EE:2:84, EE:2:107 EE:2:120, and EE:2:129) and three of the Class III sites (AZ EE:2:109, EE:2:116, and EE:2:117) also have heterogeneous material compositions. Therefore, the hypothesis that occupational factors have contributed to variation in material composition must be rejected.

Instead, variation in material composition is much more easily explained by source proximity. For example, the assemblages from AZ EE:2:76, EE:2:77, EE:2:105, EE:2:107, EE:2:116, EE:2:117, and EE:2:120 are heterogeneous, and are very similar to one another. All of these sites are located in close proximity to either of two major drainages, Barrel or South canyons (Fig. 5.38) in which a wide variety of materials is available. Sites AZ EE:2:84, EE:2:113, and EE:2:129 also have heterogeneous assemblages, but differ from the sites mentioned above in having higher percentages of metasediment. These sites are located within a few minutes walk from one another, near the confluence of the drainages of Barrel and McCleary canyons. The similarity in material composition of the assemblages from these sites, and especially their greater percentages of metasediment, suggest that a source of this material is located nearby. More specifically, metasediments may be

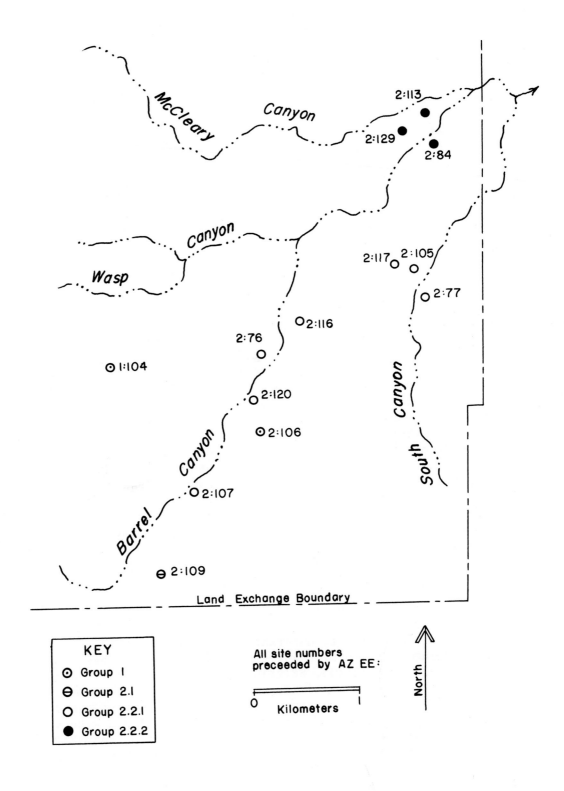

Figure 5.38 Map of the Rosemont area showing site locations and the material type composition group.

more abundant in the alluvial gravels which make up the ridges on which
these sites are located. Alternatively, these materials may be carried
downstream by the McCleary or Wasp canyon drainages from a source or
sources above the sites. Therefore, the differences in material
composition between these three sites, as a group, and the other sites
discussed so far may indicate that the inhabitants of AZ EE:2:84,
EE:2:113, and EE:2:129 had immediate access to a slightly different
range of materials than did the occupants of AZ EE:2:76, EE:2:77,
EE:2:105, EE:2:107, EE:2:116, EE:2:117, or EE:2:120.

        AZ EE:2:106, EE:2:109, and EE:1:104, unlike all others, are
located farther from major drainages. As a result, the material
compositions of the assemblages from these three sites reflect the use
of materials which were immediately available on the ridges and slopes
surrounding the sites, rather than the use of the wider range of
materials available in the major drainages. For example, the high
percentage of silicified limestone at AZ EE:2:109 simply reflects the
fact that cobbles of this material are common on the ridges near this
site. In a similar fashion, the dominance of gray green quartzite in
the assemblages from both AZ EE:2:106 and EE:1:104 reflects the
abundance of this material on the ridge slopes and in minor drainages
surrounding these sites. Interestingly, AZ EE:2:106 is not located
much farther from the Barrel Canyon drainage than is AZ EE:2:107, yet
substantial differences in material diversity exists between the
assemblages from these two sites. This suggests that, while the
inhabitants of AZ EE:2:107 used the range of materials present in
the drainage of Barrel Canyon, the inhabitants of AZ EE:2:106 were
apparently unwilling to walk even a comparatively short distance to take
advantage of these same materials. Instead, they used the quartzite
which was immediately available on the ridge slopes and in the minor
drainages surrounding the site.

        The lack of substantial variation in material composition among
assemblages from major provenience classes within the same site suggests
that spatial patterns of reduction, use, and discard have acted to
homogenize the assemblages.

        Finally, it is noteworthy that only six obsidian artifacts were
recovered from the ANAMAX-Rosemont Hohokam sites. Of these, only the
Type 2 projectile point shown in Figure 5.11y is definitely of Hohokam
manufacture. The other five obsidian artifacts include three
preceramic-style projectile points, a single small proximal flake
fragment, and a small unworked nodule. While the last two may have been
used by the Hohokam, it seems likely that their presence at AZ EE:2:105
was originally associated with the Archaic occupation of the site area
(Huckell 1984a: 92).

        In summary, the Rosemont Hohokam relied almost exclusively on
immediately available materials for the manufacture of stone tools.
Intersite variation in material type composition is most reasonably
interpreted as reflecting differences in source proximity and does not
appear to be related to differences in occupational factors.

While the analysis has demonstrated substantial variation in material type composition, it has also shown that variation in some of the assemblage characteristics examined, including material texture, scraper size and retouch extent, and platform lipping and edge alteration on debitage, is essentially nonexistent. The general lack of variation in material texture among all analyzed collections simply means that the inhabitants of different sites selected materials having basically similar properties for the manufacture of stone tools, although the range of petrologically defined rock types varied considerably from site to site.

The consistently very low occurrence of platform lipping further indicates that hard-hammer percussion is the dominant reduction technique reflected in the analyzed assemblages, and that soft-hammer percussion was probably not used with any regularity at any of the sites. The assemblage from the sheet trash deposit at AZ EE:2:129 is an exception to this generalization. Evidence that soft-hammer percussion was used to produce some of the artifacts in this assemblage will be explored in greater detail in the interpretation of variation in tool type proportions.

Variation in scraper size and retouch extent was identified as potentially related to differences in occupation intensity. It was suggested, for example, that lithic materials may have been more thoroughly reduced at more intensively occupied sites than at less intensively occupied sites. If this were true, one might expect that scrapers from more intensively occupied sites would have been subjected to more repeated cycles of modification and use before discard, and should therefore be smaller and more extensively retouched, than those from less intensively occupied sites; however, the demonstrated lack of variation in size and retouch extent among scraper assemblages from sites of all occupational classes indicates that this hypothesis is incorrect. These formal attributes of scrapers, at least, provide no evidence that reduction intensity differed according to variation in occupation intensity.

It was also suggested that a greater need to use lithic material to its full potential might contribute to differences in the frequency with which unmodified flakes and fragments were used as tools. In particular, it was hypothesized that unmodified debitage might have been used more often at intensively occupied sites than at less intensively occupied sites. Once again, however, lack of variation in the occurrence of edge alteration attributes which can be securely attributed to use, rather than postdeposition destructive forces, indicates that this hypothesis is also incorrect, and that unmodified debitage was used with approximately the same frequency at sites of all occupational classes.

So far, this discussion has addressed only one assemblage characteristic (material type composition) which shows substantial intersite variation, and several others, including material texture, scraper size and retouch extent, and edge alteration attributes, which show essentially no intersite variation. Between these extremes of

magnitude of variation, the analysis has shown that the remaining
assemblage characteristics, including artifact category proportions,
complete flake size and cortex, striking platform type, and tool type
proportions, also tend to show restricted ranges of variation, but
suggests that some of this variation may be at least statistically
significant. It should now be clear that the identification of
statistically significant variation is often a tedious and difficult
undertaking when dealing with characteristics which show only limited
variability. Interpreting the archaeological significance of this
variation is an equally challenging task. This problem will be
approached using a table which summarizes the essential characteristics
of the assemblage by occupational site classes. The basis of this
approach is the assumption that variation in any one attribute which
appears to be patterned with respect to variation in any other attribute
or attributes, or with respect to occupational site classes, is both
archaeologically meaningful and interpretable. Variation which remains
highly unpatterned will be considered insignificant to the extent that
it cannot be interpreted using the theoretical constructs presented at
the beginning of this chapter, or by modifications of these constructs.
It is freely acknowledged that theoretical orientations and analytic
approaches other than those used here can be applied to the data under
consideration, and that some other approach might permit stronger
inferences.

        Variation in artifact category proportions, complete flake size
and cortex, striking platform type, and tool assemblage diversity is
summarized for each site and, where applicable, for intrasite
collections, by occupational site class in Table 5.50. The occupation
site classes used in this table are those defined at the beginning of
this section. The collections from AZ EE:1:104 and AZ EE:2:122 were not
included in any of the above analyses. The numbers given under
"artifact category proportions" refer to dendrogram groups defined in
Figure 5.33 as a result of the cluster analysis of percentages of
complete and split flakes, proximal and medial-distal flake fragments,
nonorientable fragments, cores, and hammerstones. Group 1 assemblages
tend to have higher percentages of whole flakes and lower percentages of
flake fragments, especially medial-distal flake fragments, than do Group
2 assemblages. Group 1 collections are also distinguished from Group 2
by slightly higher percentages of cores and hammerstones. Although the
assemblage from AZ EE:1:104 was not included in the cluster analysis, it
has been assigned to Group 1, based on a subjective evaluation of its
similarity to other Group 1 collections. Two measures of complete flake
size are provided. The mean flake thicknesses repeat those given in
Table 5.24, but are arranged by occupational site class. The terms
"small," "medium," and "large" refer to the flake size classes
previously defined on the basis of nonoverlapping 95 percent confidence
intervals for mean flake thickness. Variation in complete flake cortex
is also expressed in two ways in Table 5.24. The number given for each
assemblage under "percent cortical" is the percentage of all complete
flakes which showed some cortex, in contrast to those which were
completely noncortical. The terms high and low under "cortex group"
refer to Cortex Groups 1 and 2, respectively, which were defined on the
basis of the triangular-coordinate diagram shown in Figure 5.35. Letter

590 Kenneth C. Rozen

Table 5.50

ARTIFACT CATEGORY PROPORTION GROUP, COMPLETE FLAKE SIZE AND CORTEX,
STRIKING PLATFORM TYPE GROUP, AND TOOL ASSEMBLAGE DIVERSITY
FOR EACH SITE AND ANALYZED COLECTION, BY OCCUPATION CLASS

Occupation Class	Site Number	Collection Code	Artifact Category Proportion Group	Mean Complete Flake Thickness	Complete Flake Size Class	Percent Cortical Flakes	Cortex Group	Platform Type Group	Tool Assemblage Diversity
I	AZ EE:2:105	105SF	2	5.5	Small	32.9	Low	I	High
		105FP	2	5.3	Small	38.5	Low	F	High
		105EX	1	6.9		40.0	Low	F	High
		105BP	2	5.0	Small	32.3	Low	I	High
	AZ EE:2:113	113SF	2	6.4	Medium	47.4	High	I	Intermediate
		113FP	2	6.7		40.3	Low	I	Intermidiate
		113EX	2	6.5	Medium	40.0	Low	I	Intermediate
		113BP	2	6.6	Medium	35.7	Low	I	Intermediate
	AZ EE:2:76	76SF	2	5.5	Small	39.3	Low	I	High
		76FP	2	6.5		51.5	High	F	High
		76EX	1	6.5		59.2	High	I	High
		76ST	2	5.5	Small	37.6	Low	C	High
II	AZ EE:2:77	77SF	1	6.7	Medium	50.6	High	C	Intermediate
		77EX	1	5.1	Small	35.3	Low	I	Intermediate
	AZ EE:2:129	129SF	1	6.4	Medium	32.0	Low	I	Low
		129EX	2	6.9		38.1	Low	F	Low
		129T	2	5.3	Small	34.6	Low	F	Low
	AZ EE:2:84	84SF	2	6.1	Medium	53.6	High	C	Low
	AZ EE:2:107	107SF	1	6.5	Medium	30.3	Low	C	Low
	AZ EE:2:120	120SF	1	6.2	Medium	23.4	Low	F	Intermediate
III	AZ EE:2:106	106SF	1	7.6		46.2	High	C	Low
	AZ EE:2:109	109SF	1	7.0		40.0	Low	C	Low
	AZ EE:1:104		1						Low
	AZ EE:2:117	117SF	1	8.0	Large	57.7	High	C	Low
	AZ EE:2:116	116SF	1	5.9		43.3	Low	C	Low
	AZ EE:2:122								Low

codes, representing the three platform type groups shown in Figure 5.36, (assemblages in which faceted platforms are more numerous than cortical platforms, F, those which have the highest percentages of cortical platforms, C, and an intermediate class, I) appear in the platform type column. Variation in tool assemblage composition is described in terms of "high," "intermediate," and "low" assemblage diversity. These terms correspond to groups of assemblages which have been previously defined as having heterogeneous, intermediate, and homogeneous tool compositions. The assemblage from the sheet trash deposit at AZ EE:2:129 is excluded because it is unique in its high percentage of regular bifaces. Complete flake size and cortex, and platform type data are unavailable for AZ EE:1:104 and AZ EE:2:122. Again, the assemblage of floor artifacts (FLOOR) contains artifacts from all site classes.

Table 5.50 may be used to examine the extent to which variation among the flaked stone assemblages is patterned with respect to occupational site classes. Simple inspection of this table identifies several general trends. One of the clearest of these trends can be seen in the distribution of artifact category proportion groups by site class. In particular, assemblages with lower percentages of complete flakes, cores, and hammerstones, and higher percentages of flake fragments (Group 2) appear to be largely confined to sites belonging to Occupation Class I (AZ EE:2:105, EE:2:113, EE:2:76). In contrast, assemblages showing higher percentages of complete flakes, cores, and hammerstones, and lower percentages of flake fragments (Group 1) are more often members of Occupation Classes II and III. Several exceptions to this pattern should be noted. Among the assemblages from Occupation Class I sites, the extramural feature assemblages from both AZ EE:2:76 and EE:2:105 are members of artifact category proportion Group 1, not Group 2. Conversely, among assemblages from Occupation Class II sites, the structure fill assemblage from AZ EE:2:84, and both the sheet trash and extramural feature assemblages from AZ EE:2:129 are members of Artifact Category Group 2.

Table 5.50 also suggest that there is some tendency for tool assemblage diversity to be patterned by site occupation class. Sites yielding evidence of the most substantial and intensive occupations (Class I) have tool assemblages which are either high or intermediate with respect to diversity. Occupation Class II sites are either intermediate or low in tool assemblage diversity, and the composite tool assemblage from all occupation Class III sites, combined, is low in diversity. These observations suggest that, in comparison to smaller, less intensively occupied sites, sites representing more substantial and intensive occupations are characterized by a wider range of tool types.

Inspection of the flake size data will show that there is a slight tendency for flakes to become larger with increasing occupation intensity. This pattern is most evident in comparing Occupation Classes II and III, and is least pronounced between Classes I and II. The distribution of the three striking platform groups by site occupation classes suggests that cortical platforms tend to be most common among assemblages from Class III, and to a lesser extent, in assemblages from Class II sites. The distribution of all three platform type groups appears to be highly unpatterned between occupation Classes I and II.

Finally, Table 5.50 shows that percentages of cortical flakes do not appear to vary in any patterned way in relation to site occupation classes.

Having identified these general trends, we may now evaluate their archaeological meaning in greater detail. At the beginning of this chapter it was suggested that variation in proportions of complete flakes and flake fragments may reflect differing emphases on core reduction (primary reduction) and tool manufacture (secondary reduction), or in more general terms, differences in reduction intensity. More specifically, it has been shown that certain kinds of tool manufacture yield debitage assemblages which tend to have lower percentages of complete flakes, and higher percentages of flake fragments. In contrast, core reduction may tend to produce relatively more whole flakes, and fewer flake fragments. Therefore the distribution of the artifact category proportion groups by occupation classes seen in Table 5.50 could mean that secondary reduction is more strongly evident among assemblages from Class I sites than it is in assemblages from Class II and III sites, or that in more general terms, reduction was more intensive at Class I sites than at Class II and III sites. However, it was also noted that inferences about technological variation based on differences in artifact category proportions are strongest when they can be supported by independent data. If for example, the differences between the two assemblage groups distinguished by the cluster analysis reflect differences in the object or intensity of reduction, one would expect that variation in flake size and cortex and platform type should be strongly patterned by membership in the two dendrogram groups. Therefore, if assemblages belonging to Artifact Category Proportion Group 1 are more strongly representative of core reduction, or less intensive reduction in general, than Group 2 assemblages, and conversely, if Group 2 assemblages reflect more secondary reduction or more intensive reduction, flakes from Group 1 assemblages should be consistently larger and more cortical than those in Group 2 collections. In addition, we might also expect cortical platforms to be more common among Group 1 collections in comparison to those of Group 2, and that faceted platforms should be more common in Group 2 assemblages than they are in Group 2 collections.

A review of Table 5.50 will show that inferences about technological variation among sites of different occupation classes can, in fact, be made in some instances on the basis of patterned associations of artifact category proportions, flake size and cortex, and striking platform type. For example, among Occupation Class III sites, the assemblages from both AZ EE:2:106 and EE:2:117 belong to Artifact Category Proportion Group 1, and tend to have large, cortical flakes. In addition, these two assemblages are among those showing the highest percentages of cortical platforms. In contrast, the structure fill, floor pit, and borrow pit assemblages from AZ EE:2:105, and the structure fill collection from AZ EE:2:76 are all members of Artifact Category Proportion Group 2, and tend to have small, noncortical flakes. These assemblages are either intermediate with respect to proportions of cortical, plain, and faceted platforms, or tend to show relatively high percentages of faceted platforms. These observations suggest that these assemblages from AZ EE:2:105 and AZ EE:2:76, both of which are Occupation Class I sites, may be the result of more intensive reduction, or are more strongly representative of secondary reduction than are the assemblages from AZ EE:2:106 and AZ EE:2:117. The characteristics of those two Occupation Class III sites suggest a stronger emphasis on core reduction, or at least less thorough core reduction.

While some technological differences can therefore be seen among sites of different occupation classes, it also appears that the degree to which variation in flake size and cortex, and striking platform type is patterned by artifact category group membership is not great, even though group membership is nonrandomly distributed by occupation class. For example while most assemblages from all three Occupation Classes III sites (AZ EE:2:105, EE:2:113, and EE:2:76) are members of Artifact Proportion Group 2, flakes in all assemblages from AZ EE:2:113 tend to be larger than those in most assemblages from AZ EE:2:76 and AZ EE:2:105. Like the collections from AZ EE:2:106 and AZ EE:2:117, the assemblage from AZ EE:2:109 tends to have large flakes and a high percentage of cortical platforms. While all three of these sites are members of Occupation Class III, and Artifact Category Proportion Group 1, flakes from AZ EE:2:109 tend to be less cortical than those from either AZ EE:2:106 or EE:2:117. Further, the assemblage from AZ EE:2:116, also a member of Occupation Class III and Artifact Category Proportion Group 1, not only has fewer cortical flakes than the assemblages from AZ EE:2:106 and EE:2:117, but its flakes also tend to be smaller than those from any of the other three Occupation Class III sites.

To more clearly evaluate the extent to which variation in flake size and cortex, and striking platform type is structured by membership in the two artifact category proportion groups, the data for those attributes given in Table 5.50 were rearranged according to group membership. This rearrangment is shown in Table 5.51, which lists mean flake thickness, percentage of flake showing cortex, and platform type group for each assemblage by dendrogram group membership. Average mean flake thickness, and the average percentage of cortical flakes are also given for both groups. This table indicates a slight tendency for flakes in Group 1 collections to be larger and more cortical than those of Group 2 collections. Cortical platforms also appear to be somewhat more prevalent among Group 1 collections than among Group 2 assemblages, and there is a slight tendency for faceted platforms to be relatively more common in Group 2. All of these tendencies are very weak; the ranges of variation for both mean flake thickness and percentages of cortical flakes overlap to a great extent between the two groups, and the average values for both variables differ very little between groups. Further, the slightly higher average mean flake thickness and percentage of cortical flakes for Group 1 almost certainly reflects a few extreme values for both variables among the assemblages contained within this group. Similarly, the degree of patterning of platform type groups by artifact category proportion groups is far from compelling. In general then, variation in complete flake size, and cortex, and platform type group is not clearly nor strongly structured by membership in the artifact category proportion groups.

Table 5.51

MEAN FLAKE THICKNESS, PERCENTAGE OF CORTICAL FLAKES,
AND PLATFORM TYPE GROUP BY ARTIFACT CATEGORY PROPORTION GROUP

Collection Code	Mean Flake Thickness	Percent Cortical	Platform Type Group
Group 1			
Floor	6.5	51.4	3
105EX	6.9	40.0	1
77EX	5.1	35.3	3
106SF	7.6	46.2	2
76EX	6.5	59.2	3
120SF	6.2	23.4	1
109SF	7.0	40.0	2
107SF	6.5	30.3	2
117SF	8.0	57.7	2
116SF	5.9	43.3	2
129SF	6.4	32.0	3
77SF	6.7	50.6	2
Mean	6.6	42.5	
Group 2			
76ST	5.5	37.5	2
129EX	6.9	38.1	1
113FP	6.7	44.4	3
129T	5.3	34.6	1
105FP	5.3	38.5	1
113EX	6.5	40.3	3
76FP	6.5	51.5	1
105BP	5.0	32.3	3
84SF	6.1	53.6	2
113BP	6.6	35.7	3
113SF	6.4	47.4	3
105SF	5.5	32.9	3
76SF	5.5	39.3	3
Mean	6.0	40.5	

Platform type groups:
1 – Collections with relatively more cortical than faceted platforms

2 – Collections with relatively more faceted than cortical platforms

3 – Collections which are intermediate between Group 1 and 2 with respect to the proportions of cortical and faceted platforms

Therefore, while differences among some of the assemblages with respect to artifact category proportions and flake attributes suggest that relative emphases on primary and secondary reduction, or in more general terms, reduction intensity, may have varied slightly among sites of different occupation classes, the lack of patterned variation in flake attributes by artifact category proportion groups indicates that the nonrandom distribution of assemblages by artifact category proportion group and occupation class is not due to substantial technological variation.

Additional evidence that the artifact category proportion groups do not reflect any appreciable variation in reduction intensity, and accordingly, that reduction was generally no more intensive at Occupation Class I than Class II and III can be found in percentages of nonorientable fragments. As noted earlier, the results of one recent study (Rozen 1981) suggest that the percentage of nonorientable fragments tends to increase as reduction becomes more intensive. A review of Table 5.23, which shows mean percentages of artifact categories for the two dendrogram groups, indicates that the mean percentages of nonorientable fragments for Groups 1 and 2 are nearly identical.

Finally, still more evidence of the lack of substantial technological variation between these groups can be seen in the magnitude of the variation which is responsible for group differentiation. In purely subjective terms, the differences between Groups 1 and 2 with respect to mean percentages of complete flakes and flake fragments are not robust, as one might expect if major technological variation were responsible for group differentiation. To provide a stronger basis for this assertion, the results of the present study can be compared to those of the author's analysis of 23 assemblages from the St. Johns area in east-central Arizona (Rozen 1981). Those assemblages were very diverse in age, representing both Archaic and ceramic period occupations and came from a wide variety of site types, including sites with permanent architecture, sites with temporary structures, simple sherd and flaked stone scatters, and quarry sites. A cluster analysis of those assemblages was performed, using the same artifact categories and clustering algorithm used here. The result of that analysis was a dendrogram in which the first group distinction occurred at a merge level of approximately 60. A review of Figure 5.33 will show that the distinction between Group 1 and 2 among the ANAMAX-Rosemont Hohokam assemblages occurs at a merge level of about 20. One way to think of this comparison is that there is only a third as much variation among the ANAMAX-Rosemont assemblages as there was among the St. Johns collections. This observation should not be surprising in view of the temporal, technological, functional, and cultural diversity of the St. Johns assemblages; the Rosemont assemblages, in contrast, are all from Hohokam sites having permanent architecture and representing a relatively short period of time.

If, as has been concluded here, the dendrogram groups do not represent significant technological variation, other explanations for the nonrandom distribution of assemblages by dendrogram groups and occupation classes must be sought. The most realistic of these explanations involves the interaction of variation in occupational factors, the extent to which assemblages reflect either the selected products or unwanted by-products of reduction, and intrasite spatial patterns of refuse disposal. For example, even though the object and intensity of lithic reduction does not appear to have differed by occupation site class, assemblages from Class I sites may tend to have lower ratios of whole flakes to flake fragments than assemblages from Class II and III sites because artifacts may have been subjected to more manipulation, both intentional and unintentional, on relatively more intensively occupied sites. In short, flakes at AZ EE:2:76, EE:2:105, and EE:2:113 may have been more frequently stepped on and kicked around, and had hammerstones and manos dropped on them more often than did flakes from the other sites. This simple explanation has some merit, but it is not entirely satisfactory because, in many cases, there is no reason to believe that sites of different occupation classes differed in terms of the numbers of people present per unit area at any given time. A comparison of two of the Class III sites, AZ EE:2:106 and AZ EE:2:109, and AZ EE:2:76, a Class I site, will illustrate this point nicely. All three of these sites are located on ridge tops, are of approximately the same size, and have nearly equal numbers of house pits. Because the number of people present at AZ EE:2:76 was probably no greater than the number of occupants at either AZ EE:2:106 or AZ EE:2:109, it seems unlikely that the rate of flake breakage due to postdetachment destructive factors would have been any greater at AZ EE:2:76 than at the other two sites. Therefore, occupation intensity alone cannot fully explain the patterned distribution of assemblages by artifact category proportion group and occupation class, in the sense that the term "occupation intensity" has been used thus far. Instead, it is likely that the two dendrogram groups reflect differences in the extent to which assemblages are composed of either the selected products of reduction, or the unwanted by-products of all activities involving the manufacture, use, and refurbishing of flaked stone tools. More specifically, the higher ratio of complete to broken flakes character-istic of Group 1 assemblages, and the lower artifact densities at sites which produced these assemblages suggest that Group 1 collections are more strongly representative of the selected products of reduction. In contrast, the lower ratio of complete flakes to flake fragments typical of Group 2 assemblages, suggests that unwanted items are relatively more abundant in these assemblages. Further, the high artifact densities typical of the Group 2 collections strongly suggest that these assemblages consist of items which were gathered together and disposed of collectively.

With this interpretation, an explanation for the patterned distribution of assemblages by occupation class and dendrogram group can be found in differences in the occupational histories of the sites, and in the manner in which refuse was discarded. All three Occupation Class I sites saw long occupations in which pit houses were built, occupied, and abandoned, and new pit houses constructed. Nearly all of the analyzed collections from these sites are members of Artifact Category Proportion Group 2, because abandoned house pits were habitually used as trash dumps by the occupants of actively inhabited pit houses.

In contrast, most Occupation Class II and III sites have much shorter occupation spans, and have produced comparatively little evidence of repeated cycles of pit house construction and abandonment. In some cases, we may even suspect that all pit houses were occupied contemporaneously, and were simultaneously abandoned, never to be occupied again. As a result it seems reasonable to propose that Occupation Class II and III sites have lower artifact densities and assemblages which are more representative of the selected products of reduction, rather than refuse, because trash was more commonly dumped on the slopes surrounding the sites than in vacant house pits or other currently unused features.

AZ EE:2:129 is unlike all other Occupation Class III sites because it has a long occupation span (Table 5.49). It is gratifying to note that two of the assemblages from this site are also anomolous to Class III--and Class II sites as well--because they are members of Artifact Category Proportion Group 2, rather than Group 1. Therefore, it now appears that artifact category group membership, interpreted here as reflecting differences in the extent to which assemblage represent refuse, is more strongly correlated with occupation span, than it is with anything else.

So far, this discussion has focused on the interpretation of artifact category proportions and flake attributes as these data reflect differences in the object and intensity of reduction, differences in the extent to which assemblages represent refuse, the manner in which trash was disposed of, and the occupational histories of the sites. For the most part, this interpretation has been conducted at the intersite level of comparison; however it will be worthwhile to briefly examine the extent to which artifact category proportion group membership is patterned among assemblages from major intrasite provenience classes, other than structure fill. The composite assemblage of floor artifacts (FLOOR) is a member of Artifact Category Proportion Group 1. This would be expected if Group 1 assemblages are, in fact, more representative of selected products of reduction, rather than refuse, and if the artifacts contained in this assemblage are usable items which were left on pit house floors at the time of their abandonment. A review of Table 5.51 will show that the extramural feature assemblages from AZ EE:2:76, EE:2:105, and EE:2:77 are all members of Group 1. Note that at AZ EE:2:76 and AZ EE:2:105, only the extramural feature collections belong to Group 1. These observations suggest that extramural features at all three of the above-mentioned sites were not used as trash dumps, as were the vacant house pits at AZ EE:2:76 and EE:2:105. While this suggests that the former assemblages may therefore be composed primarily of the selected products of reduction, the possibility that certain kinds of items were deliberately discarded in these features cannot be discounted. For example, in comparison to Group 2 assemblages, the higher percentages of hammerstones and cores characteristic of Group 1 assemblages in the case of the above-defined extramural feature collections, could mean that cores and hammerstones were intentionally discarded in roasting pits to serve as heat-retaining objects along with other, unmodified rocks. The extramural feature assemblages AZ EE:2:113 and EE:2:129 are members of Group 2; thus no clear patterning of assemblages from this provenience class is apparent with respect to artifact category group membership.

All three of the floor pit assemblages (76FP, 105FP, and 113FP) are members of Group 2, as are the structure fill assemblages from AZ EE:2:76, EE:2:105, and EE:2:113. Therefore, there is no reason to believe that the contents of floor pits differ from structure fill assemblages in the extent to which they represent trash. Similarly, the borrow pit collections from AZ EE:2:105 and EE:2:113 are members of Group 2, as are the structure fill assemblages from these sites. This simply means that the inhabitants of these sites dumped their garbage in any large, vacant depression, regardless of its original function.

Interpretation of Variation in Tool Type Proportions

By far the most distinctive of all the tool assemblages under consideration is that from the sheet trash deposit at AZ EE:2:129. This assemblage is unlike all others in that regular bifaces are very common, and are second to only scrapers in relative frequency. Many of these bifaces appear to have been broken during manufacture, and all have flake scar morphology suggesting soft-hammer percussion. Frequencies of faceted platforms and platform lipping in the debitage collection from this deposit are higher than in most other assemblages, suggesting that tool manufacture is strongly represented. In addition, approximately 20 complete flakes and proximal flake fragments showed patterned combinations of certain attributes, including faceted platforms, platform lipping, flake curvature, and flake scar orientations on exterior surfaces, which clearly indicate that these items were produced as a result of soft-hammer percussion biface thinning.

As the discussion of previous research indicates, soft-hammer percussion biface manufacture is not a common aspect of Hohokam flaked stone technology. This, and the near absence of pottery in the sheet trash deposit at AZ EE:2:129 suggests that much of the material contained in this deposit was of preceramic age. In order to determine whether the flaked stone assemblage represented either a rare case of Hohokam soft-hammer biface reduction, or a mixture of Hohokam and Archaic artifacts, a single radiocarbon date was obtained from a piece of charcoal recovered from the base of the deposit. This analysis yielded at date of 1550 $\pm$ 190 B.P. (A-3558), between A.D. 210 and 590, which is interpreted here as transitional between the preceramic and ceramic period temporal horizons, and between the late Archaic and Hohokam cultural horizons. As noted in Chapter 3, this date is similar to one obtained from a known late Archaic site, AZ EE:2:50, along Pantano Wash (Huckell 1982). In all likelihood, the relatively strong emphasis on soft-hammer biface manufacture seen in the assemblage from the sheet trash deposit at AZ EE:2:129 is due to a mixture of late Archaic (San Pedro) and Hohokam artifacts.

With regard to the remainder of the tool assemblages, some tendency for assemblages from the more substantially occupied sites to be more diverse in tool composition than those from sites which have yielded evidence of much less substantial occupation has already been noted. It will also be recalled that the distinction between diverse and homogeneous tool assemblages is based primarily on the presence or absence of certain kinds of small implements, most notably preforms, projectile points, drills, projections, and wedges. On the basis of these observations, it is tempting to infer that a wider range of activities involving stone tools was conducted at the more substantially occupied sites than was carried out at the less intensively occupied sites, and that there is therefore some evidence for functional differentiation among the sites.

Before accepting this interpretation, several factors that may affect tool assemblage composition, but which are unrelated to site function, must be considered. The first of these concerns tool assemblage sample sizes, and the frequencies with which the above-mentioned tool categories occur in general. Projectile points, preforms, drills, projections, and wedges are nowhere common, even among assemblages of diverse tool composition. It is therefore unlikely that these items will be represented in small samples. A review of Table 5.50 will show that only the Occupation Class I sites (AZ EE:2:76, EE:2:105, and EE:2:113) have tool assemblages of more than 100 items. Tool sample sizes for Class II and III sites are all less than about 50 items. Therefore, the lack of tool assemblage diversity among Class II and III sites probably reflects nothing more than poor sample sizes. A second factor unrelated to site function which may affect tool assemblage composition is the value which was attached to certain kinds of tools. For example, it seems reasonable to assume that tools whose manufacture involved a greater investment of time and effort, such as projectile points and drills, may have been more highly valued than tools which could be made more quickly and easily. Therefore, hammerstones and scrapers may have been more often left behind on sites which were occupied for short periods and quickly abandoned, than were projectile points. In contrast, the probability of a projectile point being broken and discarded as trash may be greater at sites which were occupied for long periods than at sites which comparatively briefly occupied. In view of these considerations, it would be imprudent to conclude that variation in tool assemblage diversity reflects functional differences in sites of different occupation classes.

Perhaps the only exception to this lack of demonstrable variation in tool assemblage composition can be found in comparing the assemblage from AZ EE:2:113 with those from both AZ EE:2:76 and EE:2:105. Because all three of these sites have tool assemblages containing well over 100 items, we can be certain that the differences among these sites with respect to percentages of regular bifaces, preforms, and projectile points is significant. It will be recalled, for example, that the assemblages from both AZ EE:2:76 and EE:2:105 have higher percentages of these kinds of tools than does the assemblage from AZ EE:2:113. This suggests that the manufacture of small bifacial implements, especially projectile points, was a more frequent activity at AZ EE:2:76 and EE:2:105 than at AZ EE:2:113. I am further inclined to believe that this difference in emphasis on the manufacture of small bifacial tools is largely responsible for slightly, but statistically significantly larger flake size at AZ EE:2:113 than at either AZ EE:2:105 or AZ EE:2:76. While the difference between AZ EE:2:113 and AZ EE:2:105 and EE:2:76 is both clearly significant and interpretable, no explanation for this difference is apparent.

A final observation on tool type proportions, concerns the distribution of projectile point types by site. AZ EE:2:76 yielded the widest range of Hohokam projectile point styles, consistent with its position as the site with the longest ceramic period occupation span. AZ EE:2:76 differs from other sites which yielded substantial numbers of projectile points (AZ EE:2:105 and EE:2:113) because elongate points with serrate blades, and abruptly laterally expanding, convex or straight bases (Type 3) are the dominant type. As was noted in the tool type descriptions, this style is not commonly reported in the literature. At AZ EE:2:76, this style may represent the idiosyncratic preference of small group of people. At two other sites along Barrel Canyon, AZ EE:2:107 and EE:2:120, located upstream from AZ EE:2:76, Type 3 points were recovered from structure fill. On the basis of ceramic evidence, the occupations of these two sites appear to be confined to the middle Rincon phase, as it has been defined and used elsewhere in this report (Deaver, Chapter 4; Ferg, Chapter 10). Therefore, Type 3 points may be diagnostic of this time period in the Rosemont area. It is also interesting to note that the Type 3 point from AZ EE:2:120 is nearly identical to several points from AZ EE:2:76 in all aspects of style and technique of manufacture. It is tempting to speculate that all of these points were made by a single artisan.

Preceramic projectile points were found at AZ EE:2:84, EE:2:105, EE:2:109, and EE:2:113. The San Pedro points from AZ EE:2:84 and EE:2:109 were found during surface-stripping excavations and selective surface collections, respectively. Because of the contexts in which they were found, these preceramic points cannot be securely associated with the Hohokam occupations of these sites. Similarly, 8 of the 17 Archaic points from AZ EE:2:105 were found in contexts which cannot be clearly attributed to the Hohokam occupation; however, the remainder (9), and those (5) from AZ EE:2:113, were found in feature fill deposits which are clearly Hohokam in origin. Occurrences of Archaic projectile points in ceramic period contexts are not unusual throughout the Southwest, and simply mean that projectile points were scavenged from Archaic sites by later groups. Though AZ EE:2:105 yielded a wide range of Archaic projectile point styles, the dominant forms (Types 8 and 9) are of late Archaic age. The relative abundance of these points probably reflects the presence of a late Archaic site (AZ EE:2:128) northwest of the ballcourt. Finally, it will be recalled from the projectile point descriptions that corner-notched, stemmed points (Type 10) originate in late preceramic horizons, but persist into the ceramic period in the Mogollon culture area. The relatively strong representation of San Simon branch Mogollon pottery at AZ EE:2:113 opens the possibility that the three Type 10 points from this site may not represent Archaic "pick ups," but instead, may either have been manufactured at AZ EE:2:113, or imported to the site in the same manner in which Mogollon pottery was brought to the site.

Conclusions

The Rosemont Hohokam relied almost exclusively on immediately available materials for the manufacture of stone tools. Substantial variation in material type composition among assemblages from different sites simply reflects differences in the kinds of materials which were available in close proximity to each of the sites, and is not related to differences in the nature of site occupations. In comparison to material type composition, all other assemblage characteristics examined tend to show much more restricted ranges of variation. Detailed analyses of artifact category proportions and flake attributes have shown that some of the sites may differ slightly in the relative emphasis on core reduction and the manufacture of small, bifacial tools. In general, however, the technology which prevailed at the ANAMAX-Rosemont Hohokam sites was essentially uniform. With the exception of small, pressure-flaked implements, this technology involved hard-hammer reduction of immediately available, medium-textured materials producing a wide range of tools, the most common of which is a diverse group of unifacially retouched flakes which have been referred to here as scrapers. Although the sites exhibit a wide range of variation in nonassemblage characteristics including artifact densities and numbers of structures, extramural pits, and burials, there is little, if any evidence that the thoroughness with which materials were reduced varied according to differences in occupation intensity. Similarly, there is little evidence in variation in tool type proportions to suggest that the range of activities involving flaked stone tools differed to any appreciable extent from one site to another. Probably the single most illuminating result of this analysis is that assemblages with slightly higher at proportions of whole flakes to flake fragments tend to be most common sites with short occupation spans, while assemblages with slightly lower proportions of whole flakes to flake fragments prevail at sites with long occupation spans. Rather than reflecting technological variation, the strong correlation of proportions of whole flakes to flake fragments with occupation span reflects an interaction of three factors: (1) differences in the extent to which assemblages represent either the selected products of reduction, or the unwanted by-products of manufacture, refurbishing, and use; (2) differences in the manner in which trash was disposed of, as dictated by; (3) differences in the occupational histories of the sites.

Discussion

Despite the fact that the sites differ greatly with respect to nonassemblage characteristics, there is very little evidence for functional differentiation, either in terms of the way in which lithic material was reduced, or in the range of activities for which flaked stone tools were used. The apparent lack of variation in the thoroughness with which material was reduced suggests that once a permanent structure appears on a site, reduction intensity reaches a

threshold beyond which it no longer varies. Therefore, while we may
reasonably expect to see substantial technological variation between
sites with and without permanent architecture, the results of this
analysis suggest that we are unlikely to see major technological
differences between sites with structures, even when comparing a site
with 2 pit houses with one having 32 pit houses. This observation is
consistent with the results of the Gila Butte-Santan study (Rice 1979)
and the Salt-Gila Aqueduct flaked stone analysis (Bernard-Shaw 1984).
The apparent lack of variation in the tool assemblages suggests that the
activities which occurred at the sites were all very similar. These
activities are undoubtedly related to the maintenance of groups of
people living in permanent or semipermanent villages. It is important
to realize that the lack of variation in tool assemblages from the
ANAMAX-Rosemont Hohokam habitation sites does not necessarily mean
that the occupants of these sites pursued the same activities in the
drainages and on the ridges which surrounded them. That is, the
location of certain sites in particular areas may in fact be related to
differences in site function (that is, with what the people were doing);
however, the evidence for this functional differentiation is not likely
to be seen in the flaked stone assemblages from the habitation sites
themselves, but at other, associated sites without architecture, where
those tasks were undertaken.

Problems and Directions for Future Research

A wide variety of problems can be identified with the ANANAX-
Rosemont Hohokam flaked stone analysis. Some of these difficulties
pertain to the replicable observation of some of the attributes which
were examined. The presence or absence of platform lipping, and the
presence or absence of use-related microflaking were especially
difficult to record consistently. Other problems concern the
application of some statistical techniques to certain kinds of data.
Some objections might be raised regarding the manner in which Spearman's
ranked correlation coefficient was applied or the use of means, rather
than medians, as measures of central tendency for flake metrics. In the
long run, however, I believe that these problems are relatively minor,
and do not seriously affect the validity of the interpretations which
have been offered.

A somewhat more serious problem concerns the tool typology. It
will be noted, for example, that many more types were defined in the
theoretical discussion than were found to be useful in the analysis of
assemblage variation. The large number of types which were originally
defined is symptomatic of the frustration encountered in attempting to
provide adequate formal descriptions of assemblages which lack those
patterned attribute combinations on which intuitively discernible types
might be based. This problem is likely to recur whenever such
assemblages are examined. Defining large numbers of tool categories

will do little harm as long as they are not accorded unwarranted significance, and as long as typologies are designed so that categories can be collapsed into more meaningful combinations.

As regrettable as they are, the problems mentioned above, as well as others which will undoubtedly come to light through critical examination of this study, are relatively minor in comparison to two more general problems which can be identified. The first of these more serious problems is that the ANAMAX-Rosemont flaked stone analysis has yielded comparatively little new information about Hohokam prehistory in exchange for the great investment of time, money, and effort it required. Conceivably, this sobering observation could mean that some major aspect of the analysis, such as its research questions, theoretical orientation, or interpretation was basically unsound. Hopefully, most readers will find little justification for these potential criticisms and instead, will conclude that the small amount of new information gained probably reflects certain fundamental limitations of the analyzed assemblages. In particular, the restricted range of variation seen in the Rosemont assemblages has been interpreted as reflecting the fact that all of the assemblages were produced by essentially the same kinds of activities. It is my guess that we are likely to encounter a similar lack of patterned variation wherever simple hard-hammer-percussion-produced assemblages from Hohokam habitation sites are compared.

If this is true beyond the Rosemont area, then I seriously question whether additional analyses of such assemblages, using approaches comparable to that which was used here, are likely to tell us much more about Hohokam prehistory than we already know. While such assemblages are by no means without research potential, especially if they can be compared to assemblages from other kinds of sites (sherd and lithic scatters, agricultural sites, and so forth), the amount of information to be gained through intensive quantitative analysis of assemblages from only habitation sites may be so slight that such analyses may be inappropriate. In retrospect, therefore, the most serious criticism of this study is that it did not take advantage of the full range of site types present in the study area.

Finally, the most critical problem encountered concerns the accomplishment of the analysis within the temporal and monetary constraints of the ANAMAX project. Despite the best efforts of, and frequent communication between all individuals involved, this analysis was in many respects not accomplished within project limitations. In retrospect, it is now clear that the scope of this effort was far out of proportion to the available resources. Probably the best indication of this is the fact that an analysis of assemblages from 41 pit houses, using essentially the same approach, was also conducted; however, limitations of time and space preclude their presentation and interpretation here. The most obvious lesson to be drawn from this observation is that the scope of the analysis should have been drastically narrowed early in the project. While I doubt that anyone

would disagree with this often repeated observation, the fact remains
that the problems of completing sound archaeologial research within such
limitations (both within and outside contract archaeology) are both
widespread and persistent. I am therefore inclined to believe that the
root of this problem lies much deeper than mere adjustment of the
research scope undertaken in individual analyses. Instead, the problem
seems to be caused by a basic lack of consensus about what is and is not
good, or at least minimally adequate research. To ignore this problem
by saying that such a consensus is inherently unattainable is to deny
that research standards exist. In fact, all reasearchers employ
personal standards concerning the quality of their work. That these
standards are sometimes relatively higher or lower, or simply different
in some cases, is not the relevant issue. The point is, they exist, and
should be used as the basis for developing some common notion about what
analyses such as this one should represent. I believe that such a
consensus, though difficult to achieve, is not only attainable, but is
absolutely essential.